Gramsci Contested

Historical Materialism
Book Series

Editorial Board

Loren Balhorn (*Berlin*)
David Broder (*Rome*)
Sebastian Budgen (*Paris*)
Steve Edwards (*London*)
Juan Grigera (*London*)
Marcel van der Linden (*Amsterdam*)
Peter Thomas (*London*)

VOLUME 250

The titles published in this series are listed at *brill.com/hm*

Gramsci Contested

Interpretations, Debates and Polemics, 1922–2012

By

Guido Liguori

Translated by

Richard Braude

BRILL

LEIDEN | BOSTON

Library of Congress Cataloging-in-Publication Data

Names: Liguori, Guido, author. | Braude, Richard, translator.
Title: Gramsci contested : debates and polemics, 1922-2012 / by Guido Liguori ; translated by Richard Braude.
Other titles: Gramsci conteso. English
Description: Leiden ; Boston : Brill, [2022] | Series: Historical materialism book series, 1570-1522 ; volume 250 | Includes bibliographical references and index.
Identifiers: LCCN 2021052528 (print) | LCCN 2021052529 (ebook) |
  ISBN 9789004270169 (hardback) | ISBN 9789004503342 (ebook)
Subjects: LCSH: Gramsci, Antonio, 1891-1937–Influence. | Communism–Italy–History. | Socialism–Italy–History.
Classification: LCC HX289.7.G73 L5413 2022 (print) | LCC HX289.7.G73 (ebook) | DDC 335.43–dc23/eng/20211028
LC record available at https://lccn.loc.gov/2021052528
LC ebook record available at https://lccn.loc.gov/2021052529

Typeface for the Latin, Greek, and Cyrillic scripts: "Brill". See and download: brill.com/brill-typeface.

ISSN 1570-1522
ISBN 978-90-04-27016-9 (hardback)
ISBN 978-90-04-50334-2 (e-book)

Copyright 2022 by Koninklijke Brill NV, Leiden, The Netherlands.
Koninklijke Brill NV incorporates the imprints Brill, Brill Nijhoff, Brill Hotei, Brill Schöningh, Brill Fink, Brill mentis, Vandenhoeck & Ruprecht, Böhlau Verlag and V&R Unipress.
All rights reserved. No part of this publication may be reproduced, translated, stored in a retrieval system, or transmitted in any form or by any means, electronic, mechanical, photocopying, recording or otherwise, without prior written permission from the publisher. Requests for re-use and/or translations must be addressed to Koninklijke Brill NV via brill.com or copyright.com.

This book is printed on acid-free paper and produced in a sustainable manner.

Contents

Preface to the Second Edition IX
Preface to the First Edition XII

1 Gramsci in the Writings of His Contemporaries (1922–38) 1
    1 The Liberal History of a Sardinian Communist 1
    2 Off the 'High Road' 5
    3 The Sentence 6
    4 Prison 12
    5 Death 15
    6 'Antonio Gramsci, Leader of the Italian Working Class' 19
    7 'An Irreparable Loss' 23
    8 Between Carducci and Pascoli 26

2 The Identity and Tradition of the Party (1939–47) 30
    1 Gramsci and Togliatti 30
    2 The 'New Party' and the Intellectuals 33
    3 'Gramsci's Politics' 40
    4 Politics and Culture 49
    5 Between Croce and Marx 52

3 Diamat and the *Notebooks* (1948–55) 57
    1 The Cold War and the *Prison Notebooks* 57
    2 Gramsci's 'Anti-Fascism' 63
    3 Interpreting the *Notebooks* 65
    4 Dogmatic and Non-dogmatic Marxisms 70
    5 Dissonances 75
    6 The History of the Italian Communist Party 79
    7 A Legendary Comrade 84
    8 First Evaluations and New Perspectives 89

4 Gramsci and the Italian Road to Socialism (1956–59) 94
    1 1956 94
    2 'Too Few Gramscians' 99
    3 Gramsci's Relevance 104
    4 Gramsci and Leninism 107
    5 The Rome Conference 110
    6 The 'Return to Marx' 116

7 The Future City 117
  8 The Debate on Italian Unification 121

5 **From the 'New History' of the Communist Party to the Crisis of Historicism (1960–69)** 124
  1 The Late Togliatti 124
  2 The 'New History' of the Italian Communist Party 129
  3 Three Biographies 132
  4 The *Giovane Critica* 137
  5 The Crisis of Historicism 141
  6 Gramsci and Civil Society 148
  7 The 'Historicisation' of Gramsci 152
  8 Within the International Communist Movement 155
  9 Historicism and the Communist Party 156

6 **The Golden Age (1970–75)** 162
  1 Gramsci Back on His Feet 162
  2 Workerism and Americanism 165
  3 Gramsci and the Soviets 167
  4 The Concept of Hegemony 168
  5 The Primacy of the Political 172
  6 Gramsci's Marxism 175
  7 Gramsci and the State 178
  8 Gramsci and the 'New Left' 181
  9 The 'Gerratana Edition' 189

7 **The Apogee and Crisis of Gramscian Culture (1976–77)** 191
  1 The Pluralism Debate 191
  2 Hegemony and Democracy 193
  3 The Frattocchie Seminar 198
  4 The Florence Congress 202
  5 The Crisis 206

8 **Ten Years of 'Blackout' (1978–86)** 209
  1 The Crisis of Marxism 209
  2 Gramsci and 'Organicism' 210
  3 Prediction and Praxis 213
  4 Intellectuals and Power 218
  5 Interpretations of Hegemony 220
  6 In the 'Factory' of the *Notebooks* 223
  7 Gramsci, Religion, Catholicism 226

9 Between Politics and Philology (1987–96)   233
   1 Gramsci and the Communist Party in 1987   233
   2 Gramsci in the World   236
   3 The Fiftieth Anniversary of a 'Classic'   238
   4 Gramscians and Post-Gramscians   242
   5 Between Politics and History   246
   6 A Post-communist Gramsci   248
   7 Gramsci, Togliatti, Stalin   253
   8 Gramsci, Tania, Sraffa   258
   9 Towards a New Edition of Gramsci's Works   260

10 Liberal Democrat or Critical Communist? (1997–2000)   266
    1 National and International   266
    2 The Return of Civil Society   270
    3 Taylorism and Fordism   274
    4 Gramsci's Method   277
    5 The Story of a Prisoner   280
    6 Gramsci Contested at the End of the Millennium   283

11 Gramsci in the Twenty-First Century (2000–08)   288
    1 For Gramsci   288
    2 Gramscian Research   294
    3 Gramsci's Translatability   301
    4 Renewed Interest   306
    5 Gramsci and Politics   311

12 Gramsci's Return (2009–12)   318
    1 New Working Tools   318
    2 On the 'Philosophy of Praxis'   326
    3 Gramsci's 'Fortune'   334
    4 Creative Uses   337
    5 Stories and Histories   341
    6 The Political and Theoretical Journey of the Prison Years   346
    7 The Future Gramsci   355

Bibliography   359
Index of Names   376

Preface to the Second Edition

In 1991 the Italian Communist Party, Gramsci's party, ceased to exist. Over the 1990s, liberal democratic culture gained a position of *hegemonic* importance, including on the Italian left: liberal figures such as Ignazio Silone and Carlo Rosselli won the day and were even compared to Antonio Gramsci, not to mention people whose ideas were even less similar. For several years it seemed that the Sardinian communist risked disappearing from public view altogether, so much so that it has often been noted that Gramsci was being studied far more outside of Italy than in his home country. In truth this was only partly the case.

Fallen from grace in the eyes of both the political class and the majority of intellectuals, Gramsci's position in Italian culture could not have descended much further. But in the fifteen years following the sixtieth anniversary of his death in 1997, around 180 volumes (both books and monographs) came out that were either about him or published his works, around one per month – including many large publications, especially in the first few years of the twenty-first century.

There are a range of explanations for this phenomenon. In the first place, it had been widely accepted that Gramsci represented a giant of twentieth-century thought, and he had become the most studied modern Italian author in the world. Gramsci's fortunes outside of Italy from the 1980s and 1990s increased considerably not only in places where the left is more present (e.g. South America), but also throughout the English-speaking world, in British and American universities, as well as being drawn upon by African-American and Bengali intellectuals. This diffusion of Gramsci and the *globalisation* of his fame, naturally had a positive effect on his fortunes in Italy itself.

A second reason that prevented Gramsci from being entirely drowned out in Italy was the development of historical-philological studies in the 1990s that came out of the Gramsci Foundation's national edition of his writings (the *Edizione nazionale degli scritti di Antonio Gramsci*), which utilised newly released archival material in Moscow as well as new research relating to various figures in Gramsci's life. It also drew on research on the diachronic organisation of the *Notebooks* and the impact of that 'great and terrible world' on their contents, research that has gradually provided a new context for the prison works.

Last but not least, a *resistance* was mounted to this dangerous removal of Gramsci, conducted by groups, organisations, activists and individual teachers – both in and outside of the academy – who opposed this forgetting of the Sardinian Marxist. In this context, the establishment of the Italian Sessions by the Italian section of the International Gramsci Society (IGS) in 1996 was of great importance, contributing to the organisation of seminars and conferences, the collation of new editions and, beginning in 2001, seminars on the language of the *Notebooks*, encouraging a new collective process of studying the prison writings free from the burdens of prior interpretations, forming a new generation of Gramsci scholars.

This book – now in its second edition (expanded to include studies from 1997 to 2012) – includes an account of those interpretations and discussions of Gramsci which have taken place in Italy over these past fifteen years.

The first nine chapters that formed the first edition in 1996 have been altered as little as possible, with the exception of the ninth section of Chapter 9, which has been largely reworked, while the tenth section of the same chapter has been removed. For the rest, some notes have been added or completed, and corrections have been made to errors of printing and formatting. There are also additions relating to some essays that have been unjustly ignored, and a few opinions have been revised. I think the only significant modification is my re-evaluation of the previously under-estimated existence of a long distance exchange between Gramsci in Turi and Togliatti in exile; in the previous edition, I had favoured the hypothesis that Togliatti had wanted to break off relations with Gramsci in 1926.

Three chapters have been added on the development of Gramsci studies in the years following 1996. My reconstruction of the years 1996–2005 is the result of work undertaken in collaboration with Chiara Meta in our jointly-authored *Gramsci: Guida alla lettura* (Milan, Unicopoli 2005). Some of the opinions expressed there been partly revised in the new chapters. This is also the case for the many reviews and essays that I have written over the years for various journals, as well as for the website of the International Gramsci Society. The new chapters follow the design of the first edition, in which we decided to prioritise critical discussions whose impact is central to current interpretations.

Many friends have read whole chapters or parts of them, providing precious advice even if I have not always followed it. Aside from Chiara Meta, I extend my deepest gratitude to Lea Durante, Eleanora Forenza, Fabio Frosini, Raul Mordenti, Giuseppe Prestipino and Peter Thomas for their indispensable *dialogical* role. It is not merely a formality to say that the responsibility for the final product is mine alone.

My thanks also goes to the participants of the seminars on the interpretation of the *Notebooks* organised by the IGS Italia, whose collective work I have drawn upon for many years.

This book is dedicated to Carlos Nelson Coutinho, a friend who is with us no more. The intensification of his illness and his eventual passing away in

September 2012 interrupted a conversation which we had maintained at a distance for many years, 'along the internetted road', as he put it. Throughout the work of drafting the new chapters of this book I missed his advice and criticism but I believe that his significant contribution is present nevertheless, through the way he enriched my reading of both Gramsci and his interpreters over the years. Thank you, Carlos.

Preface to the First Edition

Antonio Gramsci is one of the most well known Italian authors in the world today. In his introduction to a collection of essays on the subject, Eric Hobsbawm (who was the first to really note this fact)[1] recently re-emphasised the magnitude of Gramsci's fortunes outside of Italy.[2] The American historian John M. Cammett has put together a bibliography of writings about Gramsci published between 1922 and 1993, which includes more than 10,000 titles.[3]

After a long phase of 'bad fortunes', interest in and debate regarding the author of the *Notebooks* seems to have been rekindled – including in Italy. This is despite the paradoxical fact that in the 1980s, exactly when Gramsci was becoming increasingly famous abroad, the Sardinian thinker was generally ignored in Italy itself. Lately even the political heirs of his torturers have attempted to put forward their own clumsy claims to his legacy, attempting to insert Gramsci into their own political family tree.[4]

To my mind, such efforts, although clearly instrumental, are only possible because while it is the case that Gramsci has become something of a *nome celebre*, a subject for polemical journalism, perhaps even a myth in some select areas of Italian politics and culture (though not very large ones, to tell the truth), his life, work and thought are not really understood or widely studied. The reason for this lies in the difficulty of approaching a body of work which comes across as disorganised and complex, labyrinthine and still significantly 'open'. The critical literature is not of particular assistance in this regard. Instead, the myriad of accumulating and overlapping interpretations and re-interpretations that have been produced over the decades are equally difficult to decipher, containing their own theoretical presuppositions and political motivations, thus providing their own additional obstacles rather than helping one in approaching the author himself.

The present work, therefore, hopes first and foremost to be a map for making one's way through the great book of Gramsci interpretation – the thousands of articles, essays and volumes that today comprise the *bibliographia*

---

1 Hobsbawm 1987.
2 E.J. Hobsbawm in Santucci 1995.
3 Cammett 1991, Cammett and Righi 1995. There is also an online version, periodically updated and including around 20,000 titles, on the website of the Fondazione Istituto Gramsci: *Bibliografia gramsciana*, edited by J.M. Cammett, F. Giasi and M.L. Righi.
4 For a critique of this position and an indicative bibliography, see Pistillo 1996.

gramsciana – by providing a volume dedicated to the Italian debates, one that complements similar work which has already been undertaken in other geographical contexts. There is an obvious difference however, in that Gramsci's presence is far more rooted within the history of his own country than elsewhere, meaning a history of interpretations of Gramsci in Italy must inevitably leave some issues *uncovered*, perhaps to the dissatisfaction of some of the protagonists. It is clear that the current work leaves some disciplines of study insufficiently analysed and under-represented, despite having been influenced by the author of the *Notebooks*. It is worth noting, in fact, that it is perhaps impossible to give an account of the repercussions of Gramsci's legacy through all of the developments within the different specialist lines of inquiry. We have chosen therefore to privilege the theoretical-political reflections and focus on *particular* studies (from historiography to literary criticism, from the study of Southern Italy to cultural anthropology and pedagogy) when such studies have taken on a significance which is of interest not only to the relevant specialists in those fields.

In any case, due to the peculiar fact that Gramsci was not only an intellectual or a philosopher or a politician but all of these things together, the history of the debates around Gramsci are not only a history of the reception of his thought but also of the story of Italian culture, in particular of the culture of the Italian left, its different phases of evolution and its intellectuals.

Without exception, all of the exponents of the most importance fields in twentieth-century Italian culture have grappled with Gramsci, whether to praise or condemn him. The reconstruction attempted in these pages shows how, throughout the period of time examined herein, there are two different interpretations of Gramsci that have frequently been opposed to each other. If it were not quite so hackneyed a formula, the title might have been *The Two Gramscis*.

First, there is the communist reading – whether in line with Togliatti, against him or in reaction to him. In their cultural and political turns, in fact, Italian communists have always proposed different, renewed readings of Gramsci, which has proven to be a litmus test for the transformations that have characterised the history of the Italian Communist Party. From 'the leader of the working class' and the party of antifascist martyrs, from the father of 'the politics of unity' after the war, a 'great Italian' and 'great intellectual', through to the inspiration for the Italian road to socialism; from the exponent of traditional national culture to the ambassador of Italian communism throughout the world and emblem of Eurocommunism; to the critical communist, and in the end the point of departure for a new possibility of being a communist after the crisis of 'real existing socialism'.

Alongside these we find another, equally varied but nevertheless distinct series of interpretations. This is the liberal-democratic, liberal-socialist, *pragmatic* interpretation, which relies on a different but consistently revived emphasis that, faced with a *communist* Gramsci, proposes a liberal and libertarian one, more intellectual than politician, frequently the yardstick by which to measure (negatively, and almost always uncharitably and prejudicially) his comrades in the party and in struggle. This line of interpretation again contains great diversity within itself, ranging from Gobetti and Prezzolini through to Croce ('as a man of thought, he was one of us') and right up to the supporters of the post-communist Gramsci of recent years.

How come there is this *contested Gramsci*, libertarian and Cominternist, councilist and Leninist, liberal and man of the party, intellectual and militant, communist critic and critic, *ante litteram*, of communism?

Of course, there have been plenty of episodes of patent instrumentalisation (not all of which have been abandoned). But even these were only possible by beginning from a shared factual starting point; they did not come from nowhere. At the basis stands the extraordinary richness and complexity of Gramsci's thought, whose conceptual repertoire can be – and continues to be – drawn on from different sides with very different objectives. This is without doubt a positive fact, perhaps the best proof of a thinker's greatness.

Gramsci is thus shown to be *more advanced* than nearly all of his interpreters, and also more problematic and more open. Due to the peculiarity of his biography (the gap represented by his arrest and his parallel affirmation of Stalinism; the fact that his work was to be known better after his death than in life, in times and places profoundly different from those in which it was conceived; the specific characteristics of being inextricably both intellectual and politician) has contributed to the possibility of these quite different readings.

Due to a complex weave of historical reasons, therefore, Gramsci perhaps represents a theatrical stage on which struggling elements have played out their battles for hegemony in Italy and the Italian left. His destiny has been that of being both an ideological weapon and a piece in the game, a 'protagonist' in the confrontation and a *locus* of different forces, projects, theoretical hypotheses and politics. It is for these reasons that, for the most part, the present work does not try to affirm or demonstrate the greater or lesser theoretical plausibility of the different interpretations of Gramsci under examination, but instead attempts to measure their meaning and historical significance objectively, in order to represent their greater or lesser validity *from within*.

This book is the product of continued study, not without interruption, over a considerable number of years, in the course of which some parts of it have been published in different articles which I would like to note: *Gramsci negli*

PREFACE TO THE FIRST EDITION

scritti dei suoi contemporanei, in *Critica marxista*, 1986, n. 4; *Dieci anni di studi gramsciani in Italia (1978–1987)*, in *Critica marxista*, 1987, n. 2–3; *Tradizione e indentitá di partito in Togliatti interprete di Gramsci*, in *Critica marxista*, 1988, n. 3–4; *Apogeo e crisi della cultura gramsciana in Italia*, in *Democrazia e diritto*, 1991, n. 1–2; *Il centenario gramsciano nella stampa italiana*, in *IG Informazioni*, 1991, n. 1; *La prima recezione di Gramsci in Italia (1944–1953)*, in *Studi storici*, 1991, n. 3; *Le letture di Gramsci nel dibattito della sinistra dopo il 1956*, in *Studi sorici*, 1992, n. 2–3.

I would like to express my gratitude to the journals in the aforementioned citations, and to their editors (Aldo Tortorella, Aldo Zanardo, Pietro Barcellona, Giuseppe Vacca, Francesco Barbagallo) for having supported me through the generous scholarly examination of my work. All the articles in question have been more or less significantly revised and modified, not only in their form for the sake of publication in a larger volume, but also in how they were originally conceived. If on one hand they might seem outdated in terms of their opinions and evaluations, on the other hand I would like to refer the reader back to them if they should desire a more specialised analysis, the kind from which I have needed to partially distance myself in the attempt to offer simultaneously a synthesis and an overview.

In particular I must thank Valentino Gerrantana, who read and discussed my work attentively with the greatest competence and meticulousness. Many thanks also to Joseph Buttigieg, Domenico Losurdo, Giorgio Lunghini, Carlo Montaleone and Antonio A. Santucci for reading the manuscript and encouraging me to publish it.

CHAPTER 1

Gramsci in the Writings of His Contemporaries (1922–38)

1 The Liberal History of a Sardinian Communist

Leafing through the bibliography on Gramsci that Elsa Fubini has put together and set in chronological order,[1] one quickly notices that the first important evaluation of Gramsci was written by Piero Gobetti. This is not only because he dedicated several pages of interest to the Communist leader in 1922,[2] in a moment in which (as Togliatti would later recall), 'Antonio Gramsci's own political strengths and his capacity to lead were recognised only by those to whom he was closest',[3] but also because it was thanks to Gobetti's influence that the name of Gramsci circulated at that time among other important, non-Communist exponents of Italian culture, such as Prezzolini and Guido Dorso. There was nothing accidental about this: they reflected both the reasons for objective convergence between the youth of the *Ordine Nuovo* and those groups of intellectuals more sensitive to a renewal of twentieth-century Italian culture, as well as the early results of that peculiar Gramscian attention to the issue of the relation to intellectuals which later would have very different repercussions. Indeed, in the light of this importance, one cannot help but notice in these earliest tentative interpretations a singular anticipation of the fate to which Gramsci's fortunes would be subject for a long period after Liberation, when so many non-Communist intellectuals would end up claiming that, to use Croce's words, 'as a man of thought, he was one of us'.[4]

Others have reconstructed the complex relation between Gramsci and Gobetti.[5] It will suffice here simply to focus our attention on the specific places in which the young 'liberal revolutionary' spoke about Gramsci. Sketching an image of a Turin on the cutting edge of the processes of industrialisation, the

---

1 See Fubini 1969 and Fubini 1979.
2 See P. Gobetti, *Storia dei comunisti torinesi scritta da un liberale*, in *La rivoluzione liberale*. 1922, issue 7; P. Gobetti, *Uomini e ideee. Gramsci*, in *La rivoluzione liberale*, 1924, issue 17; and the essay *I comunisti* in Gobetti 1924. Now all in Gobetti 1960 (to which edition I will make future references).
3 Togliatti 2001, p. 283.
4 Croce 1947, p. 86.
5 See above all Spriano 1977.

location in which a workers' movement was fomenting in 1922, Gobetti did not hesitate to claim that 'the theory of this new intellectual and economic reality was being attempted by a group of obscure youngsters',[6] i.e. the promoters of the *Ordine Nuovo* and Antonio Gramsci foremost among them. His big idea was the factory council: simultaneously an organism for educating the working class in how to govern the factory and the state, and also the means of organisation for the current struggle. For Gobetti, following Pareto, this saw the creation of a new power, a new *hierarchy*, in order to promote an 'aristocracy from below',[7] moving towards 'a state that might know how to solve the bourgeois crisis and confront the unresolved problems inherited from Unification'.[8]

Two years later, in 1924, in an article dedicated to the communist leader on the occasion of his election to parliament, and anticipating the image of Gramsci as intervening in Parliament and forcing 'the Fascist members of parliament into collective silence though his slight and subtle voice', Gobetti claimed that 'Gramsci is more than a tactician and a combatant, he is a prophet'.[9] On this occasion, Gobetti also provided a more human sketch of Gramsci (one which would be reprised and amplified in *La rivoluzione liberale*) and in which Gobetti's affected moralistic style was amalgamated with moments of a more complex description. 'Antonio Gramsci', he wrote, 'has the head of a revolutionary; his figure seems to have been constructed through will alone ... the mind has overwhelmed the body'.[10] This is a Gramsci who has been physically remade in the process of leaving his 'provincial' condition. And this *will* was, for Gobetti, not only a fact of his character, but also of his politics and culture:

> He has that kind of passion for categorical and dogmatic clarity one finds among dreamers, a passion that blocks sympathy and communicative ease [...] behind an ethical concern of his political program lies a dry rigour and cosmic gravity that does not concede a single moment of leniency.[11]

---

6   Gobetti 1960, p. 281.
7   Gobetti 1960, p. 288.
8   Gobetti 1960, p. 293.
9   Gobetti 1960, pp. 645 and 647.
10   Gobetti 1960, p. 1001. This image will be taken up again, and with the same words, in Germanetto 1931. [Translator's note: titles are generally left in the original Italian, with exceptions for Gramsci's works (where translated) and where the sense of the text is lost without translation.]
11   Gobetti 1960, p. 1004.

Indeed, in line with Gobetti's idea that the youth of the *Ordine Nuovo* were the inheritors of the bourgeois revolutionary tradition of Unification, behind this description of Gramsci one can make out a kind of Robespierre, so central to the traditional iconography.

One might say that Gobetti constituted a kind of mediator between the *Ordine Nuovo* and Prezzolini, as is shown by two letters written in these years. In the first, dated 25 June 1920, the young liberal wrote to Prezzolini about the movement of the factory councils, along with a brief and admiring portrait of Gramsci. Divided though he was

> between his studies and political propaganda ... he himself brought together the night workers who could not study, and he did so through bringing them closer to culture, sincerity, morality; he did all this disinterestedly, humbly ... even if he was not generally known, he had a huge influence throughout socialist circles, and the Turin section followed his lead.[12]

In his small volume of 1923, *La coltura italiana*, Prezzolini wrote again about the *Ordine Nuovo*, describing them as seeds of a future 'new socialist world' and insisting on the importance of the movement of the factory councils, seeing a 'Bergsonian creation' in their working-class membership. There is another aspect to this, however, which is more important to emphasise: an evaluation of the shift from 'cultural' activity within the *Ordine Nuovo* to something more strictly 'political', which began with the founding of the Communist Party of Italy (PCd'I). Prezzolini wrote:

> having had the chance to produce a newspaper and then throwing themselves into militant politics seems to me to have smothered this small group's creativity, along with their accompanying original genius and beliefs, as is so often the case. For their Party it will surely be a plus. As a reader, I am quite bitter about the fact.[13]

---

12   Prezzolini 1971, p. 19. In a second letter to Prezzolini the following year, Gobetti proposed to edit a small volume of Gramsci's writings for *La Voce*, which would bring together 'his more important articles on the factory councils. If you want, there will also be an introductory preface' (Prezzolini 1971, p. 42). The proposal was not to be taken up.

13   Prezzolini 1923, p. 122. In the second revised edition, Prezzolini wrote of the youth of the *Ordine Nuovo*: 'Their morals, founded on the concept of the necessity of struggle, allowed them to understand the revolution as sacrifice, the life of a communist as a kind of mission, and propaganda as the basis for a heroic conception of existence. This brought them close to idealism, and in the early years they happily cited Croce and Gentile, from studies on which they had built'. Prezzolini 1930, p. 161.

It is an opinion which Gobetti shared in his own book in 1924. Gramsci and Togliatti shared the same cultural background as Gobetti, 'based in the bourgeois culture that developed in the first fifteen years of the twentieth century':[14] Croce and *La Voce*, Salvemini and Einaudi, Sorel and Mosca. To understand how their positions diverged, one can turn to Togliatti's review of Prezzolini's volume:

> There has always been a line of separation, an abyss, between our culture and our lives. 'Intelligence' is always separated off from the other faculties either because it is kept apart, either because it is unable to understand the necessity of an organic bond between all forms of life, or because it is unable to translate into practice a unity which has been achieved and demonstrated in the mind.[15]

What radically separated the youth of *Ordine Nuovo* from the liberal thought in which they had been in contact during their development was that Gobetti and Prezzolini essentially still judged matters from the standpoint of the *separation* of 'Italian intelligence' from the national scene, according to which the foundation of the PCd'I constituted a rupture, one that could not be easily smoothed over.

One position which was close to Gobetti's, but also original in its insistence on the 'Southern question' (developed from the ideas of Salvemini and Fortunato), was that of Guido Dorso, whose *Rivoluzione meridionale* – 'Southern Revolution' – came out in 1925, edited by Gobetti himself. It included an interpretation of 'Gramsci's inherent Marxism', connected both to the movement of the councils and, above all, to what he called the passage from Marxism to Leninism, from workers' revolution to the peasants':

> The merit of this revision should be almost entirely attributed to Gramsci, who knew ... how to bring together the essential elements of Leninist thought ... This young, well-read Sardinian, having being the first to show the true dialectical motion of the Italian crisis through the theory of the factory councils, was then the first to discover the kernel of the Italian problem in the development of the agrarian question.[16]

---

14 Asor Rosa 1975, p. 1442.
15 Togliatti, *La 'intelligenza' italiana*, in *Il lavoratore*, 23rd May 1923; now in Togliatti 1967b, p. 490.
16 Dorso 1925, p. 203. In a negative review of Dorso's book (in *Il lavoro*, October 1st 1925), Giovanni Ansaldo also criticised Gramsci, an episode mentioned in the *Prison Notebooks* (Gramsci 1975, pp. 48 and 2485).

In a work on this very matter (*Alcuni temi della quistione meridionale*) Gramsci had underlined the importance of stabilising a positive relationship between groups of liberal intellectuals.[17] In this sense, Gobetti and Dorso, leaving aside the merits of their positions, thus represented the most interesting figures in Italy at the time.

2 Off the 'High Road'

If liberal writers appreciated Gramsci for the heterodox basis of his political theory, this was also a reason for scandal and polemics within the Communist Party itself. This is shown in an article by Ruggero Grieco from 1924, published by Bordiga in *Prometeo*, of interest to us here because it falls into the period of transition between the Bordigist current and that of the new leading group which Gramsci formed around his own political positions.[18] Grieco, who collaborated closely with Bordiga, approved of working in the 'centre' of the party – a position in which he differed from Bordiga himself. In this situation, the article on Gramsci hosted by *Prometeo* in its second issue necessarily reflected the contradictory position of its author, caught as he was between cohering to the theses of the 'left' Bordigists on the one hand and the 'centrist' position which was opening up on the other – positions between which there was a growing and problematic divide.

Grieco referred to Gramsci's cultural background, the influence of Croce and Gentile; and he observed how Gramsci had 'arrived at Marx via the cathedral of Hegel', and therefore would 'arrive at Marxism, in a sense, in the same way in which Marx had arrived at it'. Grieco did not believe this however to be the 'high road', that is, the outlining of 'the deterministic laws that guide wage workers (the scientific work of communist acolytes)':[19] an obvious conclusion, as its author was already dependent on a form of economistic Marxism which he would hold in common with Bordiga for the greater part of the Second and Third Internationals, and against which Gramsci would struggle, as his main theoretical battle, while in prison. Rejecting the 'slanderous' figure of an interventionist Gramsci at the beginning of the First World War (though forming the hypothesis that on such questions the young Sardinian had 'some doubts') Grieco recalled the experience of the *Ordine Nuovo* which, notwithstanding its 'traces of idealism', had to be given credit for going beyond its initial results.

---

17 Gramsci 1978 [1926].
18 Spriano 1967, from p. 291.
19 R. Grieco, *Gramsci*, in *Prometeo*, 1924, n. 2, p. 29.

It was here, however, that an echo of polemic resurfaced more strongly, as the young Turinese group had opposed Bordiga's journal, *Soviet*. The experience of the councils of the Turin proletariat, Grieco wrote, 'perhaps distracted Gramsci and his group from a more comprehensive vision of the general problems of the Italian proletariat, the results of which prepared the defeats of the 1920s'. Their work in provoking the revolutionary energy of the masses of Turin nevertheless 'failed to identify the organ of coordination, synthesis and leadership: that is, the revolutionary party'.[20] These are positions which return time and again in the debates of those years when one reconstructs the historiography. We will see how Togliatti, when speaking about Gramsci, will respond to the thesis that Grieco expresses here. He will also repeat the attempt to describe the leading Sardinian as 'the learned', 'erudite Marxist', sketching out a purely intellectual figure, just as he had been portrayed – in a more vindictive manner – in the pages of *Prometeo*.

3 The Sentence

Between 28 May and 4 June 1928, although scheduled for the previous summer, the special court in Rome opened the so-called 'great trial' of the leaders of the PCd'I, concluding with Gramsci's sentencing to more than twenty years in prison. Between September 1927 and September 1928, articles and news on the '*procès monstre*' in Rome and about the Communists detained in Fascist prisons appeared in *La Correspondance internationale*, the bulletin of the Comintern in Paris, written in French and signed by Ercoli, Leonetti and Trostel.[21] Of these articles, only the first (Leonetti's, dated 24 September 1927) contained any specific reference to Gramsci, describing the story of his imprisonment and above all the extremely precarious condition of his health, put under strain as it was by his transferral and lack of any proper treatment. As the title indicated, according to Leonetti, *Antonio Gramsci se meurt de faim* – 'Antonio Gramsci is dying of hunger'. This method of campaigning to support the leading prisoners also inspired a letter from Piero Sraffa (signed 'An Italian in England') in

---

20   R. Grieco, *Gramsci*, in *Prometeo*, 1924, n. 2, p. 30. In a letter from March 27th 1924, Gramsci wrote to Togliatti: 'I still have not read Grieco's article in *Prometeo* about me: however in March 1923, after the arrests, I did read an article in *Lavoratore* which I think is also by Grieco, which contained appraisals which seem to me completely erroneous'. Gramsci 1992, p. 295.

21   *La Correspondance internationale*, 1927, issues 98, 100, 122; and 1928, issues 50 and 103.

the *Manchester Guardian* on 24 October 1927,[22] as well as an anonymous note which appeared in *La Correspondance internationale* on 12 May 1928, entitled *Le vie de Gramsci et de Tulli est en danger* – 'The lives of Gramsci and Tulli are in danger'. These alarms regarding the prisoner's health, a moment in which Gramsci would show his strength,[23] nevertheless lack any evaluation of Gramsci or his activity as a leading Communist. There is one important exception: the article which Togliatti wrote for *Lo stato operario* in October 1927, which began the long series of his contributions, continuing up until 1964, specifically dedicated to the figure of the Sardinian leader.

The article in question is entitled *Antonio Gramsci un capo della classe operaia (In occasione del processo di Roma)* – 'Antonio Gramsci, a leader of the working class'. The report begins by confronting the issue of the intellectual and political management of the Gramscian 'legacy' which Togliatti formed out of Gramsci's arrest and sentencing. It has been argued that the relation between the two leaders is 'not so much a chapter, but rather a watermark that one can clearly read running across a large part of the history of the Communist Party'.[24] Theirs is a complicated personal and political history, a long distance from the hagiographic image of perfect identity which has been commonly composed ever since the 1930s. It lasted from the university years to those of the *Ordine Nuovo*, through the split at Livorno, and continuing into the complicated process of the formation of the new group of leading Communists. The few months following this, between 1925 and 1926, represented the moment both of greatest proximity and greatest distance: the preparation of the Lyons conference, an act that came close to a refounding of the party, as well as a political (and also human) clash over attitudes towards the struggles within the Russian Communist Party. The relationship between Togliatti and Gramsci, if not interrupted, was nonetheless profoundly muted after this point, a transformation that was compounded by the impossibility of a direct exchange between the imprisoned Gramsci and Togliatti, first head of the party and then of the international Communist movement.[25]

---

22   'An Italian in England', (P. Sraffa), *The methods of fascism*, October 24th 1927, now in Gramsci 1965, p. 913. On the background to the publication of Sraffa's letter, see Potier 1990, pp. 41–2.

23   In a letter to his wife dated April 30th 1928, Gramsci wrote: 'My health is good enough. I know via judiciary and prison authorities that many inexactitudes have been published on my account: that I died of hunger, etc etc. This is very upsetting for me, because I know that in such matters there is no need to make things up, nor to exaggerate'. Gramsci 1996, p. 186.

24   Spriano 1980, p. 87.

25   The form and content of the long-distance conversation between Gramsci and Togliatti

Togliatti's article from 1927 ought to be read within this context, one that helps us to understand (aside from the homage paid to Gramsci) his difficulty in laying out their recent political positions. Togliatti wanted to propose a historical tradition that might sustain the leadership and thus consolidate the approach of the PCd'I which he had achieved with so much difficulty after its Bordigist 'early period' – but in a moment in which Togliatti was not yet the undisputed leader he was to become in the 1930s:

> The history of out party is yet to be written. Whoever comes to write it and wants to understand the fundmentals of its historical formation as the vanguard of the working class *over and above all the particular political and organisational moments*, must give a special place of honour to Antonio Gramsci.[26]

In an autobiographical note which explicitly recognised a political primogeniture, he added that:

> without Gramsci, the progress we made in 1924 and beyond would not have been so quick. He overcame that resistance that some of us still felt, and provided our central leadership with a unity and homogeneity, and the whole party gathered around him.[27]

The struggle against Bordiga returned nonetheless. Gramsci had to deal yet again with the old accusations of 'intellectualism'. The victory of Marxism was in departing from Hegel and claiming the 'high road', 'the road by which Karl Marx and Friedrich Engels had come to socialism and historical materialism', the only road which understood how 'the soul of the Hegelian and Marxist dialectic' could join with that 'sense of history of all that is real' which had characterised Gramsci's early thought.[28] And it was, finally, the Bordigist thesis on the gaps in the movement of *Ordine Nuovo* which Togliatti refuted, claiming that:

---

has been recently reconstructed in Vacca 2012. But also see Vacca and Rossi 2007; Rossi 2010. On the relation between the two leaders of the Communist Party allow me also to recommend my introduction to Togliatti 2001. Also, on the exchanges of letters of 1926 and a full contextualisation, see Vacca 1999.

26 Togliatti, *Antonio Gramsci un capo della classe operaia (In occasione del processo di Roma)*, in *Lo stato operaio*, 1927, n. 8. Now in Togliatti 2001, p. 41 (my emphasis).
27 Togliatti 2001, p. 43.
28 Togliatti 2001, p. 42.

it was in the propaganda for the factory councils in 1919–1920 that the seeds and development of all the principles and doctrines of the party were to be found – not the party as a sect or as a barracks or any other pseudo-military organisation, but of the party as an organised section of the working class, a part of it, irrevocably bound to it, the leader of the proletariat in every moment of its history.[29]

This was a clear political position, one that only a year after the break of 1926 would have sounded like a *defence* of Gramsci and an important reaffirmation of his (far from certain) 'leadership' in the eyes of the Russian Party and the International.[30] It was also the beginning of a historical tradition which privileged the formation of a new collective identity of a party that, in some ways, still had to overcome the 'extremism' of its Bordigist phase. It was an attitude which had to be continually restated, even at the expense of evading urgent matters of current political debates and positions.

With the sentencing of the Sardinian leader and the *de facto* 'succession' of Togliatti to the top of the party[31] came a more difficult period, as far as the relation between Gramsci and the PCd'I was concerned. This difficulty became apparent through the events following the letter of 1926, the international Communist movement's 'turn' in those years, and the consequent acquiescence of the Italian party.[32] With respect to this last point it is worth noting that Gramsci registered his own dissent even from within his imprisonment in Turin. In the discussions that took place in 1930 with other detained Communists, Gramsci

---

29   Togliatti 2001, p. 43.
30   See, on this and in on general on the relation between Gramsci and Togliatti, Agosti 1996, from p. 110.
31   Togliatti was to be elected secretary of the Communist Party only at the 5th Congress of the party, immediately following Liberation. In the 1930s there were various different successors to the position of Secretary, while Togliatti worked within the ranks of the International.
32   In July 1929 the 10th Executive of the Comintern imposed on the member parties the political doctrine of 'social fascism', already prepared by the 6th Congress. In this position Togliatti, in harmony with Gramsci's positions, tried to resist the imposition (see the text of his intervention, which appeared under the title *L'orientamento del nostra partito nelle questioni internazionali*, in *Lo stato operaio*, 1928; for the reconstruction of the episode see Fiori 1991, pp. 29–30.) At the 10th Plenum, Togliatti and Grieco finally tried to defend the 'politics of Lyons' and the 'popular', non-sectarian character of the antifascist struggle, but had to capitulate under pressure from the International and the position in which the small Pcd'I found itself, exiled and persecuted by a triumphant Fascism. Togliatti declared on this occasion: 'Is it right or wrong to put these questions ...? If the Comintern says that it isn't right, we will do it no more; each of us will think these things and speak of them no more'. (See the reconstruction of the entire episode in Ragionieri 1976, p. 703 onwards).

held that a democratic phase was necessary in order to find a way out of Fascism. Gramsci's profound dissent from the politics of the party spread quickly among the detained Communists throughout Italy, and already by March 1931 Umberto Terracini informed the 'centre' of the party of this fact.[33] This fundamental difference added to another, growing difference in Togliatti and Gramsci's personal relations; furthermore, there was the matter of Gramsci's general approach, for it was understood he had little inclination for illegal activities. Above all, communication between the prisoner and his main political interlocutors continued through a 'circle of virtue' put in place by the PCd'I and the International: Piero Sraffa and his sister-in-law Tania Schucht guaranteed order within the line of communication through a complex system of copied letters sent to the top of the party.[34] What remains clear is that from the moment of his arrest, Gramsci and Togliatti's activities were now placed on different levels.[35]

One should certainly not miss the significance of the fact that Togliatti – as well as Leonetti, Ravazzoli and Tresso, 'the three' who openly opposed the 'turn' (and were consequently expelled) – called on Gramsci to defend and strengthen their respective positions. For example Leonetti, in the meeting of the political section on 28–29 August 1929, explicitly opposed Gramsci's position to Togliatti's,[36] heralding a form of argument destined to be reprised many times over and utilised as a political weapon. Togliatti himself published *Stato operaio* ('Workers' state'), a collection of Gramsci's writings – both previously published and otherwise[37] – the first issue of which, in January 1930, featured the essay given the title 'Some Themes on the Southern Question',[38] which referenced the heightened struggle against the 'three' for the first time.[39] The

---

33 See Terracini 1975, p. 71.
34 See Vacca 2012 and Canfora 2012.
35 As has been noted, Gramsci's suspicions were increased by the "strange letter" from Grieco in 1928: see Spriano 1977, from p. 25 onwards, and below pp. 319, 327, 333, 454–5.
36 See Ragionieri 1976, p. 422.
37 See *Stato operaio*, 1927, issues 3 and 6; 1928, issues 3 and 10; 1929 issue 1; 1930 issue 4; 1931, issues 3 and 4.
38 Gramsci's manuscript bore the title *Note sul problema meidionale e sull'atteggiamento nei suoi confronti dei comunisti, dei socialisti e dei democratici*. See the critical edition edited by F.M. Biscione in *Critica marxista*, 1990, issue 3.
39 For Giorgio Amendola the publication of this essay by Gramsci was 'a political act whose value we must not underestimate. At the centre of Gramsci's essay was the theme of the alliance of the working class with the peasantry and the working population of the South. The development of the argument, the emphasis on the function of intellectuals, went against the schematism introduced in the communist International in the struggle with

reprinting of the essay on 'The Program of the *Ordine Nuovo*'[40] was also significant, recalling the preceding argument against Tasca, and was issued along with other accounts by protagonists of the factory occupations of 1920; it was published on the occasion of their tenth anniversary, of which Gramsci spoke in almost apologetic terms.[41] Another essay by Gramsci was also published in March–April 1931, and in June an article appeared by Amendola which cited the Sardinian Communist and openly espoused the importance of his work.[42] In the same month (while in Paris to celebrate the tenth anniversary of the PCd'I) Egidio Gennari praised the leading role which Gramsci had played between 1924 and 1926, years in which he was apparently confirmed as 'the head of the party'.[43] After this there is an interruption in references to the imprisoned leader, an interruption which lasted around two and a half years, ending in November-December 1933 with an article by 'Luigi Gallo' (Longo's pseudonym) entitled 'Centralism, federalism, autonomy'.[44] In the meantime there had been abortive projects to publish Gramsci's writings under the title 'The Factory Councils and the Workers' State' – which we know about thanks to correspondence between Togliatti and Tasca,[45] as well as the plan for a 'Notebook of *Stato operaio*' on occasion of the tenth anniversary of the PCd'I, for which Togliatti planned to write an essay on the *Ordine Nuovo*.[46] Instead an article by him appeared in the same magazine, titled 'Our Experience' (La nostra esperienza), which made no mention of Gramsci whatsoever, nor of *Ordine Nuovo*.[47] Without doubt, in all these cases, the omissions are as meaningful as the results, and evidence the now dominant climate in the international communist movement, and the impossibility of conserving within it a secure place for the political and cultural specificity of a party like the PCd'I, especially on a historiographic level. It was indeed precisely this terrain of historical reconstruction

---

the "turn" ... Gramsci clearly reaffirmed, with the publication of the thesis on the Southern questions, the validity of that political legacy which he had always tried to defend'. Amendola 1978, p. 185.

40 *Lo Stato operaio*, 1930, issue 4.
41 V. Bianco, *La organizzazione militare rivoluzionaria durante l'occupazione*, in *Lo Stato operaio*, 1930, issues 11–12.
42 A. Gramsci, *Necessità di una preparazione ideologica di massa*, in *Lo Stato operaio*, 1931, issues 3–4; and Amendola, *Con il proletariato o contro il prolerariato?*, in *Lo Stato operaio*, 1931, issue 6.
43 See the account of Gennari's speech in *La celebrazione del X anniversario del Pcd'I*, in *La vie prolétarienne*, June 25th 1931.
44 *Lo Stato operaio*, 1933, issues 11–12.
45 Ragionieri 1976, pp. 383–5 and pp. 723–4.
46 Ragionieri 1976, pp. 723–24.
47 *Lo Stato operaio*, 1931, issue 1.

in which Stalin directly intervened, with his famous article 'On the Subject of Some Questions on the History of Bolshevism', which *Lo stato operaio* reproduced in its entirety in December 1931. It must also be said that if Togliatti and the PCd'I were not able to publicise the bond they actually held with a leader who during this period was classified as a heretic, as was evidently the case with Gramsci, they did manage – in the years in which four members of the political office hostile to the turn were expelled (i.e. Ignazio Silone and the 'three' already mentioned above) – to maintain a simple *silence*, maintaining their connection with Gramsci as much as they could: an umbilical cord which remained as vital and revocable, if not as strong, as the *iron bond* with the USSR.

4   Prison

It is not until we reach 1933–1934 that we find a new series of interventions and articles about Gramsci. Two circumstances converged: the decline of the 'social Fascism' thesis, the gradual closing of the gap between the Communists and the Socialists, resulting in the pact of unity of action in 1934 and the politics of the Popular Front in 1935; and, at the same time, news regarding the situation of the leading Sardinian's health, which was becoming extremely concerning. The rumour of Gramsci's death circulated among the anti-Fascist opposition abroad; the organ of the *Concentazione antifascita*, 'La libertá', published an alarmed text on 23 March 1933 titled: 'Gramsci dead in prison?'. The newspaper *La vie prolétarienne*, printed in Italian as 'the organ of the French Communist Party', put out a series of calls for mobilisations to 'force Fascism to free Gramsci'.[48] It was signed by '*l'opposition de gauche du Parti comuniste italien*', and on 21 April even Leonetti, one of the 'three', sent an article for a united mobilisation in support of Gramsci to *La Vérité* – a Trotskyist newspaper – reprinted by *La Libertá* (4 May) and *Avanti!* (6 May). The Socialist newspaper (which on 4 March had already published an anonymous paragraph in which the attention given to Gramsci by the *Concentrazione repubblicana* during the Matteotti crisis was juxtaposed to the 'sterile sectarianism' of Togliatti during the period of social Fascism)[49] followed-up the reprint of Leonetti's letter with a note by

---

48   *Il fascismo vuole assassinare Gramsci*, in *La vie prolétarienne*, April 5th 1933; and moreover: *Salviamo Gramse e Thaelmann*, in *La vie prolétarienne*, April 12th 1933; *Rendeteci Gramsci*, in *La vie prolétarienne*, May 1st 1933; *Viva Gramsci*, in *La vie prolétarienne*, May 21st 1933. The first moment of concerned voices came out in the daily of the PCF, *L'Humanité* (in the issues of March 26th–28th and 30th).

49   See *Da Gramsci a Ercoli*, in *Avanti!*, 1933, issue 10.

Angelo Tasca supporting the necessity of defending the detained anti-Fascists irrespective of any divisions within the party, but not without also claiming that 'Palmiro Togliatti, Stalin's lackey, is without doubt boycotting the actions in support of Gramsci due to his hatred of the Communist opposition which the latter had organised'.[50]

Communist sectarianism of the 1930s is, however, another topic. Nevertheless, it is not true that the PCd'I failed to fight for Gramsci's liberation and that of other detained anti-Fascists, even if it did so after a little hesitation.[51] The second issue of *Azione antifascista* in June 1933 was dedicated entirely to the imprisoned victims of Fascism: other than Gramsci, there were articles on the socialist Pertini and the anarchist Lucetti. On this occasion, Athos Lisa, Velio Spano, Mario Montagnana, Ruggero Grieco and the socialist Eugenio Bianco made interventions in support of Gramsci.[52] The articles, both biographical and commemorative, do not mention any of the post-1926 disagreements.

It was in this context that, in the August 1933 edition of *Giustizia e libertà*, the most interesting essay of the period appeared: 'Gramsci and the *Ordine Nuovo*', by 'Fabrizio', a pseudonym for Umberto Calosso, who stated that he wanted to describe Gramsci without falling into a 'funereal elegy'[53] (that is, without sparing criticism). Gramsci's particularity, claimed Calosso, was to have conceived of revolution not 'as a frontal attack, but as an explosion of the seeds from within. Gramsci saw these seeds, the wealth of the future, in the factory commissions'.[54] For him this represented both the high point of Gramsci's project and also its limitation: the elaboration of a form of creative proletarian organisation, useful for the 'constructive needs' of activity but unsuited to the particular historical phase, failing to match up to the rhythm of the development of the hastening crisis, which required speed for the mobilising of the masses in preparation for the defeat of Fascism. According to Calosso, this was why the experiment of *Ordine Nuovo* had 'ended up as a "mythology of the concrete", losing sight of the vital work of the moment'.

---

50 Alfa [A. Tasca], *Antonio Gramsci muore. Difendiamo la vita dei carcerati politici*, in *Avanti!*, 1933, issue 19. For the works of Claudio Natoli, see below p. 364.
51 On the campaign for Gramsci's liberation organised by the Pcd'I, the attempts to liberate other imprisoned leaders and, more generally, on the relations between Gramsci in prison and his party, see Pistillo 1989.
52 See *Azione antifascista*, 1933, issue 2.
53 Fabrizio [U. Calosso], *Gramsci e l' 'Ordine Nuovo'*, in *Quaderno di 'Giustizia e libertà'*, 1933, issue 8, p. 71.
54 Fabrizio [U. Calosso], *Gramsci e l' 'Ordine Nuovo'*, in *Quaderno di 'Giustizia e libertà'*, 1933, issue 8, p. 73.

The majority of writings about Gramsci in these years continued to be strictly bound up with biographical points and political contingency, that is, with either immediate polemic or antifascist hagiography. In 1934 Romain Rolland, an intellectual who Gramsci had held in high regard at the time of *Ordine Nuovo*, put out a booklet called 'Antonio Gramsci: Those Who Are Dying in Mussolini's Prisons'. Rolland emphasised the originality of the idea of the councils, even downplaying the importance of the influence of the October Revolution, recalling Gramsci's political and cultural depth, a man 'who never separated philosophy from politics'.[55]

In the same year there was an interesting polemic in the columns of *La nostra bandiera*, the PCd'I's weekly newspaper printed in France. In February an essay appeared by a young activist, Nicola Potenza, who, having met Gramsci in Rome in summer 1924, provided a description of his recollections, juxtaposing him to 'those luminaries who understand everything at once, who "intuit" the reason for everything in flashes of ... genius, and discharge rounds of "synthesised ideas" as if from a machine gun'.[56] Gramsci prevented himself from resolving issues in such a schematic manner, claimed Potenza, multiplying the problems instead, questioning everything before arriving at a synthesis. Two issues later, the paper hosted an apology titled 'On Our Gramsci (Addendum to an Apology)' signed by 'G'. (probably Ruggero Grieco, known at the time as Garlandi). The tone of the article made it clear that this was an official correction to be taken heed of. Potenza's description, wrote 'G'., 'is not the Gramsci that we know; this is not the Gramsci who is "leader of our party"'. In this light one cannot understand how Gramsci was not just a leader, but above all a 'Communist leader'. Nor did Grieco find it acceptable for Gramsci to be seen as an intellectual capable only of 'filling his comrades' heads' with nothing but doubts and problems. For him it was essential, rather, that Gramsci '*went to the school of the working class*'. Above all, his real merit was in having pressed on the levers of power and in fact 'Gramsci's error (if there has been one) was that he did not *immediately* see the importance of forming a Communist Party', even though his experience with the working class of Turin had allowed him to reject the errors of the 'Bordigist' leaders. Gramsci, therefore, was above all 'a man of the party'. Without the Party, Gramsci 'is something else entirely ... something that does not interest us'. In the final analysis, Potenza's error lay in a 'liberal conception of the Party', the understanding that every militant could critically rethink every directive of the Central Committee rather than showing discip-

---

55   Rolland 1934.
56   N. Potenza, *Che cosa era Gramsci per noi giovani*, in *La nostra bandiera*, 1934, issue 24.

lined obedience; and his veiled accusation of the current leadership as being (in distinction to Gramsci) empty and pretentious 'luminaries'.[57]

This authoritative reply from 'G.' is interesting first of all for its mention of Gramsci's 'error', which took up the tradition of the polemic against the Bordigists, that is, the undervaluing of the matter of the Party in the period of the *Ordine Nuovo*, which we have already seen in Grieco's writings in 1924 and which Togliatti had repeated in 1927. Secondly, one notes the emphasis on Gramsci as 'man of the party', a typical interpretation provided by the Communist Party before the Second World War, which was to be revoked only in the context of a 'New Party', when Gramsci was represented instead as the 'inheritance' of all Italians. Among the Communists themselves there remained, however, a remarkable disparity of opinion over Gramsci and the concept of the party, as we will see in Togliatti's writings of 1937–38.

Over the years of the Popular Front, Gramsci once again took up his role as protagonist in the history of the PCd'I, and Grieco was able to write, even in the pages of *Stato operaio* (in which the name of Gramsci had been ignored for a considerable number of months) that 'we have taken the road opened up by Gramsci and developed his study of the *Italian situation* of the proletarian revolution and that of our country',[58] claiming that it was Gramsci's development of this 'second phase' that had culminated in the Lyons Congress, transforming the theoretical and political framework of Italian communism.

5   Death

Gramsci died on 27 April 1937. The official press reported the news on the 29 April,[59] and returned to the subject the following day, juxtaposing the manner of Gramsci's death – 'his last days spent in a sunny clinic in Rome' – to the Italians accused of Bordigism who had been disappeared in the USSR.[60] An article signed by Mussolini reprised the argument a few months later, claiming that

---

57 'G.', *Sul nostro Gramsci (Postilla a una 'apologia')*, in *La nostra bandiera*, 1934, issue 26. Two weeks later, in the same journal (which in the meantime had changed name), Potenza gave the ritual self-criticism in a new contribution called *Gramsci capo del nostro Partito (Per stroncare le speculazioni)*, in *La bandiera dei lavoratori*, 1934, issue 2.
58 R. Grieco, *Il carattere internazionale della rivoluzione proletaria e le 'particolarità nazionali'*, in *Lo Stato operaio*, 1935, issue 7. (My italics).
59 *La morte dell'ex deputato Gramsci*, in *Il Messaggero*, 29th April 1937.
60 *Una sparizione e una morte*, in *Il Messaggero*, 12th May 1937. Canfora claims that this article could not have been written by Mussolini. Canfora 2012, pp. 123 onwards.

Gramsci, after a brief period of confinement in prison, was allowed to reside in a clinic in either partial or complete privacy. Furthermore, he died by disease and not by lead, unlike those generals, diplomats and high-ranking communists in Russia whenever they show even the smallest dissent from Stalin – and which would have taken out Gramsci too if he had gone to Moscow.[61]

The news of Gramsci's death in the antifascist and Communist press contained a very different tone of course: 'Our Comrade Gramsci Is Dead' wrote *l'Humanité* on 28 April. The leader was commemorated by Bruno Buozzi, Carlo Rosselli and Egidio Gennari during a demonstration in Paris on 22 May.[62] The organ of the Comintern, *La Correspondance internationale*, provided a profile of the disappeared leader, mainly recalling his contribution to the founding of the PCd'I on the basis of a platform 'which Lenin, at the 2nd Congress of the Communist International, had characterised as the closest to the Bolshevik position'.[63] The text was translated for *Stato operaio*, which published messages from the central committee of the PCd'I, the International and other party Communists alongside some extracts on Croce from Gramsci's prison letters and the first part of Togliatti's essay 'Antonio Gramsci: Leader of the Italian Working Class'.

The 'two leaders' – Gramsci in prison and Togliatti at the head of the party and the International – was a formula which had already been introduced in 1936.[64] On the occasion of Gramsci's death, however, this combination was officially reintroduced, partially reviving what had by then become a classic, stereotypical formula of the Communist movement.[65] The words of the Central Committee remembered Gramsci as 'the founder of the Communist Party in Italy', 'beloved leader of our Party', 'the greatest Italian of the century', adding that 'Palmiro Togliatti (Ercoli), leader of our Party, is his greatest student'. They emphasised that the Sardinian leader, beneath his political image, had also been the first to deal with 'the problem of the unity of the Italian people, of the

---

61 *Altarini*, in *Il popolo d'Italia*, 31st December 1937; now in Mussolini 1959, vol. xxxix, p. 45. An article to the right of this note by Mussolini was provided by an Italo-American anarchist newspaper, which published a sketch of Gramsci as an odious privileged communist, in cahoots with the other communists. See E. Taddei, *Di ritorno*, in *L'adunata dei refrattari*, December 4th 1937. On Taddei and his version of anti-Gramscian calumny at the beginning of the Communist Party, see Canfora 2012, pp. 131 onwards.
62 *Il comizio per Gramsci*, in *Giustizia e libertà*, May 28th 1937.
63 *La Correspondance internationale*, 1937, issue 19.
64 *I nostri capi sono i capi della classe operaia italiana*, in *Il grido del popolo*, April 4th 1936; see Spriano 1977, p. 107.
65 See Ragionieri, *Introduzione* in Togliati 1967a, p. xiv.

proletariat of the North and the farmers in the South and on the islands, of the intellectuals and of all the different layers of the suffering, labouring people', as well emphasising his merit in having led the work of the 'Bolshevikisation' of the party.[66] 'The highest farewell of the Communist International' was signed by the internal executive committee of the Comintern but the text was probably written by Togliatti alone. Here again the necessity was emphasised of synthesising the figure of Gramsci with the tradition bound to the names of 'Marx, Engels, Lenin and Stalin', in a ritual homage; Gramsci 'was educated in the ranks of the Communist International, in the school of the Party of Lenin and Stalin', he was 'faithful to the Communist International and its Party down to his very last breath'.

Such expressions, which are also present in Togliatti's essay, were not only a sign of adhesion to the living canons of the leaders of the Comintern; they were also part of a political operation put in motion by Togliatti to safeguard Gramsci's name and bind him to the International, as well as to shore up the specificity of a political tradition which a few months later Togliatti himself would have to defend against the same group now directing the PCd'I. In 1938, immersed in a new wave of Stalinist repression, under the criticism of the International and in Togliatti's absence, the Comintern had expelled many leading Communists from the Central Committee of the Italian party (Berti, Grieco, Di Vittorio). In a meeting of the secretariat on 12 August 1938, they took a public position against Gramsci's letter of 1926, the existence of which Tasca had recently made public in France. Togliatti opposed the decision, nipping in the bud a revision of Gramsci's positions, an act that would certainly not have been possible without a little historiographical reconstruction.[67] This was an important episode that indicated both that Gramsci was still a leader with an air of heresy around him and that Togliatti's move to claim Gramsci's legacy was nevertheless still up for debate.[68] It also shows that, at least in part, Togliatti's political position continued to be connected to a certain dynamic of evaluating the direction of the Pcd'I in terms of how it developed after its Bordigist period, a phase to which Gramsci was still the key.

L'Unità, secretly distributed throughout Italy, published some of the homages to Gramsci penned by exponents of the international Communist move-

---

66 *La morte di Antonio Gramsci*, in *Lo Stato operaio*, 1937, issues 5–6.
67 On this episode, see Spriano 1977, pp. 118–121.
68 Once he had read the *Notebooks*, Togliatti understood that it would be necessary to adequately 'manage' Gramsci's legacy, in which there were moments of collision with Stalinist Marxism. See Vacca, *Introduzione*, in Daniele 2005, in particular p. 25 (letter from Togliatti to Dimitrov, April 25th 1941).

ment. In all these writings, repeated and reprinted many times over, he was celebrated both as a martyr to anti-Fascism and as a 'leader' of the Communist Party. After the 7th Congress of the International, Gramsci had become one of the 'great prisoners' of Fascism and Nazism, referred to in demonstrations and commemorative speeches. The majority of the communist contributions that followed Gramsci's death remained squarely in this framework. The main exception was without doubt Togliatti's own essay, written in Moscow in 1937,[69] published in part in the aforementioned issue of *Stato operaio* and then in its entirety for the first time in the volume *Gramsci*, issued in Paris on the occasion of the first anniversary of the death of the Sardinian leader.

We must pause briefly on this essay as it records a speech Togliatti gave in Moscow only one month after Gramsci's death, given at a demonstration commemorating International Red Aid on 27 May 1937. The text of the speech was published in Russian in a booklet put out some months later. It does not add much to the article issued simultaneously in *Stato operaio*. It is significant however, that Togliatti did not hesitate to celebrate his disappeared friend in the presence of an audience in Moscow, at the very moment when a new darker stage of Stalinist repression was taking shape and the trials against the 'Trotskyist' opposition were beginning. In this context, Togliatti provided an essay which described the kind of party Gramsci had fought for, one that did not fall into the Bolshevik-Stalinist canon. Indeed, he seemed to echo the position of Potenza, the very same who in 1934 had had to submit to the severe reprimand of G.'s authority. Gramsci, Togliatti wrote, had defeated

> the false ideas held by the renegade Bordiga … who did not believe it was necessary for a good Communist to do anything other than carry out orders passed out from the centre. Above all, Gramsci was concerned with his comrades' education. He wanted to teach them to conduct themselves autonomously in political struggle, on the basis of Leninist principles – a knowledge of the facts and their connection to the working class.[70]

---

69 Although usually considered to have been written between Moscow and Paris, Togliatti's article, as Michele Pistillo has claimed on the basis of new documents, was probably 'written in its entirety before he left Moscow (the end of May, beginning of June 1937)'. See Pistollo 1991, p. 119, regarding the introduction to the text of the Moscow conference by Togliatti on Gramsci on May 27th 1937.

70 Togliatti, *In memoria di Antonio Gramsci* [1937], in Togliatti 2001, p. 56. This polemic against the Bordigist conception of the party was also covered in the simultaneous article for *Stato operaio*.

This was yet more proof of fidelity to a political tradition on which, even in the darkest moments of Stalinism, Togliatti would never renege, and to which he tried to provide some political space and a 'right of citizenship' within the international Communist movement, despite the inevitable contradictions imposed by history.

6 'Antonio Gramsci, Leader of the Italian Working Class'

It is difficult to overemphasise the importance of Togliatti's essay in the context of the history of reading Gramsci, and the process of the formation of that collective political identity which Togliatti would forge for the 'New Party' by privileging a historiography that recognised the necessity of unifying the full cultural heritage and political experiences that had flowed into the Communist Party during the Resistance and in the first years following the Liberation. The 1937 essay does not constitute the final structure that Togliatti's interpretation of Gramsci would take in the years following the war but important moments are present nevertheless, above all the concern to present Gramsci as a 'man of the party', which we have already mentioned. This bears witness to an approach that was aimed more at the reinforcement of a political identity than the deployment of that hegemonic project which would become possible only after 1944. However, in this essay Togliatti began to fight for his old comrade to become the central figure not only of the history of the first period of the PCd'I, but of Italian Marxism more generally, initiating a cultural operation that appears still more exceptional when one considers that he was not yet aware of the *Notebooks*[71] and thus based his opinions solely on Gramsci's work prior to his arrest and on those letters which he had had the opportunity to read.

On the one hand, Togliatti located his Gramsci among a series of the victims of Fascism (from Matteoti to Amendola, from Gobetti to Gastone Sozzi). At the same time he was connected to a tradition of *great men*, 'those persecuted by the ruling class of our country': Dante, Bruno and Campanella, as well as Galilei, Mazzini and Garibaldi. The vital difference, however, was that Gramsci had not only expressed the needs of the people but had also had the strength to lead a

---

[71] Exactly when Togliatti eventually did read the *Notebooks* is a matter of controversy. According to Ambrogio Donini, this was in Barcelona in Autumn 1938 (Donini 1975, p. 475). Giuseppe Vacca suggested instead that it was not until he was in Moscow in 1939 (Vacca 1994). In any case, in Barcelona, Togliatti would have only *begun* to leaf through Gramsci's folios.

struggle against exploitation; he was not only a *rebel* but also 'a revolutionary of modern times', educated by the working class and nourished by the writings of Marx, Lenin and Stalin. He was, in other words, 'the first true and consistent Marxist' in Italy, and therefore had possessed the knowledge to unite 'the theory and praxis of revolution, the study and interpretation of the facts of society, with a connection to the masses and the daily political activity of organising', establishing and leading a Communist Party. Gramsci, therefore, and not Labriola (as many would come to say in the 1950s), was the first 'complete' Marxist in Italy. Gramsci, added Togliatti, unlike exponents of other antifascist groups, 'was not "intellectual" and "studious", a "writer" in the sense which his posthumous eulogisers would have us believe. Above all, Gramsci was and is a man of the Party'.[72]

Outlining Gramsci's life, Togliatti laid emphasis on the fact that Gramsci had been educated in the 'school' of 'a young, intelligent, revolutionary proletariat of great concentration'. A precious school, thanks to which he became 'a new leader, the leader who learns from the masses', next to which Togliatti established the other great *source* for his reconstruction: 'the lessons of Lenin ... of Bolshevism and of the great socialist October Revolution'.[73] The experience of the factory councils and the period of the *Ordine Nuovo* seemed to have been born out of the dialectic between these two elements in the Sardinian leader's development. In that period, the struggle for power did not follow a pace laid down by the will of the workers' organisations. The shortcomings consequently raised around the question of the party thus found a reply within that very situation:

> from the very first moment of their creation and development, Gramsci brought the factory councils together through the creation and development of a network of political organisations, i.e. 'communist groups' capable, after a while, of leading the movement of the councils and radically renewing the socialist party.[74]

Notwithstanding the defeat, 'the question of the driving force of the Italian revolution and the peasant question, as a corollary to the problem of the dictatorship of the proletariat, had already been proposed and correctly answered by the proletariat of Turin, under Gramsci's guidance',[75] with an emphasis very different from 'Bordiga's orthodoxies'.

---

72 Togliatti 2001, p. 63.
73 Togliatti 2001, p. 72.
74 Togliatti 2001, p. 76.
75 Togliatti 2001, p. 77.

For Togliati, the theses developed at Lyons and in the *Southern Question* were already present in the Gramsci of the *Ordine Nuovo*: the working class as

> the first and only, truly *national* class, capable of resolving all the problems which the bourgeoisie and the bourgeois revolution had left unresolved, and of eradicating every form of exploitation, misery and oppression.[76]

In the beginning, Gramsci was unable to struggle against both the reformist centre and against Bordiga. Only the permanence of the Soviet Union in 1922–23 had allowed Gramsci to become a true 'leader'. This was a historical point which was to be cited frequently after the war in a great deal of Gramscian hagiography, tending to ignore the fact that the real founder of the PCd'I had not been Gramsci but Bordiga. For Gramsci, Togliatti explained,

> the Italian working class required the creation ... of a Communist Party which was not a sect of pretentious doctrinaires but a section of the working class, both a vanguard and a part of the masses, bound to the class, capable of feeling it and interpreting its needs.[77]

Notwithstanding a little manipulation, this reconstruction of the foundation of the PCd'I and of the struggle for the new Gramscian political direction grasped the core of the matter. The internal strife in 1926 and 1929–1933 was left out: this was the price paid not so much on the altar of strengthening Togliatti's political position but to safeguard Gramsci's legacy through the maelstroms of Stalinism. Gramsci was, therefore, inserted into the centre of a new strategy of antifascist unity mounted by Togliatti in the context of the new stage of the 'Popular Front':

> In his last years, having received news of the decisions of the 7th Congress of the International, all of his thought was directed towards the search for a way to create an antifascist popular front in Italy ... His basic idea was that after fifteen years of a Fascist dictatorship that has disorganised the working class, it is not possible for the class struggle against the reactionary bourgeoisie to develop around those same positions at which the proletariat had arrived in the period immediately following the Great War.

---

76 Togliatti 2001, p. 78.
77 Togliatti 2001, p. 81.

A period of struggle for democratic freedoms is indispensable, and the working class must bear this struggle in mind.[78]

Even without referring to the arguments of the 'turn', Togliatti attributed to Gramsci a belief in the necessity of struggling 'for democratic freedoms' in order to defeat Fascism. And, consequentially, Gramsci also became the harbinger of that new content which democracy and socialism were now given, however cautiously anchored in the particular situation created by 'fifteen years of ... dictatorship'. The rise of a different and fuller notion of democracy would only emerge after the Second World War.[79]

The question of to what extent the first steps in this direction were really taken by Gramsci, or instead were derived from Togliatti's own autonomous, original ideas, is a question to which there is perhaps still no satisfactory answer, even if there have been many discussions. The *umbilical cord* which bound Togliatti to Gramsci, the political and cultural roots they held in common, Gramsci's ideas from 1923 onwards, his opposition to the 'turn' – an opposition that was to a certain extent vindicated through the failure and rejection of the politics of 'social Fascism' – all this constituted the premise *sine qua non* of Togliatti's positions, which continued to be developed with creativity and formal originality, first within the ranks of the International and the experience of the war in Spain and then still more importantly, later, in Italy. Gramsci and Togliatti lived (and therefore acted politically) in epochs which were contiguous but different nevertheless. The break, which arose from around the time

---

[78] Togliatti 2001, p. 89. According to the claim, of the necessity of this 'indispensable ... period of struggle for democratic freedom' that which 'the working class must bear in mind' (that is, the Gramscian proposal of the 'constituent') had caused Gramsci many problems with other communists detained in Turi, in the years of the 'turn'. Angelo Rossi and Giuseppe Vacca (Rossi and Vacca 2007) have laid great importance on Gramsci's proposal, which emphasised the character of the break with respect to Soviet communism. Moreover, the fact that in 1937–8, Togliatti could recall in this mode the scope of Gramsci's indications, in my view puts their thesis in perspective. In Gramsci's final years, the theme of the 'constituent' was actually returned to by the Pcd'I, no longer having a *heretical* character. See Spriano 1977, pp. 108 onwards.

[79] In the volume from 1938 titled *Gramsci*, together with the complete version of Togliatti's essay and other contributions of a memorialising character, an introductory article was also published by Grieco which made the point of the elaboration of the PCd'I from the 7th Congress of the International, insisting in particular on the moment of the national struggle for democracy, as 'it is impossible for the Italian working class to struggle for socialism if it is not also the champion of the struggle for the reconquest of all democratic freedoms. It is this which Gramsci never tired of repeating in the final years of his life'. Grieco, *Anniversario*, in Togliatti 1938, p. 12.

of Stalin's self-acclamation, and from Gramsci's arrest and sentencing, was so strong that there is little point in writing a history of 'what ifs'. The fact remains that it would not be correct to claim that those communists who were advancing down the road of combining socialism and democracy in the international panorama (even after Togliatti) all belonged to Gramsci's party.

7 'An Irreparable Loss'

Recalling Gramsci as 'a man of the party' constituted a polemical response to other contributions which appeared in the anti-Fascist press reporting his death.

The newspaper *Giustizia e libertà* emphasised Gramsci's importance and the role he had played, republishing extracts from Gobetti and Calosso's article of 1933 and claiming Gramsci as 'not only the head of the Italian Communist Party' but also 'the beloved leader of the Italian proletariat, the greatest exponent of revolutionary thought, one of the greatest, most noble Italian intellectuals'.[80] The claim that Gramsci was a leader of the proletariat even before being leader of the PCd'I was also present in an article signed by Pierlandi, which appeared in issue no. 22 of the same publication: 'Some saw Gramsci as the leader of the Party; but I know how to pay homage to this great man, now passed away ... it is important to say that Antonio Gramsci was not the leader of a party ... but a master and a teacher, the great teacher of the Italian proletariat'.[81] The idea of Gramsci as godfather to the entire left was even present in a commemorative speech given by the anarchist Camillo Berneri on the CNT-FAI radio in Barcelona, in which he saluted

> the brave intellectual, the tenacious and dignified militant who was also our adversary, Antonio Gramsci, convinced as we are that he added his voice to the edification of a new order ... a modern political and social arrangement in which society and the individual are fruitfully harmonised in a collective economy and within a true and connected political federalism.[82]

Giustizia e libertà reproduced extracts from the *Ordine Nuovo* and 'The Southern Question' in issue no. 19. In the same issue there was also an essay by

---

80   *Lento assassinio*, in *Giustizia e libertà*, 1937, issue 18.
81   Pierlandi, *Antonio Gramsci nei ricordi di un operaio*, in *Giustizia e libertà*, 1937, issue 22.
82   Berneri 1964, p. 238.

Angelo Tasca ('Recalling Gramsci and Gobetti') and a second essay ('An Irreparable Loss: Antonio Gramsci') was published in *Il nuovo Avanti* on 8 May. In the former, Tasca first evoked some traits of Gramsci's character destined to be reprised often: his studies on linguistics, his 'Socratic' relation to the workers, the importance of the councils. He concluded by comparing Gramsci to Gobetti, on the basis of 'a common tendency to define freedom as concrete and universal', claiming that

> if the socialist movement renews itself and, rediscovering its unity, sets itself the most important tasks which lie ahead, it cannot do so without clarifying and understanding the secret of the collaboration of these two men, finding a synthesis of socialism and freedom within the new period of history into which we have entered.[83]

In the second essay, Gramsci was described as 'the most profound and coherent theorist of "Sovietism"'.[84] But more importantly, Tasca reproduced significant passages from two of Gramsci's letters. In the first letter, sent from Vienna in January 1924, Gramsci had claimed the lack of a single unifying politics in the original group of the *Ordine Nuovo*, expressing a harsh judgement towards that uncertainty which characterised Togliatti in the phase of his split from Bordiga.[85]

The second was the infamous letter sent to the Bolshevik party in 1926. It is not difficult to imagine the political repercussions which these 'revelations' (which is what they were at this point) had on relations both within the leading group of the PCd'I itself and between it and the higher ranks of the International in turn. The following year Tasca was to publish the letter of 1926 in full, adding a brief introductory note in which he observed that: (a) Gramsci based his recognition of the leading role of the Russian party 'only on the condition that the unity of its centre remain neither compromised nor destroyed'; (b) that the letter also contained a reference to the theory of the hegemony of the proletariat, 'which did not result from an *a priori* investiture ... but was derived from the class's ability to win over the collective spirit'; (c) that the letter, even if originally forwarded by Togliatti to its recipients, had no practical outcome, as in reality the International was always 'an appendix to the Russian state', and

---

[83]   A. Tasca, *Ritorno a Gramsci e Gobetti*, in *Giustizia e libertà*, May 7th 1937, now in *Rivista storica del socialismo*, 1966, issue 29, p. 159.

[84]   A. Tasca, *Una perdita irreparabile: Antonio Gramsci*, in *Il nuovo Avanti*, 1937, issue 19, now in *Rivista storica del socialism*, 1966, issue 29, p. 152.

[85]   See the letter in Togliatti 1971, pp. 181–84.

the real problem that lay ahead was a 'socialist unity' that might cut the 'umbilical cord' connecting individual Communist Parties to the motherland, that is, to the Russian Bolshevik Party and the Soviet state.[86]

Tasca's interventions were part of a series of articles that appeared after Gramsci's death penned by members of groups that had been defeated in the internal struggles of the PCd'I. Among them, two in particular are worth mentioning. The first, 'The Proletarian Martyrology of Antonio Gramsci', appeared anonymously in the Bordigist journal *Prometeo*, reprising some classic examples of the Bordigist critique of Gramsci, the *Ordine Nuovo* group and the new direction of the PCd'I in 1923–24. The article criticised Gramsci's cultural emphasis, the influence of Salvemini's thought, his interventionism and his not having immediately realised the scope of the October Revolution.[87] According to this essay, Gramsci had never been a 'leader' of the proletariat but in reality had first doubted the role of the Party in the revolutionary process, then had been 'influenced' by Bordiga, before being directed otherwise by the Comintern. Nonetheless, he had at least had the merit of criticising the Bolshevik majority in 1926 and 'perhaps, with the full knowledge of all the errors of the past ... would have understood the importance of rejoining the revolutionary proletariat'.[88]

The other essay, by Pietro Tresso (one of the 'three' expelled in the period of the 'turn'), was published in the Trotskyist paper *Lutte ouvrière*, and reflected a very different point of view, defending Gramsci's positions in the context of the struggle against Bordigism and their absorption into the theses of the anti-Stalinist opposition. Tresso thus claimed that 'Gramsci's entire activity, his entire conception of the development of the party and of the workers' movement was opposed to Stalinist absolutism'.[89] In doing so he did not only make reference to the letter of 1926, but also claimed that between 1931 and 1935 'Gramsci's moral and political rupture with the Stalinist Party was complete'. According to Tresso, Gramsci had at this point been 'officially removed as *head*

---

86 See A. Tasca, *Una lettera di A. Gramsci al Partito comunista russo*, in *Problemi della rivoluzione italiana*, 1938, issue 4, pp. 25–26.

87 A. Tasca, *Il martirologio proletario di Antonio Gramsci*, in *Prometeo*, May 30th 1937, now in *Rivista storica del socialismo*, 1966, issue 29, p. 147.

88 A. Tasca, *Il martirologio proletario di Antonio Gramsci*, in *Prometeo*, May 30th 1937, now in *Rivista storica del socialismo*, 1966, issue 29, p. 148. From the same press came another more Bordigist article: V. Verdaro, *Antonio Gramsci*, in *Bilan*, 1937, issue 42, now in Peregalli 1978.

89 O. Blasco [P. Tresso], *Gramsci (Un grand militant est mort.)*, in *La lutte ouvrière*, 1937, issue 44, now in *Rivista storica del socialismo*, 1966, issue 29, p. 162.

of the Party', and that, according to 'comrades recently in prison' he had been 'excluded from the Party'. We are here confronted for the first time with the circulation of a 'rumour' that was to be taken up many times and become a well-known and remarkably consistent controversy all the way through to the 1970s and 1980s, despite a series of historical reconstructions showing it to be entirely unfounded.

8 Between Carducci and Pascoli

From 1938 onwards there were a handful of editorial initiatives to publicise and popularise Gramsci, at least among anti-Fascists and exiles, and above all in France: *Antonio Gramsci: Témoignages*, published in French and edited by the *Entente Internationale pour la defense du droit, de la liberté et del la paix en Italie*, compiled brief contributions from French intellectuals and reprinted extracts from writings and speeches by Rolland, Togliatti and Carlo Rosselli. *L'hanno ucciso!* ('They Killed Him!') edited by Red Aid Italy, compiled reprinted accounts of various kinds about the Sardinian leader, with an introductory note by Giuseppe Gaddi:

> A fallen soldier. An Italian. The greatest among them. A LEADER. The leader of Italian communists, Italian workers, of the whole Italian people: Antonio Gramsci ... After he had spent ten years of prison, the Hapsburgs finally returned Silvio Pellico to the land of the living. But after a decade of torture, today's tyrants have maliciously denied Antonio Gramsci's family even the body of their beloved.[90]

From this moment on[91] there was a series of minor interpretations of the late leader, aimed at ordinary activists and sympathisers of the workers' movement, that is for an uneducated public, one more easily reached through sentiment than political motivations. This was an *oleographic* and hagiographic treatment, one that would come to assume particular importance in constituting the 'New Party', but which in 1938 had already found an important foundation in the publication in Paris of the volume *Gramsci*, continuously reprinted and

---

90 G. Gaddi, *Ancora un caduto*, in *L'hanno ucciso!*, s.l., Edizioni della solidarietà, 1937, p. 5.
91 Elements of the popularisation of Gramsci's figure were present even in the years immediately prior to this, but it is from the moment of his death onwards that they were to become a real 'line' in their own right.

later distributed in Italy after Liberation. Aside from an introductory essay by Grieco and the essay by Togliatti which we have mentioned above, the book also contained ten commemorative articles, written by activists who had known Gramsci personally.

Togliatti's article also contained elements of this *oleography* of Gramsci (together with typical hagiographic expressions about Stalinism, which were difficult to avoid in this period). The most detailed passages were the descriptions of moments in prison and of Gramsci's illness, such as the moment of his transferral

> from one prison to another, bound in manacles and heavy chains, kept in the filthy mobile cages in which men are buried alive, forced to stand between its four walls, unable to move, crammed into a goods train or left in an abandoned railway station, burning in the high heat of Summer or reduced to an icicle in Winter, left in the wind, rain and snow.[92]

Almost a small piece of literature. But from out of the atrocities of the prison regime and his sickness, and the physical deformities he had received through beatings, emerged a Gramsci depicted with little respect for historical truth, shown instead as the great proletarian 'leader'. This Gramsci – a 'son of poor farmers', 'a son of the people and a rebel' – was woven into the familiar figures of popular tradition (Dante, Mazzini, Garibaldi) and with descriptions of an 'an enlightened, energetic, secure leader'.[93] It should be noted therefore that Togliatti's own essay did not leave out the predominant element in the populist hagiography of Gramsci ('Gramsci the good man') which would become so relevant after the war. Here Gramsci was of course viewed in very positive terms, but closer to the tones of Carducci than those of Pascoli (who provided other contributions in the same volume):

> All his life was subject to a will of iron. He radiated energy, serenity, optimism; he knew how to impress upon himself the harshest discipline of work, but he was also capable of enjoying life to the full, in all its aspects. As a man, he was an atheist, enemy of every hypocrisy, a merciless critic of every falsity, of every fake sentiment, of every effeminacy.[94]

---

92 Togliatti 2001, p. 59.
93 Togliatti 2001, pp. 62–64.
94 Togliatti 2001, p. 86.

All these traits were partly true, but organised and presented in a way so as to make the late leader more of a mythical hero than a man of 'flesh and blood'. This was even more clear in other contributions to the same volume. In an article by Amoretti, for example, Gramsci was more than a 'leader, he was a "master"', who embodied

> so many of our feelings and emotions ... all of our conscious political life, the sense of discipline and devotion to the Party, all of that which is good in us ... his physical body had to be of an extraordinary kind, the kind of geniuses and heroes, the kind of new men, superior to every contradiction, with which one cannot be joyous nor in pain, nor disgraced, nor fortunate – but only a great flowing path winding into great depths, with soul and mind in serenity.[95]

Gramsci was presented, among other aspects, as a 'friend of the workers and farmers, of all labourers, of all the exploited', propelled forward in struggle by his sympathy 'for the suffering of humanity, the mother in the family, the hungry, the homeless sons in rags'.[96] He 'knew how to be both comrade and leader, friend and teacher',[97] even appearing sometimes just like 'one of those children whom he loved and who instinctively felt a connection to him, with great fidelity and adoration'.[98]

Yet these memorial essays also contain elements that are useful for understanding the life and thought of the Sardinian leader: his 'Socratic' teaching method, the ability to speak with the workers, the attention to all aspects of the life of the proletariat; as well as some partial accounts of the troubles he met in prison at the time of the 'turn', when Gramsci

> was outraged at the superficiality of some of his comrades who, in 1930, had declared the imminent fall of Fascism ... and who claimed that the Fascist dictatorship would transition immediately into the dictatorship of the proletariat.[99]

Despite this, these writings are above all examples of the reconstruction of Gramsci in which elements of history and of hagiographic exultation remain

---

95   G. Amoretti, *Con Gramsci sotto la Mole*, in Togliatti 1938, pp. 63 and 66.
96   G. Parodi, *Gramsci con gli operai*, in Togliatti 1938, p. 104.
97   R. Montagnana, *La sua grandezze e la sua semplicità*, in Togliatti 1938, p. 129.
98   F. Platone, *Antonio Gramsci e l''Ordine Nuovo'*, in Togliatti 1938, p. 152.
99   G. Ceresa, *In carcere con Gramsci*, in Togliatti 1938, p. 116.

too tightly bound together to be separated. We will return to this hagiography of Gramsci, so widely diffused between 1945 and 1956, which was to become an important factor in the context of the reconstruction of a culture of 'popular Communism' at least up until the 1960s.

CHAPTER 2

The Identity and Tradition of the Party (1939–47)

1   Gramsci and Togliatti

Landing in Naples on 27 March 1944, after eighteen years of exile, Togliatti established profound change in the politics of the Italian Communists, known as the 'Salerno turn'. It was not only an institutional question that was confronted and resolved in a different manner; it was the entire politics of the Communist Party – the PCI[1] – as well as its culture and approach, a change that more or less represented a break. The novelty of Togliatti's politics was recognisable above all in the concept of the 'New Party' and an emphasis on the *democratic* and *national* character of the activity of the Communist Party.[2] The first results of Togliatti's new magazine, *Rinascita*, centred on the national significance of the Italian Communist struggle. In December 1945, at the opening of the 5th Congress of the Party, a congress for its total renewal, Togliatti indicated Gramsci as the starting point of this long journey: a small 'fighting minority' had become

> the resilient nucleus for a new kind of party, a national party as Antonio had seen it some twenty-five years ago. This profound thinker, a man who represented the Italian workers' movement, cautioned us that there was no possibility of developing the Party if one does not know how to leave behind sectarian manoeuvring and turn one's attention to the real problems of the nation, that is, the Party must know how to set down roots in the historical terrain on which it must work. Gramsci's instructions have not fallen by the wayside.[3]

The plan proposed at the 'Salerno turn' in reality had its roots in other events related to Togliatti's activities in the 1930s: the period of the Popular Front, the experience of the Civil War in Spain, his reflections on the new character of Fascism and of mass society. Even in that period in which the strategy of the international communist movement and Gramsci's reflections in prison did

---

1 The Communist Party of Italy (PCd'I) had changed its name, assuming that of the Italian Communist Party following the self-implosion of the Communist International in June 1943.
2 See Natta 1984, p. 24 onwards.
3 *Quinto Congresso*, in *Rinascita*, 1945, n. 12, p. 257.

indeed converge, it is important not to underestimate the real differences, and how the Gramscian 'war of position' did not in truth concern the anti-Fascist struggle but rather a wider strategy to think through new kinds of anti-capitalist struggle and the transition to socialism. Moreover, the characteristics of the politics that Togliatti deployed at Salerno – an entirely new situation – differed from Gramsci's on at least two main points: the mass party, different from the Gramscian party of cadres, which was still Leninist and related to the Third International;[4] and above all the emphasis on pluralism and political democracy.[5] This said, it remains true that Gramsci's prison writings had opened up a new page for the Communist movement, emphasising consensus and the 'structural' limitations of force.

One can probably claim with safety that Togliatti had realised, in a general sense, a Gramsci-inspired politics as much as his own realism would allow within the limits of a post-Yalta world. Highlighting the moments of *discontinuity* between Gramsci and Togliatti should not cover over the elements of continuity, which certainly did exist and are important – but they do need to be recalled in order to understand the reasons behind a certain post-war *utilisation of* Gramsci.

What did Gramsci represent in 1944? Not only to Italians, but to Communist Party activists and the partisans who fought in the Gramsci Brigades?[6] For most, he was simply unknown. In the best instance he was a martyr, a hero and an example. Gramsci was above all remembered as a victim of Fascism who died in the prisons of the regime without ceding to his enemies. Togliatti, citing Gramsci in a speech given in Moscow on 26 November 1943, had described him as 'the founder and leader of the Communist Party' who had 'already in 1924' launched 'its call for unity of all healthy powers of the nation against Fascism'.[7] Fuelling the leaders and militants in exile who had seen the emotion provoked by his passing, 'the legend of the life and death of Antonio Gramsci has transformed into a desire for struggle, into a capacity for sacrifice, into a declaration of resistance at all costs'.[8] Perhaps the image of Gramsci handed down by liberal democratic intellectuals such as Dorso and Gobetti had not been entirely forgotten; but one is dealing here with a small elite, active but not plentiful.[9] The

---

4 See Gruppi 1984, p. xxxix.
5 See Natta 1984, p. 31.
6 On the partisan units named after Gramsci, see Santarelli 1991, pp. 33–34.
7 Togliatti 1979, p. 367. Gramsci was also recalled in the theoretical journal of the Communist Party which was published in New York: see Montagnana 1942 and Berti 1943.
8 Amendola 1967, p. 12.
9 A reference to this thread of transmission of Gramsci's figure and thought is made in Garin 1974, p. xix. But also see Santarelli 1991.

memory of Gramsci, in the end, after twenty years of dictatorship, remained marginal, both among the masses and among that young generation of intellectuals who had passed in a few years from 'left' Fascism to antifascism and then frequently into the militia in the ranks of the Communist Party. Why therefore – and this is the crux of the matter – did Togliatti make Gramsci the central point of reference for the politics and culture of the Communist Party? Was it a necessary step? And which were the most important reasons? In my view this needs to be understood as a *choice*, in the sense that in 1944 Togliatti could have 'turned the page' without reneging on Gramsci as a figure, but while finding another source of ideas and symbols around which to construct an identity for the Party, to legitimate its politics: anti-Fascist unity, the Resistance, progressive democracy, the myth of the USSR. All of these elements were present in the work of constructing a *culture* for the party but frequently passed through the *filter* of Gramsci, the real 'cornerstone' of the novelties which Togliatti was trying to construct.

What were, then, the motivations that determined this choice? Above all, they stemmed from Togliatti's own history and culture, the old friendship, that common cultural and political background invoked so many times, the separate but not divergent reflections during the 1930s: certainly a complex and non-linear relation, with ups and downs, but also with deep roots, ones not easily discarded. Additionally, there was the necessity of providing the Communist Party with a history: this was a party which went from five or six thousand militants in July 1943 to sixty or seventy thousand members by December 1945,[10] with all the problems encountered by a party transforming itself from a network of cadres into a mass organisation, but without a unified historical tradition or theory. Next to this, there was the desire to grasp the peculiarity of Italian Communism, of asserting (without breaking from the USSR, even at the price of levelling out some quite different cultural moments) that political line to which Togliatti had adhered as well as a balance of power, both internal and external to the international Communist movement which, following the 7th Congress of the Comintern, had allowed him to propose the possibility of an entirely new project, emphasising a separation in terms of the theoretical traditions of Marxism-Leninism and Stalinist ideology. Furthermore, on a quite different level, there was an attempt to find common ground with intellectuals – to unify the anti-Fascists among them, and to win a frequently right-wing society over to the left – by making Gramsci a *great intellectual*, 'one of the great geniuses of today's Italy'.[11]

---

10   See Sassoon 1980, p. 34.
11   Togliatti 1949.

It was a peculiar trait of Togliatti (as well as a limitation) that he often introduced new and important elements within political activity without emphasising their novelty nor the break with the past, proceeding instead through a process of *accumulation*, preferring to provide a sense of that *continuity* (above all in relation to Gramsci) which constituted the central aspect of his historicism.

In the end, Togliatti 'exalted' Gramsci but frequently deviated from his thought; he made the Sardinian leader the genesis of Communist politics in Italy at the expense of highlighting that it was he, Togliatti, who was the initiator of many of its most important changes and innovations. The choice of a certain *utilisation* of Gramsci's legacy was therefore on the one hand in continuity with Togliatti's political choices of the previous decade, while on the other it was determined by the necessity of providing a unified historical tradition to a mass of new members, and of finding common ground with antifascist intellectuals. Togliatti's mission was to give a historical tradition to the subaltern classes in order to provide an ideal form of autonomy for a progressive historical bloc and to bring together a class of antifascist intellectuals by providing them with an example of a 'great intellectual' whom they might follow. For these reasons it is not always easy to separate Togliatti's creation of a tradition from the development of his own ideas, which in some respects went *beyond* Gramsci (while in many others, nonetheless, lagging behind the *Notebooks*). The fact remains however that in presenting 'Gramsci's politics' as the *true* politics, Togliatti committed himself to what was in some ways an arbitrary historiography, but one which at the same time provided an anchor for the 'New Party', overcoming resistance from those cadres and leaders who felt closer to the myth of the USSR and insurrectionist fantasies.

2   The 'New Party' and the Intellectuals

The Communist Party's relationship with intellectuals remained complicated by the vibrant differences among the intellectuals themselves, above all in terms of ideology. As well as the old Crocean antifascism, which was present most of all in the central South and politically already quite diverse within itself, there were also the young intellectuals who had come out of 'left Fascism', not infrequently destined to become functionaries and leaders of the Communist Party, and Northern intellectuals who were closer to other European cultural experiences, again with many internal variations (from Banfi to Vittorini, from Luporini to Geymonat). And this is not to mention that large layer influenced by Gentile, that gathered up so many different experiences in its folds but which could not be made explicit due to its *unpresentable* character in that historical moment, deriving as it did from a philosopher 'on the other side of the barricades'. The unifying factor of this complex weave was clearly not to be found on ideological grounds but in political history, signified fundamentally by the defeat of Fascism. The *Program* with which Togliatti opened the first issue of *Rinascita* in April 1944 provides a sufficiently accurate snapshot of the situation:

> The adhesion of more and more groups ... of elements deriving from the middle classes of society and within the top level of intellectuals and flowing into the Communist movement, is one of those facts which bodes well for the future of Italy. We cannot hide from ourselves the fact that this adhesion is motivated today more by moral and political prestige, as much national as international prestige, than by profound convictions.[12]

The conclusion traced out by Togliatti was the need to intensify the spreading and the study of Marxism in Italy. There would be other roads which the relation between Communists and intellectuals could take in the immediate future however. In fact, the main problem which arose in those years was providing an explanation of Fascism, something for which Croceanism turned out to be entirely inadequate. Croce considered the two decades of Fascism as a kind of *parenthesis* within Italian history,[13] an accidental phenomenon, alien to the fabric of the nation. Such a thesis constituted a comfortable alibi for those fighting for the continuity of the old culture and for liberal society,[14] but could never satisfy anyone with a real interest in understanding what had actually taken place. In this regard, Italian Marxism could claim a stronger tradition of interpretation, already outlined in the 'Lyons Theses' and the 'Southern Question' (which *Rinascita* republished in 1945) and which was then further developed, with both consistency and internal complexity, in Gramsci's *Notebooks* and Togliatti's 'Course on the Opponents' of 1934.[15] In a speech given in Moscow on 26 December 1943, Togliatti had already stressed how the imprisoned Communist leader 'was profoundly rethinking the history of our country, searching for the roots of the Blackshirts' poisonous regime within the reactionary tra-

---

12   *Programma*, in *La rinascita*, 1944, n. 1, p. 1 (the text is given only in the first issue). See also the analysis by Lucio Lombardo Radice in the same journal the following year: *Rinascita*, 1945, no. 9–10, p. 217.
13   See Croce 1944, pp. 55–6.
14   See Garin 1966, pp. 521–2.
15   Togliatti 2010; but also Togliatti 2004.

ditions of the Italian ruling classes'.[16] Gramsci and Togliatti's interpretation of Unification and of the history of Italy over the previous century and a half – characterised by an *absence of revolution*, a capitalism in retreat, the division between North and South, a *weak hegemony* which, despite popular and proletarian advances after the Great War, gave way to a Fascist reaction – would be repeated by the secretariat of the Communist Party and in the *Report* of the 5th Congress of the party, held in Rome from 29 December 1945.[17] Indeed, in an editorial in the second issue of *Società*, the Crocean interpretation had already been rejected:

> We do not accept this idyllic conception of the modern history of Italy, one that views Fascism as a passing and casual aberration, like a foreign body violently introduced into our social organism. Fascism did not just fall from the sky, Fascism was not the envious gift of a hostile divinity, Fascism was not 'the invasion of the Hyksos': Fascism was born in the bowels of our own society.[18]

Alongside the problem of the interpretation of Fascism was that of the role played by intellectuals, of their function in society and politics – a subject which would very soon come to be the grounds for much confrontation and collision. If, after the Resistance, the majority of Italian intellectuals could not but feel, in a more or less explicit manner, responsible for the old idealist culture, many were nonetheless reluctant to entirely leave Croceanism behind, inasmuch as it had represented the theoretical form in whose mould they had been formed, and a moment of refusal of (if not struggle against) Fascism. Above all, one of Croce's central points had contributed to the strengthening of the peculiar character of an 'Italian mentality' and its place within national life: the *distinction* and separation of culture from other aspects of social and political life. Even in 1945, Croce, in criticising the proximity of political and cultural writing to each other, still claimed the necessity of a separation between the two 'approaches' – 'because one is a contemplative, theoretical part of critical science, while the other is practical, that is, animated by pragmatic passion'. For

---

16 Togliatti 1979, p. 367.
17 Togliatti 1979, pp. 185–7. Giuseppe Bedeschi has emphasised the importance of the Gramscian interpretation of Unification in Italian culture of the post-War period in Bedeschi 1983, pp. 9–11. On the 5th Congress of the Communist Party see Martinelli 1995, chapter 1. On Gramsci's 'presence' there, p. 41.
18 *Situazione* in *Società*, 1945, no. 1–2, p. 5. The parallel between Fascism and 'the invasion of the Hyksos' had been proposed by Croce in a speech given at the Teatro Eliseo in Rome on 21st September 1944.

Croce, cultural magazines and newspapers had to be 'kept outside of political and economic conflicts'.[19] Communist political culture posed an explicit alternative to this mode of conceiving the relation of intellectuals with society. It is no coincidence that journals like *Rinascita* and *Società* began their activity by affirming the *non-separation* of politics and culture, the necessity of involving intellectual forces in the political and moral reconstruction of the nation.[20] In Togliatti's 'Program', this need was also sustained through an affirmation of a principle which was at the same time an indication of an interpretation of Marxist method:

> We ought not raise up artificial or hypocritical barriers between different national spheres of activity – economic, political, intellectual. We do not, nor do we hope to, separate ideas from facts, the course of thought from the relations of material forces, politics from economy, culture from politics, individuals from society, art from real life. Our strength, the strength of Marxist doctrine, lies in this unitary conception of the world.[21]

Togliatti had made this same argument against the separation of intellectuals from the first half of the 1920s.[22] Now he reprised it as a critique of Croce and Croceanism. Even if, for structural reasons, Croceanism could no longer be the ideological form of bourgeois hegemony, it was nevertheless the dominant ideology of non-Marxist anti-Fascism[23] and therefore an appropriate target, not just a 'comfortable' one. The very first issue of *Rinascita* published some of 'Antonio Gramsci's Opinions on Benedetto Croce' – *Guidizi di Antonio Gramsci su Benedetto Croce* – clearly extracted from letters written in the prison in Turi between April and June 1932. The argument follows the role developed by Croce in his confrontation with Marxism, his *revisionism*, the concept of hegemony, the history of nineteenth-century Italy, 'Transformism', and the break between Croce and Gentile.[24] Almost as if to clarify exactly to whom these pages were addressed (that is, intellectuals of a Crocean background who were tarrying with the Communist tradition), this was followed by a profile of Gramsci taken from Gobetti's *La Rivoluzione liberale*. A little further on there was a review by

---

19   Croce 1945, pp. 111–2.
20   See the editorial notes opening the two journals, titled respectively *Programma* and *Situazione*. On the relationship between Togliatti and Croce see De Giovanni 1977.
21   *Programma*, p. 1.
22   See above, pp. 22–3. Also see Vacca 1976, pp. 39 onwards.
23   See Asor Rosa 1975, p. 1592.
24   See *Guidizi di Antonio Gramsci su Benedetto Croce*, in *La rinascita*, 1944, issue 1, pp. 7–10.

Togliatti of Croce's 'Towards a History of Communism as a Political Tendency', in which the Neopolitan historian was treated like a Fascist collaborator.[25] The motives for this open, violent polemical confrontation with Croce were recalled by Togliatti self-critically during a meeting of the Cultural Commission of the Communist Party in 1952:

> In order for Marxism to penetrate into Italian culture we essentially have to engage in confrontation, or so we used to say [in 1945], a confrontation with Croceanism, that is, with the cultural current of idealism. In the course of the struggle for liberation, and even before, under Fascism, we were nonetheless allied with many intellectuals who clearly held to this cultural current ... It was therefore necessary to make some distinctions, to avoid placing everything and everyone in the same box. [Of course] there was also discontinuity, bitterness, unnecessary capitulation, oscillations between pure propaganda and wider cultural activity, contradictions even.[26]

The real limit, however, was that arguing against a 'protagonism of the intellectuals' did not shift into questioning the *status* of *great intellectuals* who were outflanking the workers' movement. If for Gramsci the question of the intellectuals was a problem related above all to the hegemonic apparatus and forms of cultural organisation, for Togliatti it was seen first and foremost on the ideological level, a change in the horizon of ideas.[27] Yet while it is true that Togliatti held to a certain 'privileging of intellectual elites'[28] it is not the case that he failed to recognise 'imbalances of knowledge and understanding', of the 'distance between privileged and subaltern layers of society'.[29] In reality, Togliatti did not ignore these *imbalances*: if anything he regarded them too pessimistically, unchangingly. The *traditional intellectual* as deployed 'on the left' ended up occupying the same position as that which they had in liberal society and ideology. Intellectuals thus entered into a new kind of Transformism,[30] triggering a *break* represented by the Resistance, and Gramsci – as we will see – constituted

---

25 See P. Togliatti, *Benedetto Croce – Per la storia del comunismo in quanto realtà politica*, in *La rinascita*, 1944, issue 1, p. 30. In the following issue the journal published a letter of apology from Togliatti to Croce for the tone used in his review. See P. Togliatti, *Lettera a Benedetto Croce*, in *Rinascita*, 1944, issue 2, p. 31. On this episode, see Ajello 1979, p. 23 onwards.
26 Togliatti 1974, pp. 195–6.
27 Vacca 1976, p. 114 and Vacca 1984, p. 232.
28 This, for G.C. Ferretti (Ferretti 1992, p. 105), was a trait he shared with Vittorini.
29 Ferretti 1992, p. 106.
30 See Paggi 1970, p. xiii.

one of the main bases for this process, thanks to a one-sided interpretation of his work which favoured above all the confrontation with Crocean intellectuals.

In this context, the fundamental axis of Communist political culture was that which came to be defined generally as 'Marxist historicism': they denounced the aporias, the insufficiencies, the conservative outcomes of Crocean culture, but nonetheless accepted its terrain and questions; it reduced the anti-Croce 'to an overturning of the historiographic tradition while nevertheless maintaining the *category of historiography* as the central link in the Communist Party's cultural effort'.[31] If, in this manner, predetermined arenas of research and criticism became privileged, above all the fields of historical study and artistic production, the study of Italian society (changes within which, in a few years, would come to 'surprise' an unprepared left) was neglected. This was due to the perpetuation of a Stalinist view on the impossibility of the development of real capitalism exactly at that moment when neo-capitalist dynamics were about to assert themselves. This error of judgement, which constituted perhaps the main limit of 'Togliattian Marxism', appeared all the more serious given that in Gramsci's *Americanism and Fordism* a different reading of capitalism was available, one more clearly anti-Stalinist. It is no accident, therefore, that this text was left to gather dust, extraneous as it was to the *stadial* vision to which the communist held. Indeed, Felice Platone's preface of 1949 was protecting the reader from considering the *contemporaneity* of Gramsci's analysis.[32]

Certainly historicism, if it on the one hand laid emphasis on moments of continuity rather than rupture (in terms of the relationship with intellectuals), on the other hand allowed emphasis to be laid on the particularity of the Italian situation, justifying the politics of the Communist Party,[33] the democratic turn, the 'ideology of reconstruction',[34] without putting in question its solidarity with the international Communist movement. Togliatti worked on different levels of articulation,[35] choosing to *speak* in a range of languages and with a range of interlocutors, advancing a form of theoretical political activity which he knew would both strengthen the 'New Party' and grasp the peculiarities of 'Italian

---

31   Vacca 1976, p. 112.
32   'Today ... we have before our eyes a Fordist country quite different from that which Gramsci knew'. Platone, *Prefazione* to Gramsci 1949, p. 15.
33   Cesare Luporini wrote: '*historicism* seemed the only interpretation of Marxism perfectly adequate to and corresponding with the politics of the party, to the strategic line. To the line, that is, of antifascist unity, of the Salerno turn, of the Constituent, and perhaps of the vote on article 7'. Luporini 1974, p. xxix.
34   See Luperini 1971.
35   See Ciliberto 1984, p. 137.

Marxism'. In other words, a form that would deepen a democratic awareness, preventing the isolation of the working class and stabilising relations with traditional intellectuals. This was no easy task, and would become a fundamental moment for the interpretation of Gramsci, even at the cost of at times confusing 'the effective content of Gramsci's thought' with Togliatti's own particular reading.[36]

Of course, one might also consider that Togliatti's political culture was limited in over-estimating Croce's influence. Scholars remain divided over the effective strength of the Crocean 'hegemony'. For some, Croce's antifascism had already been defeated before the collapse of Fascism, in a society which had already become a mass society.[37] And even if 'across those two decades, the political hegemony of Fascism', according to Garin, 'could not be matched by the Crocean cultural hegemony',[38] the sunset of one would necessarily mean the waning of the other. The fact remains however that Croce, having held a position of pre-eminence within both Fascist and antifascist culture for over twenty years, was not able to maintain a position of particular strength upon Fascism's fall. It is also necessary to consider the influence of Gramsci's interpretations of Croce given that although they were penned before and during prison, they were only made known and distributed after 1944–45.[39] No less important is the distance of time between the first polemic on Croce, in 1943–44, and the perpetuation of the situation through to the first years of the 1950s, at which point one might criticise the political culture of the Communist Party (and their reading of Gramsci) for lingering on a *target* that was now out of date.

The problem of whether or not Croce was central as an antagonist therefore constituted an important point of difference within the circle of Communist intellectuals. According to Luporini, this was one of the main causes of divergence between the 'first run' of *Società*, whose editors saw the 'Croce question' as already stale, and Togliatti's *Rinascita*.[40] Vittorini's *Politecnico* was no less dif-

---

36 Luporini 1974, p. xxviii.
37 More radically, Ciliberto contested the 'myth' of Crocean hegemony, claiming instead that the philosopher was, from the end of the 'Great war', 'a solitary, isolated man' (Ciliberto 1982, pp. 15–16).
38 Garin 1966, p. 500.
39 Luporini identified this aspect of the reception of Gramsci's thought in Luporini 1973, p. 1605. For a general thematic approach to the problems which derive from the diffusion of the conceptual work as read in different periods, see Garin, 1978, pp. xii–xiii.
40 Luporini recalled: 'between us and *Rinascita* there were moments of friction: Togliatti wanted to build a bond with Croceism in his review, a seminar, as well as a polemic, which to us, more drastic and impatient as we were on this matter, seemed inopportune and anarchronistic'. Ajello 1979, p. 71.

ferent in its outlook, including on this aspect. Not coincidentally, these three journals became the symbol of plurality, of the richness of contradictions of post-War communist culture. Togliatti's polemic against Vittorini arose from his old mistrust of the *separation* of the intellectuals,[41] but also for a particular kind of democratic culture – European, American, foreign to the national tradition. *Società*, while differing from Togliatti for the reasons already given, was more distant still from Vittorini, opposing its own programme of 'continuity' to the 'new culture' of *Politecnico*.[42] These different positions did not find a way to coexist. Nevertheless, the fact that in 1945, at the 5th Congress, the party sanctioned the possibility of adhering to only basic agreement over its political program, agreeing not to be bound by any ideological choices,[43] was a fundamental turning point. From this freedom of orientation came the necessity of forming a theoretical political tradition around Gramsci, one that could unify the heterogeneous cultural currents present within the Communist Party. If unity could not be guaranteed *a priori*, on the level of a formal, statutory bureaucratic dogmatism, it was all the more important to appear to guarantee it around an interpretive *tradition* of the history of the party and its theoretical development.

3   'Gramsci's Politics'

Togliatti referred to Gramsci in the first speech he gave upon his return to Italy at the end of March 1944, given to the Neopolitan Communists on 11 April: 'The best of us, Antonio Gramsci, departed this life in prison, tortured, brought to a premature end by monstrous Fascists under the direct orders of Mussolini'.[44] Following this, on 30 April the entire third page of *l'Unità* (southern edition) was dedicated to 'the 7th anniversary of the death of Antonio Gramsci'. At the top of the page, between two articles by Togliatti – one still signed with his Comintern pseudonym, Ercoli, and the other left unsigned – was a photo of the Sardinian leader, with a small biography detailing his family origins ('from the smallest bourgeoisie'), his university studies (spent among 'hardship and

---

41   On the polemic between Vittorini and Togliatti see Vacca 1976, p. 30. The criticism of Vittorini's *split*, noticeable in many quite different authors, is symptomatic of the reading of the bond between politics and culture prevelant among communist intellectuals in the 1970s. See, other than Vacca 1976, De Giovanni 1977, p. 301 and Asor Rosa 1975, p. 1602.
42   See Di Domenico 1979, p. 33 onwards; and Ciliberto 1982, p. 323 onwards.
43   Togliatti, *Rapporto al V Congress*, pp. 220–1.
44   Togliatti 1984, p. 8.

deprivation'), his joining of the Socialist Party, the *Ordine Nuovo*, the foundation of the PCd'I and the struggle with Bordiga, his imprisonment and his death. On the same page of *l'Unità* there was also an account from Sandro Pertini on 'Gramsci in prison', which recalled the period spent in Turi:

> When Gramsci was in Turi we were all close friends. It was a joy for us to live next to him. Gramsci continued to work, write, speak with his comrades, teach, and then he would write some more. He read a lot, and was very sick but always calm and followed everything that was going on with the utmost attention. He advised comrades not to view things superficially, and he could not but smile when faced with certain predictions and opinions.[45]

This last reference must have sounded a little obscure to the majority of readers, but not to Togliatti and other leaders who remembered the divergence between Gramsci and the party with regards to 'predictions' of the ultimate collapse of the Fascist regime and of capitalism with it, prophecies that not only had made Gramsci 'smile' but had provoked his bewilderment and even aversion.

Togliatti's two articles were titled 'Gramsci's Politics', signed by Ercoli, and 'Gramsci's Written Legacy', unsigned but of an equally certain attribution.[46] In the first, Togliatti recorded that 'among the last words which Gramsci passed on to me ... were the necessity for us to make a "national" politics'. Foreseeing the fall of Fascism, Gramsci had encouraged the continuation of 'the politics which he had begun in 1919 and continued in 1924, which we had brought forward in order to fully resolve the question of the true unity and rebirth of the Italian nation'.[47] In fact, as Togliatti explained, by the period of the *Ordine Nuovo* and the factory councils in 1919, 'Gramsci's politics had been founded on an integral vision of specifically Italian problems, starting with the harshness of the class divide' particularly visible in the North of the country 'and up to the social decomposition' in which the bourgeoisie kept the South. For him

> the national function of the working class ... consisted in making all levels of the working population aware ... of the necessity of combining their labour power with that of the proletariat ... In 1924, when Gramsci took the political leadership of our party directly into his own hands, this was

---

45   S. Pertini, *Gramsci in carcere*, in *l'Unità* (Southern edition), April 30th 1944.
46   Thanks are due to Luigi Cortesi for realising the importance of these two articles. Cortesi 1975.
47   Togliatti 2001, p. 9.

> the central idea. [Indeed, now] is it only by following 'Gramsci's politics' – that is, beginning with clear alliance of the middle strata of the countryside and the city, coming to their defence, vindicating their demands and radically righting the wrongs done through all parts of our country ... that the working class can manage to fulfil its task. In this moment, in which a new period in the history of our country is beginning, we feel truly the spirit of Gramsci is there to guide us. He created our party. He determined the national role of the proletariat in the struggle for its emancipation. He foresaw the resurrection of our country.[48]

This was the first article by Togliatti dedicated to Gramsci after his return to Italy. Here, 'Togliatti's politics', or rather the 'politics of Salerno', and the basic line regarding Gramsci which would remain prevalent throughout the period after the War, are joined together in exemplary manner. It is a politics of unity, of the national role of the working class, of reconstruction. And it is a reading of Gramsci aimed at providing a birthplace of legitimacy for this politics, picking out a red thread which starts neither with the reflections in prison nor from the centrist phase, but – according to Togliatti – all the way back in 1919, in the experience of the *Ordine Nuovo*, from which came a draft of an 'anti-workerist' interpretation which would be affirmed many times over. And without *overtly* referencing the contrasts with 1926 or with the 'turn', Togliatti – though not without some effort – managed to praise a basic line of thought through which he played out the possibility of rooting the Communist party in the new situation being created at the end of the War.

The second article, 'Gramsci's Written Legacy' provided the first piece of news about the prison writings of the incarcerated Communist. Togliatti wrote:

> The principle theme [of the *Notebooks*] is the 'history of intellectuals', by critically examining the role that intellectuals have played as an instrument for the ruling class to maintain their dominance over the popular classes, along with the rebellion of certain great thinkers against this role and the relation of Italian thought to history ... an entire notebook is given over to the thought of Croce, the secular pope ... whose dictatorship over the twentieth-century intelligentsia has covered up and enabled the dictatorship of the reactionary bourgeois caste within the economic and political order.[49]

---

48   Togliatti 2001, p. 48.
49   Togliatti 2001, pp. 44–45.

He announced that everything was to be published, even 'the prison letters to his wife, sister-in-law and children', in order to make 'this rich material of study [available], a true revelation for all those who did not know Gramsci personally'. The announcement of the intention to publish Gramsci's writings was not new. It went back to at least 1937–38.[50] The catalogue of the new publishing house *Nuova Biblioteca*, dated 7 June 1944, announced the coming publication of 'all the writings of Antonio Gramsci', to be edited by Palmiro Togliatti. According to an account by Carlo Bernari, the project was to be executed under the supervision of Felice Platone on the invitation of Delio Cantimori.[51] This idea was also not followed through. It would still be some years before one could read Gramsci's writings, and instead Togliatti's essay from the 1937 Roman edition of *l'Unità* was reprinted (the shorter presentation is dated 'April 1944'), while a reprint of the whole of the 1938 issue appeared later that year.

Gradually moving up the peninsula as it was liberated, Togliatti continued to present Gramsci to communists members – 'for the most part young and recently politicised' – in the speeches with which he explained the 'national' politics of the Communist Party. At the Brancaccio theatre in Rome, on 9 July 1944, he invoked the celebrated response of Gramsci given to the judges in the special Fascist court: 'There will come a day when you will bring Italy into catastrophe, and it will fall to us communists to save our country'.[52] In the speech at Florence on 3 October 1944 he recalled Gramsci's sacrifice, describing him as 'the leader of our Party'.[53] At the beginning of 1945 the Northern edition of *l'Unità*, printed and distributed secretly in the occupied areas (which bore under its masthead the text 'Founder: Antonio Gramsci' from its first issue in 1943) published a photograph of Gramsci accompanied by a brief article on the Party and an extract from an article by Togliatti from 1937, in which Gramsci was said to have united 'the great Italians': Bruno, Campanella, Galileo, Mazzini and Garibaldi.[54] In April 1944 two small works on Gramsci were secretly published in the occupied North. The first, edited by Eugenio Curiel, was a reworking of Togliatti's essay from 1937 which appeared in *Lo Stato operaio*. The second, by Leo Valiani, appeared in the series *Quaderni dell'Italia libera* (the name of the newspaper of the *Paritio d'Azione*) along with a monograph dedicated to

---

50   See Spriano 1977, p. 111. Fundamental for all the events of the first edition of Gramsci's writings is Daniele 2005, including Giuseppe Vacca's introduction.
51   See C. Bernari, *Gramsci entra nel catalogo*, in *l'Unità*, April 1st 1977. Bernari's editorial may have been, however, the product of Cantimori's generous idea rather than an actual project.
52   Togliatti 1984, p. 74.
53   Togliatti 1984, p. 96.
54   See *l'Unità*, (Northern edition) January 10th 1945.

Gobetti and Tosselli. Valiani's essay, entitled 'Antonio Gramsci: The Origin of the Revolutionary and Antifascist Movement of the Italian Proletariat' (*Antonio Gramsci: Le origin del movimento rivoluzionario e antifascista del proletariato italiano*), like Franco Momigliano's work 'The Factory Commissions' of the previous year, demonstrated an interest in 'Actionist' elements (i.e. democratic and liberal socialist) around the movement of the *Ordine Nuovo*, demonstrating an attempt to use Gramsci to oppose the Communist Party's politics.

In the second issue of *Rinascita* in February 1945, Togliatti reprinted the entirety of *The Southern Question*, with the famous pages on the role of Benedetto Croce and Giustino Fortunato, 'the most hard-working reactionaries on the peninsula'. However, the attack on Neoidealist philosophy was not the main reason for the reprinting of the essay in *Rinascita*, but rather its anti-determinist stance. Ernesto Buonaiuti – the great historian of Christianity and proselytiser of modernism who died in 1946 – had claimed in *Epoca* that Gramsci's method of analysis was 'not Marxist' because more attention was given to superstructure than the base (unlike, for the author, the example of Antonio Labriola): an emphasis destined to be followed a great deal in Gramsci's contextualisation. A polemical note appeared in response to these theses, unsigned but attributable to Togliatti, in the third issue of *Rinascita*. What was at stake, fundamentally, was Gramsci's Marxism, with respect to which Togliatti attempted to distance him from Labriola, in whom – he said – was present 'a tendency towards a kind of unilateral interpretation, limited to and fatally founded on the doctrines of scientific socialism … Antonio Gramsci, who studied Labriola carefully and was a pupil of the real meaning of his words, corrected this errant tendency', with a dialectical conception of the relations 'between an economic situation and a socio-political one'.[55] It was this *anti-determinism* which made Gramsci's Marxism distinct: the understanding of a system of mediations that passed from the 'economy' through to 'cultural and intellectual currents' allowing 'an active intervention, by an organised vanguard, to alter historical development'. This is why, therefore

> Gramsci's Marxism was a living Marxism. It was effective, it provided an orientation for thousands upon thousands of people and organised them into action; it created a party; it provided the Italian people with instructions in their struggle for emancipation.[56]

---

55 Togliatti 2001, p. 97.
56 Ibid.

The eighth anniversary of Gramsci's death fell on 27 April 1945. *L'Unità* published an editorial by Velio Spano carrying the title 'Gramsci Is Still With Us' and announced 'a people's pilgrimage' to the tomb of the Sardinian leader. The next day the newspaper reported that 'fifteen thousand Roman workers lined up in front of the Antonio Gramsci's funeral urn. The Party gathered around comrade Togliatti honours the first leader of the Italian working class'. *L'Unità*, under the title 'Antonio Gramsci's Teachings Remembered With Emotion by Togliatti' (*L'insegnamento di Antonio Gramsci nella commossa rievocazione di Togliatti*), published the speech Togliatti had given at the English cemetery in Porta San Paolo, to which Gramsci's ashes had been translated. Speaking on the day after Liberation, Togliatti based his recollection 'of our comrade and dearest friend ... my teacher and educator' on praise for the Resistance and the question of a 'new political direction' within the country. The sketch of Gramsci, 'hero and martyr', depicted him as 'physically weak, broken throughout his body, ill, denied all of those things which are called the pleasures of life'; and remembered how 'though weak, he turned to the weak', working and struggling for them, even while in prison, leaving

> to us, his disciples, friends and comrades ... – to the Party which is the fruit of his labours, the result of years and years of meditation and study over the destiny and history of our country – to us he left his works, which – once we have published them – will dumbfound the intellectuals of Italy with the profundity of his thought, the precision of his analysis, the audacity of their conclusions.[57]

If the example of hero and martyr was the first thing with which the workers were presented, if 'the flag of liberty and socialism' passed to the Communist Party, in which 'the spirit of Gramsci lives on, the teachings of Gramsci live on, as does the soul of this great freedom fighter, of this great Italian', then an equal position was given to Gramsci's *words*. Togliatti described him an as example to be followed by 'young intellectuals' and by all of those who, as victims of ancient prejudices, still thought of the working class and the Party as lacking ideas or limited by a set of narrow-minded economic demands.

The message which the invocation of Gramsci was meant to convey, therefore, from the earliest of Togliatti's essays and speeches, was meant to go beyond the militants of the Communist Party, moving outwards to address all Italians, including those, in south-central Italy in particular, where the experi-

---

[57] Togliatti 2001, p. 101.

ence of the Resistance was not so broad and intense, for they proved to be more doubtful of and indifferent to the Communists and their democratic, national vocation. The politics of antifascist unity, which Togliatti would emphasise throughout the historical period after the War, found a fundamental point of reference in Gramsci. In the speech given at the San Carlo Theatre in Naples on 29 April 1945, speaking of the years 1923–26, Togliatti claimed:

> Throughout the period, Gramsci's central idea for political activity was unity: unity of the workers' parties in the struggle for the defence of democratic institutions and for the rescinding of Fascism; unity of the workers' parties with the democratic forces that they began to organise particularly in the South; unity of the mass of socialist workers with the mass of Catholic workers in the cities and countryside, unity of workers, unity of workers and citizens, unity of manual and intellectual workers, all with the goal of forming a great bloc of national forces on the basis of which it would be possible to block the streets from the ultimate advance of Fascism and – as is still possible – to save our country.[58]

Here we have an interpretation which certainly brings out that strong *tendency* of Gramsci's 'centrist' direction, now manoeuvred to the forefront by Togliatti. Rather than focussing on the years 1924–26, here the political line of *unity* was partly based on Gramsci's prison reflections, which pointed to the objective of a Constituent Assembly and the restoration of democracy. Togliatti forced this history to some extent but nevertheless remained within a tradition and methodology which was also Gramsci's own, even if this had little or nothing to say, from the middle of the 1930s, about the entirely new situation that would be created in the decade following the defeat of Fascism. Obviously the question of *what is to be done?* was now all on the shoulders of Togliatti, but this last invocation of Gramsci served to establish a political tradition that was neither economistic nor subversive.

In the emphasis on unity in that moment, even Togliatti's attitude towards Croce seems to have abandoned its harshest tone. Gramsci had shown

> that the new idealistic Italian culture represented a step forward in the development of our national culture ... that it was not possible to simply take a negative attitude towards this new intellectual current. Instead he claimed that in confronting this philosophical school we must carry out

---

58 Togliatti 2001, p. 115.

an operation analogous to that which Marx and Engels had undertaken in their own time when, in confronting Hegelian logic, they performed what they themselves called the overturning of the Hegelian dialectic, that is, of the abstract ideological schema constructed by Hegel, and made of it the most complete guide for understanding the development of the real dialectic within things, within the conflict of the classes, within society itself.[59]

He then touched on the working class, and the intellectuals of the vanguard as 'heirs to all those who have been a positive and progressive force for the development of our country's culture'. And the call had fallen

> on the intellectual classes in the Southern provinces who are particularly plentiful and active. The moment has come in which they must turn towards a new world ... in which they must collaborate with the great masses of manual labourers and take the concrete problems of our reconstruction to heart.[60]

The idea of *overturning* would come to dominate the history of Marxism in Italy for at least two decades. But the glances thrown in the direction of the 'Crocean' intellectuals would not be passed over without response, as we will see.

In the early post-war period, Togliatti's interpretation of Gramsci attained a final coherence. In a speech on 27 April 1947 at Cagliari, when the moment of the unity of the anti-Fascist forces was coming to an end, Togliatti chose to make Gramsci the (primarily moral and cultural) basis for the fullest possible marshalling of social and political forces. In sketching out the background of Gramsci's character, his childhood and youth in Sardinia, he described the beginnings of his reflections on 'the Southern question' as the conclusion to his own vivid personal experiences. Gramsci's 'kernel of thought', said Togliatti, lay in the fact that, for the first time in Italy, Socialism had become 'not only a movement of the exploited classes in a struggle for the betterment of their conditions of existence' but 'the motor for the renovation of all Italian society ... a liberating and progressive national movement'.[61] The Communist Party, therefore, was faithful to the thought of Gramsci,

---

59   Togliatti 2001, p. 111.
60   These last claims are contained in the second part of the speech, which *l'Unità* reported on 1 May 1945 with the title *Nello spirito di Gramsci sulla via della rinascita. Togliatti commemora Gramsci a Napoli.*
61   Togliatti 2001, p. 123.

> who wanted the Party of the working class ... to be a profoundly national Party, one which would never separate the cause of workers, farmers and labourers from the cause of all the classes who contribute to the life and prosperity of the nation, one which would know how to bring together the struggle for the emancipation of the workers with the struggle for the renovation of the life of the nation as a whole.[62]

Formally revoking the claim of Gramsci's *partiality* by which, ten years previously, he had commended the work of the Sardinian leader,[63] he now directed himself not to dispersed groups of exiled anti-Fascists but to the entirety of the Italian people. Togliatti declared:

> Woe betide us, we Communists, if we were to believe that the legacy of Antonio Gramsci is ours and ours alone. No, this legacy is for everyone, for all Sardinians, for all Italians, for all workers who fight for their emancipation, whatever their religious faith or political beliefs may be.[64]

This 'Gramsci for all', contrary to the long-standing 'left wing' polemics of the 1960s and 1970s, was an important moment in the struggle for a hegemony which Togliatti believed to be more open-ended than it was in reality. For, some months later, with the definitive end of the unity of anti-Fascist forces, a historical period would close and would change Togliatti's reading of Gramsci. The interventions analysed here bring out two elements: firstly, that of the *continuity* on which Togliatti, not without some efforts, constructed the legitimation of his political line, above all within the party; and secondly the use of Gramsci as a common ground for a range of political and cultural forces, in order to indirectly legitimise the Communist Party both within democratic public opinion and throughout the intellectual classes, primarily in the South. The unilateral character present in this *utilisation* of Gramsci does not negate the value of the far-reaching cultural operation, one carried out more openly and clearly in the years of the Cold War.

---

62 Togliatti 2001, p. 124.
63 See above, p. 19.
64 Togliatti 2001, p. 128.

4 Politics and Culture

Gramsci's name slowly began to circulate beyond the core of the Party. The edition of the weekly paper *Riscossa* in Sassari on 23 April 1945 was dedicated to the Sardinian Communist and, aside from the editorial by Francesco Spano Satta, included biographical notices and accounts by Giuseppe Sardo (*Davanti al Tribunale speciale*) and Michele Saba (*Antonio Gramsci e Attilio Deffenu*, on the proximity of the young Gramsci to the island's anti-protectionist movement).[65] On 10 June, Parliament commemorated Mattotti, Giovanni Amendola and Gramsci, three MPs who had been victims of Fascism. The commemoration of Gramsci was delivered by Ruggero Grieco.[66] In July the anti-Fascist review *Mercurio* hosted a short profile of Gramsci signed by Mario Berlinguer, which remembered how he, as a member of parliament in Amendola's tendency, had become acquainted with Gramsci in the parliament chamber in 1924 and, although defining him as 'the greatest Communist thinker since Lenin', added: 'We believe that Antonio Gramsci, if he were alive, would emphasise and fortify the democratic direction already revealed in his final writings'.[67] In 1945, moreover, two authors re-examined and commented on the essay on the 'Southern question': Guido Dorso repeated Gramsci's thesis in an appendix to a reprint of *Rivoluzione meridionale*[68] and Salvatore Francesco Romano dedicated his attention to it in his *Storia della questione meridionale*, an anthology by means of which the Sardinian leader's essay was revived for the public.[69]

As for the Communist newspapers, or those within a 'Communist environment', the first issue of *Società* featured a review by Augusto Levi of the volume *Gramsci* (originally published in 1938 but republished in 1945 by *l'Unità*) in which the author, in line with Togliatti's interpretation, treated the figure of Gramsci as a 'prophet' of a 'unitary pact against Fascism for the reconstruction of democratic freedoms' who held to 'the necessary promise of all true Socialisms'.[70] *Rinascita* published a fragment by Gramsci on *Insegnamento classico e riforma Gentile* – 'Teaching the classics and Gentile's reforms' – advertising that this was 'the first part of a prison notebook by Gramsci which has come to public attention. It is part of a work on the role of intellectuals in society, the

---

65 See *Riscossa*, 1945, issue 17.
66 See *Discorso dell'onorevole Grieco*, Rome: Tipografia della Camera dei deputati, 1945 (other than Grieco, speeches were given by Vittorio Emanuele Orlando, Giuseppe Romita, Raffaele De Caro and Ivanoe Bonomi).
67 M. Berlinguer, *Gramsci*, in *Mercurio*, 1945, issue 11, pp. 29–30.
68 See Dorso 1945.
69 See Romano 1945.
70 A. Livi, *Gramsci*, in *Società*, 1945, issues 1–2, pp. 317–21.

publication of which is forthcoming'.[71] Six months later, the review featured a full report of the notebooks on this theme (*Relazione sui quaderni del carcere. Per una storia degli intellettuali italiani*) by Felice Platone, who – under Togliatti's direct supervision – was preparing the prison writings for publication. Platone's essay is important for revealing the full range of problems that Gramsci confronted while in prison, which now entered the public domain for the first time with a wealth of particulars and information. Platone did not limit himself to simply providing news on the range of Gramsci's legacy and the difficulties presented by the publication, or the numerous philological and chronological problems, or the contents of the notebooks, Gramsci's plan of work, its title, and the numerous arguments collected therein. Additionally, he also provided a key to its interpretation, insisting on the theme of the intellectuals, on the contents of the *Notebooks* dealing with the 'problems posed by the *Ordine Nuovo* in the years 1919 and 1920': Gramsci's problem, from that time on, was that of 'renovation, state and culture, of creating a state and a national, popular culture, and selecting new groups of leading intellectuals from the popular masses'.[72] It was the *break* represented by the *Ordine Nuovo* in the history of Italian intellectual culture that, according to Platone, provoked the necessity of Gramsci's struggle against Croce's conservative positions. Thus in 1946 the schema by which Platone was editing the future thematic edition of the *Notebooks* did appear to be advancing in the direction of a reconciliation of Gramsci's thought with those established analyses that fostered a *traditional* relationship with intellectuals.

Interest in Gramsci's writings grew from this moment on. Accounts multiplied, as did the hagiography (on which more will be said below). Letters and unedited extracts were published, along with memorials and commentaries. For example Franco Rodano, in *Rinascita*, referred explicitly to Gramsci on the *Southern Question* in discussing the relations with Catholics, emphasising Gramsci's novelty: the consideration of the 'Vatican question' not as a religious problem but as a political problem of the masses as represented by Catholics, with respect to which Gramsci had taken an attitude that remained fundamentally within the Socialist tradition.[73]

There were other interpretative hypotheses within the Communist Party (in a remarkably diverse, if not divergent, fashion) that ran alongside Togliatti's and

---

71 See *Rinascita*, 1945, issues 9–10, p. 209.
72 F. Platone, *Relazione sui quaderni del carcere. Per una storia degli intellettuali italiani*, in *Rinascita*, 1946, issue 4, p. 87. As has been shown in the previous pages, the reading of the *Notebooks* as reflections on the role of intellectuals in this history of Italian society was to remain always present and repeated by Togliatti and *Rinascita*.
73 See F. Rodano, *Quesione vaticana*, in *Rinascita*, 1946, issues 11–12, p. 297.

that were already being outlined before the publication of the *Letters* in 1947. Elio Vittorini effectively began the discussion by publishing a small anthology of letters in *Politecnico* ('by kind permission' of Einaudi publishers), preceded by an introductory note, titles and an editorial program designed to provide a key to interpretation. It was probably a coincidence that these pages were published around the same time as the famous letter by Togliatti in *Politica e cultura* that signalled the beginning of a break between the Milan group and the Communist Party, a letter that, according to Vittorini, was published when *Politecnico* 'was just going to press'.[74] Nevertheless, Vittorini's Gramsci certainly focussed on cultural autonomy and the role of intellectuals. Gramsci, Vittorini wrote,

> could be more acutely 'political' thanks to his ability to find the cultural motivations behind every question, rather than reneging upon them. By these means, Gramsci claimed for the arts and poetry the importance of aesthetic as well as historical evaluations, and thus went further than every other great revolutionary ... For us, in every way, in all problems, he has the last word. And I do not say this only for 'Italian communists'; I say this for communists in general, as well as for all Italian intellectuals.[75]

The final annotation ('And I do not say this only for "the Italian communists"; I say this for communists in general') appears to anticipate the fundamental problematic conjuncture not only of Togliatti's theoretical political evolution (the relation between 'Italian life' and 'the national life of Socialism')[76] but more generally the *alterity* of Gramscian Communism as far as its place in the international Communist movement was concerned. Aside from this, the passages chosen by Vittorini show a non-conformist Gramsci who criticises the 'so-called theory of historical materialism', that had 'made a kind of "hidden God" out of "economic structures"'. Vittorini's Gramsci is attentive to the autonomy of the aesthetic sphere, a theorist of the expansion of the concept of the intellectual, heterodox in claiming that 'psychoanalysis is correct'. It is also interesting to note that Gramsci, for the first time since the internecine struggle of the 1920s and 1930s, now became – clearly if still not explicitly – a *contested object* within the Communist Party.

---

74 *Politica e cultura. Una lettera di P. Togliatti*, in *Il politecnico*, 1946, issues 33–34, p. 3.
75 e. v. [E. Vittorini], *Lettere dal carcere*, in *Il politecnico*, 1946, issues 33–34, p. 5.
76 See P. Ingrao, *'Via italiana' o 'vie nazionali al socialismo'? Riflessioni sull'internazionalismo di Togliatti 1956–1964*, in *Critica marxista*, 1985, issue 4.

5   Between Croce and Marx

The publication of the *Prison Letters* in 1947 was a literary as well as political event, and they were awarded the Viareggio Prize for literature in the same year.[77] Gramsci's character and personality, above all in terms of culture and politics, impressed itself on public opinion, the rewards of the *popular* form in which it had been decided to begin the diffusion of Gramsci's legacy, and the decision to publish through Einaudi – a 'fellow traveller' – instead of the less widely distributed Party press.[78] Some of the critics later turned against this edition of 1947[79] and indeed it is easy to spot its basic limitations: the intervention of the Stalinist censors who had imposed the omission of extracts referring to Bordiga, Trotsky, Rosa Luxemburg and the 'left opposition'. Of the 428 letters published in the later edition of 1965, 119 were published for the first time (although, it should be said, some were only found after 1947).[80] These political and methodological limits do not, however, invalidate the importance of this moment of Gramsci's introduction into Italian culture. This was, in itself, a brave move: in a climate of the already mounting Cold War, Gramsci marked out the originality, autonomy and diversity of the Italian Communist Party in relation to the international communist movement, signalling the start of a presence which would impress itself in all spheres of culture. Togliatti's basic decision to publish Gramsci, making him the unitary and cohesive basis of the 'New Party' – despite the contradictions inherent in the Italian Communist Party's strong link with the international Communist movement – represented a *choice* which was in many ways irreversible. Togliatti was aware of the fundamental process which such an operation would put in motion, contributing to the formation of an Italian Communism significantly different from the tradition of the Third International and a typical Stalinist party.

---

[77]   See *Il Premio Viareggio alle 'Lettere dal carcere'*, in *l'Unità*, August 19th 1947. On the events which led up to the assigning of the prize and on the first editions of Gramsci after the war see Chiarotto 2011.

[78]   On the proposition of the publication of the *Notebooks*, see Cesari 1991. The agreement with Einaudi was finalised in May 1945. Thus the manuscripts were to be edited by a 'special commission designed by the Communist Party' (Vittoria 1992, p. 20).

[79]   See above all Sechi, *Le 'Lettere dal carcere' e la politica culturale del Communist Party* [1965], now in Sechi 1974.

[80]   On the reasons which made the publication of many of Gramsci's letters objectively difficult in 1947, for various reasons (resistance from his family, protection of those still living, missing conclusions, including many texts, etc), see Vacca 1994, p. 126 onwards. Much more critical in this respect is Canfora 2012, p. 164 onwards.

There was no lack of attempts to oppose Gramsci to his own Party, praising the disappeared revolutionary for fighting for a different legacy. On one hand, there were certain small Socialist currents, such as those which revolved around the journals *Iniziativa socialista* and *Europa socialista*, who claimed Gramsci's legacy for themselves either *in toto* or in part, underlining how 'the Communists' derivation of today's political struggle from Gramsci has been entirely arbitrary'.[81] *Iniziativa socialista* recalled the Gramsci of the *Ordine Nuovo*, whose teachings had been 'abandoned and betrayed' by the Communist Party. In *Europa socialista*, Ignazio Silone was full of praise for the Sardinian leader, in which 'the young generations' could see 'perhaps the only teacher for a generation who have remained for too long in an era without teachers'.[82]

But above all it was Benedetto Croce who picked up the baton of counterposing Gramsci to the Communist Party. Reviewing the *Letters* in *Quaderni della 'Critica'* he wrote: 'As a man of thought he was one of us', preceding to list the characteristics which marked out Gramsci's thought as welcome within the school of Neoidealism: 'The renewed concept of philosophy as a speculative and dialectical tradition, and not simply positivist and classificatory; the full historical vision; the unification of erudition with philosophising; the vibrant sense of poetry and art in their original sense. And at the same time, an openness to the ability to recognise all ideal categories in their positivity and autonomy', everything therefore that could set Gramsci up against 'Stalin's philosophical catechism', thus commenting that 'today's Communist intellectuals ignore Gramsci's example far too much'.[83] With the publication of the first of the notebooks – *La filosofia di Benedetto Croce* – in the following year, the Neopolitan philosopher had to make a quick retreat, maintaining that his attitude, 'which derived fundamentally from politics and the Party', was too headstrong: the principle of 'practical necessity' postulated by the materialist dialectic impeded Gramsci from searching 'for that which he had declared to be non-existent, that is, thought and truth'.[84] For a moment, however, Croce's position on the *Letters* caused a stir, partly because it was so widely diffused by

---

81 *Gramsci*, in *Iniziativa socialista*, 1947, issue 8, p. 1. The article, unsigned, can be attributed to Lucio Libertini (see Santarelli 1991, p. 45).
82 *Antonio Gramsci*, in *Europa socialista*, 1947, issue 11, p. 9. The article, again unsigned, can be attributed to Silone as editor of the review. In the same volume Franco Lombardi countered the 'liberal' communism of Gramsci to that of the Communist Party.
83 Croce 1947, pp. 86–8.
84 Ibid. It should also be said that the Communist Party did not miss the difficulties and – to use the critical words of Delio Cantimori – 'ruthlessness towards the critique of Croce' contained in the first volume of the *Notebooks*. See the letter of Cantimori to Giulio Einaudi of 1947, in Turi 1990, p. 197.

the daily papers, seemingly demonstrating its political rather than theoretical character.[85] Togliatti replied to the philosopher with an unsigned, ironic and harsh polemic in *Rinascita*: Benedetto Croce, Togliatti wrote,

> has fired off his last cartridge in the struggle against Communism ... when we present Gramsci to him, a Communist, the founder of our Party, a colossus of thought and action, a martyr fallen in the furthest trenches of humanity, he stops playing his silly game and blurts out 'Yes, this is a great spirit and a great man, but you lot are different!' ... To live up to the immortal example of this leader is precisely the task we have set for ourselves. Don Benedetto is welcome to try, if he still can, to live up to this example as well, i.e., among other things, an example of intellectual sincerity and clear-headed historical and philosophical investigation, contemptuous of every quack who attempts to justify contradictions which are unclear but nevertheless 'pragmatically' and politically useful.[86]

The polemic against Croce was nonetheless made in the thick of a discussion with those more or less important Croceans who seemed to be moving away from the master and towards the Communist Party, not infrequently by way of Gramsci, whether directly or indirectly. Ranuccio Bianchi Bandinelli, commemorating Gramsci in Naples on 28 April 1947, spoke on behalf of those 'intellectuals adhering to the Communist Party ... indebted to Croce for an entire part of our intellectual and cultural formation', who were nonetheless no longer able 'to follow Croce to the ultimate political consequences of his thought'. Bianchi Bandinelli added that Croce had, in the best way,

> accompanied us along a long road, up to a closed door, which we know opens onto another world ... the world of tomorrow ... Faced with this closed door, Gramsci's frail form reaches out to us, proffering a bundle of his disordered papers scrawled in the solitude of prison so that, under his watch, we might find within them the key to pass over into the beyond.[87]

Another distinguished scholar and pupil of Croce, Luigi Russo, left the liberal camp for the *Partito d'Azione* and therefore the Communist Party, above all that

---

85 The newspapers which published the essay by Coce were *Il giornale, Risorgimento liberale* and *La patria* (see Bertelli 1980, p. 226).
86 *Antonio Gramsci e don Benedetto*, in *Rinascita*, 1947, issue 6, p. 152.
87 Bianchi Bandinelli 1962, p. 242.

'current' which he defined as 'Gramsci's style of Crocean Marxism'.[88] Celebrating the Sardinian leader at the *Scuola Normale Superiore* in Pisa on 27 April 1947, on Togliatti's invitation, Russo underlined Gramsci's bond to Croce (a scholar on a par with Hegel, De Sanctis, Marx, Engels and Lenin), as well as claiming that Gramsci

> knew Croce's justified criticisms of that doctrine [Marx's 'historical materialism'] very well and acknowledged that the best of it was already in the past, in the philosophy of spirit, for after the wave of positivism the word 'materialism' must have appeared to him much debased in ethical and political historiography.[89]

This foray with 'left Croceans' was taken further still in the Communist press. In the same issue of *Rinascita* in which he responded acerbically to 'Don Croce', Togliatti published a forcefully philo-Crocean essay by Gabriele Pepe (who had abandoned the Liberal Party in 1946) which claimed Gramsci's attitude towards Croce was that of 'a disciple who critiques the master', from whom he had assimilated 'the most profound historical spirit'.[90] Similarly, in *Società*, Gramsci was presented, perhaps more generally throughout rather than in any single contribution, as the central link between intellectuals and the masses, an idea that permeated the entire first series of the journal, even while preceding the publication of the *Letters*.[91] And it was in *Società* that Carlo Muscetta replied firmly to Croce, noting ironically how 'the news that the *Prison Letters* had not put Croce to sleep' was satisfying enough – because, according to a 'verified' story reported by Muscetta, Croce had woken up his daughter to read them to him, 'due to the genuine enthusiasm which those fragments had moved in him'. Muscetta added that 'many literati felt in some way authorised to praise Gramsci "the writer", safe in the knowledge that this was the role that allowed him to be "recognised" and eventually even "prized"'.[92] But in the same issue the journal published a 'Small Note on Gramsci and Croce' by Paolo Alatri (another ex-Actionist, like Muscetta) recalling how 'Neoidealism and historical

---

88   Ajello 1979, p. 97.
89   L. Russo, *Antonio Gramsci e l'educazione democratica in Italia*, in *Belfagor*, 1947, issue 4, p. 402.
90   G. Pepe, *Antonio Gramsci – Lettere dal carcere*, in *Rinascita*, 1947, issue 6, p. 165.
91   See, for example, the essay in which Cesare Luporini introduced his translation of a fragment of Hegel, *Libertà e destino*. See Luporini, *Un frammento politico giovanile di Hegel*, in *Società*, 1945, issue 3.
92   C. Muscetta, *Le lettere dal carcere di Antonio Gramsci*, in *Società*, 1947, ssue 5, p. 697.

materialism' were doctrines 'cut from the same cloth, that is, from modern secular thought' and thus 'Croce and Gramsci held much common ground'.[93] This thesis must have embarrassed the editors of the journal, for a note was added to Alatri's essay stating that it was not possible 'to take on board all of the Croceanisms which remain in here'. Gramsci's anti-Idealist battle – as was noted some years later by Giuseppe Carbone, author of the first review dedicated to the debate on Gramsci[94] – was not only often misunderstood, but also turned on its head, as there were frequent attempts to assimilate his own thought into the schema and theses of Croce. Yet while Carbone's essay ended up as proof of the vast terrain that remained common to many Gramscian Croceans, he had not considered the possibility of another, similar reading of Gramsci. For Guido Morpurgo-Tagliabue, Gramsci had tried to build a bridge 'between Croce and Marx', an enterprise destined to fail because 'history as ethics' and 'history as economics' remain inherently irreconcilable, one being an idealist and conservative historicism while the other is materialist and innovative: Gramsci was left in the middle of the crossroads, a member of neither tradition of thought.[95]

93   P. Alatri, *Una noterella su Gramsci e Croce*, in *Società*, 1947, issue 5, p. 680.
94   G. Carbone, *Su alcuni commenti alle Opere di Antonio Gramsci*, in *Società*, 1951, issue 1.
95   G. Morpurgo-Tagliabue, *Gramsci tra Croce e Marx*, in *il Ponte*, 1948, issue 5, pp. 492–38.

CHAPTER 3

Diamat and the *Notebooks* (1948–55)

1   The Cold War and the *Prison Notebooks*

The period between 1947–48 and 1953 saw a 'partial suspension'[1] of the 'politics of Salerno', as well as significant changes within cultural politics and the relation between the Communist Party and intellectuals. The Cold War, the break in the anti-Fascist alliance, the foundation of the Cominform (September 1947) and the defeat of the Popular Front in the election of 18 April 1948 transformed the situation drastically in the space of a few months, including in terms of Togliatti's 'politics of Salerno' and the 'New Party'. All the Communist strategies seemed to have been founded on the hypothesis of a long period of collaboration between the democratic parties. The analysis of Fascism as an epochal phase, and Togalitti's political *pessimism*, meant that he feared the possibility of a return to a form of non-democratic bourgeois hegemony. The originality of the Communist Party in the years of the 'Cold War' did not lessen but the contradictions between 'Italian life' and the stern adhesion to the USSR allowed for a re-emergence of the harsh decisions of Stalin and Zhdanov within the Communist Party – including for Togliatti.

In terms of cultural politics, the deeply contradictory nature of the Communist Party's position in these years became still more evident. On the one hand the Communists tried to create stronger alliances to deal with the isolation they were risking by maintaining their link to the Soviet Union. The wave of clerical and covert manipulations that surrounded the elections meant that the Communists objectively became the champions of liberty and culture, so that *Unità*, among others, wrote that 'we are the liberals of the twentieth century'[2] and Togliatti edited a collection of *Essays on Tolerance* by Voltaire,[3] protesting 'the abolition of the holiday of 20 September, voted for by the majority of parliament'.[4] This new phase did not lack important consequences for theoretical

---

1 Asor Rosa 1975, p. 1591.
2 O. Pastore, *I liberali del secolo XX*, in *l'Unità*, August 31st 1948.
3 'Between Enlightenment rationality and Marxism the difference is without doubt very great ... But in that there remain those within it, as with Enlightenment scholars, who are animated by the greatest faith in man and his faculties, the employment of his weapons of thought in order to open a new era of humanity's renewal, we cannot but recognise it is a precursor'. Togliatti 1984, p. 521. [1949].
4 Roderigo di Castiglia [P. Togliatti], *L'abolizione del XX settembre*, in *Rinascita*, 1949, issue 6.

developments: the struggle against Croce lost momentum,[5] partly due to the increasingly obvious inadequacy of the Neopolitan philosopher faced with the post-liberal society that was being formed. There was not, however, a matching new development of Marxist theory and its classic texts, nor an analysis of the new Italian society. Instead, emphasis was laid on the necessity to connect with a national democratic tradition that Italian Marxism had inherited – above all along the axis of De Sanctis/Labriola – with Gramsci as the hinge between the two. Thus if in 1945 Togliatti had spoken of a clean break in the relation between Labriola and Gramsci[6] after 1947–48 he would instead speak about their *continuity* and Gramsci would be claimed as 'Labriola's greatest pupil and continuer'.[7]

The reasoning for this emblematic claim was provided by Mario Alicata in *Rinascita* in 1948: it was an error to judge the 'phenomena of a disbanded ideology' as the result of political opportunism. One might dismiss 'certain simpletons and superficial enthusiasts, yet many writers and artists have tried to come to terms with themselves through their own language – it is not possible to throw off a habit like a sweaty and threadbare shirt'. In passing through the emotions dictated by the era of the Resistance, leaving behind the hope of building a democratically advanced (if not Socialist) society vanished, and the intellectuals turned to being more 'traditional'. If it were absurd – as Gramsci had written – to think that intellectuals could '*as a mass*, break with the whole past and put themselves on a new ideological level', then according to Alicata it was necessary to skip over the 'incomprehension' of intellectuals on the cultural level, for one could not just impose on them 'our ideological sphere', i.e. Marxism. It was necessary instead

> to continue the construction of the broadest possible cultural front, which might eventually include ... even those who (while we ourselves will not tolerate the most backward positions) are not disposed to see certain elements of traditional Italian culture sacrificed – I will not say elements of cultural freedom as such – those elements that are part and parcel of the life and history of our Nation.[8]

---

5   D. Sasoon (*Togliatti e la centralità del parlamento*, in *Critica marxista*, 1985, issue 1) has shown how the battle of Togliatti against the 'fraudulent laws' relied for the most part on the conceptual arsenal of classic liberalism, See also De Giovanni 1977, p. 275.
6   See above, p. 71.
7   Togliatti 1974, p. 324. Togliatti's reflections on Labriola were not without their own oscillations and developments. See A. Zanardo, *Togliatti e Banfi sulla via di Labriola al marxismo*, in *Critica marxista*, 1986, issue 5, p. 139 onwards.
8   M. Alicata, *Una linea per l'Unità degli intellecttuali progressivi*, in *Rinascita*, 1948, issue 12, p. 454.

On the other hand, however, next to this democratic calling, entirely Zdhanovist attitudes deepened and permeated through these years, transforming all convictions that 'the party which leads the great work of construction of a new society, of a Socialist society, as well as being responsible for organising the largest section of society, must also organise within the artistic and cultural spheres'.[9] It was this side of the relations with the USSR in which 'Roderigo de Castiglia' (Togliatti's pseudonym) remained a prisoner of those conciliatory attitudes, compliant with the 'politics of Salerno' and the 'legacy of Gramsci'. Naturally Togliatti himself also thought exactly the opposite, and therefore that 'one could not truly understand Gramsci without Stalin and Zhdanov'. Thus Emilio Sereni, minister for culture in the Communist party in these years, explained that:

> It is enough to simply recall some of the recurring themes in Gramsci's work, even though they are often cited: culture and its leadership, understood as the struggle against spontaneity; pedagogy and morality, understood as the intimate relation between theory and praxis, the overcoming of 'Guicciardinian man'; Marxism as a philosophy of the masses, as something entirely new, as a qualitative leap in the history of human thought; finally, of the gnoseological value of the socialist edifice.[10]

This was a period full of the risks of isolation and Stalinist entanglements. It was in these leaden years, if not years of lead, those between 1948 and 1951, that Gramsci's *Prison Notebooks*[11] were published by Einaudi, the political and cultural event which would contribute the most to the formation of the mod-

---

9   Roderigo di Castiglia [P. Togliatti], *Orientamenti dell'arte*, in *Rinascita*, 1949, issue 10, p. 454. Togliatti's claim, in an argument with Massimo Mila, is emblematic because it is in direct opposition to that of the USSR. On the polemic with Mila see Gruppi's introduction to Togliatti 1974, pp. 26–29. On Togliatti and the Communist Party's Zdhanovism, see Ajello 1979, p. 235 onwards.
10 Sereni 1949, p. 9.
11 *Il materialismo storico e la filosofia di Benedetto Croce* came out in 1948, and *Gli intellettuali e l'organizzazione della cultura* and *Note su Machiavelli, sulla politica e sullo Stato moderno* came out the following year, *Risorgimento* and *Letteratura e vita nazionale* in 1950, and *Passato e presente* in 1951. At first the 'plan of publication' of the prison writings was made by Felice Platone in a slightly different way. See Gerratana 1989, p. 66. He speculates also about a quite different publication 'by Einaudi, of the writings focused on intellectuals, different from *Unità* that had a more immediate interest to a more or less specialised stratum of readers' (ibid.) Fabrizio Onofri also proposed a 'diplomatic edition' and a 'popular edition' of the *Notebooks*, 'which worked to maximise the readership and render it accessible to the greatest number of readers'. Gerratana 1989, p. 68.

ern identity of the Communist Party, definitively forming the foundation of a notable *diversity* in the panorama of the parties bound to the Third International. The timing, therefore, was a courageous choice, one that did not fail to provoke – at least in some of the older circles – a phenomenon of disorientation, as Alessando Natta witnessed:

> I was at the college [the central college of the Communist Party in Frattochie], as a student, in 1949, when the first volume of the *Notebooks* came out, *Historical Materialism* [The Philosophy of Benedetto Croce], and I remember very well the disturbing effect it had, in particular on our teachers ... they had a different training, which made it very difficult to understand Gramsci's Marxism.[12]

The Notebooks, in fact, inflicted 'a decisive blow to every mechanistic embarrassment of Marxism',[13] impeding the flatness of *Diamat* and proposing 'innumerable extremely difficult questions', as Cesare Luporini recalled:

> [the problem was] how to interpret the book, how to identify and interpret the different levels on which the notes were arranged, how to gather together the fundamental theoretical principles, how to trace them to their roots. And it did not only deal with a particular period of Italian and European history, with revolution and class struggle in itself, but it also dealt with a history that was to remain mysterious to us still for a long time ... and it was precisely these texts which seemed the most enigmatic: those on the history of the party that Gramsci supported, and that had come together in the Resistance ... What was the real link between Gramsci and Leninism? And could one make all this richness flow back into the accepted structures of Stalinist Marxism which seemed so lucid in their simplicity but in which, in the end, it seemed quite difficult to move ... conceptually?[14]

Togliatti was, moreover, quite aware of the 'rupture' which the *Notebooks* constituted with respect to the Marxist-Leninist orthodoxy. In a letter written in the Soviet Union dated 2 April 1941 and addressed to Dimitrov, the leader of the Comintern, Togliatti maintained that:

---

12   See A. Natta's conclusions in De Giovanni, Gerratana and Paggi 1977, p. 274.
13   Togliatti 1974, p. 31.
14   Luporini, *Introduzione*, p. xxviii.

Gramsci's *Notebooks*, almost all of which I have already studied closely, contain material that can only be used after some careful work. Without such treatment, the material cannot be used, and there are even parts which, if they were to be used in the form in which one finds them now, might be of no use to the party.[15]

We can thus see that in 1941 Togliatti had not only studied the *Notebooks* but had also already understood the problematic consequences which their publication might bring. The thematic divisions chosen by Togliatti, a kind of 'montage' of the chronological arrangement, were the means by which he rendered them suitable (if not entirely, taking on board Natta and Luporini's accounts) to both Soviet orthodoxy and the Gramscian legacy, angling the interpretation of the latter in the direction of 'national peculiarity' and not towards the disputes within the international workers' movement of the 1920s and 1930s.

Naturally what appears clear in hindsight could only have been vaguely understood in the years in which the arduous formation of a *communist identity* proceeded to accumulate often heterogeneous material for itself, held together by politics more than theory. The subdivision of Gramsci's prison writings on a thematic basis, while being open to a philological criticism – and certainly also tainted by that censorship frequently mentioned in relation to the *Letters* – thus had the merit of dramatically helping their diffusion and cultural impact. As for the intellectuals, they came to grasp a classic subdivision of knowledge and 'that form of traditional intellectual understanding which Gramsci had entirely overcome'.[16] What was lost, or rather deliberately left in the shadows, was the link between the prison writings and the history of the Communist movement.

The effect of the break which the *Notebooks* had within the panorama of Italian culture was nonetheless enormous, instigating a profound revaluation in all disciplines, from literary history through to political thought. In general one might indeed say that 'the recognition in these fields ... was itself of a national character',[17] as Gramsci had hoped for, above all in the return to historiographical study: from Unification to the Southern question, through to the history of intellectuals. Moreover, it was Togliatti himself who pushed

---

15   See Vacca's introduction to Daniele 2005, p. 25 (letter of April 25th 1941 from Togliatti to Dimitrov).

16   N. Auciello, *Il partito nuovo e la sua capacità intellettuale*, in *Rinascita*, 1975, issue 25, p. 34. Nonetheless also see the balanced judgement of Gerratana in his preface to Gramsci 1975, p. xxxiii.

17   Gramsci 1975, p. 866.

matters in this direction. In his contribution to the meeting of the national Cultural Commission of the Communist Party on 3 April 1953, Togliatti had already emphasised the necessity of Marxist research into Italian history and the valorisation of the progressive thread running through Italian cultural tradition.[18] Not by accident, this appeal was to become the dominant line from 1956 onwards, even if by 1952 the connection between the choice of cultural politics and the necessity of keeping some distance from the dogmatism of Stalinism was already clear:

> The Soviet Union has provided us with an important example of the creation of a socialist culture. The task which now falls to us is thus the creation of an Italian socialist culture ... A socialist culture is, in fact, one that is socialist in content but national in form ... For an Italian socialist culture, Giordano Bruno and Galileo Galilei have greater importance than they do for other countries ... Certainly we must tell educated Italians about Belinsky's thought [but] it is the thought and limitations of Franceso De Sanctis that we must discuss in this area first and foremost. Likewise ... Antonio Labriola remains the first person who established the roots of our culture in the mid-nineteenth century, immediately opening up the way to the progressive thought of the master road to Marxism. The importance of Gramsci in the development of Italian culture seems to me so vital precisely because he knew how to move steadily in this direction and through this same method. From the first years of university, I recall, he had mastered the classics of Marxist thought which were then available in Italy, that is, Marx, Engels and Labriola. And later he knew Lenin and Stalin as well. In his *Prison Notebooks*, however, when he examines the various currents and expressions of Italian culture, you never find a pure negation or an abstract comparison between reality and model. Instead, there is always the attentive and objective analysis of all the positions of thought and culture which interest him, which he breaks up into their elements, showing their origins, the relations to positions in the real world, the contradictions, the inconsistencies.[19]

Gramsci's method and Italian tradition thus became the search for a meeting point with a national culture. But this was also the method and means to create some distance from a Stalinist, Zhdanovist model without at the same time

---

18   See Togliatti, *Intervento*, p. 201 onwards. On this also see Vacca 1984, pp. 232–33.
19   Togliatti, *Intervento*, pp. 200–2.

defining an open break which would have been politically unsustainable (and this is often forgotten by those who stress how this edition of the *Notebooks* may have *downgraded* an alternative strategy for the whole Communist movement to a reflection on a particular *national* reality). These aspects represent in those years two sides of the same coin, impossible to separate without a polemical force which would necessarily remove all the complexities, even at times the contradictions, from the politics of both Togliatti and the Communist Party.

2   Gramsci's 'Anti-Fascism'

Between 1948 and 1953 Togliatti made two interventions both of which need to be discussed here: the commemoration in 1949 at the University of Turin and the speech at Bari in 1952.[20] Turning to the first, Togliatti was certainly moved by the location and audience of where he gave the speech. He focussed in particular on Gramsci's cultural background, invoking the climate in which his education had taken place: after the period of positivist supremacy, Neoidealism had 'freed us of so much provincialism and banality' but had also 'raised up yet more problems, without resolving them'.[21] Next to this existed the contradictory activities of both Croce and Gentile, who took up irrational, decadent, aestheticised positions.

> Distance was growing between the intellectual currents of the country and the life of the people, that is, the real life of the nation, which Gramsci discovered was typical to Italian history ... Antonio Gramsci's thought was formed in this crisis, a crisis out of which, through him, came the impetus to action and which he, indeed he alone, has shown the road by which to overcome and resolve that crisis.[22]

The overcoming of the crisis was possible for Gramsci (and for Togliatti) by turning to 'the history of men, the matrix of all that we know and can know'[23] and 'by helping people rediscover the unity of being and thought, helping them

---

20   See *Pensatore e uomo d'Azione* and *L'antifascismo di Antonio Gramsci* in Togliatti 2001. From 1951 there is also the short writing by Togliatti published in *Il Ponte* on *Gramsci sardo*, now in Togliatti 2001 as well, with interesting annotations on the young Gramsci and his linguistic and glottological studies (to which reference was also made at the Turin conference).
21   Togliatti 2001, p. 137.
22   Togliatti 2001, p. 139.
23   Togliatti 2001, p. 132.

find this unity in concrete history, in concrete struggles to transform and renew this country, creating new economic and social relations therein'.[24] If, therefore, the *Ordine Nuovo* was 'born in the University of Turin', this was possible only because there was also another reality there, that of the workers' movement (the meeting with which Togliatti recalled in a rapid but impressive manner) and, following this, the decisive impact of the Bolshevik Revolution. Togliatti's recollections of Gramsci ranged from the separation between the *intellectuals and the people* in the beginning of the twentieth century to the break represented by the *Ordine Nuovo*, to the tendency of a new closer relation between 'manual and mental labourers' in the difficult years of the Cold War: this is the meaning of the Turin speech, leaving aside the nevertheless important and much noted differences between the interpretation of the role of intellectuals in the very different contexts of the *Ordine Nuovo* and the 'cultural alliance' in the years after the War.

The Bari conference of 1952 on 'Antonio Gramsci's Anti-Fascism' was still more filled with varying historical, political and theoretical arguments, the interweaving of which constituted one of the sharpest moments of Togliatti's reflection in those years on the struggle of the Communist Party against the tendency 'to return to a reactionary hegemony of the old type, extinguishing all forms of democracy'.[25]

Togliatti's speech began from a historical basis, noting the lateness with which many anti-Fascist forces had been marshalled, and followed the history of ideas through an examination of the concept of freedom and the distinctions (while explicitly referring back to De Sanctis) between the liberal tradition (freedom as method) and the democratic tradition (freedom as substance). It was by recalling and deepening this democratic tradition of De Sanctis and Gobetti that Gramsci was able to demonstrate the existence of 'a practical instrument of dominance and social hegemony' within liberal ideology and Fascism's 'violent enactment of the traditions of the ruling class, rendering the rise of the working classes impossible'.[26] He thus delineates the important difference of interpretation between Croce and Gramsci: for the former, 'Fascism was "an intellectual and moral disease which was not only classist but also an emotional one, affecting human imagination and will"'.[27] For the latter, however, it had a very precise class content and could therefore only be fought by the workers' movement. This different conception of Fascism relied

---

24   Togliatti 2001, p. 143.
25   Togliatti 2001, p. 180.
26   Togliatti 2001, p. 167.
27   Ibid. The citation is also dealt with in *Chi è fascista?*, in Croce 1945b.

on a fundamental difference of method: according to Croce, '"research which tries to find the causes of evil in a previous age, even though manifested in the one following" is dangerous and must be criticised'.[28] Gramsci, on the other hand, as well as combating vulgar Marxism and its banalities, 'not only investigates and shows in the full history of the past the premises and conditions of the present, but sees the development of the present within the past, the seed already contained within it'.[29]

The reaffirmation of the relation between Gramsci and the national democratic tradition, specifically in Marxist history; the *reduction* of Croce to the protagonist of bourgeois hegemony and a spectator incapable of grasping the scale of its reformulations; the conception of Fascism as a contemporary current, 'always present, dangerous and menacingly looming over us'[30] – it was the interweaving of these elements which made the Bari conference of 1952 perhaps the most total expression of Togliatti's theoretical reflections in the period of the battle against the electoral changes (the so-called 'fraudulent law') of 1953. The epochal importance of the 'anti-Fascist strategy' – for Togliatti far more than for Gramsci himself – was based on the assumption that Fascism is a constant potential tendency within capitalism, and therefore the democratic anti-Fascist revolution a necessary and irrevocable stage in the struggle for socialism.

3 Interpreting the *Notebooks*

With the publication of the *Prison Notebooks*, reflections on Gramsci broadened and deepened. Perhaps on the basis of the *Letters* alone the moral stature of the Communist leader – along with the general climate established after the War – had resulted in a unity which misrepresented his thought. But if, in the context of the Cold War, the debate on Gramsci still had its Manichean overtones in relation to those writings which were gradually made available from 1948 onwards, there were now studies which – whether accepting or rejecting Gramsci's theses – demonstrated a clear desire to judge him productively, without prejudice. In the Catholic sphere, for example, Felice Giannattasio condemned Gramsci's research without apology, while at the same time recognising the existence of a *common enemy*:

---

28 Togliatti 2001, p. 170. This citation is dealt with in *Di un libro sulla libertà in Italia*, in Croce 1948.
29 Togliatti 2001, p. 171.
30 Togliatti 2001, p. 178.

> If it were sufficient to demonstrate the errors of one's adversaries in order to demonstrate the truths of any given doctrine, then Gramsci would perhaps have succeeded, and it certainly is not for us to contest the validity of some of his criticisms of idealism and materialism. But every attempt to critically defend the philosophy of praxis clashes fatally with his fundamental presupposition, which emphasises praxis over theory ... and this being the case, it remains closed in a blinkered *vital impetus*.[31]

From this viewpoint, Marxism was not able to be the bearer of values and *conscience*: and Gramsci's Marxism therefore entered back into the category of economic determinism, that is of materialism, from which it nonetheless seemed to want to take some distance. A very different tone was taken up in comments by Gianni Baget Bozzo in the journal *Studium*, who outlined the differences separating Gramsci from Stalinism:

> All of Gramsci's work is the negation of cultural dogmatism: his is a concrete historical investigation, an interpretation of reality based on the canons of empirical nature, which for him do not belong to any metaphysics.[32]

Baget Bozzo therefore tried to salvage those materials which could be utilised regardless of any dispute over the *fundamental ends* of their respective visions of the world, an attempt to establish a theory of politics in Gramsci's work. The autonomy of the political act, intuited by Machiavelli and elaborated philosophically by Croce, became a 'central moment of human language' for Gramsci. And with Gramsci, Baget Bozzo overturned the traditionally negative Catholic interpretation of Machiavelli, promising a new political theory for the Church.

The liberals, however, engaged in more fervent criticism. Carlo Antoni in *Mondo*, for example, wrote – in relation to the Gramscian interpretation of Unification – that Gramsci's thought suffered from his having been the 'leader of a party', and thus aimed only 'at providing a historical perspective for his Party's program', treating the problem of the 'Southern agrarian question' anachron-

---

31 F. Giannattasio, *Gli sviluppi italiani della filosofia della prassi*, in *La civiltà cattolica*, 1949, issue 1, pp. 69–70. [Translator's note: 'vital impetus' is a reference to Bergson, *L'Évolution créatrice*.]
32 G. Baget Bozzo, *Gramsci e la fondazione della teoria della politica*, in *Studium*, 1951, issue 3, p. 145.

istically. Here Gramsci failed because 'the political task overtook the scientific work: Jacobinism won out over historicism'.[33]

Aldo Garosci made similar arguments in his review for *Passato e presente*. Gramsci's writings were not 'philosophical writings, nor did they contain an original theory for an effective recreation of Marxism'.[34] Garosci underlined the influence of Gentile, concluding that Gramsci's 'dogmatism ... muffled the liberal direction of his theory'.[35] The same author, two years later, in 1954, would temper his judgement, confirming its central thesis nevertheless in an essay significantly titled 'Totalitism and Historicism in Gramsci's Thought'.[36] Here Garosci underlined the positive influence of Croce, who on the one hand had proposed the 'absolute historicism' entailed by negating the more *materialist* aspects of Marxism, but on the other wrote of the insuperable limits which such a historicism found in the concept of the 'rule of liberty' and in the dream of a 'regulated society', a society with neither contradictions nor history. In the heat of the polemic against Gramsci's 'totalitism', Garosci denied, in the end, even the existence of an ethical political moment, one which he had at first judged positively but then dismissed as merely the instrumental means to 'gather intellectual forces together' and then 'subdue them'.

Croce himself, moreover, explicitly took up Antoni's theses to put an end to 'a game that has gone on far too long', that is, to clear up that misunderstanding which had made Gramsci into an intellectual and thinker capable of opening up new horizons of research. As the philosopher wrote in 1950:

> Gramsci was not able to create a new kind of thought and fulfil the powerful revolution which has been attributed to him because – as Antoni has put it quite rightly – his intention was simply to establish a political party, a calling which has nothing to do with disinterested truthful research.[37]

The Neoidealist philosopher would intervene again in 1952 to forcefully reject the proposal of a cultural, historical line running from De Sanctis to Gramsci, one which had found resonance after the publication of the third volume of the *Notebooks*, 'Literature and National Life'.[38] For Croce, there were no affinit-

---

33   C. Antoni, *Il Risorgimento di Gramsci*, in *Il Mondo*, 1949, issue 8, p. 8.
34   A. Garosci, *Antonio Gramsci – Passato e presente*, in *Il Ponte*, 1952, issue 7, p. 1022.
35   A. Garosci, *Antonio Gramsci – Passato e presente*, in *Il Ponte*, 1952, issue 7, p. 1023.
36   See *Totalitarismo e storicismo nel pensiero di Gramsci* in Garosci 1954.
37   B. Croce, *Un giuoco che dura ormai troppo*, in *Quaderni della 'Critica'*, 1950, issues 17–18, p. 231.
38   For other communist interpretations see M. Alicata, *Gramsci e De Sanctis*, in *La voce del Mezzogiorno*, 1951, issue 7, p. 4 and C. Salinari, *Il ritorno di De Sanctis*, in *Rinascita*, 1952, issue 5, p. 292.

ies between the two authors: the dyad De Sanctis/Gramsci was an 'intervention' by communists who believed 'in the power of making facts simply by repeating words monotonously *ad infinitum*'.[39] The contention around De Sanctis returned, on the political level, in the particular versions of the bond claimed between democracy and socialism in those years. The search for a link between Marxism and democratic culture was pursued, for example, by Valentino Gerratana in an argument made explicitly against Croce in an article in *Società*: the alternative – wrote Gerratana – was due to 'a counter-posing of contents, rather than a substitution of Croce's interpretation of De Sanctis for a Marxist or Gramscian interpretation'. If anything, Gerratana claimed, for Gramsci 'it was Marxism that had been influenced by De Sanctis'. For not only was it true that Marxism inherits the best of past traditions; also

> it must face a similar task today in confronting nineteenth-century democratic thought, the task of renewing the human substance of culture and freeing it from the fetters of old superstructures in a period of profound social transformation.[40]

Through De Sanctis, therefore, light could be shone on those aspects of the *militant critic* which Croce had dismissed, thus radically transforming De Sanctis in order to make him homogeneous with Croce's own critical discourse. This operation obviously contributed to the creation of a new strain of ideology which, on the level of aesthetic criticism, seemed to combine, in Gramsci's name, Verga, De Sanctis, Zhdanov, Lukács, Neorealism, Realism, popular nationalism, etc. – in sum, all those usually heterogeneous elements which combined to form the aesthetic of *metellismo*.[41] This was one of the many different products (today cast in a very bad light) of the thematic recalibration of the *Notebooks*.

In 1951 Giuffré issued the first monograph by Nicola Matteucci, 'Antonio Gramsci and the Philosophy of Praxis'. For Matteucci, Gramsci's work consisted in substituting the three classic 'sources' of Marxism (German philosophy, English political economy, French political theory) with authors coming from the Italian tradition, with the goal of making it acceptable to Italian – first and foremost Crocean – intellectuals. As such 'Hegel and the French Revolution were substituted with Croce and Machiavelli ... allowing for the emergence of

---

39   B. Croce, *De Sanctis-Gramsci*, in *Lo spettatore italiano*, 1952, issue 7, p. 294.
40   V. Gerratana, *De Sanctis-Croce o De Sanctis-Gramsci? (Appunti per una polemica)* in *Società*, 1952, issue 3, pp. 498–9.
41   On these themes see Ajello 1975, chapters 7 and 10.

a philosophy of praxis derived directly from the Italian cultural tradition'.[42] In this work of *translation*, Gramsci gave life to a profoundly original perspective, uniting different Leninist themes (the party, hegemony) with the refusal of Bukharin's economism (thanks to Croce's influence). 'This was no mere meeting of Croce and Lenin, or a Croce who explains Lenin, or a Lenin who criticises Croce' claimed the author, 'but a synthetic development, a qualitative leap for all Italian culture'.[43] Nonetheless, Matteucci was less disposed to positively welcoming the effort of *synthesis* provided by Gramsci, keeping his distance from the political and ethical level of his thought. Not only was Gramsci homogeneous to Lenin (for the anti-deterministic re-evaluation of subjectivity) but went beyond him, by comparing 'the modern Prince to the categorical imperative, the absolute bearer of good and evil, the only criteria of virtue or wickedness, aligning himself with the theses of Stalin and Zdhanov'. For the Party, Stalinism lay 'at the centre of man's life', and Matteucci opposed it to a 'modern secularism' that did not want to substitute 'freedom of conscience for the "divinity" of the Party – a kind of secularism deriving from a reaction against all those intermediaries between man and divinity, the prioritising of a form of reasoning that implies tolerance and therefore liberty'.[44]

Some of the questions debated by Matteucci returned again in the articles which originally appeared in *Critica sociale* and were later collected in a small work put out in 1955, which Rodolfo Mondolfo dedicated to 'Gramsci and the philosophy of praxis'. One of the protagonists of the Italian Marxist debate at the turn of the century, Mondolfo had reprinted the 1908 *anti-metaphysical* reading of Marx provided by Antonio Labriola. As well as deriving from positivism, his work was above all an attempt to devise a conception of Marxism which would overcome fatalistic determinism on the one hand and overly subjective voluntarism on the other. In purely philosophical terms therefore, he wanted to refute any unidirectional relation between subject and object, man and environment, thought and action, underlining the reciprocal bond of the dialectical relation. In his 1955 booklet, Mondolfo – now 72 years old – did not deny the elements which accommodated his interpretation with that of Gramsci, because 'he, as much as myself, felt the influence of Labriola so strongly'.[45] In contrast to Matteucci, Mondolfo thus pointed out the continuity not only of the *pars destruens*, i.e. in opposition to common enemies, but also the fact that such

---

42   Matteucci 1951, pp. 18–19.
43   Matteucci 1951, p. 157.
44   Matteucci 1951, p. 74.
45   See Mondolfo 1955, p. 25. On Mondolfo's Marxism, see Bobbio's introduction to Mondolfo 1968.

oppositions arose from common ground, from exactly that of the *philosophy of praxis*. The 'contradiction' which Mondolfo noted in Gramsci was moreover more political than theoretical: the adhesion to Leninism, the *subjectivism* of a 'Bolshevik' model that was also reconstructed in the *Notebooks:* 'the idea of a revolution that pushes along the times, obeys a negative conception of historical maturity', one which looks to backward situations (the 'weak links') rather than to the existence of 'conditions, elements and constructive forces'. And this inevitably provided the basis for Jacobin misconstruals and Stalinist deformations.[46]

For the most part, this resumed an argument from the 1920s, founded on Mondolfo's interpretation of Leninism as not recognising signs of 'the immaturity of the historical conditions' in the *subjective immaturity* of the masses.[47] Gramsci's adhesion to Leninism had been read by Mondolfo as 'contradictory' because 'there also exists a profoundly Marxist Gramsci, one who rises up with us against that of the Leninists and Stalinists',[48] as would be demonstrated in the concept of the 'historical bloc' aimed at overcoming divisions between rulers and ruled, intellectuals and the people. Meanwhile, for Mondolfo, the role which the Bolsheviks came to assign to elites rendered the reabsorption of these distinctions and juxtapositions by the masses impossible. In terms dear to Gramsci (and to the tradition of the philosophy of praxis), Mondolfo wrote that 'the educator ought not superimpose himself dictatorially on those being educated ... he must not demand from them a conformism which, as such, can never be "active": the education of freedom cannot be made through authoritarian and despotic means, but only through those of that very same freedom itself'.[49] While not always traversing theoretical and historical political planes very clearly, Mondolfo nonetheless undoubtedly summarised some of the problematic and highly debatable moments of Gramsci's legacy.

4   Dogmatic and Non-dogmatic Marxisms

The price paid in those years to 'Marxist-Leninist' orthodoxy is visible in the writings of many Communist authors. In the first issue of *Società* in 1948, Emilio Sereni provided a singularly important contribution, destined to be repeatedly reprinted and cited, providing a new point of reference for those interpreta-

---

46   Mondolfo 1955, p. 60.
47   Mondolfo 1955, p. 39.
48   Mondolfo 1955, p. 61.
49   Mondolfo 1955, p. 58.

tions of Gramsci which were less inclined to hark back to traditional democratic thought. Sereni began by remembering how 'at college, Gramsci did not stand on the side of Croce and idealist criticism, but with the working class'.[50] This allowed the Sardinian leader to have a real criticism of Neoidealism: he (and not Labriola) was in fact the first Italian Marxist, and his thought represented 'a leap' with respect to our national culture. On the fundamental basis of the theory of hegemony, Gramsci had become connected to Lenin and thanks to this Italian culture had finally re-established 'its living and productive link with the science of the vanguard, with the most progressive and modern currents of global thought'.[51] Warning against 'hasty interpretations and superficial alterations' (even if 'in good faith'), Sereni also cautioned against interpreting the *Notebooks* 'without reflecting on their vital link with Gramsci's organisational activity in the factory councils, the founding of the *Ordine Nuovo* group and his subsequent founding and leadership of the Italian Communist Party'.[52] These were moments in an uninterrupted political struggle, 'a weapon of that struggle'. Sereni emphasised historical, theoretical claims that had indeed been left aside in those years despite their veracity. Nevertheless, the *political* meaning of this emphasis is clear enough, inasmuch as connecting Gramsci to a national specificity also allowed him to provide a certain theoretical, political autonomy (even if only relatively) from Stalinism. If the 'kernel' of Gramscian ideas was found in the theory of hegemony (not incorrectly), then making this the connection between him and 'vanguard knowledge' (i.e. Stalinist Marxism-Leninism) would have meant also hollowing out not only Gramsci but the entire development of an 'Italian road'.

To be precise, this was not so much an *attack* on the Togliattian line as a juxtaposing of 'Stalinist' and 'Gramscian' lines within a general context that downplayed the more original parts of 'Salerno' era politics and culture. Yet there were those – such as Sereni – who went further still in their search for an organic homogeneity among all the positions supported by the Third International, positions that included different focuses, potentials and directions. Togliatti had relied on this *diversity* in the period immediately after the War, using Gramsci as the inspiration and standard for his *own* political project. (And it is worth noting that even in the darker years of the Cold War, Togliatti would never lose sight of this 'Gramscian originality'). As for the rest, the combination of Gramsci and Stalin was present in many authors of a quite different

---

50 Sereni 1948, p. 10.
51 Sereni 1948, p. 27.
52 Sereni 1948, p. 20.

character from Sereni, those more attentive to Gramsci's national specificity – such as Mario Alicata and Lucio Lombardo Radice.[53] The influence of Soviet Marxism-Leninism could be felt in other positions that more explicitly imitated 'Diamat', i.e. the 'dialectical materialism' to which Gramsci was not only an outsider but which he had even openly criticised. The biologist Massimo Aloisi attempted to 'analyse Gramsci's thought in relation to ... natural sciences and the gnoseological problems to which they are connected'.[54] Aloisi took up the theme of the *objectivity* of nature, his thesis being that Gramsci, engaged in criticising both Croce and scientific positivism, had left space for some margin of ambiguity in his critique of idealism. However, not wanting to speak badly of Gramsci, Aloisi took recourse to an almost Byzantine logic by which

> Gramsci laid out the correct critique of Bukharin's positivism, but clearly one cannot simply substitute Crocean idealism with some other form of idealism. A reader not familiar with Gramsci might fall into some form of idealism if he were to forget the reality (and therefore historicity) of a world before the appearance of man and on which the existence and history of man depends ... We must hold to a dialectic of nature which has nature itself as both the beginning and end of dialectical human thought. One such formulation is of course dialectical materialism, which is to be found in the thought of Antonio Gramsci.[55]

A reader of the *Notebooks* could be helped along in an erroneous interpretation therefore by Gramsci himself, for while he had managed to effectively combat positivist positions, this was at the risk of being misunderstood as adhering to idealism. If Aloisi expressed some concerns, others went still further in the course of the debate. This was the case with Armando Borrelli, who spoke of 'Gramsci's residual idealism' and the 'idealistic elements dispersed among the materialist ones'.[56] This was nevertheless still a minority position: more space would be given over to the polemic against Gramsci's 'idealism' from the end of the 1950s when it was taken up by the 'school of Della Volpe' and subsequently by Althusser.

---

53   See M. Alicata, *Antonio Gramsci – Gli intellettuali e l'origine della cultura*, in *Società*, 1949, issue 1; and L. Lombardo Radice, *Una strada nuova*, in *l'Unità*, 11th September 1948.
54   M. Aloisi, *Gramsci, la scienza a la natura come storia*, in *Società*, 1950, issue 3, p. 385.
55   M. Aloisi, *Gramsci, la scienza a la natura come storia*, in *Società*, 1950, issue 3, p. 409.
56   A. Borrelli, *Scienza, natura e storia in Gramsci*, in *Società*, 1951, issue 1, p. 105. In this issue there were also contributions from Francesco Albergamo, Armando Borrelli, Omero Bianca and a reply from Aloisi.

In 1950, however, the Fondazione Gramsci was established with the aim of promoting the publication of Gramsci's writings and the close study of his works.[57] Under the direction of Ambrogio Donini, and in keeping with the 'Zhdanovism' of Sereni's cultural work in the Communist Party, the society found itself working within the same contradictions that Togliatti had encountered in his thematic editing of the *Notebooks*. On the level of 'cultural activity' the Party seemed stuck on a model which considered intellectuals as allies in mobilising support for the USSR and global peace. After the 7th Congress of the Communist Party (1951), Communist cultural politics partly overcame this Zhdanovist position by electing Carlo Salinari as secretary of the cultural commission. The following year, he would provide a self-critique on the work undertaken over the preceding period, making his own reference to Gramsci:

> We did not succeed in creating an instrument that might inspire enthusiasm for research and study in our country, the kind of fervour that we lack in other fields in our national culture. And even though we had the possibility of doing so, we failed to provide a platform on which to mobilise Italian intellectuals in order to inspire them in taking their research in a new direction: the works of Antonio Gramsci. This is the nucleus around which all the problems of Italian culture today will be focussed. Antonio Gramsci quite clearly represents the point of departure for a new Italian cultural movement, not just for Communist intellectuals, but for culture as a whole.[58]

In a yet more acute moment of the 'Cold War' and the strong link with the USSR, Togliatti's *anti-sectarian* choice in the cultural sphere provided a clear indication, the return to a fundamental decision, the 'politics of Salerno' – a politics that was by now perhaps *obfuscated* but not entirely denied.

In 1953 the first proposal for a conference on Gramsci organised by the Fondazione Gramsci was not followed through,[59] perhaps due to a 'conflict

---

57   For this history of the Fondazione Gramsci, from 1954 called Istituto Gramsci, see Vittoria 1992.
58   *Estratti del rapporto presentato dal compagno Carlo Salinari, responsabile della sezione culturale centrale*, in *Per una cultura libera moderna nazionale: Documenti della Commissione culturale nazionale. Roma, 3 aprile 1952*. Rome, no date, p. 26.
59   See *Progetto per il 'Convegno di studi gramsciani'* in Vittoria 1992, pp. 267–270. In the *Progetto* are previews of Togliatti's general remarks and of the three sessions (Gramsci and the history of Italy, modern thought, literature), with remarks from, respectively, Gastone Manacorda, Grieco and Platone; Donini; Muscetta.

of interests' between Togliatti and Donini.[60] The latter wanted above all to argue against the 'false conception' of a Gramsci 'who writes and speaks of the problems of the working class outside of the concrete struggle against opportunism'.[61] He returned therefore to that description of Gramsci as 'leader of the Party' which we saw had dominated the 1930s, but which was now opposed to the Togliattian description of Gramsci as a 'great intellectual' and the legacy of all Italians.

At the end of 1954 the Fondazione Gramsci was the scene of another important cultural controversy. Invited by Donini to introduce a meeting of historians, Arturo Colombi became the protagonist of a harsh reprimand aimed at those Communist historians (Gastone Manacorda first among them) who, with their 'scientific' activities, refused to take on board the 'militant' model represented by Stalin's. In his speech, Colombi criticised historians for utilising Gramsci and his 'terminology' – not without its 'idealist strands' – 'with the aim of making our theory more palatable for people who are scared to confront the clean and precise terms of Marxism-Leninism'.[62] Colombi's speech provoked reaction and protest from historians, as much in relation to the propositions and method of their own work as care for the 'pensive and purposeful' character of Gramsci's own language.[63] But above all he provoked a harsh letter from Togliatti to Donini, in which the secretary of the Communist Party claimed that

> if in Italy today ... we have managed to establish enough contacts in, and penetrate into, the cultural world, that has depended on the fact that we avoided judging matters from afar, and instead tried to develop our own capabilities; that we prioritised and carried out objective research. At the same time, however we did not simply reject – nor, worse, ignore – that which came to us from different quarters. Instead, we have engaged in debates without pretending that we are infallible. This is also, moreover, one of the reasons for the great success of Gramsci's work: that in the end it arrives at the fiercest of criticism but always following the enemy closely, with scrupulous philology and true scholarship.[64]

---

60 Vittoria 1992, pp. 23–6.
61 Vittoria 1992, p. 24.
62 A. Colombi, *Orientamenti e compiti della storiografia marxista in Italia*, typescript, p. 25.
63 Vittoria 1992, p. 56. Also see p. 48 onwards for the reconstruction of the episode.
64 Vittoria 1992, p. 275.

The error, for Togliatti, was that Gramsci had appeared only in the last pages of Colombi's contribution: 'Gramsci began the Marxist historiography of our country ... it would be better to start with Gramsci and continue his novel investigation of historiography'.[65] Colombi's polemic on Gramsci's 'language' provoked a very strong criticism:

> Gramsci expressed himself like the scholars of the times and of his country, without nevertheless conceding anything to the substance of their opinions ... In every country Marxism must know how to fight on the grounds of national culture, in its traditions, in its mode of being and self-development, if it wants to become an active and determining part of this development.[66]

Here the cornerstones of the struggle for a *national* culture re-emerged. In the context of the time, for the Communist Party this meant being as independent from the USSR as possible. Moreover, this 'historiographic' polemic came at the time of the struggle against Secchia, who would leave the 4th Conference of the organisation defeated (January 1955). In 1955 Alessandro Natta became director of the Istituto Gramsci: the process of renewing the Communist Party was thus begun *before the earthquake of 1956*, and of course Gramsci was called upon to play out his role at the highest level.

5   Dissonances

Gramsci's legacy produced results that went in many directions, setting down deep roots and opening up new horizons of research, above all in those of the historiography of Unification[67] and a revision of the 'Southern question'.[68]

---

65   Vittoria 1992, pp. 275–6.
66   Vittoria 1992, p. 276.
67   See G. Manacorda, *Una visione nuova del Risorgimento italiano*, in *l'Unità*, 31st August 1947; G. Manacorda, *Il 'Risorgimento' di Antonio Gramsci*, in *Società*, 1949, issue 2; F. Platone, *A. Gramsci: 'Il Risorgimento'*, in *Rinascita*, 1949, issue 4.
68   See M. Alicata, *Gramsci e il Mezzogiorno*, in *l'Unità*, 27th April 1952; F. Ferri, *Questione meridionale e unità nazionale in Gramsci*, in *Rinascita*, 1952, issue 1. A study is needed in order to evaluate the influence of Gramscism on the politics of the Communist Party in the South and on the journal *Cronache meridionale*, which would be on Amendola, Alicata, Chiaromonte, Napolitano. Against Gramscianism there was on the other hand the journal *Nord e Sud*, edited by Francesco Compagna, inspired by Croceanism and liberalism, on which see Ajello 1979, p. 328 onwards.

Another field in which the *Notebooks* provoked a debate of no small account was cultural anthropology, leading on from Ernesto De Martino's essay 'Towards a History of the Subaltern Popular World' published in *Società* in 1949. An intellectual in the Crocean mould, but already distanced from his teacher through his *The Magical World* of 1948, De Martino made use of some of Gramsci's ideas, deriving them from the publication *Historical Materialism* rather than the 'Observations on Folklore', an essay published only in 1951 in the volume on *Literature and National Life*. De Martino began with a critique of *bourgeois* ethnology, which considered the world 'after Eboli' as 'ahistorical', *natural* and immutable due to its 'subaltern' existence. The author claimed that today, on the other hand, 'the popular masses are fighting on the world stage in order to enter history, to overturn the very order that keeps them as subaltern'.[69] De Martino connected the idea of the peoples of the Third World with the 'subaltern strata' of 'hegemonic countries', and therefore cited the unavoidable problems of the 'barbarisation of culture and habits' emerging along with 'the eruption' of the masses into history, citing in defence Gramsci's thesis on the contamination of Marxism with 'popular conceptions' ('vulgar materialism'). While these 'reactionary' elements needed to be used in politics and used to a positive end, 'high traditional culture' faced the task 'of *historicising* the "popular" and the "primitive", of dealing with the archaism of historical passion', passion that must in the end lead to the 'popular modern reform' heralded by Gramsci.

With this fundamental moment of *historicisation* of the popular world, no longer reading it as *nature* but as a product of bourgeois cultural hegemony, De Martino developed an idea which could not but provoke the reactions of Gramscian intellectuals. *Società* published a review by Cesare Luporini who, while appreciating the anti-naturalist critique, contested the thesis of the 'barbarisation' of culture as the 'irruption of the masses into history' and in particular the pertinence of invoking Gramsci; for him, De Martino had not understood that the forced 'alliance' of Marxism with tendencies such as 'vulgar materialism' was a residual act, one that would be eliminated by the extension of working-class hegemony through the cultural spheres.[70] For Luporini the origin of this misunderstanding lay in the fact that De Martino had not understood 'the particular function of the working class' and the role of its 'organised vanguard': on the one hand, the concept of 'the subaltern popular world' was clearly too

---

69 E. De Martino, *Intorno a una storia del mondo popolare subalterno*, in *Società*, 1949, issue 3, p. 149.
70 C. Luporini, *Intorno alla storia del 'mondo popolare subalterno'*, in *Società*, 1950, issue 1, pp. 99–100.

indeterminate (slipping into populism, that is); on the other, De Martino's work lacked a vision of the role of a revolutionary party engaged in the passage – in Gramscian terms – from a 'subaltern culture' to a 'hegemonic culture', with all that this includes for the *transformation* of the working class which becomes a leader through leading, a transformation which Marxism, as the most advanced theory, must render possible. In other words – casting aside the chaff of the times – Luporini reprimanded De Martino for a *static* vision of society, one which does not allow for the possibility of change: a classic Marxist critique of cultural anthropology in subsequent years.[71]

The polemic continued in *Società*[72] as well as flowing over into the daily press.[73] With the publication of Gramsci's 'Observations on Folklore', De Martino changed his own position, criticising the author of the *Notebooks* for not having grasped the progressive potential of popular culture, what De Martino called *progressive folklore*.[74] Aside from the specific aspects of the ethnological debate, this introduced the Gramscian concept of *subaltern culture* into the discipline, necessarily defined through its relation to *cultural hegemony* and, by these means, the assumption of class divisions in society. This was a strand of thought destined to be taken up and developed in the following decades.

There was no lack of attempts to interpret the *Notebooks* in an original manner, including within political theory proper. For example, the essay by Vezio Crisafulli on 'State and Society in Gramsci's Thought' emphasised an element destined to be much repeated:

> The most general establishment of the work that Gramsci proposed to develop ... necessarily invoked the problem of the state, in fact representing a new and extremely suggestive attempt to explore it *from within*.[75]

This was, for Crisafulli, the key to Gramsci, deriving from the problems of the Soviet revolution and, above all, from those of the 'revolution in the West'. Starting from the assumption that the 'recognition of national character' demanded by the complexity of civil society represented 'the final and essentially political

---

71   For the international fortune of the Gramscian concept of the subaltern which would really take off from the 1990s, see below, p. 301 onwards.

72   E. De Martino and C. Luporini, *Ancora sulla 'storia del mondo popolare subalterno'* in *Società*, 1950, issue 2.

73   See the articles by L. Anderlini, F. Fortini, A.M. Cirese and others in *Avanti!* Now in Pasquinelli 1977.

74   See E. De Martino, *Il folklore progressivo*, in *l'Unità*, 28th June 1951; and E. De Martino, *Gramsci e il folklore*, in *Il calendario del popolo*, 1951, issue 7.

75   V. Crisafulli, *Stato e società nel pensiero di Gramsci*, in *Società*, 1951, issue 4, p. 583.

objective of Gramsci's prison research',[76] Crisafulli arrived at the theme of hegemony, highlighting its connection with Lenin's studies but also the concept's peculiar originality: 'the state as all of society', that is, the balance of forces between the classes confronted concretely as *the problem of the state* in itself. For him, the conclusion of Gramscian research lay in that which, in the 1960s, would come to be defined as the 'expansion of the concept of the state'. For Crisafulli this was the discovery that 'the state is not *only* the political-juridical apparatus of the dictatorship of the dominant class, but *also* the "private apparatus of hegemony"'.[77]

Crisafulli's essay has the merit of reviving an otherwise outdated interpretative voice. The fact that it remained an isolated attempt, without significant repercussions, demonstrates the influence of the process of editing Gramsci's work, a process that framed the cultural politics of the Communist Party in those years. There were other *anomalous* voices, including among Communists. The article on 'Antonio Gramsci and Cultural Responsibilities' that Remo Cantoni published in *Studi filosofici* in 1948 was in some ways unconventional, but it was also representative of a position – that of the group gathered around Banfi – that attempted to resist the closures of the Cold War and the flattening out under Zhdanovism without nevertheless claiming a continuous line between 'De Sanctis/Labriola/Gramsci'. Cantoni attempted to emphasise Gramsci's *critique*, the impossibility of reducing him either to the dogmatism of common sense and scientific positivism or to a vulgar Marxism and naïve realism. Gramsci was more concerned with 'understanding matters than making summary moral judgements', viewing Marxism 'as a dynamic cultural process that will always produce new cultural syntheses'.[78] The reprisal of Gramsci's polemic against the vulgarisation of Marxism and dogmatism seemed to represent an indictment of Stalinism above all. In combating Marxism's *vulgarisation* – the author added – Gramsci had wanted 'to solder the intellectuals to the masses', advancing the claims of 'democratic philosophy'; he was a firm believer in the continual role of change within a society that desires and is committed to its self-transformation. By including the struggle against dogmatic Marxism, the confrontation with modern culture, and the new relations of the intellectuals to the masses, Cantoni's reading of 'Gramsci's critical and humanist historicism' staked out a greater distance from the Soviet model than any

---

76   V. Crisafulli, *Stato e società nel pensiero di Gramsci*, in *Società*, 1951, issue 4, p. 590.
77   V. Crisafulli, *Stato e società nel pensiero di Gramsci*, in *Società*, 1951, issue 4, p. 601. On the 'expansive concept of the state' see below p. 178 onwards.
78   R. Cantoni, *Antonio Gramsci e le responsabilità della cultura*, in *Studi filosofici*, 1948, issue 2, p. 141. On Cantoni see Montaleone 1996.

other interpretation. These perspectives were as distant from each other as 'hegemony' was from 'dictatorship':

> A culture becomes hegemonic not through a compulsory process but a historical one. The principle of hegemony is by nature both ethical and political, the result of a struggle in which there is no possibility of fraud or abuse, because it deals with the creation of a new 'common sense', a renewed 'common good'.[79]

A convincing position, especially in the face of the continuing developments within the reality of Soviet socialism.

6   The History of the Italian Communist Party

In the first half of the 1950s these polemical positions were played out through interpretations of the history of the Communist Party. The deliberate attempt in those years, among communist activists and Party members, to form a historical consciousness in terms of the birth and development of the Party was advanced through the second volume of *Quaderno di 'Rinascita'*, dedicated to 'Thirty years of the Communist Party', published in April 1952 and edited by Togliatti. The volume contained around forty essays, dedicated to either periods or protagonists selected from throughout the history of the Party. The chosen formula itself, that of a plurality of essays in place of a holistic reconstruction, perhaps softened the edges of the project's official form but it also left space for partiality and ambiguity. Nevertheless, the instructions given to the authors by Togliatti (published by *Rinascita* in 1970) had far more negative implications, tending as they did towards a biased reconstruction of the interpretation of those 'historic minorities' on both the right and the left that had come out of the defeat of the internal struggles of the 1920s and 1930s.[80] It was Togliatti's vein of 'Stalinist historiography' which bore the brunt of the cultural climate of the international Communist movement, becoming in truth something very far from Gramsci's own thought, which thought it had

---

79   R. Cantoni, *Antonio Gramsci e le responsabilità della cultura*, in *Studi filosofici*, 1948, issue 2, p. 163.
80   See *Il piano di Togliatti per il 'Quaderno' dedicato al trentesimo del PCI*, in *Rinascita*, 1970, issue 48, where we read on p. 21: 'One can see clearly and objectively from the exposition the infamous Bordigist doctrines, made only in a way which was critical and destructive'.

contained a stinging and harsh polemic on reality, and had never falsified it. Already in 1938, in one of the historical conjunctures that saw the PCd'I depend more and more on Stalin's USSR, and already shocked by the violent 'purges', Togliatti had written: 'In 1930 [Gramsci] introduced into the prisons the indicative phrase "Trotsky is the whore of Fascism"'.[81] It was a claim without any basis and is today entirely unjustifiable. But worse still was the re-emergence of this approach between 1948 and 1953, in yet another confirmation of that *suspension* of the 'politics of Salerno' of which we have already spoken.

Turning to the *Quaderni di 'Rinascita'*, the history of the Party was now territory designated as *off limits* for historians who wanted to exercise a 'craft' of their own. The result was a weak reconstruction full of omissions, particularly in relation to the 'first period', that of the Bordigist current. An essay signed by Giuseppe Berti, contesting the theoretical political positions of the first real leader of the PCd'I, brought together a series of insults typical of Stalinist propaganda, including the claim that after the conquest of the Party by the group led by Gramsci, 'Bordigism and Trotskyism were united in a single front of Fascist and bourgeois agents, traitors and spies'.[82] The treatment of the 'rotten opportunist' Angelo Tasca was no better, nor that of Silone or the 'three' (Leonetti, Tresso, Ravazzoli) who had opposed the 'turn' of 1929.

As for Gramsci himself, many referenced him consistently, along with Togliatti, in the struggle against Bordigist 'extremism' and right-wing 'opportunism', and among these articles and writings of various tones we should note a unique contribution (and this itself is a fact not easily explained away) by Felice Platone on the *'Ordine Nuovo'*, largely dedicated to the Sardinian leader.[83] Following precise instructions from Togliatti,[84] the author underlined the richness and limits of the group's project. Drawing on previous essays by Togliati, Platone paid particular attention to the young Gramsci's cultural background and refuted the accusations of voluntarism and spontaneity so often attributed to the group of young Turinese communists. Even if there were elements of interest, such as the references to the divergence between Gramsci and Togliatti

---

81 P. Togliatti, *Antonio Gramsci capo della classe operai italiana*, p. 88.
82 G. Berti, *La natura controrivoluzionaria del bordighismo*, in *Trenta anni di vita e lotte del PCI, Quaderni di 'Rinascita'*, 1952, issue 2, p. 63.
83 F. Platone, *L''Ordine Nuovo'*, p. 35.
84 On the *Ordine Nuovo*, Togliatti wrote that 'the critique is touched upon by me in the essay on Gramsci's death and by others, if you want. It must not, however, be destructive, but conclude with a lack of experience, the tiring search for the correct path'. *Il piano di Togliatti per il 'Quaderno' dedicato al trentesimo del PCI*, in *Rinascita*, 1970, issue 4, p. 21.

in 1920, the essay mainly repeated the line already noted, a repetitive celebration and hagiography which remained one of the more negative moments in the history of the Communist cultural politics over the Stalinist years.

Works that attempted a reconstruction of the historical events of the Communist Party in radical opposition to the 'official' interpretation nevertheless often contained distortions as well, however. They attempted to *rewrite* the history of the Communist Party from the viewpoint of those sections of the Party (the 'right' of Tasca and the 'left' of Bordiga) that had been defeated in the long internal struggle of the 1920s. The first of these was the *Storia del Partito comunista italiano* by Fulvio Bellini and Giorgio Galli, which appeared in 1953, and which is remembered for being the first attempt at an organic reconstruction of the history of the Communist Party. For all its very real merits, it was nonetheless tainted by its unscientific *picture-book* style and its research put into doubt by the lack of references to sources and some garish inexactitudes. These failures, however, are also testament to the entirely pioneering character of the work, in a situation characterised by a lack of sources – the archives were closed to the public – and an overly cautious self-censorship among the circle of Communist leaders. It was no accident that the main Communist historians avoided dealing with the history of the Communist *Party*, leaving this terrain almost entirely open to *unscientific* contributions of the party leaders.

Without hiding their sympathy for Bordiga, the authors at least had the merit of emphasising for the first time the importance of the role that the Neopolitan engineer had plated the Livorno split until the Congress of Lyons. From the Congress of Rome of 1922, Bellini and Galli maintained, there were 'differences of orientation among those who formed the majority of the party and in particular among Bordiga's abstentionist current and the group around the *Ordine Nuovo*'.[85] It was only during his Moscow trip that Gramsci put some distance between himself and Bordiga as far as the relation with the International was concerned. Gramsci appeared therefore as 'the Moscow man', who had inserted himself into the process of the bureaucratisation of the international Communist movement, conquering the leadership of the PCd'I with the aid of 'bureaucratic, coercive systems'. 'Today the official historiography makes Antonio Gramsci the precursor, the founder, the leader of the Communist Party from the incandescent days of Livorno onwards', while 'in reality, from a strictly political point of view, the figure who was dominant far longer ... from the national conference at Como onwards' had been Bordiga.[86]

---

85   Bellini and Galli 1953, p. 52.
86   Bellini and Galli 1953, p. 191.

As for Gramsci, the book took an interest in him only up until his arrest. He was described as a figure with an 'enormous talent for sharp thought and a fighting tenacity', but they also attributed to him 'quite general omissions that undoubtedly characterised his personality and which appear quite negatively when seen from a political point of view'.[87] In substance this was the old Bordigist line that Gramsci was 'an intellectual of the classical mould, with all the virtues but also with all the defects of a petty bourgeois intellectual, not excluding the tendency for *petite-bohemian* pretensions'.[88] While Togliatti was cited as representative of the official image of Communist hagiography, he was not described as having had any important disagreements with Gramsci, neither at the time of the *Ordine Nuovo*, nor in the period of the distancing from Bordiga, nor above all in 1926. Even though the authors cited the (at the time, misunderstood) letter of the feud within the Bolshevik party, published in France by Tasca in 1938, they did so only to highlight the 'uncertainty' of the whole of the PCd'I's towards the struggle within the ranks of the Comintern.[89] In the work of Bellini and Galli, therefore, there was no place for reflections on the *sectarian* limits of the 'first phase' of the PCd'I and the successes of the 'new party': on the contrary, the authors claimed that the Communist Party had become a large party not thanks to but in spite of Gramsci and Togliatti's line, in that exact moment – that of the armed struggle and the Resistance – in which the masses did not, according to Bordiga, have 'any kind of democratic illusions'. Despite their questionable thesis, the book remains important in indicating the gaps, delays and omissions in a historiography that was being partially created by the Communist Party itself.

While these were the criticisms confronting Togliatti's current from one side, on the other side there were Angelo Tasca's essays from 1953. Although interesting inasmuch as they display the account of one of the protagonists, as well as the reconstruction itself, one cannot ignore the political positions of the author. A leader at the top level of the PCd'I until his expulsion in 1929 (and frequently in open conflict with Gramsci from 1920 onwards),[90] after a painful political experience Tasca had taken a position during the Cold War of irrevocable anti-Communism, in the conviction that 'Togliatti's "democracy" was and remains an expedient, simply a long tactical respite in the struggle for the tri-

---

[87] Bellini and Galli 1953, p. 16.
[88] Bellini and Galli 1953, p. 129.
[89] Bellini and Galli 1953, p. 210, note 1.
[90] In the writings examined here Tasca claimed that Gramsci had overvalued the Turin movement of the councils, ignoring traditional forms of working-class organisation, first and foremost the union.

umph of totalitarianism in Italy'.[91] On the historiographic level, Tasca radically opposed the thesis which held that the *Ordine Nuovo* was the fulcrum around which the genesis of the PCd'I turned, emphasising instead the pre-eminent role of Bordiga from the Rome Congress onward (opposed only by himself and Graziadei);[92] and so here Gramsci was in fact made part of the Bordigist majority:

> one still found strong traces of 'Bordigism' in the politics of the Party up until 1926, even after the Congress of Lyons in which Bordiga was 'defeated'; the exile of the Party leadership was necessary for the Bordigists to be removed.[93]

In parallel with this thesis on Gramsci's (and above all also Togliatti's) 'Bordigism', Tasca underlined the often-noted points of divergence between the positions of the two Communist leaders:

> The theoretical and practical fidelity of Togliatti to Gramsci is a myth. Togliatti was in conflict with Gramsci, as seen from the documents, on at least three questions: the factory councils, on which he 'joined Tasca' from the summer of 1920; his position on 'Bordigism', which he followed up until the spring of 1924; and the nature of the relations of each with the International and the Russian leaders.[94]

He ended up, therefore, radically denying Togliatti's interpretative line, citing documents (among them the letter of 1926) which were then either unknown or little noted, or recounting episodes which had either been struck from or diminished in the historiography of the Party: Gramsci and Togliatti's 'interventionism', the councilism of the *Ordine Nuovo*, the conflicts within the group, the attempted meeting between Gramsci and D'Annunzio, the difficulty which came with the creation of the Gramscian 'centre', the conflicts within the ranks of the Communist Party of the Soviet Union and the International. Tasca broke the *monopoly* over the history of the Communist Party that the leading group

---

91   A. Tasca, *Una storia del Partito comunista italiano*, in *Critica sociale*, 1954, issues 2, 3 and 4, now in Tasca 1971, p. 218. This volume also contains a review of the book by Bellini and Galli which appeared in *Critica sociale*, and of the essay 'I primi dieci anni del Partito comunista italiano', which Tasca had published in 1953 in six issues of *Mondo*, numbers 33–8. The citations are to this edition.
92   Tasca 1971, p. 126.
93   Tasca 1971, p. 218.
94   Tasca 1971, p. 150.

had maintained, at the same time slowly introducing a more scientific and fact-driven reconstruction, one that would be developed over the 1960s on Togliatti's own initiative.

7 A Legendary Comrade

Up to this point we have examined the works of intellectuals and political leaders. It would be an error to claim that these were only of interest to the political class and men of culture. One of the most important aspects of the 'New Party' was its ability to raise the cultural bar for all communist activists, inviting them to participate in a new 'world view' and to measure themselves against the complex problems of society. For the first time, those masses who had usually been extraneous to political life would become conscious of their own forces and their real social function. For the first time, the masses would be occupied in a great task of cultural expansion, learning to read the newspaper of the Party press, and to discuss it too.[95] For post-War Italy, this provided the first occasion of cultural education being offered to the poorest classes within the party, which now took on a role comparable to that of obligatory scholastic instruction and, consequently, of *mass media*, supporting and putting forward an alternative to the expansive Catholic organisations.

The contributions examined above reached an audience much wider than one formed simply from political and intellectual elites, especially the discussions which appeared in *l'Unità*, the party newspaper. Other articles, above all those of a memorialising and autobiographic tone, also appeared from the first years after the War in highbrow newspapers. One could perhaps say that there was a double publication of Gramscian writings, one for the intellectuals and another 'for a less specialised layer' of leaders.[96] The alternatives which appeared showed important differences. In this manner Gramsci, across multiple lives, came to occupy a central position for the culture of the whole party and the masses which it influenced, and even if this method might seem somewhat 'backward' today (bound as it was to populist intentions), it was nonetheless within the objective limits of a pre-determined formula, one due above all to the bringing together of some typically Stalinist tropes with distinctly populist stresses. Gramsci thus came to be presented via these stereotypes in order to both facilitate the deciphering of his works and propagate an uncrit-

---

95   Cf. on this point L. Gruppi, *Introduzione* to P. Togliatti, *La politica culturale*, p. 19.
96   See above, p. 90.

ical, mythical acceptance, especially among the popular classes. Gramscian *hagiography* was introduced at least from 1937–38 in Togliatti's own essays and discussions. The volume *Gramsci*[97] was reprinted repeatedly after Liberation and was accompanied by other recollections from imprisoned comrades such as Mario Garuglieri and Gustavo Trombetti, whose writings appeared in *Società* and *Rinascita* respectively. The profile sketched by the former, although not lacking some more clearly political arguments (deriving from the conversations held in the penitentiary in Turi), tried above all to reconstruct the figure of Gramsci in his daily life. Gramsci became poor, he understood the humble, he knew how to teach them but also how to learn from them. He was 'a teacher even while dying', refusing to ask for anything which might be seen as capitulation. He was even physically redeemed and idealised: Gramsci was 'ugly and deformed, but for those of us who were close to him, he was beautiful'.[98] A more delicate subject of this reconstruction of prison life related to the conflict between Gramsci and the other detained Communists over the 'turn'. Garuglieri did indeed mention some 'quarrels' but attributed these to the small privileges allowed to Gramsci and from which were derived 'petty resentments'.[99] This was quite different from the explanation provided by Trombetti: 'Fascism was definitely not about to fall, and in these conditions Gramsci lashed out at anyone who maintained that Italy was an immense powder keg, threatening to explode if a "match" were to touch it'.[100] In order to describe this political conflict, even if a somewhat dampened one, the author superimposed another kind of explanation still further from the truth:

> Gramsci was a passionate man, who loved his imprisoned comrades without pretensions or theatrical demonstrations, and they reciprocated with equal affection. But one small, haggard group of renegades, some of whom were in the service of OVRA [Organisation for Vigilance and Repression of Anti-Fascism], went to the point of throwing ... a rock at him; it must have weighed around a kilo ... Gramsci didn't pay much attention however, knowing that it was OVRA pulling the strings.[101]

---

97 See above, p. 50 onwards.
98 M. Garuglieri, *Ricordo di Gramsci*, in *Società*, 1946, n. 7–8, p. 691. This essay and others were then republished in stand-alone publications for the purpose of wider disemination.
99 Ibid., p. 699.
100 G. Trombetti, *In cella con la matricola 7047 (Detenuto politico A. Gramsci)*, in *Rinascita*, 1946, n. 9, p. 233.
101 Ibid., p. 234.

In any case, Trombetti added, 'there were men who, in a period in which there was not a single Communist comrade in Turi' acted in order to defend the 'beloved' leader. The episode of the throwing of the rock was also recounted by Antonio Arcari, who interviewed two Communist militants who had been imprisoned with Gramsci, Ceresa and Piacentini, for *Il Calendario del popolo*. Gramsci

> had enemies including among his comrades in prison: anarchists and Trotskyists. Following their principle that the revolution begins ... with the murder of the bosses, they threw a huge rock at him while he was relaxing with a game of chequers with Ceresa, which fortunately did not hit him.[102]

The story touched on the usual themes of a *Socratic* Gramsci, of his persecution in prison, etc., recounted in pious, populist tones with particular intensity, depicting Gramsci as 'simple, intelligent and good'. In the same edition of the *Calendario*, under the title 'A Great and an Exemplary Life' [*Grandezza ed esempio di una vita*], there was also a text described simply as 'a radio transmission made on the tenth anniversary of his death', which reconstructed – with a series of rapid flashbacks – some moments in Gramsci's life, not without also focussing on the letters by which the prisoner entertained his eldest son. The theme of 'Gramsci and children' and Gramsci's 'paternalism', was given some centrality in *Rinascita* by Antonio Meocci, for whom Gramsci's typical 'moral sentiment' was born from two 'needs': 'a great love for the family, and an extension of this feeling out into a sense of greater responsibility, to a great concern with "the better part of the self", duty, mission, an ideal'.[103] Nor was Gramsci spared comparison with 'that sentimental father, Marx', because 'just like Marx, Gramsci "knew how to be a child with children"'.[104] Eugenio Reale in *Unità* also claimed that, 'aware of the coming end, he busied himself with listening to the words of his sons'.[105] The author compared Gramsci to Silvio Pellico: from the letters of both flowed the image of peaceful and serene men – but whereas in Pellico this was explained by Christian faith, for Gramsci this came from an 'earnest faith in the true creed'.

---

102 A. Arcari, *Pensiero lotta e martiro di Antonio Gramsci*, in *Il calendario del popolo*, 1947, n. 3, p. 54.
103 A. Meocci, *Gramsci e i bambini*, in *Rinascita*, 1951, n. 8–9, p. 420.
104 Ibid., p. 402.
105 E. Reale, *Umanità di Antonio Gramsci*, in *l'Unità*, 27 April 1947.

The precarious parallels with Christianity were taken up once again and expanded by Gian Carlo Pajetta, again in *Unità* – but this time accompanied by a tentative historical explanation – in an article titled 'A Legendary Comrade' [*Un compagno nella leggenda*]: the author compared Gramsci and the Communists to Jesus and the first Christians, explaining and justifying the birth of the *myth* of Gramsci in the light of the birth of the *myth* of Jesus among the first exiled and persecuted Christians.

> If Antonio Gramsci had simply been a scholar, he would now be no more than a historical figure, to be read about in political handbooks and essays ... But he was also a *man*, a master in the old sense of the word and thus he entered into legend, thus he lives forever; and it is not only his teachings which will be handed down, but all his words, all the moments of his life which might be kept for us and for those who come after us.[106]

This very clear instrumentalisation of Gramsci can be explained through reference to relations with the Italian culture of the time, which had a *counter-altar* in the ecclesiastical propaganda focusing on manifold 'apparitions' of the Virgin and saints who were inciting a struggle against Communism. This instrumentalisation was not only accepted but also vindicated as part of the construction of a 'vision of the world' present not only in theory, but in the imagination, emotions and sensations. It would be wrong to ignore the importance of these aspects in certain historical contingencies. The fact remains that this work of mythologisation crushed that Gramscian sensibility which Luigi Russo had recalled when he said that he did not want to call Gramsci a 'martyr', 'as he would have been disturbed by this thoroughly anti-theoretical word'.

Next to these fairly frequent writings, and to the memoirs of certain older militants of the Communist Party, in which the figure of Gramsci came to be added without much addition to the usual hagiography,[107] there were also essays that explicitly recorded the background of the Communist cadres: 'The Italian Communist Party', the twelfth issue of the Party's correspondence course, was issued in 1950 and the 'Short Course: Gramsci on the Struggle of the

---

106   G.C. Pajetta, *Un compagno nella leggenda*, *l'Unità*, 15 May 1947.
107   See M. Montagnana, *Ricordi di un militante* (Milan: Fasani 1947) and above all G. Germanetto, *Memorie di un barbiere* (Rome: E.Gi.Ti, 1945). On this latter work and the editing undertaken in relation to the first edition in Russian of 1930 and the first edition in Italian of 1931, see Luigi Cortese, introduction to A. Tasca, *I primi dieci anni del Pci*, pp. 19–21. The moments of self-censorship introduced into the work were designed above all to minimise Bordiga's role.

Italian Communist Party for a Socialist Italy' the following year. These works represented simplified reprisals of texts and theses already noted. Although not of a different general structure, a nonetheless more articulate example, which aimed to be published in different places, was Lucio Lombardo and Giuseppe Carbone's 'Life of Antonio Gramsci' published in 1952. According to the authors the book aimed at 'being a first attempt at collating and publishing documents, testimonies and recollections that will allow for the reconstruction of the life, thoughts and struggle of Antonio Gramsci, leader of the Italian working class'.[108] The result, however, was the same reconstruction as had already been established in party publications, cleansed of every residual criticism. The fundamental axis of the book was the relation of friendship and collaboration between Gramsci and Togliatti. The Communist Party, it was claimed, had emerged directly out of the *Ordine Nuovo*, and 'Gramsci and Togliatti had waged a fierce and energetic struggle' against the *historical accident* of the Bordigist leadership.[109] The Party thus arrived at a politics of 'popular and anti-Fascist unity' by 1924, a politics it had not abandoned since. The figure of Gramsci provided was the usual iconographic canonisation, expunging every problematic moment (the disagreements with Togliatti, the relation to the Party during the prison years) and accentuating every *popular* trait (above all mentions of his early poverty and the sacrifices made for his family life). The picture which resulted was so dull that even *Rinascita*, in a review by Platone, had substantial reservations:

> one cannot close the book without wanting a more profound and complete study of the issues treated therein. The mind of the reader is presented with many questions which demand responses, ones that could be answered only if a much more expansive labour had been undertaken and with different intentions. Some points, nevertheless, could be easily cleared up, even in a work such as this.[110]

---

108   L. Lombardo Radice and G. Carbone, *Vita di Antonio Gramsci* (Rome: Edizioni di cultura sociale, 1952), p. 258.
109   Ibid., p. 107.
110   F. Platone, *L. Lombardo Radice – G. Carbone: Vita di Antonio Gramsci*, in *Rinascita*, 1951, n. 1, p. 551. Another biographical contribution that ought to be noted is that by D. Zucaro, *Vita del carcere di Antonio Gramsci* (Milan and Rome: Edizioni Avanti!, 1954). The small volume reconstructs the events following Gramsci's arrest in detention, prison and finally at the medical clinics in Formia and Rome, bringing together acconts by doctors, prison guards and ex-prisoners. The political debate held inside places like Turi is entirely ignored however.

Its omissions notwithstanding, Lombardo Radice and Carbone's book was widely read in the 1950s, becoming the main instrument for the dissemination of Gramsci's life and work – a fact which in itself indicates the limits of the work undertaken by the leading Communist circles to make Gramsci known to the masses of militants and sympathisers in the years between the end of the War and the 'turn' of 1956.

8 First Evaluations and New Perspectives

The years between 1953 and 1956 constitute a difficult period to interpret in the Communist Party's history. The death of Stalin and the defeat inflicted by the 'fraudulent laws' of 1953 marked the end of an epoch, a fact much clearer today than it was then. Very few could have imagined the events of the 'unforgettable 1956', when the Stalinist legacy unravelled. Nonetheless it would have been easy to predict a general evolution of Italian politics in the context of the defeat of FIOM in the FIAT union elections in 1955, which symbolised the setbacks experienced by the union (and the Communists) in the collective social economic transformation underway in the country.

This was also a turning point for interpretations of Gramsci. With the conclusion of the publication of the *Notebooks* in 1951, Einaudi began to publish the pre-prison writings in 1954, starting with the volume *The Ordine Nuovo (1919–1920)*. On the one hand it seemed time for an assessment of the presence and experience of Gramsci within Italian culture; on the other this opened up a new chapter in the study and interpretation of the writings from the period of the *Ordine Nuovo*.

An overview of Gramsci's biography was attempted by Gastone Manacorda and Carlo Muscetta in drawing up a report on the first ten years of the journal which they had edited, *Società*. Manacorda and Muscetta complained of a certain utilisation of Gramsci by those who were satisfied only with 'useless recollections and comfortable approximations', pushing for 'more rigorous references'.[111] The article claimed that Gramsci's vision was of an *unseparated* culture: after an initial move in this direction represented by the period of anti-Fascism and the Resistance, the authors believed that there had in fact been a return to old defects, in the form of abstract cosmopolitanism and withdrawal from the 'true national tradition'.

Togliatti's own review of the *Ordine Nuovo* volume of Gramsci's writings in 1954 centred on the strong connection between history and politics. Indeed, it

---

111   See G. Manacorda, C. Muscetta, *Gramsci e l'unità della cultura,* in *Società*, 1954, n. 1, p. 1.

is this text in which Togliatti's *historicism* emerges with greatest clarity, relating not only to an interpretation of Gramsci but to the theoretical foundation of the entire politics of the Communist Party. The specificity of this historicism, beyond the profound differences that distanced it from many other versions, lay not so much in the conviction of the superiority of historical knowledge but in the belief that the historical and social reality represented a process with a determinate end, an end which gave the process meaning and rendered it intelligible. Yet Togliatti's account of a 'history which, like thought and action, can move towards those destinations which must be reached'[112] left little space for doubting the theoretical form that Togliatti's Marxism was now taking. The relation between history and politics as defined by Gramsci and the Italian Communists was immediately clear – in the article of 1954 – as the origin and reason for the success and development of the Party, as the true element of superiority in the confrontation with the enemy.

> The Communists have experienced the history of their country as knowledge and action ... They have drawn on the unresolved problems of history and through their activity have acquired the consciousness of the necessity and possibility of resolving them.[113]

Moreover, for Togliatti praxis became not only a moment of action as guided by historical consciousness, but a moment of consciousness *tout court*, in such a manner as to give his Marxism a decisively *anti-theoretical* character:

> We understand by labouring. It is in and through practical activity that we become aware of the structures of the real world, of economic relations, of social and political relations, of their laws and tendencies of development, and consciousness in its turn can fine tune this activity, rendering it adequate to the course of events.[114]

Togliatti presented Gramsci's capacity to understand the nature of Fascism and to foresee the possibility of its development already in the years of the *Ordine Nuovo* as an example of this method. But above all Togliatti's essay made a clear contribution by problematising the consolidated image of Gramsci as a scholar, a lonely, isolated man, '*für ewig*'. Through reclaiming the connection between

---

112   P. Togliatti, *Storia come pensiero e come azione*, in *Rinascita*, 1954, n. 11–12, now in Togliatti 2001, p. 191.
113   Togliatti 2001, p. 190.
114   Togliatti 2001, p. 188.

politics and history, Togliatti denied any kind of gap whatsoever between the *Ordine Nuovo* and the *Notebooks*, between the 'political' Gramsci and the 'historical' Gramsci, opening the road (although it would only be traversable after de-Stalinisation) to the contextualisation of Gramsci's work and biography. Not only did 'the writings penned in the midst of battle, in 1919 and the years after, contain ... the themes and theses which sustained the prison work' but 'all of the prison works are no more than a deeper and clearer vision of that which had been brought to light in the preceding period of ardent participation in real struggle'.[115] The link between the writings of the *Ordine Nuovo* and those of the prison period put the latter in a more precise political context: 'The prison writings are not therefore outside of the political struggle which came before them; rather, they are an integrated part, their crowning glory'.[116]

If Togliatti's essay prepared the way for a 'discovery' of Gramsci's political activity before his arrest and a rereading of the *Notebooks* which was more attentive to his historical political context, in the immediate moment Togliatti nevertheless opposed any interpretation of a 'young Gramsci' as different from or counter-balancing the imprisoned Gramsci. At the same time, the publication of the *Ordine Nuovo* writings meant that the interpretation of the prison works had to be revised. An emblematic example was the review published by Roberto Guiducci in the first issue of *Ragionamenti*, a small journal that brought together intellectuals such as Amodio, Caprioglio, Fortini, Armanda and Roberto Guiducci, Momigliano, Pizzorno. This was certainly a heterogeneous group but one united by a tendency to develop a *new* Marxism, one for whom the Gramsci of the 'red biennial' (1919–20) was an important reference (alongside Lukács and Adorno): the *Ordine Nuovo* was read as the organ of the councils, as the theorisation of the road to the soviets, as a call for the self-organisation of the masses, an alternative not only to the unions but also to the Party. These themes were considered relevant because

> the problem of direct representation, the problem of the connection between instruments of the workers, of the unions and of the Party, between the organs of Parliament and those of the class, between cultural and political positions seem today all but resolved.[117]

The Trotskyist theorist and leader Livio Maitan also weighed in on the writings of the *Ordine Nuovo*. Though in part reprising some of the previous critiques

---

115   Togliatti 2001, p. 185.
116   Togliatti 2001, p. 188.
117   [R. Guiducci], *L'Ordine Nuovo*, in *Ragionamenti*, 1955, issue 1, p. 4.

of Gramsci,[118] Maitan's small volume recognised the positive role played by the Sardinian leader in post-WWI Italy for having recognised the double necessity of constructing the 'revolutionary party', as well as the councils as organs of the masses' self-governance (even if there were still *productivist* ambiguities) and above all in having substantially welcomed the ideas of the Third International. Yet Maitan's main concern was to show 'the clear contrast between Gramsci's positions and those of the current leaders of the Communist Party',[119] above all inasmuch as this concerned the idea of the 'national function of the working class', which for Gramsci would be a 'national class' because it represented 'the interests of the vast majority of the "nation"', and was therefore destined to guide its revolutionary activity, while in Togliatti the same concept had only been employed 'with collaborationist intentions' during the phase of 'reconstruction'.[120]

However, for the most part the publication of Gramsci's writings from his political activity in the 'red biennial' was to lead to a reframing of those interpretations which were more clearly instrumentalised and connected to contemporary matters. There were calls from different sectors for a less casual and less manipulative interpretation of Gramsci, one that was truer to the texts and their contexts. The evaluation of the first stage of Gramscian interpretation was bound up with an evaluation of the effects of a decade of liberal democratic culture after the fall of Fascism. There had been plenty of disruptive moments, dissatisfactions and disputes, as emerged in an article by *Contemporaneo*[121] which tried to summarise how much had happened 'after Gramsci', as the title of Romano Bilenchi's contribution put it. But it was Noberto Bobbio who provided an overview that lay aside any concessions to rhetoric or optimism:

> Gramsci indicated important subjects of research. If we had managed in these years to develop a positive direction in our culture some of these subjects would have been reprised and examined. What happened instead? Italian Marxists have made Gramsci into an inventory of five or six formulae by which everything can be explained, and his books have

---

[118] See L. Maitan, *Gramsci e Trotzky: la speculazione di un intellettuale staliniano*; L. Maitan, *Gramsci ignorava le reali posizioni di Trotzky*; L. Maitan, *Ancora su Gramsci e Trotzky*: all in *Bandiera Rossa*, 1951, issues 5–7.

[119] Maitan 1955, p. 7.

[120] Maitan 1955, p. 31.

[121] See M. Cesarini and F. Onofri (eds.), *Dieci anni. Inchiesta sulla cultura italiana*, in *Contemporaneo*, 1955, issue 24, p. 1. There were a great deal of contributions from intellectuals and politicians from this issue of the journal onwards.

become a mass of maxims and verses cited for arguments *ex auctoritate*. He could have been an important stimulus for new work; instead he is becoming a justification for old laziness.[122]

The strong criticisms advanced by Bobbio divided the communists. On the one hand Alicata advanced a kind of official defence of the work which had been undertaken[123] while Renato Guttuso admitted that

> the interpretation of Gramsci today, including by many progressive and even Marxist scholars, often tends to be 'reductive' ... What developments have followed from the mass of suggestions, citations, indications, which the work of Antonio Gramsci contains? ... I believe there are very serious self-criticisms to be made.[124]

The call for a self-critique represented the deep sense of unease felt as it began to dawn that many matters were about to start unravelling.

---

122   N. Bobbio, *Il nostro genio speculativo*, in *Contemporaneo*, issue 24, p. 2.
123   See M. Alicata, *Gli ottimisti e i pessimisti*, in *Contemporaneo*, issue 30.
124   R. Guttuso, *Il coraggio dell'essere*, in *Contemporaneo*, issue 25, p. 7.

CHAPTER 4

Gramsci and the Italian Road to Socialism (1956–59)

1   1956

For the history of the international Communist movement, the year 1956 represents a date of fundamental importance, opening up a new phase in relations between different parties, their theoretical and political positions and their own sense of identity. According to a now celebrated definition,[1] the 'unforgettable 1956' was when thousands of Communists found that so many of their already brittle beliefs simply crumbled away. It was the end of both a myth and of an example. In finding its certainties removed, the monolithic character of the international Communist movement entered into a crisis, reopening theoretical political research and debates. As others have said, it marked the passage from Marxism to Marxisms.[2]

The news of Khrushchev's revelations and the dramatic events in Hungary were occasions far too explosive not to have also put into crisis that *historicism* which everyone found it all too easy to explain and relate to. Faced with a moment of crisis, it demonstrated all its limits. Togliatti showed an extraordinary capacity for Party leadership[3] and strategic rethinking but he failed to avoid a backlash from the dramatic events in Hungary, paying a high price for not having foreseen, or for not having had the courage to recognise, that the Hungarian uprising – even if in a vague way – expressed 'a need for freedom and popular and workers' leadership'.[4] And while the popular base of the party tended to cling to the leading group, one that in itself was not substantially

---

1   Ingrao 1977, p. 101 onwards.
2   Asor Rosa 1975, p. 1625.
3   Two historians critical of Togliatti and Togliattism nonetheless come to the same conclusions: 'Would the Communist Party have maintained its social roots if it had broken from the "iron bond"? Historians and political scientists who have posed the problem all say that they could not have: perhaps the result would not have meant the dissolution of the Communist Party, but certainly a remoulding of its power ... it is possible that the limits and bonds which Togliatti established to pursue a radical renovation ... did provide a solution [to the crisis of the party in 1956]'. Flores and Gallerano 1992, p. 117.
4   Ingrao 1990, p. 90.

damaged,[5] the intellectuals broke off relations with the Communist Party, who had undoubtedly constituted its greatest moment of strength. The crisis of the Soviet model reverberated across Marxism, evidenced in the substantial incapacity to respond to the accusation that Bobbio had advanced against Della Volpe two years earlier, when he had claimed that only liberalism had known how to express the 'permanent necessity ... for a struggle against abuses of power'.[6]

Yet again, discussions around Gramsci were closely connected to this 'turn' in communist politics. From the very start, Togliatti invoked Gramsci in the most important political documents of 1956. In his 'report' to the central committee on 13 March, for example, at the first meeting after the 20th Congress of the Communist Party of the Soviet Union, he claimed that

> Our task has consistently been the search for an Italian road to Socialism. In my opinion, this this was also Antonio Gramsci's task. In all of his political activity, especially in the final period of his life, he was interested in providing and translating – or, better still, converting – the lessons of the Russian revolution into the Italian context.[7]

This invocation of Gramsci and the need to maintain his ideas in order to follow the 'Italian road' was also raised at the all-important meeting of the central committee on 24 June. Togliatti opened a session of the congress with the following words:

> We are fortunate to have a party founded by Antonio Gramsci. In all of Western Europe, I believe he was the thinker to have made the greatest and most profound single contribution to the development of Marxist teaching over the past 50 years, and he did so on the basis of a full understanding of the conditions of our country. We must remain bound to Gramsci in all of our teaching.[8]

Later, in discussing the theory of the dictatorship of the proletariat, Togliatti claimed that: 'Gramsci said that "Every state is a dictator". This claim remains valid and true'.[9] Nonetheless, he also added that the thesis of the inapplicability

---

5 Spriano 1986, pp. 205–16.
6 Bobbio 1955, p. 170.
7 Togliatti 1984b, pp. 110–11.
8 Togliatti 1984b, p. 152.
9 Togliatti 1984b, p. 167.

of the bourgeois state apparatus to the construction of a socialist society had already been revised by the Communist Party, and with regards to 'the form of the exercise of power', the USSR did not need to serve as a model because different historical conditions allowed for variations in the exercise of power itself. Therefore, of the three elements that described the theory of the dictatorship of the proletariat (every state is a class dictator; the role of bourgeois state apparatus; the form of the exercise of power), Togliatti kept a firm hold on the more general and analytical aspect, and used Gramsci's authority in order to bolster it.

Furthermore, the report he gave to the Eighth Congress of the Italian Communist Party's traced the party's ability to incorporate the ideas derived from the Twentieth Congress of the CPSU as deriving from the 'perfect preparations laid by Antonio Gramsci's thought' (as well as deriving from the turn of 1944).[10] In general, Togliatti attempted to draw on Gramsci's *method* as a way to reject the errors that communist parties had made in their conception of power. An analysis of reality, adherence to the tendencies in which it manifests, and an anti-dogmatic spirit: these were the hallmarks which had informed the *Theses of Lyons*, a set of principles to which 'we must always remain faithful, which liberate us from the challenges of schematicism'.[11]

In the Eighth Congress, Togliatti was not the only one who referenced Gramsci. On the one hand there was Giorgio Amendola: with an ambitious emphasis on continuity, he emphasised the thread which bound the Congress 'directly ... to those premises which Antonio Gramsci posed 35 years ago'.[12] On the other hand, Gramsci was consistently brought up by various exponents of the 'internal opposition', which the leading group of the Communist Party continued to deal with in 1956 by relying on old methods.[13] Antonio Giolitti, for example, cited Gramsci repeatedly, inducing Giorgio Napolitano to note that the Sardinian leader was not simply a flag to be brandished against others, but 'that he is the figure to whom we must all of us refer'.[14] Giolitti's reference to Gramsci was, however, far from generic. Aligning himself with an interpretive thread that derived from Gramsci's younger writings – a line which would fare better in 1958 and the 1960s – Giolitti cited the Gramsci of the *Ordine Nuovo*

---

10   Togliatti 1984b, p. 185.
11   Togliatti 1984b, p. 208.
12   Partito comunista italiano 1956, p. 466.
13   'On the political level whoever tried to push themselves out from the margins, for example Fabrizio Onofri or Antonio Giolitti, was knocked squarely back with what was still a Stalinist reaction.' Spriano 1979, p. 200.
14   *VIII Congresso del Partito comunista italiano. Atti e risoluzioni*, Rome: Editori Riuniti, 1957, p. 251.

on the relation between the revolutionary process and the organisation of the class at the site of production:

> the working class's leading role must make itself felt first of all in the process of production, and conquer political power from this starting point. The essential element is therefore that which Gramsci described as the self-consciousness workers gain *as producers*.[15]

While not exempt from those more traditionally *reformist* elements that would soon come to dominate his ideas and determine Giolitti's switch to the Italian Socialist Party – itself already entering a long period of centrism – this *councilist* viewpoint proposed an important change in direction for the Communist Party.

Togliatti's reply took to heart this an attempt 'to find the best interpretations of our party's founder's thought'. Togliatti claimed that:

> Gramsci did indeed say that the basis of the revolutionary process must flow from within the process of production. None of us reject this claim. We know quite well, nonetheless, beginning from this point, what happened in 1919 and 1920. It was on the basis of this very claim that Gramsci ... developed a great revolutionary movement within the political sphere.[16]

Not only had Gramsci argued strongly against reformists, he added, but he also never claimed that the productive process could set of a transition to socialism without the active intervention of the revolutionary party.

It ought to be no surprise that, in dealing with the consequences of Stalinism, Giolitti and other young members attempted to entirely rethink forms of communist politics in a councilist direction, a kind of return to square one. What was surprising, however, was the modesty of these attempts, which in many instances were destined to devolve quite quickly into a way into government: perhaps, consequently, demonstrating the insufficiency of the councilist hypotheses when confronted with the problems of a society that was becoming increasingly 'complex'. As far as interpretations of Gramsci were concerned, the main issues of debate between politicians and intellectuals on the left were already taking form in the new situation created by 1956. One of the Com-

---

15 Ibid., pp. 230–1.
16 Ibid., pp. 235–6.

munist Party's real limits was its inability to guarantee this debate within its own structures, despite Giolitti's appeal to the Congress during his contribution when – again via a reference to Gramsci – he underscored the need 'not just for a review of democratic centralism but for a correct understanding of what it means, and its real application'.[17]

Giolitti's ideas were presented more holistically in a small work titled *Riforme e rivoluzione* (Reform and Revolution), again filled with invocations of Gramsci. Here Giolitti focused on the Gramscian concept of hegemony, distinguishing it from that of the dictatorship of the proletariat: for him, Gramsci 'showed the working class another way to conquer and exercise power, one adequate to a situation entirely different from that described in the theory of the dictatorship of the proletariat'.[18] The working class 'began to exercise its leading function in the productive process and therefore created the conditions for the democratic conquest of political power within a bourgeois state economically developed and bound to democracy'.[19] As far as his interpretation of Gramsci was concerned, Giolitti's positions here are close to the theses of another leading Communist intellectual who broke from the Communist Party in 1956, Fabrizio Onofri. In essays gathered together in his *Classe operaia e partito* (Working Class and the Party), he stated among other claims that 'Gramsci's conception and experience of the factory councils (a conception which was no less than the reflected light of Marxism) is the kernel which resolves the problems that continue to confront the workers' movement and the struggle for socialism in Italy today'.[20] There are many pages here which deal with Gramsci's *inspired* vision, posed in response to the problems of socialist transformation, while also maintaining that he had shown where the obstacles and real limits lay ahead for the communist movement. A full response to these historical and theoretical aspects, and ultimately to the issue of 'Gramsci and Leninism', would be attempted a little later on by Togliatti. Nonetheless, a reply to the political problems posed by Giolitti came soon enough from the Vice-Secretary of the Party, Luigi Longo, with a pamphlet in which he rejected, in scholastic mode, the juxtaposition of the concept of hegemony with that of the dictatorship of the proletariat.[21]

Behind the terminological entrenchment of the Communist leader thus lay the beginning of a polemic that was destined to continue for another twenty

---

17   Ibid., p. 231.
18   Giolitti 1957, p. 29.
19   Giolitti 1957, p. 32.
20   Onofri 1957, p. 296.
21   See Longo 1957, p. 36. On the polemic between Giolitti and Longo see Barbagallo 1992.

years. In the immediate moment, the real point of insurmountable discord between Longo and Giolitti seemed to form around the different models for the party which each derived from their respective theoretical and strategic proposals. Whereas Giolitti's inquiry encouraged the formation of 'a minority, free to sustain its opinions and become the majority',[22] Longo replied that this was a 'luxury' that the proletarian party could not allow.[23] It is not surprising, therefore, that the *dissident* Giolitti would soon no longer find space within that party.

2 'Too Few Gramscians'

In his report to the Eighth Congress, Togliatti also referred to Gramsci in relation to difficulties encountered by Italian Communists following the events of 1956, particularly in relation to the question of intellectuals.[24] The year marked an end to an entire era of cultural politics and theoretical research. The end of the Cold War and the rigid logic of its respective camps, as well as the loss of any firmly established certainties, also meant the end of a fairly widely held belief in the class nature of those ideologies, and the non-independence of ideas and intellectuals within class conflict. The Communist Party came up against the limits of its politics of 'conquest' of 'traditional intellectuals' in terms of a political ideological alliance and 'commitment', and its undervaluing of the problem of intellectuals as a stratum, as a *mass*, and of the social forms of cultural organisation. Simultaneously, some of the fundamental theoretical elements of Italian Marxism entered into crisis, the specificity of which also proved to be the bond that, now severed, gave way to so much uncertainty. The relaunching of the 'national road' paradoxically also signalled the need to abandon precisely those cultural politics and theoretical tradition that had formed the linchpin of the 'national tradition'. *Historicism* was not only insufficient as an explanation for the dramatic events in the East, but had even covered up how much had changed – and was changing – in Italian society. In facing up to the moments of rupture in the mode of production and a more 'American' form of life, the confrontation with Croce was found to have become outdated.

---

22 Giolitti 1957, p. 45.
23 See Longo 1957, p. 71. 45.
24 See Togliatti 1984b, p. 221. For a reconstruction of the intellectuals confronting the facts of '56, see Ajello 1979, p. 359 onwards; Asor Rosa 1975, p. 1620 onwards; and the introduction to Vacca 1978.

One of the more important moments of discussion of these themes was the debate hosted by the journal *Contemporaneo* between March and July 1956.[25] It began before Khrushchev's revelations, demonstrating the fact that a revision of these fundamental cultural political problems was already in play before the events in Eastern Europe. The chaotic and multifaceted discussion focused on two main points: the problem of the relation between politics and culture, i.e. between intellectuals and the Party; and the errors and backwardness of Communist cultural politics over the preceding decade. In many contributions this last element turned into an evaluation of 'Gramscianism' more than of Gramsci himself, or rather, as many contributors put it, of the 'Gramsci-Togliatti line'. Luciano Barca argued that the left intelligentsia could

> fight more directly against the backwardness of cultural and political positions rather than fighting modern ideological battles ... might directly aim at resolving problems which twenty years of stagnation have only deepened, rather than new problems which have gradually arisen from new contradictions within capitalism.[26]

In terms of cultural politics, Barca's critique was hard-hitting: he claimed that the alliance between Marxist and 'democratic' intellectuals had frequently resulted in Marxism being compromised by other philosophical and ideological tendencies, renouncing its original, critical moment. The bond between intellectuals and the working class had become 'a sentimental and at times mythical ... merely folksy'. And, inevitably, he also claimed that interpretations of Gramsci had encountered many limits:

> All of this might have ensured an intelligent use of that enormous legacy that Antonio Gramsci handed down to us. If Italian left intellectuals have made contributions, this was due to Gramsci – they were working alongside him and with his most direct inheritors. But ... surely we must admit that far too often Gramsci's work has been split up? That he has been read and received only through extracts and quotations? Gramsci of the *Ordine Nuovo* has too often been separated from that of the factory councils, or the Gramsci of the *Southern Question* from the author of the *Notebooks*. The effect has been the fragmentation of a unity which should never have been broken, introducing nothing but confusion.[27]

---

25   The debate is recounted in Vacca 1978.
26   L. Barca, *Economia in primo piano*, in Vacca 1978, pp. 31–2.
27   L. Barca, *Economia in primo piano*, in Vacca 1978, p. 34.

Many communist commentators underlined the inadequacy of the reception of Gramsci's thought within the Communist Party itself. Italo Calvino thus claimed that 'Gramsci is impressed upon Italian culture even outside of our movement, through his claims and his language; but we have failed to understand his dry, tense, all-consuming intensity, a way of thinking which always pushes cultural creation onward'.[28] Or we can turn to Paolo Spriano, according to whom even the 'Gramscian concept of the intellectual' had 'not been absorbed by or made headway into the workers' movement'.[29] It was thus precisely in the communist sphere itself that he recognised little or nothing of the Gramscian tradition, and did not hesitate to say so. In a contribution significantly titled 'Too much idealism', Ludovico Geymonat levelled an accusation at the entirety of cultural politics:

> Faced with new philosophical tendencies, we limited ourselves to merely *praising* Gramsci's thought, whose work – while undoubtedly fertile – belongs to a phase of cultural development quite different from our own, a fact which is far from the author's own fault ... And though it takes extraordinary work, and exacting editions, to understand the writings of any great thinker, it is important to recognise that this is not the same as undertaking research that might go beyond Gramsci's own problems. The influence of the idealist current on Italian culture has been so profound that Gramsci's teachings, however precious, do not seem sufficient in themselves to overcome it.[30]

Aside from the communists, Gramscian or otherwise, there were other openly critical positions in the debate, including from socialist intellectuals associated with the journal *Ragionamenti* (Guiducci, Pizzorno, Fortini and Scalia). The debate began with a polemical note in *Contemporaneo* relating to various criticisms penned by Guiducci. In the contribution after this note, Pizzorno focussed for the most part on what he perceived to be the limits of 'Gramscianism':

> There can be no doubt that the Italian left has been witness to less Marxist dogmatism and Talmudism than elsewhere. Nevertheless, this partial freedom from repeating dry formulae was granted only by renouncing every serious aspect of research or expansion into modern culture, in

---

28 I. Calvino, *Nord e Roma-Sud*, in Vacca 1978, p. 28.
29 P. Spriano, *La società civile*, in Vacca 1978, p. 153.
30 L. Geymonat, *Troppo idealismo*, in Vacca 1978, p. 49.

Europe and beyond, retreating instead into the search for a national tradition. It was a provincial timidity of Gentile's fashion ... even Gramscianism has provided a cover and refuge for this timidity. And that is not even to mention the continuing influence of Spaventa, a truly pathological phenomenon that is emblematic of the question more generally.[31]

However, the main theses that bound Guiducci's group together concerned the *organisation of intellectuals*. Fortini, for example, wrote that it was an error to believe that one could form a 'Marxist culture' within a traditional cultural organisation. New means had to be devised, along with '*the work of political intellectuals* and their *specific* political work inasmuch as they are producers of a particular culture'.[32]

These barbed polemics, which had the merit of implicitly anticipating by a decade the importance of 'hegemonic apparatuses', naturally concluded with a 'Proposal for a Marxist cultural organisation in Italy' based on the arguably Gramscian idea of the self-organisation of intellectuals.[33] The vindication of a cultural sphere in conflict with the Party was not, however, supposed to take Gramsci as its exponent: the 'organised autonomy of culture' was meant to recall instead the positions of *Politecnico* and its *liberal* approach.[34]

Turning to the debate in *Contemporaneo*, there were interesting interventions from two leading communist intellectuals, Rossana Rossanda and Mario Alicata. Rossanda confirmed that behind the question of the relation between politics and culture, there actually lay the real problem of

> a certain political insufficiency. In other words, it seems to me that Italian Marxist culture has actually suffered from the politics of the workers' parties as much as it has enjoyed their positive aspects.[35]

Cultural limitations, that is, were bound directly to political limitations, and both have evidenced that a political change was necessary in order to guar-

---

31   A. Pizzorno, *Aver coraggio*, in Vacca 1978, pp. 122–3. [Translator's note: Bertrando Spaventa, 1817–1883, one of the principle Italian Hegelians of the nineteenth century. His works were in turn reprinted and studied by Gentile].
32   F. Fortini, *I politici-intelletuali*, in Vacca 1978, p. 43.
33   See *Proposte per una organizzazione della cultura marxista in Italia*, supplement to *Ragionamenti*, 1956, issue 5–6, p. 11. But also see the essays and articles from 1954–56 collected in Guiducci 1956.
34   For an interpretaton of the history of *Ragionamenti*, see Asor Rosa 1975, pp. 1627–28; and the introduction to Vacca 1978, p. x onwards.
35   R. Rossanda, *La ricerca e la politica*, in Vacca 1978, p. 183.

antee democratic freedoms in those parts of the country that had not been helped through the advances made by the Italian bourgeoisie, both structurally and ideologically. It was no accident, Rossanda added, that the previous decade had seen defeats 'in Turin and Ivrea', i.e. in the industrialised North. For Rossanda, this was the real problem that required attention. This fact had to be discussed, as it had been at the basis of Communist strategy since the War. For her, the contradictory position which Togliatti saw between cultural research and politics was no more than a fiction because, as Rossanda claimed, in the real context of intellectual and political struggles these spheres co-existed and indeed had the same level of *responsibility*.

Mario Alicata, head of the Communist Party's cultural policy from 1955, provided the concluding notes to a discussion that had gone on for more than three months. His contribution was a general one, showing a shift in communist cultural politics that emphasised its *lay* elements (as we would say today), focusing on structural elements of cultural organisation, beginning with schools.[36] As had been the case with the *Ragionamenti* group, Alicata's contribution responded to the issue of intellectuals in substantially organisational terms. But the aspect which concerns us more here was his judgement of communist cultural politics over the post-War period and the way in which Gramsci had been utilised in those years. Alicata rejected

> the opinion of those who seem to be claiming that the deficiencies in the party's cultural policies derive from the common heritage of Spaventa, De Sanctis, Labriola and Gramsci ... There is an obvious contradiction between the claim that this has been the party's prevalent tendency in terms of cultural policy, and the other claim that the prevalent line was Zhdanov's, to which it is quite opposed. But to be quite clear about matters, we should also admit that if the former line was indeed pushed with force, I do not really see why efforts to identify an Italian tradition of advanced and Marxist democratic culture is meant to have in itself been an obstacle to the continued development and improvement of a Marxist analysis of modern Italian society.[37]

For Alicata, as for Rossanda, the deficiencies of the party's cultural policies derived from the limits of the party's politics more generally. And these were identified in the 'obstacles', 'timidity' and 'backwardness' that were blocking the

---

36   M. Alicata, *Troppo poco gramsciani*, in Vacca 1978, p. 202.
37   M. Alicata, *Troppo poco gramsciani*, in Vacca 1978, pp. 200–1.

path of the 'Italian road to Socialism ... the most creative, original and indicative content of which lay in Gramsci's work'.[38] Alicata therefore claimed it was necessary to return to

> Gramsci's bold teachings ... we ought not criticise ourselves for having been too Gramscian but for not having been Gramscian enough, and for having held to too 'scholastic' an interpretation of our great and least scholastic Marxist thinker ... And who for this very reason, here and there, is still recognised as a heretic.[39]

In the great turn of events sparked by the 'unforgettable 1956', therefore, even the least iconoclastic continued to invoke Gramsci's thought as anti-dogmatic, potentially even heretical. The previous interpretative model, though officially defended, now lost its force. Gramsci had been freed from the hall of mirrors in which he had been trapped for a decade.

3   Gramsci's Relevance

1956 constituted a watershed in the history of Gramsci interpretation. The figure of the 'great intellectual', heir to the nation's democratic culture, ceded to a vision which placed Gramsci in the context of his own political activity, and his leadership role. Different elements flowed together into this new interpretation. In 1955, with the initiation of the publication of Gramsci's writings prior to his arrest, renewed attention was given to issues that had previously been left to one side, allowing Gramsci 'the activist' to emerge, a leader and theorist of the organised workers' movement. The emerging 'new Marxism' or 'critical Marxism' took an interest in the 'young Gramsci' while also remaining suspicious of – and rejecting – 'Gramscianism' or 'Gramscian-Togliattian' ideology. What it took from Gramsci was his mental curiosity, his anti-dogmatism, his critical research, his methodological propositions and radically 'anti-Stalinist' contributions. The end of Stalinism and the Cold War created a climate within the left that was generally more favourable to free historiographic inquiry: the influence of the Third International, and the assumption that the history of the Communist Party was the privileged location for the training and legitimation of leadership, was fading. But above all, Gramsci's reflections on *why*

---

38   M. Alicata, *Troppo poco gramsciani*, in Vacca 1978, p. 201.
39   M. Alicata, *Troppo poco gramsciani*, in Vacca 1978, p. 204.

the revolution in the West had been defeated made him an important point of reference for study and debate, not only in Italy but in all advanced capitalist countries. With 1956 the problem of the modes and forms of the transition to socialism had to be reconsidered, and new theories needed to be provided. Gramsci became the theorist of the different roads to socialism, 'of the different forms which the dictatorship of the working class assumes in its different phases, and can assume in different countries'.[40]

Togliatti's writings on Gramsci during 1957–58 can be seen as a single corpus characterised by a unified attempt to respond to the new demands posed by the national and international situations; his interpretation now focused on the connection between Gramsci and Leninism. Moreover, in order to restore a more historically determinate interpretation to Gramsci's works, these writings assumed a very specific political and cultural significance, confined to the debates and polemics following the 'unforgettable 1956'. Being 'Leninist' meant, above all, remaining within a revolutionary tradition that had a life outside of Stalin or at least diminished his role, in an attempt not to throw out the peculiarities and *raison d'etre* of the Communist movement along with the bath water. But to be *'Leninists'* and to grasp 'Gramsci's Leninism' also meant reiterating that *councilist* reading of Gramsci which frequently developed into a rough and ready critique 'from the left' of Togliatti's own line. Being Leninists, in the end, also meant being 'nationalists' in a new way: it meant taking up the creative moments of Leninism which Gramsci had established on the basis of the distinction between 'East' and 'West' (war of position, hegemony, historic bloc), and combining it with an 'assessment of the national situation' similar to that which Lenin had conducted in Russia. It meant equipping oneself with the tools necessary for the new struggle for hegemony in Italy and the West.

But for Togliatti it was not enough that one be simply a 'Leninist'. It was also necessary to follow Gramsci in *translating* 'Leninism' out of the Soviet Communist tradition and into an Italian one. Thus from 'Gramsci and Leninism' he derived a broad theoretical political perspective, a development that could even be *autonomous* of Italian Communists, founded on Gramsci and now rendered historically feasible. In this sense it is true that, in commemorating the twentieth anniversary of Gramsci's death, 'Togliatti emphasised his differences from Lenin'.[41] But put together these two points comprised the fulcra of Togliatti's argument, referencing both Lenin and the originality of the

---

40   Togliatti 2001, p. 233.
41   Vacca 1991, p. xxxiii.

line between Gramsci, himself and the Communist Party. Both formed aspects of the Communist leader's attempt to overcome the potentially fatal crisis of 1956, his attempt to forge a continuity of innovative ideas within the communist tradition as a whole, and not only the Italian one. Arguably this manoeuvre remained in the dark for a long period, overshadowed by other attempts to focus on Gramsci as part of a purely 'Leninist' horizon. Yet it ought to be remembered that at this point Togliatti took an important step along the road of reading 'Gramsci according to Gramsci', and not surprisingly this interpretation was to become a point of reference within the 'Gramsci debate' over the coming decades.

In an extraordinary meeting of the Central Committee (i.e. a *political* meeting) on the occasion of the twentieth anniversary of the death of the Sardinian leader, Togliatti gave an important speech on the 'contemporary relevance of Antonio Gramsci's thought', explicitly stating the need to overcome the idea of a *national* Gramsci. His work may have been concentrated on the history of Italy, yet Gramsci was nevertheless

> aware that the mature transformation of our country was occurring within the framework of a greater movement pushing capitalism towards its final demise, generating the necessary conditions for a new society on a global scale. His Marxism thus remains new and relevant precisely because it followed on from Lenin's own great discoveries, because it was guided by Lenin's actions.[42]

Togliatti denied that the young Gramsci – the councilist Gramsci – 'had ignored the need for the wilful organisation of the workers' vanguard'. As well as through specific citations, 'this supposition is refuted by the fact that the problems of the organisation of the factory councils were debated within the Party, resolved in these very meetings, and the fact that the new party emerged from the framework of the council movement'.[43] Without a party 'the working class cannot become the state' because it would never become a strong and socially diverse bloc under the leadership of the workers. The loss of a revolutionary party and the formation of an alliance between the proletariat and other social strata had defeated the factory councils. For Togliatti, it was precisely this failure that demonstrated the historical necessity of the split at Livorno. Togliatti knew full well that the particularity of the relation between party and move-

---

42 Togliatti 2001, p. 197.
43 Togliatti 2001, p. 207.

ment had its own problems, but the fact remained that he could not ignore a dichotomy within Gramsci's work between two inescapable moments of what was, in truth, a revolutionary dialectic.

Togliatti's speech also made explicit reference to 1956, claiming that Gramsci provides 'a guide to understanding the problems arising ... now that the deformities produced by the Soviet regime have become apparent'.[44] What was important, he argued, was to maintain the 'substance' of the Soviet social model, a model which 'in the long term' would be *necessary* in order to move beyond the 'deformations connected to the name of Stalin', and in order to revive 'the basic necessity of democracy and legal security'.[45] Structure and superstructure thus appeared bound by a *necessary* relation: a profound understatement of the disastrous consequences which we can see with the benefit of hindsight. Yet this was a trait common to the Marxism of the time and did not pertain to Gramsci as such. Indeed, in his strenuous defence of the USSR, Togliatti was *lagging behind* Gramsci.

4   Gramsci and Leninism

On 11–13 January 1958 the Istituto Gramsci held the first conference of Gramsci studies in Rome, an important moment in the attempt by Italian Communists, following the *trauma* of 1956, to reopen a dialogue with democratic, non-Communist sections of Italian culture, as well as to better define a *political culture* that might support the strategy sketched out by Togliatti after the Twentieth Congress of the Communist Party of the Soviet Union. The new interpretative mode proposed by Togliatti[46] was clear enough: studying the relation between Gramsci and Leninism meant making his political activity an 'object of investigation' in itself. Togliatti claimed that:

> Doing politics means acting to transform the world. Each person's true philosophy is contained within their politics, along with that very substance of history that – for any individual engaged in a critical awareness of the world and the work that falls to him in the struggle to transform it –

---

44   Togliatti 2001, p. 206.
45   Togliatti 2001, pp. 206–7.
46   The Togliattian contribution was outlined in two texts, one printed, distributed in the form of 'points', and the other read in the usual running of affairs. The first is 'Il leninismo nel pensiero e nell'azione di A. Gramsci (Appunti)' and the latter 'Gramsci e il leninismo'. Both now in Togliatti 2001.

remains the substance of his moral life. It is within his politics than one must seek the unity of Antonio Gramsci's life. It is his politics that must be both the point of departure and arrival.[47]

The strength of Gramsci's theory thus lay in its context. Gramsci, Togliatti claimed, could only be understood by those who remained aware 'of the concrete moments of his activity' and of how to see 'an adherence to every doctrinal formulation and general claim' within these concrete moments.[48]

This interpretation placed Gramsci on a new level: his 'national' existence was given an international panorama, the real context within which his theories had been developed and situated. Even Gramsci's inquiry into the role of intellectuals, for a long time seen as the main theme running through the *Notebooks*, 'contains a fundamental Leninism', becoming a moment of reflection on the *engagement* of intellectuals, 'an essential part of the Leninist doctrine'. It was only thanks to Lenin and the October Revolution that these ideas had become available throughout the world, initiating Gramsci's research. It was in this manner that Togliatti claimed to demonstrate that 'the appearance and development of Leninism on the world stage was the decisive factor in the evolution of Gramsci both as a thinker and as a political activist'.[49] This became the decisive claim in Togliatti's new interpretation from 1956 onwards. It was an interpretation which also contained a drastic simplification, covering up the content of Gramsci's thought prior to his encounter with Lenin, a problem which would only be corrected in the studies of the 1970s; yet at this point in time it represented an important step forward in leaving behind the Gramsci of the thematic editions of the *Notebooks*, the 'great intellectual' – at turns philosopher, historian and literary scholar, etc. – outlining instead the figure of a great thinker of the Communist movement, one member of an international discourse who reached his real theoretical maturity in the context of a specific moment, a historically determined position. This new interpretative position *began to create the need* for a new critical edition of the *Notebooks*. The problem was noted initially by Gastone Manacorda at the Rome conference:

> Whoever studies Gramsci's works encounters great difficulties, arising from the manner in which the edition of the *Prison Notebooks* was put together. I thus propose that a new edition should soon be prepared, one

---

47   Togliatti 2001, p. 213.
48   Togliatti 2001, p. 16.
49   Togliatti 2001, p. 239.

which might faithfully respect the chronological order of the *Notebooks'* composition as much as possible, as well as the arrangement which the individual fragments have in each *Notebook*.[50]

The dynamic between Lenin and Gramsci, however, was not only an 'Italian translation of Leninism' but a dialectical and creative development. Lenin represented, moreover, a figure who had emphasised the importance of individuating the historical diversity in which revolutionary struggle concretely occurs and therefore the range of forms which such a struggle might, and indeed must, assume. Gramsci had developed this idea by describing the shift from 'war of manoeuvre' to 'war of position'. It was a framework that contained moments of both continuity and innovation. For example, for Togliatti the moment of continuity seemed to lie in the theory of hegemony, which did not contradict the Leninist theory of the dictatorship of the proletariat.[51] The concept of the party demonstrated moments of difference, however: a year previously, Togliatti had claimed that Gramsci's work 'grafted directly' onto Lenin's, but with an original form by which the party was conceived as a 'collective intelligence'.[52] For Togliatti, continuity and development were tightly woven together, disallowing the possibility of a one-sided version of those issues dealt with by both Lenin and Gramsci. It was in this way that Togliatti attempted to fashion the relation between Lenin and Gramsci in order to face the international communist movement:

> It would have been absurd to ask the proletarian revolution to create a parliamentary regime, especially in a country in which parliamentarianism had never existed. But in other countries, where parliaments have managed to have some democratic content, as a mode of consultation and of the expression of the will of the people, they can also provide the means by which to resolve the problem not only of how to express the people's will but also of how to make active participation in the running of economic and political life accessible to the working masses. At the same time, maintaining the working class's access to power necessitates a continuing extension of forms of direct democracy.[53]

---

50 G. Manacorda, *Intervento*, in Cessi et al 1973, pp. 512–13.
51 See Togliatti 2001, pp. 232–3. Here Togliatti emphasised that in Gramsci 'the difference between civil society and political society is methodological rather than organic'.
52 Togliatti 2001, p. 207.
53 Togliatti 2001, pp. 260–1.

In the end 'Gramsci's Leninism' meant rediscovering politics in all spheres, challenging the Communist movement to find new strategies for confronting new historic situations as they were being formed. At the same time, it also meant refusing to renege on its own past, fashioning history to meet the needs of current *praxis*. The most important moment in Lenin's work was thus the identification of a revolutionary doctrine.[54] Togliatti thoroughly rejected the focus being laid on 'Gramsci's councilism'. For him it was the Moscow trip of 1922–23 and not the 'red biennial' that represented the decisive moment in the formation of Gramsci's thought, as successive studies would reaffirm.[55] Yet his fierce polemic overemphasised Lenin's role in Gramsci's thought. The intellectual honesty of his research came into conflict with his attempt to resolve this complex question, one which even today has not been definitively resolved, i.e. the interrelation between Gramsci's national background, the studies and experiences of his youth, his creative assimilation of Leninism and the influence of the Bolshevik exemplar. Last but not least there was also Gramsci's development of the Southern question, which Togliatti claimed rather curtly was 'of Leninist derivation',[56] while in a second presentation he highlighted the influence (mediated by Salvemini) of the 'rationalist and positivist historiography' without which Gramsci 'could not have developed his thoughts on the alliance of the Northern working class with the Italian peasant masses, particularly in the South'.[57]

5   The Rome Conference

Aside from Togliatti's own contributions, there were many other interesting contributions to the 1958 Rome conference. Each of the other three essays was provided in two separate versions. Aside from Roberto Cessi's essay on historiographic questions, about which more will be said below, the other interventions shared similar subject matters, such as the essays by Eugenio Garin on 'Gramsci in Italian culture'[58] and Cesare Luporini on 'Marxist philosophical methodology in A. Gramsci's thought'.[59]

---

54   Togliatti 2001, p. 220 onwards.
55   Togliatti 2001, pp. 218–19.
56   Togliatti 2001, p. 27.
57   Togliatti 2001, pp. 251.
58   E. Garin, *Antonio Gramsci nella cultura italiana* and E. Garin, *Gramsci nella cultura italiana*, both in Cessi et al 1973.
59   C. Luporini, *La metodologia filosofica del marxismo nel pensiero di A. Gramsci*, and C. Luporini, *La metodologia del marxismo nel pensiero di Gramsci*, both in Cessi at al 1973.

Garin's contribution played the role of the *prosecution* in the 1956 debate on *cultural tradition*, not only in terms of the 'privileged relation' Gramsci had with Croce but also in terms of the problems Gramsci derived from responding to other tendencies in national thought. However, Garin claimed that Gramsci was in no way a *Crocean* as such, but reduced himself to *Croceanism* only in order to enter into a dialogue with a philosopher who represented the 'most important (and most dangerous) voice in Italian life'.[60] Garin defended Gramsci's choice to measure himself against the most advanced culture of his time: 'Salvemini and Gobetti's adoration was much more "abstract" and "doctrinal" than Cattaneo's "concreteness"'.[61] For both Togliatti and Garin, Gramsci was not a 'scholar' but a politician, focused on finding 'a unique, workable position for Italy'.[62] Though surely not an entirely wayward judgement, this was nonetheless one-sided, leading to a criticism of Gramsci for having chosen to situate himself on the same conceptual level as Croce even while inverting the philosopher's conclusions. This made not only Gramsci and his criticism of Croce the target of polemic but also a line of *Gramscian* criticism that had remained unaltered despite the extent to which the panorama of Italian cultural had been transformed, ignoring the analytical content that lay in Gramsci's thought, of a potential richness and importance for a largely new situation. It was Togliatti's *interpretive turn* of 1956–58 which finally overcame the question of the link between Croce and Gramsci, opening up a new horizon of research, beginning to clarify how Gramsci engaged with Italian Neoidealism on his own terms and above all how he had perceived the more advanced moments in the confrontation between capitalism and socialism, searching for new solutions for the Communist movement after the defeat of the 1920s.

Even though the reasons to present an *anti-Croce* had for the most part been exhausted, the figure was resurrected by Cesare Luporini, though not without noting the importance of Gramsci's achievements and his important methodology (in term of his 'ability to translate languages') within this role. In contrast to the Gramscian-Crocean *clichés* of the 1950s, both of Luporini's contributions reflected on the depth of Gramsci's thought, starting with the fundamental concept of the philosophical originality of Marxism as a fully autonomous science, both a method and a vision of the world.[63] Rehearsing the history of Marxism, Gramsci had taken from Marx the concept of *praxis* (from the 11th *Thesis on Feuerbach*) and a specific interpretation of the link between structure

---

60　Cessi et al 1973, p. 9.
61　Cessi et al 1973, p. 10.
62　Cessi et al 1973, p. 404.
63　Cessi et al 1973, pp. 38–9.

and superstructure (from the Preface to *A Contribution to a Critique of Political Economy*) in order to underline the theoretical and historical importance of the latter of these two terms.[64] The 'Leninist' concept of hegemony was considered to be a development of these two points, an evolution which raised the situation of the consciousness of the masses to the highest point, perceived as the problem of their cultural unity (and it was thus that the notion of 'common sense' became central to Gramsci).[65]

Luporini emphasised Gramsci's distance from the 'version of Marxism' in which historical materialism was intertwined with dialectical materialism, which in substance 'tended to ignore man's existence in the world'.[66] Distancing himself from Diamat nevertheless opened up the problem of Gramsci's *historicism* and his relation to materialism (though one could also say that it also opened up the problem of Luporini's adherence to a historicist framework that was substantially more political than theoretical).[67] For Luporini it was only by making reference to 'sensible human praxis' that Marxism could be protected from falling into the errors of 'metaphysical materialism' and thus remain true to Marxism as the philosophical 'meeting of naturalism and humanism'.[68] Here, Gramsci mitigated naturalism rather than humanism. The question was that of the 'complex objective connection ... between *nature* and *history*'.[69] Gramsci's thought, though not lacking in 'oscillation and uncertainty', managed to safeguard the objective character of reality by constantly anchoring itself in history and humanity. Luporini was disturbed by the 'Gramscian resolution of *man in history*' by which the 'component of nature' within Marxism had been lost.[70] Luporini rejected this conclusion, claiming that *human nature*, in Gramsci as in Marx, had to be the *presupposition* of human history: 'man remains still, insuperably, *nature*', but a nature 'embedded in human historical sociality'.[71] What lay behind this solution was the very real limitation that had been reached by the historicist interpretations within Italian Marxism, which had used Gramsci as its main theoretical prop. The 'return to Marx' begun in Italy in 1956 would follow a road of polemicising against Gramsci, a polemic frequently reprised through the 1960s. Even here it must

---

64 Cessi et al 1973, p. 39.
65 Cessi et al 1973, p. 40.
66 Cessi et al 1973, p. 458.
67 See the introduction to Luporini 1974.
68 Cessi et al 1973, p. 459.
69 Cessi et al 1973, p. 460.
70 Cessi et al 1973, p. 461.
71 Cessi et al 1973, p. 457.

be said that the target was no doubt *Gramscianism* more than Gramsci himself; after the season of theoretical-political (and historiographical-political) polemics in the 1960s, a section of anti-historicist Marxism would converge around Gramsci once again, proposing an interpretation prepared to deal with the appropriate theoretical coordinates.

It is clearly not possible to mention here all of the contributions presented at the 1958 conference. I will return to the historiographical debate later. The contributions more specifically dedicated to questions of aesthetics and literary criticism are beyond the limits of this study (those from Dal Sasso, Petronio, Seroni and Della Volpe). For those who want to deepen this or that aspect of Gramscian thought, it is not enough to merely cite those essays and contributions which – for varying reasons – ought to be kept in mind: from the note by Noberto Bobbio on dialectic to that by Umberto Cerroni on the relation between state and civil society, from the re-proposing of doubts regarding Gramsci's relevance by Ludovico Geymonat to the valuable and pioneering study by Aldo Zanardo on the Gramscian critique of Bukharin's *Programme*, and from the observations on 'historicity' by Fulvio Papi to the study of his relation to Hegel by Livio Sichirollo. Aside from their individual merits, the general value of these contributions and many other presentations given at the Rome meeting lies in the fact that they inaugurated a deeper study of Gramsci's work: work that until then often been glanced over, cited, accepted or reject – but rarely studied in a scientific manner.

First, we will limit ourselves to examining the main themes debated in those years, the most *relevant* being, first and foremost the question of Gramsci's *councilism* (within which one can see, though still only roughly, the beginning of a reflection on different ways of interpreting the concept of hegemony), present above all in the contributions by Alberto Caracciolo, Paolo Spriano and Valentino Gerratana. Secondly, there were those questions relating to 'Gramsci's Marxism' raised by Mario Tronti and others. Caracciolo and Tronti would also be among the contributors to the edited collection *La città futura* ('The Future City') issued in 1959.

Beginning with the question of Gramsci's councilism, Caracciolo made two different interventions which did not entirely overlap. In the first he connected Gramsci's exposition of the councils to 'the more genuine Marxist concept of the Communist state as the state of producers, as a training ground of self-governance, a site for the encouragement and re-evaluation of an emerging political and civil society'.[72] The author insisted on the differences on

---

72   A. Caracciolo, *A proposito di Gramsci, la Russia e il movimento bolscevico*, in Cessi et al 1973, p. 100.

this issue between Gramsci and Lenin, between 'the movement of the *Ordine Nuovo* – everything generated, articulated and self-organised from below' and 'the tendency of the Russian soviets towards greater centralisation'. Gramsci had misinterpreted the real role of the soviets in the Soviet Union, idealising them as libertarian and anti-Jacobin. The Turin councils differed from them entirely, both in terms of control over the productive process as well as their role in workers' self-government. In his second intervention, however, Caracciolo seemed to take a step backwards: Gramsci was a Leninist and for this very reason could not have left the moment of the councils unexplored, as it was a moment typical of Lenin's thought as well. The difference between the two revolutionary leaders therefore lay within a shared 'conviction, a shared participation in experience, instruction and elaboration, all of which Lenin had brought to that historical moment'.[73] For Caracciolo this remained true even if there was a difference between 'the Leninism of his own time' and 'the Leninism of today, that is, the Leninism of the epoch of Stalin'.

Paolo Spriano and Valentino Gerratana also contributed to the debate on the councils. Having recognised the important project of the Turin proletariat over the first two decades of the century, Spriano claimed that Gramsci's activities in the period of the *Ordine Nuovo* had more than once resulted in a 'theoretical systematisation of the council as the fundamental, *state* organ of the new proletarian order'. For him, Gramsci had been interested

> in making the masses aware of that which he called 'new theoretical values' ... the workers' council was, therefore, a kind of school for political preparation, an expression of leading consciousness in a moment in which ... *preparation was necessary*, a moment in which power was the decisive problem.[74]

In opposition to this partial *mythologising* of the *Ordine Nuovo*'s councilism as a means of counter-balancing the Communist Party's *Togliattianism*, Spriano saw the 1920s as an example that emphasised the return of the Communist movement to a kind of *virginity* that had been lost with Stalinism. Diverging from the historians of the Communist Party who insisted on the contingent character of the experience of the councils (while nevertheless sustaining its basic lessons), Spriano described the councils as 'conceptually indispensable,

---

73   A. Caracciolo, *Intervento*, in Cessi et al 1973, p. 568.
74   P. Spriano, *Intervento*, in Cessi et al 1973, pp. 540–1.

including in the forms gradually produced through a shifting reality, through a dialectal continuity between consciousness and spontaneity'.[75]

Valentino Gerratana, while claiming the centrality of the concepts of 'war of position' and of 'hegemony' in Gramsci's thought, nonetheless maintained the necessity of 'recognising the [national] context that Gramsci identified and in which he operated, in order to be aware of the changes that have taken place since his own epoch, so that the aims of the workers' movement can be adjusted appropriately'. Gerratana claimed that:

> For this reason, it would be absurd – as it seems to me Caracciolo has done in his own contribution – to pick out one particular institution arising historically in a moment of determinate struggle of the Italian workers' movement – that is the 'factory council' in the movement of the *Ordine Nuovo* – and turn it into the focus of Gramsci's thought, the unique foundation of his Leninism. Certainly one should not dismiss forms of the factory council that arise and develop in a similar manner within other historical situations. Yet this can lead to a somewhat abstract analysis that ends with a formal analogy without deepening the concrete historical function to which such institutions respond in different periods.[76]

Caracciolo's error, according to Gerratana, thus derived from an insufficient effort to contextualise, from a partial reading of Gramsci that failed to identify the crystallisation of this or that moment and lost the 'rhythm of thought in development'. The Communist readings, in the end, tended to relativise the project of the councils; ultimately the council experience did not find a defence within the framework of Togliatti's post-War strategy. Those who did express such a defence were, on the theoretical-political level, labelled as being to the *left* of Togliattism and the 'Italian road to Socialism'. The terms of this discussion would be continuously revived up till the end of 1960s, and constituted the terminology by which Marxists were invited to rethink the appropriate strategy and instruments of struggle in the light of the events of 1956.

---

75 P. Spriano, *Intervento*, in Cessi et al 1973, p. 541.
76 V. Gerratana, *Intervento*, in Cessi et al 1973, pp. 591–2.

6 The 'Return to Marx'

The second issue that returned to the centre of discussion following 1956 was the theoretical standing of Marxism itself. An initial consequence of the general crisis of 'Marxist historicism' was a 'return to Marx', i.e. a return to the direct study of the classics of Marxism, with an attitude which was either openly or implicitly critical of the *historicism* which had been prevalent up to this point. In this context, the work already undertaken for years by Galvano della Volpe in his polemical line against Hegelian Marxism was to have a wide resonance. It does not seem accidental that Della Volpe, careful not to openly contradict the opinions of the Communist Party but nevertheless engaged in a positive contribution on the definition of its theoretical political identity, participated in the Rome meeting with a contribution on *aesthetic* problems, thus refusing to play the role of an explicit critic of the theoretical line derived from Gramsci (who was never 'his' author).

Della Volpe's positions were nonetheless drawn on quite openly by the young Mario Tronti, who – assimilating Gramsci into Hegelian Marxism and drawing on Lukács texts in *History and Class Consciousness* in particular – claimed that, in line with the Hungarian philosopher, 'Marx is the continuation of Hegel; Marxism is the *conclusion* of Hegelianism, its fulfilment, the *real* Hegelianism' and that for Gramsci, 'Marxism is the *reformation of the Hegelian dialectic*; it is the final positive conclusion of the various attempts made by Italian idealism to revise and update the logical instrument of the Hegelian method'.[77]

For Tronti's version of Gramsci, both Croce and Gentile had retreated from Hegel, having carried out a 'reactionary reform' in the tradition of Vico, Spaventa and Gioberti, one that was paradoxically 'not Hegelian enough': for them, the work of Marxism had to consist in *concluding and completing* Hegel. Referencing Della Volpe and emphasising the methodological break between Hegel and Marx, Tronti claimed that 'Hegel has no need of being concluded; Hegel is already the conclusion. It is exactly this conclusion that Marx rejects'.[78] For Gramsci, the philosophy of praxis was not only a question of terminology but an element of his thought that showed that he never settled for a purely idealist position. What remained outside of Tronti's interpretative horizon, however, was Gramsci's effort to oppose a Marxist and positivist determinism, precisely due to his confrontation with Croce. Dramatically resolving the same issue which we have already seen had arisen for Luporini, Tronti claimed that for

---

77   M. Tronti, *Alcune questioni intorno al marxismo di Gramsci*, in Cessi et al 1973, pp. 311–12.
78   M. Tronti, *Alcune questioni intorno al marxismo di Gramsci*, in Cessi et al 1973, pp. 312–13.

Gramsci 'the first element is becoming ... Objectivity tends to disappear into an intersubjectivity ... praxis tends to become the *primary reality*'.[79] Tronti agreed on the Gramscian (and Labriolan) thesis according to which Marxism represents an original and autonomous theory. But for him the novelty of Marxism with respect to all preceding philosophy (and this was another important point of distance from Luporini) remained exactly in its not being only *philosophy* but in presenting itself as *science*.

Tronti's posing of these questions at the Rome meeting may have isolated him a little. The same questions, the same problems (the crisis of historicism, the link between Hegel and Marx, Marxism as science) would nonetheless *explode* in the first half of the 1960s as central problems of Marxism, and not only in Italy: the period of the greatest peak of Della Volpe's studies and of Althusser's anti-historicism corresponded with the greatest regression from Gramsci's legacy. It should nevertheless be remembered that – although this argument was theoretically distant from Della Volpe – identifying 'absolute historicism' with Lukàcs's own historicism (or with that of other 'Hegelian Marxists') was an erroneous and shortlived maneouvre, as will be seen better further on in relation to Althusser. It had only been possible because of an interpretative tradition that was only now being left behind.

7   The Future City

In 1959 Feltrinelli published the essay collection *La città futura* [The Future City] edited by Alberto Caracciolo and Gianni Scalia. The book gathered together contributions on a range of aspects of Gramsci's thought. The authors[80] – who while not holding to a single point of view as such, in general belonged to an intellectual sphere which, following the events in Hungary, had rejected the party's 'orthodox' cultural perspective – were engaging in new research that often benefited from the *revisionist* battle undertaken first by the journals *Ragionamenti* and *Passato e presente*. Their contributions to research on Gramsci's life and work was therefore characterised in general by a refusal of the interpretations advanced by Togliatti's circle, i.e. a rejection of the assimila-

---

79   M. Tronti, *Alcune questioni intorno al marxismo di Gramsci*, in Cessi et al 1973, p. 316.
80   Emilio Agazzi, Ezio Avigdor, Alfeo Bertondini, Alberto Caracciolo, Carlo Cicerchia, Armanda Guiducci, Roberto Guiducci, Luigi Rosiello, Gianni Scalia, Giuseppe Tamburrano, Mario Tronti. A reduced edition was printed in 1976, by the same editors, containing only the essays by Agazzi, Cicerchia, Roberto Guiducci, Tamburrano and Tronti, with a preface by Franco Fergnani.

tion of Gramsci into any particular theoretical school. The two editors claimed that 'Gramscian thought represents an original act, with which one can agree or disagree: it is not, we believe, a link in a chain, either in the Idealist tradition or the more recent "historical materialist" tradition of Stalinism'.[81]

Of the many contributions which made up the volume, here we will only make reference to those most closely connected to the cultural and political debate of the time. We cannot focus properly on Caracciolo's essay, although the author proposed a reconstruction of the events internal to the Socialist Party and summarised its interpretative presuppositions. Carlo Cicerchia's opening essay, 'The relation to Leninism and the problem of the Italian revolution', however, constituted something like a 'counter report' to Togliatti's discussion of the same issue in Rome. For Cicerchia, Gramsci's Leninism was in reality traceable to the analogous functions performed by the two revolutionaries in their own countries. The similarity lay in their shared effort to adhere to conditions in their respective national situations,

> in having exercised a sharp Marxist critique of various political and philosophical conceptions that had long remained at the core of the workers' movement; in struggling against a dominant culture; in having known how, through the work of a political leader, to clarify the true tasks of reform for the proletariat in a given situation. This is where Gramsci's Leninism lies and not where one might wish to see it, i.e. in the function of the party: for Gramsci, the party is an instrument of hegemony and not, as Lenin was inclined to think, of dictatorship.[82]

Based on these reflections, Cicerichia opposed the interpretation proposed by Togliatti in 1958, countering this Gramsci to a 'studious interpreter of the needs of the nation'. In some ways this was a regression, although it did not entirely go so far as to revert to a thesis of a 'Leninist Gramsci', one that would have risked flattening out some of the more original moments in the *Notebooks*.

We do not need to say much more about Mario Tronti's essay than that which we have already said in relation to his contribution to the Rome conference. The kernel of his interpretation remained the same: Tronti framed Gramsci within the Italian philosophical debate, finding precedents for his thought in Labriola and Mondolfo, Croce and Gentile, claiming that the 'philosophy of praxis' did

---

81 a.c., g.s. [A. Caracciolo, G. Scalia], *Premessa*, in Caracciolo and Scalia 1959, pp. 9–10.
82 C. Cicerchia, *Il rapporto col leninismo e il problema della rivoluzione italiana*, in Caracciolo and Scalia 1959, p. 15.

not constitute a terminological *ploy* but represented a proposal of substance. Coming from an idealist background, Gramsci had pushed the issue to its very limits. And though it remained unresolved, Gramsci could no longer be of help, for the true research into an autonomous and original Marxism (if it were to evade the rocks of 'the philosophy of praxis' and 'dialectical materialism') now had to be steered in the direction of 'a Marxism which raises itself up, quite simply, as a *science*'.[83]

Another contribution of a similarly philosophical tone was that by Emilio Agazzi on 'The Philosophy of Praxis and the Philosophy of Spirit'. Here, an adherence to Croce's program (secular and immanent concepts; historicism) and a criticism of his incapacity to adhere to them constituted the two aspects that remained at the basis of Gramsci's attitude towards Neoidealist philosophy. The programmatic, anti-speculative moments in Croce did not follow from the facts, it was claimed: rather, his philosophy represented the ideology of a socially determined group. Agazzi confronted the question of Gramsci's *utilisation* of Neoidealist philosophy, in order to confront and correct the assumptions of a deterministic Marxism, thus reaching an entirely original position: 'concrete unity of theory and praxis does not mean their conjunction in a metahistorical link but the practical conditions of theory', not in a Crocean sense where

> every problem is borne out of a given historical situation that requires 'clarification', but in a much more determinate and concrete sense, in which *theory arises out of solutions to determinate practical problems* and constitutes itself as such in its own formal structure, so as to allow a solution to move over into praxis itself.[84]

The unity of theory and praxis was therefore reached only by means of a unity of philosophy, history and politics: such a position constituted a rejection of Croce's positions, the unveiling of the ideological character of the separation which he had made between politics and culture.[85] Agazzi, however, also seemed to recognise some worth in this separation, at the point at which

---

83   M. Tronti, *Tra materialismo dialettico e filosofia della prassi. Gramsci e Labriola*, in Caracciolo and Scalia 1959, p. 171. Here is not the place to delve into how this hoped-for mode for Marxism ('as a science') was in reality anything but 'simple'.
84   E. Agazzi, *Filosofia della prassi e filosofia dallo spirito*, in Caracciolo and Scalia 1959, p. 217.
85   Neither in Agazzi's contribution, nor in many others of these years examined here, was the relationship between Gramsci and Gentile's philosophies discussed or thematised, which remained for a long time a source of the *Notebooks* which could not be named.

he deduced from the Gramscian theory of hegemony the belief that Gramsci wanted to accentuate – in relation to Lenin – 'the relatively autonomous character of culture', the necessity that it articulate its own institutions, and that the 'cultural front' could not be absorbed into political struggle immediately.[86] Agazzi's considerations may have seemed obvious: aside from the most fervent Zhdanovists (who had by now been defeated), no one on the Italian left after 1956 really denied the *relatively* autonomous character of culture. The problems arose when one tried to deepen an understanding of the character and limits of this so-called 'relativity'. In terms of Gramscian discourse, the point of Agazzi's position was to reject Togliatti's thesis concerning the methodological (and not ontological) character of the distinction between civil society and political society, in that for Agazzi only the former constituted the appropriate space for intellectuals and culture.

Mention should also be made of the very original contribution made by Giuseppe Tamburrano, which anticipated many of the theses sustained in his book on Gramsci that came out in 1963. Tamburrano's thesis was simple: 'Gramsci was a Leninist in the years before prison but overcame Leninism; he overcame the politics which he had held to in the preceding years, through a process of reflection during the nights spent in prison'.[87] For him there were in fact 'three Gramscis': the Gramsci of the articles of *Il grido del popolo*, which 'still maintained a faith in the democratic struggle of the proletariat'; he of the *Ordine Nuovo*, who tended towards the theory of insurrection; and the Gramsci of the *Notebooks*, who had been forced to rethink the problem of power after the failure of the revolutionary moment. Tamburrano's sympathies lay with this last Gramsci. For him it was this Gramsci who had understood that coercion alone is not enough to explain the dominance of a class, who questioned his own 'conceptions of the world', who stressed hegemony and the search for consensus rather than dictatorship. The novelty of this interpretation lay in bringing together some *selected* aspects of Gramsci (and in this partiality were also its limitations) while over-emphasising others (through which Gramsci would seem not to differ from traditional democratic viewpoints) and radically simplifying others (the reduction of the idea of revolution to that of insurrection, reminiscent of 1848 and entirely different from how Gramsci had understood it). In doing so, Gramsci was not stigmatised as a reformist, but praised for being so.

---

86 E. Agazzi, *Filosofia della prassi e filosofia dallo spirito*, in Caracciolo and Scalia 1959, p. 225.
87 G. Tamburrano, *Fasi di sviluppo del pensiero politico di Gramsci*, in Caracciolo and Scalia 1959, p. 117.

8 The Debate on Italian Unification

Historiography was another important feature in the collective reflection on Gramsci's work in the late 1950s. I will not attempt here to reconstruct the influence which the *Notebooks* would have on Italian historiography more generally. Nonetheless, the debate in those years on the Gramscian interpretation of Italian Unification in particular must be mentioned, above all following the important critical comments on Gramsci and Gramscian historiography that had been made by Rosario Romeo. The ripples of the ensuing debate transcended an audience of specialists and became one of the central moments in which Gramsci's work entered into a critical dialogue with Italian political culture.

Of the four presentations at the meeting of Gramscian scholars in 1958, it was Robert Cessi's contribution that focussed on 'Historicism and Problems on Italian History in Gramsci's Work'.[88] Aside from analysing the methodological presuppositions of Gramscian historiographical research (history and historiography, objectivity and subjectivity, historicism), Cessi also focussed on the Gramscian interpretation of Unification as a bourgeois revolution in which the role 'of the peasants, workers, and the lower class' was described as 'subaltern'. Cessi's essay avoided the points that had formed the object of Romeo's explicit disagreement. These points, which aimed to revise the Gramsci-inspired histories of the 1950s, had emphasised the basic limits of Gramsci's thesis that Unification had represented a 'failed agrarian revolution'.[89] Gramsci, Romeo claimed, had read the victory of the moderate wing as resulting from the inability of the *Partito d'Azione* to mobilise the farmers even while interpreting their socio-economic objectives; that is, it resulted from the absence of a truly Jacobinite party. Revising the liberal historiography (Croce, Antoni, Chabod), Romeo advanced two main objections to Gramsci's thesis. The first was that Gramsci's judgement did not derive from the real situation of the objective historical moment of analysis as such, but rather from 'an abstract moral and political ideal, to which one arbitrarily presumes real history as it happened must accommodate itself'.[90] The posing of a different form of (Jacobin) rela-

---

88 R. Cessi, *Lo stoicismo e i problemi della storia d'Italia nell'opera di Gramsci*, in Cessi et al 1973.

89 See R. Romeo, *La storiografia politica marxista*, in *Nord e Sud*, 1956, issues 21 and 22. The article was republished together with another essay on *Problemi dello sviluppo capitalistico in Italia dal 1861 al 1887* (in *Nord e Sud*, 1958, issue 44), which consituted the *pars costruens* of the critique of Gramsci: see Romeo 1959.

90 Romeo 1959, p. 21.

tions between city and countryside was, for Gramsci, the model of the relation between workers and peasants as it had been proposed in the first decades of the twentieth century. For Gramsci, there were no other possibilities for a revolutionary solution in the period of Unification. Furthermore, Romeo rejected the idea that an agrarian revolution, even an imagined one, could have had a more 'progressive' character than the solution effectively reached under the hegemony of the moderates. This was not only for internationalist reasons (a Jacobin revolution would have created anti-Italian sentiment throughout the powers of Europe)[91] but also because

> in the historic conditions of Italy at the time, an agrarian revolution would have represented a force running contrary to the tendency which had (more or less) determined capitalist accumulation – at the peasants' expense – in the majority of the countryside of the North and Centre of the peninsula for over a hundred years.[92]

According to this interpretation, due to its late historical development, in the nineteenth century Italy was still in a phase of sharpening antagonisms between the peasant masses and the bourgeoisie, deep in a process of primitive accumulation at the expense of the countryside (a phase which France had already surpassed by the time of the French Revolution, making the Jacobins a potential 'solution' to the problem).

There was a range of Marxist historians present at the Rome meeting of 1958 who tried to compete with each other over these questions while all directly engaged in the work of developing Gramscian theses.[93] In the end it was Renato Zangheri who presented the most articulate objection to the thesis proposed by the liberal historians. He claimed that Gramsci was perfectly aware of the differences between the situations in eighteenth-century France and nineteenth-century Italy, and he had himself repeatedly recalled these differences – from the 'international situation' to the historical interval between the 'Italian revolution' and that of France. The reference to Jacobinism did not imply a historical parallel, an ideal model by which to judge Unification, but rather the elaboration of a political category. For Gramsci, 'Jacobinism' meant

---

91 Romeo 1959, p. 22.
92 Romeo 1959, p. 38.
93 I am referring to R. Zangheri, *La mancata rivoluzione agraria nel Risorgimento e I problemi economici dell'Unità*; G. Manacorda, *Intervento*; and G. Candeloro, *Intervento*, all in Cessi et al 1973. Romeo's theses discussed above caused a wide debate, among which see above all L. Cafagna, *Intorno al 'revisionismo risorgimentale'*, in *Società*, 1956, issue 6.

Cromwell as much as Robespierre, Machiavelli and Lenin as much as Gioberti – i.e. anyone who, in different times and historical situations, tried to unite 'the leading national forces ... with the popular masses and the peasants in particular'.[94] Gramsci's hypothesis relating to the existence of an alternative to a moderate process of Unification, dominated by a revolutionary bourgeoisie, had in truth been much more cautious than the version outlined by Romeo. Gramsci did not start from the existence 'of an "objective" possibility of revolution' but tried to investigate and explain the causes for an *absence of Jacobinism* in the movement for Unification. Zangheri delicately contested the economic history advanced by Romeo, in particular in relation to the process of primitive accumulation as derived purely from ground rent (with the consequent diminution of the role exercised by both government spending and external capital).

Giorgio Candeloro and Gastone Manacorda's contributions again took up Romeo's thesis as a point of polemical reference. The former claimed the possibility of continuing to develop the historical theory begun by Gramsci, in order to test the theses on the ground, to see their value and limitations through a confrontation with an effective reconstruction of the relation between the really existing classes during Unification. For him the real limits of Marxist historiography lay in not being sufficiently grounded on this basis. Manacorda, for his own part, contested the hypothesis of the commencement of the peasant question in the period following the First World War and therefore of its instrumental superimposition onto the problem of Unification. The problem of the lack of agrarian reform and the backwardness of the South was felt to derive from the democratic currents of the previous century, passed onto Gramsci through Salvemini. Even if Gramsci had proposed the problem in new terms, claimed Manacorda, a solution had become possible only after the First World War.[95] As with Zangheri, Manacorda unpicked Romeo's accusations against the Gramscian historiography as well as Gramsci's own: it was not Gramsci who had read the past in an arbitrary way, according to the political needs of the present, but Romeo and other liberal critics who caricatured the historical process for strictly ideological, political reasons, clearly constructing through historical research an apology for the current situation via the historical process that had produced it.[96]

---

94   R. Zangheri, *La mancata rivoluzione agraria nel Risorgimento e I problemi economici dell'Unità*, in Cessi et al 1973, p. 372.
95   G. Manacorda, *Intervento*, in Cessi et al 1973, pp. 508–9.
96   Among the more important reiterations of Romeo's thesis was that of P. Togliatti, *Le classi popolari nel Risorgimento*, in *Studi storici*, 1964, issue 3.

CHAPTER 5

From the 'New History' of the Communist Party to the Crisis of Historicism (1960–69)

1   The Late Togliatti

Over a period of just over a decade, from 1954 onwards, the publication of Gramsci's pre-prison writings meant that the public was able to read a body of work much more closely connected to his activities as a militant journalist and political leader.[1] This also had an effect on the changing cultural climate within the Communist Party after 1956. The publication of the correspondence and documents relating to the creation of the new leading group of Communists in 1923–24 (edited by Togliatti and introduced with his important essay on the historical background) proposed a new historical periodisation.[2]

Togliatti's new approach post-1956 took central place in historical research. In turning a critical eye on the episodes and figures of the history of the Italian and international Communist movement,[3] Togliatti attempted to redefine the party's identity, to a certain extent removing it from the sanctified pedestal on which it had been raised. Freeing this historical reconstruction from the direct influence of politics, Togliatti encouraged and theorised a 'historiographic revolution':

> In writing the history of the workers' movement – especially that of the party through which it acts, which it comprises and leads – I consider it a grave error to try and demonstrate that the party and its leadership have

---

[1] Gramsci's works appeared as *L'Ordine Nuovo* (*1919–1920*), *Scritti giovanili* (*1914–1918*) and *Sotto la Mole* (*1916–1920*), published by Einaudi in 1954, 1958 and 1960. In 1961–62 the correspondence on 'the formation of the leading group of the Communist Party' came out, on which more will be said. There were then two important anthologies: Gramsci 1963 and Gramsci 1964, containing much unedited material. In 1965, again from Einaudi, the new edition of the *Lettere dal carcere* was published, edited by Caprioglio and Fubini, revising and integrating the edition of 1947, with 119 new letters. Einaudi published Gramsci 1966 and this was soon followed by the writings from 1914–26, edited by Spriano: Gramsci 1967b.

[2] See Togliatti, *La formazione del gruppo dirigente del Partito comunista italiano nel 1923–24* [1961], in Togliatti 2001. The collection in which it was originally published, *Annali Feltrinelli 1960*, was amplified and republished the following year by Editori Riuniti.

[3] Beyond the writings on Gramsci also see Togliatti 1964.

always made the right choices, in the best possible way. This is the conclusion one reaches if one represents our history as an unbroken series of triumphs. But this is a false representation, far from the truth and even contradictory to it ... No doubt the correct path was always looked for with intelligence and the faith of a good fighter. But the correct solutions were only gleaned ... through hesitation, debate and errors, sometimes by first following the wrong path, one that perhaps did not respond to the real situations lying ahead of us and the tasks that had to be undertaken.[4]

It was by beginning from this thesis that, over the following years, communist historians would turn to the history of the Communist Party and the workers' movement, by producing work that was certainly always 'militant' in its intentions if heterogeneous in its outcomes, but at the same time work which could not be contested for its scientific engagement. An important intervention was his introductory essay to the correspondence between Gramsci and Scoccimarro, Terracini, Leonetti and himself, along with papers by Terracini and Tasca, and articles by himself and Gramsci, all material which for the most part had not been previously published, provided by the Tasca Archive and the Archive of the Communist Party. Togliatti used the opportunity to fill in gaps in current knowledge, shed light on areas previously cast in shadow, explicate elements and evaluations otherwise indicated only in citations and undertones, and consequently overturn critical judgements in new ways, in forms that were less demonising and generally more balanced both in terms of analysis and evaluation. More than anything perhaps this provided a lesson in style, one which was to have a strong influence on activity throughout the ranks of the Communist Party. Togliatti accused the Bordigist current of having limited the potential of the struggle of the subaltern classes, pushing them 'into a narrow corner that limited their potential'.[5] The limits of Bordigism here were those very same ones that Togliatti had underlined so many times before: the party as 'organ' – rather than 'part' – of the class; a method that starts from abstract principles rather than the real situation; a rejection of every possibility of political mediation, of every alliance, of every intermediary objective; the inability to distinguish between different adversaries; the party's activity reduced to propaganda; discipline as no more than a formal attitude. 'The vanguard becomes a sect, steeling itself away in preparation for the moment in which the masses will come over to their position, at which point it will then be ready to lead

---

4   Togliatti 2001, pp. 280–1.
5   Togliatti 2001, p. 269.

them to a final victory'.[6] This picture of the 'first period' of the Communist Party was not substantially new. There was novelty, however, in Togliatti's admission that

> the entire Party welcomed this as the correct and pragmatic direction ... some comrades, like Terracini and Togliatti, finally capitulated to a sectarian concept of the party and its function; under Gramsci's leadership they had not only followed a very different working aim but he had made a contribution to the development of quite different concepts and had been inspired by them during important activities.[7]

Gramsci himself, moreover, had explicitly avoided bringing his criticisms into the political arena for a long time. Togliatti recorded the contrasts between the Bordigist leadership and that of the International, hypothesising that Gramsci's reticence – the kind shown at the Congress of Rome in 1922 – derived from the fact that he did not see any alternative to the leading group holding office in that moment. Only in 1923–24 did Gramsci manage to win over a new leading group to his own position, and only at the Lyons Congress of 1926 did this anti-Bordigist line form a majority (at least in formal terms, one should add).

The years 1923–24 constituted a break in the intellectual and political life of the Sardinian leader. Gramsci, hypothesising that the bourgeoisie would liberate itself from Fascism, advanced 'the real hypothesis of a democratic future, one that the workers movement and the Communist Party must be ready to confront'.[8] This first hint of liberal democratic values should not be exaggerated however, nor is this the right place to discuss its validity, which I would argue remained tactical above all. Yet beyond any merits or flaws in this position, Togliatti's historical approach remained a central part. It is worth noting in relation to this the fact that it was *Rinascita* that, throughout the 1960s, hosted documents, letters and analyses relating to the historical events of the Communist Party, including significant episodes such as the publication of the exchange of letters from 1926 on the internal struggles of the Russian Communist Party[9] and Athos Lisa's memoir on the conflicts between Gramsci and other

---

6 Togliatti 2001, p. 271.
7 Togliatti 2001, pp. 191–92.
8 Togliatti 2001, p. 287.
9 See *Gramsci al Comitato centrale del Pc(b). Togliatti a Gramsci (1926: sulla rottura del gruppo dirigente del partito bolscevico)*, in *Rinascita*, 1964, issue 22. The text of Gramsci's letter, formerly published only by Tasca, was included in Gramsci 1964. *Rinascita* published it along-

communists detained in the penitentiary in Turi in relation to the 'turn' and the Constituent Assembly,[10] as well as memoirs by Lay and Trombetti.[11] Nor, in this context, ought the facts provided by Paolo Spriano be forgotten, to which we will return.

In reviewing the anthology of *Ordine Nuovo* documents edited by Spriano, Togliatti disputed some of those elements typical of Spriano's 'councilist' interpretation of Gramsci, rejecting his undervaluation of the party during the 'red biennial'. In Togliatti's view, this underestimated the fact that Turin represented a very advanced but nevertheless limited location within Italy of that period.[12] For Gramsci the revolution could certainly not resolve itself in the creation of a party dictatorship, but it was also the case – again according to Togliatti – that for Gramsci the party remained an irreplaceable instrument in the 'new historic consciousness of the workers'.[13]

Togliatti's final essay on Gramsci was a small article published in *Paese sera* on occasion of the publication of a volume entitled '2000 Pages of Gramsci', only a couple of months before Togliatti's death in Yalta. He took the occasion to propose a self-critique of the relation between Gramsci and the party intellectuals and leaders (himself first of all) who had interpreted Gramsci's work primarily in relation to the needs and concerns of the Party itself – of its own work and practice:

> Perhaps with the passing of the time, which has shed light and shadows over many events long passed ... I am far more certain today, as I gradually read over the pages of this anthology, which run through so many different aspects ... that Antonio Gramsci ought to be placed under a more vivid light, one which transcends the historical event of our party.[14]

---

    side a response from Togliatti from 1926, as well as a letter from Togliatti to Ferrata which not only recognised the authenticity of the letter, but also added that in a successive missing letter Gramsci had rejected Togliatti's arguments. For a not always convincing critique of these events, and of the entire management of the publication of Gramsci's letters, see Canfora 2012.

10   See A. Lisa, *Discussione politica con Gramsci in carcere*, edited and with comments by F. Ferri in *Rinascita*, 1964, issue 49. This is the 'whole text' of 1933 as sent by the author to the 'Centre' of the PCd'I. On the limits of Lisa's memory, see Rossi 2010, p. 79 onwards, and Vacca 2012, p. 120 onwards.

11   See G. Lay, *Colloqui con Gramsci nel carcere di Turi*, in *Rinascita*, 1965, issue 8; and G. Trombetti, *'Piantone' di Gramsci nel carcere di Turi*, in *Rinascita*, 1965, issue 18.

12   Togliatti 2001, p. 302.

13   Togliatti 2001, p. 303.

14   Togliatti 2001, p. 308.

One certainly cannot ignore the implicit message aimed at both scholars and militants here: Gramsci should not be limited to the foundation of 'the Italian road to Socialism', but had sufficient depth to *withstand* more general reflections, a situation made more urgent by the profound crisis of the international Communist movement (and Togliatti was aware of this, as his *Yalta Memorial* would demonstrate). Further still, there was Gramsci's important ability to give expression to traditions and cultures different from those which he had witnessed directly, as was to become evident from the 1990s onward, when the legacy of the Sardinian communist would be read, studied and *translated* (including culturally) throughout the world.[15] Indeed, Togliatti seemed to return to the *leitmotif* of his own post-War writings, reprising the idea of Gramsci the 'great Italian', inasmuch as he claimed that: 'I cannot find in the history of the last century of our country a single figure who is his equal, not since the great men of Italian Unification'.[16] The tone seemed to be dedicated to bringing to the surface not so much Gramsci the political theorist and militant as Gramsci the 'man', a dramatic example of the tension between theory and praxis, between personal limitations and the struggle to overcome them:

> Antonio Gramsci represents the critical consciousness for a hundred years of our country's history. For all too brief a period of time, and only in select disciplines, his judgement and activities have become part of our history. Today they are present in our party's political research, i.e. its theoretical and practical positions. But comrades you must excuse me if I say that for me this is not of the greatest importance. What matters above all is the meeting of thought and action in which all of the problems of our time are present and woven into each other. This also means a moment of contradictions, I am well aware; yet these are contradictions that find their solution not in a quiet game of scholastic formulae but in the affirmation of an inexorably logical reasoning, within the ruthless search for the truth and the hard work of constructing a new human character, in the struggle not only to understand but to transform the world.[17]

For the *late Togliatti*, therefore, the deepening difficulties and contradictions, most of all within the international Communist movement, did not give rise to the possibility of a formulaic, superficial reconciliation but the necessity for

---

15   See Filippini 2011.
16   Ibid.
17   Filippini 2011, pp. 219–220.

a further *burst* of revolutionary subjectivity so as to understand the new situation, the struggle to overcome it and its limitations.

Thus concludes – with a glance to the future – what we might call Togliatti's great book on his old comrade, a book written over an arc of 37 years. Without this book, written on paper but all the more so in praxis, Gramsci – the Gramsci which the whole world knows today – would probably never have existed. And for this reason, beyond the limitations and contradictions within Togliatti's *interpretation*, any judgement of it that fails to take into account this fundamental fact can only remain partial and erroneous.

2   The 'New History' of the Italian Communist Party

We have already mentioned Paolo Spriano's contribution to the work of understanding the history of Gramsci and the Communist Party. His interest began before Togliatti's essay of 1960,[18] and developed instead within the context of that 'revolutionary historiography' which was rooted in 1956 and more explicitly developed through the publication of papers on the formation of the leading group around Gramsci. Through his research, Spriano advanced an interpretative model which moved beyond the history of the Communist Party. To explain the central points, we must make reference not so much to his celebrated 'History of the Italian Communist Party' (*Storia del Partito comunista italiano*) but to his other writings that focussed specifically on Gramsci, more apt for examining the specific problems concerning the Sardinian leader.

Two motivations seem to have characterised Spriano's interpretation: an emphasis on the councilism of the 'red biennial', and the missing link he identified between the prison writings and the period preceding them. The introduction to his anthology on the *Ordine Nuovo* reconstructed the variegated cultural climate in which the journal had been founded and developed. The names of Croce, Labriola, Salvemini, De Sanctis and Renato Serra found company alongside others from outside Italy: from Rolland to Barbusse and Péguy, from Lunacharsky and *Proletkult* to Sorel and De Leon. What brought this heterogeneous collection of stimuli together, confounding and overcoming the influence of the great 'bourgeois' thinkers, was – for Spriano – the October Revolution. It was from this that one could understand the 'turn of the *Ordine Nuovo*', i.e. the fundamental establishment of the factory councils. 'Gramsci's Leninism' – clearly distancing himself from Togliatti's own reading – was inter-

---

18   See above all Spriano's introduction to Gobetti 1960, and Spriano 1960.

preted by Spriano as intimately bound up with the Soviet alternative: 'What Gramsci saw as paramount in the Leninist conception of revolution was the necessity to immediately construct the foundations for a new state'.[19] Here again the Gramscian emphasis on the councilist movement was inserted into a fully international panorama, one which, in different ways, embraced both Russia and Germany, Hungary and England. But this Gramscian interpretation of Lenin was perhaps a little *one-sided*, aiming only at evaluating the issue of the councils. There was still a marked difference between the two Communist leaders – 'a distinction', as Spriano wrote in 1967, 'that remained important even after the period of the *Ordine Nuovo*'. In Lenin there was always an

> awareness of how, at a certain moment in the revolutionary crisis, the need arose for an element of leadership from above, i.e. the party, whereas in Gramsci what prevails is the attack on the enemy-state *from below*, the *molecular process* by which one can create dual power, the search for *new institutions* and expressions of the masses, beginning with the workplace.[20]

In his conception of the party, Gramsci's specificity was traced back to the 'real movement of the councils'.[21] The great questions of the red biennial had not been raised in vain: without the factory workers' trust, 'the conception of a new party of the working class would not have arisen as anything structurally different from that of a normal socialist party'.[22]

Even while he did demonstrate a more general change in his interests, Gramsci's political activity after Livorno did not signal a real break from the preceding projects; although Gramsci's political leadership was now part of the theoretical and political sphere of the Third International, it remained within the discourse and analyses of the international communist movement. As Spriano wrote:

> Over the period of Gramsci's activities as a politician – in the decade of his 'legal' activities, that is – there is nothing which gives reason to believe that he interrogated the problem of democracy in terms any different from those of the Third International, but rather that he saw within it a representative regime of *political democracy*, a historical terrain on which

---

19   See Spriano's introduction to Gramsci 1963, p. 53.
20   P. Spriano, *Gramsci dirigente politico*, in *Studi storici*, 1967, issue 2, p. 231.
21   Spriano in Gramsci 1963, p. 63.
22   Spriano in Gramsci 1963, p. 90.

to move towards socialism. We are in 1916–26, not 1936–46. It would not be correct to credit Gramsci with Togliatti's ideas. When Gramsci speaks of a democratic phase, he speaks about it in a rigorously Leninist sense, a critical sense, keeping in mind the development of the revolution as Lenin analysed and universalised it, anxious to shorten the democratic intermediary period as much as possible.[23]

For Spriano, it was only once in prison that Gramsci's thought moved onto a different level, in reaction to the 'constant pressure to begin from the experience of the *great defeat* and understand its root causes'.[24] The victory of Fascism forced Gramsci to develop his consideration of the relation between democracy and socialism, the idea of an alliance without any residual instrumentality and the assumption of a *national* element, as indicated by his reflections on the Constituent Assembly. But in this way he was 'already far beyond those conclusions he had reached in the "legal period" and the Lyon theses; at this point we certainly do find him in agreement with the views of the Communist Party under Togliatti's leadership, especially as far as the 1930s are concerned, and the new conception of political democracy'.[25] The missing link detected here between the 'legal period' and the prison writings was to provoke confusion and polemic among historians, most of all among communist ones.[26] This confusion was fair enough, as Spriano's interpretation is not particularly convincing in its proposal of a *fragmented* Gramsci, with a watershed of *before* and *after* his arrest, reread in the light of the *successive* development of the Communist Party. Such evaluations aside, however, Spriano's intervention remained an important attempt at a historical reconstruction of the events of the Communist Party, not an *official* one but nevertheless an interpretation that was *internal* to the Party – one that helped the conclusions of Togliatti's 1960 essay to reach a wider public, first and foremost among party activists. As for its merits, Spriano's reading strongly emphasised Gramsci's councilist moment and, at the same time, the break between the 'two Gramscis', which seemed able to provide a rounded description of the Sardinian leader, both for a 'democratic' public (to whom he recommended reading the *Notebooks*) and – if unknow-

---

23   P. Spriano, *Gramsci dirigente politico*, in *Studi storici*, 1967, issue 2, pp. 249–50.
24   P. Spriano, *Gramsci dirigente politico*, in *Studi storici*, 1967, issue 2, p. 251.
25   P. Spriano, *Gramsci dirigente politico*, in *Studi storici*, 1967, issue 2, pp. 254–55.
26   See above all Paggi 1970, pp. xvii–xxii. For a more general criticism of Spriano's *Storia del Partito comunista italiano*, see E. Ragionieri, *Problemi di storia del Partito comunista italiano*, in *Critica marxista*, 1969, issues 4–5, and L. Paggi, *La ricerca storica marxista nella lotta teorica del partito*, in *Rinascita*, 1972, issue 4.

ingly – for that cultural circle around the 'New Left' which was forming in the 1960s and for whom the experience of the factory councils – elevated to the level of a paradigmatic revolutionary mythology (accompanied by a 'councilist Gramsci') – was to become a central moment for their own political ideology.

3   Three Biographies

One of the new aspects that marked out the reprisal of the historical study of Gramsci and the Communist Party in the 1960s was the publication between 1963 and 1966 of a series of monographs in a predominantly biographical mould, penned by three non-Communist scholars – Giuseppe Tamburrano, Salvatore Francesco Romano and Giuseppe Fiori.

As well as reconstructing Gramsci's personal and political journey, Tamburrano attempted to provide an original interpretation of the main theoretical drives that characterised his thought. His Gramsci was clearly 'split' into three periods. The first phase covered the years 1919–20, in opposition to the Communist Party line which Tamburanno accused of 'altering Gramsci's thought' in order to emphasise the role of a party – a role that in his opinion had demoted Gramsci to 'a secondary role'.[27] Tamburrano revisited Gramsci's ideas on the factory councils as fundamental to proletarian democracy and as historically non-contingent tools for workers' self-government. With the end of the 'red biennial' the centrality of the councils lessened in Gramsci. This was then followed apparently by a 'Third Internationalist' period, in which the 'New Party' became central, a party that could 'only function and survive through an iron discipline and a centralised democracy'.[28] This 'Leninist Gramsci' obviously received little sympathy from Tamburrano, who pointed instead towards a recovery of the original ideas from 1926, even if developed on a very different foundation than in the years of the *Ordine Nuovo*. A profound revision of all the developments preceding his arrest – Tamburrano claimed at least – had led Gramsci not only to investigate the causes which had seen Fascism claim victory but also search for the possibility of a 'national road to socialism', which Gramsci derived from the new phase of 'socialism in one country' now in use in the Soviet Union; finally this also led him to reflect on the 'degenerations of Soviet power in the USSR'.[29] The peculiar trait of this 'third phase' was the development of a theory of hegemony that differed from the Leninist and Third

---

27   Tamburrano 1963, p. 70.
28   Tamburrano 1963, p. 71.
29   Tamburrano 1963, p. 175.

Internationalist versions, thanks to which Gramsci overcame a 'schematic' theory of the dictatorship of the proletariat and of the state as 'dictatorship by one class'. The dominant class had to be ready 'to exercise its hegemony on the level of civil relations, i.e. to obtain the "active consensus" of the mass of citizens'. Gramsci thus came closer to 'liberal theories by which free society is founded on the principle of replacement, i.e. the rotation of leading groups'.[30] Taking his lead from Bobbio's ideas on the double meaning of the term 'dictatorship' (as supremacy of a class and as the authoritative form of such a supremacy, in opposition to the 'democratic' form),[31] Tamburrano claimed that in Gramsci's prison writings the theory of hegemony was 'a democratic theory which posits the active consensus of the governed'.[32] Gramsci, in conclusion, emphasised the search for consensus, on the moment of education, on the search for alliances and abandoned the hypothesis of the proletarian 'dictatorship', which belonged instead to the classics of Marxism and in particular to Lenin.

Tamburrano evinced a certain recklessness in only drawing on some select points about the theory of hegemony contained within the *Notebooks*, allowing himself to demonstrate an unusual – and implausible – version of Gramsci, one that was divorced from his own time. Nevertheless, the author's book did serve to anticipate a discussion about hegemony and democracy that would be reprised in the 1970s. His originality lay in assimilating Gramsci to the socialist and social-democratic current of the European workers' movement, making the *Notebooks* a socialist, rather than communist, alternative to Stalin's USSR, providing an interpretation 'to the right' of Togliatti in a moment in which Italian socialists – faced with the experience of the centre left – were intensifying their critical activity against the politics and culture of the Communist Party.

A more purely biographical mode was adopted by Salvatore Francesco Romano, whose own book came out in 1965 in the series 'The Socialist Life of New Italy', a set of biographical profiles of 'illustrious Italians' published by UTET covering figures from Crispi to De Gasperi and from Croce to Giolitti. Romano's hefty work was, however, a little too inclined to resolve problems in Gramsci's life and work through recourse to a psychological journey as a 'young Sardinian' conditioned in a decisive way by the physical, environmental, economic and social conditions of his infancy and youth. Nor were all periods of Gramsci's life investigated with equal weight, to the extent that the final

---

30   Tamburrano 1963, p. 236.
31   N. Bobbio, *Democrazia e dittatura* [1954], now in Bobbio 1955.
32   Tamburrano 1963, p. 260.

result appeared extremely imbalanced, providing surprisingly little information about the Sardinian period and the years following the Rome Congress of 1922, and practically ignoring the decade spent in prison. The most interesting part was Romano's description of the years between 1911 and 1916, with the reconstruction of Gramsci's cultural interests as a student (i.e. his studies of linguistics, his passion for theatre, his journalism, the question of the relation between thought and action) and as a young socialist militant (his views on Mussolini on the eve of the Great War and the problem of intervention).

Giuseppe Fiori's biography, however, was the most important of the three. Although of course it had its own limitations and gaps, it was the first work to propose a reconstruction of Gramsci's life that was neither hagiographic nor coloured by any particular ideological preconception. Given the context of the time, it managed to provide a significant reconstruction of the arc of Gramsci's life, moving from his youth in Sardinia to a reconstruction of the prison years and the *political* tensions that motivated him even in this last phase of his life. Its limits lay in a lack of contextualisation within the more general horizon of the workers' movement in Italy and – more importantly still – internationally. It also failed to contextualise events within the history of Italian socialism and the Third International or the political events of the Moscow period, focussing instead on the human and sentimental events of his biography. The most beautiful and clearly novel aspect of Fiori's work was the reconstruction of the first twenty years of Gramsci's life in Sardinia: this drew on a significant collection of first-hand accounts and provided information on his economic, social and political context. This not only meant that various residual mythological and hagiographic elements about Gramsci's familial and social provenance could finally be left to rest, but also that the importance of Gramsci's Sardinianism in the development of his thought was finally examined. This included the debate around Sardinian independence, Gramsci's first contact with socialism through his activities in Cagliari, and his earliest journalistic ventures. If the question of Gramsci's Sardinianism and his vision of regional autonomy did not fail to stir up some debates,[33] there was nevertheless another aspect of Fiori's research which provoked still more heated reactions: his argument relating to Gramsci's position on the 'turn' of the PCd'I while he was in prison, and the expulsion of the 'three':

---

[33] See U. Cardia, *Il sardismo rinnovatore del primo capo del Partito comunista italiano*, in *Rinascita sarda*, 1966, issue 9, and G. Fiori, *Non ho taciuto né omesso nulla*, in *Rinascita sarda*, 1966, issue 10.

Gramsci had to face the fact that plenty of political bridges had been burned. His political isolation did not only bring an end to his practical activity – removing him from his old comrades in struggle, leading to a delayed and often vague knowledge of political problems and their origins in debates within the International and the national communist parties, in the first place the Italian one – but something worse still. The final position of the International ... no longer corresponded to Gramsci's own views, and he did not feel the necessity to correct his own position in response.[34]

The Sardinian leader, that is, did not agree with the Social Fascism thesis but remained convinced instead of the need for a democratic, bourgeois phase after Fascism and the constitution of a broad range of alliances. Gramsci's disputes in prison were well known but Fiori's book emphasised the conflict that would later emerge between Togliatti himself and the 'centre' of the PCd'I, emphasising the lull in relations between Gramsci and the Party over a longer period and the possibility that this represented an irreparable break. Antonio's brother Gennaro – wrote Fiori – had invited Togliatti to speak with Gramsci in prison in order to inform him of the expulsion of the 'three' and explain the positions taken. In an interview with Fiori prior to his death in October 1965, Gennaro Gramsci had revealed that his brother's position 'was in line with Leonetti, Tresso and Ravazzoli: he could not support their expulsions, rejecting the new line of the International and claiming that Togliatti had agreed in haste'.[35] Fearing that his brother's dissent would have worsened his experience of political isolation, on returning to Paris Gennaro had apparently lied to Togliatti and assured him of Gramsci's support. The book ends at this point.[36] Responding to Umberto Cardia, who had initiated a long debate in the newspaper *Rinascita sarda*, Fiori argued against the Communist Party ('the Party's contemporary interests conditioned the current research') and claimed that

> the ideas of the 'three' *were Gramsci's ideas*, and the 'three' were expelled for holding to them. Gramsci, in other words, shared all of the reasoning

---

34 Fiori 1966, pp. 287–8.
35 Fiori 1966, p. 292.
36 Gennaro's mission and his 'secret report' which he gave to the highest ranks of the Communist Party on his return from Turi would only become clear forty years after the publication of Fiori's book. See Vacca and Rossi 2007, p. 56 onwards and p. 207 onwards.

held by the 'three' against the suicidal Stalinist position to which Togliatti adhered (without much conviction I believe).[37]

On a political rather than historiographical level, therefore, Fiori unearthed the question of the relation between Gramsci and the Communist Party in the prison years or, to be precise, in the years of the 'turn'. For Fiori, with the introduction of the policy of the 'popular front', the Communist movement and the PCd'I had returned to being in line with Gramsci's own analysis and instruction. The Communist Party's position on this historiography was set out in an unsigned editorial in *Rinascita* that recalled the historical context of the facts:

> Togliatti and other comrades struggle under extremely difficult conditions ... To stand on the breach, in a world awaiting war, with Fascism dominating in Germany and Italy, with the workers' movement broken and dispersed in the West, with growing difficulties in the Soviet Union – there was nothing easy about such a situation. It does not seem correct, therefore, to speak of a banal disagreement between Gramsci and Togliatti ... but rather of different fields of vision, different conditions, and not so much simply a matter of opinion.[38]

These 'different conditions' undoubtedly influenced Gramsci and the 'centre' of the PCd'I in different ways. But to reduce everything to this would mean to evade all discussion about moments of *discontinuity* between Gramsci and the Communist Party, of which there was more than was readily admitted, when we look at the contributions which the historical debate had made since 1956. There was a *historicist* culture that weighed down this still fiercely defensive approach, one that laid the utmost value on 'continuity'. The real argument which saw the evolution of Gramsci's political positions in prison, nevertheless, was not the undoubted opposition to the 'turn', but the relation between the prison writings and the politics of the popular front. Fiori's thesis on this question was clear enough: Gramsci's positions, already at the moment of the Lyons theses, had anticipated this policy. We will see how in the following years

---

[37] G. Fiori, *Non ho taciuto né omesso nulla*, in *Rinascita sarda*, 1966, issue 10, p. 10. According to the *Rapporto Gennaro* (Vacca and Rossi 2007, p. 207 onwards), Gramsci would not have objected to the expulsion of the internal opposition which was connected to the Trotskyist oppositions, while he would have criticised the 'turn' determined by the new political line of 'class against class' (or of 'social Fascism') imposed on the Italian Communist Party by the International.

[38] *Gramsci e il partito tra il 1929 e il 1937*, in *Rinascita*, 1966, issue 31, p. 14.

this would come to provide different responses to the social democratic link between Gramsci and the workers' movement from the 1930s. The discussions around the continuity and discontinuity between Gramsci and his party was to focus, for the most party, on this issue.

4   The *'Giovane Critica'*

The depth of the 1960s historiographical debate on Gramsci and the Communist Party continued in the positions put forward by a group of scholars who collaborated on the *Revista storica del socialismo* – a group which, even if not without its internal differences, showed a particularly polemical and iconoclastic attitude in relation to Gramsci. This historiographic aversion to Gramsci was a direct consequence of their hostility towards the politics of the Communist Party throughout its long period under Togliatti's leadership. But it was also a refusal of the cultural roots that lay under these politics, now countered by a sympathy for the 'socialist left' (i.e. by Morandi and Panzieri) and a nostalgic recollection of Bordigism. The kernel of these historiographic and political ideas lay in questioning Togliatti's cultural framework and a homogenous reading of Gramsci: in this sense they participated in a general cultural movement (from the 'workerism' of the journals *Quaderni rossi* and *Classe operaia* to the critique of 'anti-Fascism', 'populism', etc) that prepared the way for the 'culture of '68'. In different ways, the need was felt for a shift in focus onto class conflicts within advanced industrial society. But in the 'Bordigist' version of 'New Left' culture that went on to form itself around the opposition between workers and capital (which, in a certain sense, reprised the old 'class against class'), the conceptual range proved to be infinitely poorer and more backward than that of theoretical workerism, as partial as it may have been.[39]

Turning to the studies published in *Rivista storica del socialismo*, we can begin with the work of Stefano Merli on 'The Origins of the Centrist Leadership of the Italian Communist Party' from 1964. Dating Gramsci's partial distancing from Bordiga's positions to 1923, and limiting this to the question of obedience to the directives of the Comintern, Merli aimed at a re-evaluation of Bordiga's role, arguing that up to this point he had held full control over the Party (with the exception of Tasca's 'right-wing'). For Merli, the axis around which the new

---

39   On many of the questions just mentioned, see Istituto Gramsci 1972. On the same themes also see Alcaro 1977, which is full of interesting references to the passage from 'anti-historicism' to the practical politics of the groups leading into 1968.

centrist leadership was constituted proposed a new workers' and peasants' government as 'an answer, within the democratic and anti-Fascist context of the working class and its allies, to the incapacity of the bourgeoisie to form itself into a single block, as Fascism had shown'.[40]

A more mature re-evaluation of Bordiga's role was published the following year by Luigi Cortesi. Seeing a missing link between the experience of the factory councils and the period of the birth and early years of the PCd'I, Cortesi depicted a Gramsci who refused to submit to the influence of Bordiga and indeed moved towards 'Leninism' (of whom the author seemed to accept a formalistic interpretation à la Bordiga) only *after* the defeat of the factory councils. The Rome Congress had seen the undisputed hegemony of the Neopolitan leader and in the *Theses* produced 'the final great Communist document on the hypothesis of a fundamental permanence of revolutionary motivations'.[41] It was in the period 1923–24 – with the constitution of the new leading group around Gramsci – that Cortesi identified the beginning of 'a political tradition which would constantly inspire the Communist Party up until today, including a gradual tendency not only to overturn Bordiga's findings but even to break away from a Leninist framework'.

The continuity between Gramsci and Togliatti, therefore, was drastically reaffirmed, even if under a new name. Another backdating of this political line was given by Andreina de Clementi, for whom there was a substantial continuity between the Gramsci of the councils and of the successive period up to the split of Livorno. In both cases Gramsci's ideas were 'neither Marxist nor Leninist' but liberal democratic. She argued that 'the origins of the Gramscian theory of the party, of its "national" and "mass" character' lay in the Turin years, since 'the Leninist notion of the party was alien to Gramsci's theories both before and after Livorno, the consequence of an instrumentalising interpretation that places Gramsci outside of Marxism'.[42] The 'national function of the working class' was, for de Clementi, the non-class position (the authentic *red thread*) that connected the Gramsci of the Communist Party to the *Ordine Nuovo* and through to the 1960s. Bordiga had the merit, the author claimed, of having stressed the conquest of political power, thus recalling Lenin, while Gramsci had actually misunderstood the character of the Russian soviets, which were

---

40 S. Merli, *Le origini della direzione centrista nel Partito comunista d'Italia*, in *Rivista storica del socialismo*, 1964, issue 23, p. 621.

41 L. Cortesi, *Alcuni problemi della storia del Partito comunista italiano. Per una discussione*, in *Rivista storica del socialismo*, 1965, issue 24, p. 158.

42 A. de Clementi, *La politica del Partito comunista d'Italia nel 1921–1922 e il rapporto Bordiga-Gramsci*, in *Rivista storica del socialismo*, 1966, issues 28–29, p. 138.

political organs of the dictatorship of the proletariat and not – as was the case, on the contrary, for the *Ordine Nuovo* – instruments for the control of production. Gramsci was democratic, inter-classist, moralist, economistic (sic!), idealist, distant from Marxism and Leninism, standing fast to a liberal conception of the state: for de Clementi, he was wrong even when he was right, as in the case of his 'prediction' (as the author defined it) of Fascism, which 'might only superficially be seen as the result of an analysis more rigorous' than Bordiga's, characterised as it was by a significant under-evaluation of the phenomenon.[43]

Stefano Merli returned to Gramsci in 1967 in the pages of *Giovane critica*, in particular on the relation between Gramsci and communist *politics*. Lucio Colletti, drawing on ideas from Fiori's biography, had claimed that from a *Leninist* point of view (i.e. from the conviction of the possibility of a proletarian revolution in Italy) it was impossible to understand Gramsci's opposition to the 'social Fascism' thesis through popular frontism and the defence of 'bourgeois democracy' in opposition to Fascism. Yes, this was a politics of alliances but with two different directions, two different hegemonies: a proletarian revolutionary perspective (Gramsci's) and a bourgeois, Stalinist, reformist one in Togliatti's case, i.e. the Popular Front. It was a case of Gramsci *versus* Togliatti in Colletti's view.[44] Arguing against attempts to *use* Gramsci as an alternative in opposition to the positions of the Communist Party, Merli located the Sardinian leader instead within a framework of 'international Stalinism', in which 'he does not represent an alternative to but an affirmation of the central conception of revolution through democratic stages as developed in Western countries'.[45] But by this point Gramsci was considered to have been superseded, for the workers' movement was well beyond *statism*, horizons posed by both the Second and Third Internationals and beyond which Gramsci was no longer able to pass. The author 'accused' Gramsci of having chosen 'a politics of alliance against a class-based one, and a politics of democracy against that of socialist revolution'.[46] In this framework – Merli claimed – the autonomy of the class disappeared, and the party took on an 'all consuming' dimension. Merli concluded that

---

[43] A. de Clementi, *La politica del Partito comunista d'Italia nel 1921–1922 e il rapporto Bordiga-Gramsci*, in *Rivista storica del socialismo*, 1966, issues 28–29, p. 156.

[44] See L. Colletti, *Antonio Gramsci e la rivoluzione in Italia*, in *La sinistra*, 1966, issue 1.

[45] S. Merli, *I nostri conti con la teoria della 'rivoluzione senza rivoluzione' di Gramsci*, in *Giovane critica*, 1967, issue 17, p. 63.

[46] S. Merli, *I nostri conti con la teoria della 'rivoluzione senza rivoluzione' di Gramsci*, in *Giovane critica*, 1967, issue 17, p. 68.

in Gramsci the concept of the *revolutionary break* is substituted for that of a *revolution in two stages, of revolution without revolution* ... The 'direct struggle for power' is placed in an undefined second period which will need to arise *necessarily* from the organised and political reinforcement of the Communist Party.[47]

Merli's theoretical and political proposal was 'classism', posed as an alternative to the Gramscian concept of hegemony. While opposing Gramsci and Togliatti he reserved his positive remarks for Morandi and Panzieri's 'left socialism' (the context out of which 'workerism' derived). In the same years, arguments similar to Merli's were already to be found in Asor Rosa's *Scrittori e popolo* ('Writers and the People'), which in the world of literary and cultural criticism had had the same iconoclastic intentions which the *Rivista storica del socialismo* had had for historical research. Asor Rosa levelled his own arguments against the Togliattian tradition of anti-Fascist unity and democratic revolution.[48] In an attempt to demystify the *populism* that had characterised much of Italian culture since Unification, Asor Rosa denied the importance of the question of hegemony and alliances, such as in his interpretation of the Resistance, for example.[49] The inter-classist alliance prevalent in the Resistance, which represented the *containment of the advances of the working class*, had only developed after the fall of Fascism. For Asor Rosa this represented the final role of popular and national politics in the Communist Party, given the consistency of a political line which, thanks to Gramsci, had arrived at the 'Italian road to socialism' only by passing through the politics of the Popular Front, anti-Fascist struggle, and 'national reconstruction'. Asor Rosa's reading of Gramsci was based on the premise that 'what unites Gramsci's writings is the thread of democratic thought running through the nineteenth century'.[50] This was reference above all to Gioberti, from whom Gramsci had derived the concept of the 'national-popular' – a concept that, for the author, was opposed to the class-based positions of the *Ordine Nuovo*, in which there had instead been an attempt 'to theorise and establish institutions genuinely comprised of the workers, in a state fundamentally comprised of classes'.[51]

---

47 S. Merli, *I nostri conti con la teoria della 'rivoluzione senza rivoluzione' di Gramsci*, in *Giovane critica*, 1967, issue 17, p. 70.
48 On these matters an important writing to note is F. Fortini, *Mandato degli scrittori e fine dell'antifascismo*, in Fortini 1965.
49 See Asor Rosa 1965, p. 192.
50 Asor Rosa 1965, p. 260.
51 Asor Rosa 1965, p. 259. The term *nazional-popolare*, used by Asor Rosa to describe so much of post-War Gramscianism, is never found in Gramsci, who always wrote *nazionale-popolare*.

While there can be no doubt as to the populist connotations within the whole of post-Resistance and Neorealist literature (even if founded on a very vague notion of 'the people'), it is difficult to understand how this supports Asor Rosa's reading of Gramsci and the *Notebooks*, in which 'popular' culture is never praised uncritically but always seen as a starting point from which to commence a process (one which moves from subaltern to hegemonic culture) at the end of which such subaltern culture above all others would be truly transformed. This was in opposition to populists, for whom, as Asor Rosa himself emphasised, the 'people' represents a static model to be praised as they are.

In my own opinion, this confusion results from an interpretation that put all the emphasis on Gramsci's *historicism*: having focused all his attention on the present reality, Gramsci left any vision of possible transformation to the blurry margins. Yet once again Gramsci was moved aside and his place taken by the political aims of the Communist Party, that peculiar link between democracy and socialism that Togliatti wanted to maintain; the strategy of the 'war of positions' – derived from Gramsci but not without some *adjustments*; the relation of continuity and the 'legacy' claimed by the Italian communists between the socialist movement and the democratic tradition, between Marxism and 'bourgeois culture'. Indeed, for Asor Rosa, all culture was and could only be 'bourgeois'. Not only was there not, in his view, any space for the struggle for hegemony: here we are also much closer to the most mechanist reading of Marxian theory as 'dominant ideology' (which we also find in Althusser). In so doing, he was certainly very far from an authentic reading of Gramsci.

5   The Crisis of Historicism

Though of vast importance for historiography, studies on Gramsci in the first half of the 1960s did not have the same effect on theoretical work. On the one hand, the new cultural climate overtook that 'Gramscian' historicism which had been so prevalent in the previous decades; on the other hand, it tried to fill in a gap left by Gramsci, or a certain Gramsci, with a glance all the way back to Marx. The crisis of 1956 brought to light theoretical differences which had existed before but less explicitly, particularly in the philosophical debates that appeared in the columns of *Rinascita* over 1962.[52] These juxtaposed the 'historicists' to 'the Della Volpe school', beginning with an evaluation of Nicola Badaloni's book *Marxism as Historicism*. Arguing against Lucio Colletti's ideas,

---

52   The most important contributions are now collected in Cassano 1973.

Baladoni stressed the *objective* character of contradictions and the validity of the dialectical method. Marx's *Capital* was founded on the principle by which contradiction pointed towards 'human praxis, which alone can be entrusted with the possibility of *sublation*'.[53] This was a restatement of the usual principle underpinning Italian Marxism, which Badaloni reprised through an explicit reference to Gramsci:

> If it is true that in Gramsci's teachings the objective situation is characterised not only by the presence of capitalism but also the force of its *contradictions* ... Then it is also true that the methodological explorations of the real course of events must also be present in the philosophical sphere. Research and methodical awareness is the main road towards Marxist hegemony in Italy.[54]

It is not possible to reconstruct here the 'debate of 1962',[55] which did not focus directly on Gramsci (a fact in itself significant). Nonetheless it has to be noted that it resulted in a substantial re-shuffling of the cards, interrogating the use of the concept of *contradiction* within Marxist historicism, attempting to reassess that the thesis of supposed *backwardness* according to which Italian capitalism was not at the correct stage (almost by definition) to be overcome.

The polarisation of the debate between those on the left who 'accentuated the backwardness of Italian capitalism, its resistance to reform and those, on the other hand, who emphasised changes in productive organisation, the elements of development',[56] found expression in the printed debate on historicism hosted by *Rinascita* in the context of the Eleventh Congress of the Communist Party (January 1966). The discussion began with an article by Rossana Rossanda (then 'head of cultural affairs') who attempted to create an open dialogue between Marxism and other cultural tendencies of the time, from the artistic Neo-avant garde to the main schools of 'bourgeois' philosophy, in order to try and recuperate those vast areas of modern culture which had been left outside of 'Marxist historicism' in the 1940s and 1950s, as well as in order to advocate a modern, secular conception of Marxism. In her article 'Political Unity and Cultural Choices', Rossanda deftly showed the limits to Togliatti's

---

53 Badaloni 1962, p. 232.
54 Badaloni 1962, pp. 208–9.
55 For a reconstruction of the 'debate of '62' and the roles of its main antagonists, Della Volpe and Cesare Luporini, see my own work on the subject, in Liguori 1996b.
56 Ingrao 1977, pp. 153–54.

political and cultural hypothesis (the 'great historicist tradition'), which 'did not bring together those links that had already been forged between national development and the development of European culture'. In her view, Togliatti undervalued certain currents and tendencies that were destined to become important. Instead, Rossanda emphasised the necessity to look for 'a bond between Marxism and the ideal, social experience of the advanced capitalist West in all its complexity ... Was it not the case that Gramsci had already recognised this need?'[57] It was the return to an old *querelle* which had already emerged in 1945–47 and had been reprised in 1956. The confrontation with other democratic currents – as Luciano Gruppi wrote in response to Rossanda – had not been impeded by the historicist tradition, but by its insufficient development. For Gruppi, the tradition begun by De Sanctis and Labriola, and further developed by Gramsci and Togliatti, was

> the authentic thread of Marxism, with the principle of praxis at its centre, maintaining a relation between subject and object neither through flattening out the former nor by ignoring the latter ... this long tradition, demonstrated definitively in the *New Party*, cannot be reached through a deterministic vision of the historical process, nor through speculative development and the application of the laws of dialectic to history. It must be reached, rather, through 'things in themselves' (Togliatti), from the 'real movement' (Marx), from their contradictions – and here is where the dialectic truly lies. And it will be reached only if one grasps the role of the subject, of the *Party* – not by opposing reality to models for the future but by suggesting solutions for today, always bearing the principle of *praxis* in mind.[58]

Gruppi's historicist Marxism referenced Gramsci and that interpretative line which read Gramsci through the axis of subject, party and praxis. For Gruppi, the *New Party*, by '*doing politics*' – which, according to the Togliattian expression, meant stressing the creative moments connected to the real situation of the Communist Party during the 'Salerno turn' – shared with this historicist tradition and with Gramsci himself a conception of historical reality as a set of 'individual' facts that cannot be generalised, with respect to which party and subject interacted by constructing an appropriate interpretive apparatus *within*

---

57 R. Rossanda, *Unità politica e scelte culturali*, in *Rinascita*, 1965, issue 34, p. 22 of the supplement *Il contemporaneo*.
58 L. Gruppi, *Palmiro Togliatti: cultura e metodo*, in Cassano 1973, p. 255.

praxis (and one could explain this in turn through the Togliattian tendency to support concrete political choices with a kind of generalisation and theorisation which was not only explicitly methodological but even rule-based). Rossanda's reply tried instead to emphasise the very real differences between Marxism and historicism:

> Labriola and Gramsci entirely accepted the Marxist, materialist and dialectical conception of history ... according to which every fact or idea ought not be interpreted simply in terms of its origins, and how its past prefigures the future, but through its structural relations – as fully mediated as they are, i.e. the social relations of production. It is this that makes history not a succession or accumulation of unrepeated and meaningless moments – nor therefore, of empiricist politics and idealist teleology – but the intelligible expression of a social dynamic, the laws of which are objective, knowable and therefore also changeable.[59]

Rossanda's anti-historicism (in opposition to so many in the years to come, as we will see with the case of Althusser) did not lead her to a negative judgement of Gramsci. Rather, she wrote that:

> Labriola and Gramsci do not differ in their relation to this fundamental fact of Marxism. They developed it to its peak as an instrument for the interpretation of our society and of the mediations between 'structure' and 'superstructure', between social and historical laws.[60]

Instead, even if it was only hinted at, there was a proposal here for a different interpretive key to the author of the *Notebooks*, which – at this level of elaboration at least – risked representing a reductive version of Gramsci's Marxism, its idiosyncrasy and innovations. Nevertheless, it began to become clear that as the crisis of Marxist historicism deepened, it was also freeing up theoretical and political energies. Cesare Luporini's studies should also be seen in this light, since Luporini quite profoundly revised his positions after the 'discussions of 1962', as well as in the context of those structuralist currents which were making Althusser's presence felt within Marxism. In his contribution to *Rinascita*, Luporini wrote that:

---

59   R. Rossanda, *Marxismo e storicismo*, in Cassano 1973, p. 260.
60   Cassano 1973, pp. 260–1.

> *Capital* is not a historical investigation, and even less is it *historicist*, methodologically speaking. Its field of reference is 'current society'. It takes pure social formation (the 'system of mercantile economy') as its starting point, the purity of which has never existed in historical reality ... Historical empirical material is indispensable to the construction of that model but its presence is always that of a variable within determinate limits ... *Capital*'s method is thus not in fact a historicist one. It is, rather, a structuralist method, in line with the canons of historical materialism.[61]

For Luporini, only an analysis which began with this *system* would be able to provide a non-empiricist foundation for the historical dimension, so as to uncover the specific historical nature of an event and the structural dimension by which to understand it. For Gramsci himself, Luporini recalled, the term 'historicism' was clearly an Idealist derivation, a part of the framework of that 'work of recuperation' by which Neo-idealism had drawn on historical materialism. 'In his propositions, Gramsci went far beyond this ("complete" historicism, "absolute" historicism)'. But for Luporini 'Gramsci nonetheless reopened the problem of history and *historical character* within a Marxist framework'.[62] With a nod to his own times (which in the cultural sphere were riding the structuralist wave), Luporini summarised the path towards a new reading of Gramsci, reclaiming a connection to Marx in opposition not only to 1950s historicism but also – one should add – against Bobbio's own interpretation, which would soon re-propose Gramsci as 'the theorist of the superstructure'. Nonetheless, Luporini's contributions to the discussions of 1962 left contradictions and dialectics in the shadows, maintaining a certain embarrassment in relation to a reading of Gramsci's Marxism that did not want to 'abandon' the historicist tradition of which it was still very much a part, and which still awaited its own rediscovery and renewal. The anti-historicist polemic and its connection to a political struggle brought the terms of discourse to their extremes, as was clearly the case in Lupoini's intervention at the 'Congressional Tribunal' of *Unità* in 19 January 1966, a few days before the opening of the Eleventh Congress of the Italian Communist Party;[63] and still more so in an intervention by Rossanda which appeared at the same moment in *Rinascita*, in which she claimed that 'different ways of understanding Marxism have brought forth different methods of interpreting our society: a "materialist" vision that lays emphasis on the structure, and a "historicist" vision of political processes, of

---

61   C. Luporini, *Una visione critica dell'uomo*, in Cassano 1973, pp. 276–77.
62   C. Luporini, *Una visione critica dell'uomo*, in Cassano 1973, p. 282.
63   See C. Luporini, *Una battaglia culturale e politica*, in *l'Unità*, 19 January 1966.

the superstructure'.[64] Mario Alicata replied, not without basis, that laying out matters in such a manner ignored the concepts of the historical bloc and of hegemony which not only Gramsci and Togliatti but also Lenin himself had opened up as new paths in revolutionary theory and activity.[65]

Beyond the arguments made at the congress, a general shift was underway that began to be felt throughout Italian Marxism. The 'return to Marx', an insistence on Marxism as a science and anti-historicism all relegated Gramsci to second place – when he was not explicitly perceived as an 'adversary', that is. This was the case with the *early* Althusser,[66] who resolutely criticised the Sardinian Communist for his 'historicism'. In *For Marx*, Althusser had initially recognised the originality and importance of Gramsci's studies: 'the theory of the specific power of superstructures ... is, for the most part, yet to be developed ... Who has *really* attempted to develop Marx and Engels's line of thought? I can only think of Gramsci'. The *Notebooks*, for Althusser

> touch on all the basic problems of Italian and European history: economic, social, political and cultural. There are also some completely original and in some cases genial insights into the problem of the superstructure. Also, as always with true discoveries, there are *new concepts*, for example, *hegemony:* a remarkable example of a theoretical solution in outline to the problems of the interpretation of the economic and the political.[67]

Perhaps the French philosopher's fight against the 'Hegelian' conception of the dialectic was not necessarily in contradiction to the Gramscian re-evaluation of the superstructural moment as contained in the concept of hegemony and the historical bloc. Yet in his subsequent work Althusser assimilated Gramsci into a (decidedly heterogeneous) group of 'Marxist Hegelians', including Mehring, Rosa Luxemburg, Korsch and Lukács (and the polemic did not spare Della Volpe and Colletti either, along with its immediate target, Sartre).[68] Althusser held that every historicism – including Gramsci's 'absolute' historicism – contained an 'expressive' conception of social totality (i.e. deriving from a single foundation), annulling the differences within it – as well as an 'ideological' conception of theory, reduced to the immediate consciousness of experience. This

---

64   R. Rossanda, *Un programma politico per la cultura*, in *Rinascita*, 1966, issue 4, pp. 37–38.
65   See M. Alicata, *Il nostro dibattito sulla cultura*, in *l'Unità*, 1966, issue 23.
66   For a chronology of the various phases of Althusserian thought, see Mancina 1977.
67   Althusser 1969, pp. 113–14 (including footnote; Ben Brewster translation).
68   See Althusser and Balibar 1997 (Ben Brewster translation), p. 314.

attempt to make Gramsci's historicism appear as a variation on Hegelianism was no doubt forced – in a similar manner as Bobbio's studies would attempt a little later, in the meeting at Cagliari in 1967. Nevertheless, it was clear that Althusser *the theorist* detected in Gramsci a lack of an 'epistemological break' or *dividing line* without which religion, philosophy and Marxism could all be considered – as the *Notebooks* said – 'conceptions of the world'. In any case it should be pointed out that Gramsci did indeed move in an opposite direction from the Althusserian definition of historicism, re-evaluating the superstructural moment without eliminating (in a Hegelian manner?) the differences internal to that which he called 'the historical bloc'.

Althusser would later abandon the rationalist schema based on the dichotomy of ideology and science, reconsidering theory as at least partly historically determined. From this re-evaluation of 'politics' would arise a re-evaluation of Gramsci and the link between philosophy and politics. The events of May '68 meant that all those French institutions which had previously been seen through the lens of 'consensus' were now seen through that of 'repression', making it possible to grasp the fallacy of various theoretical extremes, and putting Althusser's own reflections on the concept of hegemony back into the centre, 'translated' into the terms of the question of French philosophy in his essay *Ideology and Ideological State Apparatuses*.[69] The Gramscian 'apparatus of hegemony' was used here to 'expand' (as was said back then) the concept of the state, no longer seen simply as a repressive machine. Furthermore, the theory of hegemony emphasised the identification of those *apparatuses* that were particularly suited to its purposes, thus also emphasising the fact that hegemony had its own *materiality*, availing itself of particular institutions (schools, churches, etc.).

There are important objections to this study to be made, beginning with the linguistic-conceptual turn in Althusser's work itself. But fundamentally the difficult relation between Althusser and Gramsci lies in the inevitable collision between the concept of hegemony and that of 'dominant ideology', in which a mechanical version of the Marxian thesis expels dialectics from the realm of superstructure. This version does not in truth leave any space for class struggle within the ideological state apparatuses, even if Althusser himself claimed otherwise. How might a class become a *ruling* class, a *leading* class, in a Gramscian sense, if it has not yet become a dominant one? The fact remained nonetheless that Althusser's studies contributed to shifting the focus onto Gramsci's theory of the state and power, a theory which would become central to the debates of the 1970s.

---

69   See Althusser 1971.

6 Gramsci and Civil Society

The marking of thirty years since Gramsci's death, in 1967, provided an opportunity for a wave of commemorative editorial projects and studies, including the Second International Meeting of Gramscian Studies held on 23–27 April. This represents an important moment in the history of Gramsci studies, in which the interpretation of the author of the *Notebooks* as a 'great intellectual' was significantly galvanised. With the exception of Ernesto Ragionieri's essay and the subsequent debate, the general tone of the Cagliari conference, its organisation (importantly including the subdivision of the contributions and discussions on a rigid and traditional disciplinary basis: history, philosophy, pedagogy, the study of Southern Italy, etc.) all contributed to making the 1967 meeting an effective reply to those new tendencies moving within society and culture, and not only in Italy. Here was a bitesize Gramsci for all seasons, more the 'great writer' of democracy than a *revolutionary* leader and thinker, someone suited for being abstractly compared with other giants of thought than understood within the concrete events of his time.

Not that the reasons for this organisation of the Gramscian congress were not evident: much water had passed under the bridge since 1956. The Communist Party had regained strong relations with democratic culture, and the usual prestigious names – including Garin, Bobbio, Galasso and Sapegno – signalled a renewed esteem, a range of figures capable of a dialogue with Gramsci's Party (even if with important internal differences). And yet the main outcome of the convention was not in truth an adequate response to the transformations of the 1960s. There was too much polemicising against the new interpretative strands (in particular structuralism and Althusserianism), implicitly reaffirming the historicist view. It provided an interpretation of Gramsci – or rather, a series of interpretations of Gramsci – that frequently attempted to explain his historicising position instead of recognising his originality and validity, in the end 'neutralising' him rather than recounting his conceptual categorises so as to test their viability in the various historical and contemporary contexts. On the eve of 1968, the Gramsci who was offered to the new generations and new layers of intellectuals – not only via the Cagliari congress but also through the simultaneous publication of numerous monographs of *Critica marxista* – was more the Gramsci of those interpretations prevalent in the years following the Second World War than the Gramsci who had been claimed in the 1960s as the theorist of hegemony, the Communist leader who tried to rethink the strategy of the workers' movement. He was still a 'Gramsci for all'[70] who would

---

70   This line comes from R. Paris, *Il Gramsci di tutti*, in *Giovane critica*, 1967, issues 15–16, a polemical commentary on the Cagliari meeting.

nonetheless not have enjoyed the meeting between the traditional left and the 'new movements' which had already been glimpsed and which were to be confirmed in the subsequent years.

Between the many contributions made at Cagliari, the one which was most discussed and exercised the greatest influence was without doubt the speech given by Noberto Bobbio, *'Gramsci e il concetto della società civile'* (Gramsci and the concept of civil society): without claiming Gramsci to be outside of the Marxist tradition, the Turinese scholar strongly emphasised the motives of his *autonomy* from it (which many would nonetheless read as *distance* and 'rejection'). This was identified through a particularly close reading of the concept of civil society, situating the Communist leader in a more general history of political thought in which, with a clever play of approaches and responses, Gramsci ended up being simply one of many other Hegelian writers. In this way Bobbio, on the pretext of not 'embalming' Gramsci, as he put it, and through a work of fairly forced historical contextualisation, managed to make the Communist leader a *classic*, outside of any particular time and space and above all distanced from the problems of the present.

On the central concept of 'civil society', Bobbio claimed, Gramsci derived much less from Hegel than from Marx. In Gramsci and in Marx (unlike in Hegel) 'the active and positive moment of historical development' was not in the state but in civil society. But while for Marx such an 'active moment' was structural ('the real home and stage of every history'), for Gramsci it was superstructural; civil society was to be understood 'not as "the web of material relations" but rather the web of ideological, cultural relations'.[71] And this – claimed Bobbio – was because Gramsci derived the his own concept of civil society 'not from Marx, but clearly from Hegel', and from a Hegel *different* from that which Marx had created: 'the Hegelian concept of civil society which Gramsci had in mind is not the system of needs (on which Marx built his concept), that is, economic relations, but the institutions which regulate them'.[72] Both Marx and Gramsci, therefore, had started from the ambivalent Hegelian concept of civil society, but read it in different ways. The consequences of this repositioning were important: for Marx, the 'theatre of history' was the structure, the economy; for Gramsci it was the superstructure, culture, the labour of ideas. Gramsci thus becomes – according to this reading – the fundamental passage to the re-evaluation of subjectivity (not determined by the 'economic structure', as Gramsci had written in 1918, but 'the interpretation which one makes

---

71   N. Bobbio, *Gramsci e la concezione della società civile*, in Rossi 1969, i, p. 85.
72   Rossi 1969, i, p. 87.

of it').[73] Gramsci was, therefore, for Bobbio, above all the *theorist of the superstructure*, not because he had provided appropriate attention to this aspect of reality, nor because he had grasped its increasing importance in the modern world, but precisely because of the meaning that the ethical and political had in his theoretical system, which was fundamentally different from that which it held for Marx and Marxism. Consequentially, just as the relation of structure and superstructure had been inverted, so too the twin concepts of institution and ideology were overturned.[74] At the same time, the concept of hegemony was read by Bobbio as being without 'political direction', and instead having a 'cultural direction'.[75] For the Turinese philosophy, this was the key distinction between Gramsci and Lenin: in the first, the moment of force was subordinate to that of hegemony, in the second the two moments came forth at the same time. In the first the conquest of hegemony preceded the conquest of power, in the second it accompanied and followed it.

Bobbio's reading focussed on a thesis of *revoking* the relation between structure and superstructure which Gramsci had made with respect to Marxism, and found a wide public. Croce's cry – 'as a man of thought, he was one of us' – was implicitly repeated, embedding the Communist leader in the great tradition of liberal thought, and that dichotomous pairing of state and civil society on which Bobbio's thesis was founded. Such a reading, nonetheless, could only be provided if one had a very simplified vision of the relation between structure and superstructure, in Marx as much as Gramsci, and without considering the intrinsically reductive character of this celebrated spatial metaphor in terms of the interpretative model of society advanced by Marx. In order to build his thesis, therefore, Bobbio had to take for granted a *mechanistic* reading of the relation between structure and superstructure, in which one of the two terms (usually the former) became the strong and immediate determination of the other level of reality *in the last instance*: 'the platform of every history'. Togliatti, already in 1958, had underlined the *methodological* and not *organic* nature of this distinction,[76] to which Gramsci himself had called attention, proposing the concept of the 'historical bloc'. Undoubtedly, as Togliatti again had noted in 1958, in Gramsci there was certainly a *primacy* given to subjectivity, to the political, but in a sense quite different from that emphasised by Bobbio. Gramsci is the antipode of every economism and determinism, advancing a profound

---

73 A. Gramsci, *Utopia* [1918] in Gramsci 1984, p. 205; Rossi 1969, p. 89.
74 Rossi 1969, i, p. 90.
75 Rossi 1969, i, pp. 94–5.
76 Togliatti 2001, p. 258.

rethinking of the deterministic *structures* of Marxism. But his attempt to construct a theory of politics and of ideological forms always *began with Marx*, not from a "counter-reformation" of Marxism. Rather, the historical developments in the relation between economy and politics of the twentieth century – broadly borne out of the state's intervention in the sphere of production, into the work of organisation, promotion and rationalisation by which politics is related to and, to an extent, produces society – burst out into Gramsci's Marxism. In 'returning' to Hegel, Gramsci in reality utilised the elements of Hegelianism which allowed him to show the new place of the state in the economy. Bobbio did not grasp this fundamental element in the Idealist formulations of his essay, in which he moves from doctrine to doctrine, from theory to theory, without any reference to the real context. The liberal democratic tradition tried yet again to render Gramsci homogeneous with all the intellectuals who preceded him, dissolving the real contours of his historical figure, that bond between theory and praxis that represented the key to understanding his real significance.

Bobbio's essay gave rise to many reactions at the Cagliari congress. There were some scholars, like Irving Fetscher, who welcomed Bobbio's contribution, in particular in terms of the connecting of Gramscian ideas not only to Marx but also to Lenin. Luciano Gruppi, however, diminished the difference between Gramsci and Lenin, claiming that for both the concept of hegemony was understood as simultaneously the moment of dominance and of leadership, even if Gramsci had emphasised the latter. Valentino Gerratana recalled the richness of Gramsci's investigation of the superstructure, nevertheless pointing out Gramsci's own observation that in more developed capitalist countries '*civil society* has become very complex and resistant to the catastrophic "eruptions" of immediate economic factors'. On the one hand, in fact, Gerratana claimed that 'the substance of the Marxian analyses of the separation between civil society and the political state in the process of the formation of the modern state and modern bourgeois society ... seem to me a fundamental and integral part of Gramsci's thought'. On the other hand, he identified with precision how the difference between the concepts of civil society in Marx and in Gramsci 'shows above all else the fact that the kind of civil society that concerned [Gramsci] ... was no longer that which had occupied Marx'.[77]

Jacques Texier demonstrated his critical take on Bobbio's work first in Cagliari and reprised the same line the following year in an essay that appeared

---

77 V. Gerratana, *Intervento*, in Rossi 1969, i, p. 172.

in *Critica marxista*.[78] Texier proposed that the fundamental category through which to disentangle the conceptual mesh of the *Notebooks* was not that of 'civil society' but rather the 'historical bloc': one needed to start from the dialectical unity of the structure and superstructure in order avoid falling into either deterministic economism or subjectivism. Bobbio had made Gramsci into a Crocean in the very moment in which he perceived civil society as simply a set of ideological relations, and thus also saw intellectuals as the true 'motor of historical becoming'.[79] Not only did civil society have an economic content for Gramsci, Texier pointed out, but the concept of hegemony itself had an economic foundation, as well as socio-economic content. The struggle for hegemony is the struggle for power, and superstructural activities have a class character, arising out of those contradictions that Marx had identified as central to modern history.

7   The 'Historicisation' of Gramsci

For Eugenio Garin, the re-evaluation of the superstructure, and therefore of culture and intellectuals, was central to Gramsci's thought. But he did not then distance Gramsci from Lenin, or juxtapose the two thinkers, as Bobbio had done. On the contrary, Garin praised the relation between these two *theorists of subjectivity*.[80] His contribution at Cagliari was dedicated to 'Politics and Culture in Gramsci (the problem of intellectuals)'. His contribution to the meeting in Rome ten years earlier had focused on the issue of *cultural tradition*. Now, however, the more interesting part of Garin's contribution concerned the reconstruction of the problematic between intellectuals in the full arc of Gramsci's experience. Garin demonstrated the important role which the Communist leader had assigned to 'raising consciousness' within political struggle, from the years of the *Ordine Nuovo* onward, and to 'Enlightenment' and therefore to intellectuals; to demonstrate this, Garin focused on the *Southern Question* and the analytical novelties which had contributed to Gramsci's interpretation of the different roles played by cultural figures in different epochs; he distinguished between the different kinds of intellectuals that Gramsci had brought to light, and on their roles in the *Notebooks*. Garin claimed, in summary, that 'the problem of intellectuals' was 'the fulcrum around which

---

78   J. Texier, *Gramsci teorico delle sovrastrutture*, in *Critica marxista*, 1968, issue 3.
79   J. Texier, *Gramsci teorico delle sovrastrutture*, in *Critica marxista*, 1968, issue 3, p. 87.
80   *Discorso di Eugenio Garin*, in Rossi 1969, i, p. 29.

everything turned',[81] not only in the prison writings but in all of Gramsci's work – the product of a man who was indivisibly both theorist and political leader.

Garin noted the importance of situating Gramsci's historicism within the Italian and European cultural contexts of his lifetime. In the *Discorso* of 1969, Garin had already begun to work on a strong defence of Gramscian historicism, arguing (more or less explicitly) against the full range of anti-historicist positions which, as we have seen, had been proposed by Marxists over the 1960s.[82] This polemic clearly outshone many of the other contributions; indeed, it constructed the general background for the entire conference. Natalino Sapegno, for example, proposed 'the problem of literature' and in what was clearly an argument against Asor Rosa's *Writers and the People*, claimed it was absurd

> to measure Gramsci's merits against a model derived from later, entirely different perspectives on culture and activity; instead, a more methodologically justified approach would take into account more seriously the cultural conditions in which he actually worked.[83]

Not only was Gramsci strongly *reduced to* (and not *inserted into*) the context in which he worked; this also smoothed over his differences from the traditions of liberal democratic thought. Both of these directions found their greatest support in Giuseppe Galasso, in his *Gramsci e i problemi della storia italiana*, which had a particular focus on Italian Unification, situating Gramsci in relation to the liberal, Crocean historiography. Galasso referred primarily to the positions put forward ten years earlier by Romeo in terms of the formation of market capitalism in Italy, claiming that these were really the positions of a much later historiography. 'What is needed' claimed Galasso, 'is a total historicisation of our discussions about Gramsci, a proper awareness of the framework of the problems and attitudes by which people have moulded ... and adapted him, and made him their own'.[84] Gramsci, therefore, was not to be confused with those scholars who had 'put Unification on trial' – which moderates had interpreted merely in terms of *Gattopardismo*, neglecting, for example, other substantial forces that were working *against* Unification. For Galasso, Gramsci's work con-

---

81   E. Garin, *Politica e cultura in Gramsci (il problema degli intellettuali)*, in Rossi 1969, i, p. 65.
82   On this see also E. Garin, *La formazione di Gramsci e Croce*, in *Praxis rivoluzionaria e storicismo in Gramsci*, Critica marxista – Quaderni, 1967, issue 3, p. 123.
83   N. Sapegno, *Gramsci e i problemi della letteratura*, in Rossi 1969, i, p. 265.
84   G. Galasso, *Gramsci e i problemi della storia italiana*, in Rossi 1969, i, pp. 307–8.

tained an 'unresolved tension' between 'strictly reasoned historiography' and a *political* critique of the left at time of Unification. Criticising this attitude, Galasso underlined how, furthermore, 'the image which Gramsci gave us of the world of Unification does not diverge ... from the image consolidated by the dominant historiography of the liberal tradition, from Croce to Omodeo, from Chabod to Maturi'.[85]

Galasso seemed to be saying that Gramsci had long been made into 'one of us', to repeat the famous Crocean invocation, a process the echo of which could still be heard twenty years later in Cagliari. Gramsci was thus the result, if an anomalous one, of the liberal historiographic tradition. (And this was also shown, for Galasso, by the fact that Croce's critique of the *Notebooks* focussed on the *political* sphere, precisely not on that of *historiography*). But Gramsci believed – as Galasso recognised – that political activity must emerge from historical understanding, and he thus criticised Unification 'in a context which is no longer the contemporary one'.[86] This was consequentially a political reflection, as well as representing 'a politics *constructed* scientifically, namely the scientific critique of all that has been'.[87]

The reactions to Galasso's contribution at the same congress were dominated by a strong emphasis, among the Gramscian historians, of a final and effective overcoming of the liberal historiography, i.e. of the old accusations that Gramsci had projected onto Unification the political problems of the period following the First World War. What prevailed therefore was a *recognition of recognition*: Galasso had recognised the *scientific* weight of Gramsci's historiographical research (as well as its political ends). There were then those who, like Procacci, correctly emphasised that Galasso was forcing Gramsci's thought to synchronise with the Crocean tradition, leading to his failure to see the overturning of the ethical and political conception of history undertaken in the *Notebooks*. Today it seems clear how mistaken Galasso was, as well as how radically unfair, in not properly considering the historical-theoretical categories which constituted the pivot of Gramsci's thought (hegemony, passive revolution, organic crisis, etc.). In this sense, even while Galasso's essay is full of interesting insights, today it appears incapable of glimpsing the most evident and productive hallmarks of the prison writings.

---

85   Rossi 1969, i, p. 331. [Translator's note: 'Gattopardismo': referring to Tomasi di Lampedusa's novel *Il Gattopardo*, the relevant theme of which is the insubstantial nature of the reforms introduced by Italian Unification.]
86   Rossi 1969, i, p. 341.
87   Rossi 1969, i, p. 340.

8   Within the International Communist Movement

In the context of a relatively homogenous series of presentations, in which Gramsci was still immersed within a dialogue with the liberal tradition around Unification, Ernesto Ragionieri's contribution set itself apart for its attempt to place Gramsci in the real historical and political context in which his ideas developed. While Bobbio drew Gramsci closer to Marx and Hegel, and others assimilated him to Croce and his followers, Ragionieri remembered the need to explicate Gramsci in his entirety, including in the *Notebooks*, by beginning from the facts of his political activism, and therefore from the October Revolution and his relation to Lenin. Today this view might seem somewhat reductive: successive studies have shown not only how Gramsci was situated on this horizon, but also how some central characteristics of his conception existed prior to the meeting with Bolshevism, and then continued after this moment. Nonetheless, in the context of the ongoing attempt to interpret Gramsci not as an original thinker (with elements of his thought already formed prior to 1917) but instead as a *Crocean* who had, fundamentally, remained as such even after his meeting with Lenin, Ragionieri's attempt (under the guidance of Togliatti's indications) to consider the thought of Gramsci in the light of his also having been 'a man of action' constituted an extremely important step forward. This importance derived from the way in which Ragionieri dragged Gramsci back out of the abstract horizon to which he had otherwise been abandoned. He recalled the Lenin of the 'United Front' – a figure who was present in Gramsci's mature writings both before and after his arrest – and understood the decisive role played by 'Gramsci's journey to the Soviet Union between 1922 and 1923'.[88] It was precisely in this period that

> the tactics of the 'United Front' – which Gramsci had already either rejected or limited to a purely syndicalist arena of political activity – were entirely reconsidered. More than a simple conversion or recantation, the moment represented a general modification in the terms of debate.[89]

This represented a profound understanding of the 'stabilisation of capitalism' and the new importance Gramsci had assigned to the 'national question', which provided his original conception of the difference between East and West, hegemony and the war of positions. The prison writings thus appeared as the

---

[88]   E. Ragionieri, *Gramsci e il dibattito teorico nel movimento operaio internazionale*, in Rossi 1969, i, p. 116.

[89]   Rossi 1969, i, p. 119.

continuation, in a new context and by new means, of the work of excavation and reconstruction of a revolutionary theory which he had already begun in his years at the centre of the PCd'I. As we have noted, this hypothesis initiated new discussions throughout Communist historiography. For example, in his own contribution at Cagliari,[90] Paolo Spriano grasped the fundamentals of the most accurate interpretation: the break between the period 1917–26 and the prison years was show primarily – as far as the terms of the actuality of revolution and political democracy were concerned – through Gramsci's reconsideration of Lenin's influence, the importance of the factory councils during the 'red biennial', etc. This was an interpretative position which understandably had an implicit political consequence as well: if the 'revolutionary' period had been submitted to a process of self-critical reconsideration during the prison years, then Gramsci had already seen the importance of choosing a 'democratic' road for Italian Communists; i.e., he had already turned the page, fundamentally, in the 1930s, as far as the October Revolution was concerned. For Spriano, Gramsci was thus distanced from Leninism in order to reaffirm a unified thread running through successive developments within the Italian Communist Party.

9 Historicism and the Communist Party

As the same time as the Cagliari conference, the Party's theoretical journal *Critica marxista* issued a monograph on the subject of *Prassi rivoluzionaria e storicismo in Gramsci* – 'Revolutionary Praxis and Historicism in Gramsci' – which frequently referenced both the political debate and the surrounding cultural issues. The small volume opened with an essay by Giorgio Amendola, 'Rereading Gramsci', which argued against the tendency in the 1950s to read the author of the *Notebooks* through either an 'extreme' set of political positions or, alternatively, 'social democratic' ones. Amenodola rejected the attempt to break the link of continuity between Togliatti and Gramsci, emphasising the post-War Togliattian reading, i.e. focussing on a 'national' and 'anti-Fascist' Gramsci. He re-contextualised every episode and rejected every interpretation which might imply any distance between Gramsci and policies later followed by Italian Communists, including the polemic of 1926 and the disagreements over the 'turn'. Amendola's Gramsci was historicist, trapped within a vision that held on to a particular theoretical conception and political line, in the conviction that 'with Gramsci, we must trace the consciousness of true historical value from a

---

[90] See P. Spriano, *Intervento*, in Rossi 1969, i, pp. 180–82.

historical consciousness'. Aside from the general problems of forced continuity and Party chauvinism throughout this exasperated mode of writing, the intervention also shows an explicit connection to the political struggle of the preceding years, culminating in the Eleventh Congress of the Communist Party.

Defining Gramsci's thought as 'ideologically anti-Fascist', the author wrote that:

> With the Eleventh Congress, the Communist Party has underlined its work of building a single Party of the working class which will, under new conditions, safely place Italy on the road to socialism. This Party cannot but refer back to Gramsci, as it is he who showed us the path of an anti-Fascist revolution, and cannot but find in Gramsci's thought the basis for its program.[91]

Putting Gramsci forward as the 'spiritual' father of *the whole* Italian left did not gain traction, and indeed ten years later Communists and Socialists would be fiercely divided over Gramsci's legacy, as we will see. Amendola was attempting to defend Gramsci in his role as 'the father of anti-Fascism', in tones that recalled the interpretation put forward by Togliatti in the early 1950s but abandoned after 1956.

An article by Alessandro Natta further focussed on the theme of the Party, here in the *Notebooks*, beginning with a polemic against those interpretations of Gramsci which opposed the Communist Party. But unlike Amendola, Natta rejected the idea that the history of the Communist Party could only contain continuities, refusing to accept that the Gramsci of the 1930s could be defined as 'seemingly anticipating every political line which the Communist Party would take in historical contexts entirely different from the struggle for liberation from Fascism'.[92] Having reconstructed the character of Gramsci's ideas on the Party (i.e. as deriving not only from the classic conceptions of Lenin but also from 'the facts of the concrete experience of power, of the direction taken by the Communist state and Party, which Gramsci interpreted critically')[93] Natta lucidly insisted on the *differences* running through Gramsci's vision of the party and Togliatti's 'New Party'. The novelty of Togliatti's version derived from the political line begun at Salerno. It was a radically new situation, claimed the author, in which 'the necessity of *hegemony* was more pressing

---

91   Amendola 1967, p. 44.
92   Natta 1967, p. 51.
93   Natta 1967, p. 64.

than that of *dictatorship*':[94] the mass character of the Party had been founded on a different idea of power, on new forms of organisation and leadership, on a conception of collective organism that 'did politics'. Natta added:

> No doubt we are still acting on the terrain of the concrete idea of hegemony. But the novelty of major importance which led to the 'New Party', it seems to me, arose precisely from his having identified the central problem of *hegemony* as that of the link between *democracy* and *socialism* and in having built an entire politics of alliances and unity on this basis. The *democratic* character of the party therefore takes democratic goals and methods as the essential strategic terms for the advance towards socialism.[95]

The Togliattian party, for Natta at least, was developing as Gramsci wanted and even went *beyond* his horizon, taking the concept of hegemony to its logical end, fully situated in an awareness of the importance of political democracy.

The concept of hegemony as an indivisible unity of leadership and dominance was the subject of a series of reflections by Luciano Gruppi, who traced its genesis back to the rejection of determinism in the young Gramsci. The concept of hegemony was the scarlet thread which ran through all of the Gramsci's work, from the experience of the factory councils through to the *Southern Question* and the *Notebooks*. It was the main contribution of Gramsci to Marxism, a *selective* reception of Leninism both in terms of philosophy and politics: this account privileged the Lenin of hegemony and cast aside the Lenin of *Materialism and Empirocriticism*. Gruppi's critique of this latter work centred on the principle of objectivity and the theory of consciousness as 'reflexive', arguing that Lenin had only demonstrated one of two moments present in the theory of hegemony: 'the claim is exactly that of objectivity, without which the revolutionary initiative is a voluntarist and arbitrary act; what is lost, or lost in the distance, is the other moment: that of the creativity of knowledge, the reciprocal dialectic between *being* and *consciousness*'. It was, for Gruppi, the active function of the vanguard to regretfully admit, on the political level, the contrary of that which occurred in various moments of Lenin's own elaboration (for example in books such as *Two Tactics of Social Democracy* or in the *Philosophical Notebooks*), in the light of that which Gramsci described, even if Gramsci's own ideas did sometimes, Gruppi admitted significantly, fall 'into the dangers of idealism or even positions which are idealist *tout court*'.[96]

---

94   Natta 1967, p. 76.
95   Ibid.
96   Gruppi 1967, p. 85.

The Gramscian concept of hegemony came to be proposed not only in terms of political theory, but also in arguments with Althusser, i.e., in epistemology. Gruppi, attentive to the problem of the balance between the two moments of the dialectic of subject and object in arguing against structuralism, perhaps ended up himself privileging one of the two sides, i.e. the subject. In trying to establish a distinction between Marxist and idealist historicism, the author saw how the notion of structure allowed 'not only the identification of basic (economic) material, of the historical process, but also avoided the total relativisation of historical events'. The Marxist method could thereby be defined as concerned with both genesis and structure, in that 'The identification of the *synchronic* moment of the structure ... is never separated from the search for origins of social forms'.[97] Gruppi's argument, concerned not so much with structuralism in general as with Althusser's Marxism, in the final analysis levelled the accusation of a mechanistic conception of the relation between structure and superstructure, the very antithesis of the conception of hegemony and of the role that it assigned to the subject. It was the subject, and not the 'relations of production', or the *relations* between subjects, for Gruppi, which was the true theoretical and practical centre of politics and history in Gramsci. But the polemic against this 'excessive' Althusserian anti-subjectivism, notwithstanding the attempts to find a certain balance between *synchronic* and *diachronic* analyses, ended up reaffirming an interpretation of Gramsci which did not value the fact that in the *Notebooks* the subjective beginning, while resting on the 'search for origins', had been supported by a 'political science' (with the creation, or creative utilisation, of such concepts as 'balance of forces', 'hegemonic apparatus', etc.) which contained a fundamentally *non-historicist* approach.

The *Quaderno di Critica Marxista*, which emphasised the political-cultural inferences and moments of the *continuity* between Gramsci and the Communist Party, was clear enough on this aspect: Marxist historicism was still the theory of the majority of the leading group and intellectuals of the Party, even if in the membership it did not have an *official* position (and Togliatti himself, in the discussions of 1962, abstained from every direct intervention on this matter).

In his own contribution on *Gramsci storicista di fronte al marxismo contemporaneo* Nicola Badaloni reaffirmed a reading of Gramsci as a theorist of subjectivity and formed his argument first and foremost against Althusser's anti-historicism. For Badaloni as well, the evaluation of Gramsci's Marxism

---

97   Gruppi 1967, p. 91.

began from emphasising the role of the 'collective man' and the 'collective will of modern man'.[98] The Gramscian re-evaluation of the *subject* (and therefore of culture and intellectuals) showed itself in his effort to translate 'the entire historical field in terms of *ideas/will*'.[99] Class struggle could therefore be read as the struggle of the will, and the struggle for hegemony as the disassembling and re-aggregation of a series of 'concrete individual wills' removed from a dominant field of 'exploitative wills' and inserted into a 'different system of values'. Another important aspect of Gramsci's Marxism was what Badaloni identified as an emphasis on the historical basis of ideology, an element of *realism*, i.e. the 'ability to return to values within the framework of historical possibility'.[100] 'Utopian' and 'realist' elements were indivisible in Gramsci: 'collective revolutionary will ... restores *possibility* to that which for others would simply be *utopia*'.[101] Badaloni's interpretation of Gramsci focused on the problem of the role of autonomy that the superstructure played in the *Notebooks*, trying to respond to those (such as Althusser) who sustained the impossibility of translating elements of the 'historical field in idealist-voluntarist terms'.[102] Grasping the empirical origins of theory and opposing the Althusserian pairing of theory and ideology as truth and error, Badaloni wanted to reclaim the validity of the Gramscian conception, focussing on the 'relation of theory and practice'.[103] And yet, in mediating the confrontation with the anti-historicist current, Badaloni also tried to avoid the danger which the theoretical-political historicist tradition was nearing: *voluntarism*. Marxist historicism and voluntarism, for Badaloni, were separated through the capacity to grasp the limits of capitalist development on a *theoretical* level and of the possibility of intervening – i.e. the possibility of revolutionary activity:

> A solution which does not take account of the limits, impediments and contradictions internal to a socially determined economic system would be voluntarist; it would entail putting forward a solution which is disconnected ... from the real possibility of concretising an active collective will, as Gramsci emphasised.[104]

---

98   Badaloni 1967, p. 98.
99   Badaloni 1967, p. 99.
100 Badaloni 1967, p. 103.
101 Badaloni 1967, p. 97.
102 Badaloni 1967, p. 99.
103 Badaloni 1967, p. 113.
104 Badaloni 1967, p. 116.

Badaloni's words seem to refer to the *Quaderni Rossi* and the theory of workerism (*operaismo*) which had achieved some relative fortune with the masses in those years: the distinction between a 'voluntarism without limits' and 'voluntarism' as the will to change began from the awareness of the 'objective side' of matters. Badaloni's formulations might appear convincing but would nevertheless find short thrift from the 'movement of '68'. Based on a philosophy of *immediacy* – and in this sense, by a *lack of Gramscianism* – it was precisely on this point that the movement would find its major theorical-political limits.

CHAPTER 6

The Golden Age (1970–75)

1   Gramsci Back on His Feet

The 1970s represented the moment of the greatest development, both quantitatively and qualitatively, of Gramsci's fortunes in Italy. To understand this quantitatively, it is enough simply to glance over Elsa Fubini's chronological bibliography, as well as the quantitative analyses made on the basis of John M. Cammett's *Bibliografia gramsciana*.[1] The *qualitative leap* which can be perceived in the study of Gramsci between 1970 and 1977 – and thus even before the new 'critical edition' of the *Notebooks* (1975) could have made any real impact – was determined by *environmental*, political and cultural-political factors, as well as influences more closely related to historiographic research and theoretical reflections. On a general level, the long wave of 1968 determined a cultural period favourable to ideas and thinkers from the Marxist tradition. Marxist research and thought was widespread in Italy in those years, through the raising of the 'Communist question' and along with it the categories and challenges of Gramscian thought.

These favourable conditions were grafted onto those factors already present in the preceding decade: a new attitude to the history of the Communist Party, a crisis of the historicist tradition, and a simultaneous construction of new disciplines (anthropology, linguistics, etc.), as well as the publication and gradual diffusion of Gramsci's earlier writings, i.e. those before his arrest. The demand for a theory of transformation in Western capitalist countries, combined with reflections on historical theory, interrogated these texts in innovative, emancipated ways. This formed a period in which theory and politics, even if not without some effort, found a constant point of reference in Gramsci, in the end making him the most widely-read and globally-discussed modern Italian writer.

Leonardo Paggi's 1970 monograph on the young Gramsci (*Gramsci e il moderno principe* – 'Gramsci and the Modern Prince') marked the beginning of a new decade of studies on the Sardinian author.[2] Explicitly departing from

---

1   Fubini 1979, pp. 427–31; Cammett 1989.
2   Paggi 1970 (the 'second volume' of Paggi's intellectual biography of Gramsci – with the title *Le strategie del potere in Gramsci* ('Strategies of Power in Gramsci') – would only be published decades later, in both its formal and substantial points of view essentially a separate work).

Togliatti and Ragionieri's theses, Paggi rejected every interpretation of Gramsci that was not founded in historical facts, and criticised those attitudes of the past that had been too inclined to see only moments of continuity between the Communist thinker and the successive policies of his Party. He situated Gramsci on the one hand within the situation of the national and international workers' movement and on the other within the world of those intellectuals (and not only Italian ones) who had contributed to the forming of his thought prior to the October Revolution. Paggi claimed that one could only read the *Notebooks* 'if they were related to specific political experiences and events' and therefore it was necessary 'to retrace the stages of his political journey'.[3] Thus 1916–18 was situated as 'the designing of a program of thought which ... one still finds in his general line of thinking later on, even in much later writings'.[4] Even the great event of the Russian Revolution did not change the preceding 'structures of thought' but only inscribed them onto a different political horizon. As such, there were indeed in Gramsci 'moments of substantial continuity' in cultural and intellectual spheres, alongside moments of profound innovation in politics, which found a real turning point and final stability in 1924–26. 'One can thus see in Gramsci's work a series of successive strata, cutting across every fundamental intuition, which over the years were always enriched with new and more complex meanings'.[5] Paggi therefore rejected a chronology of Gramscian thought founded on a clean break between the 'councilist' period (which supposedly dominated the foundation and early years of the PCd'I) and the final years of the prison period. In the years of his youthful experience and studies – which could not be reduced to Neoidealism, as had so often been claimed – Gramsci had developed a perspective which was to last a lifetime: the sharpening of a 'revolutionary historicism', a conception of the autonomy of Marxism, and a new analysis of the relationship between state and society, removed from crude dualism. Paggi's detailed analysis, although labouring somewhat in order to paint the full sense of the motion of Gramscian thought, nonetheless offered points of undoubted interest: we ought to remember the pages on the influence exercised by the journal *Voce* and Serrati's impact on the young Gramsci, the analysis of the agreements and disagreements between them and Rosa Luxemburg, the reading of Michels, Sorel, Bergson and Labriola, the influence of French culture, the early reflections on the Southern question, on Unification, and on intellectuals.

---

3   Paggi 1970, p. xv.
4   Paggi 1970, p. xxix.
5   Ibid.

A few years later the same author provided a reading of Gramsci which was both more organic and more systematic, in an attempt to define a 'general theory of Marxism'.[6] One can already detect a thesis which was far from obvious, to say the least: that *all* of Gramsci's elaborations represented a coherent theoretical system, a thesis which radically opposed the subjection of Gramsci's legacy to traditional scientific divisions. This represented a penalty being paid for the previous period which had presented an excessively organic vision of an intrinsically 'open' body of work (as would appear more evident still from the 'critical' edition of the *Notebooks* a few years later).[7] What was emphasised here, on the other hand, was the *rupture* which the Gramscian version of Marxism had represented for the philosophical and intellectual tradition. For the Sardinian thinker, Marxism represented (as Paggi emphasised) not so much a philosophy among or in the mould of others, or juxtaposed to them, but a radical innovation departing from all previous conceptions of philosophy and theory. There were two versions of the essential alterity – Marxism as 'absolute humanism' and as 'absolute historicism' – by which Gramsci's conception had been absorbed into traditional philosophical discourse. For Gramsci, Paggi noted, one could not interrogate humanity in general, the essence of human nature, if this was removed from the social relations of production, from the divisions of class and from class struggle. In opposition to the substantial philosophy of the *first* Althusser (against whom, in this essay, Paggi established a fruitful if implicitly *contradictory* attitude), Gramsci's *absolute historicism* was thus the moment of greatest break, and not of continuity, from tradition: not only did it represent a critique of Croce (whose historicism had expelled the element of class from the historical-philosophical sphere, even though this was the fundamental element), but also the discovery of the real, intrinsic limits of philosophical discourse. Once this discourse accepts that 'the extant limits of thought are the limits of the extant world', it turns into a 'theory of contradictions', which can only be overcome through the transformation of social relations. Philosophy is no longer enough: praxis becomes a necessity.

Reaffirming the autonomous character of Marxism and the break from all preceding philosophy, Paggi also demonstrated Gramsci's conception of the distance that Marxist theory maintained from science:

> Science, according to the naturalistic model, is a science of facts. Philosophy, critique, renders these facts transparent so that we can see through them, beyond them, to possibility, but only the possibility of a new series

---

6 Paggi 1974.
7 Cf. Gerratana's criticism of Paggi, *Note di filologia gramsciana*, in *Studi storici*, 1975, issue 1.

of facts. The verification of this possibility falls completely outside of its field. In this sense, Gramsci says, it can make predictions only within these limits.[8]

Here the space for praxis lay in the ability to modify 'not particular facts in the world, but the actual limits of the world itself'. In this way, Paggi showed new moments beyond the *Notebooks:* the identification of a *field of possibilities* in which subjects and their activity could be measured. The concept of prediction is substituted, therefore (according to Gramsci) with that of *objective possibility*, the reality of which is understood only by entering into political activity.

In Paggi's reconstruction Gramsci's thought posited itself in relation to Leninism as Lenin had posited himself in relation to Marxism: not as a scholastic repetition, but as a creative development. With the concepts of hegemony, historical bloc, passive revolution and his conception of dialectics, Gramsci was not only a theorist of the revolution in the West. He had tried to explain both East and West, the 'revolution against *Kapital*' and that (to be made) against capital *tout court*, elaborating a *unitary* theoretical model which had since been broken down and read only in partial and limited ways by Togliatti and the dominant Marxist historicism.

2   Workerism and Americanism

Franco De Felice's book on *Serratti, Bordiga, Gramsci*, like Paggi's own volume, largely focused on the *first* Gramsci, i.e. on the two crucial years following the October Revolution and the end of the Great War. The author examined the figures of these three leaders with the aim of measuring them by the Socialist tradition on the one hand and by the horizons newly opened by the Revolution on the other. De Felice showed the abstract character of the 'red biennial' through the question of the peasant masses: seeing the 'poor farmers' in a slow process of their *proletarianisation*[9] not only prevented Gramsci from seeing 'the real movement, set on other objectives', but made the link between workers and farmers not so much an actual political outcome as simply an object of propaganda. Gramsci's ideas thus faced the limitation of 'not providing any objectives for the peasants other than collective management of the land'.[10] What would emerge was a typically workerist error: despite not having a purely

---

8   Paggi 1974, p. 1354.
9   De Felice 1971, p. 330.
10 De Felice 1971, p. 332.

proletarian conception of the revolutionary process, Gramsci had apparently projected the institution of the factory councils onto the ('fundamentally workerist') organisational level of different social strata.[11] The unification between these strata could happen only on the political level, while Gramsci fell into the sin of economism. For De Felice, the Sardinian leader underestimated the role of political power in this period of his writing, assuming that the decisive battle would be played out in the heart of the process of production. On the basis of a conviction in the 'actuality of revolution', the analysis of enemy forces had not been sufficiently *differentiating*. In the period of the *Ordine Nuovo*, Gramsci apparently still moved 'along the horizon of the Second International: the real expression of this was the fact that the leading role of the working class was not resolved'.[12]

For De Felice, furthermore, Gramsci's conception of the party – compared with and opposed to Bordiga – ended up being very close to Lenin's own, at least from 1920 on. There was not, therefore, a break between the Gramsci 'of the councils' and of 'the party': 'Gramsci's thought during the biennial cannot be resolved into a councilist hypothesis'. Rather, the council was inserted into a framework of a 'general conception of revolution, which had the state as its point of general unification and the masses as the historically determined identification of the social protagonists of the revolutionary process'.[13]

It should be noted, however, that in a brief essay that came out in *Rinascita* in 1972, De Felice returned to Gramsci in order to recall with greater emphasis one of the final theses of the *Notebooks*, 'Americanism and Fordism', which was still much misunderstood.[14] Starting from the decision to read *all* of Gramsci in the light of his political life, De Felice knew to explicate the link between Gramsci's recognition of 'Americanism' and the strategy of the 'war of positions'. The 22nd *Notebook* was supposed to contain all the central questions of the *Notebooks*: the new relations between the 'economy' and 'politics', the recognition of the 'emplacements' of power, the widespread forms that hegemony takes. The more that De Felice identified the possibility of seeing the very centre of Gramsci's prison reflections in the note on 'Americanism and Fordism', the clearer it became that this represented an interpretation not so much of the 'past' as of the foundation for a theoretical political discourse addressing the 'present'.

---

11 De Felice 1971, pp. 338–9.
12 De Felice 1971, p. 344.
13 De Felice 1971, p. 22.
14 F. De Felice, *Una chiave di lettura in 'Americanismo e fordismo'*, in *Rinascita* (supplement *Il contemporaneo*), 1972, issue 42.

3   Gramsci and the Soviets

Between 1970 and 1973, Massimo L. Salvadori made a range of contributions to the historicisation of Gramsci's thought, paying particular attention to the 'red biennial' and what the author – opposing De Felice's thesis – identified as the main horizon that Gramsci formed in those years, one which thereafter was never far from his thought: *councilism*.[15] Salvadori proposed this interpretation in three main moves: the unitary character of Gramsci's works; the defining character of the soviet, containing all the successive developments of his thought; and finally the centrality of the question of subjectivity in his revolutionary interpretation of Marxism. For Salvadori, this *sovietism* was not only a choice entirely made in the context of the dilemmas posed by the October Revolution, but also the means by which to critically assess the level of real democracy in contemporary society, to direct a *politically* valid proposal towards the present. Although formed with a specific political orientation, Salvadori's research managed to place Gramsci in the actual context of his contemporary international debate. The choice of the democracy of the soviets during the 'red biennial' represented a *complete break* from the democracy of the bourgeois parliament, a clearly Leninist choice motivated by the conviction that revolution was 'on the agenda'. The space opened up by the disappearance of this hypothesis – Salvadori sustained – was taken up by the question of the party, but Gramsci nonetheless never abandoned a particular way of understanding the relation between the vanguard and the masses, i.e. he continued to see the masses as the true revolutionary *subject*. This was later confirmed in the *Notebooks*, even when Gramsci overturned his opposition to parliamentarianism.

Within these basic theses, themselves open to discussion (especially that of Gramsci as consistently councilist), Salvadori sometimes forced positions and situations in order to sketch out a corresponding figure. It was certainly true that 'in all his ways of treating the question of democracy, Gramsci gave scant attention to certain technical problems of the management of power'[16] and that, taking for granted the possibility of proletarian democracy, these questions emerged in the moment in which 'one passes over to the problems of the

---

15   Cf. Salvadori 1970 (and second edition of 1973). In the first edition, among other contributions, there were three essays on Gramsci, republished in the second edition along with three new essays which held, either entirely or partly, to the same argument. The second edition of Salvadori's book would be published again thirty years later, as Salvadori 2007 (with an introductory essay by A. d'Orsi).

16   Salvadori 1970, p. 24.

functionality of the bodies of the new democracy and the revolutionary party'.[17] But Salvadori considered the revision of the experience of the soviets in the *Notebooks* in a manner which attributed far too much simplicity to Gramsci, claiming that Gramsci believed that the masses within the soviets could only reinforce communist positions, thus giving the party an important pedagogic function.[18] This reading, which essentially turned Gramsci into a determinist, for whom the path to communism had the character of *necessity*, gave rise to interpretations of Gramsci as a supporter of a 'harmonious' society, of which more will be said below.

4   The Concept of Hegemony

The 1970s not only witnessed a significant development in the historical contextualisation of Gramsci, but also in the theoretical excavation of his main categories of thought (already present in the works of the authors mentioned above). One of the first contributions on in this regard was Giorgio Nardone, in his volume *Gramsci's Thought* (*Il pensiero di Gramsci*), an attempt to create a formal system for Gramsci's work, which Nardone argued contained a strong unity throughout. For him, Gramsci's discourse was philosophical because his writings 'try to formulate a final modality of being', interrogating the world 'through a radical and philosophical discourse'.[19] Opposing this to the 'abstractions' of both positivists and idealists, i.e. anyone for whom 'the existence of abstract entities dominate history' (e.g. Nature, Idea, Divinity, Reason), Gramsci claimed that history is 'entirely practical activity', uniting 'will and subjectivity', structure and superstructure, past and future. Here, absolute immanence becomes the philosophical kernel of Gramsci's approach. Gramsci did not oppose 'metaphysics' with 'science' but with 'praxis in action'.[20] Gramsci's historicism was not imprisoned by any *a priori* schema, Nardon claimed. The dialectic of necessity and freedom represented the only possible access to human freedom.[21] One can agitate for its realisation but not predict it. One can struggle towards a determinate goal even while knowing that 'failure is possible: there is no certain *a priori* outcome either to political struggle, nor to the truth which the philosophy of praxis claims for itself'.[22]

---

17   Salvadori 1970, p. 51.
18   Salvadori 1970, p. 52.
19   Nardone 1971, p. 13.
20   Nardone 1971, p. 522.
21   Nardone 1971, pp. 15–16.
22   Nardone 1971, p. 18.

Following in Bobbio's footsteps, Nardone stressed that the site of this political struggle was civil society. It was here that Gramsci had developed the struggle for hegemony,[23] in which the subject in a real sense is the 'social group', the 'masses', in relation to which the Party is 'of partial and intermediary value' and not of 'final or original value'.[24] For Nardone, the centrality of *class* represented the centrality of civil society itself: just as the Party is the *instrument* of the former, so the state is that of the latter.[25] The Party is necessary to the class in order to allow 'historical initiative', in order to enact its hegemony. Politics is *everything*, but the subject of politics is not the Party but rather the 'masses': 'an important element in the Gramscian conception of the Party is its radical dependency on the masses or, more immediately, on the determined social group which it "expresses"'.[26]

But even if the 'masses' were considered by Gramsci to be the subject whose political activity was truly foundational, that was not enough (for Nardone) to free the Gramscian Party from the shadow of its totalitarian ends. This thesis was claimed by the author in explicit reference to the idea of hegemony, in contradistinction to the educational, pedagogic function of the Party (on which was based the dialectical relation of Party and mass), and distinct from its role of 'assimilating' and prefiguring values destined to be claimed in a *totalising* manner.[27] Gramsci's totalitarianism, while negated on the level of the philosophy of history, was therefore identified by Nardone as the *outcome* of political activity.

The same risks of totalitarianism were underlined (but starting from a liberal democratic position) by Gian Carlo Jocteau in an essay on the concept of hegemony in Gramsci and Togliatti.[28] Jocteau defined the concept of hegemony as including the following characteristics: it is both leadership and dominance (from which derived the slippery slope of opposing *hegemony* to *democracy*); it is bound to the fundamental *autonomy* of classes; and it refers to a comprehensively '*totalitarian*' political project (which explains the centrality, in the *Notebooks*, of 'intellectual and moral reform'). For Jocteau, the alliance

---

23 Nardone 1971, p. 128: 'Hegemony exists ... when one determined social agent (a social group, a party, elites of various kinds, cities, nations) is the ruling principle for another ... when the activity of one group is exercised over another not in the form of "dominance" but through "intellectual and moral leadership"'.
24 Nardone 1971, p. 91.
25 Nardone 1971, p. 152.
26 Nardone 1971, p. 90.
27 Nardone 1971, pp. 136–7.
28 Jocteau 1973, n. 1. To the same author we also owe a reconstruction of the early interpretations of Gramsci: Jocteau 1975.

with democratic tactics in Gramsci's works was only a temporary moment in this 'totalitarian' project, and entirely explainable from within it. The passage from 'East' to 'West' had brought a great awareness of the complexity of the idea of taking power and the important tactical expression of democracy, but had not changed the fundamental strategies: it was only with Togliatti that Gramsci's 'democratic' doctrine had become a holistic transition from the struggle against the bourgeoisie to the struggle against the most backward part of it (anti-Fascism) and with that, full acceptance of political institutions.

The interpretation of Gramsci that Bobbio had proposed at the Cagliari congress was supported by Hugues Portelli, the French author of *Gramsci et le bloc historique*, originally published in 1972 and translated into Italian the following year.[29] He argued that a certain *vulgarisation* had led Gramsci's central concept (the historical bloc) to have been seriously misunderstood, speaking of a 'historically dominant bloc' rather than a 'new historical bloc'.[30] In this way, he used the Gramscian term solely to designate social blocs, opposed to and in struggle with each other. In Gramsci's discourse, indeed, the historical bloc included 'both the subaltern classes and the hegemonic system'.[31] It is therefore both structure and superstructure, and the problem presented is that of how, in a given situation, the relation of the classes come to be configured in the form a determinate ideological and political situation. If from one side, for Portelli, Gramsci seemed to distance himself from Lenin inasmuch as he saw society as the state, i.e., more as hegemony than as dictatorship ('Gramscian hegemony' is based on civil society and its politics',[32] which was, according to Portelli, the opposite of Lenin), on the other side it was claimed that Gramsci had innovatively unified and *integrated* Marx (society) and Lenin (state). Creating a new historical bloc meant, therefore, to make a new hegemonic system, so as to usher in a clash between hegemonic systems. The fundamental problem was obviously the relation between structure and superstructure, and the central role was given to intellectuals, because it fell to them to ensure the link by which a historical bloc might go beyond its *physiological* limits. As such,

---

29 Portelli 1973.
30 The reference was above all to G. Napolitano, *Il 'nuovo blocco storico' nell'elaborazione di Gramsci e del Partito comunista italiano (A proposito di alcune tesi di Roger Garaudy)*, in *Rinascita*, 1970, n. 12. Also see E. Sereni, *Blocco storico e iniziativa politica nell'elaborazione gramsciana e nella politica del Partito comunista italiano*, in Storia politica organizzazione nella lotta dei comunisti italiani per un nuovo blocco storico, Critica marxista – quaderni, 1972, n. 5.
31 Portelli 1973, p. 92.
32 Portelli 1973, p. 74.

Bobbio's argument on the primacy of the *ideological* was reaffirmed, helping to advance an interpretation of the phenomena of the new dislocation of the intellectuals demonstrated from May '68 onwards.

An interpretation of a quite different kind was provided in those years by Luciano Gruppi, starting with the problems of the connection between the concept of hegemony and the Leninist tradition.[33] Opposing Bobbio's reading, Gruppi derived the concept of hegemony in Gramsci from the structural contradictions identified by Marx and Lenin's re-evaluation of subjectivity. Throughout Lenin, Gruppi claimed, 'hegemony means first and foremost the role of leadership',[34] while in Gramsci, although this reading is also present, what prevails is a vision of hegemony as both leadership and dominance.[35] Gruppi's emphasis showed an oscillation which indeed could be traced back to the *Notebooks*, where sometimes 'hegemony' is opposed to 'leadership' while at other times Gramsci uses the couplet of 'leadership-dominance', speaking of 'supremacy' as the hegemonic function *in toto*. In reality, Gruppi claimed, the specificity of Gramsci's concept of hegemony seemed to be derived from the role that the *Notebooks* assigned to ideology as 'a conception of the world': 'hegemony is the attempt to construct a historical bloc, i.e. to create a unity of politically diverse social forces and to try and bring these together through a conception of the world which it describes and spreads'.[36] However, linking hegemony and ideology, without demonstrating the *forms* and *apparatuses* by means of which it forms a 'vision of the world' – i.e. without demonstrating the role of the state – risked reintroducing other aspects of Bobbio's idealist reading, even while this was precisely the main target of Gruppi's argument.

Gruppi then searched for a definition of the concepts of hegemony and the historical bloc in the long story of Togliatti's post-War interpretation, posing the theme of hegemony as 'the problem of the national function of the working class'.[37] Gruppi's argument fails to be convincing, inasmuch as it interprets hegemony as little more than a version of Lenin's 'dictatorship of the proletariat', here adapted to the different context in which Gramsci worked. In so

---

33 Cf. Gruppi 1972, in which the author published a lecture series given at the Istituto Gramsci in Rome between October and December 1970. The origins of the work explains its partially popular character, and perhaps also some of the excessively schematic reasoning.
34 Gruppi 1972, p. 21.
35 Gruppi 1972, pp. 21 and 76.
36 Gruppi 1972, p. 99.
37 Gruppi 1972, p. 78.

doing, Gruppi translated the concept into 'the Italian road to Socialism', reducing it to a bare minimum and perhaps even eliminating all of the *discontinuities* along this road.[38]

5 The Primacy of the Political

The interpretation advanced by Nicola Auciello,[39] in opposition to Bobbio's thesis at Cagliari in 1967, emphasised how the concept of hegemony had a fundamentally economic basis for Gramsci. Auciello's reading differed from Gruppi's, however, in that he saw the essential moment as consisting in leadership (not of leadership and dominance in combination), here meaning political and moral, intellectual leadership. The analysis of the concept of hegemony for Auciello was bound up with the analysis of the concept of the state: 'Gramsci identified in the function of "hegemony" the new features of the modern state and the terrain within which, in a dynamic way, the relations between the bourgeoisie and the subaltern class flows'.[40] With the bourgeoisie the state became an 'educator'. Hegemony is the form specific to the process by which the 'state becomes' the foundational class. In Lenin the state was still something extraneous to society, whereas

> Gramsci initiated a direction of research that went beyond this dichotomy, outlining a vision capable of rediscovering the state within civil society itself, as a complete articulation of mediating elements (bureaucracy, parties, etc.) which those classes that maintain power attempt to base within the popular masses.[41]

For Gramsci – as Auciello emphasised – the state was 'the entirety of the practical and theoretical activity by which the ruling class not only justifies and maintains its dominance but also manages to obtain the active consensus of the governed'.[42] These and other claims advanced

---

38   It is not possible to deal here with some of the relevant contributions which, along with their quite specific attention to pedagogy, contain interesting interpretative hypotheses on Gramsci's work in general, and the theory of hegemony. Cf. Gramsci 1967a (edited by G. Urbani), Manacorda 1970, Gramsci 1972 (edited by Manacorda), Broccoli 1972 and Ragazzini 1976.
39   Auciello 1974.
40   Auciello 1974, p. 66.
41   Auciello 1974, p. 67.
42   Gramsci 1975, p. 1765. (*Prison Notebooks*, notebook 15, paragraph 10).

the identity of the concept of the state with the entirety of superstructural activity and in particular with the role of dominance and hegemony as real functions, distinct but never separate from historical reality itself, which is the state in its organic and integral sense.[43]

What was clear to Auciello was that Gramsci's concept of hegemony was much more comprehensive and had greater potential than Lenin's. In outlining a new concept of the state in the *Notebooks*, Gramsci had pointed not only to a moment of unity but also carried out a profound innovation within Russian revolutionary thought. It was this novelty that Togliatti had consistently drawn upon, and which constituted the 'scarlet thread' which allowed Auciello to identify a living theoretical tradition within Italian Communism, one based on the *primacy of the political*.

Auciello's interpretation can be seen as part of a school of thought represented above all by Giuseppe Vacca who, in his contemporaneous *Saggio su Togliatti e la tradizione comunista* – 'Essay on Togliatti and the Communist Tradition' – advanced an interpretation of Gramsci as the founder of an 'Italian tradition' which itself represented a 'development and continuation' of Leninism. For Vacca, Gramsci's role in relation to Lenin was represented as '*a beginning*, that of a great creative mediator and not of an imitator'.[44] The attention to the question of alliances, to the 'protagonism of the masses' and the '*democratic, popular* and *gradual* character of the proletarian revolution',[45] taken from late Lenin, had a defining impact on the formation of Gramsci's revolutionary concepts, determining the development of the concept of 'hegemony' and of 'anti-Fascist revolution'. With the guidance of Lenin's late writings, Gramsci had reconceived the relation between democracy and socialism in the context of a theory of transition to a different time period. This was not a linear process suited for all situations. The identification of partial objectives, of a democratic and anti-Fascist character, was still seen in the 1920s as an *instrumental* means toward the final objective of the dictatorship of the proletariat. Despite certain limitations, Gramsci's interpretation of Leninism prior to the prison years started from the 'definition of the *national* character of the *transitions* to Socialism'.[46] These were the particularities of the social structure and of the formation of the Italian state, creating the terrain on which concrete forms of hegemony could be expressed.

---

43   Auciello 1974, p. 93.
44   Vacca 1974, p. 78.
45   Vacca 1974, p. 55.
46   Vacca 1974, p. 149.

Vacca's book thus laid down some important interpretative distinctions: (a) the importance of Lenin and the Leninist horizon for other aspects of Gramsci's thought, (b) the strong continuity between Gramsci and Togliatti, (c) the primacy of the political, inasmuch as 'the class struggle, for the first time, poses the problem of the state, catalysing the entire life of the workers' movement, reclassifying its theoretical tradition, its strategic positions and forms of organisation'.[47] On the level of *theory*, Vacca added, Gramsci translated class analysis into political analysis, putting the state at the centre.

The 'primacy of the political' had a range of meanings in Vacca's book. Above all else it meant social reality itself, in which 'the logical and historical primacy of political forms' is the primary motor, indeed the *producer* of social reality, inasmuch as the political determines 'the modes of decomposition and recomposition of the masses'.[48] Furthermore, the state was 'the protagonist of the masses'; 'the *primacy of the political* ... is also a *historically determined social fact* ... The logical primacy of the political is therefore the consequence and reflection of a new historical reality, itself historically determined'.[49]

Gramsci had 'put the state at the centre of his historical analysis', and thus it came to be inscribed into the historical theory of Leninism: this was not so much a move 'from Marx to Marx' (or rather, the return to the social protagonist after the 'political parentheses' provided by Lenin) as a focus on the *epochal character* (in the epoch of the transition from capitalism to socialism) of the state form and of the party form, the true subjects of history. The masses were the protagonists only '*because* they were always more *organised*'[50] and connected into the *forms* which manifested the true determinate forces of a historical process.

Vacca's arguments responded to Bobbio's pretext of reproducing a dichotomous vision of the relation between state and society on the one hand, and politics and society on the other – even in an epoch characterised by new forms of reciprocal relations, intersections and osmosis. But this foundation of a *tradition* turned on the relation between Gramsci and Togliatti, without recognising the moments of discontinuity and embedded in a version of Leninism (even if in a creative manner). This resulted in a *totalising* theory that tended towards anachronism. The analytical innovations and arguments attempted to demonstrate the coherence of the theoretical, political ideas of the Italian Communist Party, here depicted as democratic and revolutionary from the very

---

47 Vacca 1974, p. 119.
48 Vacca 1974, p. 120.
49 Vacca 1974, p. 510.
50 Vacca 1974, p. 515.

start, drawing on Togliatti's *symptomatic interpretation*, one that emphasised certain parts of his own development and history. In opposition to those attacks on the Communist Party from the *left*, from 1968 onwards, Vacca's *political* argument was an attempt to make theoretical proposals which could bridge the gap between the Italian Communist Party and the young anti-capitalist movement of the 1960s by, on the one hand, relaunching the tradition of Italian Communism and crediting it with revolutionary content, while on the other offering 'the '68 generation' the possibility of democratic engagement.

6   Gramsci's Marxism

These very different interpretations of Gramsci had an important effect on scholars of Italian Marxism more generally, right up to the highest level. For example, in 1975 Nicola Badaloni provided some interpretations which went in an entirely different direction from Vacca's. For Badaloni, 'Gramsci's Marxism'[51] implied a combination of different elements that, however original, showed the influence of Sorel right from the start. Gramsci had then met Lenin and this had been a definitive moment for him – but for Badaloni, Gramsci could not be *reduced* to Lenin because the meeting had happened when the Italian Communist already had a consolidated intellectual formation and theoretical goal. This background took prevalence over his nevertheless fundamental meeting with Leninism, and constituted the peculiar traits of Gramscian Marxism. The Sardinian thinker had taken from Sorel a conceptual tradition which extended from Hegelianism and anti-positivism through to an aversion to reformism, and included the idea of the historical bloc and 'popular nationalism', intellectual and moral reform, the critique of democracy, councilism and the exaltation of the 'classes of producers'. Traversing this conceptual web, Gramsci had inherited from Sorel a kind of 'primacy of the social', which was modified but never lost in the meeting with Lenin and his 'primacy of the political'. Gramsci aimed instead for a *recomposition*, both in theory and in praxis, of these two sides of Marx's thought, focusing on the figure of the *producer*, the subject of a new political culture and a new technical productive knowledge.[52] Badaloni's focus on the theme of the 'producer'[53] implied a rejection not only of Bobbio's inter-

---

51 Badaloni 1975.
52 Badaloni 1975, p. 67.
53 Badaloni 1975, p. 103. 'In this juxtaposition of the *producer* and the *wage worker* lies the kernel of Gramsci's Marxism. Within it he summarises the essential moment of Marx's analysis of capitalist, bourgeois society'.

pretations, which had made Gramsci a 'theorist of the superstructure', but also of Vacca's, who saw Gramsci above all in the light of the category of the 'primacy of the political'.

For Badaloni, Sorel's 'spirit of scission' remained the original moment of the young Gramsci's councilism, inasmuch as it introduced the question of the historical bloc: it was this, Badaloni wrote, that 'Gramsci derived from Sorel. Its specific character in relation to contemporary Leninist problems must be emphasised'.[54] To point to the *subjective side* of the productive forces, to the development of the consciousness of the working class, to the intransigent struggle of *transformism*, to a conception of Marxism as an original and autoumous theory, meant for both Sorel and Gramsci (and Lenin) to search for an exit out of the crisis of Marxism at the turn of the century. Nevertheless, it also meant – and here they departed from Lenin – that the development of the productive forces did not contain in itself an objectively progressive meaning. With the Russian Revolution, Gramsci grasped that the separate nature of the 'new fundamental class' would not only preserve that class itself, but posed the task of a real 'substitution of dominance'.[55] The 'spirit of scission' continued to hold a place within Gramsci's ideas even while he distanced himself from Sorel over the question of hegemony and the role of intellectuals. In response to Sorel's scornful opinion of the 'democracy of intellectuals' as always mimicking the attitudes of the elite in terms of power, Gramsci – here reflecting partly on Lenin's understanding of alliances – theorised 'democratic situations' as 'transitional' situations and, furthermore, as the terrain of hegemonic struggle. Nevertheless, Badaloni warned that Gramsci differed from Togliatti in that 'he had not managed to conceive of democracy as the entire political site of historical transition'.[56] Gramsci saw in democracy the fading of old social forms, rather than the rising of a new one: it would be left to Togliatti (and here was an important moment of *discontinuity*) in the post-War period to make it *the* place of transition. Nevertheless, the distance from Sorel was real enough: through a confrontational encounter with Croce, Gramsci had assisted Marxism's passage to the ethical-political sphere.

Badaloni's book was in tune with a vital part of the 1968 *Weltanschauung* ('from Marx to Marx'). This explains the significant downplaying of the problem of the state in Gramsci, both in terms of the question of intellectuals and in relation to the economic productive sphere. Nevertheless, its merit lay in underlining the importance of not reducing Gramsci to Lenin, as well as in

---

[54] Badaloni 1975, p. 60.
[55] Badaloni 1975, p. 101.
[56] Badaloni 1975, p. 128.

noting the limits of Togliatti's interpretation of 1958. This provided an image of Gramsci as a theorist of *communism* (that is, of a concept more radical than Togliatti's *socialism*) not just *in Italy* nor only in *the West*, but in the perspective of an emergence of a new tendency *ab initio* in *the East* as well.

In terms of the discussion of Gramsci's 'sources', mention should also be made of the claims of another central representative of Italian Marxism, Cesare Luporini, who advanced an entirely different interpretation of the link between Sorel and Gramsci:

> If Sorel 'influenced' either Gramsci or Togliatti's intellectual backgrounds, this was part of an experience that was completely exhausted and resolved during the period of the *Ordine Nuovo*. (Gramsci raised the question of Sorel in very different terms in the *Notebooks*.)[57]

For Luporini, therefore, Gramsci's work perhaps pays 'homage' to Sorel (who had supported the October Revolution) but – at the time of *Ordine Nuovo* – he was not an 'influence' as such.

Luporini's comments constituted a polemical appendix (arguing against Leo Valiani) to an essay published in Einaudi's series on the history of Italy, entitled *Il marxismo e la cultura italiana del Novecento* – 'Marxism and Italian Twentieth-Century Culture' – focusing on *Ordine Nuovo* and noteworthy for its thesis on the 'profound break' between Antonio Labriola and Gramsci.[58] In Gramsci, Luporini claimed,

> It is difficult to distinguish how much he derived directly from Labriola (probably not much), how much he later derived from his experience in political and intellectual struggle (and therefore, fatally, the limits of this experience), and how much was objectively a resurfacing, in circumstances of profound historical change, of irresolvable problems of Italian society and of the Italian working class. Inasmuch as this defines the relation between Labriola and Gramsci, it suggests discontinuity and rupture.[59]

---

57   C. Luporini, *Autonomia del pensiero di Gramsci e di Togliatti*, in *Rinascita*, 1974, n. 9, p. 33. This was a reply to an article by Leo Valiani (*L'Italia con gli occhiali di Marx*, in *L'Espresso*, 1974, issue 1), which included an overview by Luporini signed 'c.l.' and entitled *Il rapporto con Sorel*.
58   Luporini 1973.
59   Luporini 1973, p. 1587. One ought to remember that already in 1963 Gerratana had written that: 'Even in the development of Gramsci's personality, in the youthful period, as with the experience of the *Ordine Nuovo* and the early period of the Communist Party, one

This was in itself an important break from the *Togliattian* axis of the 1950s (the thread running through De Sanctis, Labriola and Gramsci), even if it should be noted that Luporini's essay referred only to the period of *Ordine Nuovo* and the author himself stressed that, following this, an extraordinary development can be found in Gramsci and Togliatti's thought, culminating in the 1920s in the *Theses of Lyons* and above all in the essay on the Southern Question. For Luporini, therefore, the Russian Revolution had posed the centrality of the issue of the state for *Ordine Nuovo*. In this Gramscian meeting with Lenin, Marx had been 'rethought' within the urgency of struggle and the changing situation in the context of Fascism.

7 Gramsci and the State

At the end of the 1960s one of Althusser's main assistants and collaborators, Nicos Poulantzas, had already tried to apply the French philosopher's methodological observations to the study of 'politics' and the state in the situation of the capitalist mode of production. Such attempts at establishing a Marxist political science clearly set Poulantzas on a path that would cross with the road once taken by Gramsci. Maintaining the positions of the 'first Althusser' throughout, and therefore on the other side of the gap (to which we have already referred) between the concept of (dominant) ideology and the Gramscian concept of hegemony (traversing class contradictions), Poulantzas replicated his teacher's approach, divided between viewing the Gramscian concept of the historical bloc as a *historicist* unity, amenable to a truly Marxist Hegelian 'expressive totality',[60] and recognising in it many other 'discoveries', for example the role of intellectuals[61] and the discussion of 'Caesarism'.[62]

In relation to the concept of hegemony, Poulantzas reproached Gramsci for having privileged *consensus* and ignoring the importance of *force*[63] and for having made the concept of hegemony into a 'strategy of the working class', maintaining that the class can lead by becoming politically dominant. It was an error (and certainly not Leninist!), according to Poulantzas (in accordance with his functionalist training) to think that a class could impose 'its concep-

---

cannot really detect Labriola's influence ... Instead he was clearly and deeply influenced by Labriola's work in the later writings'. Gerratana 1972, pp. 157–8.

60 Poulantzas 1975a [1968], p. 252.
61 Poulantzas 1975b [1974], pp. 218 onwards.
62 Poulantzas 1971 [1970], *passim*.
63 Poulantzas 1975a, p. 287.

tion of the world', conquering 'the position of ideological dominance before the conquest of political power',[64] when for Lenin, as Poulantzas claimed, even after taking power for the working class, the dominant ideology 'continued to be that of the bourgeois and petit-bourgeoisie for a long time'.[65] In this way, equating hegemony to ideological dominance, Poulantzas not only lost sight of Gramsci's discovery of the *material* nature of ideology,[66] but even the main insight of Gramsci's political theory, i.e. the fact that the subaltern classes are also subjects who struggle for hegemony; indeed, that hegemony is *the* class strategy by which the subaltern attempts to rule.

It was another of Althusser's students, however, who put Gramsci to more advantageous use: Christine Buci-Glucksmann, author of *Gramsci e lo Stato* (*Gramsci and the State*), which had a certain success in Italy, where it strongly oriented the debate around Gramsci just as the 'communist question' was developing, along with the Communist Party's need to confront the question of the state. Buci-Glucksmann rejected Althusser's *theoretical* judgement upon Gramsci's historicism: 'The historicity of Marxist philosophy ... has nothing to do with an expressive concept that is entirely social in its outlook'.[67] The author reread the categories of the *Notebooks* in a way that was liberated from every idealist hypothesis (i.e. those advanced by Bobbio), underlining therefore how Gramsci had wedded the concept of hegemony to that of apparatus ('hegemonic apparatus') – schools, church, libraries, journals, newspapers, etc. Unlike the Althusserian 'Ideological State Apparatus' – and functionalism ('integration') and the Weberian argument of 'legitimation' more generally – Buci-Glucksmann singled out that the 'hegemonic apparatus' was not unitary, but encompassed contradictions. Still bound to a kind of Leninist orthodoxy which ran through the Althusserian school, Buci-Glucksmann saw a '*continuation of Leninism*' in Gramsci, specifying nevertheless that to 'continue' did not mean to 'apply' Leninism in different historical conditions, but to 'translate' and 'develop' it.[68] For her there were not 'two Gramscis' but *three*: 'the prison writings [have] their beginning deep within the "great turn" of 1923 and in the self-critical reflection of that time'.[69] The concept of hegemony 'was already there in a *practical way* in the experience of the *Ordine Nuovo*, and theoretically

---

64   Poulantzas 1975a, p. 258.
65   Poulantzas 1975a, p. 259.
66   On this, see C. Mancina, *Introduzione* to Althusser 1977, and C. Mancina, '*Il fronte ideologico*': *ideologie e istituzione statali in Gramsci*, in *Prassi e teoria*, 1980, issue 7.
67   Buci-Glucksmann 1976 [1975], p. 386.
68   Buci-Glucksmann 1976 [1975], p. 23.
69   Buci-Glucksmann 1976 [1975], p. 225.

appeared ... from 1924',[70] finally arising in the essay on the Southern Question. The first *Notebook* of 1929[71] had already dealt with the concept of hegemonic apparatus. But whereas in the Southern Question hegemony was (potentially) attributed to the proletariat, in the first *Notebook* it represented above all, in Buci-Glucksmann's view, the praxis of the dominant classes. In the *Notebooks*, therefore, the appearance of the concept of 'hegemonic apparatus' was mediated through 'an analysis of hegemony in terms of the state'.[72] Gramsci rejected every *instrumental* vision of the state, such as that which reduced it purely to a tool by which a class exercises its will. From 1917–18, the state had been for Gramsci 'not an instrument external to the class, but had played a role in the constitution and unification of the class itself ... the separation of economy and politics ... is an *effect* of the capitalist mode of production'.[73] Gramsci thus rejected every organic distinction between the state and civil society, but the two terms were nevertheless still not identical to each other (as in Gentile's version of the totalitarian state). The 'integral state' therefore did not mean that the state 'is everything' (as, according to Gramsci's famous statement, it was 'in the East' where civil society was not particularly developed). 'The expansion of the state', wrote Buci-Glucksmann, 'is accomplished ... through the *incorporation* of hegemony and its apparatus within it'.[74] It represented, therefore, the terrain of struggle for the working class in the epoch of a new equivalence between the economy and politics. On such terrain, a double 'war of positions' takes place: for the hegemonic classes in terms of 'passive revolution', and for the working class and their allies in terms of the development of their own 'passive antirevolution' to escape subalternity.[75]

Buci-Glucksmann's book, as I have already said, was entirely in line with the debate on the *problematic* of the Eurocommunist parties in the mid-1970s, the major limits of which lay in a basic *orthodoxy* typical to Althusserianism, above all in relation to Lenin. This orthodoxy made it difficult to fully accept the novelty of Gramsci's ideas, and to see how his innovative reading of the state – which Buci-Glucksmann fully recognised – had radically changed the terms of

---

70 Buci-Glucksmann 1976 [1975], p. 17.
71 Buci-Glucksmann was the first author, even if only in the final phase of her work, to benefit from the new critical edition of the *Notebooks* by Gerratana, and the possibilities the editions made available to periodise Gramsci's prison thought.
72 Buci-Glucksmann 1976 [1975], pp. 63–64.
73 Buci-Glucksmann 1976 [1975], p. 161.
74 Buci-Glucksmann 1976 [1975], p. 90.
75 See C. Buci-Glucksmann, *La classe operaia e lo Stato*, in *l'Unità*, 27 April 1977. Also see the contribution by the same author to the congress of Gramscian studies held in Florence in 1977, discussed below.

the revolutionary process and the relation between democracy and socialism. Buci-Glucksmann grasped that

> the war of positions ... breaks with the lyrical illusion of the great day. Nonetheless, it does not suppress the necessity of the conquest of political power and, therefore, the state. Under different conditions and in different ways one needs, quite simply, 'to break' the state; only that the state which needs to be broken is a state already quite different, deprived of its historical basis, wounded in its mechanisms and hegemonic apparatus, mediating a new balance of forces favourable to the people.[76]

This conceptual novelty was mixed with an already outmoded language, an indicator of legacies that were yet to be overcome. Its merit remained in having reread Gramsci in an original way, with the lens of the traditional functional structuralist, contributing to some far-reaching innovations (bound to an analysis of the *form* of bourgeois hegemony) on which a historicist Marxism could never focus.

8 Gramsci and the 'New Left'

A broad discussion of Gramsci's thought also took place within what was called the 'extra-parliamentary left' in 1968 and the 'new left' later on. There was a double approach here. One side saw in Gramsci the roots and symbols of an 'Italian road to socialism' harking back to Togliatti. Accusing the Italian Communist Party of being revisionist in theory and reformist in practice, this negative attitude towards Gramsci was thus a polemic against both past and (perhaps above all) present, constituting the *raison d'etre* of such political subjects. We are dealing here, really, with the old 'Bordigist' attitude, reprised by groups and intellectuals from different backgrounds and organisations, even those really quite distant from Bordigism such as *Potere Operaio*, *Lotta Continua* and, later, *Autonomia Operaia*, part of the legacy of the theoretical *operaismo* of the 1960s. Nor did such groups evaluate Gramsci directly: they had no choice but to be anti-Gramscian, for at least two reasons. One was the importance of adopting an approach in opposition to the Communist Party. Another was the incompatibility between Gramsci's *operaismo*, which focused on the figure of the *producer* (that is on workers qualified not only by their political consciousness

---

76   C. Buci-Glucksmann, *La classe operaia e lo Stato*, in *l'Unità*, 27 April 1977, p. 331.

but by the task of replacing the *management* of the factory itself, so as not to interrupt the process of production) and the new *mass worker* of the kind that the new *operaismo* claimed existed in Italian neo-capitalism at the end of the 1950s: an unskilled worker, the mythical bearer of a rebellious, egalitarian and anti-productivist energy veering on Luddism.

In the 'extra-parliamentary left' there was another attitude, however, according to which, in their process of radically criticising the Communist Party, Gramsci represented a revolution *betrayed* by his successors – one which had to be recovered. This was the Trotskyist position (to which we have already referred), whose devotees confirmed their traditional attitudes at the end of the 1960s[77] without any noteworthy variation. This current included the radicals of *il manifesto* (first a monthly and then daily newspaper, as well as an organised political group); disciples of Pietro Ingrao; other 'Marxist-Leninist' groups such as *Avanguardia Operaia* (who then flowed into *Democrazia Proletaria*); and finally other 'Chinese-influenced' intellectuals and scholars, such as Maria Antonietta Macciocchi.

The evolution of a *workerist* tendency can be seen above all in the approach of Alberto Asor Rosa, who after having been one of the protagonists of the *left* criticism of the Communist Party in the 1960s became a member of the Party (along with Mario Tronti and Massimo Cacciari), nevertheless conserving a specific 'autonomous' cultural physiognomy, even if one that was constantly evolving, which kept open the channels of communication and *seduction* for a young generation of intellectuals and militants coming out of the politics of '68. In the 1970s, the author of *Writers and the People* changed his interpretative viewpoint. In an essay from 1971, Asor Rosa maintained a critical judgement on Gramsci for having 'overestimated the role played by intellectuals'. Asor Rosa's interpretation came, nonetheless, from a *historicist* reading of Gramsci, in which the link between present and past emerged from a conscious level of politics and activity, condemning the 'philosophy of praxis' as a mask for a substantial stagnancy, only just covered over by an illusory ideology of progress:

> It is necessary to conceive of the people as 'an amorphous element of the masses', as a collection of 'simpletons', if one wants toto attribute intellectuals with the task of ethical and pedagogical education. Yet an intellectual who has been formed in such an ideological manner *always* tends to see the people as standing away from him, as 'an amorphous ele-

---

77   Cf. S. Corvisieri, *Gramsci contro Stalin*, in *La sinista*, 1967, issue 6, and Corvisieri 1969.

ment of the masses', as a collection of 'simpletons'; and similarly he sees conceptual political activity itself as fundamentally the art of convincing, directing and raising up the 'masses'.[78]

Gramsci was thus supposed to have been the means (to put it in a Gramscian terminology) towards a kind of 'passive revolution': *progressive* intellectual groups (with everything which that word meant for the author of *Writers and the People*) accepted Gramscian discourse only 'because such a recognition allowed them to claim their *own* hegemony over the historical bloc and therefore within the party'.[79] Aside from its qualities as an interpretation of Gramsci this was not an argument entirely deprived of truth. Yet in the *Notebooks* themselves – in the categories of 'passive revolution' and 'organic intellectual' (opposed to the 'traditional intellectual') – one can find the very material for its counter-argument.

Asor Rosa's evaluation of Gramsci in the context of the rich history of Italian culture over the previous hundred years was less drastic, published in Einaudi's 'History of Italy' in the mid-1970s. This contained a negative judgement in terms of many aspects central to Gramscian developments, from the 'intellectual and moral reform' and 'absolute historicism', through to the conception of culture as 'moral life'. On the question of the role of intellectuals, as central to Asor Rosa as it was to Gramsci, the author seemed to show an interest in the new relationship between intellectuals and politics proposed by the Sardinian communist, as well as between intellectuals and the party: 'Gramsci's discovery was that politics is also an intellectual activity, that politicians are also intellectuals'.[80] And still more, that the activity of intellectuals

> passes, in order to remain vital, through politics; it represents an integral part of being the Prince, a direction to which intellectuals contribute as politicians and as experts. The historical bloc of the working class understands that intellectuals are an integral, decisive element. Only within the historical bloc can they play a role which is neither subaltern nor parasitic. Gramsci proposed them with nothing less than the possibility of participating in their own *leadership*.[81]

This change of perspective, if nothing else, seems to grasp the complexity of Gramsci's thought, during that bright period in the mid-1970s when there were

---

78   Asor Rosa 1973, pp. 570–71.
79   Asor Rosa 1973, p. 572.
80   Asor Rosa 1975, p. 1565.
81   Asor Rosa 1975, p. 1566.

still relations between the Communist Party and intellectuals, traditional or otherwise. Notwithstanding his continued negative judgement on Gramsci's cultural politics, Asor Rosa recognised that Gramsci had attempted 'to overturn the cultural hegemony in our country'.[82] It was no small admission for someone who had begun from a vision which had seen Gramsci as simply the continuer of a much deplored 'national tradition'.

Almost all the reasons for a certain *anti-Gramscianism* on the left in this period can be found in an essay by Giacomo Marramao which appeared in *Quaderni Piacentini* in 1972. In reality this was a kind of *overview* of the main reasons to criticise Gramsci from the left, especially those already examined in contributions by Mario Tronti (busy with a reading, following Della Volpe, of Marxism as science rather than as ideology) and Stefano Merli (who provided a definitive polemic against Gramscian theory as a theory of 'revolution without revolution') as well as, above all, a volume which appeared in West Germany in 1970 by Christian Riechers, *Antonio Gramsci: Marxismus in Italien*.[83] For Marramao the 'situation of the class' had demonstrated 'in practical, factual terms, the necessary process of detaching itself from Gramscian analysis':[84] it was, in other words, the passage from the artisan worker to the mass worker, from an archaic capitalism to a *neo-capitalism* and the consequent new composition of classes within society, which invalidated the analysis provided by the author of the *Notebooks*, an analysis which read Italian capitalism only in terms of 'backwardness' and from which came the consequences attributed to the politics of the Communist Party's version of democracy and anti-Fascism after the War. Gramsci's ideas, for Marramao, did not represent a 'qualitative'

---

82 Asor Rosa 1975, p. 1567.
83 Riechers' book (translated into Italian with little notice, first in 1975 by Thélème and then in 1993 by Graphos in Genoa, with a preface by A. Peregalli) had some small fame, not only in Germany, as a re-reading of Gramsci which was in tune with the point of view of the 'movement of '68'. It was in reality a reprisal of old anti-Gramscian ideas (diverse among themselves, but here mixed together) associated with Tasca, Bordiga, Tronti and Asor Rosa. Gramsci – beyond being gradually tainted by a Mussolini-style interventionism, of being part of the 'intellectual clique associated with Croce and *La Voce, in partibus infideliam*' (Riechers 1975, p. 59), tainted by idealism and with little actual understanding of Marxism and Leninism, etc. etc. – above all was one of the original thinkers of the abhorred 'Italian road to socialism'; he was thus accused of being the creator (from 1914) of the theoretical operation which substituted class with (Italian) nation as the *subject* of historical activity. Based on such a premise the Communist Party, from the *Lyons Thesis* onwards, according to the author, could not but explicitly become 'the executive organ of the real development of the Italian nation' (Riechers 1975, p. 93).
84 G. Marramao, *Per una critica dell'ideologia di Gramsci*, in *Quaderni piacentini*, 1972, issue 46, p. 74.

leap as far as the Marxism of the Third International was concerned.[85] The Sardinian communist had never *broken* 'from the ideological forms of bourgeois political consciousness' (representative democracy, abstract equality).[86] He had reduced *critique* to *translation*. He had ignored the Marxian *critique of political economy*, considering Ricardo only from a philosophical point of view and taking from classical economics only 'the *value of labour* inasmuch as it is the motor of development, of progress'.[87] Gramsci, in the end, was not a Marxist, but an idealist. He had not shown any *discontinuity* with the 'progressive doctrines of bourgeois thought'. His theory, merely another chapter in 'intellectual and moral reform', had constituted the necessary grounds for the *political proximity* of the Communist Party to the bourgeois parties.

Aside from an inability to distinguish Gramsci from the gradual *interpretation* of his work by the Communist Party and its modernist attempt to form a political science around it, Marramao's contribution represented – if perhaps in unusually negative terms – part of a well-ploughed field: the relation between Gramsci and the critique of political economy. On this point the author indicated Gramsci's distance from central dimensions of Marx's theory such as the labour theory of value. However, recognising this and theorising the 'non-Marxist' character of Gramsci's thought are clearly entirely different matters.[88]

The more general polemic against Gramsci was demonstrated in a book by Tito Perlini titled *Gramsci e il Gramscismo*, on the one hand devoted to separating Gramsci's 'responsibility' from that of Togliatti, but only in virtue of 'the moral and political work' that rendered Gramsci 'qualitatively heterogeneous from Togliatti, to the hypocrisy and ambiguity of the political substance within his thought and, in general, every form of opportunism therein'.[89] On the other hand, frequently with reference to the interpretative theses of Merli and Riecher, Gramsci was attributed with 'macroscopic errors of an all-embracing evaluation which constituted the arena from which all of his theoretical and political aberrations derive, and which have found expression in Togliattian opportunism and the revisionism and reformism of the Italian Communist

---

85 G. Marramao, *Per una critica dell'ideologia di Gramsci*, in *Quaderni piacentini*, 1972, n. 46, p. 78.
86 G. Marramao, *Per una critica dell'ideologia di Gramsci*, in *Quaderni piacentini*, 1972, n. 46, p. 84.
87 G. Marramao, *Per una critica dell'ideologia di Gramsci*, in *Quaderni piacentini*, 1972, n. 46, p. 86.
88 For this argument, see nonetheless Gramsci 1994, and the *Introduzione* by G. Lunghini.
89 See Perlini 1974, p. 53.

Party'.[90] The fundamental error which Gramsci had undertaken, for Perlini, was that of having accepted the 'inevitability of socialism in one country'. From here derived 'the pre-eminence of the national framework', the reduction of the class struggle to the 'democratic' context and the anti-Fascist alliance, etc. In revising the revolutionary positions of the 'red biennial', Gramsci had provided the basis from which Togliatti's 'opportunism' would inevitably emerge.[91]

Those currents within the 'new left' attempting to *recuperate* the Sardinian leader and his thought into a contemporary 'revolutionary' vision are of greater interest to us however. The Gramsci presented by *il manifesto* demonstrated the need, in the current social and political dialectic, of stressing *class* rather than *party*. Togliatti's post-War 'new party', wrote Luigi Pintor for example, embodied less of that 'distinctive trait' which distinguished the experience of *Ordine Nuovo*, i.e. a 'reference to the factory as the *national territory* of workers' self governance',[92] and the relation between party and class as it had been presented in the Theses of Lyons. It was *councilism* (and Gramsci the councilist) which *il manifesto* recognised as the theoretical political way forward. In her introduction to a conversation with Sartre in the same issue, Rossana Rossanda wrote that 'Gramsci's experience in Turin is completely anchored in the hypothesis of the maturing of the class as a direct political subject', with regards to which the party was 'one instrument, but not the only one, of political expression. The class has no need of mediation; it is already formed in the councils, in the class's recognition of itself as a revolutionary alternative, a new society *in the making*'.[93] In the *Notebooks*, therefore, 'the accent is misplaced: it falls on the vanguard, the Prince'. In Gramsci there was thus an 'itinerary' that conditioned the historical passage he was living through, a shift in accent from council to party. The relaunching of a strong councilist hypothesis, on the back of a vast political wave which was redrawing the relationship in Italy between classes and forms of political and union initiatives – but which the *'manifesto'* group, in comparison with others, evidently overestimated – was reproposed by Lucio Magri. Magri identified an important distinction between those who, on the basis of Lenin and Gramsci – but also on the basis of a certain 'left' Gramscianism of the kind found in Italy after 1956 – saw the councils as the 'political

---

90   Perlini 1974, p. 55.
91   Perlini reopened the argument over *The Southern Question* started in Capecelatro and Carlo 1972, who had criticised Gramsci for having incorrectly understood the South as a feudal and pre-capitalist society, due to his 'industrialist' standpoint, which equated capitalism and industrial development. This was one aspect of the more general argument against Gramsci as a theorist of the backwardness of Italian capitalism.
92   L. Pintor, *Il partito di tipo nuovo*, in *il manifesto*, 1969, n. 4, p. 23.
93   R. Rossanda, *Classe e partito. Da Marx a Marx*, in *il manifesto*, 1969, n. 4, p. 45.

institutions of the masses, instruments of a direct anti-capitalist struggle',[94] thus rejecting the character of an immediate political subject as such. Magri did not fail to advance a criticism of Gramsci that focussed on the 'consciousness of producers', blaming the councils for the distraction of self-management and undervaluing the problems of state power. On the contrary, Magri wanted the councils to 'initiate the critique and confrontation of the "consciousness of the producers"', expressing 'the criticism of the factory class and the class of the real social division of labour'.[95]

Giorgio Bonomi's small book *Partito e rivoluzione in Gramsci* should also be situated in this context of the publications of the 'new left'. Bonomi perceived a radical break between Gramsci and Togliatti 'the revisionist'. Indeed, Bonomi defended Gramsci's 'Leninism', or rather, a conception of hegemony in which 'dominance' had no less relevance than 'leadership', arguing against those who 'reduced class power to a pure ideological consensus'.[96] Nor, according to Bonomi, did he abandon a vision of the class character of the state, the necessity of a *violent* revolution for its 'disintegration', with the objective of heralding in the dictatorship of the proletariat.[97] The 'war of positions' should not be read, for Bonomi, as the equivalent of a 'democratic' or 'peaceful road': the difference between 'East' and 'West' was in fact reduced here to a tactical variation, different means of reaching the same goal. What remained therefore of Gramsci's *specificity*? Only 'the importance of the ideological struggle' which, moreover, he shared with Mao.[98]

The reference to Mao was also present, in a more pronounced and ultimately misleading way, in Maria Antonietta Macciocchi's work, an author whose *Per Gramsci* found a certain success (both in France, where she lived, but also in Italy) aimed at a wide audience of activists among the 'new left' as well as scholars. These scholars, however, would not have been impressed by a discourse characterised by frequently erroneous versions of Gramscian thought, which ignored huge historical and geographical distances. It was precisely these elements, however, that allowed the text to find common ground with a certain audience of activists, to whom a 'Maoist' Gramsci was offered, described in a simplified and comprehensible language, charged with passion. Macciocchi's book was also partly an argument against the Communist Party: Togliatti had 'diluted' the power of an alternative inherent in Gramsci's views (councils and

---

94 L. Magri, *Una risposta a Ingrao*, in *il manifesto*, 1970, n. 1, p. 38.
95 L. Magri, *Una risposta a Ingrao*, in *il manifesto*, 1970, n. 1, p. 44.
96 Bonomi 1973, p. 37.
97 Bonomi 1973, p. 48.
98 Bonomi 1973, p. 73.

proletarian democracy vs bourgeois parliamentary democracy).[99] Gramsci was defined as 'the Marxist thinker who offered the greatest theoretical instruments for the examination of a revolution which, as with the Chinese Revolution, constantly demonstrates a search for hegemony'.[100] To overcome the 'old China' it had been necessary to enact a true 'intellectual and moral reform', begun in 1919, which alone made possible the new state of 1949: more than thirty years of 'the struggle for hegemony', according to Macciocchi, had confirmed the Gramscian thesis by which one could and must lead even before the conquest of state power. The book attempted to advance a host of historical parallels (even ending with a collection of iconographic similarities)[101] including a comparison of Gramsci's working method in prison and that 'in which Mao worked for a long period, closed up in Yenan'.[102] On the more properly theoretical level, it is hard not to see how in the conception of Mao's dialectic (both in respect to the social dialectic and that which concerned the relation between party and the masses) the moment of *negation* could be assigned to the search for *force*, assuming strongly *destructive* features. The Maoist dialectic of the 'one divided into two', which becomes 'one' through the destruction of the other 'half', was very distant from the heartfelt tones in which Gramsci spoke, in the celebrated letter of 1926, of the dangers inherent in the internal struggle of the Bolshevik leading group. And it was also very different on the question of socialist democracy, for example in Gramsci's note on 'black parliamentarianism'. Macciocchi's *Per Gramsci* remained therefore above all a document of its times, a record of the great Maoist *infatuation* of those years which, in this case, formed a work far from any acceptable standards of academic rigour.[103]

---

99   Macciocchi 1974, p. 48.
100 Macciocchi 1974, p. 228.
101 Macciocchi, in relation to well known photographs of the young Gramsci, spoke of a 'head which emerges from a stern uniform with a closed collar, which cannot but make one recall Mao's own portrait'. Macciocchi 1974, p. 37.
102 Macciocchi 1974, p. 203.
103 Another result of the reflections on Gramsci within the political cultural sphere of the 'new left' can be seen in Cambria 1976, a novel rethinking of the relation between Gramsci and the Schucht sisters – his wife and sister-in-law – through a 'neo-feminist' view of the relation between the 'personal' and 'political'. The author also published many letters by Giulia and Tania, till then unedited. The role of the three Schucht sisters will be studied more carefully within Gramscian studies from the 1990 and the studies by Aldo Natoli. See Natoli 1990 (especially p. 334), Schucht 1991 (with preface by G. Gramsci and an introduction by M. Paulesu Quercioli). Also cf. L. Durante, *Guilia*, and *Tania*, entries in Liguori and Voza 2009, M.L. Righi, *Gramsci e Mosca tra amori e politica (1922–1923)* in *Studi storici*, 2011, n. 4; Vacca 2012. On the reconstruction of the world of Gramsci's family life also see Paulesu Quercioli 1991, Gramsci Jr 2008 and Gramsci Jr 2010.

9   The 'Gerratana Edition'

The publication of the *Prison Notebooks* in the 'critical edition of the Istituto Gramsci, edited by Valentino Gerratana' (as printed on the frontispiece of the four volume work issued by Einaudi in 1975) represented a culminating moment to the 'golden age' of Gramsci's legacy in Italy in the first half of the 1970s. The work of reconstructing the Sardinian thinker in relation to the unfolding political and historical events of the time, the rich debate on his conceptual apparatus, the growing diffusion of his writings before arrest[104] – these were given a final and important impetus by the new publication. It was immediately recognised that Gerratana – and the team under his leadership and training – had made a qualitative leap in the study of Gramsci's thought. The old thematic edition was assigned to the shelf, along with the interpretation it had implied. The result was the definitive acknowledgement that Gramsci's work in prison was not 'disinterested' and *'für ewig'* (i.e. 'timeless', as the author had described his own 'programmatic' position, but not without caution),[105] but instead was connected with the theoretical and political struggles of and within the international Communist movement. Already by 1958, as we have noted, Togliatti had claimed that the 'continuous thread' of Gramsci's work was to be found 'in the real activity which begins from the questions of his youth and then slowly developed up to the rise of Fascism, his arrest and even after that'.[106] And it had been Togliatti himself who had promoted and encouraged the critical edition of the *Notebooks* as far back as 1962.[107] The new edition, Gerratana wrote in his comprehensive preface to the volume, was inspired by the 'need to offer an instrument for interpretation that allowed readers to follow

---

104 The volume of Gramsci's writings published in 1974 (A. Gramsci, *Per la verità*), edited by Martinelli, included Gramscian articles which had appeared in the socialist and communist press, for the most part unsigned, and which had escaped previous research and were thus excluded from the corpus of the complete works published by Einaudi. It is also worth mentioning the *Scritti 1915–1921* edited by Caprioglio (Gramsci 1968). On the problems for Gramscian studies relating to Einaudi's publication of the pre-arrest writings, see the Introduction to Gramsci 1974; V. Gerratana, *Note di filologia gramsciana*, in *Studi storici*, 1975, issue 1; and, more recently, F. Giasi, *Problemi di edizione degli scritti pre-carcerari*, in *Studi storici*, 2011, issue 4; M. Lana, *Individuare scritti gramsciani anonimi in un* corpus *giornalistico. Il ruolo dei metodi quantitativi*, in *Studi storici*, 2011, issue 4.

105 Gramsci 1965, p. 56 (letter to Tania of 19 March 1927). On the different meanings attributed to the Gramscian *'für ewig'*, see J. Francese, *Sul desiderio gramsciano di scrivere qualcosa 'für ewig'*, in *Critica marxista*, 2009, issue 1; E. Forenza, *Für ewig*, in Liguori and Voza 2009; Vacca 2012, pp. 108–9.

106 See Togliatti 2001, p. 214.

107 Vittoria 1992, pp. 152–53 and p. 242n; Vacca 1994, p. 125.

the rhythm of the developments unfolding across the pages of the *Notebooks*. This edition therefore attempts to avoid any interpretative hypothesis, instead trying to remain within the framework of the interpretative flow of Gramsci's own thought'.[108] To this end, Gerratana presented the *Notebooks* according to the chronological order of their composition 'reconstructed on the basis of objective findings', reproducing both the notes of the first and second draft in their original ordering, as well as the marginal and intra-linear notes in the manuscript, without any *obvious* manipulation or censorship. The critical apparatus was nonetheless kept quite separate from the text, collected together in the last of the four volumes in which the *Notebooks* were published, trying not to interpose *distractions* between the reader and the material which might allow space for erroneous interpretative interventions.

In comparison with the previous thematic edition, the immediate impression was the 'fragmentary character' of the *Notebooks*. Gramsci, as Gerratana observed, did not write through aphorisms: instead, the *fragmentary* character of his writing presupposed a strong unified plan. The style was not external to the content, but was a functional aspect of Gramsci's thought: open, problematic, anti-dogmatic. The new version was a philological restoration which opened the road 'to a true *theoretical restoration*',[109] and inherently impeded the possibility of any partial and *absolute* interpretations, demonstrating the richness of the *Notebooks* instead and the very fact that Gramsci had rejected the 'method of apodeictic doctrinality'.[110] The critical edition thus clearly constituted a *qualitative leap*; from this point on, that could not be ignored by anyone who truly wanted to read Gramsci – even if reading him would now require greater effort in general. Not all the problems of the *Notebooks* had been entirely resolved of course, from a philological point of view. For example, the sequence of the notebooks was calculated by the date on which each volume was begun, even though Gramsci often worked on the different notebooks at the same time, and did not always proceed from one page to the next, meaning that in reality the problems of dating each note remained. This would be raised a little later,[111] but was destined to become a real subject of debate only in the 1980s and '90s. The fact remained, however, that Gerratana's 'critical edition' represented a point of reference for study of the *Notebooks* which has still not been surpassed, and indeed serves as a model of critical work and rigorous philology.

108   Gerratana's preface to Gramsci 1975, p. xxv.
109   V. Gerratana, *La ricerca e il metodo*, in *Rinascita*, 1975, issue 30 (insert *Il Contemporaneo* entirely dedicated to the critical edition), p. 11.
110   V. Gerratana, *La ricerca e il metodo*, in *Rinascita*, 1975, issue 30, p. 13.
111   See Francioni 1977, pp. 369–94.

CHAPTER 7

The Apogee and Crisis of Gramscian Culture (1976–77)

1 The Pluralism Debate

The years 1976–77 represented the moment of maximum expansion – and, immediately afterwards, the beginning of a long decline – in the electoral fortunes of the Italian Communist Party, as well as in the diffusion and effect of Gramsci's work in Italy. This was no coincidence: as we have repeatedly seen, the activity of the Communist Party had been the most important vehicle for the spreading of Gramsci's thought; simultaneously, Gramsci's thought had been the main *medium* through which the Communist Party had managed to speak to different generations and audiences of both intellectuals and activists. This was a difficult relation to maintain which, in the years considered here, suffered a build-up of tension in the context of national elections: for the first time since 1947, the Communist Party made a real advance, and consequently had to evaluate the theoretical problems arising from (to use the language of the times) the 'the working class making the state'. The political and social crisis of the 1970s was widely interpreted, rightly or wrongly, as a *crisis of hegemony* and as *the struggle for hegemony*, as the process of substituting the declining hegemony of the bourgeoisie with a new workers' hegemony. This fact, together with those internal to historical-theoretical research, managed to export Gramsci out of the more or less restricted circles of specialists and into not only the world of militants on the left and the unions, but also a still wider world of the *mass media*, of political classes and public opinion. The debate on Gramsci reached this point at the same time as the fortieth anniversary of his death, in 1977, a point in many ways without precedent, characterised by an overlapping of very different tones: theoretical research and contemporary politics, high culture and mass culture, militant ideology and academic debate, party strategy and political science. It is easy to understand how, in such a context, there was a constant risk of excessive politicisation, even of instrumentalisation. But there were also important political and cultural possibilities.

The merit of having started the 'pluralism debate' fell to Noberto Bobbio, a debate which constituted the immediate and most influential background to the theoretical-political discussions of 1977. On one hand, Bobbio presented a liberal democratic philosophy, yet again arguing that Communists had an important role as interlocutors in the meeting between theories of democracy and of the state.[1] On the other hand, in the new situation created after the election of 20 June 1976, Bobbio's position assumed an objectively novel character within a context where political energies and intellectual interests were multiplying in order to block the possibility of the Communist Party actually entering into the arena of government. In a speech given to a meeting of the socialist journal *Mondoperaio* in July 1976, Bobbio stressed the fundamental differences between socialist and communist identities which prevented their amalgamation, speaking of a 'lay conception of history opposed to a totalising conception ... in which there is no room ... for the new Prince to whom Gramsci attributed the work of transforming society'.[2] Two months later in September, Bobbio published two articles in the newspaper *La Stampa*, which together formed a discussion around pluralism and the Communist Party, in which he advanced the thesis of essential contradictions between the kind of pluralism professed by the Communist Party and the non-pluralism of its 'cultural matrix'.[3] He clarified this in a subsequent interview in *Repubblica*:

> Gramsci speaks of class having hegemony through the party that represents it ... he compares the party to the 'Prince', considering it to be a historical protagonist with a mission of unifying, of eliminating all contrary elements. Now, how could a prince, who is by definition singular, allow multiplicity? ... If we claim that pluralism is necessary in this moment and in this society, we also have to renounce the concept of a hegemonic party.[4]

In order to construct his argument, Bobbio had to posit that the political culture of the Communist Party was still that of the PCd'I in the 1930s; that Gramsci was not a particularly *original* author, the theorist of civil society who had been illuminated in the 1960s, but simply an *imitator* of Leninism. Pietro Ingrao, then President of the Chamber, was quite right in replying that the pluralism which the communists were emphasising was that of Article 3 of the Italian Consti-

---

[1] The reference is to the discussion between Bobbio, Della Volpe and Togliatti in 1954 on 'democracy and socialism', as well as to the more recent debate on 'the Marxist conception of the state', which took place in 1975–76 in the columns of *Mondoperaio* and *Rinascita*. Cf. Bobbio 1955, and also N. Bobbio, *Il marxismo e lo Stato*, Quaderni di Mondoperaio, 1976, n. 4.
[2] N. Bobbio in Coen 1977, p. 247.
[3] Cf. N. Bobbio, *Che cos'è il pluralismo* and *Come intendere il pluralismo*, in *La Stampa*, 21 and 22 (respectively) September 1976.
[4] N. Bobbio, *Al "Principe" non si addice la repubblica*, interview by R. Balbo in *la Repubblica*, 24 September 1976.

tution and that one had to be aware of 'certain schematic reductions which yesterday made Gramsci all for spontaneity and "councilism" while today ... presenting him as preaching party totalitarianism'.[5] It is nonetheless interesting to note how, further on in the article, Ingrao recognised that even Gramsci would not suffice any more, as the contextual transformations in the intervening period had broadened out anti-capitalist social elements and forces, laying the 'rational roots' for the Communist Party's pluralism.

2 Hegemony and Democracy

The polemic between Ingrao and Bobbio on pluralism anticipated in no small way the themes which would animate the debates on the Italian left in 1977, marked by the 'year of Gramsci'. The discussion which unfolded in *Mondoperaio* between October 1976 and May 1977 represented, for the most part, a reprise of Bobbio's discourse on the intrinsic and authoritative meaning of the concept of hegemony, and therefore of the illegitimacy of the communists to govern without rescinding their own theoretical and historical roots and homogenising themselves into the socialist tradition. The debate in *Mondoperaio* began with two articles, by Furio Diaz and Massimo L. Salvadori respectively. If the first gave an overview of the entire arc of the history of the Italian Communist Party, maintaining, in the end, the thesis of its significant distance 'from the Soviet model',[6] Salvadori's own analysis focussed more specifically on Gramsci and the 'Communist interpretations' of his thought, which

> tended to suggest a reading according to which Gramsci had undertaken a kind of theoretical 'about turn', starting from Leninism but in the end fully developing a 'theory of hegemony', the path of the Communist Party's real strategy, based on an emphasis on 'pluralism', political democracy, the dialogue between diverse political forces, and a strategy of reform.[7]

But if one could really demonstrate a hypothesis of continuity between Gramsci and the Communist Party of the times, Salvadori objected, then the Communist Party would have to be seen as merely a wing of Leninism, because Gramsci's theory of hegemony would be none other than a *tactical variation* of Bolshevik strategy and democracy in a transitional phase, necessary in order to

---
5 P. Ingrao, *Il pluralismo*, in *La Stampa*, 7 October 1976.
6 F. Diaz in Coen 1977, pp. 39 and 31.
7 M.L. Salvadori in Coen 1977, pp. 33–34.

'gather forces' after Fascism, when the 'final assault' on the Winter Palace was still on the horizon. Only after the war, according to Salvadori, did the Communist Party take note of the balance of forces on an international level, and repudiate the 'functional link' between war of manoeuvre and war of position. But we are dealing now with this discontinuity being made explicit, the renouncing of that 'Catholic wisdom' by which 'everything had been "adapted" and nothing "changed"',[8] and the recognition that the Communist Party of Eurocommunism and of the acceptance of political democracy had always been closer to Kautsky than to Gramsci.

Salvadori was justified in claiming that one could not find the entire development of the history of the Communist Party in Gramsci: there was no explicit acceptance of political pluralism, even if the notes in the *Notebooks* on 'Caesarism' and 'black parliamentarianism'[9] denounced the inherent dangers of a single party regime. Nor was there, in the Sardinian Communist's thought, a fully non-instrumentalised version of democracy, especially given that he was writing from within a Fascist prison and that democracy as known by the workers' movement up till then had very well-defined class limits. On this basis, and from the obvious movement which, in the four decades following his death, had shifted the Communist Party *beyond* Gramsci, it is important to consider how simplified Salvadori's version of hegemony was. Salvadori saw hegemony as merely a tactical variation on Leninism because he ignored that in the *Notebooks*, before it was a strategic proposal, hegemony had been a category for the interpretation of reality: there is always a class hegemony, which can show itself in either single or multiple party systems. The war of position was not an instrumental variation destined to give way to the 'frontal attack' as soon as the conditions were right, an obligatory choice imposed by the processes of massification of politics and the diffusion of that hegemony which Gramsci was the first to understand.

Salvadori was in part right to denounce the *bad historicism* of the Communist Party, which had at times hindered the Communists from maintaining a beneficial relation with Gramsci, i.e. they took too long to understand the modernism of his analysis of the new relation between economy and politics, and consequently had erected upon this supposed basis a strategy of 'historic compromise' which actually had very little to do with the author of the *Notebooks*. Throughout, the idea of a democratic Communist Party, which had severed itself from its Gramscian roots, was not so different from those who similarly

---

8   M.L. Salvadori in Coen 1977, p. 52.
9   Cf. G. Liguori, *Cesarismo* and L. La Porta, *Parlamentarismo nero*, in Liguori and Voza 2009.

found evidence for the democratic unreliability of the Communist Party in the *continuity* of its history. In both cases this relied on a substantial misunderstanding of the novelty that Gramsci represented not only at the beginning of the Italian Communist tradition but, in some aspects, in anticipation of it.

In the debate which played out in the pages of *Mondoperaio*, there was a broad agreement among the majority of interventions: the Gramscian concept of hegemony 'posed itself as the premise of the dictatorship of the proletariat, and not as an alternative to such a dictatorship', because 'the fact that Gramsci was a Leninist was never contested by anyone'[10] (Bobbio); hegemony was 'an integration and development of the concept of the "dictatorship of the proletariat"'[11] (Colletti); an authoritative pedagogy arising from the nineteenth century, a project which was 'anti-democratic, "totalitarian" even, in a technical sense'[12] (Galli della Loggi); a variation on Leninism and therefore 'essentially and irredeemably *totalitarian*'; a mythical and religious conception, the most mature version of 'totalitarian communism', of 'gnostic Marxism'[13] (Pellicani). Galli della Loggia's essay, in particular, should be noted as one of the more *negative* assessments of Gramsci by democratic liberals: if a party is 'democratic', he argued, it could no longer hold a 'conception of the world', because 'democracy does not know how to – nor can it – take care of the formation of individual conscience. Consciousness instead remains at the mercy of two uncontrollable forces ... the market and the unconscious'.[14] Here one does not need to speak of 'hegemonic struggle', because the 'political sphere' passes over 'from a sphere of consciousness to that of interests',[15] or rather, as became clear in the 1980s of triumphant neoliberalism, the mediation of corporativism dominated by the logic of exchange. Gramsci, a figure of nineteenth-century culture who 'remained throughout his life an *Italian* intellectual and a *Southern* intellectual, was in the end too Italian and Southern to really see the world',[16] and could not have imagined the 'democratic capitalism of the masses, its mechanisms and citizens'.[17]

These harsh judgements did nonetheless face a few dissonant voices, above all that of Roberto Guiducci,[18] faithful to the reading of a *councilist* Gram-

---

10 N. Bobbio in Coen 1977, p. 55.
11 L. Colletti in Coen 1977, p. 63.
12 E. Galli della Loggia in Coen 1977, p. 86.
13 L. Pellicani in Coen 1977, pp. 102 and 107.
14 E. Galli della Loggia in Coen 1977, p. 89.
15 E. Galli della Loggia in Coen 1977, p. 90.
16 E. Galli della Loggia in Coen 1977, p. 88.
17 E. Galli della Loggia in Coen 1977, p. 89.
18 R. Guiducci in Coen 1977, pp. 187–99.

sci which he had provided since the 1950s, along with Giuseppe Tamburrano, again faithful to that image of a Gramsci who, in the *Notebooks*, had created a democratic, and not Leninist, conception of politics.[19] But these were minority positions which did not change the general form of debate. It was concluded by a round-table discussion which brought together three socialist intellectuals (Amato, Diaz and Salvadori) and two communist intellectuals (Gerratana and Spriano).[20] If the socialist side repeated theses and positions which had already emerged over the course of discussion, the interventions by the two communist scholars included disagreements which were also important for their interpretation of the Gramscian legacy. On one side Gerratana, having confirmed the compatibility of 'a pluralistic reality with exercising some form of hegemony',[21] also claimed that Gramsci and the Communist Party excluded – both in *short and medium terms* – the passage to a society free of class contradictions, but could not have excluded 'the long-term perspective of both Gramsci and Marx', which would have risked

> altering the concept of political struggle itself, which lies at the heart of the communist tradition, in which political struggle is not bound only to the solution of immediate problems of a strictly political nature, but is written into the general project for social transformation with a universal character and which represents, in a sense, the utopian element within communism.[22]

Paolo Spriano's intervention went in a quite different direction, starting from the claim that

> we are entering a phase in which political democracy ... begins to appear as the terrain on which the working class and its allies are not only managing to freely develop the class struggle, but are ready to begin building – as Salvadori has noted – a new state and society. This is a historical element very different from that of Gramsci's time, a period in which he could not have imagined an experience of this type, one able to move in open seas, so to speak. Gramsci helps us with this, but we have need of

---

19   G. Tamburrano in Coen 1977, pp. 131–38.
20   G. Amato, F. Diaz, V. Gerratana, M.L. Salvadori and P. Spriano (roundtable) in Coen 1977, pp. 199–222.
21   Coen 1977, p. 202.
22   Coen 1977, p. 211.

others – although to be honest no one can help us, because we are living in a situation which is, in many ways, entirely new.[23]

Thus Spriano, in opposition to Gerratana, claimed to renounce the concept of transition and replace it with 'a concept of the democratisation of society towards socialism'.[24]

These different and diverse readings of Gramsci from two extremely prestigious *Gramscian* intellectuals in the Communist Party require a couple of brief comments so that they can be fully contextualised and understood. The first relates to a form of political discussion among Communists which was still underway in the 1970s, a discussion that was not always explicit – indeed it was often allusive, evading obvious differentiations, characterised by a common acceptance of the same political proposal but out of which came different 'interpretations'. According to the theory of 'democratic centralism', the exchange of views through such representatives allowed for the sharpening of political meanings within the cultural debate. From this point of view, the diversification of readings of Gramsci and relation with Gramsci could be defined as symptomatic of the divisions which had characterised Italian Communism in the first half of the 1960s. Between the 1950s and 1960s the development of Italian society had made the Gramscian analysis of the processes of capitalist modernisation more important. But the victorious line coming out of the Eleventh Congress of the Communist Party (1966), the first congress after Togliatti's death, had rejected the interpretation of the national situation in terms of its *backwardness*, a reading which later would be found to underlie even the proposal of the 'historical compromise'. In the 1970s, therefore, although now within a new environment and in the context of different arguments and problems, the old *querelle* between 'backwardness' and 'modernity',

---

23   Coen 1977, p. 206.
24   Coen 1977, p. 218. This was also shown in the two books which Spriano published in 1977 on Gramsci. The first, *Gramsci e Gobetti. Introduzione alla vita e alle opere*, suggests through its title alone [Gramsci and Gobetti: An Introduction to his life and works] an interpretative key to Gramsci (as antifascist and a 'great Italian'), in concordance with author's theses as we have just explained. The second book, *Gramsci in carcere e il partito*, represented an important piece of historical research disproving the myth of a *split* between Gramsci and the PCd'I during the 'turn' of 1929, research which caused a great deal of further studies and polemics on the subject of the book's title [Gramsci in prison and the party]. On this theme, and on Gramsci's life more generally, important information is to be found in Paulesu Quercioli 1977, which contains 40 'rememberances' of the communist leader, from Sardinia to prison, a work bringing together many of the protagonists who had known Gramsci in very different times and places.

the necessity of a 'qualitative' or 'quantitative' development, was reprised in the interpretation of the 'Italian situation', in relation to which, for example, Pietro Ingrao asked if it might express 'a *"backwardness"* with respect to solutions and methods that had already been tried and tested, or an exasperated and paradoxical *anticipation* of the problems that were currently maturing in other countries as well'.[25]

Salvadori's 'provocation', and that put forward by other intellectuals within *Mondoperaio*, therefore, brought to the surface enquiries and differences among Communists, differences that also included the strategic consequences of a proposal – the historic compromise – which had now become an inescapable fact for everyone in the Party. Moreover, in the small debate which played out among those Communists close to Salvadori,[26] matters tended to become concentrated within the seminar organised in the session of the central school of the Party and the cultural session of the Central Committee of the Communist Party held in Frattocchie in January 1977.

3   The Frattocchie Seminar

The conclusions to the seminar on 'Hegemony, the Party and the State in Gramsci' were provided by three talks given by Leonardo Paggi, Valentino Gerratana and Biagio De Giovanni.[27] Paggi's speech on Gramsci's pre-prison thought began by replying to the issue of liberal socialist culture and focussed on Gramsci's novel analysis of Lenin and the crucial theme of the state. The author recalled the Sardinian leader's comments on Marx's *The Civil War in France*: while Lenin had read this text above all as an argument on the 'break' from the machinery of the state, Gramsci had underlined the argument around the 'self-government of the producers'. The conquest of the state was for Gramsci, as for Marx, the final moment of a long process and the overcoming of 'bourgeois democracy', which could occur only after the overcoming of the market. Even if the Sardinian leader had already understood that the 'correspond-

---

25   Ingrao 1977, p. 9.
26   For a positive assessment of Salvadori's thesis, see L. Gruppi, *Insomma, s'è sbagliato anche lui. E allora diciamolo*, in *l'Espresso*, 1976, n. 49 (the same author downplayed his evaluation in *L'esigenza di una nuova guida*, in *Rinascita*, 1976, n. 50.) Socialist arguments against this thesis came from Ingrao (*Discutendo su questa 'parolaccia' che è l'egemonia*, in *Rinascita*, 1976, n. 48), C. Mancina (*Egemonia, dittatura, pluralismo: una polemica su Gramsci*, in *Critica marxista*, 1976, issue 3–4) and B. De Giovanni (*Dietro la polemica sull'egemonia*, in *Rinascita*, 1977, issue 1).
27   The acts of the conference are collected in De Giovanni et al 1977.

ence between production and politics does not function without mediation, its effects are filtered through the fullness of history'.[28] In any case, if the question of pluralism was not dealt with in Gramsci, there was the proposal of a democracy richer than that of bourgeois society, which could therefore not be accepted as the *unique* source or benchmark of democratic possibilities.

But it was in the *Notebooks* that the Gramscian concept of hegemony clearly reached its mature form. Gerratana called attention to how varied and diverse the modes and forms of hegemony were in late Gramsci, in terms of the social forces which evoked it. A class which struggled to end all exploitation could not pursue forms of hegemony 'which maintained only agreements by proxy, that is, in agreement with subaltern alliances'.[29] The proletariat, for Gramsci, had to *transform* the principle of hegemony, changing and innovating the relevant institutions and instruments. Simultaneously, Gramsci's party had to have an *active* character, educational and autodidactic, not passive or focussed on delegation.

Biagio De Giovanni's talk was dedicated to *Gramsci e l'elaborazione successiva del partito comunista* – 'Gramsci and the Subsequent Development of the Communist Party'. In an essay published in *Critica marxista*, the author had already contributed to the debate on Gramsci and pluralism. According to him, the Sardinian Communist had recognised the new character of the 1930s, the diffusion of politics and hegemony within society, and developed the only response adequate to the Communist line. The new relation between the state and economy repositioned the masses, which 'had always been formed most directly on the level of the society, meeting the state in the "immediacy" of its own productive forms'.[30] This massification of politics and the broadening out of hegemony established the basis for the pluralism that the workers' movement had made its own. 'But we need to be clear', De Giovanni insisted, 'the struggle for social recomposition remains at the centre of our strategy. Without this, the workers' movement loses its real identity and the real reason behind its *political* essence'.[31] Above all, De Giovanni's article demonstrated the distance between Gramsci and Lenin and provided an explanation for the new form of the party in relation to the state. The category of 'recomposition', however, was more problematic, and was argued in Frattocchie and elsewhere to entail *organicism*, a term that gave rise to much discussion and argument. In his speech, De Giovanni shifted the focus onto the problem of the relation between

---

28 L. Paggi in De Giovanni et al 1977, p. 31.
29 V. Gerratana in De Giovanni et al 1977, p. 50.
30 B. De Giovanni in De Giovanni et al 1977, p. 44.
31 B. De Giovanni in De Giovanni et al 1977, p. 52.

continuity and break between Gramsci and the Communist Party. On the issue of the party, for example, he claimed that, in defining the party as 'a democracy which organises itself', Togliatti had overcome the Gramscian concept of parties as a 'nomenclature of classes'. If Togliatti could be attributed the merit of 'having rethought the function of the party and the relation between party and state',[32] then the proposal of the 'historic compromise', for De Giovanni, returned to

> an interpretation of the Italian situation seen through the struggle for hegemony. In this sense, Gramsci's relevance is quite profound ... Gramsci's relevance today is central to our political research ... how can we, today, rediscover the central nucleus within the theory of hegemony? The strategy of the historic compromise offers the general basis of this answer, since ... it clarifies – overcoming a residual error – that *today the hegemony of the workers' movements must come through the recognition of political pluralism*. The proposal of a long period of the leadership of Italian society, which has so many aspects today ... is destined to take us much further than our present analysis of political pluralism.[33]

De Giovanni's entire speech polarised a good deal of the debate. It expressed a point of view already well determined by the theory, history and politics of Italian Communists, in which some would read an emphasis overly influenced by the political preoccupations and needs of the present moment. In Cesare Luporini's words, De Giovanni's reconstruction contained a 'pointedly organicist tendency',[34] in which many moments of rupture and contradiction were overlooked, and in which moments of error and lack of direction were similarly never recognised. Luporini also opposed the particular use of the term 'recomposition' (which, at least in a philosophical sense, evoked the reconstitution of an original unity which has been lost and needs to be reconquered); for him, too much space was given over to the *political* dimension, both with respect to the socio-economic environment and to the theoretical dimension; and also (together with Gruppi, Ingrao and others) a purely negative conception of the definition of parties as 'class nomenclature'.

Other interventions, revoking any affinity with De Giovanni's claims and methodology, emphasised the need for communists to have an autonomous

---

32 B. De Giovanni in De Giovanni et al 1977, p. 67.
33 B. De Giovanni in De Giovanni et al 1977, pp. 71–72. Again, it was the 'process of social recomposition' which was the lens by which to understand the communists' pluralism. De Giovanni et al 1977, p. 74.
34 C. Luporini in De Giovanni et al 1977, p. 169.

version of democracy. Giuseppe Vacca, for example, developing the argument around 'social recomposition', on which he agreed with De Giovanni, outlined the possibility of wedding pluralism to the self-government of the producers. If it were true that hegemony and pluralism were compatible (concepts which operated on different levels: the transformation of the '*class basis of the state*' and of the 'concrete explication of *government* and political leadership'), then it was also true that the pluralism of Italian Communists could be contained entirely 'within the processes of "political democracy" experimented with up till now'. In the Italian context in particular, pluralism 'as connected positively to elements of *mass democracy* as already developed in our country ... does not coincide with, but is nonetheless not in contrast to, those democratic processes' so dear to Bobbio.[35]

Even Pietro Ingrao, in his own contribution, spoke of *hegemony in pluralism*: as a consequence of the new arc of anti-capitalist forces deriving from the epochal transformation of the 1920s and 1930s, Communists had to recognise that the influence of such forces in the struggle for socialism 'did not occur in a form of consciousness' appropriate to the workers' movement.[36] It is easy to see in such claims the potential for a *reform of the concept of hegemony* (the articulation and specificity of anti-capitalist forces, the revitalisation of the role of the party, the development of mass democracy), the basic elements of which Gerratana had shown in Gramsci himself, and which – on the level of politics strictly speaking – the Communist Party grasped far too late in that fateful year of 1977, with dire consequences.[37] Moreover, Ingrao saw a constant attention to forms of self-government in Gramsci's work: it fell to Communists, Ingrao claimed, to avoid that the parties flatten out into one, and a loss of their ability to 'understand the new needs which mature in the depths of society'.[38]

Paolo Spriano's intervention contained an extremely transparent reference to contemporary events, which showed above all that there was a *self-critical* dimension of Gramsci in the *Prison Notebooks*, a need 'to overcome the isolation of the working class which had led to its defeat'.[39] That is, in prison Gramsci had tried to correct those errors of leadership committed, according to Spriano,

---

35   G. Vacca in De Giovanni et al 1977, pp. 119 and 125.
36   P. Ingrao in De Giovanni et al 1977, p. 242.
37   I cannot describe here all the social and political events which are evoked by the year 1977 in Italy. It is enough to recall that in this year a deep fracture was finalised between the traditional workers' movement (the Communist Party and the unions) and a vast, heterogeneous young anti-capitalist movement which came to be defined then, in a way which was effective if debatable, as a *second* society (Asor Rosa 1977).
38   P. Ingrao in De Giovanni et al 1977, p. 253.
39   P. Spriano in De Giovanni et al 1977, p. 141.

in 1924–26 (anti-socialism, isolation of the PCd'I, politics of direct confrontation), encompassing everything within the 'insistent exaltation of the *antagonistic autonomy* of the party against all other parties'.[40] After the war of position lasting 30 years – Spriano concluded – it was necessary to finally act on the fact that the contemporary situation was no longer that of Gramsci's era, but rather one 'which requires that the masses relate to the state, within the state, which presents a qualitative difference: there is a process of transformation underway'.[41]

The Frattocchie seminar, of which necessarily only a brief account is provided here, was characterised by the intersection and overlapping of very different levels of discourse. It was not without some divergence: along with that which has already been said, for a long period the differences between the right and left wings in the Communist Party concerned above all the method of understanding the link between theory and politics, their relation to each other within a mutual sphere but with their own specificity, as well as basic judgements on the strategy of the historic compromise. Beyond this, one should also note how the invocation of Gramsci was present above all among that section of Communist leaders and intellectuals who shared an interpretation of political struggle as *the struggle for hegemony* and theories for developing instruments and hypotheses of *transition*, i.e. with a *strong* assimilation of the main categories of Gramscian thought. The scenario of *transition* was widely considered to be a credible one, even if in reality the processes had already begun which were to determine a more moderate development through the 1980s.

4   The Florence Congress

The 'Gramscian year' began with the Frattochie seminar and concluded with the international conference organised by the Istituto Gramsci of Rome – held in Florence in December – on the question of 'Politics and History in Gramsci'. In his opening speech, Nicola Baldoni underlined the difference from the analogous meeting held ten years previously in Cagliari: the arguments of the 1960s (between *historicism* and *structuralism*) and an interpretation of Gramsci that had been trapped in a network of reference points more usually left to 'contemporary culture' had now been left behind. The Florentine convention presented itself instead as a culmination of that direction of research post-1967

---

40   P. Spriano in De Giovanni et al 1977, p. 143.
41   P. Spriano in De Giovanni et al 1977, p. 146.

which, so Badaloni claimed, had 'brought to light the "political question" and more specifically that of the state'.[42] Another speaker, the English historian Eric Hobsbawm, noted how 'the main contribution made by Gramsci to Marxism' lay in 'his original contribution to the field of Marxist political theory'.[43]

The basic idea that characterised the volume of contributions[44] published ahead of the convention was in effect an attempt to provide a reading of the *Notebooks* as the fundamental place for a new 'political science', based on a broad concept of the state and passive revolution, connected to the more traditionally studied concepts of hegemony and the historical bloc. In these circumstances, for example, De Giovanni's contribution began by emphasising the diffusion of the phenomenon of politics and the state, which 'touched directly on the reorganisation of the world of production'.[45] This was not, therefore, the line Bobbio had proposed ten years previously at Cagliari, in an inversion of the classic Marxian analytical couplet: here Gramsci had understood the decreasingly rigid separation of state and civil society; the importance ascribed to the 'superstructure' derived from the new role of politics within the economy and hegemony more generally in society. From the analyses of these real processes 'the new political science' had been born. It was with Gramsci that 'the "internal" character of the contradictions' had begun to be understood:[46] the diffusion of the state in society had changed the relation between state and the masses, making the former the *terrain* of struggle.[47]

Converging with De Giovanni's salient points of analysis, Giuseppe Vacca showed the concatenation of Gramsci's conceptual apparatus, the links that brought together the concepts of passive revolution,[48] war of position and hegemony. Gramsci's distance from the Third Internationalist tradition was attributed above all to his abandonment of the *instrumental* conception of the state: the relation between the state and the ruling class was not linear, and the latter was not a 'subject gifted with organic consciousness'. The 'concrete form of the state' emerges from the specific mode in which, in each individual instance, the hegemonic class has managed 'to organise the entire substance of

---

42 N. Badaloni in Ferri 1977–1979, ii, p. 18.
43 E.J. Hobsbawm in Ferri 1977–1979, ii, p. 37.
44 See the 'printed acts' in Ferri 1977, vol i.
45 B. De Giovanni in Ferri 1977–1979, i, p. 231.
46 B. De Giovanni in Ferri 1977–1979, i, p. 251.
47 B. De Giovanni in Ferri 1977–1979, i, p. 254.
48 The category of 'passive revolution', at the Florence convention, was the subject of many praiseworthy studies, such as the contributions of Buci-Glucksmann, De Felice and Mangoni. Cf. the explanation attempted by Bodei, also at the Florence convention.

the relations between governed and governing'.[49] Hegemony, therefore, is the concrete mode of how every form of state operates. This kind of attention to the specific form of hegemonic constitution (from which derived the importance of intellectuals) also determined the conclusion that the form of the 'workers' state' could not constitute itself except by passing through 'a differentiated process'. This was not a process, therefore, of substituting one instrument for another, political class for political class, but of creating the conditions by which a new ruling class could emerge from the world of production and name itself as such.

I have focussed on this contribution (albeit briefly) not because there were no other equally laudable interpretations from the point of view of the study and understanding of Gramsci,[50] but because the axis of reasoning which I have tried to reconstruct seems very close to the 'spirit of the times', to the problems and dilemmas which were most passionately debated. One needs, therefore, to explain how in theory Communist politics came to be situated entirely on the terrain of the state, and whether this did not also mean reneging on the transformation of social and political relations. The situation of Italian Communists was at that time determined by the contradictions between the politics of *compromise* and *solidarity* with the political forces, and the impulses and hopes of *radical alternatives* which were emerging from the social body. In his own intervention at the convention, Remo Bodei advanced the hypothesis that the full analytical space given over to the category of passive revolution in the 'printed material' reflected the fact that one could sense above all the *limits* of the possibility of 'advancement' open to the workers' movement, and therefore 'the most serious historical and class-based situations', the obstacles, the dangers of regression, 'all those elements which emerge through reflecting on the crisis and different forms of passive revolution'. Passive revolution could also assume, for Bodei, 'the aspect of joint responsibility ... of the organisations of the working class for the mismanagement of a crisis which has become endemic and ungovernable'.[51] The debate in Florence, in effect, not only allowed those preoccupations connected to the dramatic phase of political struggle to become visible, but also showed that too great an emphasis had been laid on the state and its processes of 'state expansion', and not enough on the mediations between the theoretical and political discourses, determining the phenomena of 'statolatry' (Gramsci's term) rather than the 'socialisation of the political'. This seems to be the sense in which Badaloni recalled that 'the

---

49   G. Vacca in Ferri 1977–1979, i, p. 472.
50   Cf. for example the 'printed acts' by Badaloni and Bodei in Ferri 1977–1979, p. i.
51   R. Bodei in Ferri 1977–1979, ii, pp. 229–30.

nucleus of Gramscian reflection lies in a single question: how is it possible, in a historical epoch which seems manifestly to depend on the expansion of the state, to begin the process of its reabsorption into civil society, into the self-government of the masses?'[52] Such contradictions could not be resolved, for Badaloni, except through 'a liberation of the power and responsibility of civil society, a discovery of individual and collective creativity'.[53]

The intervention by Arcangelo Leone de Castris went in the same direction, contesting the fact that one could reduce 'Gramsci's political theory to a science of the universality of political mediation ... reducing the notion of hegemony to that of political hegemony, the universality of political mediations, the absolute rationality of the leadership of statist government'.[54] Claudio Pavone laid out the dangers of combining the Gramscian category of the state with a dehistoricised concept of civil society, forgetting in the processing its 'bourgeois' character, and thus running the risk of distorting Gramsci and utilising him for political operations quite alien to his own intentions.[55] Claudia Mancina recalled how, in reporting 'the debate on Gramsci as it is today, in the contemporary form of communist politics', one can run the risk of making the *political* ends more important than *history*, for example by retrospectively seeing in Gramsci a *contemporary* conscience critical of Stalinism, which in Gramsci could only have been, if anything, embryonic.[56]

This preoccupation with the anachronistic contemporaneity of the debate over Gramsci brought to the surface, therefore, the question of the period's relation to the Sardinian Communist. The *Notebooks* did, as Leonardo Paggi confirmed, provide some 'prefabricated solutions for today; there is, indeed, a quite full awareness of the quality and horizon of the problems'.[57] And even Aldo Tortorella, at the time representative of the Communist Party's cultural wing, brought attention to a 'normative conception of theory',[58] emphasising instead the popular nature of the relation established by the Communist Party with its own tradition. In line with the validity of these concerns, the problem was that of knowing if the key Gramscian categories would help to *interpret* the great change which capitalism was undergoing, those 'entangled problems of the public and private', as Pietro Ingrao put it, 'which stand before us,

---

52   N. Badaloni in Ferri 1977–1979, ii, p. 22.
53   N. Badaloni in Ferri 1977–1979, ii, p. 35.
54   A. Leone de Castris in Ferri 1977–1979, ii, p. 105.
55   C. Pavone in Ferri 1977–1979, ii, p. 112.
56   C. Mancina in Ferri 1977–1979, ii, pp. 154 and 157–58.
57   L. Paggi in Ferri 1977–1979, ii, p. 169.
58   A. Tortorella in Ferri 1977–1979, ii, p. 241.

and which are fundamentally changing the relation between the state and the masses'.[59] Ingrao's response (and that of the whole congress) was affirmative, even if there clearly remained an awareness of the fact that 'the experience of our times is quite different from Gramsci's thought',[60] above all in the conception of the party. Gramsci as a 'theorist of transition', therefore, overlapped with the research and developments of those in the Italian Communist Party who were not content with managing the existing situation, and genuinely feared the spectre of 'passive revolution'. As I have tried to show, there were contrasts and differences in this camp, but also a united vision, a collective concern and a political culture which, despite everything, continued to view Gramsci as an irrevocable point of reference.

5   The Crisis

In this greatest moment of the expansion of Gramscian cultural politics there was, nonetheless, an abrupt turn, the beginning of a sudden crisis destined to undermine the whole edifice. As always, this event was foregrounded in reasons which were both direct and indirect, both specific and general. It is easy to see how in the course of the events of 1977 the political framework was rapidly changing. With 'national solidarity' and the so-called 'politics of sacrifice', the Communists took on shared responsibility for the measures of the economic recession, measures which hit their own social base most of all. What interests us here is that even this 'two phase politics' was accompanied, more or less explicitly, by a particular interpretation of Gramsci, which had the abruptness, but also the steadfastness, of 'popular convictions'. At the beginning of 1978, in a well-known interview conducted by Eugenio Scalfari, Luciano Lama – General Secretary of the largest Italian trade union and member of the Communist Party – claimed that 'the union should propose a politics of sacrifice for the workers', even while acknowledging the fact that 'an economic system does not include independent variables', as the trade union movement of the time considered *salaries and employment* to be, according to Lama.[61] The union, that

---

59   P. Ingrao in Ferri 1977–1979, ii, p. 209.
60   P. Ingrao in Ferri 1977–1979, ii, p. 212.
61   L. Lama in Russo 1978, pp. 22 and 24. This small volume brought together many contributions and interviews with politicians, trade unions and 'opinion makers'. It is worth recording here at least the position of Guido Carli, then president of Confindustria, on the topic of hegemony and pluralism, which shows the breadth of Gramscian themes and terminology, and also that of Bobbio, who explained, with a noteworthy difference of accent

is, gave up its intransigent defence of the interests of salaried workers, opting instead to put their hopes in increasing accumulation, investment and therefore boosting employment. Excluding a true 'change of policy', which Lama explicitly rejected,[62] the union's line nevertheless showed the imprint of a certain reading of the theory of hegemony: the working class first had to lead by entering into power and renouncing its own corporative interests in favour of social alliances. In fact Lama claimed: 'When you have to give up on your own "particular" objectives in favour of noble ones, even while those who are called upon to make such sacrifices do not see the concrete benefits, you rely on an elevated political and class consciousness ... The working class must take the brunt of the national problems'.[63] On which, some days later, Eugenio Scalfari would comment that Lama's position 'represents the working class's correlating obligation for hegemony over the rest of society'.[64]

This reading of the concept of hegemony does not find any real basis in Gramsci: the 'politics of two phases' is an example of a false dialectic, one that does not see how 'each part of the dialectical opposition must seek to be entirely its own self and throw all of its political and moral "resources" into the struggle'.[65] One ought to remember therefore that, in confronting this culture of exaggerated mediation, a gaping hole was left in place of *immediacy*, of the 'everything and now', or the 'needs', or hyper-subjectivism, of desire, of the critique of reason and of a history which unites the different paths of the political and trade union left on the one hand and subjectively *antagonistic* layers (the 'second society', to use Asor Rosa's phrase) on the other. The limit to the Communist understanding of Gramscian culture was first in noticing too little of the real processes which had begun to so profoundly change within society (which demanded at the very least a rapid 'reform' of the concept of hegemony, so as to allow the working classes to not forget its true alliances in the moment in which it began its great numerical and political decline); and in second place in flattening out Gramsci in terms of the political *necessities* of the present moment, cramping his thought within the confines of the 'historic compromise'. There was above all a culture prevalent in the Communist Party – which can be invoked summarily through the slogan 'politics of sacri-

---

from his 1976 intervention, how 'hegemony means to lay claim to a system of values which belong to a group or class which conquers hegemony: there is no reason that these values cannot be those of freedom and pluralism'. Russo 1978, p 184.

62   L. Lama in Russo 1978, p. 28.
63   L. Lama in Russo 1978, pp. 27 and 29–30.
64   E. Scalfari in Russo 1978, p. 33.
65   Gramsci 1975, p. 1768.

fice' – of dealing a strong blow to the Gramscian culture *on the level of common sense*. Still more, the defeat of the Communist Party opened the door to a neo-conservative offensive of a planetary dimension. The working class, defeated on the political field, was now dethroned from the heavens of theory too. The neo-functionalist paradigm of 'complexity' replaced the 'hegemonic clash', the irreducibility of 'differences' sounded a radical critique of any idea of 'social recomposition'. Which is not to set aside, in the decade following 1977, the value laid on Gramscian studies. But the debate around Gramsci would no longer be at the centre of the theoretical and political scene. The terminological abandonment of analysis in terms of 'struggle for hegemony' itself evidenced the rise of a different hegemony. The need to reform the concept of hegemony would be recognised only several years into the crisis and after the near dissolution of Gramscian culture among the masses, as well as within the Communist Party itself.

CHAPTER 8

Ten Years of 'Blackout' (1978–86)

1   The Crisis of Marxism

'A blackout', 'a low season', 'off stage', 'an eclipse': these were some of the metaphors used in 1987 to emphasis Gramsci's ebbing fortunes in Italy between 1978 and 1986. 'Almost no one reads his writings anymore', lamented Paolo Spriano at the beginning of 1986.[1] There was an element of truth in this complaint: in the 1980s, there was no longer any *debate* over Gramsci. After 1977, the Sardinian author had simply stopped being a necessary *site* of confluence and argument for anyone, on the left or otherwise, who wanted to understand the problems of *actual* theory and political culture. Gramsci was no longer the *language*, the metaphor, the 'hegemonic' terrain, at least in Italy – even if elsewhere there were nonetheless, as we will see, important studies of his life and thought. At the end of the 1970s, the failure of the Communist politics of 'national solidarity' and the beginning of the 'crisis of representation' brought a historical period to a close. At the same time, the 'crisis of Marxism'[2] was fed by the obvious crisis in 'real existing socialism'. But the 'crisis of Marxism' was also that of a culture which had proposed a monocentric interpretation of reality: a single subject, the working class, able to 'unify' society, constituting both the 'standpoint' by which to understand it (the point of reference for a full politics of alliances) and the attempt to construct a process of social *recomposition*. If, as many hypothesised, there was no longer a 'centrality of workers', if the 'differences' (whether 'corporativisms', or those processes which rendered society ever more 'complex') no longer allowed any hypotheses of social reunification, what remained of the concept of hegemony? There were new theories of power in fashion, new readings of politics and society – from Weber to Foucault, from Schmitt to Luhmann – which overtook and replaced Gramsci's own. This had a certain weight among intellectuals, disappointed with the outcome of the political conjunction of the 1970s in which so many had been heavily involved, but who had then felt the need to turn their attention to a culture which was *separate* from their previous work. This cultural reflux was bound up not only

---

1   P. Spriano, *Ma è davvero esistito Antonio Gramsci?*, in *l'Unità*, 26 January 1986.
2   Elements for an evaluation of Gramsci's fortunes in relation to the 'crisis of Marxism' are also recounted in the introduction to Santucci 1987.

with the disappointing political defeat but even more so with the new processes of revolutionary information technology and new class composition it brought with it. These were the factors which, together, heralded a 'low season' in Gramsci's fortunes.

This result, it bears repeating, should be understood in terms of Gramsci's *political* fortunes. For however much concern there was from specialised studies and research, the 1980s did not register a real *deficit*. Above all there was the gradual emergence of results deriving from the 'Gerratana edition', on the one hand allowing the clarification of references to the historical, political facts which underlay Gramscian concepts and on the other helping one to follow the *rhythm* of his thought, the 'open' character of his reflections, the multiplicity of readings and interpretations which were made possible, as is always the case with a great author, by the richness of his own reflections and questions, a richness with few equals.

2   Gramsci and 'Organicism'

Liberal democratic and liberal socialist culture took advantage of the 'crisis of Marxism' and Gramscian culture, in which the interpretation of Gramsci was characterised by a *leitmotif* of Gramsci as 'absolutist', 'totalitarian', 'organicist'. Among the protagonists of the debate on the 'crisis of Marxism' in Italy first place was given to Noberto Bobbio. In the 1978 edition of the journal *Belfagor*, he turned to the role of Gramsci in relation to the Marxist theory of the state and transition, asking what theoretical lacuna in Marxism had allowed the emergence of an 'absolutist' end in 'socialist states', thereby assimilating Gramscian strategy (and the theory of hegemony) to the theoretical practical solutions experimented with in the environment of, or beginning with, the Third International. For Bobbio the fundamental problem in Gramsci – a problem which was first and foremost *political* and only then *theoretical* – was the strategy for conquering power. Furthermore, Bobbio added, the question of power and its abuses, of it limits, had not only remained outside the Marxist tradition, but also 'the political and juridical culture of Italy, in the horizon of which Gramsci had been formed'.[3] An acceptable observation if one thinks only of the young Gramsci, but lacking any account of the difference between (to put it in Gramsci's terms) the author who focussed on the insurmountable separation between governed and governing, between intellectuals and masses (a

---

3   N. Bobbio, *Gramsci e la cultura politica italiana*, in *Belfagor*, 1978, issue 5, p. 289.

large part of the 'political and juridical culture of Italy' and especially of the 'elites'), and indeed the author who believed in and struggled for the overcoming of this separation and indeed made it the centre of his entire programme (i.e. *Ordine Nuovo*).

A different angle was taken up by another liberal democratic author, Paulo Bonetti,[4] for whom the relation between Gramsci and liberal culture could be both overturned and brought forward: Gramsci criticised the liberal Italian state for its incompletion and its deep connection to the 'heroic phase' of liberal capitalism, above all the ethical moment necessary to found a new society. The situation of the councils, the centrality of the factory and of the producer was none other than a transfiguration of the liberal idea of the primacy of civil society. For Bonetti, therefore, the mature Gramsci had theorised a society which was politically and culturally *monistic*, totalitarian, characterised by the end of conflicts, an absence of democracy, and even the topic of hegemony had always in truth meant the search for consensus. But all this reasoning seemed to have erroneously arisen from an ideological imagination of an 'original capitalism', entirely focused on morality and *ethos*.

For Massimo Salvadori the fundamental category by which to understand Gramsci was *totality*. Gramsci had considered the revolutionary process as total separation and total recomposition. 'Separation of the revolutionary parts in the old society, anticipating *in nuce* the process of recomposition in a new society by means of a revolutionary struggle'.[5] Marxism, the party and the state had all been present in Gramsci in a totalising fashion. Unlike other socialist critics however, Salvadori did not indicate Gramsci's totalitarianism in order to indirectly criticise Communist politics: he claimed that the 'Eurocommunist' party had already gone far *beyond* Gramsci. Whereas for Gramsci the frame of reference had been the international revolution, the reunification of the 'two paths' (East and West, the war of positions being a simply tactical variation), for the Eurocommunists the revolution of socialism in the West was present in a way entirely autonomous and different from the perspective of the Soviet world. The Eurocommunists, democratic and pluralist, could thus no longer refer back to Gramsci, nor make full use of 'parts' abstracted from the 'whole': the importance of consensus, the critique of party bureaucracy, the confrontation with other philosophies, the nationalisation of struggle. In Salvadori's view, this *distancing* from Gramsci (and from Lenin), as well as the consequent *approximation* to Kautsky, had to be explicit in order to complete the process of the Communist Party's democratisation.

---

4   Bonetti 1980.
5   Salvadori 1978, p. 44.

Silvio Suppa's reflections went in a different direction, dealing with the relation between Lenin and Gramsci,[6] emphasising on one hand the peculiar character of the Sardinian Communist's thought in continuity and discontinuity with the Italian Socialist tradition, and on the other his bond to the international Communist movement. For Suppa, this meant inquiring into the perspectives which lay behind the specific 'historical language' of both Lenin and Gramsci, a language by which they 'shared membership in the epoch of proletarian revolutions and the social subject that brought them into political activity'.[7] Simplistically, the author compared a specific and complex notion of the *political* (which would find its mature and more accurate expression in the *Notebooks*) and the 'war of movement' as a pure imitation of the Soviet model which Gramsci abandoned after the failure of the factory occupations. In Gramsci, the councils were important seeds for the development of the idea of hegemony[8] as well as the 'protagonism of the state'. In the contingencies of the post-War period, nonetheless, the crises of capitalism and the old liberal classes brought these two moments into conjuncture with the search for 'a new form of struggle and organisation'.[9] In Gramsci's political theory, the councils constituted a general response to capitalist crisis, irreducible to a specific fact of the reality of the factory, but instead representing the possibility of 'coagulating other new social occurrences, those necessary for the idea and construction of socialism'.[10]

A more traditionally philosophical reading of Gramsci was provided by Lucio Colletti in the framework of a historical reconstruction of Marxism,[11] subdividing it into categories of 'dialectal materialism' (Plekhanov and Lenin in the wake of Engels, but also Kautsky and Max Adler) and 'Western Marxism', of a Hegelian and historicist derivation (Lukács and Korsch, but also Gramsci). Like Lukács, Colletti noted, Gramsci had criticised Bukharin's 'vulgar Marxism' and his concept of science, itself derived from a model of the natural sciences. For Colletti, Gramsci's philosophical opinions, strongly influenced by Croce, contained a decisive critique of materialism (dialectical and otherwise), science, sociology and common sense. The 'crisis of Marxism' in its epistemological form therefore seemed irrelevant as far as Gramsci was concerned, because ... he had never been a Marxist, but a left idealist.

---

6 Suppa 1979.
7 Suppa 1979, p. 11.
8 Suppa 1979, p. 218.
9 Suppa 1979, p. 16.
10 Suppa 1979, p. 17.
11 Colletti 1979a and Colletti 1979b.

Leszek Kołakowski's contribution was also part of a much fuller reconstruction of the history of Marxism (and more relevant than that proposed by Colletti). Kołakowski's general thesis, indicated by the title of his work – *Main Currents of Marxism: Its Origins, Growth and Dissolution* – had many aspects in common with those arguments advanced by exponents of the new *vogue* for liberal socialism. Kołakowski also emphasised the distance between Gramsci and Lenin: a party 'subordinate' to the class; revolution as a process of the masses and not as 'coup d'etat'. A more profound difference was identified in the philosophy of knowledge: if Marxism were not part of a scientific conception which could be developed *separately* from intellectuals, then the party could not be born or sustained *outside* of the class, nor could it be considered a receptacle of 'scientific socialism'. Gramsci's writings therefore 'could serve as a basis for an alternative model of communism', showing, that is, an 'independent attempt to form a communist ideology and not a mere adaptation of the Leninist formula'.[12]

Franco Sbarberi's work on Gramsci also focussed on those arguments about 'totality' and 'organicism' so precious to the authors already examined above: for Sbarberi, Gramsci had fought for an 'organic', 'integrated and harmonious society'. The young Gramsci had already had a conception which the author defined as 'councilist organicism': the future society would be organised on the basis of a 'great mechanical workshop', and the 'factory as a microcosm of the future city' would be the fulfilment of a 'thirst for totality, a lay religion, a new ethical political morality which Gramsci developed in his early years as a journalist'.[13] In the *Notebooks* this totalising organicism, which had already been present in the early period, was explicitly completed through his conception of a monistic and self-sufficient Marxism, the party and the state. At this point Gramsci's adherence to Lenin had apparently been near total.

3   Prediction and Praxis

If the liberal socialist critics provided a reading of Gramsci designed to emphasise the bonds with a *totalising* Marxist tradition and based on a philosophy of history destined to flow into a 'harmonious society', a contrary interpretation which wanted to make Gramsci into the bearer of an *open* Marxism showed how in the *Notebooks* there was a political science which hinged on the concept

---

12   Kołakowski 2005, Chapter 4. For an extended consideration of Kołakowski's interpretation of Gramsci, see Liguori 1996c.
13   Sbarberi 1986, p. 26.

of 'prediction'. Nicola Badaloni's essay *Gramsci: la filosofia della prassi come previsione* – 'Gramsci: The Philosophy of Praxis as Prediction' – (which appeared in Einaudi's *Storia del marxismo*) offered a 'comprehensive' reconstruction of Gramscian thought, perhaps the most complete among those that came out of the 1980s, stretching from the young period through to the *Notebooks*. In the youthful period the revolutionary process was, for Gramsci (according to Badaloni), 'filled with the intellectual and moral capacities' of the members of the new class 'as both its presupposition and effect'. Such a process, therefore,

> is comprehensible more as the foundation of new principles than as the historical emergence of events. From here derived the appearance (and in part also the reality) of an important idealist argument in which principles exist so as to forge a path and anticipate facts which otherwise remain undetermined.[14]

Predicting *the facts* is thus impossible; even Marx predicted only 'usual moments, the general modes of new formations', not the *exceptional* situations, as was verified in Russia. The 'prediction' of a 'new order' had focussed on the socialising tendency of the working class and the cultural and productive expansion which this allowed. But Gramsci had underestimated the ruling classes' capacity for counter-offensive. After the failure of the factory occupations, he had had less faith in the *inevitable* victory of the producing classes. Badaloni reconstructed the fundamental moments in the evolution of Gramsci's analysis while also insisting on the moments of discontinuity and revision. The broadening of Gramsci's theoretical strategic horizon was recognised in the reconsideration of the new role of intellectuals, which opened up 'a new field of prediction and therefore of action ... Gramsci had found in the positioning of the intellectuals the new strategic line'.[15] The *Notebooks* represented the search not so much for a 'why' of the defeat (analyses which had already been made before, at Lyons and in the essay on the *Southern Question*), but the tactical, strategic hypothesis of reigniting the struggle. The hegemonic ability of the 'new producers' could emerge only if one realised a process not of 'conquest' but of the 'transformation' of the intellectual strata, not for an alliance of 'producers' and 'intellectuals', but for their 'increasing fusion'.[16] If the economy remained 'in the last instance, the determining factor', there could only be a

---

14 Badaloni 1981, p. 253.
15 Badaloni 1981, p. 268.
16 Badaloni 1981, p. 337.

weak predictive capacity for the new role of any 'subjective' and superstructural components and the new combinations of politics and economy which it determined. For this reason, Gramsci's Marxism could be considered, instead, as

> a method of 'prediction' in determinate conditions, some of which are not 'given', but constructed, or able to be constructed, through organisation ... This development is 'predicted' only in as much as it is accompanied by a strong organisation of the will. Left to their own devices, matters can develop other propensities.[17]

There was no space, in this reconstruction, for a philosophy of totalising history, neither for a prefiguration of outcomes nor stages in the course of history. As Gramsci had written, 'only the struggle can be foreseen'.

The concept of 'prediction' had already been dealt with by Claudia Mancina in her essay of 1980. Gramsci had proposed the development of a methodology that jettisoned both idealist exaggerations of the subject and determinism, the latter representing a more dangerous threat within the Communist movement. Again, the starting problem was that of the passage from the structural moment in which the 'relations of force' were expressed in relation to subsequent 'ideological' and 'political' moments. If only ideological forms allowed one to understand the economic conflict and how to fight it, it was significant that this could be developed 'only inasmuch it has been *activated* by subjective forces (i.e. *actors*). That is, when the relation of forces has been developed to its full extent'.[18] The specificity of Mancina's analysis led to a decisively 'morphological' reading of Gramsci, emphasising the non-arbitrary relation between *objective* (or necessary) and *subjective* (or possible) situations:

> There are no historical laws other than *tendencies*: basic directions taken by forces, in which political action can intervene to bend them. And this is not an alien, external intervention, but a potential (a capacity to transform) already included within the arena of forces ... Thus Marx's stable laws are not natural laws, or regularities, but definitions of a dialectic within which subjective activity is a constitutive part ... Politics, therefore, is ... the capacity to make a solution emerge (a synthesis) that was not entirely present before – a possible, rather than neces-

---

17 Badaloni 1981, pp. 335 and 337.
18 Mancina 1980, p. 42.

sary, motion; and to some extent it is unpredictable, in the sense that there is always a difference between the subjective project and objectively attained syntheses.[19]

For Mancina, Gramsci did not reject with this the existence of 'natural' laws in society, but circumscribed the primacy of the moments of the 'balance of forces', that 'structural' relation that constituted the ultimate horizon of political ideological activity, the 'evaluatory criteria of its realism'. The historical process therefore was read as 'the conflictual link – and in this sense, also dialectical – between necessity and possibility. The *play* between these poles represents the locus of class politics'.[20] The balance of forces 'are not *calculable*, because they are always *in play* (which is a game of wills)'. Prediction 'consists in *programming the correct intervention in the game*'.[21]

In an attentive reconstruction of Gramsci's conception of history from the youthful period through to the *Notebooks*, Renato Zangheri insisted on the anti-teleological and anti-fatalist aspect of Gramsci's thought. Zangheri described Gramsci's process as a conquest of a position equidistant between youthful idealistic voluntarism and a form of determinism prevalent in the Marxist tradition (and not absent from Marx himself). In Gramsci 'history and design' opposed one another. 'Human history', wrote Zangheri, 'is not contained in its premises, but established through its dialectic of freedom, breaking every previous constitutive schema'. The fundamental principle on which he based this mode of historical conception, derived from the Marxian *Theses on Feuerbach*, was the dialectic

> of human will, of the sublation of praxis, the transformation of society. Gramsci was thus a theorist well attuned to a historical materialism which situated its problems and resolved their contradictions in the heart of revolutionary praxis, as 'antithesis' and 'beginning', as the 'moment of conquest'.[22]

The category of *praxis* therefore lay at the centre of this reading, in which the difficult Gramscian balance between anti-voluntarism and anti-determinism appeared oriented to take distance above all from the latter factor.

---

19 Mancina 1980, pp. 45–6.
20 Mancina 1980, p. 47.
21 Mancina 1980, pp. 50–1. Also see Mancina 1980b, which focuses on the idea of *materiality* in ideology, read via Althusser as the site of the constitution of the subject.
22 Zangheri 1983, p. 22.

Biagio De Giovanni worked on both 'prediction' and 'praxis' in these years. In an essay from 1981 the author began by restoring the 'Gramscian' party with its legitimacy, i.e. its 'knowledge. The strength of this knowledge lies in *prediction*, in *anticipation*'.[23] There were two meanings of 'prediction' here: (scientific) anticipation and (political) prefiguration, which tended to combine into a single *praxis* which tried to determine a particular outcome of the historical process. 'The party's knowledge of prediction' was understood by De Giovanni in a very strong sense ('the historical execution of prediction'), removing any chance of a philosophy of history simply because the claim – and this was the decisive aspect in Gramsci – of a 'sense of the world' cannot be realised as *laws*, but only through the role which the party manages to carry out in the modern war of position.

In the following years De Giovanni continued his Gramscian reflections above all through the *leitmotiv* of 'praxis' and 'the philosophy of praxis', in an approach that came close to Gentile (and Del Noce), that 'formalist Marxism' which had been the main protagonist of the 1970s. Paraphrasing De Giovanni (according to whom 'Gramsci's Marx was Marx the philosopher'),[24] we might say that De Giovanni's Gramsci was precisely Gramsci the *philosopher*: after the excesses of politicisation of the 1960s and the evident *disappointment* emanating from the sudden historic defeat of the Communist Party and communist culture, De Giovanni's attention to the category of *praxis* was paradoxically a return to philosophy, even if this was a philosophy which had to understand its transformation into the political sphere in order to realise itself. The philosopher of praxis, claimed De Giovanni, had grasped 'how to transform philosophy into politics without in the process forgetting that it is, indeed, philosophy'.[25]

Gramsci was thus torn away from the horizon of a reconceived strategy and the foundation of a political science so as to be, yet again, plunged into the waters of national tradition,[26] in which *discontinuities* were not overlooked (for example, with Labriola) but in which the strongest intermediaries were identified in Croce (explicitly) and Gentile (more surreptitiously, and yet more profoundly, for those who were concerned with the *form* of Gramsci's philosophy). De Giovanni's reading would emerge gradually over the 1980s as the one most emblematic of the new 'philosophical' and 'meta-political' period which would take hold of Gramscian culture for the best part of a decade.

---

23   De Giovanni 1981, p. 53.
24   De Giovanni 1985, p. 26.
25   De Giovanni 1985, p. 12.
26   Also cf. De Giovanni 1983.

4   Intellectuals and Power

Another question repeatedly considered to be central in interpreting Gramsci was the 'question of intellectuals'. Viewing matters from this perspective, and in the framework of a much fuller reconstruction on the subject of 'Marxism and intellectuals' more generally, Giuseppe Vacca reconstructed a comprehensive overview of Gramsci's thought, interpreted as a theory of politics (based on Marx's general theory of history).[27] This was against a line which had shifted entirely homogeneously between Kautsky, Adler and Lukács, and in contradistinction to the *ideological conquest* of intellectuals. Instead, Vacca proposed another 'tradition', one constituted by Labriola and Gramsci. From this he reconstructed an original conception of the state and hegemony: Gramsci had rejected every instrumental conception of the state, describing instead a conception of it as a *process*, 'by which the ruling class ... managed to obtain the active consent of the governed'.[28] The functions of state classes manifest according to the ways in which they split up and organise hegemonic functions in general. Gramsci did not intend intellectuals to be 'conquered' by the party; instead the party provided 'the setting for the *centralisation of various leading and fundamental functions in the development of hegemony* on behalf of the direct producers'.[29] The party was *part* (a decisive one) of the processes of hegemonic development. The history of parties, for Vacca, returned to the realm of the history of hegemonic form and had to be *translated back into* the history of intellectual groups, the state and management. The question of the party needed to be re-understood and reabsorbed into that of intellectuals. The problem of the relation between socialism and the intellectual was resolved (in Gramsci) through the ways in which the workers' movement developed their own hegemony. The decisive political problem was 'the organisation of expertise' which takes place within the state, alongside the relations in which one struggles Gramsci went along with this perspective – this was at the basis of his approach to the entire 'Marxist tradition'. The new scientific model had to begin from the understanding that the natural scientific model could not be transposed into the sphere of social history. The philosophy of knowledge and political theory could not continue to hinge on the issue of 'prediction', inasmuch as the social sciences do not identify 'causal links' between occurrences, allowing the prediction of successive occurrences.

---

27   Vacca 1985 (republished in *Critica marxista* from 1983).
28   Gramsci 1975, p. 1765.
29   Vacca 1985, p. 122.

Instead, they identify *tendencies* that function within the historical process: 'regular tendencies' define the limits in which political action can effectively operate:

> The awareness of the rules and dynamics of a historically determined social system (namely the *necessities* imposed by *current* dynamics) delimit the realm in which well-defined collective ends become *possibilities*.[30]

In 1984 Leonardo Paggi brought out the 'second volume' of his intellectual biography of Gramsci,[31] which reflected and incorporated various aspects of the debate on the 'crisis of Marxism': how the question central to the reflections of the left, in the 1980s, ceased to be that of *revolution* and became instead the forms of and limits to *power*. Thus the passage of the period of transition from Gramsci's youthful phase of *Ordine Nuovo* (which lay at the centre of Paggi's first volume) to the Gramsci of the Moscow trip and the struggle for the forming of a new leading Communist group was accompanied by a shift in his thinking, from the former question to the latter. Paggi argued that during his Moscow trip Gramsci had been deeply influenced by the leading group of the International and the Bolshevik party, through the Fourth Congress of the Comintern, the last to be held under Lenin's leadership (this was the Congress of the 'united front' and of the stabilisation of capitalism). More generally, the influence of the late Lenin was particularly decisive for Gramsci, who insisted on the inability of the October Revolution to be repeated and the problems of the combination of forces and consensus (after Krondstadt), which gave sustenance to the argument on hegemony. Gramsci matured within this complex experience (the problems of power in the USSR *after* the revolution), leading to his overcoming both a Bordigist influence and providing the underlying logic of the politics of *Ordine Nuovo*. On the other hand, in the following period (Gramsci was in Vienna from 1923), he not only rethought the Bolshevik experience but also reflected on the victory of Fascism in Italy, going *beyond* Lenin (according to Paggi), and indeed attributing the label of 'Leninism' to thoughts and positions which were substantially post-Leninist, not only in their conception of the party but also in the theory of the balance of forces, going to the very heart of political science.

---

30   Vacca 1985, p. 126.
31   Cf. Paggi 1984. The first part of Paggi's research came out under the title *Gramsci e il moderno principe. I. Nella crisi del socialismo italiano*.

As for activity associated with the *Ordine Nuovo*, Paggi emphasised both the deep revision of some of its principles (the role of the superstructure, the new conception of the intellectual as organiser), and the permanence of other *constants*, brought together through the term 'Sorelism', a term which (opposed to the other 'Leninist' factors) denoted nevertheless more a theoretical category located within Gramsci's conceptual systems than a point of reference to the French thinker. Through it, he wanted to bring attention to the element of 'the refusal of delegation' by the 'producing class', the conviction that the class could and had to express a mode of political activity alternative to that of the bourgeoisie (and the Second International). What was stressed in Gramsci, for Paggi, was an unresolved oscillation between Lenin and Sorel, between *political science* and *the critique of politics*. This also indicated many of the *contemporary* aspects of Gramsci's thought, emphasising central questions for the debate of those years: the complexity of power, the search for consensus, the impossibility for the horizons of human liberation to be exhausted within the political sphere.

5   Interpretations of Hegemony

Alongside the question of how to manage Gramsci's 'legacy', another recurrent argument around his interpretation focused on the sources, that is, on the process of the formation of his conceptual instruments. To begin with there was Perry Anderson's book,[32] which essentially pivoted on an examination of the concept of hegemony, whose genesis the author reconstructed from the Russian left at the end of the nineteenth century and then in the context of the Bolsheviks and the Comintern. Originally used to designate the role of the working class within bourgeois revolution, the term, with one of those Gramscian 'semantic displacements' which Anderson emphasised, was used in the *Notebooks* with reference to the ruling class and, still more, with a 'powerful cultural emphasis'. Gramsci, in the end, was not so much interested in the 'politics of alliances' of the proletariat as much as the 'structures of bourgeois power in the West'.

---

32   See Anderson 1977. The Italian title – *Ambiguità di Gramsci* (1978) – had a slightly different meaning from the original 'Antinomies of Antonio Gramsci'. For a historical philological reconstruction of the term and concept of hegemony (including in Gramsci), see Vivanti 1978. For the meanings which the term assumed in the *Notebooks*, see G. Cospito, *Egemonia* in Liguori and Voza 2009.

Anderson reconstructed various uses which Gramsci made of the concept of hegemony in the *Notebooks*, his employment of analogies and juxtapositions with other categories, the use of the categories of the state and civil society, of 'war of position' and 'war of manoeuvre', of 'East' and 'West', etc. Starting from those terminological points of interest, of which there are many, it should be said however that Anderson never established a positive relation with Gramscian texts, remaining a little *to one side* of all the analytical and strategic innovations of the *Notebook*: the passage from East to West, the enlarged concept of the state, the *methodological* character of the separation between state and civil society were not included because Anderson, in the end, was not convinced that 'October', that type of revolution which represented a *break*, was so far off and could not be repeated. The book became therefore an examination of whether Gramsci was a revolutionary or a left reformist; in the end the Sardinian communist had 'failed' because he believed (at least, Anderson claimed he believed) that the essence of bourgeois power lay in its cultural supremacy, which meant that the working class could take up the leadership of society without conquering and transforming the state. In this the 'conquest of the state' meant, for Anderson, 'insurrection'. He thus gives the impression of always remaining to one side of Gramsci and the Gramscian overcoming of the instrumental conception of the state.[33]

Turning to the theme of hegemony and the problem of 'sources', one of the more original pieces of research was Franco Lo Piparo's *Lingua intelletttuali egemonia in Gramsci (Language, Intellectuals and Hegemony in Gramsci)*. For Lo Piparo, Gramsci's sources were not to be found either in Marx nor Lenin, but in the linguistic studies undertaken during his 'university apprenticeship'. Indeed, the study of language was one of many aspects to the young Gramsci's thought, the originality of which owed much to this study of comparative philology, as was claimed by Tullio De Mauro in his *Preface* to Lo Piparo's volume, in which he claimed that 'without reflection on the nature and function of language, the entire structure of Gramscian theory could not have been built, and the central notion of "hegemony" would not have had its particular physiognomy, indeed, perhaps it would never have been formed'.[34] Lo Piparo reconstructed the argument of Gramsci's teacher, the glottologist Bartoli, against the naturalistic, fatalist, determinist materialism of Neo-grammatics, according to which linguistic changes are found within physiological changes; i.e. against a mechanical mode of thought by which 'historical processes are determined and

---

[33] For an accurate argument against Anderson's thesis, see G. Francioni's essay *Egemonia, società civile, Stato* in Francioni 1984.

[34] T. De Mauro, *Preface* to Lo Piparo 1979, p. v.

guided by laws independent of will and the conscious and organised intervention of men'.³⁵ Gramsci's anti-determinism was thus born in the arena of Bartoli's struggle against Neo-grammatic positivism. The young Sardinian would also be influenced by another thesis from philology, that of 'linguistic consensus', according to which languages could be extended beyond their original confines thanks not to a 'dominant politics', but to a 'spontaneous process' of the population, which they possessed only if the new language was the means of transmission for a civilisation possessing 'spiritual superiority'.³⁶ Lo Piparo claimed, therefore, that if it were true that before 1924 the terms 'hegemony' meant in Gramsci above all 'supremacy' and 'dominion', the new meaning of the term was already present in the preceding relation to linguistic terminology of 'prestige' (in the linguistics of the second half of the nineteenth century, 'prestige', 'hegemony' and 'dictatorship' were all semantically equivalent terms). The young Gramsci used the term 'prestige' in his writings as a functional part of the same semantic area as 'hegemony': one term constituted the terminological precedent of the other. Here therefore the question of language was not, for Lo Piparo, one of many present in Gramsci (even if these were all bound together, in the mature reflections, to that of intellectuals and the state): rather, there was a unique conceptual chain which connected language, culture, intellectuals, nations and state. For Lo Piparo, the history of language, in Gramsci, brought the hegemony of an intellectual strata and the processes of state formation into one whole.

Giuseppe Prestipino provided an interpretation of the concept of hegemony which did not rely on any argument about 'sources', in a book which helped bring focus to an important juncture in Italian communist thought.³⁷ The place of hegemony, claimed Prestipino, is the state, but the terrain on which the hegemonic party acts is also civil society. Hegemony, that is, represents the capacity demonstrated not by a class as such, 'but a class ... in the process of becoming the state, the ability to create a maximum level of consensus in the arena of civil society, within the necessary constructions of the law'.³⁸ Hegemony, therefore, is a constraint supported by consensus, 'the functional relation between the state and civil society'. This interpretation of the concept of hegemony relied

---

35 Lo Piparo 1979, p. 80.
36 Lo Piparo 1979, p. 91.
37 Cf. Prestipino 1986. It is also worth nothing Prestipino 1979, which nonetheless cannot be examined here because, more than an intepretative contribution, it was an attempt to plunge the depths of Gramsci's theoretical science, beyond Marx – i.e. as that author wrote, 'to propose Marxist research without the safety belt of the classic reinterpretations'.
38 Prestipino 1986, pp. 41–2.

on the 'twin levels' present in the political institutions of the West: state and civil society. If hegemony seemed to be the relation between these two levels of politics, Prestipino concluded (aware that these conclusions were not explicit in Gramsci) then hegemony and pluralism were not incompatible: pluralism was simply civil society's mode of existence.

6   In the 'Factory' of the Notebooks

The investigative works which we have examined above were the first results of the archaeological activity made possible thanks to the new critical edition of the *Notebooks*. The edition also allowed for a deeper study of Gramsci's working method and the problems which this had for his interpreters. For example, in an article from 1987, Gerratana asks if there was

> something in Gramsci's *forma mentis* ... something particular to the internal structure of his prison work, which meant that it was necessarily *incomplete*, in a strong sense of the term ... I think we can say that indeed there was, if we think about the dialogical nature of his philosophical mentality.[39]

Gramsci, in fact, spoke explicitly about 'a new kind of philosophy', of a 'democratic philosophy', convinced of the necessity of a *reciprocal* influence between the self and 'cultural environment' in which one acted. He was thus a theorist who desired a dialogue but was constrained into a monologue. The incompleteness of the *Notebooks*, Gerratana hypothesised, was therefore perhaps functional 'for a future meeting with a desired interlocutor', as Gramsci warned, but this went along with the potential for new research and new interpretative instruments, bringing original conclusions to the surface.

Attilio Monasta began his own work on the basis of this new edition of the *Notebooks*,[40] criticising Platone and Togliatti's previous edition not so much for its censorship (which was of a form in keeping with their historical period) but rather for the thematic subdivisions and disciplinary hierarchy imposed through the thematic arrangement of the publication: from philosophy to political history through to literature and art. Monasta studied how the *Notebooks* had been cut up and stuck together again in the first edition, through an invest-

---

39   Gerratana 1987, p. 11.
40   Cf. Monasta 1985.

igation into the recurrence of three key words or concepts: intellectuals, hegemony, education. His result was an active denial of the *Notebooks*' fragmentation and a recognition instead of their fundamental coherence as analyses of the role of the intellect, the critique of the traditional function of intellectuals and the proposal for a new kind of intellectual.

Michele Ciliberto also made a very particular use of the new possibilities offered by the 'Gerratana' edition, analysing moments of a process of *rewriting*, as evidenced by many of the notes. The author carried out a lexicographical analysis, emphasising the important substitutions which frequently occurred between the first and second versions. For example, if in one note Gramsci had emphasised the link between Hegel and Marx, in rewriting he emphasised the autonomy of Marxism both from Hegelianism and from Neo-idealism. Ciliberto observed that around 1930 Gramsci changed his attitude to the cultural tradition then prevalent in Italy: 'The rethinking of Hegel's influence on the genesis of practical philosophy belongs definitively to the past of Croce and Gentile'.[41] Such a concept of 'practical philosophy' was, the author claimed, the fruit of Labriola's own studies, but was also there in relation to the new reading of the politics of the state which emerged in the 1930s. In the second version, for example, Gramsci had reconstructed the bond between Hegel and Marx: 'Marxism' and 'the philosophy of history' were substituted for 'practical philosophy' and 'the history of philosophy', because the first two expressions indicated two 'closed' conceptions of Hegel and Marx's doctrines, 'revealing an undervaluation and lack of understanding of politics'. This labour of rewriting in the *Notebooks* was also connected to the politics of the 'turn', which Gramsci criticised. From that point on, he had developed the need for a less schematic approach, one more capable of finding alliances. The theme of *praxis*, of 'doing politics', and the necessity of alliances (with anti-Fascist parties) was accompanied, according to Ciliberto's hypothesis, by a critique of their cultural tradition, partly to safeguard the 'diversity' among Communists themselves. As well as the political necessity of alliances, Gramsci also stressed the political strategic independence of Communists and therefore emphasised a critical rethinking of the bourgeois cultural tradition, from Vico to Croce. In the end, for Ciliberto, those semantic variations which Gramsci introduced in the course of rewriting his work (those which Gerratana had called the 'C Texts') were not stylistic but rather theoretical and political choices, demonstrating processes of development within the conceptual universe of the *Notebooks*.

---

41   Ciliberto 1982, p. 273.

It is easy to see how the 'critical edition' of Gramsci's prison writings gave rise to a series of studies based on a very precise examination of the entries, of their close reciprocal relation and the historical developments by which Gramsci continued to reflect on and with respect to which he came to modify some of his ideas. This kind of research meant that every entry in the *Notebooks* needed to be dated with still greater precision. Gianni Francioni had already pointed out this necessity from 1977 onwards,[42] and in a book from 1984 stressed the insufficiency of the chronological criteria in the 'critical edition'. The numbering of the *Notebooks*, in fact, had essentially been based on a chronological sequence that ran from the moment in which each notebook was *begun*, excluding any exact dating of many of the notes contained therein – *in primis* those in the notebook of 'miscellaneous notes' – given the fact that Gramsci often worked on more than one notebook at a time when in prison, or went back to fill up spaces which he had previously left blank.[43] Although contesting some of Gerratana's choices, Francioni recognised that 'the criteria adopted in the critical edition seem substantially correct'. He sustained nonetheless that, despite the best editorial intentions, Gramsci's text had not been reproduced as Gramsci had written it. Recognising the impossibility of '"splitting up" the composite materials of the notebooks in order to decompose the notes in individual manuscripts and then recompose them into a perfect montage arranged in the chronological order in which Gramsci composed them in the gradual process of writing up',[44] Francioni proposed instead 'a kind of map that would allow the reader to orient themselves more easily within the labyrinth of the *Prison Notebooks*', in relation to Gerratana's reproduction of the manuscripts.[45] In the end, he proposed a critical examination of 'the Gerratana edition', with the hypothesis (and in turn this too was to be critically examined) of further corrections and the inclusion of a chronology of the prison notes on the basis of a historical-philological archaeology. At the beginning of the 1990s, as we will see, these questions were raised yet again, with some proposals that went in a radically different direction.

---

42 Cf. Francioni 1984.
43 Also now see Francioni's essay *Come lavorava Gramsci*, in Gramsci 2009, p. i.
44 Francioni 1984, p. 21. It is interesting to note how the metaphors chosen by Francioni and Ciliberto as titles for their works would converge on similar visual analogies: *officina* (workshop) and *fabbrica* (factory).
45 Francioni 1984, p. 21.

7   Gramsci, Religion, Catholicism

A significant number of the interpretations from this period can be encapsulated under the heading 'Gramsci and the Catholics' or, to provide a fuller sense of the question, 'Gramsci and religion'. After the first establishment of post-War positions, there were many contribution in the 1960s which dealt with this perspective in a variety of ways: from Giorgio Nadone's book (about which we have already spoken)[46] to Hugues Portelli's work on the issue,[47] or the monograph by Francesco Saverio Festa[48] – all the way to some of the speeches and interventions at the Florence conference.[49] There was thus no novelty in the fact that the world of Catholicism was paying attention to Gramsci, or to religious phenomena in relation to Gramsci more generally. In the years between 1978 and 1987, nevertheless, there were numerous contributions from a wide range of voices, taking interpretative and thematic positions of which only some can be recounted here. First among these, however, was the much-read interpretative contribution by the Catholic traditionalist philosopher Augusto Del Noce, without doubt the contribution destined to wield the broadest influence among all the Catholic interpretations.

Del Noce advanced his interpretation in the context of his thesis about the 'suicide of the revolution', a negative, destructive moment for traditional values, without any creation of a positive new order; for him, revolution meant only 'a collapse back into the old order, but now completely deconsecrated'.[50] The revolution which killed itself was therefore, for Del Noce, one that stalled at the first moment of *contestation*, unable to produce anything but *nihilism*. There were two elements of Gramscian interpretation which the Catholic philosopher proposed: the link between Gentile and Gramsci, and the Gramscian conception of religion. Long ignored by critics, with few exceptions,[51] – above all for *political* reasons, but not these reasons alone[52] – the influence of Gentile

---

46   See above, pp. 292 onwards (from around note 41 of this chapter).
47   Portelli 1976.
48   Festa 1976.
49   Among the 'printed acts' see those of G. de Rosa and G. Galasso, and among the intervention see those by G. Baget Bozzo, E. Fattorini and R. Orfei.
50   Del Noce 1978, p. 6. Beyond the *Introduction*, the most interesting part of the book are the chapters on *Gentile e Gramsci* [1975] and *Gramsci, o il suicidio della rivoluzione*. On Del Noce also see Serra 1995.
51   See M. Tronti in Caracciolo and Scalia 1959, and Orfei 1965.
52   Del Noce himself noted how the *Notebooks* lacked an 'anti-Gentile' even though Gramsci had claimed that an 'anti-Croce' could not but take heed of the philosopher of 'actual idealism'.

on Gramsci had been increasingly invoked from the 1970s onwards. In this sense (second only to Del Noce's study examined below), Giancarlo Bergami's book on *Il giovane Gramsci e il marxismo* – 'The Young Gramsci and Marxism' – was pioneering.[53] But the thesis of Gentile's profound influence over Gramsci came from Del Noce's reconstruction of a theoretical tradition which derived from Gentile and was articulated by Mussolini, Gobetti and Gramsci alike, manifesting a substantial continuity, according to the author, between Fascism and anti-Fascism. For Del Noce, Gramsci had supported the possibility of a return from Croce to Marx by starting from the idea that Croce's philosophy was none other than an attempt to translate Marxism into a speculative philosophy. But the philosophy by which Croce had attempted this 'translation' was not that of Marx but of another 'philosophy of praxis', i.e. Gentile. Gramsci, searching for the Marx in Croce, had (without recognising it) stumbled across Gentile, despite the important historical and logical place which Gentile's philosophy had in relation to Crocean philosophy.[54]

If on the one hand Del Noce brought Gramsci and Gentile together, on the other he focussed on the critique which Gramsci advanced both of Croce and Gentile, with respect above all to the link between religion and philosophy.[55] Del Noce argued that for Gramsci both of the neo-Idealist philosophers had the flaw of having harboured the idea of religion as a philosophy of the masses, an idea which implied the separation of intellectuals from the masses and which, for the Catholic thinker, relied essentially on the division of classes within society ('division' in the sense of a medieval 'organic society'). Incorporating the 'experience of his younger thought' into the *Notebooks*, and influenced by his reading of Croce's *Storia d'Europa*,[56] Gramsci proposed instead the absolute negation of transcendental religion. The task of Marxism was to substitute religion with a holistic secularism, until then restricted to a bourgeois elite, thus restoring the organic unity between intellectuals and the masses. The destruction of religion for Gramsci, according to Del Noce, had to come about through historicism, 'unveiling' religion as a historical residue. This differed from Marx, because for Gramsci the disappearance of religion was a condition, not a consequence, of a future classless society. Del Noce claimed: '[Gramsci's] total break with Christianity is not therefore scientific but religious: communism is

---

53 Bergami 1977, in which the author nonetheless circumscribed the influence of Gentile on Gramsci's early years.
54 Del Noce 1978, p. 156. For a critique of this interpretation of the bond between Gramsci and Gentile, see Losurdo 1990.
55 Del Noce 1978, p. 310.
56 Del Noce 1978, p. 176.

the reaffirmation of religion in an already entirely secularised world'.[57] In this *radical Croceism*, there was therefore a moment of real distance from the contemporary situation and the relation between religion and philosophy. Gramsci's communism, for Del Noce (which was in turn influenced by the opinions of Bordiga and the 'Bordigians', Riechers and Perlini) could not truly overcome the 'bourgeois world', but only 'complete it', transforming revolution into modernisation, 'as the complete disassociation of the bourgeois spirit from Christianity',[58] that is, the completion of secularisation. This too was a 'suicide of the revolution', the renunciation of the possibility that a new world can replace the old one.

Nor did Del Noce spare Gramsci the accusation of 'totalitarianism'. Such an idea was connected to the 'total' revolution: the passage of a society (founded on a theological conception, whether transcendent or immanent) to a completely secularised version meant the transition from one *totality* to another. Gramsci's totalitarianism, therefore, derived from his wanting to substitute one 'religion' for another. At this point, however, Del Noce's discourse risked being intrinsically contradictory. On the one hand, the totalitarianism inherent in revolutionary action did not seem to move in the direction of the process of that desacralisation of the modern world which concerned him so much, because in searching to substitute one religion for another Gramsci had also tried to restore the 'organic world' which the bourgeoisie had destroyed. On the other hand, Gramsci was part of the movement for the 'suicide of the revolution', not so much breaking with the bourgeois world but cooperating with it and furthering its work of desacralisation.

Del Noce's interpretation of Gramsci was in many ways erroneous, starting with his interpretation of the *Notebooks* as an example of 'actualism': not of the *identity* between theory and praxis as Gramsci quite clearly said, but of *unity*; his discourse developed not on the level of philological metaphysics, but political history – in the end, two entirely different set of problems.

Furthermore, there was a certain confusion regarding Gramsci's 'new faith', in reality an opposition to determinism precisely due to its implication of 'fidelity', a warning against the danger of any form of 'faith' in Marxism beyond a necessary initial phase. The Catholic philosopher's interpretation of Gramsci, therefore, seems to be wholly overestimated. There is another point of interest in his discourse however: in reality Del Noce, in speaking about Gramsci, was speaking about the political cultural processes of Republican Italy and in par-

---

57   Del Noce 1978, p. 181.
58   Del Noce 1978, p. 321.

ticular those of the 1960s and 1970s. Del Noce defined *contestation* (an eminently 1960s term) as the 'transforming of revolution into dissolution'.[59] One can see that the philosopher's elaboration was a reply to the upheaval experienced by the traditional cultural order culminating in 1968, read here as a process of definitive *modernisation* of Italian society. The Gramscian (or Togliattian) strategy of 'revolution by erosion' (or 'revolution without revolution', as Del Noce repeated, citing the left critique of Gramsci which had polemically thus renamed the theory of the war of position and the struggle for hegemony)[60] seemed to him at the time an idea destined to be defeated, even self-defeating: a resounding case of 'passive revolution'.[61] The philosophy of praxis thus became, in a Bordigist sense, the genetic flaw dragging down the Communist Party, the basic element undermining any possibility of constructing an effective alternative to bourgeois society. But this questionable idea, albeit worth discussion, really has more to do with the history of Italian Communism than of Gramsci.

The accusation of 'totalitarianism', of 'the totalitarian conception of politics', particularly in reference to the 'modern Prince', was also levelled against Gramsci by a group of critics 'deriving from the Catholic world', who shared a 'love for democracy as a firm guarantee of the fundamental rights of human beings'.[62] These were the authors of two volumes edited by Virgilio Melchiorre, Carmelo Vigna and Gabriele De Rosa, whose rich writings dealt with many Gramscian issues. Melchiorre's work was particularly useful for reconstructing – even if from a critical standpoint – the Gramscian conception of religion and for establishing a profitable confrontation with it. Starting with Croce, Gramsci had considered religion a 'necessity', an ideology which expressed real human needs but in a 'childish' way. Gramsci had differed from Croce, however, by expressing doubts about the possibility of overcoming such mythical forms of identity consciousness without making recourse to a new immanent 'faith', basing himself on Sorel's thought. Melchiorre's reasoning, therefore, allowed him to explain Gramsci's elaboration without returning to that easy method of reading Gramsci as 'totalitarian', instead deepening the discourse on the materialist conception of ideology which Gramsci developed by expanding on Sorel.

Another moment of interest was Melchiorre's explanation of the reasons for which Gramsci opposed religious conceptions. These he traced to the fact that fundamentally every religion had 'a dualist conception of reality', from which

---

59   Del Noce 1978, p. 186.
60   See above, p. 185. around Chapter 5, fn. 39.
61   Del Noce 1978, pp. 189–90.
62   Melchiorre et al 1979, i, p. 11.

derived the claim of 'the objectivity of the external world'.[63] It was not, for the author, that Gramsci denied the existence of another reality beyond that of man, but that he discounted the existence of an 'objective world'; he rejected the possibility of speaking 'of a stand-alone reality', beyond any intersubjective formulation, because the acceptance of such a gnoseological dualism, which permeates common sense, came for him to be identified as 'the legitimation of man's passive insurmountably', the ultimate basis of every ideology of the *status quo*. The recourse to these gnoseological references allowed Melchiorre to find an 'opening' in the confrontation with Gramscian ideas, by historicising them: Gramsci had confronted a profoundly 'Hellenised' model of Christian religion, i.e., a dualistic one. In confronting the 'more recent theological conscience, which has distanced itself from every Hellenistic dualism, emphasising instead the Biblical God of historical engagement',[64] one could share Gramsci's critique inasmuch as it took aim at an inadequate form of religiosity – indeed, his critique was a means to search for a more authentic form. (Nonetheless, from Gramsci's immanentist point of view, it is difficult to speak of that 'participatory transcendence' to which some proponents of contemporary theological thought refer).

The most exhaustive treatment of the argument came from Tommaso La Rocca's book *Gramsci e la religione*, which attempted to conduct an overview and interpretation of Gramsci's many discussions of religion, including in the period preceding his imprisonment. Gramsci's ideological intransigence against religion, La Rocca claimed, related only to some (albeit central) aspects of Catholic doctrine – transcendence, dualism, the realist conception of consciousness – while some positive elements were grasped in their role in the Reformation in relation to the birth of capitalism and more generally to the historical *necessity* of religious discourse. Central for this understanding of Gramscian analysis of relation was the category of 'common sense', an analysis with which the author agreed. Marxism was seen as the final result of a general process of replacing Christianity with immanence and secularism. Marxism, La Rocca claimed, was for Gramsci the inheritance of the Reformation, which in turn was seen as the culmination of a process, a *red thread* which also included Early Christianity and heretical movements. Through this thread of Christianity, Gramsci 'had not disdained from naming the "good sense" of Christianity,

---

63　On this, see Di Meo 1986, pp. 171 onwards, which notes that, in relation to the problem of 'real objectivity', Gramsci had argued not only against Bukharin's *Essay* but also the philosophical realism advanced by neo-Thomism. Cf. the writing discussed below, on this theme, by Cesare Luporini.

64　Melchiorre et al 1979, pp. 125–26.

its "clear nucleus of common sense which is worthy of development and coherent unification".[65] An inheritance, therefore, which like neo-Idealism could be seen as 'a historical process still in motion, by which to produce a new, necessary philosophical and cultural synthesis'.[66]

The reference to the category of 'common sense' had already been made central in an essay by Cesare Luporini from 1979.[67] It proposed that Gramsci was interested in religion as a 'social ideology', in the active and unifying role which it had for the *subjectivity* of groups and social movements, and that Gramsci was interested in Catholicism above all for its attempt to not separate 'intellectuals' from 'the normal people'. Furthermore, he claimed that for Gramsci, while the Church tended to perpetuate such a distinction, Marxism instead had to bring a superior conception of life to 'the normal people'. The Church wanted to keep normal people within the bounds of 'common sense': it was 'common sense' and not religion which was the 'enemy' that had to be fought (even if religion was always seen as an element of common sense.) Luporini clarified how Gramsci's basic aversion to the Judaeo-Christian creationist tradition was, as we have seen, an aversion to the 'naïve realism' of popular common sense, and how such opposition, in the spheres of gnoseology and epistemology, also had a side connected directly to Marxism and the formation of a collective will. This could be seen in the conception of a Christian tradition as reconstructed through the 'system' which Bukharin provided for Marxism, contributing to a dangerous fatalism, a *faith* in the unchangeable future of Socialism, useful in historical moments of defence but a serious obstacle when the revolutionary class had to pose itself the task of becoming hegemonic and therefore of leaving behind every attitude of Messianic expectation. On this basis, among others, Luporini built a synthetic but magisterial reconstruction of many aspects of 'the religious question' in Gramsci, and the interconnections which together signalled another point in Gramsci's development in the *Notebooks*, which Luporini originally identified as 'Gramsci's most profound moment of confrontation and clash with religion'. Gramsci wrote:

> From the 'philosophical' point of view, what is unsatisfactory in Catholicism is that fact that, in spite of everything, it insists on putting the cause

---

65 La Rocca 1981, p. 85.
66 I cannot focus here on some of the works relating to the theme of 'Gramsci, religion, Catholics' which would be interesting to analyse properly. But I recommend in particular the article by V. Fagone in *La civiltà cattolica*, 1978, issues 3066, 3074 and 3079, Pierini 1978 and Vinco 1983. I also refer the reader to Liguori 1987.
67 Luporini 1979.

of evil in the individual man himself, or in other word that it conceives of man as a defined and limited individual. It could be said of all hitherto existing philosophies that they reproduce this position of Catholicism, that they conceive of man as an individual limited to his individuality and of the spirit as being this individuality. It is on this point that it is necessary to reform the concept of man.[68]

Behind this argument on the 'cause of evil' therefore was that of the conception of man, in whom, for Gramsci, society was 'necessarily implicated'. As Luporini explained, 'individuality is not dissolved but included as "a central knot" of complex relations ("other men", "nature"), both active and passive, obligatory and wilful, systematically intertwined on the one hand, historically rooted on the other'.[69] It was in these terms that Gramsci was first and foremost opposed to religion – indeed, to all religions – and in which he struggled for intellectual and moral reform.

---

[68] Gramsci 1965, pp. 1344–5; English translation in Gramsci 1971, p. 353.
[69] Luporini 1979, p. 84.

CHAPTER 9

Between Politics and Philology (1987–96)

1 Gramsci and the Communist Party in 1987

In 1987, the recurrence of a 'Gramscian year' (by this point a tradition) provided Italy with a certain *contradictory* view of the author of the *Notebooks*, cutting across the Communist Party and the intellectuals connected to it. This tradition reflected the diversification in ideas and politics then current among Italian communists, rarely in an explicit form, but nonetheless now close to exploding in the final crisis of 1989. Within the Communist Party there were therefore those who worked to make the 50th anniversary of Gramscianism an occasion to relaunch Gramsci and his historical legacy in the Party, though without neglecting the necessity of profoundly reforming it. There were others, indeed, as we will see, who were content to make Gramsci into a residue of the past, an aspect which belonged to a historical moment that had already been left behind.

Among these initiatives we ought to recall the intervention by Alessandro Natta, Secretary of the Communist Party, who inaugurated the 'Gramscian year', and whose talk stands out for its strongly political tone.[1] Natta highlighted how even in the context of so many new factors, Italian communists had to remember the 'lessons' of Gramsci, emphasising above all the self-critical capacity of the Communist Party and its knowledge of how to change along with reality itself. Natta placed Gramsci at the beginning of a 'varied tradition' of communism, especially in relation to Leninism:[2] in relation to Gramsci the party had effectively taken an ulterior path, above all in terms of the conception of the party itself. But the theory of hegemony was placed in a direct relation to the principal character of Italian communism, its formation of a 'democratic communism' entirely *alternative* to the project of the Third International. 'There is no contradiction between hegemony and democracy, but the understanding of how one can establish a direction of the state and a politics of a fuller consensus ... the perspective of hegemony understands that the socialist transformation is democratic, or it is no transformation at all'.[3] One sees here a *strong* vindication of the Gramscian legacy in the context of the substantial

---

1 Cf. Natta 1987.
2 Natta 1987, p. 19.
3 Natta 1987, p. 24.

novelty of the Communist Party's political choices, not always recognisable in other interventions even when they were aimed at strengthening Gramsci's legacy.

Another of the more interesting projects within the communist sphere was the monographic issue dedicated to Gramsci by *Jonas*, the journal published the FGCI, the Party's youth organisation, the spirit of which was best represented by Mario Tronti's article. Tronti wrote against the 'reduction of politics to small manoeuvres and petty bartering, against spectacle and illusion, against market and exchange, against the defence of single or group interests, rather than a politics of great social forces'[4] – that is, against all the years of the *low tide*, of the distancing from politics and the triumph of the *spirit of capitalism*, invoking Gramsci's 'hatred of the indifferent'. Tronti's rediscovery of Gramsci was not, however, a revision of the critical theory he had elucidated at the end of the 1950s. The Gramsci who he recalled with so much effect here was the *voluntarist* Gramsci of the youthful period, and the figure of great moral standing who emerged in the *Prison Letters*: 'Theory and practice, thought and action, the realm of choice, revolutionary will, cultural conscience of the reasons for real action and its acceptance of all the consequent points of praxis: these are the coordinates of Gramsci's personality'.[5] This was, therefore, Tronti's version of an example for the youth, a Gramsci who came down more to 'feeling' than 'thinking', a mode which for the author still held within it a 'communist hope'. Yet Tronti no longer spoke of Gramsci's thought or of this figure as a theorist, effectively relegating him to the past.

In another monograph put out by *Critica marxista* significantly titled *Oltre Gramsci, con Gramsci* – 'Beyond Gramsci, With Gramsci' – the defence of Gramsci's *relevance* was accompanied by an emphasis on his *method* more than on his *content*. For example, the director of the journal, Aldo Zanardo, introduced the issue by explaining that though Gramsci still had to be a point of irrevocable reference for the Communist Party, it was necessary to warn that

> the roots and nutriments of the culture of the left is not, nor can it be, merely a reflection on Gramsci. Nor can it be this reflection taken to its limits. Yesterday's thoughts, however relevant and prescient, cannot adequately sustain the identity which the culture of the left must have today. No return to the origins, no single moment of our origins, can provide us with the sufficient means to decipher and confront the problems of today.[6]

---

4   Tronti 1987, p. 9.
5   Tronti 1987, p. 8.
6   Zanardo 1987, p. 6.

Moreover, Gramscian thought itself, Zanardo continued, 'pushes us towards a culture of the left which is not only a comment on, or application of, a pre-defined set of classics'.[7] Gramsci did not only examine real *things* rather than books and theory, but saw reality with an attitude free from preconceptions, refusing to reduce everything to the confines of pre-existing categories.

Even if there were many concrete moments of Gramsci's work that still showed through (in particular, the references to a Leninist and the Third Internationalist communist culture) for Zanardo the methodological lesson of the Sardinian intellectual and leader could nevertheless be taken on its own, both in terms of its delineation of a distinctly *analytical* interpretation of the world, and in the act of defining, for an *organic* intellectual, a role in opposition to any defeatism: in Gramsci the unity of interpretation

> and praxis is not 'ancillary' to praxis ... The intellectual and the specialist must produce knowledge; they must agree on an appropriately decisive praxis, explaining its reasons rather than providing support for an activity which has already been decided upon.[8]

Other leading communists did not fail to join the camp of defending a non-dogmatic, open relation to the Gramscian tradition: thus Aldo Tortorella emphasised what he believed to be the 'fundamental intuition' of the author of the *Notebooks*:

> the protagonists of the struggle for hegemony are not social stratifications, categorised according to their position in the system of production (that is by income, quantity of power, etc.) but are subjective forces with conflicts among themselves, each one a bearer of a theory of society and the state ... founded on the endeavour to interpret reality.[9]

Similarly Giuseppe Chiarante emphasised the 'anti-economistic' aspects of Gramscian thought, carrying out an earnest, all-encompassing self-critique of the Communist Party's journey and its relation to the Sardinian leader, stressing how intellectual and moral reform had frequently been 'the object of analysis and speechifying' but had 'rarely been the arena for effective political projects'. It was from this claim, indeed, that the Communist Party had to begin to lay the

---

7   Zanardo 1987, p. 7.
8   Zanardo 1987, p. 9.
9   Tortorella 1987, p. 313.

road 'for the overcoming of an essentially productivist and quantitative vision of development and instead to concretely begin the construction of a different kind of society'.[10]

2 Gramsci in the World

Beyond the activity of the leading group of the Communist Party, there was another factor which marked the 50th anniversary of Gramsci's death: the realisation in Italy of quite how vast the fame, awareness and *fortune* of Gramsci was throughout the world, in quite different cultural and historical contexts, from Western Europe to Latin America, from the United States to the Eastern bloc. It was certainly not a homogeneous fortune: sometimes limited to the academic sphere, at other times marked by an all too easy use of Gramscian categories for immediate, polemical political ends. But even so one must remember a single astonishing fact: that while in his own country Gramsci had risked being assigned to oblivion, or being relegated to a mere defeated trace of the past, in the rest of the world the Sardinian communist was becoming the most well-known and studied Italian thinker in modern history. An important indicator of this phenomenon was provided by *Il contemporaneo*, the supplement to *Rinascita*, in an issue dedicated to 'Gramsci in the World', in which Eric Hobsbawm summarised the tone:

> The list of world authors most frequently cited in the international literature of arts and humanities contains very few Italian names, of which only five were born after the sixteenth century. This list includes neither Vico nor Machiavelli, but it does mention Antonio Gramsci. His being cited, of course, does not guarantee knowledge or even basic understanding of the author in question, but it does indicate a certain intellectual presence. Gramsci's presence in the world, fifty years after his death, is undeniable.[11]

In effect, the *Rinascita* supplement contained a clear significance: Gramsci was now present, in different forms and ways, in the political culture of America and many European countries. And in different ways: in France and Spain, his presence was bound up with the fortunes of the left, or of components of leftist forces that evoked his legacy or turned to the *Notebooks* to arm them-

---

10   Chiarante 1987, p. 64.
11   Hobsbawm 1987, p. 23.

selves with a theory that maintained some distance from the communism of
the Third International, and in order to sustain the ability to connect socialism
and democracy, the overcoming of capitalism and the search for consensus.
In Great Britain and West Germany as in the USA, Gramsci's fame was more
rarefied, limited to a *high culture*, to the academic world or to that of a political elite, and thus less dependent on the ebb and flow of the fortunes of this
or that political party. The previous ten years in Latin America (if not without
significant exceptions) had seen a shift from an alleged 'war of movement' to
a phase of conscious 'war of position' and this democratic stabilisation had
greatly favoured the diffusion of Gramsci's works.

The return of Gramsci's fortunes in the world can also be made clear simply
by scrolling through the lists of celebratory events, conferences, debates and
educational conventions organised on the occasion of Gramsci's fiftieth anniversary outside of Italy, including 'London, Moscow, Athens, Stockholm, Bud-
apest, Paris, Tokyo, Ljubljana, San Paolo, Adelaide, etc'.[12] This book does not
aim to delineate the impact of Gramsci's thought outside of Italy. The awareness of this fact represented, nevertheless, a further tool for those in the country
of Gramsci's birth to counteract his virtually being relegated to the archives, a
situation which could be attributed to

> a progressive ebb in civil tensions, a wide disinterest in the battle of ideas
> and politics, the absence of any 'spirit of scission' and the growth of a
> new conformism, deepening the crisis of thought, including Gramscian
> thought.[13]

In October 1989, the Fondazione Istituto Gramsci in Rome organised a congress in Formia on *Gramsci nel mondo*[14] – 'Gramsci in the World' – providing
an unprecedented representation of the most well-known Italian author's fortunes and reception across five continents. A no less important part of the
Formia congress was the presentation of the 'provisional version' of the *Bibliografia gramsciana*, finalised by the American historian John M. Cammett,
which collected together around 6,000 titles of publications in 26 languages
on the life and work of Gramsci.[15] Of these 6,000 titles, 3,681 (62%) were in
Italian, 842 (14%) in English, 250 in French, 203 in German and 200 in Russian.

---

12   Santucci 1989, p. 25.
13   Santucci 1989, p. 27.
14   Cf. Righi 1995. I also refer you to Liguori 1989.
15   Cammet 1989.

The same issue was to be revisited in the mid-90s in the essay collection edited by Antonio Santucci on 'Gramsci in Europe and America'.[16] This did not constitute only an updating of the *panorama* of Gramsci's international fortunes, but also provided a useful instrument for understanding which roads had been followed by Gramscian thought in theoretical contexts quite different from those in which it had been formed. For example, the development of the concept of 'common sense' in the Birmingham department of Sociology had provided 'Stuart Hall with a powerful analytical instrument' for his 'characterisation of Thatcherism as "authoritarian populism"'.[17] Similarly, there was the influence that Gramsci had often had on American intellectuals connected to the pragmatist tradition, such as Stanley Aronowitz and, above all, Cornel West.[18] In his *Introduction* to the volume, Hobsbawm wrote:

> Gramsci survived that political conjuncture which provided the basis for his first international success. He survived the European Communist movement itself. He demonstrated his independence from the highs and lows of ideological fashions ... He survived being closed in that academic ghetto to which so many other thinkers of 'Western Marxism' seem destined.[19]

3 The Fiftieth Anniversary of a 'Classic'

Naturally, the panorama of commentary on Gramsci and his work also included negative evaluations, though it should be said that these did not so much signal invidious attitudes as the relegation of the Sardinian communist to a gallery of 'founding fathers', as inoffensive as they are illustrious, and far enough away to no longer be an object of contestation. Typical of this was the attitude of those who remarked that Gramsci was irredeemably in the *past*. Lucio Colletti wrote:

---

16   E.J. Hobsbawm in Santucci 1995. The book, apart from Hobsbawm's introduction, also contained essays by A. Tosel (France), F. Fernández Buey (Spain), D. Forgacs (Britain), I. Grigor'eva (Russia), J. Buttigieg and F. Rosengarten (USA), C.N. Coutinho (Brazil) and O. Fernández Díaz (Latin America).
17   D. Forgacs in Santucci 1995, pp. 67–8. See below, p. 298 onwards.
18   F. Rosengarten in Santucci 1995. On this argument I can also refer you to my own essay, *Dewey, Gramsci e il 'pragmatismo neogramsciano' di Cornel West* [1996], now in Liguori 2006.
19   E.J. Hobsbawm in Santucci 1995, p. x.

Almost the entirety of the left in Italy today declares itself to be reformist ... It is indeed a fact – that is, an observation, not a negative assessment – that Gramsci was never a reformist ... the half century which separates us from him has not been traversed in vain ... those decisions that the Communist Party has taken have, despite whatever words they utter, signalled an almost irrevocable break.[20]

Others drew on the question of his 'classic figure' to argue for the lack of Gramsci's relevance. For Aldo Schiavone, for example, Gramsci was 'a great classic of political thought. Like Machiavelli, Hobbes, Max Weber ... Today we cannot but see and judge his failures, just as we judge the failures of the classic liberal tradition, of Locke and the fathers of European liberalism'. For this reason the remaining relation between Gramsci and the Communist Party of the 1980s was, for Schiavone, 'a modest one. And it could not be anything but; today we can no longer find a single one of Gramsci's political instructions in the entire basis of the Communist Party's politics'.[21]

Schiavone was not only an intellectual within the Communist Party, he was also – for seven years – director of the Fondazione Istituto Gramsci. Understandably, the international congress of Gramsci studies traditionally organised by the institute (notwithstanding the compromises and necessary mediations within an already broken and divided communist arena) resented the attitudes of its highest leader, whose attitude indeed represented the tip of an iceberg. The acts of the convention on 'Morals and Politics in Gramsci', organised by the Fondazione Istituto Gramsci in Rome, 24–26 June 1987, on the occasion of the fiftieth anniversary of the death of the Sardinian thinker, were never published: a fact which perhaps indicated the problematic nature of the results of the meeting for the majority of that world which was looking to Gramsci. Examining the progress of the convention (as much as is possible),[22]

---

20   L. Colletti, *Addio a lui e a Turati*, in *L'Espresso*, 8 March 1987, p. 107.
21   A. Schiavone, *Compagno Nino, addio*, interview by L. Borgia, in *Il Mattino*, 18 April 1987. On the topic of Gramsci's 'classic nature' also see the counter argument by Gerratana: 'If "classic" is an interpretation in its *own time* which remains true *for all time* ... if "classic" means an author who is worth rereading and reinterpreting in the light of new needs and problems, then indeed one could say that Gramsci today deserves the title of "a classic author"'. Gerratana 1987, p. 10.
22   Only abstracts of the conference were published, in *Il Contemporaneo*, the supplement to *Rinascita*, 1987, issue 30, entitled *Come rileggiamo Gramsci. A cinquant'anni dalla sua scomparsa*. (Herein *Contemporaneo* 1987). A full outline of the ideas in Zanardo's speech appeared in *Critica marxista*, 1988, issue 5, under the title *Gramsci e la concezione della vita morale*. As for the works distributed before the conference, the presentations by S. Veca,

what is striking is how much the axes had radically changed since the analogous meeting of 1977, when a contemporary *relevance* was pushed too far, presenting Gramsci not only as a political theorist but also at times a point of reference for current political processes. This time, the convention as a whole presented a *meta-political* and academic reading of the author of the *Notebooks*, framed as a classic of philosophy, distanced from every possibility of contemporary relevance and, at times, even from historical contextualisation. This attitude – the meta-political and philosophical *styling* of this reading of Gramsci – was not always supported by the simultaneous claims that there had been a total break between the author of the *Notebooks* and the Communist Party 'in the 1980s': even if the proponents of this second attitude could not but welcome with open arms this meta-political viewpoint and could quite easily use it to support their own convictions. A purely philosophical approach to Gramsci was not in itself a regrettable project: it dealt with one of the many possible ways of relating to an author of extraordinary richness and complexity. But privileging such a reading in that moment signalled an orientation which had already been determined, one which was increasingly underlined throughout the 1980s, and could hardly be accidental.

Among the paladins of the new meta-political interpretation of Gramsci, the primary position, as we have already seen, fell to Biagio De Giovanni, who in his opening speech proposed that any reading of the *Notebooks* should focus on the relation of Gramsci to Italian idealism: not Lenin and the October Revolution, but a philosophy which claimed 'its autonomy from the immediacy of historical development'.[23] Among other claims, De Giovanni proposed that:

> The philosophy of praxis is an alternative idea to historicism ... Its alternative character, one might say, is to be found within the folds of the concept of historicism, and foremost in that point in which the *historicised* philosophy of praxis is itself collected within and not external to the course of its life. In this manner, the philosophy of praxis finally reduces itself to the annulling of every historicist tendency, because it is exactly this self-understanding which annihilates that historicism which was *always* beyond historicisation.[24]

This was, therefore, Gentile more than Croce, as Actualism 'indirectly represents "a triumphal re-evaluation of the philosophy of praxis"'.

R. Bodei and G. Vacca have not survived.
23 B. De Giovanni in *Contemporaneo* 1987, p. 19.
24 B. De Giovanni in *Contemporaneo* 1987, p. 19.

This *philosophical* reconstruction included other contributions which continued a deconstruction of the *Notebooks*. The second presentation, by Giacomo Marramao, focussed on the 'meta-political' character of Gramsci's reflections, and his being 'a classic in a purely twentieth century sense. In the sense, that is, of the impossibility of a system', closing the gap between the Sardinian thinker (through the 'optimisation of the relation between activity and ends, and his reflections on the essential link between technics and politics') and authors such as Weber, Schmitt and Jünger. Gramsci had in fact created – according to Marramao – 'a historical anthropology of cultural structures' which he brought together not only outside of 'the ideological orbit of the workers' movement and the communist movement of his times' but also 'of the framework of an epistemological "self-understanding" of Marxian theory itself'.[25] A theorist of the crisis of modernity, therefore, more than of hegemony, here Gramsci was combined with aspects of twentieth-century culture outside of his legacy, privileging points of view that, even if more or less plausible, were nonetheless quite distant from debates within the Communist International and even from the development of a Marxist historical and political science. In its place came models from biological sciences (Ciliberto),[26] or Freud and psychoanalysis (Mancina).[27] This emphasised that tendency, which some have argued can be framed as the 'postmodern', which considered Gramsci to be simply one author among many, one *commodity* among many available in the *supermarket* of culture, whose ideas could be conveniently combined with others, without cautioning the reader or listener that Gramsci had battled fiercely against those very authors by whom he was now *contaminated*, and from whom he had accordingly kept his distance or even marked his complete departure.

There were, however, also voices and positions not animated by the prominent preoccupation with *saving* or *burying* Gramsci, but which equally concurred with his extrapolation from the real problems in which he was immersed. Badaloni, for example, remembered the 'struggle against passivity' of the masses and the individual at the centre of Gramscian thought.[28] Gerratana read the relationship between politics and morality in the *Notebooks* as the necessary ethical choice for those who wanted to lead the struggle for hegemony on behalf of the masses, as it was impossible to struggle for this through the *immoral* methods of the dominant elites.[29] Luisa Mangoni returned to the

---

25 G. Marramao in *Contemporaneo* 1987, p. 20.
26 M. Ciliberto in *Contemporaneo* 1987, pp. 26–27.
27 C. Mancina in *Contemporaneo* 1987, pp. 21–22.
28 N. Badaloni in *Contemporaneo* 1987, pp. 16–17.
29 V. Gerratana in *Contemporaneo* 1987, p. 28.

fundamental concept of 'passive revolution'.[30] Tronti claimed the necessity of 'understanding' – more than hurriedly judging – the metaphor of the 'modern Prince', by which Gramsci intended the 'collective strength, will, ability and knowledge of the social political body'.[31] Zanardo, who focused attention on the Gramscian search for a realisation of man beyond – and rendered superfluous by – the political (in harmony, moreover, with an important suggestion by Marx) did not uproot Gramscian *utopianism* from the real context of the balance of forces in which it was born.[32] The overall message of the convention remained this: on the fiftieth anniversary of his death, beneath the *crust* of his universal embalming – and even thanks to this – the author of the *Notebooks*' most vital legacy risked being buried, that is, the *objective* reading of modern social conflicts bound to the adoption of a determinately critical point of view and consequent praxis.

4   Gramscians and Post-Gramscians

In 1987 there were many other scholarly meetings of which it is impossible to give a detailed account, but of which brief mention can be made as testimony above all to the widespread interest registered around Gramsci's anniversary.

One of the most stimulating meetings was that on *Gramsci e il marxismo contemporaneo* organised by the University of Siena in April 1987.[33] Many of the talks outlined a kind of analysis which proved to be among the most convincing of those proposed in the 1980s: the limits of *democracy* known to us and the characteristics of democracy and self-governance as hypothesised by Gramsci (Nicola Badaloni); socialism as 'radical democracy' based on the logic of a civil society disconnected from the logic of capital (Jacque Texier); the proposal of an *enlarged* concept of the state and reflections on its transformation, over the span of the prison writings, into the *subject* of hegemony (Giuseppe Prestipino); the relevance of Gramsci and the ethical political element in confronting the claim of a bourgeois hegemony characterised by the tendency to collapse back into an economist, corporativist phase (André Tosel); the demonstration of the distance of the Gramscian *philosophy of praxis* from the conceptions of Croce and Gentile, in a period in which there was a tendency to

---

30   L. Mangoni in *Contemporaneo* 1987, p. 27.
31   M. Tronti in *Contemporaneo* 1987, p. 19.
32   A. Zanardo in *Contemporaneo* 1987, pp. 24–25.
33   *Gramsci e il marxismo contemporaneo*, acts from the conference organised by the Centro Mario Rossi, Siena, 27–30 April 1987, Rome: Editori Riuniti, 1990.

underestimate the distance from the latter (Domenico Losurdo) – all constituted points of departure decisive for anyone who did not wish to adhere to the fashionable thesis of Gramsci's *irrelevance*.

In September the Istituto Gramsci in Emilia-Romagna hosted a conference on 'Gramsci and the West' in Bologna, under the direction of the Communist Party,[34] perhaps more influenced by immediate political motives than other conferences (the Communist Party's decision to declare itself 'an integral part of the European left').[35] Among the contributions – which included Badaloni, Canfora, Gianni Ferrara, Spriano and Zangheri – those of greatest interest were by Mario Telò on *Notebook 22*, in which he showed the connections (and divergences) of the prison reflections on Fordist capitalism with the writings from the 1920s and those on the Third International in the following decade; and the contributions by Michelangelo Bovero and Gian Enrico Rusconi, who discussed the idea that Gramscian theory was irredeemably connected with conceptions bound to the past or vitiated by negative elements, such as to render it useless for application within the field of practical politics and government. Bovero did not only claim that the conceptual structures within Gramscian thought were 'inadequate to modernity',[36] but also that 'the structural characteristics of the prescribed Gramscian model' were formulated 'in organicist terms', repeating a *leitmotiv* of the 1980s on which we have already focused. For Gian Enrico Rusconi too there was a need to recognise that 'the concrete political references of Gramscian discourse apply to a phase of history that has been brought to a close'.[37] Gramsci had claimed that 'the parliamentary system was incapable of leading to a "regulated society"',[38] and ignored the possibility and benefits of the elimination of 'conflict' through the 'mechanisms of multiple and changing representation'. In sum, he was too distant from the reality of a 'mature pluralist society'.[39] One can easily add that in the remit of Rusconi's discussion – a point of view formulated in the context of a political and social theory then on the rise (functionalism, systems theory, theory of communicative action), which in effect assumed from the start that a society is unable to change, or the unpromising fate of such a change, given its basic political and social characteristics, its relations of leader and led, the hegemonic and subaltern classes, etc. – a thinker such as Gramsci essentially no longer made *sense*; he was incomprehensible.

---

34   Tega 1990.
35   I can refer you to Liguori 2009.
36   M. Bovero in Tega 1990, p. 189.
37   G.E. Rusconi in Tega 1990, p. 219.
38   G.E. Rusconi in Tega 1990, p. 221.
39   G.E. Rusconi in Tega 1990, p. 225.

The international convention organized by CIPEC (*Centro di Iniziativa Politica e Culturale*) in Rome on 'Gramsci and the Critique of Americanism' went in a completely different direction: this was a meeting of both scholars and activists, almost entirely dedicated to the theme of Americanism, analysed by scholars including Giorgio Baratta, Joseph Buttigieg, Mario Alighiero Manacorda, Jacques Texier and André Tosel, among others. Baratta's introductory talk focused on the centrality of Marx's 'mode of production' to Gramsci's discourse. In 'Americanism', Gramsci had grasped the basic character of the capitalism of his times – which had still not been imposed throughout the whole of the West – seeing how it embraced the sphere of production, the functioning of the state, social organisation and cultural diffusion. Gramsci had understood how to overcome the model of specialised workers, central to *Ordine Nuovo*, seeing the triumph of the machine, of automation and of the mass-worker in Fordism:

> From Turin to the entire world: the project and process of *Ordine Nuovo* was to spread out in all directions: spatially, temporally (now shown in a long, perhaps the longest duration) and qualitatively. This is the challenge of civilisation, determined by the fractious but productive contradictions of capitalism in this phase of a 'programmed economy' ... For Gramsci, Americanism represents the advanced grounds of economic and social development, and therefore the 'privileged' site of the revolution.[40]

Even if there were an awareness that in the course of the 1980s, 'American Fordism' was being overtaken by a new technological and productive revolution, the Gramsci which CIPEC's convention restored was far from the figure depicted by those who considered him to be imprisoned in another era. Here he was presented as a thinker from whom to begin to tease out a new and adequate discourse for the critique and overcoming of capitalism. In this sense, beyond the many contributions on *Notebook 22*, which here it is unfortunately impossible to even simply cite, it is necessary to mention the intervention by Roberto Finelli, who emphasised how Gramscian political philosophy negated every philosophy of history, inasmuch as

> the subject, able to provide historical initiative, is never *presupposed* but always *posed*, that is, always situated by political activity in itself, whose ... production process finishes with the genesis of subjectivity itself.[41]

---

40   G. Baratta in Baratta and Catone 1989, p. 39. The essay collection was republished in the same year in Rome by Edizioni Associate.
41   R. Finelli in Baratta and Catone 1989, p. 211.

Finelli claimed that the political in Gramsci was in reality always '*a critique of* politics', because *democratic* representation presupposes

> subjects already defined and determined according to their economic activity, whose individuality is here mediated by politics, constituting as its very beginning that which for Gramsci, conversely, was precisely an outcome and conclusion.[42]

The CIPEC convention situated itself throughout in opposition to that tendency of the cultural era which the Italian left was living through, and which was best represented by the congress which concluded this 'Gramscian year', dedicated to 'Antonio Gramsci: A Political Theorist in a 'Peripheral Industrial Country' – *Antonio Gramsci: un teorico della politica in un 'paese industriale della periferia'* – organised by the Piedmontese 'Antonio Gramsci' Institute in Turin in December, one of the most cohesive and unified meetings, practically united in claiming itself as *post-Gramscian*. It rejected the cultural and political heritage with which many had felt they needed to evaluate on the occasion of the fiftieth anniversary of Gramsci's death. For Franco Sbarberi, for example,

> the current problematising of the great utopias of the left reverberate even in the thought of Gramsci, in part dissolving it, in part relegating it to oblivion, due to the evident difficulties of continuing to recall a thinker of such 'strength' in a political moment characterised by an identity of such 'weakness'.[43]

The results of the Gramscian analyses were considered by Sbarberi to be 'far from univocal' and allowed glimpses of 'a project which in the end was unfortunately disturbing ... the complexity of modernity is read though a predominantly technical and historically transitory logic, in which the state of the future is conceived as an independent variable, simplifying the entire social process.'[44] The author repeated his theses on the *harmonious society*. Gramsci had noted, for Sbarberi, a decisive theoretical *deficit* exactly on that front, that of 'conflicted society', which now became the ideological *leitmotiv* of the neo-liberal revenge of the 1980s.

---

42   R. Finelli in Baratta and Catone 1989, p. 213. [Translator's note: *le individualtità* refers to 'concrete' individuality.]
43   F. Sbarberi, *Introduction* to Sbarberi 1988.
44   F. Sbarberi, *Introduction* to Sbarberi 1988, p. 15.

Bobbio also insisted on this reasoning: Gramsci belonged to that world of Italian culture (Mosca, Michels) which ignores all of the authors of the great liberal tradition (Locke, Constant, Bentham, Mill, Tocqueville).[45] And similarly for another speaker, Luciano Cafagna, Gramsci was the spiritual son of Papini, Prezzolini and Sorel, genetically distant from and critical of democracy.[46] With few exceptions (the contributions by Tosel and Calabi, for example) the entire Turin conference was thus oriented towards a rejection of the 'anti-democratic' Gramsci.[47]

5 Between Politics and History

The year 1988 was also witness to a full debate on Gramsci, but in reality this dealt with a political and historiographical campaign, conducted through the mass media for political ends after the rehabilitation of Bukharin by Gorbachev's USSR and the full of accusations thrown at Togliatti the 'executioner', charged for co-responsibility in the crimes of Stalinism. Gramsci was brought into the polemic with an article by Umberto Cardia published in *Unità*,[48] in which he put forward the hypothesis of an 'approach of condemnation and marginalisation' organised by the PCd'I in relation to the imprisoned leader. It is not worth focusing on the lengthy articles which the daily press devoted to this polemic, endorsing the most baseless of theses, as much as this nevertheless showed the effect of an operation designed to juxtapose a Gramsci described as exiled or expelled from the Communist Party (and perhaps 'self-enrolled' in the PSI), to a Togliatti described as his knowing persecutor. Moreover, there already exist proficient and informed responses.[49] *l'Unità* had a good try at republishing and securing wide diffusion of Paolo Spriano's book of 1977 on 'Gramsci in Prison and the Party' – *Gramsci in carcere e il partito* –

---

45 N. Bobbio in Sbarberi 1988.
46 Cf. L. Cafagna in Sbarberi 1988.
47 A question which we can at least indicate here, even if not examine fully, was that chosen by a conference on *Gramsci e la letteratura dell'Ottocento* [Gramsci and nineteenth century literature], held in Recanati 5–7 February 1988, which included many important scholars, from De Mauro to Ferretti, Guglielmi to Muscetta, Leone de Castris, Bettini, Carpi, Fasano, Gensini, Luperini. Cf. Calzolaio 1991. It is also worth mentioning Baratta and Catone 1995 (a book which for the most part derived from a conference in Urbino between 16–18 November 1987). A few years later, again in Urbino, there was a conference, the acts of which also came out in the mid-90s: Giacomini et al 1994.
48 U. Cardia, *Per Gramsci fu fatto tutto?*, in *l'Unità*, 24 February 1988.
49 Cf. A.A. Santucci, *Quel che fu fatto per Antonio Gramsci*, in *Rinascita*, 1988, issue 9.

which had already demonstrated how the hypothesis of a total break between the Sardinian leader and the PCd'I could not be sustained.[50] Some months later, in October 1988, the same newspaper published another small volume in Spriano's memory, who had passed away in the intervening period, with unedited documentation of Soviet provenance on which the historian had been working at the end of his life, related to two failed attempts by the Soviet state to liberate Gramsci by diplomatic means, first in 1927–28 and then in 1934–35.[51] The thesis that Gramsci was imprisoned by Mussolini at the behest of Togliatti and Stalin was thus shown to be entirely unfounded.

The debate on the relations between the incarcerated leader and his comrades in the Party was reignited a few months later with the publication in February 1989 of Luciano Canfora's *Togliatti e i dilemmi della politica* – Togliatti and the Dilemmas of Politics[52] – the theses of which were decidedly unfashionable. Canfora defended the Stalinism which Togliatti had chosen in a historical situation constrained by rampant Fascism and by the evident class limits of the liberal democratic regime, as well as his decision to continue to remain in the International Communist movement, often setting aside (if never forgetting) 'Gramsci's politics'. If he had not made this choice, he could not have contributed to the turn towards the Popular Front enacted by the Comintern in 1934–35, nor would he have been able to build the 'new party' on the basis of the democratic decision of 1944–45, with all the consequences that would follow for the workers' movement and the left, in Italy and beyond. This thesis, nevertheless, was not really discussed. All the attention was focused on the *Appendix*, entitled 'History of a Strange Letter' – *Storia di una strana lettera* – regarding three letters written to the three prisoners awaiting trial – Gramsci, Terracini and Scoccimarro – in February 1928 and signed 'Rugero' (Grieco). Grieco's letter, as we have already noted, worried Gramsci a great deal, who suspected there was a plot against him; at the same time Terracini considered the letter quite normal; the letter never reached Scoccimarro. Spriano, in his book *Gramsci in carcere e il partito*, had reached the conclusion (already advanced in the late 1930s by Sraffa) that was not some other 'nefarious' intention behind Grieco's action, but only a form of 'imprudence'. Canfora's thesis was, instead, that Grieco's letters were in reality forgeries by OVRA, who had manipulated the original letters, adding compromising phrases concerning the political situation

---

50 P. Spriano, *Gramsci in carcere e il partito* [1977], supplement to *l'Unità*, 13 March 1988. The small work also included an archival appendix corroborating the author's thesis.

51 *L'ultima ricerca di Paolo Spriano*, with essays by A. Natta and V. Gerratana, supplement to *l'Unità*, 27 October 1988.

52 Canfora 1989.

in order to provoke suspicion and division among the ranks of the PCd'I. The arguments adopted by Canfora,[53] both within his book and in the course of the full debate which followed in various newspapers, provoked a 'trial of circumstantial evidence', in which the 'prosecution' nonetheless never seemed to be able to sufficiently prove their thesis: the agents of OVRA seemed to be 'absolved' by an 'insufficiency of proof', based on the available documentation.[54] Above all, we should ask ourselves, was it really possible that, given Gramsci's wounded reaction in 1928, that no one in the upper ranks of the PCd'I would have considered it to be a police provocation? And that not one of the more than qualified protagonists of the event would have advanced this thesis of the letters' forgery over the following decades?

Moreover, the hypothesis of an anti-Gramscian plot on the part of Togliatti and the communist leaders in exile (of which Canfora's thesis was meant to be the most radical denial) did not, and does not, have even a minimal objective confirmation, as demonstrated further by a documentary book that Michele Pistillo wrote in 1989. The author therein refuted Leonardo Sciascia's argument:[55]

> there does not exist any 'objective resemblance' between the two cases. Antonio Gramsci, despite the extremely complex nature of human and political events around him, was *never* abandoned by his friends, his party, or the men who considered themselves his disciples and comrades, and who recognised and identified him, up to his death, as the 'leader' of Italian communists.[56]

6   A Post-Communist Gramsci

In November 1989, in the face of the unfolding crises of communist parties across Eastern Europe, the Italian Communist Party also began a long and tor-

---

[53]   The fact that the copy of the letter was retrived from the OVRA archives, the doubts over the handwriting, the graphic errors in Trostky's name, etc. Canfora's critics responded to these 'clues' point by point. Cf. for example A. Natoli, *Ma fu solo leggerezza*, in *il manifesto*, 25 February 1989, and A.A. Santucci, *Gli errori di Grieco*, in *Paese sera*, 8 April 1989.

[54]   Canfora himself subsequently formed other hypotheses (Canfora 2012). See below, chapter 12, around footnote 130.

[55]   L. Sciascia, *Gramsci e quella strana lettera da Mosca*, in *La Stampa*, 17 March 1989.

[56]   Pistillo 1989, p. 9. A parallel between Gramsci and Moro – generally unconvincing, and opposed by Pistillo, focused on the 'betrayal' of their respective parties – was attempted again many years later in Mastrogregori 2008.

tuous period of political debate and struggle which, in January 1991, brought the Italian Communist Party to an end after exactly seventy years of life.[57] This also coincided with the hundredth anniversary of Gramsci's birth. This fact immediately provoked a question: would Gramsci have survived the death of the party he had co-founded in 1921, and re-founded in 1926, and with whose fortunes his own legacy had been connected for so long? Certainly, Gramsci had already shown for some time that he was capable of walking on his own two legs, beyond the borders of the Communist movement and even beyond that of Marxist culture. Nevertheless, the correspondence in Italy of the relation between the fortunes of Gramsci and those of the Communist Party understandably raised the question of whether there would be space in 1990s Italy for the author of the *Notebooks*, still more in light of the fact – noted by Massimo Salvadori – that while in the past the Communist Party had always included Gramsci in its *turns*, 'now the Communist Party underwent a transformation in which the thought of the great Sardinian was no longer being actively recalled'.[58]

First of all, how did the newly-born *Partito Democratico della Sinista* (PDS) see its relation to the founder of the party on which it was based?[59] Examining the contributions which appeared in the press on the occasion of Gramsci's centenary (born on 22 January 1891) one noted how the attributions of 'revisionist' and 'dissident' (or 'heretic'), used in some articles of the supplement to *Unità* of 15 January 1991,[60] are those which give the most accurate connotation, semantically, of the interpretative line of some politicians and intellectuals favouring the transformation of the Communist Party into the PDS. The two terms – 'dissent' in the PCd'I and the 'revisionism' of Marxism – are not obviously coincidental nor necessarily bound together. But with frequent use, they began to define a single interpretative horizon, establishing a kind of implicit reciprocity on the levels of both theory and political history.

Bruno Gravagnuolo spoke of 'Gramsci the revisionist' in reviewing the volume in which Norberto Bobbio had collected together his own essays about Gramsci. For Gravagnuolo, 'Gramsci's revisionist *proprium* in relation to Marx'

---

57 Liguori 2009.
58 M.L. Salvadori, *Un intransigente grande italiano*, in *Tuttolibro*, supplement to *La Stampa*, 12 January 1991.
59 The other political formation born from the ashes of the Communist Party, the Partito della Rifondazione Comunista, in attempting to maintain some continuity with the communist tradition, while always renewing it by its own 'social logic', *naturally* conserved a positive and direct relation with Gramsci, at least on the level of 'declared intentions'.
60 Cf. *Gramsci dopo la caduta di tutti i muri*, supplement to *l'Unità*, 15 January 1991. In particular, I am referring to the articles by C. Mancina, B. De Giovanni and F. Argentieri.

as identified by Bobbio consisted in 'the idea of *civil society*'.[61] It was not perhaps accidental, nevertheless, that Bobbio himself had never in fact used the term 'revisionist' (so weighed down as it was in the history of Marxism), both because he had always rejected every attempt to evaluate Gramsci in terms of major or minor 'orthodoxy', and also because he quite clearly never wanted – with his interpretation of the concept of 'civil society' – to deny Gramsci's Marxism and his 'struggle on two fronts', i.e. vulgar materialism and Crocean idealism. Others on the other hand, such as De Giovanni,[62] identified Gramsci's 'revisionism' within the 'circuit of Gramsci, Croce and Bernstein', indicating a direction of research that seemed to stretch from Croce both out towards the class revisionism of German social democratic theory as well as a Gramscian 'revisionism'. Certainly it does not seem accidental that one could speak of Gramsci's 'originality' up to this moment in time, and then of his 'revisionism' after the birth of the PDS: this last term, which De Giovanni adopted in a strong sense, made certain claims of equivalence between Gramscianism and Croceanism in the post-War period. Against the hypothesis of a 'revisionist Gramsci', there was another Gramscian intellectual, Giuseppe Vacca, who had adhered to Occhetto's 'turn' and then the PDS, and for whom

> if there was common ground [between Croce and Gramscianism], it was that of the problems of the world in the first half of the twentieth century in general, to which Croce responded with 'the philosophy of spirit' and Gramsci with 'the philosophy of praxis', i.e., opposing positions.[63]

Others insisted on Gramsci's 'originality' in relation to Marxism, or better still that he had gone 'beyond Marxism', as Claudia Mancina titled her supplement to *Unità*, giving the term 'revisionism' a much wider sense, less referring to the debates at the end of the nineteenth century, and more therefore to another kind of 'politics'. This environment effectively gave rise to a postmodern Gramsci: 'Gramsci was a great eclectic, an omnivorous assimilator, who followed the most different kinds of suggestions without fear of contamination. And therefore he is not a classic as such', wrote Mancina, arguing

---

[61] Gravagnuolo 1990, p. 75 and Bobbio 1990. The definition of Gramsci's ideas as 'communist revisionism' was already there in L. Kołakowski. See above, pp. 212–213.
[62] Cf. B. De Giovanni, *Quando la storia volta pagina*, interview by T. Marrone, in *Il Mattino*, 15 January 1991.
[63] G. Vacca, *'Nino', il capo senza partito*, interview by M. Cozzi, in *La Gazzetta del Mezzogiorno*, 20 January 1991.

that his 'fragmentary character' instead related 'to a quite typically twentieth-century intellectual cipher (who some have called – and not without basis – post-modern)'.[64] It remained for Gianni Vattimo to compare Gramsci both to Rorty's neo-pragmatism and to a similarly imprecise 'post-modern sensibility', with respect to which, nonetheless Gramsci had to be pruned, in the manner inaugurated by Croce, of the 'dead matter' in his thought: hegemony, historical bloc, theory of the party, class standpoint, etc.[65] It is not clear what remains of Gramsci at this point, but without doubt the proposed perspective certainly appeared consonant with a 'post-modern sensibility', the critical activity of which does not necessarily need to respond to the actual facts to which it refers. Cesare Luporini, however, referred to an interpretation which went in an opposite direction:

> Today one speaks of Gramsci as an essayist, or worst still, as a failed essayist. This is not the case. His thought has a systematic quality: it is never expressed in aphoristic form (as is, to give an example immediately clear to everyone, Nietzsche's thought). No one understands this in Italy simply because it is no longer fashionable to re-evaluate systematic thought.[66]

Bobbio's intervention provided a re-reading of Gramsci relevant to the events of 1989 and the theorisation of democracy as the left's only horizon,[67] a reading that attempted to provide maximum space to everything in the *Notebooks* on the value of democracy and Gramsci's non-instrumentalised conception of it. Nonetheless, this came with the risk of an excessive abstraction from any historical theoretical context in which the Sardinian thinker could be situated, in the end perhaps calling 'democracy' that which was for Gramsci, in truth, 'communism'. It was thus important for Bobbio to rightly emphasise the 'democratic' aspects of the Gramscian legacy, having already argued throughout the 1970s for the incompatibility between the thinking in the *Notebooks* and political pluralism. This was also because there were those who continued to believe

---

64 C. Mancina, *Un grande revisionista*, in *Gramsci dopo la caduta di tutti i muri*, supplement to *l'Unità*, 15 January 1991.
65 G. Vattimo, *Gramsci come noi*, in *L'Espresso*, 13 January 1991.
66 C. Luporini, *Ma questo è un intellettuale organico?*, interview by A. Debenedetti, in *Corriere della sera*, 13 January 1991.
67 Cf. N. Bobbio, *La democrazia nei* Quaderni, in *Gramsci dopo la caduta di tutti i muri*, supplement to *l'Unità*, 15 January 1991.

that 'Gramsci moved within the arena of totalitarian political thought',[68] or that 'Gramsci never welcomes the establishment of liberal or bourgeois democracy'.[69]

A critique of a very different kind was that advanced by Gennaro Sasso. For him, Gramsci was no philosopher: at most he was 'an educated and perceptive man, but philosophy also requires long and constant study. There are great classics about which one must think for years and years. It does not seem to me that Gramsci had that kind of commitment in his engagement with philosophy'.[70] One finds here a confirmation of the low fortunes which Gramsci had in the university 'bunkers', as recalled, with his customary irony, by Eugenio Garin:

> With few exceptions, philosophy – or that which is given that name, and viewed as such in the university – was something which was also beyond him. He considered himself too connected to political positions, too opposed to those ritual problematics with which one ought to occupy one's mind. Just think of how limited he was: there is no essay by Gramsci on the concepts of Time and Space![71]

The debate over Gramsci's 'dissent' also provoked many interventions. De Giovanni, for example, emphasised that Gramsci's 'task was the construction a new object of reflection *in political solitude* which opposed *all* politically and historically determined communist thought, already begun in the judgments on the failed crisis of that rationality which constituted the Soviet experience'.[72] For Federigo Argentieri, Gramsci was the first in a long line of Italian communist leaders (Silone, Tasca, Terracini, Ravera, Cucchi and Magnani: but then why not Bordiga, Leonetti, and 'the three', Giolitti, etc?) who were distant from the Party (in time or terminology) as far as evaluation of the USSR was concerned.[73]

---

68   M. Cacciari, *Dal Risorgimento a Lenin. Le riflessioni di un totalitario*, inteview by C. Cossu, in *La Nuova Sardegna*, 18 January 1991.
69   L. Colletti, *Un raro esempio di totalitarismo illuminato*, interview by G. Lehner, in *Avanti!*, 20 January 1991.
70   G. Sasso, *Gramsci, troppo politico per essere filosofo*, interview by G. Lehner, in *Avanti!*, 20 January 1991.
71   E. Garin, *Quell'abile trovata di Togliatti*, interview by N. Ajello, in *la Repubblica*, 20 January 1991.
72   B. De Giovanni, *Intravide la catastrofe*, in *Gramsci dopo la caduta di tutti i muri*, supplement to *l'Unità*, 15 January 1991.
73   F. Argentieri, *Fu il primo dissidente*, in *Gramsci dopo la caduta di tutti i muri*, supplement to *l'Unità*, 15 January 1991.

We should briefly recap the main points of discussion which developed on the occasion of Gramsci's centenary, as it reflects well the tangle of questions posed about Gramsci in the context of the crisis of 1989, the collapse of the regimes in the East and the end of the Italian Communist Party. The substantial point, around which many different interventions turned, seems to have been that of admitting more a less a distinction between 'Communism' and 'Stalinism'. If the two terms coincided, Gramsci could at the most be considered a 'dissident'. If they did not coincide (as Rossana Rossanda claimed, for example),[74] Gramsci continued to be a 'critical communist'. The question is therefore whether Gramsci was a 'dissident', a 'heretic' (and in a broad sense, a 'revisionist') with respect to Stalinism or to Communism (and to Italian Communist), whether Togliatti was entirely within 'Stalinism', whether the entire Italian tradition was indeed a part of it, except for Gramsci *the heretic*. But if this last hypothesis were true, where did Gramsci's origins lie, so isolated and apparently *unique*? Was he too a 'Hyksos'? Or did there exist rather a strong link which united Gramsci and Togliatti (if not without discontinuities, contradictions and conflicts, due to the different *historical periods* in which these two figures lived out the greater part of their real experiences) and which provided the basis for an alternative *communist* tradition (the Congress of Lyons, the *Notebooks*, the 'New Party', the Eighth Congress of the Communist Party, the *Memoriale di Yalta*) which differed from 'Stalinism'? Within these questions lay the reasons for the periodic return not only to Gramsci but also to the relationship between Gramsci and Togliatti, and to the *use* to which Togliatti had put Gramsci. A *use* (a word which included therefore an *instrumental* relation, as I have tried to demonstrate in this work, within certain limits) which cannot be denied, but which immediately poses another question of whether this use was legitimate and beneficial.

7   **Gramsci, Togliatti, Stalin**

Beyond the more contingent polemic, some books appeared in the course of 1991 – even if with a great diversity of approaches and results – that deepened the moments of relation between Gramsci in prison and the 'great and terrible world' outside. The research became oriented towards the need to better define the relations between the author of the *Notebooks* and the dramatic political events to which Gramsci remained bound, with the goal of decipher-

---

74   Cf. R. Rossanda, *Eretico e comunista*, in *il manifesto*, 20 January 1991.

ing either those problems that had remained in the shadows for a long time, or which now seemed to require new critical examination. In the first years of the 1990s, research on Gramsci therefore became quite profoundly biographical, focusing on the exegesis of correspondence and the examination of new archival sources as they slowly became available. After the *meta-political* readings which had culminated in 1987, there now appeared a new season of research and debate over Gramsci.

Some twenty-five years after his classic biography, Giuseppe Fiori returned to Gramsci with a book composed of three distinct essays.[75] In the first of these the author confronted the question of the relation between Gramsci in prison and Togliatti, arguing for Togliatti's loyalty to Gramsci and the Lyons line at least up to the Tenth Plenum of the Comintern (5 July 1929), noting among other points how, over the course of the Sixth Congress of the International (July 1928) and then in his work *Stato operaio*, Togliatti invoked exactly those various struggles within the leading Bolshevik group which constituted the core of Gramsci's positions in 1926.[76] Fiori also convincingly demolished the suspicions which Gramsci held regarding Grieco's letter, emphasising how it had added nothing to that which the Special Court already knew regarding Gramsci's leading role, and offered an unedited and extremely unfavourable portrait of Judge Macis, who had gained Gramsci's confidence, causing doubts about his fidelity among his comrades. After the 'turn' of 1929, however, for Fiori, the substance of the relation between Gramsci and Togliatti also changed. Gramsci's writings were held back from publication long after his death. In his 1938 essay, Togliatti had presented a *Stalinist* Gramsci, profoundly falsified, and had utilised the disappeared leader in order to construct his own political legacy. In response, Fiori reconstructed the spasmodic climate of 'anti-Trostkyist struggle' which had gripped the International and the PCd'I, especially after Tasca published the letter of 1926. Is it necessary to repeat that there were plenty of high-ranking leaders who proposed that Gramsci should be put 'on trial' and publicly self-criticise the Party for its positions of twelve years earlier? Or that it fell to Togliatti to halt steps in this direction and, in his own article *Antonio Gramsci capo della classe operaia italiana* – 'Antonio Gramsci, Leader of the Italian Working Class' – to present a Gramsci who was 'acceptable' to the Comintern and Stalin? Discovering an 'Orthodox Marxist-Leninism' in Gramsci, Togliatti allowed his figure and thought to survive a period in which the PCd'I, as I have

---

75 Fiori 1991. The three essays in this volume are titled respectively: *Gramsci Togliatti Stalin*; *L'universo affetivo di Nino*; *Sardegna, le radici: Gramsci 'federalista'?* (Gramsci, Togliatti, Stalin; Nino's Sentimental World; Sardinia, Roots: Gramsci 'the Federalist'?).
76 Fiori 1991, pp. 23–24 and 259.

already emphasised, was little more than a small party of exiles, persecuted by Fascism and viewed with diffidence by many parts of the International communist movement. Translated thus, Gramsci had been recuperated by Togliatti in substance and introduced into Italian culture, beginning a long, gradual and autonomous path. Fiori, nonetheless, did not deal with all the consequent logical steps of his own accurate reconstruction of the facts: he recognised that without Togliatti's canniness, Gramsci's thought would not have survived Stalinism, but at the same time criticised Togliatti for having collaborated with the necessity of that historical contingency.

In 1991, moreover, the discovery of new documents in the Moscow archives seemed to focus the interpretative line which saw Togliatti as the true *saviour* of the Gramscian legacy: as shown in a series of articles and studies by Giuseppe Vacca, Togliatti was concerned, immediately after Gramsci's disappearance, with making him in some way 'the leader of the Italian proletariat'.[77] The publication of his writings was immediately put into motion, even if – in the dramatic years of the global conflict and the Nazi advance on the USSR – this process found met with many obstacles of different kinds.[78] Togliatti had grasped the *unorthodox* character of Gramsci's notes, their political implications, their intrinsically anti-Stalinist character, and the necessity for their publication had to be mediated through an attentive and inevitably long work of *curation*.[79]

Vacca's contribution to the interpretation of the documents which had been discovered in the Moscow archives of the International, in understanding the context of these documents, took a step back from the interpretative context which had been in place through the 1980s. The thesis could be summarised thus: already from the letter of 1926, but above all in the *Notebooks*, there was an *objective and non-contingent* critique of 'Stalinism', articulated at length in the reflections which concerned not only the concept of 'Caesarism' but also that of 'hegemony' and 'passive revolution'. In arguing with Trotsky, Vacca claimed, Gramsci had also in reality been arguing with Stalin, who – aside from the power struggle unfolding in the USSR – ended up following the 'analyses and strategic lines' advanced by his rival.[80]

77　Cf, for example, G. Vacca, *Quando Togliatti chiese le cenere di Gramsci*, in *l'Unità*, 27 April 1991, which includes a previously unpublished letter by Togliatti to Dimitrov from 21 May 1937, in which the urn of Gramsci's ashes is requested to be transported to the Soviet Union in order to pay tributes 'of particular honour to the leader of the Italian proletariat'. This essay and the ones following, that make reference to it, are nor collected in Vacca 1994.

78　See Vacca 1994, pp. 123 onwards.

79　G. Vacca, *Sì, Togliatti 'corresse' Gramsci*, in *l'Unità*, 6 April 1992, which included an unedited letter from Togliatti to Dimitrov, dated 25 April 1941.

80　G. Vacca, *L'Urss staliniana nell'analisi dei 'Quaderni del carcere'*, in *Critica marxista*, 1988, issue 3–4.

In 1989 Vacca reprinted the essay in his volume titled *Gobačëv e la sinistra europea;* if Gorbachev's 'revolution' was a daring project for the refoundation of communism and socialism after the end of the long epoch of Stalinism,[81] Gramsci had to be one of the points of reference, standing at the beginning of 'a *non-Stalinist communist tradition*'.[82] In order to rescue Gramsci, Vacca tried to show how he reached across two paths: that of the critique of the USSR contained in the *Notebooks* (about which we have already spoken) but also – and more powerfully still – that of the his conception of the state as an alternative to the Third International. Gramsci, in fact, rejected the conception of the state as an *instrument* and *expression* of the ruling class, whilst nevertheless still maintaining their coincidence *in the final analysis*, between politically and economically dominant classes. He thought that the concrete forms of individual states 'derived from the modes in which they stabilise the relations between governed and governing and how the functions of government are executed'.[83] Nor is the ruling class an 'anthropomorphic subject with a unified will and corporate interests'. Within Vacca's discussion the terms of the question of Gramsci's anti-Stalinism were perhaps over-emphasised, but the substance of his thesis seems correct: without doubt the *Notebooks* provided both the foundation for a communist hypothesis profoundly different from that of Stalin, even if a question remains over whether it is possible to attribute to Gramsci an awareness of the Stalinist phenomenon that might equal our own comprehension today.

In a book published at the end of 1991 simply titled *Gramsci e Togliatti*, Vacca finally opposed the new common sense which saw these two authors as figures of the *past*, relegated to the archives of the Italian communist tradition. The book unfashionably reaffirmed the link between the two figures, claiming a quite precise 'tradition' which did not have to mean a relation of total and direct *continuity*, but a strong and productive bond. Aside from this general aspect, it was the first of the essays of which the volume was comprised (*I 'Quaderni' e la politica del '900* – 'The *Notebooks* and Twentieth-Century Politics'), the only one dedicated solely to Gramsci, which constituted the most innovative section, but also the one destined to provoke the most confusion. This focused on two points: an interpretation of the theory of hegemony as the direct antecedent to Gorbachev's theory of 'interdependency', and a strong emphasis on the 'philosophy of praxis' as the central idea of the *Notebooks*. In Vacca's reading, hegemony became a '*program*' for the hierarchical subordina-

---

81   Vacca 1989, p. 11.
82   Vacca 1989, p. 13.
83   Vacca 1989, p. 94.

tion of power-politics ... to hegemonic-politics'.[84] Furthermore, Vacca claimed that 'the foundation of the theory of hegemony ... cannot be anything but the principle for the integration of political activity into a unified and solid theory of the development of humankind: *the principle of interdependence*'.[85] Connecting the theory of interdependence to the Gramscian theory of hegemony was a stretch, and not purely terminologically. Not only because Gramsci's world was profoundly different from our own, but also because such a theory, once it had been transferred from the level of relations with the state and those of international politics to that of politics *tout court* – and therefore a politics of the relation between classes – risked appearing (in its attempt at unity and solidarity) as one of a 'peaceful' society, in which social conflicts are approached only on the basis of a 'vision of unity and solidarity'. One can discuss if this might be possible – but this was nevertheless not the historical and theoretical framework in which Gramsci's thought was situated. For the author of the *Notebooks* there was nothing less than a profoundly dichotomous vision of the forces at play, based on class struggle, on the 'spirit of division' and aimed at conquering the passage from one hegemony to another, directly from one 'civilisation' to another: Gramsci is entirely within the culture of *revolution*, a term he profoundly redefined but on which he never reneged. By clipping the wings of Gramscian theory, strengthening it unilaterally in the direction of a politics of consensus, was there not also the risk of falling back into that interpretation represented by Bobbio and Croce (who Vacca criticised) of an entirely 'superstructural' Gramsci?

Another central point in Vacca's reasoning was that of reading Gramsci's 'philosophy of praxis' not only as struggle on a purely economic level as described by Bukharin (and reintroduced in the historical moment) but as a theory of subjectivity to construct a real theoretical *turn* within the *Notebooks*. The reasoning behind the philosophy of praxis, as we have seen, had been greatly developed through the 1980s, provided with a *broader* sense: in the philosophy of praxis, Vacca claimed, the subject produces itself, and therefore continually renews itself. Just as in Del Noce, therefore, the philosophy of praxis rejected every *given*, every *essence*. It seems important that Vacca emphasised so strongly how in Gramsci the issue was that of the autonomous philosophy of Marxism. A certain confusion remains nonetheless: this philosophy of praxis omits everything which is *given* and in which the party-subject fundamentally is not answerable to anyone except itself; thus conceived, does it not effectively

---

84   Vacca 1991, p. 13.
85   Vacca 1991, p. 86.

contain another *risk* of a kind of *transformism* or even a 'genetic mutation' of the collective subject it creates? Vacca was right when he claimed that the basic limit of Marxist culture was to have never developed a version of modernity alternative to that of capitalism. But *from what* ought this alternative criticism of capitalism be constructed? Simply responding *from the subject* seems insufficient.

8   Gramsci, Tania, Sraffa

As noted, while in prison, Gramsci's relation to the world of emotions and politics outside was largely mediated through his sister-in-law, Tania Schucht. The letters which Gramsci addressed to her were then sent to Piero Sraffa, who in turn sent them to the 'centre' of the Party, Togliatti. From the end of the 1980s various studies have been dedicated to clarifying this 'virtuous' or 'vicious' circle, according to one's point of view. This was a real *archival turn* in Gramscian studies, with the goal of acquiring and sifting through all the possible documentation on the life of the communist leader.

In 1990 Aldo Natoli published *Antigone e il prigioniero* – 'Antigone and the Prisoner'[86] – in which the author interpreted Tania's letters to Gramsci for the first time (652 letters and postcards), evaluating the character of the woman herself, who had so long been left in the dark, and the triangular relationship established between Gramsci and the two Schucht sisters (the third, Genia, remained in the background in this work).[87] A figure which both historians – and at times Gramsci himself – had always considered little more than a 'paper pusher' now acquired concreteness and was finally described in all her human depth.[88] Above all, this managed to dispel the malicious hypothesis that Tania was not Gramsci's friend but rather a Soviet 'spy': nothing about her seemed to render plausible the hypothesis that she had been a 'Bolshevik' chosen for this thankless mission. Tania's letters only appeared in Natoli's volume in selected and edited extracts, thus already filtered by a work of interpretation. A window that had long been left closed was swung open, but the necessity grew at the

---

86   Cf. Natoli 1990.
87   It was only many years later that some of the motives for Genia's hostility towards Antonio became clearer, at least in part due to an emotional relationship which ended badly. Cf. Righi 2011.
88   For a *political* evaluation of Tania Schucht, see Vacca 2012, in whose consideration Tania was, from the moment of Gramsci's arrest, his closest collaborator, working both as a secretary and as the link with the Soviet embassy.

same time for the publication of the letters written by the full range of protagonists within the 'virtuous circle', in the absence of Gramsci's papers being published in full. The publication in 1997 of the letters between the Sardinian communist and his sister-in-law through the prison years, edited by Natoli and Chiara Daniele, was thus not entirely unexpected.[89] It was a work which contributed to providing a different reasoning for the study of his papers, shedding light on the events of Gramsci's life in prison and, at least in part, interpretations of the *Notebooks*.

In 1991 Valentino Gerratana published a volume containing the letters written by Piero Sraffa 'to Tania for Gramsci'.[90] The texts of the great economist were presented to the reader in whole, without being broken up by commentary (but with an introduction by the editor): this was a collection of letters of great interest for reconstructing the network of people and situations which moved around Gramsci (beyond Sraffa and Tania, there was also obviously Togliatti). Through reading Sraffa's 79 letters, and from the precise reconstruction of the relationship between *Gramsci e Sraffa*, introduced by Gerratana, the role of the Cambridge economist in the work of Gramsci's intellectual stimulation while in prison was confirmed: for example, his sending a book of small publications, or the well-known request of help (suggested to Gramsci by Tania) when writing of a review on the *Storia d'Europa del secolo XIX* by Croce, or the very real long distance conversation (through Tania's inevitable mediation) on crucial themes such as the (weak) role of sciences in Italian culture in the early twentieth century, or the relationship between Ricardo and the 'sources' of Marx. It was exactly on this matter, however, that the dialogue between Gramsci and his friend, the great scholar of Ricardo, became hindered.[91] After this point, 'the intellectual exchange between Turi and Cambridge' was interrupted, not because of any argument between the two but, as Gerratana showed, because of the escalation of prison censorship.[92]

Sraffa's letters also seemed important for another reason: the clarification of the relationship between Gramsci and the Party, of which Sraffa was the main mediator, and in particular the episode of the 'infamous letter' sent by Grieco in 1928 and the consequent aftermath. Gerratana wrote: 'Sraffa never raised any doubts on this matter. The obsessive state of Gramsci's nervous exhaustion during this period ... left no room for other explanations'.[93] After the concession to

---

89   Gramsci and Schucht 1997.
90   Sraffa 1991.
91   Sraffa 1991, p. xli.
92   Ibid. On the divergence between Gramsci and Sraffa in relation to Ricardo and Marx, see Badaloni 1992.
93   Sraffa 1991, p. xliv.

some conditional freedoms in October 1934, Sraffa met Gramsci three times at Formia and five times in Rome. Notwithstanding Gramsci's worsening health and the problems related to the possibility of a final freedom, it is not difficult to image – Gerratana wrote – that the two had spoken of the developing political situation:

> It is certain in any case that Sraffa continued to be the intermediary between Gramsci and the centre of the Party in Paris, and that Gramsci himself was quite aware of his friend's role. In his long imprisonment, Gramsci felt isolated and suffered from this; in the grips of an ongoing disease (whether untreated or treated badly), he experienced moments of desperation and nervous exasperation, but he also knew how to overcome these difficult episodes. There was not, however, any irreparable break, and through Sraffa's mediation a stable relationship was re-established: which, among other things, is shown by the message on the question of the 'constituent assembly' which Gramsci handed to Sraffa in their final meeting (26 March 1937).[94]

Gerratana's considerations constituted a balanced position in the longstanding argument on relations between Gramsci in prison and the PCd'I. More recent work on the prison years, while proposing interpretations slightly different from those here, have been possible only due to newly acquired documents, and have not disproved the conclusions to which the *Notebooks*' editor arrived at the beginning of the 1990s.

9 Towards a New Edition of Gramsci's Works

From the end of 1990, talk of a new 'national', 'critical' edition of Gramsci's works was mentioned in the press.[95] In May and July 1991 the Fondazione Istituto Gramsci organised two seminars to put the project into motion: a new edition of all of Gramsci's writings, essentially based on the hypotheses advanced by Gianni Francioni[96] and devised by the director of the Fondazione, Giuseppe Vacca. The project was begun with the idea of

---

94   Sraffa 1991, p. xlvi.
95   Cf. Battista 1990 and Fabre 1990.
96   Other than Francioni's theses already discussed, also see the volume by the same author Francioni 1984 (see above, **p. 225**). The debate took place within the Fondazione Istituto Gramsci and above all in *Ig Informazioni*, 1991, n. 2, which published the speeches from

creating a new complete edition of Gramsci's writings, one which would have a unitary character and be up to the standard of Gerratana's edition of the *Notebooks*, including the publication of the pre-prison writings, and the letters too. There has been agreement on the proposal to regroup Gramsci's writings into a new edition in four 'parts': *a*) the pre-prison writings; *b*) notebooks; *c*) letters; *d*) critical apparatus ... It has also been agreed that the new critical edition of the *Notebooks* ought to include the notebooks of translations. Moreover, there has been an evaluation around the opportunity to publish parallel documents in the epistolary volume, for example the letters between Tatiana Schucht and Piero Sraffa, between Tatiana and the Schucht family and Gramsci, etc.[97]

The hypotheses concerning the new arrangement of the publication of the Gramscian *opera omnia* did not, in the first completed steps, meet with any dissent relating to the proposals for the first, third and fourth parts. Dissent was registered instead between those who maintained that such 'vast' ambitions for publication would in themselves affect other ideas for publications, and among those who thought instead that the 'national edition' would not render more traditional publications – e.g. of letter collections, selections, different editions – futile or damaging. Would the *Prison Letters* conserve their autonomy, their value for a wider public beyond that of simply archival papers, inevitably useful above all for specialists? For example, a useful result was Antonio Santucci's publication of the volume *Letters 1908–1926*,[98] which provided important information on Gramsci's life and activity prior to the prison years. The arguments over the publication of the *Letters to Tania for Gramsci by Sraffa* (edited by Gerratana) were also brought up by those who favoured the publication of the complete archive. And one scholar in particular – Francioni – was convinced of the need for the most complete publication possible of the material in question, drawing on the example provided by Gerratana's edition.[99] We should ask ourselves if perhaps it would have been better to complete the edition of the *Opere di Antonio Gramsci* in the Nue series put out by Einaudi, which had stalled at the pre-prison writings up to 1920.[100] The evident risk, in other

---

the meeting of the 'committee of experts' of 6 May and 3 July 1991, as well as essays by G. Francioni, M. Ciliberto, F. De Felice, V. Gerratana, L. Mangioni and G. Vacca.
97   Istituto Gramsci 1992.
98   Gramsci 1992. This was the first collection of Gramsci's pre-prison letters.
99   Cf. for example, Francioni 1992, p. 717.
100   This second series of the 'Opere di Antonio Gramsci', begun in 1980, appeared in four

words, was that of an *aristocratic* behaviour by those who, while maintaining a *critical* approach to the works of the Sardinian thinker (in itself positive and necessary), also proposed an open or undisguised contempt for every different solution regarding the publication of Gramsci's writings. The ambiguous work of reducing Gramsci to a 'classic' (comparable with Bruno, Plotinus or Vico), begun in 1987 and continued up till 1991, had found some explicit support among followers of the 'national critical edition'.[101]

In an analogous manner Giuseppe Vacca, contesting the legitimacy of a new edition of the *Prison Letters*, the most complete ever made in Italy, edited by Antonio A. Santucci for Sellerio publishing house,[102] claimed that there was no reason for a new edition of the most read Gramscian writings in the moment in which work remained to be done on the whole collection.[103] This way of thinking tended to view one of the many philological, editorial methods for presenting the Gramscian *opera* (that of the most arduous, for the lay reader) as the only valid one. But would the archives really render superfluous the selection of the *Prison Letters*, a volume which has an indisputable value and comprises a book for endless study and research? The persistent fortune and reprinting of the *Letters* in recent years clearly seem to suggest – along with many other logical and historical reasons – a negative response.

Francioni's proposal for a new edition of the Notebooks elicited even greater discussion. Aside from the question of the book of translations,[104] it was in fact the idea for a general reordering of the main Gramscian work which lay at the centre of the controversy. Francioni had identified a four-part typology

---

volumes of his writings (*Cronache torinesi 1913–1917; La città futura 1917–1918; Il nostro Marx 1918–1919*, all edited by S. Caprioglio; and *L'Ordine Nuovo 1919–1920*, edited by V. Gerratana and A.A. Santucci), was interrupted after this last volume, published in 1987. For the years following 1920, one has to refer to the collections of the two volumes published in the 'first series' of the 'Opere di Antonio Gramsci', also begun under Einaudi, in the 1950s: *Socialismo e fascismo. L'Ordine Nuovo 1921–1922* (1966) and *La costruzione del partito comunista 1923–1926* (1971).

101 For example, see M. Ciliberto and L. Paggi in Istituto Gramsci 1992. Fabio Frosini wrote on this subjectt hat 'Gramsci is not Plotinus, and never will he be so long as the world is full of inequality, injustice and conflict'. Frosini 2012, p. 68.
102 Gramsci 1996.
103 Cf. G. Vacca, '*È solo pirateria, la vera novità sarà il carteggio*' (interview by M. De Murtas) in *La Nuova Sardegna*, 24 January 1996. The title of the interview with the then director of the Fondazione Gramsci indicated the difficult context surrounding the rights to Gramsci's works which was stirred up by Santucci's edition. Once the edition had been sold out it in fact could not be reprinted following a court decision.
104 A full work on the translation of Gramsci's theoretical writings from prison was provided by Borghese 1981.

of the notebooks written by Gramsci in prison: aside from those which only concerned translation, he spoke of the *miscellaneous* notebooks, containing notes and points of various arguments; the *specialist* notebooks (according to the denomination given by Gramsci himself to the mono-thematic notebooks); the *mixed* notebooks, containing notes of miscellaneous themes, thematic sections and translations.[105] Not able to have all the notebooks in his cell at any one time, Gramsci had devised a way of dividing the notebooks according to two or three 'sections' in which to develop parallel reflections on different arguments; or to fill a preceding notebook which remained partly empty with notes relevant to different arguments from those to which it had originally been dedicated. The writing of the *Notebooks*, that is, was not executed in a chronological order. As Francioni wrote:

> The real chronological succession of the notes, therefore, traverses horizontally across the notebooks: there are moments of redaction in which there is not a connection from one notebook to the next, but of one note to another while alternating between different notebooks.[106]

Francioni recognised that it was not only impossible to exactly date every single note, but also that it would not be advisable to dismantle and recompose the notes in a chronological order – not even for the miscellaneous notebooks that formed a 'unique medley' – on the basis of a straightforward chronological criteria, because that would mean disaggregating Gramsci's text exactly at those points where he thought the author had unified it, thus splitting up blocks of notes and frequently rendering them less comprehensible or even entirely so.[107] Above all Francioni advanced a proposal of reorganisation of the *Notebooks* which distinguished the *miscellaneous* from the *specialised* (with a third part reserved for *translations*), maintaining that 'the order in which Gramsci had effectively drafted his notes does not, according to certain clues and evidence, seem to correspond to their exterior sequence in the manuscript' and that the new desired edition 'will need to re-establish the internal chronology of the notes only when the notebook in question is presented as a homogeneous whole'; while 'when a block of different notes are placed together, these need to be considered as a sum of non-homogeneous matters, each of which will then need to be brought into its place in the chronology'.[108]

---

105 Cf. Istituto Gramsci 1992, p. 89.
106 Istituto Gramsci 1992, p. 97.
107 Istituto Gramsci 1992, p. 98.
108 Istituto Gramsci 1992, p. 102.

This hypothesis thus proposed a dismemberment and recomposition of the fragments of the notebooks according to their presumed dating. Furthermore, for Francioni it was also necessary to reproduce the sections of every 'mixed' *Notebook* just as 'they appeared to Gramsci', that is, in fact, as distinct notebooks. In fact the unity of the 'mixed' notebooks would only be formal, due to contingency. Therefore, Francioni concluded, nothing prevented 'splitting up the autonomous parts at different points, on the basis of the initial date of their compilation'.[109]

Every attempt at reordering had contained a similarly philological proposal. Yet Francioni's thesis was particularly significant for how it related to *Notebook 10* which, contrary to tradition, he did not consider to be 'a monographic notebook in the proper sense': after the first six notes, Gramsci had in fact abandoned the original project. 'We are in the second half of May 1932', wrote Francioni, 'and Gramsci is no longer interested in a specific notebook on Croce's philosophy, the drafting of an "anti-Croce"'.[110] The author contested therefore the inversion of two parts of manuscript as effected in the 'Gerratana edition', in one of the few cases in which that edition, clearly believing that the second part of the notebooks had been written by Gramsci *before* the first, had enacted an *inversion of the ordering* of the text. In his *Preface* to the critical edition of the *Notebooks* Gerratana had in fact written: 'Within every notebook we have followed the path of greatest order of the material from the pages, save where it was clear that Gramsci had employed a different order' but also that 'the original page number of every notebook is given in the margin of the text'.[111] For Francioni, however, 'the occasional, contingent character' of the paragraphs on Croce collected in *Notebook 10*

> remain for the most part concealed by the Gerratana edition providing page numbers to the notes: the two-part structure, with the inversion of blocks of paragraphs, make the tenth notebook seem like a true monograph on Croce. A different system, however, would shed light on this 'weak' structure and emphasise the 'provisional nature' of these annotations.[112]

---

109   Istituto Gramsci 1992, p. 104.
110   Istituto Gramsci 1992, p. 138.
111   V. Gerratana, *Prefazione* to Gramsci 1975, p. xxxvi.
112   G. Francioni in Istituto Gramsci 1992, p. 139. It is not necessary to go into the controversy relating to the tenth *Notebook* because it interests here only for the contributions *on its method*.

This was an interpretative thesis which did not convince Gerratana however, who replied that the hypothesis of the tenth notebook as a 'montage', as advanced by Francioni, is *possible*, but is anything but certain, and to me still seems quite improbable'. Francioni, for Gerratana, was entitled to defend his proposal, 'but he cannot pretend that it is the only one'.[113] Yet Francioni's argument served the purpose of rebalancing a *querelle* which had deeply divided the research community, for it allowed one to appreciate that: *a*) Francioni's hypotheses were *hypotheses* and not certainties; nothing disallowed that if the *Notebooks* were broken up and reconstructed (or rather, *notes and sections of the Notebooks printed in a different sequence from the real one*) that new documentary acquisitions, different evaluations, other considerations would not reveal errors in these hypotheses, rendering it thus necessary to make a new edition, which in turn could be successively demonstrated to be erroneous, etc.; *b*) Francioni's 'philological turn' rested on a quite specific interpretative hypothesis: Gramsci was not particularly concerned with becoming the 'anti-Croce' while in prison, but with combating Bukharin, or rather Soviet Marxism, i.e. Stalinism. It is not important here to establish whether such a reading was correct or not. What does seem contestable, however, is the idea of offering the reader *an interpretation* of the *Notebooks* rather than an instrument designed for the discussion of the various interpretative possibilities.[114] A 'national edition' ought to offer this second kind of tool.

---

113   V. Gerratana in Istituto Gramsci 1992, pp. 66–7. Francioni would in fact largely change his mind about the tenth *Notebook*: cf. G. Francioni and F. Frosini in Gramsci 2009, vol. Xiv, pp. 1 and onwards. On this question also see N. Badaloni and V. Gerratana's contributions in Istituto Gramsci 1992, pp. 64–65 and 69–72.

114   In agreement with Buttigieg, who has claimed: 'it is not important for the 'experts' to establish once and for all how the *Notebooks* ought to be read and presented: there is a need instead to provide a working instrument which allows the reader to read and interpret the *Notebooks* in an intelligent manner'. J. Buttigieg in Istituto Gramsci 1992, p. 76. Also see below, p. 320.

CHAPTER 10

Liberal Democrat or Critical Communist? (1997–2000)

1   National and International

In 1997 there was a host of initiatives, meetings and studies dedicated to Gramsci to mark six decades since his death. These provoked often divergent readings, partly because they also had to deal with the legacy of the first decade of the Sardinian Communist's death in the context of his party's own demise. If on the one hand this provided some distance from a standpoint which had been too firmly tied up with the contingencies of political ideology, on the other hand it rejected the various political positions which had been held by the main protagonists of the Communist diaspora.

Among the many meetings of 1997, the first global convention of the International Gramsci Society ought to be singled out,[1] representing as it did an international association spread across many countries,[2] a moment for scholars and 'activists' from across the world to meet in Naples. Among the more than one hundred participants, there were scholars from Brazil, America, France, Germany, Australia, Cuba, Denmark, Romania and Russia, hailing from a range of cultural disciplines, testifying to the fact that, despite the fall of the Berlin Wall, Gramsci was still a living and indeed vital author: the only 'Marxist' other than Marx to enjoy an expanding fortune in that part of the twentieth century, a thinker who thus seemed able to help with a critical understanding of the contemporary world. The debate at the Neapolitan conference interrogated the conditions for the construction of a hegemony based on the new self-consciousness of the 'subaltern', albeit with a diversity of approaches and languages born out of the breadth and thought of the association which had organised the meeting. The reflections on democracy and the link between democracy and socialism lay at the centre of Domenico Losurdo's intervention,[3] which reconstructed the critical relation between Gramsci and elitism, highlighting an important theoretical innovation in Gramsci's writings with

---

1   Baratta and Liguori 1999.
2   Information on the foundation and early years is available in G. Baratta, *L'International Gramsci Society*, in Baratta and Liguori 1999.
3   D. Losurdo in Baratta and Liguori 1999.

respect to both Marx and Lenin: the consideration of the political not so much as that which relates to taking power, but above all as that which concerns the construction of a resilient 'new order'. Carlos Nelson Coutinho,[4] from Brazil, saw in Gramsci's original and holistic conception of democracy the development of a concept of 'collective will' often close to Rousseau's 'general will'. If indeed Gramsci had, on the one hand, adhered to a Hegelian notion of will, on the other he took from Rousseau – according to Coutinho – a conception of politics as contractual, that is, the idea of a 'regulated society' as the fruits of a collective will constructed on a consensual basis. Frank Rosengarten[5] identified in Gramsci an author who was capable of reunifying the communist and socialist traditions, democratic and communist ideals *in praxis*, invoking the historical experience of 'Real Existing Socialism' without demonising it, proceeding in an entirely new direction. Joseph A. Buttigieg,[6] also from the USA, was perhaps the first in Italy to truly add something to the Gramscian category of the 'subaltern' through the history of Indigenous Americans,[7] providing at the same time important points about the possibility for subalterns to construct a true 'counter-hegemony' on the condition of leaving behind a 'culturalist' reading of such categories. Buttigieg also cited Edward Said in his argument, a thinker who was invoked more fully by Giorgio Baratta,[8] in analysing the influence of Gramsci's thought on Stuart Hall, the main protagonists of the Birmingham School, the birthplace of Cultural Studies, as well as on the French philosopher Étienne Balibar. Baratta noted how many non-Italian authors – Said in particular but also Hall – had only a very partial understanding of Gramsci; and that this was true even for those who had not just interpreted but had *used* him, applying some of his categories in order to interpret a contemporary situation by necessity quite different from that on which Gramsci himself had reflected.

A range of other contributions was focused on the question of cultural identity, frequently in relation to processes of globalisation, even if from very different perspectives: that of the German writer Sabine Kebir, the Japanese scholar Hiroshi Matsuda, as well as Luciana Castellina, Tullio De Mauro, and the Australian historian Alastair Davidson.[9] For Davidson, post-modernism was trivi-

---

4 C.N. Coutinho in Baratta and Liguori 1999.
5 F. Rosengarten in Baratta and Liguori 1999.
6 J.A. Buttigieg in Baratta and Liguori 1999.
7 Cf. Filippini 2011, pp. 99 onwards, and below p. 302.
8 G. Baratta, *Gramsci tra noi*, in Baratta and Liguori 1999.
9 S. Kebir, *L'internazionalismo di Gramsci e I problemi odierni della sinistra*; A. Davidson, *Gramsci, folclore e autonomia*; H. Matsuda, *Stato e rivoluzione passiva in Giappone*; L. Castellina, *L'egemonia nella società dell'informazione*; T. De Mauro, *Il linguaggio dalla natura alla storia. Ancora su Gramsci linguista*. All in Baratta and Liguori 1999.

alising the Gramscian idea of the translatability of culture, turning it into a simple ratification by authority. Gramsci had been reinterpreted as a theorist of the translatability of different experiences and the construction of unity across cultural differences, on the basis of a wary but positive attitude regarding 'popular creativity'. This was as useful indicator of the confrontation underway with the contemporary problem of multiculturalism.

A great deal of space was provided at the Naples conferences to questions more closely bound to reflections on Gramsci's Marxism, and on the specificity – as Renato Zangheri put it – of the 'philosophy of praxis' being understood as a 'theory of the active subject of history',[10] to which he assigned the task of the new 'unification of (natural) material and spirit' and the overcoming of 'every interpretation of history which does not infer its criteria of analysis and judgment from history itself'.[11] For the German scholar Wolfgang Fritz Haug the philosophy of praxis represented a radical redefinition of historical materialism, reflecting its overcoming of objectivism. Gramsci was thus set alongside an extremely varied range of thinkers, from Althusser through to Brecht. Supposed similarities between Brecht and Gramsci were identified in a shared immanent vision of history that permeates through the philosophy of praxis: for Haug 'the pretexts of truth in a *strict sense*, beyond a historical one, did not make any sense'.[12] André Tosel[13] emphasised instead the possibility of reflecting on Gramscian ideas themselves and above all on their 'own contribution' to the failure of twentieth-century communism, evidenced among other matters by the limits of the relation between subject and party, as well as a certain metaphysical present in the Gramscian concept of collective subjects. Roberto Finelli (*'Gramsci filosofo della prassi'*) also considered subjectivity as the implicit result of a conception of philosophy *as* praxis, as the production of meaning: the subaltern class exists only inasmuch as it is incapable of having self-consciousness. Finelli emphasised other limits to the Gramscian concept of the (revolutionary) subject which had been overly conditioned by Neoidealism, and thus 'too voluntarist and too organic'.[14] The fact remained that subjectivity – Finelli went on to claim – had been seen by the Sardinian communist only as a *product*, a construction, and not as something *presupposed*. The principal contradiction for Gramsci was between the material conditions of how a class lives and its self-representation. From here derived the importance Gramsci had given to

10   R. Zangheri in Baratta and Liguori 1999, p. 162.
11   R. Zangheri in Baratta and Liguori 1999, p. 163.
12   W. F. Haug in Baratta and Liguori 1999, p. 94.
13   A. Tosel in Baratta and Liguori 1999.
14   R. Finelli in Baratta and Liguori 1999, p. 197.

ideology and intellectuals, even if he had apparently undervalued the ideological process of the concealment of reality and given scarce attention to the role of the *body* in the construction of the historical subject.[15] For these reasons he had remained for the most part outside of the 'Marxian critique of political economy, even if there were nonetheless some profound reflections on the organisation of the labour process (such as in the well-known pages on Fordism)'.[16]

For Aldo Tortorella,[17] it was not only Gramsci's reflections on the state which included a critique of the liberal world and Soviet socialism; fundamentally this was also present in the assumption of a new ethical principle able of preventing the risk of transforming an absolute historicism into absolute relativism. What characterised Gramsci's Marxism from other Marxisms was the continued reflection not only on *struggle*, but even more on its *meaning*. Socialism was, according to Tortorella, a limit-concept, both for Gramsci and for the contemporary left. The place of ethics in Gramsci's thought was also discussed by Domenico Jervolino, who proposed an approach that was 'hermeneutic in an essentially historical sense'.[18]

Ethics, furthermore, was an important pole for the Gramscian debate in 1997, emerging in the other conferences to which we will turn below, e.g. in Giuseppe Cacciatore's contribution to the Cagliari conference, and in Francisco Fernández Buey's contribution to the Turin conference. For Cacciatore, Gramsci 'thinks of the ethical moment in its very constitution, independently of the political dimension and the sphere of the state',[19] and thought of 'is/ought' as cutting across in history, a fact which allowed him to reinterpret political realism in a far from 'inferior' manner.[20] For Fernández Buey, Gramsci had claimed not only the 'autonomy of the political sphere' ('a principle learned from Machiavelli') but also the existence of an individual ethical level ('honesty' was 'a necessary factor of political coherence' on the basis of which political man had to be judged, in accordance with Machiavellianism).[21]

---

15   Cf. also Finelli 2012.
16   R. Finelli in Baratta and Liguori 1999, pp. 195–96.
17   A. Tortorella in Baratta and Liguori 1999.
18   D. Jervolino in Baratta and Liguori 1999.
19   G. Cacciatore in Vacca 1999, ii, p. 125.
20   G. Cacciatore in Vacca 1999, ii, p. 130.
21   Fernández Buey 1999, pp. 293–94. On this topic allow me to recommend my *Morale e 'conformismo'*, in Liguori 2006.

2   The Return of Civil Society

The tendency towards Gramsci's increasing international fame was also demonstrated at the now regular conference organised in Cagliari by the Fondazione Istituto Gramsci on the occasion of the sixtieth anniversary of his death, a convention in which there was a resounding echo of the legacy left by the Sardinian Marxist in the study of international politics. At the Cagliari conference, in fact, the most debated questions were those centring on the categorisation of 'international civil society' and 'international hegemony' in the Anglo-American world, within the context of liberal democracy. Many contributions were organised around this theoretical fulcrum, evaluating Gramsci's usefulness in the realm of a globalised political situation, as well as the Gramscian focus on the links between state and society, both national and international, and not least the note on *Americanism and Fordism*. Aside from a perspective which viewed phenomena such as globalisation and the waning political power of the state as *positive*, reflections on the *Notebooks* were also revisited, drawing on the centrality of a discourse around the new form of the twentieth-century state ('the integral state'). The most explicit intervention of this nature at Cagliari was that by Robert Cox. Unsurprisingly, he recreated Bobbio's reading and compared Gramsci to Toqueville (as did Nadia Urbinati[22] at the same conference). Cox admitted that the progressive reduction of the role of the state in the last twenty years of the twentieth century was a defeat for oppressed social groups, but derived from this a new opportunity: the relaunching of 'the full collective and autonomous action' of the subaltern. Such unity would contribute to civil society: non-governmental organisations (NGOs), volunteer associations and interstitial forms within the market related to Gramscian civil society, because in the *Notebooks* this was 'the arena in which cultural changes occur',[23] including transformations in subjectivity. On this basis, the author predicted a new participatory democracy and a 'global civil society' based on an alternative world order. Through recognising, for example, that NGOs in reality were always sustained by state subsidies and thus always relatively 'conformist', Cox saw in this heterogenous voluntarist mix (one that is external to the market) the possibility of a world alternative to capitalism. This was a clear deterioration of the Gramscian theoretical framework (which hinged on the dialectical unity of the state and society) and of the anti-institutional conception of politics.

---

22   N. Urbinati in Vacca 1999, i.
23   R. Cox in Vacca 1999, i, p. 240.

The redefinition of civil society as a unity of voluntary associations was also proposed by Jean L. Cohen,[24] for whom Gramsci had established above all the autonomy of society from the state. In an analogous manner, even if with more radical political tones, Stephen Gill[25] granted intellectuals the task of forcing the emergence of an alternative collective consciousness. Classes and parties – milestones of the theoretical work of the *Notebooks* – did not find space in such a discourse. For Marcello Montanari, Gramsci was above all the thinker of the crisis of the state, who had grasped the 'exhaustability of the progressive historical function effected by the nation state'.[26] Mario Telò also went in this direction, arriving at the conclusion that 'the modern idea of democracy transcends the figure of the nation state'.[27] Telò went further: 'there are doubts about the potential role of the state as a lever of modernisation throughout Gramsci's prison notes, even if in the end he proposed a critical acceptance of this'.[28] By shifting attention onto the undervalued role of political institutions in the prison writings and thus disregarding the distance which separated Gramsci from the mature Sorel, Telò claimed that an expanded category of the state had held no long-term strategic value. According to this theory, Gramsci's political roots lay in the pan-statist reflections of the 1930s, his view fixed on the horizon of the state's eventual transcendence; it was in the end the liberal state which he saw as 'the institutional form most suited to the kind of economic and political modernisation and internationalisation taking shape'.[29] The end of the nation state, post-national horizontal democracy, the centrality of international civil society and the recognition of the market – *in Gramsci* – were the cardinal points of this interpretation, thematised in a way which was articulated to the greatest extent in Montanari's *Introduction* to the anthology of Gramscian writings *Pensare la democrazia* – 'Thinking Democracy' – which he edited and published in 1997 for Einaudi, of which more will be said below.

Returning to the Cagliari conference, the considerations made by Anne Showstack Sassoon seemed to have played a *frontier* (or *pivotal*) role between the interpretations described above (which settled on a depiction of Gramsci as a liberal democrat) and those that were more consolidated (and critical). Sassoon carefully reconstructed the Sardinian thinker's positions on the expansion of the state from WWI onwards, attempting to shed some light on later changes,

---

24   J.L. Cohen in Vacca 1999, i.
25   S. Gill in Vacca 1999, i.
26   M. Montanari in Vacca 1999, i, p. 25.
27   M. Telò in Vacca 1999, i, p. 35.
28   M. Telò in Vacca 1999, i, p. 55.
29   M. Telò in Vacca 1999, i, p. 68.

for example volunteering, the world of *non-profits*, NGOs, the 'third sector', which for her constituted 'the new theatre of relations binding the state to the individual'.[30] It was not the case, therefore, that 'civil society' had been liberated by the withdrawal of the state, but rather that an expanded and redefined state had now arrived, by means of which the task and role of welfare in supporting the capitalist market was being redefined, a market which was itself unable to satisfy a vast range of needs.

Other interventions at Cagliari were characterised by quite different emphases, however. Michele Ciliberto, for example, stressed how one could not attribute Gramsci with a position which sustained the eventual exhaustion of the nation state. Ciliberto wrote:

> In the *Notebooks*, and on this I want to be quite clear, there is not any mechanical overturning of the primacy of the 'national' in favour of the 'international': Gramsci knew all too well that if the outlook were international, the historical process would be extremely long and tortuous.[31]

Carlos Nelson Coutinho[32] also provided a thoughtful evaluation of the link between state and civil society in the *Notebooks*, albeit in a different discursive realm, as well as on democracy and the relation between Gramsci and the philosophical tradition. Benedetto Fontana, an American, provided a much harsher critique:

> the current use of the term 'civil society', whether in the Gramscian, Hegelian or liberal sense, within the current political cultural debate, is simply a reflection of the gradual bourgeoisification of the world, of 'globalisation' and the diffusion of economic forces within the market, as well as the proliferation of private entities and groups that increasing focus on the interests of individuals.[33]

Roberto Racinaro and Remo Bodei belonged to this spectrum. The first recalled how the concept of civil society which Gramsci took from Hegel 'does not designate so much a sphere of economic relations *separate* from that of political relations, as much as a situation which does *not* correspond to the *distinctions*

---

30   A. Showstack Sassoon in Vacca 1999, ii, p. 199.
31   M. Ciliberto in Vacca 1999, i, p. 169.
32   C.N. Coutinho in Vacca 1999, p. ii.
33   B. Fontana in Vacca 1999, i, p. 290.

of the liberal state'.[34] Gramsci used the category of an 'integral state' to account for a process of political diffusion. Bodei invoked the new phenomena of the 1920s and 1930s, of which Gramsci was a very sharp observer ('the state assimilates tasks and needs by moving outside of its usual are of competence'), adding: 'There is actually kind of creeping clownish Popperism which is trying to save and defend Gramsci's legacy by turning him into a liberal'.[35] Racinaro polemically recalled the convention of the Istituto Gramsci which had been held in Florence in 1977.[36] By comparison, the Cagliari conference of 1997 included some diametrically opposed elements, almost returning to the convention of 1967 and the celebrated speech Bobbio's famous speech on 'Gramsci and Civil Society'. In 1977 the problematic of 'making a state out of the working class' (the Communist Party's search for a 'third way' towards a change in the extant political balance) had inferred a reading of the *Notebooks* which was for some far too politically constricted, but at least had been precise in its identification of fundamental categories such as 'the integral state' or 'passive revolution'. In 1997, in a very different political and cultural climate, it was not by chance that these categories had fashionably turned to civil society. From Cagliari to Cagliari, one might say.[37]

A more rigorous reconstruction of the passage of the young Gramsci 'from liberalism to "critical communism"' was that provided in Domenico Losurdo's book from 1997 for the Gamberetti press, in a small volume titled *Per Gramsci*.[38] After the young years profoundly influenced by free market exchange, by *Liberismo* and liberalism, it was in the face of dramatic historic events that the subaltern classes reached Gramsci's theoretical awareness, as well as thanks to the October Revolution and the perspectives which it opened up. For this reason, it seemed to Losurdo, to speak of Gramsci's liberalism, without any of

---

34 R. Racinaro in Vacca 1999, i, p. 378.
35 R. Bodei in Vacca 1999, i, p. 185.
36 See above, Chapter 7, part 4 (Florence convention).
37 The round table discussion was not included in the volume of the printed acts from the Cagliari conference, which was participated in by M. D'Alema (whose intervention was published in *Sole 24 ore*, 31 July 1997 under the title *Che eretico quel Gramsci liberale*), F. Gonzalez, G. Vacca, F. Palomba. The discussion focused on the risk of coopting Gramsci into a political horizon which was very far from his own, 'soliciting from him' texts beyond those necessary, which seemed a very real risk. Cf. A. Tortorella in Baratta and Liguori 1999, pp. 122 onwards.
38 Losurdo 1997. The series, initiated and directed by Giorgio Baratta, and handed over to a group of scholars in the IGS, hosted three titles – beyond Losurdo's, the first was Baratta 2003 and Capitani and Villa 1999 – before moving to the Carocci press.

the necessary specifications and contextualisations, vitiated of all respect for history and for Gramsci, simply made no sense and was merely a game of petty politics.

A *leftist* version of the same problem (that is, one anchored to the questions of class struggle and the communist horizon) arrived through the interventions in the volume *Gramsci e l'Internazionalismo* – 'Gramsci and Internationalism'[39] – the acts of a convention of the same name which took place at Lecce in October 1997. Pasquale Voza, for example, in referring to the irreversible crisis of the nation state, maintained the impossibility of stopping at Gramsci, whose positions he nonetheless scrupulously reconstructed:

> 'There is no state without hegemony': so said Gramsci in the *Prison Notebooks* ... Well today we have to admit that there is a capitalist hegemony *without a state*; without, that is, the active social and cultural mediation of the nation state. The *encasement* of this capitalist hegemony is not comprehensible within the traditional confines of the 'ideological state apparatus', but articulates and embeds itself in a theory of power and knowledge of a supranational order.[40]

For Isidoro Mortellaro, Gramsci was also above all a 'theorist of the crisis of the nation state: it is this theme which runs throughout the twentieth century',[41] while quite differently, but still at the Lecce conference, Arcangelo Leone de Castris's position focused much more attention (as Gramsci himself had done) on the unavoidable *national* paths towards a 'new internationalism' characterised by a non-capitalist hegemony.[42]

3   Taylorism and Fordism

Domenico Losurdo sympathised with the theses offered up by Leone de Castris, stressing at the Turin conference organised by the Communist Refoundation Party (PRC) in December 1997, that Gramsci had 'paid attention to the national

---

39   Proto 1999.
40   P. Voza in Proto 1999, pp. 105–6.
41   I.D. Mortellaro in Proto 1999, p. 168.
42   A. Leone de Castris in Proto 1999. In the same year, 1997, Leone de Castris also published the volume *Gramsci rimosso* (Leone de Castris 1997), arguing against the interpretative tendency which situates Gramsci on a *liberal* horizon of thorught and instead passionately invoked Gramsci as a communist and Marxist thinker.

question [as] the privileged terrain on which the struggle for hegemony develops ... the national conflict is a *form* of the conflict of society, which in certain moments becomes its most acute and concentrated expression'.[43]

The Turin convention went in an entirely different direction from the Cagliari conference, focusing on 'Gramsci and the Twentieth Century'. As was clearly stated in the preface to the acts of the conference, written by the two organisers and editors, Alberto Burgio and Antonio A. Santucci, Gramsci was considered here 'not as a classic to be embalmed, but a comrade on the streets and in battle'.[44] The conference thus presented a more directly political relation to Gramsci, at times perhaps too immediately so, even if this acted as a counterbalance to many of the moments that had emerged at Cagliari. It was an explicit approach, a political attempt to organise within a particular moment of reflection and confrontation.

One question particularly present at Turin was that of Americanism and Fordism, though perhaps here it would be better to stay 'Taylorism and Fordism', on which there were many different interpretations. From one side, Adalberto Minucci[45] and Alberto Burgio agreed on emphasising the richness of *Notebook 22*, rejecting other readings (Burgio explicitly so), most of all the interpretation put forward by Bruno Trentin,[46] who had attempted to evaluate the Gramscian position as entirely internal to an industrial and productivist culture. Against this proposal, Burgio recalled that the distinctions between machines and their 'capitalist use' was already there in Marx; thus for Burgio, 'the project of both Gramsci and the *Ordine Nuovo*, of the dialectical "scission" of Taylorism [appeared] entirely to follow from the Marxian critical project'.[47] On the other hand there was the concluding contribution by Fausto Bertinotti, who revived the critical evaluation of 'Americanism and Fordism': an 'ambiguous' and 'exploratory' thinker, Gramsci was in line with 'the science and rationale of positivist thought, or at least a wider conception symbolising the assumed neutrality of science'. Even if one cannot say that Gramsci had been 'a thinker internal to capitalist modernisation', the fact remained, wrote Bertinotti, that 'in this instance that ambiguity which usually appears so rich appears to have had a less certain effect'.[48] We cannot here that Gramsci's 'Americanism and Fordism' is a complex text and it certainly does provoke

---

43   D. Losurdo in Burgio and Santucci 1999, pp. 212 and 214.
44   Burgio and Santucci 1999, p. x.
45   A. Minucci in Burgio and Santucci 1999.
46   In Trentin 1996.
47   A. Burgio in Burgio and Santucci 1999, p. 176.
48   F. Bertinotti in Burgio and Santucci 1999, pp. 367–8.

interpretative problems, doubts and questions. A reading which views Gramsci as internal to the industrialist and productivist culture of his times is not entirely unfounded and the ambiguity of which Bertinotti spoke is indeed not entirely absent from the texts by which he justified it. A more balanced discourse and perspective would nevertheless evaluate Gramsci's text in all its complexity (and richness), which was important above all in breaking away from the ideas of stagnation and catastrophe which cut through the Second and Third Internationals, instead grasping the driving force of American capitalism. This point was also noted by Renato Zangheri in his introduction to the conference acts, which nevertheless included the observation that Gramsci 'probably undervalued the conflicts which a similar transformation provoked in the factories and in the lives of workers', and that a question remained over whether Gramsci had grasped 'the full potential for "passivity" within Fordism, and the deeply constrictive character to which the worker was subjected'.[49]

The critical theses on 'Americanism and Fordism' were also sustained though a book rich with observations not only on Gramsci but also on the social, political and metropolitan culture in which he lived and by which he was formed. This was 'The Young Gramsci and Early Twentieth Century Turin', a volume which emerged from the conference organised by the Fondazione Istitutio Piemontese Antonio Gramsci, again in 1997. Franco Sbarberi, for example, evaluated the parallels between Marx and Gramsci, claiming that the latter never grasped the kernel of the process of exploitation and alienation as understood by the former.[50] It was nonetheless Marco Revelli who relaunched with greater clarity the critique of Gramscian culture on the organisation of work. For him, Gramsci had understood perfectly well the implications of the Taylorist method, including its more *pernicious* effects on the workers:

> [He] did not hesitate to consider the passage from Fordism to Taylorism as a 'progressive' current within the industrial paradigm, making it a necessary stage in the revolutionary process. At the same time, because 'egocentric' capitalist, Fordist anthropology ... is not so different from Gramscian communist anthropology, it also created a form approximating an almost absolute productive function of man as worker, his nature absorbed as *homo faber*, and the necessity that such a nature has a corresponding 'ethics' (an absolute ethics of work). The difference seems

---

49 R. Zangheri in Vacca 1999, i, p. 13.
50 F. Sbarberi in Fondazione Istituto Gramsci Piemontese 1998, pp. 54–55.

to consist exclusively in the mode in which the internalisation of technical rationality of the factory forms a 'second nature', i.e. whether this is external and compulsory (in Fordism) or internal and participatory (in communism).[51]

Giorgio Baratta indirectly replied to Bertinotti, Trentin and Revelli's overly critical approach in his contribution to the small volume *Scuola, intellettuali e identità nazionale nel pensiero di Gramsci* – 'School, Intellectuals and National Identity in Gramsci's Thought' – acts from the convention of same name organised in Reggio Emilia. As with Burgio, Baratta saw continuity between Marx and Gramsci's reflections: those who accused Gramsci of productivism' had not taken into account the Marxian distinction between the 'material relations of production' and 'the social relations of production', clearly present in Gramsci. As Gramsci knew, for Marx these constituted – along with the 'productive forces' (workers, machines, primary materials, organisation of labour) – a 'relation' and as such a 'contradictory', not 'neutral', reality.[52]

If those readings that made Gramsci into a powerful organiser of 'labour camps' (more *ferocious* still than the capitalist factory) remain clearly unfounded for anyone who understands his human, intellectual and political biography, without doubt it is necessary to continue to uncover, under this aspect, that (supposed) *ambiguity* in 'Americanism and Fordism', starting from the premise, as Baratta recognised, that there was in Gramsci, in the *Notebooks*, an established continuity between the reflections of the *Ordine Nuovo* years and those of *Notebook 22*.

4 Gramsci's Method

In 1997 two books came out, collections of essays composed over the previous thirty years and dedicated to Gramsci by two thinkers, which in different ways, made important contributions to the study and awareness of the Marxist and communist Sardinian: Eugenio Garin and Valentino Gerratana. The first

---

51   M. Revelli in Fondazione Istituto Gramsci Piemontese 1998, p. 34. One should also note, from the Turin conference, the interventions by G. Vacca, generally converging with the ideas prevalent at the Cagliari conference of 1997, and also A. d'Orsi, on Gramsci's 'university apprenticeship', in an attempt to provide context for the formation of his thought in the Turin years.
52   G. Baratta in Capitani and Villa 1999, p. 49.

was one of the few exponents of Italian philosopher to pay continued attention to Gramsci as a fundamental author from a methodological point of view (it was not by accident that the book was called *Con Gramsci* – 'With Gramsci'), laying attention on many apparently 'minor' authors, important for the creation of an intellectual 'common sense' which had to be researched and studied if one wants to truly understand an epoch; or for the ability to grasp how the *Notebooks* might lack a 'systematic form but not a profound coherence'.[53] Garin reflected for the most part on 'Gramsci's method', on the 'argumentative strength' of his 'epigrammatic notes', and on the irrevocable 'biographical link' in the 'rapid, minute and meticulous annotations'.[54] Gerratana had spoken of a 'methodological consonance' between Garin and Gramsci.[55] The central problem that appeared from these essays (written over an arc of thirty years) seemed to turn on the relation of the historic confrontation with Croce. Gramsci's decision to measure himself against this tradition did not derive from a close adherence to the Crocean positions to the neglect of other schools, but from the intrinsic nature of Gramsci's thought, from his standing *for praxis*, even if scientifically honest and 'disinterested': Croce – for Gramsci (and for Garin) – was *the* hegemonic intellectual figure in Italy in the first half of the twentieth century in terms of the cultural sphere: throughout the twenty years of Fascism, it was inevitable that Gramsci would choose to compete with Croce.

Gerratana's book *Gramsci. Problemi di metodo* – 'Gramsci. Methodological Problems'[56] – also reprinted writings from an arc of thirty years, in part dedicated to the preparation of the critical edition of the *Notebooks* or other projects, but also to other moments of the prison writings, such as the 'self-portrait' in the letters, or the concept of hegemony, or the question of the (individual) subject starting with their 'dissolution', all very elegantly researched. The increasingly valuable rereading of the reflections which had accompanied the 'critical edition' of the *Notebooks* coincided with Gerratana's refusal to demonise the preceding 'thematic edition', which was instead appreciated for its great, historic contribution in knowing how to provide a widespread awareness of Gramsci's thought: a lesson in style and the *awareness of limitations*.[57]

---

53 E. Garin, *Gramsci nella cultura italiana* [1958], in Garin 1997, p. 45.
54 Ibid.
55 Gerratana 1974, but also see Santucci 1996.
56 Gerratana 1997.
57 On Gerratana, cf. the acts of the 2010 conference organised by the IGS Italia: Forenza and Liguori 2012.

In 1996 a text was published that was particularly attentive to Gramsci's writing and the structure of his principal work: *Quaderni del carcere di Antonio Gramsci* – 'Antonio Gramsci's Prison Notebooks' – a long essay by Raul Modernti included in the monumental *Letteratura italiana* edited by Alberto Asor Rosa for Einaudi. This work did not hold back from offering a thorough interpretation of the Sardinian thinker's ideas, perhaps hoping to draw too marked a continuation with Lenin's thought in terms of the process of 'translating' from 'East' to 'West'. Beyond the many points of great interest on this question (for example, the decisive issue of 'common sense', the issue of 'Anti-Croce', the interconnection between politics, philosophy, literary criticism and history, etc., all united through the argument of the struggle for hegemony, which Gramsci both theorised and participated in),[58] Mordenti's essay was (and remains) valuable above all because it was among the first, or perhaps the very first, to delve into the work from some other, usually less discussed viewpoints. For example, the analysis of the present in the different A, C and B texts of the *Notebooks* (according to Gerratana's nomination of the texts of the first and second drafts, and the unique draft) which relied on the progress of Gramsci's ability to work in the different episodes of his detention; commentary on the differences between 'notes' and 'points' in his 'writing toolbox', and the different kinds of writing that makes up the *Notebooks*; and the relation which Gramsci established to 'other people's arguments', on which Modernti wrote:

> when someone else's concept is referred to and adopted by Gramsci it never remains the same as it was; the force of Gramsci's argumentation completely refines the concepts used, recreating them, rendering them in effect unrecognisable and entirely original, and then proceeding to a real *incorporation* into his own discourse and reasoning.[59]

He also claimed that the 'taxonomy' of the work, though made up of fragments, was never merely 'casually' accumulated, but rather collected through a peculiar 'syntax' that needed to be reconstructed.[60] Gramsci's work, Mordenti concluded, was in many ways similar to other expressions typical of twentieth-century writing, 'in the great series of "global works" of twentieth-century European prose, all incomplete and/or fragmentary' (from Canetti to Benjamin to Musil), but nevertheless also distant from them because such a typically

---

58 Mordenti 1996, pp. 611–12.
59 Mordenti 1996, p. 606.
60 Mordenti 1996, p. 610.

twentieth-century style of writing was 'utilised by Gramsci not in order to reflect philosophically on the self and its crisis, but to speak about history, economics, sociology, politics (on the contrary, even to envision revolution in the West.)'[61]

5   The Story of a Prisoner

We have already mentioned the publication of the correspondence between Gramsci and Tatiana Schucht,[62] which opened the way to a new consideration of the Gramscian corpus of letters, above all in order to provide a more precise interpretation of the historical developments. The long introductory essay by Aldo Natoli[63] caused much confusion. Natoli reproached the communist 'orthodoxy' of having hidden Tania's letters for so long. It should be recalled however they there were open to consultation for many years in the Istituto Gramsci. If scholars such as Gerratana or Spriano had made limited use of them it had not been for a presumed 'orthodoxy' to be defended at all costs, but merely because they had (unfortunately) received little interest in general. Some of the attempts made by Natoli to reinterpret the correspondence in an *unorthodox* manner were not convincing. For example, the letter to Tania from May 1930, in which Gramsci wrote that he felt like the prisoner of 'another jail ... as a result of being cut out of not only social life, but also family life, etc. I could protect myself from the blows which my enemies rain down, but I cannot prevent those blows which arrive from elsewhere, whence I least expect them'.[64] For Natoli, Gramsci spoke here of feeling that he had been abandoned (or worse) by his Party: this is a thesis which has recently been repeated.[65] There were certainly noteworthy differences between Gramsci and the International (and the PCd'I) at the beginning of the 1930s. But immediately after the fragment just cited, Antonio added, turning to Tania: 'But there is you, you would say. And it is true, you are always very good and I love you a great deal. But these are things which someone can't just replace'.[66] This is clearly not a political comparison, but rather the desperation of a man who, among

---

61 Mordenti 1996, p. 614. Two years later the author published Modenti 1998, a volume aimed at an audience of young militant communists.
62 See above, Chapter 9, section 8.
63 A. Natoli, *Introduzione*, in Gramsci and Schucht 1997.
64 Gramsci and Schucht 1997, p. 521.
65 Lo Piparo 2012. Also see below, chapter 12, section 6.
66 Gramsci and Schucht 1997, p. 521.

other things, felt the lack of his wife and children. Again: in the letter of 24 May 1930 Tania copied two letters addressed to Antonio from her father, in which the aging Apollon explained why Giulia had not written to her husband. Natoli read between the lines a presumed disclosure of surveillance by the Soviet censors. But quite clearly there is another explanation: 'Giulia is ill, anxious, and that must be taken into account ... one cannot ask of Giulia that which one would ask of a healthy person ... is it difficult to say why anyone has not done something. Perhaps because they didn't want to, or were not able to, through negligence or lack of strength'.[67] Lack of strength then, not police surveillance. Certainly, the latter was not missing in the Soviet Union, but one frequently gets the impression that many interpreters read single phrases taken out of context in order to add value to preconceived theses which instead, according to the words themselves, rarely find justification. Gramsci, suffering both physically and mentally in prison, ended up placing the poor Giulia among his 'sentencers' (letter of 27 February 1933), allowing his family affairs and political matters to overlap, not always lucidly (as he recognised in the letter of 19 May 1930), arriving at conclusions which today appear weak and clearly without reason. There were ideas in Natoli's work which were not new, and were destined to re-emerge periodically. Still now they have not found evidence to sustain them – indeed, there have been studies which have further refuted them[68] – but they are periodically rehashed, as was the case with a book by Aurelio Lepre which came out the following year.[69] Even after the useful interpretation of the archival papers published by Daniele and Natoli there remained hypotheses unsupported by proven facts. Gramsci had certainly had a certain distance from many aspects of the Communist movement of the Third International, but he nonetheless never seemed to want to burn his bridges. The notebooks and letters had been salvaged from the start thanks to Tania (as Gerratana had first noted, in his *Introduction* to the critical edition of the *Notebooks*). And they were published and distributed in Italy, and throughout the world, thanks to Togliatti and his Party (who could also have allowed Gramsci's work to fall into oblivion). This is certain. All the rest is, in reality, merely represents conjecture that does not correspond to the facts that have been stated here.

We have focused for a long time on these questions raised by Natoli because the controversy over the relation between Gramsci and Togliatti, between Gramsci in prison and the PCd'I, and the theoretical and political evolution of Gramsci's thought while in prison, have been given a great deal of space in the

---

67   Gramsci and Schucht 1997, p. 525.
68   Vacca 2012. Also see below chapter 12 from about note 124.
69   Lepre 1998.

last fifteen years. Many of the contributions are memorable. Among the main ones in the years which we are considering here, up to the close of the century, are those of Giuseppe Vacca, who has intervened repeatedly on this matter, evaluating for himself the publication of the correspondence and unedited documents coming out of the archives of the Comintern and the Communist Party which have only recently been made available. Whether presenting the correspondence between Gramsci and Togliatti in 1926,[70] or reconstructing the crossroads between the Comintern and the Party,[71] or later examining the work of editing and interpreting the Gramscian legacy as effected by Togliatti,[72] Vacca has convincingly demonstrated that it is thanks to Togliatti that we are able to study Gramsci's thought. Moreover, the new and full collection of Togliatti's writings on Gramsci published in 2001 confirmed this point of view.[73] This is similarly documented in the several studies by Michele Pistillo and his balanced work of rectifying the historiography in contrast to those revisionist anxieties which periodically resurface regarding Gramsci and the history of the Communist Party more generally.[74] *Gramsci in carcere. La difficile verità d'un lento assassinio*, Pistillo's book from 2001, did this in relation to recently acquired documents, which further disprove the mangled 'historiographic legend' of Gramsci's arrest, of the exchange of letters of 1926 (where Togliatti behaved correctly, obtaining from his Party permission to not officially submit Gramsci's writings to the political bureau) and on the relations between the PCd'I and Gramsci in prison (who was detained and killed by Mussolini, not Grieco or Togliatti). Pistillo showed how the divergence between Togliatti in Moscow and the Italian Party (including Gramsci) developed over 1926. A good deal of the motivation for this was due to Togliatti's Bukharinism, perhaps unique among Italian communists in not exaggerating the prospect of a capitalist crisis, an error which meant Gramsci's party claimed to be witnessing a reopening of a true revolutionary phase, at the very point when Fascism was, instead, transforming itself definitively into a regime: an

---

70 Vacca 1999b.
71 Vacca 1999c, pp. 171 onwards. This volume also includes the interesting and articulate attempt to show the theoretical 'compatibility' of 'hegemony' and 'democracy', and the otherness of Gramscian theory in relation to Stalinism. Vacca nonetheless seemed to hold to, or at least tolerate, the idea that Gramsci had rescinded his own communist convictions during prison. In his more recent work however (Vacca 2012) this thesis is quite definitively rejected. (Again, see below, Chapter 12 from about note 124.).
72 G. Vacca, *Introduzione*, in Daniele 2005.
73 Liguori 2001.
74 Of Pistillo's works, beyond Postillo 1989, already cited, and Pistillo 2001, to which I am referring now, also see Pistillo 1996.

error – the undervaluation of the forces of Fascism – which had also had an important effect on the events which led to the arrest of the Sardinian communist.

There are another two full studies from the 1990s by Claudio Natoli, published as 'Historical Studies' on Gramsci's campaigns within the PCd'I and the International in 1932–1934.[75] Natoli's research constitutes an important contribution to the reconstruction of different phases of communist agitation outside of Italy on behalf of detained politicians in general and Gramsci in particular, and of their intersection both with the more general state of the Comintern and with the events of the prisoner himself. In a book which came out a little later[76] the historian turned to other events regarding the Sardinian communist, claiming that the gap between Gramsci and Togliatti – which emerged at least from 1925 and was connected to different modes of understanding the role of democracy and alliances in transition – had never entirely closed, but rather that they had had their own successive and differing moments of greater or lesser collaboration. Many questions of the *Notebooks*, the author claimed, were indeed already present in Gramsci's thinking in the 1920s.

6   Gramsci Contested at the End of the Millennium

In 1997 an essay collection edited by Salvo Mastellone came out,[77] attempting for the most part to reread Gramsci as a democratic author. This was explained in three sections: the first was dedicated to the history of interpretations of the *Notebooks* after the war, with writings by Giuseppe Vacca (on some of these interpretations), Francesca Izzo (on Luporini's Gramsci) and Paolo Bagnoli (on Gramsci's prison writings and his democratic conception of politics). The second part, beginning with an essay by Franco Livorsi on *Gramsci e la cultura politica della sinistra* – 'Gramsci and the Political Culture of the Left' – was dedicated to analyses of some of the main Gramscian concepts, with contributions from Sergio Caruso (on intellectual and moral reform), Vittore Collina (Jacobinism), Andrea Spini (intellectuals). The third part, finally, was dedicated to the confrontation between Gramscian Marxism and the democratic traditions, with essays by Mercello Montanari ('Towards Democracy: Observations on Ethics and Politics'), Corrado Malandrino (on autonomy and federalism) and Franca Papa (who emphasised the importance of the 'constituent', which in the

---

75   Natoli 1995, and Natoli 1999.
76   Natoli 2000.
77   Mastellone 1997.

following years would become more important in interpretations of Gramsci). In his *Introduction*, Mastellone did not only cover all the stages of the Gramscian debate and compare Gramsci with authors such as Bodin, Mazzini and De Sanctis, but also claimed that the Sardinian thinker's reflections – although incomplete – were based on the necessity of 'building a politics of consensus', contrasting 'Caesarism' to 'democracy'.[78]

This 'democratic' (and no longer Communist) Gramsci had been theorised in 1997 – as we have seen – by Marcello Montanari, with the full *Introduction* to the anthology on the *Notebooks* which he had edited himself.[79] Montanari in fact saw in Gramsci. in his evolution in prison, the overcoming of his original Communist positions, reaching an accord not only with a modern and open conception of democracy, but indeed an acceptance of the market and the commodity form which, after 1989, seemed indissolubly bound to democracy itself. This was not an opinion confirmed by Gramsci's texts, and the author had to force an interpretation of 'Americanism and Fordism' which saw within the meaning of 'Americanism' an 'expansion of the market' which grew 'through the regrouping of the socially subaltern, the participatory potential of political life'.[80] According to Gramsci (for Montanari) '*Americanism can generalise itself, because its idea of development is rational*'.[81] In the introduction to a volume which, a few years later, collected together essays written over a long period of time, Montanari returned to Gramsci and democracy, defending the Gramscian formula of the 'constituent', in which he saw the proposal of a new struggle for hegemony 'in a polyarchal reality', while remaining true to Gramscian democracy, leading in the end to the 'overcoming of the division of humankind into ruling and ruled'.[82] Put in these terms, the question seemed

---

78   Mastellone 1997, pp. xxxiv–xxxv. A few years later the same author, along with Giorgio Sola, gave life to an essay collection on *Gramsci: il partito politico nei* Quaderni, the culmination to a series of seminars organised from 1997 by historians of political thought and political scientists, confirming the growing interest in Gramsci at the turn of the millenium. Mastellone and Sola 2001. The volume includes essays by S. Mastellone, G. Sola, F. Livorsi, N. Antonetti, S. Mezzadra, F. Tuccari, G. Cavallari, G. Calabrò, M. Montanari and C. Carini.

79   Gramsci 1997. Some of the relevant aspects of the editor's interpretation were already present in his essay in Carini 1995, republished as Montanari 2007.

80   M. Montanari, *Introduzione* to Gramsci 1997, p. xx.

81   Ibid.

82   Montanari 2002, pp. 12–13. In this *Introduzione*, the most important problem seems to be the relation between Gramsci and Americanismo: Gramsci, Montanari writes, 'knew how to understand Americanism as a historically determined figure of the Universal; understood as a *figure* in all its rational and hegemonic potential, but also in its expansive *limitations* and frailty'. Montanari 2002, p. 16. [Translator's note: 'polyarchal' is a reference to Robert Dahl's theory of government.]

acceptable. That the category of hegemony contained within itself the potential for struggle within democracy (for socialism) is indisputable, even if this was not fully expressed by Gramsci himself. One can however actively extrapolate from Gramsci's conceptual apparatus a pluralist system, taking hold of the fact that for Gramsci democracy went beyond pluralism, described in the *Notebooks* as the movement towards the overcoming of the distinction between ruling and ruled which Montanari himself recalled.

Naturally there were in these years also very different interpretative currents, quite distant from those described above. Indeed it has often been said that Marx and Gramsci have been the two thinkers who, within Marxism, best withstood the 'fall of the Wall', continuing their consistent cultural presence. The relation between the two thinkers was the subject of a conference initiated by Giuseppe Petronio, which took place in Trieste in 1999, the acts of which were collected in the volume *Marx e Gramsci. Memoria e attualità*,[83] which outlined interesting juxtapositions of their theoretical and political categories – beginning from the claim that where one could 'compare the readings which Marx and Gramsci made of their own times as a relatively modern world, rather than *postmodern*, and the development of a process which triggered epochal change, of which the French Revolution and the coming to power of the bourgeoisie had been the essential moments'[84] – reaching through to the conclusion that Gramsci's debt to idealism, while irrefutable, was in reality less 'crucial in the final instance' than we often want to believe or pretend. In the course of the convention, Donald Sassoon compared Gramsci's Marxism to that of the Second and Third Internationals: Fabio Frosini focused on the 'return to Marx' in the *Notebooks*, while my own presentation compared the relation of state and civil society in the works of the two thinkers; Aldo Tortorella insisted on the important awareness in Gramsci, with respect to Marx, of the dangers of ethical relativism. Giorgio Gilibert advanced the hypothesis that it was thanks to Gramsci that Sraffa had known *Capital* Volume 2, which was otherwise not well known in Italy; Jacques Texier returned to the category of the historical bloc putting into relief the presence in Gramsci's writings of the Marxian discourse as a presupposition for his own ideas; while, in opposition to this, Roberto Finelli insisted on the distance of Gramsci from other fundamental Marxian categories. Wolfgang Fritz Haug, also judged the analysis of Gramsci on the productive forces to be insufficient, but appreciated the Gramscian

---

[83] Petronio and Paladini Musitelli 2001. The 1999 conference was promoted by the Istituto Gramsci Friuli Venezia-Giulia in collaboration with IGS Italia.
[84] G. Petronio in Petronio and Paladini Musitelli 2001.

philosophy of praxis as a return to a vital part of Marx and Marxism. For Giorgio Baratta, the claim that there was no strict relation between Gramsci's ideas about the economic world, Marx's own in *Capital* derived from a compromised and only partial reading of Gramsci. For Andrea Catone, Gramsci tried in the *Notebooks* to find a solution to a problem which had only been raised marginally in Marx: how, starting from the objective conditions of the capitalist relation, to effectively construct the revolutionary subject that might work for the transformation of society? Another aspect investigated at the conference was Gramsci's multifaceted analyses of language and its relation to politics, focused on by Fernández Buey. Marina Paladini Musitelli's contribution tried in turn to demonstrate how the origin of Gramsci's interest in language and method were more indebted to Marx and Marxism than, as had long been the view, to Neoidealism.

Beyond Montanari's, there were many other anthologies which came out in those years. The problem of anthologising Gramsci's writings – due to the inherited state of his works and the fragmentary nature of his writing – has always been both important and difficult, still more so with the publication of the 'critical edition' and the following increased difficulties in approaching the *Notebooks*: if for a scholar there were no shortcuts around the difficult infighting which surrounded the critical, complete edition of his writings, in prison or otherwise, it is also true that one cannot expect to *force* the uneasy struggle within the prison writings on an expanding wider public of potential readers, for whom taking first steps with the Sardinian author was becoming increasingly difficult. For these reasons, there was a strong interest in anthologies, which gave rise to important results.

In the years considered here, the anthology which was perhaps most convincing was that by Franco Consiglio and Fabio Frosini, focusing on 'philosophy and politics' in the *Notebooks*.[85] The two authors, who – as we have seen – had already brought together the Gramscian *Scritti di economia politica*, provided with this book a very useful tool, especially for universities: the anthology collates Gramscian writings into blocks of arguments, introducing each and privileging the texts of the first drafts, which are considered to be richer. The only complaint is that the book, due to unfortunate editorial events, had small circulation, and the editors did not have the means to complete the work with an anthology of the *Notebooks* along other themes, a plan which it is not difficult to see lay behind this volume.

---

85   Gramsci 1997b.

The volume *Le opere*[86] ('The Works') was also very useful for students, edited by Antonio A. Santucci and published as 'the first anthology of all the writings' of the Sardinian thinker. The book presented the texts without a contextualising or exegetical introduction, and with the critical apparatus reduced to a minimum. The choice was clearly for those who were concerned with the pre-prison writings, and showed some limitations with respect to the prison writings themselves: the passage through the *Notebooks* is too rich and complex for adequate presentation without critical apparatus or introductory notes, and thus drew on a very limited number of extracts.

Of an entirely different nature, there was the anthology *La nostra città futura* – 'Our Future City'[87] – edited a year later by Angelo d'Orsi and devoted to the 'Turin writings (1911–1922)'. The long editorial introduction on 'Antonio Gramsci and his Turin' helped to clarify this fundamental decade in Gramsci's intellectual, political and person biography, in which one moves from his formation at the university of Turin (the richness of which, D'Orsi claimed, needed to be better understood) to the definitive choice to go over to the workers' movement, and from the first Crocean beginnings to the discovery of Marxism and Leninism, into the 'red biennial' (in which, as D'Orsi wrote, one witnesses the utilisation of 'Turin as a national paradigm', and therefore the over-estimation of the 'possibility of Revolution in Italy') and right up to the foundation of the PCd'I and the visit to Moscow. The volume contained around 130 of Gramsci's writings, from the first dramatic letters to his father and the initial publications in the *Corriere universitario*, through to the more celebrated texts written in the war and the comments 'in direct relation' to the Russian Revolution, from the theorisation of the councils to the anti-socialist polemics and the first analyses of Fascism, without forgetting obviously the texts on culture, polemic, politics, the life of the city – everything that had gone into *Sotto la Mole*. D'Orsi, in other words, was not wrong in refusing to consider Gramsci in this period only as a *precursor* to the *mature* Gramsci of the prison writings, but was concerned to 'take him seriously' while avoiding teleology, studying him *in himself*, thus restoring to us a Gramsci who was anything but a *minor* author, but rather someone to be analysed and considered on a par with the Gramsci of the *Notebooks*.[88]

---

86 Gramsci 1997c. The book was republished in 2012 with the title *Antologia* and a preface by myself, through the Editori Riuniti university press.
87 Gramsci 2004a.
88 Also see D'Orsi 1999.

CHAPTER 11

Gramsci in the Twenty-First Century (2000–08)

1   For Gramsci

The opening years of the new century ushered in a new phase of Gramsci scholarship in Italy, due to many different factors: the effect of Gramsci's growing fame in the rest of the world, from the 1980s onward, had saved the author of the *Notebooks* from being entirely abandoned in his own country (as many had wanted, for overridingly political reasons, following the end of the Communist Party of Italy); the rediscovery of new documents in the archives of the former USSR; and work on a 'national edition' which was slowly getting under way in the Fondazione Gramsci, which put new intellectual energies of research in motion.

Another important reason behind this new phase was to be found in the new active collective and interdisciplinary research initiated in 2001, through a series of seminars on the vocabulary of the *Prison Notebooks* organised by the IGS Italia, which regularly brought scholars together in Rome from a range of Italian universities and cities, as well as many young intellectuals, giving rise to an important *new generation* of passionate and proficient readers of Gramsci.[1] The result of the first period of the seminar's activity was the collective volume *Le parole di Gramsci* – 'Gramsci's Words'[2] – comprised of essays by Giorgio Baratta (Americanism), Derek Boothman (translation and translatability), Giuseppe Cospito (hegemony; structure and superstructure), Lea Durante (the national-popular), myself (ideology; state and civil society), Rita Medici (Jacobinism), Marina Paladini Musitelli (*'Brescianesimo'*, the reactionary intellectuals named after the Jesuit Antonio Bresciani), Giuseppe Prestipino (dialectics) and Pasquale Voza (passive revolution). These represented thirteen of the principle key terms from the *Notebooks*, and were added to by other studies following the seminars' activity, which continued up until 2011.[3] In contrast to a

---

[1] On the seminar series in question, see the online site of the Igs Italia: www.istitutogramscisiciliano.it. In 2002 the Igs Italia founded the Premio Valentino Gerratana (the great scholar and founder of the association who passed away in 2001) awarded to unpublished essays by young scholars, won over the following decade by Roberto Ciccarelli, Chiara Meta, Eleaonora Forenza, Michele Filippini and Alessandro Errico. The essay in question, along with those of other participants in the semiar, are not collected in Durante and Liguori 2012.

[2] Frosini and Liguori 2004.

[3] Other relations discussed at the seminar are either detailed or given in full on the Igs Italia

broad tendency of 'forcing the texts' – a danger against which Gramsci himself had warned but which has too often characterised the reception of his writings – here there was a desire instead 'to reread the text with philological rigour ... to begin again from Gramsci's legacy – and from the *way* in which he had left those writings behind – freeing the work from a whole series of outdated interpretations which today risk suffocating the real spirit of the texts'.[4] The authors recognised the fact that the Gramscian vocabulary is very particular, characterised by the habit of the Sardinian thinker to immerse himself in the language and discourse of his interlocutors, so as to criticise their conclusions 'from within'. By starting from this warning, however, it was possible, and necessary, to reconstruct the diachronic nature of many of the main entries in the *Notebooks*, 'thus clarifying a theoretical drama which *through its unity* provides a credible and practical map of a thinker who otherwise risks being reduced to a bottomless well from which to draw citations in order to claim anything and sustain anyone, as has not infrequently been the case'.[5]

The volume on 'Gramsci's Words' was published in the series *Per Gramsci* on the instigation of Giorgio Baratta and promoted by the IGS Italia before being taken up Gambaretti and then the publishing house of Carocci. In the same years, Carocci also published other volumes in the series, including Giorgio Baratta's *Le rose e i quaderni* – 'The Roses and The Notebooks', originally published in 2000 by Gambaretti with the subheading 'An Essay on Antonio Gramsci's Thought' – which was reprinted in 2003, revised and expanded, with the subtitle 'Antonio Gramsci's Dialogical Thought'.[6] This was a collection of essays relating to a wide spectrum of issues and problems, in which the most interesting questions were those around the *uses* to which Gramsci had been put in different cultural realms, the importance and originality of which Baratta – with a non-dogmatic curiosity – was among the first in Italy to recognise. For Baratta, Gramsci was a *contemporary* author, attentive to the dialectic between the national and the international, and to the unity shown in a world of 'Americanism' that had already supplanted Fordism; Gramsci's thought was, for him,

---

website mentioned above. Other than the others included in Frosini and Liguori 2004, other contributions were made by Giuseppe Cacciatore, Michele Filippini, Roberto Finelli, Elisabetta Gallo and Raul Modernti, among others.

4 Frosini and Liguori 2004, p. 9.
5 Frosini and Liguori 2004, pp. 9–10. The editors added, with definitive conviction, that to 'interpret' remained fundamentally inevitable. Cf. the controversy between Coutinho and Cospito relating to *interpreting* the relation between base and superstructure as advanced by the latter. Coutinho 2004 and G. Cospito in Frosini and Liguori 2004, n. 4.
6 Baratta 2003.

characterised – as Gerratana had written – by a 'dialogic nature',[7] constantly comparing himself with one or more suitable interlocutors, contributing to the production of an *open* system of interpretations that can be constantly integrated, rethought and modernised. For Baratta this favoured a relation to *contemporary* issues (the global North and South, the importance of *spatiality* in modern culture) and interpretations of Gramscian thought such as those provided by Edward Said and Stuart Hall which, while perhaps representing interpretations that were not philologically exacting, had the capacity to utilise Gramsci so as to form original readings of present contradictions.

Already in this book – rich with thematic investigations which can only be briefly cited here (including under titles such as the people and populism, national and international horizons, pragmatism and the philosophy of praxis) – Baratta introduced the theme of 'counterpoint', a term he would develop in a following work in 2007: the musical metaphor, in the wake of Said, was meant to communicate the motion from dialectic to translatability,[8] which in turn brought Gramsci closer to different and more distant experiences – the *peripheries*, and not only in geographical or geopolitical sense – and an explosion of suggestions and points which demonstrated the author's empathy with some of those readings of Gramsci and approaches which often appeared quite unexpected, yet opening up a host of paths ahead.

In *Gramsci e la filosofia*,[9] another publication in the series promoted by the IGS Italia, Fabio Frosini began from the conviction that, 'through those results which have been laboriously reached over years of Gramscian philology' borne out of the *long wave* of the 'critical edition' of the *Notebooks*,[10] one could now gain a real understanding of Gramsci, delving into the evolution of the concepts of the *Notebooks* and their specific origins. That is, he claimed that the mode in which Gramsci's thought is structured cannot be separated from its historical development. Frosini's essay was presented in two parts. In the first he reconstructed the *making* of the *Notebooks*, providing a new hypothesis of their periodisation, subdivided into three phases. In the second part of the book, he analysed the two philosophical hinges of Gramsci's research: on the one hand the fundamental problems of Marxism, which he had tried to

---

7   Gerratana 1997 p. xiii.
8   Baratta 2007, p. 23.
9   Frosini 2003. The book co-won, along with Alberto Burgio's *Gramsci storico*, the 'International Giuseppe Sormani Price for a work on Antonio Gramsci', recently established by the Fondazione Istituto Piemontese Antonio Gramsci. The successive awarding of the prize would go in 2007 to another book from the series *Per Gramsci* by the IGS Italia, my own *Sentieri gramsciani* (Liguori 2004) an in 2011 to Thomas 2009.
10 Frosini 2003, p. 15.

remove from the grips of both materialist and idealist 'reductionist revisionism', re-establishing through the concept of praxis the bond between philosophy and politics present in Marx's *Theses on Feuerbach*. On the other hand there was the confrontation with Croce, who Gramsci wanted to 'understand and explain', without yielding to 'the claims and philosophical self-sufficiency of historical materialism'.[11] Finally, the author turned to the fundamental connection between philosophy and common sense (which had already been at the centre of the anthology edited with Consiglio)[12] and that between philosophy, politics and religion, bringing to light all the politics of the Gramscian vision of the relation between intellectuals and the mass as 'the necessity of unification, at the highest level, of the historical cultural imbalance which particularly marks modern civilisation'.[13]

Another result from the activities of the IGS Italia was the establishment in 2003 of the *Centro interuniversitario di ricerca per gli studi gramsciani* (The Intra-University Research Centre for Gramscian Studies) organised by the University of Bari and with the agreement of the Universities of Triest and Urbino. In 2004 the Centre organised a convention focussed mostly on the writings of both Labriola and Gramsci, under the conviction that the *form* of the writings was characterised by not only the 'dialogic' method of their thought, but also, as Pasquale Voza claimed in his introduction to the published volume, through the fact that of all other Marxists, these were the two who diverged the most from Marxism's mechanistic and economistic vision.[14] Gramsci's writing also constituted a model for this kind of study, through its different phases. First there was Gramsci the chronicler of Turin, in his specific cultural and political context as already outlined by Angelo d'Orsi, for whom the daily journalistic activity of the young Sardinian, 'in abandoning the sphere of party propaganda, was the first instrument of consciousness and analysis of reality'.[15] He did this, however, without ignoring communicative innovations, explained Marina Paladini Musitelli, thanks to a writing style that was rich with metaphor, and an attention which was always alive to the original meaning of words: the whole 'translates into a lexical liveliness rare in the panorama of contemporary writing and an interesting predisposition to play with the old and newer meanings of words',[16] so as to combat tired phrases, conventional thinking and ossified

---

11   Frosini 2003, p. 123.
12   Cf. see above, p. 288.
13   Frosini 2003, p. 170.
14   P. Voza in Durante and Voza 2006, pp. 7–13.
15   A. d'Orsi in Durante and Voza 2006, p. 219.
16   M. Paladini Musitelli in Durante and Voza 2006, p. 145.

common sense. Gramsci's prison style was at the centre of Lea Durante's contribution on his correspondence. There is, she noted

> a 'division of labour' between the *Letters* and the *Notebooks*: the words, in fact, are used in the former in a very fluid, winding way, communicative power given its full range in his search for answers, sometimes allowing an adjustment during the flow itself, supplementing his explanation: the phrases 'I mean/I meant to say' recur frequently in Gramsci, as he turns back on a word or expression which does not seem clear.[17]

Whereas

> in the case of the *Notebooks* the words are selected, recalibrated, at times stripping them down to the mere bones, more frequently with a richness of rich semantic charge. This does not mean that the words then become definitive: there is always an aspect of dynamism in Gramsci's vocabulary.[18]

At the Bari conference, a range of contributions focused on Labriola and Gramsci's key words, i.e. those terms that are particularly important for identifying the horizons of their thought. For Gramsci, one expression above all else, the 'philosophy of praxis', was central in the Italian Marxist tradition, and many contributors converged on its importance in quite different ways, including interventions by Roberto Finelli, Fabio Frosini and Silvio Suppa. Finelli stressed the *differences* between the Sardinian thinker and Labriola: praxis, for Labriola, was first of all *work*, the production of 'objects'; while for Gramsci it is 'the production of *subjects*, that historically collective subjectivity'.[19] From here Finelli, in line with his original reading of Gramsci,[20] derived a Gramscian re-evaluation of the concept of ideology:

---

17   L. Durante in Durante and Voza 2006, pp. 159–60.
18   L. Durante in Durante and Voza 2006, p. 160. Gramsci's language was also the focus of contributions by G. Baratta and R. Modernti in the same volume.
19   R. Finelli in Durante and Voza 2006, pp. 88–89.
20   Such a reading was largely consistent in being, in many aspects, quite critical towards Gramsci's thought, but nonetheless always original, folding out across many essays and contributions to various scholarly meetings. But I will limit myself here to commending only Finelli 2005 in which, other than contributions of which we are currently giving an account, was also published *Le contraddizioni della soggetività. Americanismo e fordismo in Antonio Gramsci*, originally given at a conference at Juiz de Fora, Brazil, in 1997.

a new conception of the content and function of historical praxis takes place in Gramsci by means of a specific and defining change in the paradigm identified in Marx and Engel's notion of 'ideology', one which in the *Notebooks* passes from a negative to a positive sense.[21]

Finelli saw an interweaving of Gentile and Croce in Gramsci. According to him, the 'philosophy of praxis' implied a different conception of subjectivity: not presupposed *a priori* as in Labriola, in line with a more traditional Marxism, but *historically posited*. Yet, aside from this necessary act of emancipation from economic determinism, there was also 'an excessive imbalance in the other direction, exactly that of an idealist view of historical practice'. For Finelli, this had then laid the basis for post-War Italian Marxism in the Gramscian mould: 'a Marxism without *Das Kapital*'.[22]

For Fabio Frosini 'praxis' in the *Notebooks* was 'always more clearly *synonymous with politics*', understood as 'the entire range of activity at work within different social relations.' On this basis, he concluded, 'the ideological character, due to its being practical in every consciousness ... becomes the political character of consciousness itself'.[23] This line of research identified the real criteria of truth in the *effects* of ideology – a point to which we will come back below when referring to Frosini's other works. In contrast to Finelli, he not only maintained the proximity of Gramsci to Labriola precisely on the issue of the philosophy of praxis, but also claimed the legitimacy and cogency of the translation of Marxism into Italy as executed by both writers.

Finally, Silvio Suppa claimed that there was a marked discontinuity between Labriola and Gramsci, focussing on the latter's interpretation of Americanism. The strong connection between thought and politics, typical of Gramsci's philosophy of praxis, appeared to be put in crisis by the objective and opaque hegemonic processes of the arrangement of production and society (Americanism) in which Gramsci identified the loss of the strength of will, of culture, of political initiative. On this basis, Suppa claimed that doubts arose in relation to the processes of passive revolution produced by these methods, 'the perception of an exceptional impoverishment of the characteristics and rules suitable for political conflict',[24] that 'hegemony borne from the factory', seeming to make the author of the *Notebooks*, a 'most lucid witness and analyst' but

---

21   R. Finelli in Durante and Voza 2006, p. 89.
22   R. Finelli in Durante and Voza 2006, p. 95.
23   F. Frosini in Durante and Voza 2006, p. 273.
24   S. Suppa in Durante and Voza 2006, p. 318. The acts of the Bari conference also included, among other contributions on the whole dedicated to Gramsci, those by B. Brunetti

also an 'helpless witness', 'dazzled by the loss of power, in this context, of an ideal and analytical operation', as was indeed fully demonstrated by the reality of the European situation.

2 Gramscian Research

The fall in the number of books on Gramsci published in Italy over the 1990s – and more than that, the minimal visibility granted to those that were published – combined with a general mistrust for the author of the *Notebooks* within political and intellectuals elites (including those in publishing houses who, across the board, now wanted to praise liberal and liberal democratic thought and, on the left, liberal socialist thought[25]) gave rise to a strange phenomenon, because at the very same moment Gramsci's fortunes were expanding abroad, along with the number of non-Italian books focussing on his thought, the mirror image of what had taken place in the 1970s. This long *embargo* was broken by the publication in Italian in 2006 of a book of essays by the leading Gramscian scholar in Brazil, Carlos Nelson Coutinho, titled *Il pensiero politico di Gramsci* – 'Antonio Gramsci's Political Thought'.[26]

Countinho – a central scholar of Gramsci in the country where his thought had had the greatest diffusion (after Italy), especially since the 1980s, both at the level of public debate and in the academic sphere – had not only worked on the transnational and Brazilian editions of Gramsci[27] and studied the concepts and development of his entire thought, but had also proposed the application of some of its fundamental categories to the history of twentieth-century Brazil.[28] Coutinho's monograph presented itself as a rigorous but lively work aimed at a public that included non-specialists. Although designed as an *introductory* work, it contained many original interpretations. For him, the centre of Gramsci's thought lay in 'politics ... the focal point of which Gramsci analysed

---

(*Gramsci, la scrittura letterria, l'analisi politica*) and di L. Mitarotondo (*Gramsci e il Rinascimento: ovvero l'eccezione politica di Machiavelli*).

25 There were also those who tried to conflate Gramsci's thought with liberal socialist thought, reading it nonetheless through a radically *left* tendency, as was possibly to do from the *late* Rosselli: cf. Vander 2002.

26 Coutinho 2006. The book was published in Portuguese in 1999, but was revised and modified for the Italian edition.

27 See below, p. 301.

28 See Coutinho 2001. The contemporary endurance of Gramsci, for Coutinho, 'results from the fact that he interpreted a world which is essentially *our own world today*'. Coutinho 2006, p. 146.

as the totality of social life, the problems of culture, philosophy, etc'.[29] This was a real 'Marxist anthology of political praxis', a reading which cut against the predominantly 'culturalist' grain, above all in the English-speaking world, which had set Gramsci's analysis of the superstructure above all other considerations. For Coutinho, Gramsci was 'a critical, heretical communist, who had thrown out the great part of theoretical units and forms of practice within so-called "historical Communism."'[30] The book reconstructed Gramsci's youthful background, the experience in the ranks of the PCd'I, up till the *Lyons Theses* and the 'letter of 1926'. He also analysed Gramsci's ideas in prison, when 'a certain "distance"' from the 'immediate historical activities' had brought him to 'widen the horizon and deepen the level' of theoretical production: 'Without rejecting being a profoundly Italian thinker ... he assumed a stature which was decidedly universal'.[31] Dialectically overcoming Leninism, Gramsci had sharpened all theoretical political categories, renovating Marxism as both a philosophy and as a conception of the world.

Alberto Burgio, in *Gramsci storico* – 'Gramsci the Historian' – also recognised in Gramsci a 'primacy of the political'. Gramsci had been convinced that 'praxis requires the kind of direction that only historical abilities can provide, i.e. a knowledge of individual episodes and the ideas within the logic of the historical process'.[32] For this reason the *Notebooks* could also be read as '*a vast history book*' and at the same time 'a book *on history*', i.e. a methodological reflection. Burgio proposed the Gramscian '"true" historicism' as anti-determinism,[33] focussing on the distinction between 'enduring an epoch' and 'making one', i.e. between history as the passing by of time without significant changes, and events that break this course, fragmenting it, splitting up its regular ordering, giving life to a 'new historical form'.[34] The author's ambition was to prioritise that which the Sardinian communist himself had omitted from the *Notebooks*, 'without adding anything to Gramsci's reflections – problems, hypotheses, concepts – which are not already present (or can only be glimpsed) in the original theoretical workings'.[35] Obviously one cannot go down this road of thought without providing a very specific *reading* or *interpretation* of Gramsci, as was clear from the title of the book. Burgio saw 'a critical theory of modern-

---

29 Coutinho 2006, p. 15.
30 Coutinho 2006, p. 148.
31 Coutinho 2006, pp. 72–73.
32 Burgio 2002, p. 15.
33 Burgio 2002, p. 9.
34 Burgio 2002, p. 20.
35 Burgio 2002, p. 3.

ity, developed on the basis of a solid belief in rationality and progress' in the *Notebooks*,[36] an equivalence between politics and statehood. The birth of the bourgeoisie as the political class had symbolised the beginning of the state in its true sense. Once political power had been conquered, the bourgeoisie had established the ability to *hegemonise* civil society, with the essential mediating function of intellectuals. This progressive and expansive progress ended nonetheless, according to Gramsci, at the end of the nineteenth century, capsizing during the extensive challenge of maintaining power in the face of the beginning of the history of the masses. This is the epoch of passive revolution and/or authoritarian tendencies.

Burgio's interest in an issue too often ignored in the history of interpretations – i.e. Gramsci's theory of history and of historiography – can also be seen in the context of the emergence of a series of approaches that came to the aid of the Sardinian author's representation. One of these was the linguistic approach, an aspect which until the 1990s very few studies had focussed on, but which today is fully accepted in the world of Gramscian studies. An example of this new tendency was the book by Derek Boothman on *Traducibilità e processi traduttivi* – 'Translatability and the Processes of Translation' – in 2004.[37] Gramsci the linguist existed not only because he had been interested in linguistic questions throughout his life, but above all because in Gramsci there were detectable elements which together made up a theory of language on a par with many other important twentieth-century versions. For Gramsci, language was an instrument of politics in the struggle to raise the consciousness of the masses, with its own roots in social activity. This was an approach absorbed through a historical social conception of semantics of terminology as advanced by his master, the neo-linguist Matteo Bartoli, on the basis of considerations by Michel Bréal and Antoine Meillet (a pupil of Bréal and a friend of Saussure). He had also drawn from Ascoli's idea of the 'substrate', for whom the formation of a unified national social economy would provide the 'substrate' for a finally unified, national language, for without such a structural unification there could be no superstructural cultural unification. Another possible source was the Russian School, as it was possible, according to Boothman, to spot traces of concepts elaborated in the 1920s by the Marxist linguist Voloshinov, a pupil of Bakhtin; on the other hand there were explicit invocations in Gramsci of other linguistic questions taken from Vailati and Pareto.

---

36   Burgio 2002, p. 286.
37   Boothman 2004.

Giuseppe Prestipino also referred to Gramsci's theory of translation but in a different sense. Remembering the proximity of the 'translator' (*traduttore*) to the 'traitor' (*traditore*), Prestipino provocatively claimed that 'no one asks how much Gramsci has been betrayed'.[38] Here, 'betraying Gramsci' meant the act of adapting his lexicon and categories into the world of today. 'I feel that the greatness of a thinker', wrote Prestipino, 'can be demonstrated to us in our unquenched intellectual thirst to interpellate and interpret, or reinterpret, his categories, putting them into conversation with theoretical and historical contexts very distant from those in which they originally arose'. Gramsci's Marxism had been thus above all *utilised*, reactivated in the face of contemporary problems, an act which was only possible thanks to the methodologically rich nature of Gramscian categories, from the links between theory and praxis to the vision of a critical and anti-determinist Marxism: these were not only *historiographic* categories, uniquely linked to the historic events in which Gramsci himself lived and with which he was concerned, but *theoretical* categories, thus applicable in the present moment as well.

The fact that historical contextualisation served to provide Gramsci a 'double foundation' on which to build analytical instruments for the present was also claimed by Rita Medici.[39] Entering into a critical dialogue with contemporary authors, such as Mosca and Pareto, who conceived of politics as an autonomous science, Gramsci had nevertheless relied above all on Machiavelli, not only as the fundamental moment in his reconstruction of Italian history from the city states to the Counter-Reformation, but also as a complex metaphor[40] by which to recompose certain theoretical moments, from 'Jacobinism' to 'state and civil society', from 'collective will' to 'ideology'.

Twenty-five years after his *Società industriale e formazione umana* – 'Industrial Society and Human Education'[41] – Dario Ragazzini returned with a new book on Gramsci, *Leonardo nella società di massa* – 'Leonardo in Mass Society'.[42] The author noted that in Gramsci the reflections on macro-problems of both structure and superstructure were accompanied by those on the micro-problems of the individual, because for the author of the *Notebooks* 'subjectivity is not *a priori* granted to everyone but is formed by and forms itself in processes'.[43] 'His concept of man', Ragazzini wrote, 'is a concept of structural

---

38 Prestipino 2000, p. 6.
39 Medici 2000.
40 Also see the author's interesting essay, Medici 1990.
41 Ragazzini 1976.
42 Ragazzini 2002.
43 Ragazzini 2002, p. 43.

relation. Consciousness is inherently contradictory. The dialectic is within man himself, as an aspect of his history and his social relations'.[44] Furthermore, 'relations ... have a relation with social structure and a historic dimension. Man can thus be called a "historic bloc." Social relations are held within forms and structures (neighbours, family, work relations, fundamental social groups, social strata, etc)'.[45] Therefore 'all of Gramsci's reflection can be read as an antidote to a mechanistic and reductivist view of society, without forgetting that it integrates and corrects that to which it responds, but without cancelling it out'.[46] Individual identity is therefore the result 'of so-called casual influxes, of the "different societies of which one is a part", which is to say the formal relations and those which fall into "indifferent judgements", both "necessary" and "voluntary", by ideologies which relate to and begin within those relations embedded over time as classes, social groups, familial and individual microhistories, in which the individual participates'.[47] Consciousness is thus 'intimately and structurally contradictory', because of the contradictory social relations in which the individual is immersed. A consciousness can be stimulated from without (the role of education), but cannot but be brought out from a nucleus within the individual, as inferred in the dialectic between 'good sense' and 'common sense'.[48]

In 2005 – one year before the author's premature death at the age of only 54 – an essay collection was published of some of Antonio A. Santucci's writings on Gramsci.[49] He had been a close collaborator of Valentino Gerratana, editor of many of Gramsci's works, author of one of the better *textbooks* on Gramsci of the 1980s (frequently republished)[50] and of many other essays and writings on the Sardinian communist.[51] With the guidance of Gerratana, Santucci had developed not only a profound awareness of Gramsci's works, but also a sober and rigorous *method*, faithful to the texts and rejecting those historiographic hypotheses advanced by conjecture alone, i.e. that lacked firm evidence. In the face of so many attempts at instrumentalisation, Santucci's work provides the example of a scholar who, while nevertheless sympathetic to political passion

---

44 Ragazzini 2002, p. 9.
45 Ragazzini 2002, pp. 99–100.
46 Ragazzini 2002, p. 67.
47 Ragazzini 2002, p. 100.
48 In relation to Gramsci's ideas on individual psychology it is worth noting the work of a professional psychologist: Ghiro 2012.
49 Santucci 2005 (with essays by E.J. Hobsbawm, A. Buttigieg and L. La Porta).
50 Santucci 1987b.
51 Some of which are collected in Santucci 2001.

and tolerant of its influence, never gave way to the temptation to forget one of those Gramscian mottoes which he loved to cite: 'the affirmation of truth is a political necessity'.[52]

Other interesting reflections on Gramsci and political economy were included in chapters of a volume by Luigi Cavallaro titled *Lo Stato dei diritti. Politica economia a rivoluzione passiva in Occidente* – 'The State of Rights: Political Economy and Passive Revolution in the West'. The author saw 'a *theory of transition*' in *Notebook 22*, one 'able to coherently think through the fact that "the old is dying, the new is yet to be born" in the capitalist West'.[53] Cavallaro focussed on the cardinal concepts of Gramscian 'political economy' claiming that 'Gramsci founded a theory of immanence capable of seeing the *coexistence of different modes of production in the historical present, each in struggle with the other for consequent hegemony*'.[54] Such conflicts between modes of production, which '*cannot but pass through the construction of new automations, of new rationalities*, which allow the reproduction of a whole society at different levels based on the emergence of new needs'[55] and attributed a central role to the state, where it was seen in the *Notebooks* as the protagonist of 'an entirely new historical period'. For Cavallaro the *welfare state* represented an autonomous mode of production coexistent with, but alternative to, the capitalist mode of production: a development which Gramsci certainly had not seen, even if the categories contained in the prison writings remained fundamental for understanding the dynamics of the years following their composition.

For Michele Martelli,[56] the confrontation with Croce was central to the *Notebooks*, both because here Gramsci had completed his reckoning with his own cultural formation, the Italian tradition in its most advanced point, and also because it provided a focus to the philosophy of praxis, maintaining a full autonomy from both Crocean idealism and mechanistic materialism, providing an 'integrated vision of the world'. Croce and Lenin – two authors central to the late Gramsci – converged in the critique of a determinist Marxism. But the Gramsci of the *Notebooks* had not failed to give due credit to philosophical idealism: Croce's new position towards Marxism (from the philosophy meeting in Oxford in 1930 onwards, an event which represented a watershed for Martelli) also represented a decisive turning point for Gramsci himself. In contrast

---

52   This is also the title of a later collection of essays by Santucci, partly on Gramsci: Santucci 2011.
53   Cavallaro 2005, pp. 120–1.
54   Cavallaro 2005, p. 125.
55   Cavallaro 2005, p. 129.
56   Martelli 2001. Also see the prior volume, Martelli 1996.

to Croce, Gramsci saw a strict connection between history and morality, even if he refused *both* Kantian abstract formalism *and* any approach that denied the responsibility of the individual, assigning all responsibility to the social sphere.

The development of Gramsci's thought regarding intellectuals over the course of his political life formed the subject of a contribution by Gianni Fresu,[57] focusing above all on the question of the construction of the Communist Party. From the *Ordine Nuovo* to the birth of the PCd'I and the affirmation of the anti-Bordigist 'centre', up till the fundamental *Lyons Theses*, the events of Gramsci's political life were reconstructed from the perspective of the theoretical and political journey of the workers' movement and the Communist movement, polemically rejecting all of those readings which had transformed Gramsci into an author external to these traditions.

In 2005 a conference took place in Naples and Salerno on that term which has become synonymous with Gramsci's legacy, 'hegemony'.[58] The meeting – organised by Angelo d'Orsi – aimed to investigate this 'controversial word' which, used in so many different contexts, and frequently in pretentious or blundering ways, risked losing any precise meaning. The contributions focussing most explicitly on Gramsci himself were those by Giancarlo Schirru, who discussed the Lo Piparo's thesis of the concept's derivation from Gramsci's linguistic education; Francesco Giasi, who confronted the topic of the Turin years and the factory councils; Anna Di Biagio, who delved into the debates in the higher echelons of the Third International; Giuseppe Cospito, who took up the notes of the *Notebooks* in which the concept was dealt with; Alberto Burgio, who emphasised the necessary link between hegemony and its economic dimension; Giuseppe Vacca, who proposed a supranational interpretation, allied with the issue of interdependence; and Raul Modernti, who focussed on the hegemonic operation effected by Togliatti. In my own contribution, I returned to the history of the polemical debates surrounding the term. Other contributors whose investigations nonetheless related to Gramsci are represented by Luigi Punzo on Labriola, Salvatore Cingari on Croce and above all Gianfranco Borrelli on Bordiga. These were three authors – Labriola, Croce and Bordiga – to whom Gramsci, in quite different ways, owed a debt in refining the concept, a term which (as the conference confirmed) had been interpreted in many ways, both by Gramsci himself and in the interpretations and *uses* to which Gramsci had been put.

---

57 Fresu 2005.
58 D'Orsi and Chiarotto 2008.

3   Gramsci's Translatability

The events of 2007, marking the sixtieth anniversary of Gramsci's death, began in Rome in April with a convention organised by the Fondazione Istituto Gramsci and the International Gramsci Society on *Gramsci, le culture e il mondo* – 'Gramsci, Cultures and the World' – focussing on those interpretations which had had the widest diffusion in previous decades outside of Italy and in particular in the sphere of *cultural studies* in the English-speaking world.[59] The volume of acts from the conference,[60] prefaced by Giuseppe Vacca and Giorgio Baratta,[61] was divided into four sections, reserved respectively for 'The use of Gramsci in Indian subaltern studies', 'Gramsci in British cultural studies', 'The presence of Gramsci in American cultural and post-colonial studies' and 'Gramsci and Said in the Islamic and Mediterranean world'. British cultural studies – a school that already spanned half a century through the works of Raymond Williams and Richard Hoggart, trailblazers of the various other *schools* represented by the different sections of the conference – was the focus of interesting reconstructions by Anne Showstack Sassoon, Ursula Apitzsch and Elisabetta Gallo, who recalled some of the aspects and fundamental problems of the school, as well as a dialogue between Baratta, Derek Boothman and Stuart Hall,[62] one of the main exponents of the 'Birmingham School'. Hall's claim was of not having so much *interpreted* Gramsci as having *used* him in the face of particular contemporary political and social phenomena – for example, in reading Thatcherism as 'authoritarian populism'. Hall's formula applied to other aspects

---

[59]   On this it is also worth noting Chambers 2006, which collated contributions from a seminar which took place a year previously in Naples on Gramsci, including essays by G. Baratta, L. Curti, L. Durante and P. Voza; and Adamo 2007, acts from a conference organised in Trieste by the Istituto Gramsci Friuli-Venezia Giulia, in which Gramsci was present above all in the essay by M. Paladini Musitelli, G. Chakravorty Spivak, G. Baratta, I. Chambers, M. Cometa, D. Forgacs and R. Mordenti.

[60]   Schirru 2009.

[61]   The President of the Igs Italia after Gerratana's death in 2001, a vibrant force in in Gramsci studies, founder of the Igs Italia and of the Terra Gramsci network, co-author of many documentaries and theatrical texts dedicated to the Sardinian thinker, and among the principle Italian scholars of the new Gramsci readings outside of Italy, Giorgio Baratta passed away in 2010. For accounts, memories and articles on his activity, see https://www.igsitalia.org in the section *In memoria di Giorgio Baratta* (accessed 26 October 2021).

[62]   After being unjustly ignored for too long in our country, the important arguments of the *Centre for Contemporary Cultural Studies* at the University of Birmingham has been recognized through two anthologies: Hall 2006a and Hall 2006b. There are various writings on Gramsci or his use in both volumes. For a critique of Hall's ideas, see Brunello 2007.

as well, defining them as 'the union between popular authority and the market', stating that he also thought 'Berlusconi to be an exponent of authoritarian populism ... by virtue of the strong connection he has established between the media, sport and entertainment, etc., those essential ingredients for the governance of a state'.[63] Hall did not fail to problematise the passage from the use of Gramscian categories in the 'national' context in which they have been born to the contemporary context of globalisation: a significant question, as all too frequently the categories of the *Notebooks* have been hastily integrated into contemporary questions without adequately thinking through their adaptability (or 'translation').

The session on the study of the Indian subaltern was also of great interest, largely for the careful reconstruction which Paolo Capuzzo gave of this historical political school, and the precise points made by Marcus Green on the question of the subaltern classes in Gramsci's work. Ranajit Guha, one of the main protagonists of *subaltern studies*, also contributed a masterful explanation of the concept's origins, the complications in the concept of power in colonial and post-colonial India and the reasons that some of the principle Gramscian categories had proved to be useful in South Asia. Guha claimed that 'Gramsci's thought possesses an openness which invites and encourages adaptation'.[64] It was undoubtedly true that the *form* of Gramsci's thought – its necessarily fragmentary nature, its unsystematic, undogmatic, dialogic character – represented an invitation to develop and adapt it to different contexts, even if it were also necessary to always understand that this work of *translation* of Gramscian thought did have to mean forgetting Gramsci's intention that through and practice transform the world, a forgetting that had been frequently risked in other continents especially.

Various aspects of the *American* Gramsci were studied in essays by Joseph Buttigieg, Renate Holub, Ronald Judy, Benedetto Fontana and Giancarlo Schirru. It was above all Fontana (an American who teaches in New York) who critically interrogated the destiny of the conceptual instruments of the *Notebooks* in a society where 'the category of class has been evicted from the political vocabulary of the radical left',[65] replaced by *issues* which seem to change according to each individual situation, without managing to find a real bond, synthesis or project that might allow them to go beyond 'corporate economics'. Fontana added a radical evaluation: 'The politics of the left, centred on

---

63   S. Hall in Schirru 2009, p. 26.
64   R. Guha in Schirru 2009, p. 31.
65   B. Fontana in Schirru 2009, p. 169.

these questions of identity, diversity and multiculturalism, instead of offering an alternative to the dominant order, is its purest reflection'.[66]

The fourth session was also of great interest: Abdesselam Cheddadi, Derek Boothman and Massimo Campanini interrogated the presence of Islam in the *Notebooks* and the presence of Gramsci in the Arab and Islamic world. Peter Mayo and Michele Brondino examined the connections between the Southern question, the question of language and the Mediterranean. Iain Chambers compared the politics of the Italian South and Orientalism, Gramsci and Said.

The Rome convention, so rich and articulate, constituted an important and much needed moment of awareness regarding Gramsci's thought as it had spread out from Italy, above all over the previous two decades. Other analogous moments followed over the 'Gramscian year' of 2007, almost as if the enormous expansion of the English language Gramscian bibliography had just been noticed and now we in Italy were attempting to hurriedly catch up with indications that had passed us by. A particularly informative intervention was the example given by the thick supplement to the newspaper *Liberazione* on 29 April, with the English title 'Gramsci Now', edited by Giorgio Baratta, Lea Durante and Eleonora Forenza, with writings by numerous other protagonists in the different readings of Gramsci throughout the world, including Timothy Brennan, Joseph Buttigieg, Edward Said, Stuart Hall, Carlos Nelson Countho, Giovanni Semeraro, Eric Hobsbawm and Raymond Williams, ending with the Brazilian singer and musician Caetano Veloso. A more challenging initiative, again in 2007, was the series of volumes titled *Studi gramsciani nel mondo* – 'Gramscian Studies in the World', issued by the Fondazione Istituto Gramsci, attempting to translate and publish in Italy the best writings on Gramsci which had appeared outside of his own country. The first volume, edited by Giuseppe Vacca and Giancarlo Schirru, focussed on a panorama of the years 2000–2005,[67] attempting to privilege those works which provided what seemed to the editors to be 'the greatest contribution to the critical deepening of basic aspects of Gramscian thought', but which also 'illustrated various aspect in the international diffusion of Gramsci's writings'.[68] This included Amartya Sen and Joseph Buttigieg, Marcus Green, Benedetto Fontana, Portantiero, Kanoussi, Adam Morton and many others – all essays which demonstrated how outside of Italy there were works and studies of a level less distant from 'Gramsci's

---

66   B. Fontana in Schirru 2009, p. 171.
67   Vacca and Schirru 2007.
68   Vacca and Schirru 2007, p. 17.

world' than that which had appeared at times in *cultural studies*, above all overseas. The following year Vacca, Capuzzore and Schirru edited another volume of international Gramscian studies, focussing on cultural debates and divided into three sections: the reception of Gramsci in British cultural studies; Gramsci and Indian Subaltern Studies; Gramsci in the recent international debate in Post-colonial Studies.[69] Other volumes in the series would come out in the following years on 'international relations'[70] and 'Gramsci in Latin America'.[71] Furthermore in 2009 an international meeting was organised at the University of Cagliari on 'Gramsci in Asia and Africa',[72] encompassing Gramsci's fortunes in the Arab world, in India and in China, as well as in studies on the subaltern and in post-colonial literature.

This vast activity of study and information in Italy on all that had happened in the world with respect to the translation, awareness and diffusion of Gramsci was necessary (if perhaps too late), in order to bridge a gap that had formed, reflecting real processes of great interest and importance. On the other hand we should not fail to raise some questions and problems. For example, in an interesting volume edited by Mauro Pala and titled *Amercanismi. Sulla ricezione del pensiero di Gramsci negli Stati Uniti* – 'Americanisms: On the Reception of Gramsci's Thought in the USA' – the American scholar Timothy Brennan provided a long list of 'those aspects of Gramsci's production most neglected in the United States', concluding that the impact of the Sardinian thinker in the American cultural realm was for the most part connected to his *heretical* relation to Marxism, reasons which to some extent were *invented*.[73] Another intellectual from the USA was Joseph Buttigieg, president of the International Gramsci Society; in the context of a convention on *La lingua/le lingue di Gramsci e delle sue opere* – 'Gramsci's Language/s and the Language/s of his Works' – which took place in Sassari in October 2007, Buttigieg lamented that one frequently found 'a Gramsci who was almost unrecognisable' among scholars in the Anglophone intellectual world, including the most prestigious among them.[74] As such he reconfirmed Foucault's observation, in a letter from 1984, that Gramsci was an author who was far more frequently cited than actually understood.[75] On the other hand, Buttigieg claimed:

---

69   Vacca, Schirru and Capuzzo 2008.
70   Vacca, Baroncelli, Del Pero and Schirru 2009.
71   Vacca, Kanoussi and Schirru 2011.
72   Baldussi and Manduchi 2010.
73   Brennan 2009, pp. 78–79.
74   J.A. Buttigieg in Lussana and Pissarello 2008, p. 226.
75   J.A. Buttigieg in Lussana and Pissarello 2008, p. 225.

Leafing through the 776 pages of *Cultural Studies* – a collection of essays by a range of authors, brought together in a single volume designed for university courses – one recognises very quickly that many exponents of this thread of research are more disposed to decipher the elements of counter-hegemonies which dwell in popular culture, rather than analyse, as Gramsci did, the reasons for the durability and elasticity of dominant hegemony. Counter-hegemonic currents are discovered in the most diverse and striking phenomena: in the spectacles and songs of Madonna, in pornography, even 'shopping' for economically disadvantaged social categories. Such a concept of counter-hegemony was never elaborated by Gramsci in his writings, and hence it would be right to consider this a pseudo-Gramscian concept. The attribution of this concept to Gramsci rests on the conviction that he was the propagator of the thesis that popular culture is itself counter-hegemonic. More than just a thesis, for the practitioners of Cultural Studies, the essentially counter-hegemonic nature of popular culture is taken as an article of faith inherited from Gramsci.[76]

The ways in which Gramsci has been received and utilised (sometimes mistakenly) in linguistic and cultural contexts entirely different from his own were also bound up with problems of the insufficient awareness of the works of the Sardinian thinker, not always translated and adequately distributed in important global languages, as noted by congress organised at Sassari, the acts of which were published as *La lingua/le lingue di Gramsci e delle sue opere. Scrittura, riscritture, letture in Italia e nel mondo* – 'Writing, Rewritings and Interpretations in Italy and the World'. To focus on the *Notebooks* alone: the 'Gerratana' editions of these had been translated in France by a prestigious publisher (Gallimard) but over a long period of time and not without problems between the Istituto Gramsci and the French editor, Robert Paris.[77] The *Notebooks* had been published in Spanish in Mexico, again by a prestigious publisher – Ediciones Era – beginning as far back as 1981; but again in this case the translation was completed over many years, and only finished in 2001 (thanks to the work of Dora Kanoussi and the Universidad Autonoma De Puebla).[78] In Germany it had been Argument Verlag and the group under the direction of Wolfgang F. Haug who had translated the critical edition, beginning in the 1990s; they had also expanded the critical apparatus and, in the

---

76 J.A. Buttigieg in Lussana and Pissarello 2008, p. 227.
77 A. Cadinu in Lussana and Pissarello 2008, pp. 197 onwards.
78 D. Kanoussi in Lussana and Pissarello 2008, pp. 237–39.

translation, 'modernised' Gramsci's language. The Portuguese edition of the *Notebooks* (the work of Carlos Nelson Coutinho, Luiz Sérgio Henriques and Marco Aurélio Nogueira in Brazil, through the Civilização Brasileira) and in English (in the USA, through Columbia University Press, with the editing of Joseph Buttigieg) had both included an important expansion of the critical apparatus in an attempt to help the non-Italian reader who lacked many points of reference obvious to a reader from Gramsci's own country. But the Brazilian edition sacrificed a great number of the notes from the first draft, while the American edition is still stalled at the translation of *Notebook 8*. The lack of an English critical edition of the *Notebooks*, which would be of great importance (and takes priority over the thematic edition, with all the limitations which it brings), has lasted for decades and has caused many interpretative problems – forcing whoever does not know the Italian language to read Gramsci through the filter of the selected anthologies.

Throughout, if the lack of a translation or the scarce reproducibility of the *Notebooks* in many important languages (those in which Gramsci has been referred to and moreover the few languages into which his works have been translated at all) has without doubt been the cause of some of the confusions in interpreting the Sardinian communist, many of the *abuses* are nevertheless connected to an overly instrumental *use* of his thought – even if the mere *use* of a thinker such as Gramsci does not necessarily betray the profundity of his though, spirit, ideas and objectives. Yet we have seen Gramsci being *used* exactly by those political and intellectual forces which he opposed ('right wing Gramscianism'). Or indeed there are even readers who (on purpose or otherwise) completely ignore the organic links within his thought, leading from analysis to strategic proposal without grasping quite how difficult it is to fully understand his line of inquiry. In conclusion, if one loses 'any connection with the horizon of meaning in which Gramsci developed his ideas, then perhaps one is no longer speaking about Gramsci, but something else entirely'.[79]

4   Renewed Interest

Many other meetings took place in Italy on the occasion of the 'Gramscian year' of 2007. One was held in Sardinia, from the end of April to the beginning of May, which included two tours around the most significant Gramscian sites

---

[79]   G. Liguori in Lussana and Pissarello 2008, p. 148.

on the island: Cagliarai, Ghilarza and Ales: the 'Gramscian journey' proposed by the Istituto Gramsci della Sardegna (27 April – 6 May 2007)[80] and the Third International Convention of the International Gramsci Society (3–6 May 2007), entitled *Antonio Gramsci, un sardo nel 'mondo grande e terribile'* – 'A Sardinian in the 'Great and Terrible World''.[81] The second meeting was especially well attended, by both Italian and non-Italian scholars, providing a varied and fascinating framework for the best international debates around and research into the Sardinian thinker, walking a line between a historical, theoretical approach and the attempts to connect Gramscian thought to contemporary politics. The sessions were dedicated to the connection between 'National/International'; the question of 'Intellectuals and Mass Society'; 'Passive Revolution and Hegemonic Struggle'; and 'Gramsci in the World Today', while two seminars were organised on the question of 'Speaking and Language' and 'Marxism as a Philosophy of Praxis'. This was a meeting which (deliberately) had no single thread, a moment of exchange between very different experiences – as is the nature of an association such as the IGS which has members from five continents[82] – of which here it is impossible to provide even a rough draft or cohesive summary.[83]

The IGS and the *Centro interuniversitario di ricerca per gli studi gramsciani* also organised a conference in Bari on 29–30 October, on *Antonio Gramsci: tra passato e presente* – 'Between Past and Present' – introduced by Pasquale Voza and with numerous contributors and discussants (including many younger scholars). The three sections were given over to 'Moral and intellectual reform and the construction of a new common sense'; 'Spontaneity and conscious direction: The formation of collective will' and 'National-International and the combinations of hegemony'.[84]

Another conference was organised in Bari in December on *Gramsci nel suo tempo* – 'Gramsci in His Times' – organised by the Fondazione Istituto Gram-

---

80 Orrù and Rudas 2010.
81 Many relations and intervention are available online, on the webpage of the Igs, in the section *Special III convegno Igs* (accessed 26 August 2012).
82 For the Igs in a global context, see the site edited by the secretary of the society, Marcus Green: www.internationalgramscisociety.org.
83 I recommend the accurate account of A. Errico, C. Meta and E. Forenza which can be read on the Igs website, under the section *Eventi gramsciani* (accessed 26 August 2012).
84 See the account of T. Bucci, which was published in *Liberazione*, 1 Novemebr 2007, but also on the Igs website in the section *Eventi gramsciani*. The contributions by A. Burgio, C.N. Coutinho, L. Durante and S. Suppa were published in *Critixa marxista*, 2008, issues 2 and 3. Durante's essay and others on Gramsci and others which have been referred to were collected along with studies on other issues in Durante 2008.

sci.[85] The title indicated the innovative formula of this meeting: there were calls to deepen individual aspects of long historical events and of scholars of Gramscian theory who were in some cases not Gramsci specialists but rather represented moments and protagonists (for example Tasca or Sraffa) in 'Gramsci's time'. These aspects were delved into with new and original research, a deepening of understanding which attempted to carry forward the state of knowledge. There were many contributions of great interest, including innovative points of reflection in the section dedicated to 'Socialism and Italy in the face of war', and also in that on the Turin years, in particular essays by Leonardo Rapone, Claudio Natoli, Sergio Soave (on Gramsci and Tasca) and Angelo D'Orsi. In the second part, on 'The Italian Revolution', interest focussed on the period from the 'red biennial' to 1926, with many contributions of note (including the contribution by Francesco Auletta and Nerio Naldi on Piero Sraffa). The third section was particularly rich, dedicated to 'The formation of the philosophy of praxis', in which special attention ought to be given to the contributions by Francesca Izzo, Roberto Gualtieri and Fabio Frosini.

In his presentation of the acts of the conference, Giuseppe Vacca wrote that this had been a scholarly convention which 'demanded long preparation and hard work to coordinate the research', 'with the objective of assessing the state of Gramscian studies in relation to the work of reconstructing the context of his thought, the network of its interactions and above all the connection between theory and biography'.[86] This was the description of a method consistent with the best studies on Gramsci over the previous decade.

Among many other conferences, seminars and meetings, we should nonetheless record that organised by the trade unions in Milan in March on 'Gramsci and Italian History';[87] the international conference (with scholars from Australia, Brazil, the USA) that took place (for the most part) at the University of Calabria on 'Gramsci in His Times, Gramsci in Our Times'; the Naples conference, in October on 'José Martì, Antonio Gramsci and Universal Culture', organised by the Cuban ambassador to Italy and the journal *Latinoamerica*; the initiatives by the Istituto Gramsci in Tuscany – the convention on 'Gramsci and the Question of National Identity' and a conference circuit – which gave rise to thick volume almost a year later;[88] and the three meetings which

---

85   Giasi 2008.
86   G. Vacca in Giasi 2008, p. 17.
87   The acts were published in Camera del lavoro 2008. A full calendar by one of the organisers and protagonists of the meeting, Marzio Zanantoni is available on the Igs Italia site, under the section *Eventi gramsciani* (accessed 26 August 2012).
88   Polizzi 2010.

took place in Turin, on the initiative of Angelo d'Orsi, among which one can single out that of 8–9 November, titled 'Our Gramsci',[89] dedicated to Gramscian research by younger scholars.[90] Particular mention should be made – again for thematic originality, one of the least debated questions in the immense Gramscian bibliography – to the convention organised in December at the Istituto Gramsci Friuli-Venezia Giulia on 'Gramsci and Science'.[91] In his *Introduction*, Marina Paladini emphasised the vast scale of Gramsci's reflections on science and his accusation that Italy lacked a sufficiently developed 'scientific mentality'.[92] Gramsci was the bearer of an epistemologically modern vision, not only combating Bukharin's objectivism, but with 'the merit of partially anticipating that interpretative line (from Popper to Kuhn) which was to dominate the history of twentieth-century epistemology'.[93] Antonio Di Meo, author of a work among the most exhaustive and interesting on this topic, recalled the 'intersubjectivity' that characterised Gramsci's position in the epistemological debate, as opposed to Bukharin's 'bloc' of 'Thomistic realism', 'common sense of the masses' and the 'vulgar materialism'. Unfortunately, Di Meo concluded, 'Gramsci's positions, simultaneously "orthodox" and innovative – seemingly paradoxically – resonated only weakly in Marxist Italian theory, including in what followed'.[94]

Finally, Gramsci was remembered by the major national institutions: parliament publicly commemorated the Sardinian communist on 17 April 2007, with contributions by Fausto Bertinoti and Mario Tronti,[95] who prepared a small work for the occasion with some of the *Prison Letters*,[96] while the President of the Republic, Giorgio Napolitano, went to Ghirlaza and gave a presentation on the volumes *Notebooks of Translations* which began to be issued in 2007 via the publication of the 'National Edition of Antonio Gramsci's Writings'.[97] These events – the conferences, publications and the article which accompanied the

---

89 An indirect product of this meeting, as one reads in the preface, was to be the volume D'Orsi 2011, in which 28 young scholars confront Gramsci with around 50 protagonists of Italian history, from Dante to Petrarch, and from D'Annunzio to Gobetti.
90 Many of these conferences are detailed on the Igs webstie, in the section *Eventi gramsciani*.
91 Paladini Musitelli 2008.
92 Paladini Musitelli 2008, p. 12.
93 Paladini Musitelli 2008, p. 16.
94 A. Di Meo in Paladini Musitelli 2008, p. 146.
95 An account is given on the Igs website, under the section *Eventi gramsciani*.
96 A. Gramsci, *Ai figli. Lettere dal carcere*, with 42 letters to Delio and Giuliano. The booklet also contained a photographic reproduction of the originals of some of the letters and also photographs of Antonio, Giulia and their children, and Sardinia and Turi.
97 See p. 324 onwards.

occasion of the seventieth anniversary of Gramsci's death – are also testament to Gramsci's relaunch within Italian culture.

More evidence of this fact was the publication from 2007 onwards of new anthologies of Gramsci's works, made available through the expiry of the publication rights. We have already focused on many of the problems connected to anthologising Gramsci.[98] In 2007 there were new, more laborious attempts to create a *general* Gramscian anthology, as well as thematic anthologies, a task far from easy if the collections were to avoid superficiality. We ought note the anthologies by Giuseppe Vacca[99] and Marco Gervasoni.[100] Aside from praise for the critical apparatus and introductions to the two volumes,[101] it ought to be said that the range of pre-prison writings in the second was much greater: Vacca's anthology provided 21 essays (150 pages of a total 300 reserved for the *Notebooks*), Gervasoni's 57 essays (250 pages, while 180 were reserved for the *Notebooks*). If the inclusion of the pre-prison works often suffered from limitations of space, the act of anthologising the *Notebooks* remained again difficult in its own way. While Gervasoni carried out a quite limited selection that was inevitably found wanting, restricting itself to only five of the notebooks (nos. 10, 11, 13, 19 and 21), Vacca's solution – along diachronic and thematic criteria – also risked creating a certain confusion through the decision to 'group together selected extracts of the "special notebooks" in specific chapters'[102] and present them to the reader with edited titles, without allowing one to find the places from which they had been extracted. The anthologisation of the *Notebooks* thus arguably not only had unsatisfying results, but the attempt had not been given adequate thought beforehand.[103] The discourse around thematic anthologies is of course quite different, which have continued to be issued with varied aims: from literary criticism to the writings on theatre, from the writings on Sardinia to a collection on Unification.[104]

---

98 See p. 283 onwards.
99 Gramsci 2007a. It is also worth mentioning another, although more limited, anthology edited by Vacca, compiled from only four Gramscian texts, and 'not for resale, available only to readers of *l'Unità*': Gramsci 2007b.
100 Gramsci 2007c.
101 Allow me to recommend my own essay, Liguori 2007.
102 G. Vacca in Gramsci 2007a, p. x.
103 In recent years there have been other anthologies, both those designed for schools (e.g. Gramsci 2008a) and *instant books* aimed at a much wider public with a limited selection of the younger writings (e.g. Gramsci 2011a).
104 Gramsci 2004b, Gramsci 2010a, Gramsci 2008b, Gramsci 2010b, Gramsci 2011b. It is also worth noting the republication of Gramsci 1972 and the now classic Gramsci 1997c, republished as *Antologia*.

In summary, the many anthologies of Gramsci which have come out demonstrate on the one hand the interest in the Sardinian thinker to a non-specialised public, and on the other the difficulties in approaching so vast a *corpus* of posthumous writings, texts that are often quite difficult to decipher without an awareness that goes beyond an initial reading.

5   Gramsci and Politics

A different confirmation of this renewed interest in Gramsci was provided by a series of books that came out in 2007 and offered an interpretative range broader than usual, and a discussion – even if indirectly – between positions that are frequently quite distant from each other. In 1999 Bartolo Anglani had published a volume on 'Hegemony and Poetry' in which he claimed that the latter term – which had only a historical, literary and artistic meaning – should not lead one to search for a Gramscian interest in an aesthetic theory, because Gramsci's discourse was entirely centred on the political dimension, on hegemonic research. Beginning with these convictions the author argued against that long history of interpretative and critical theory claiming that 'Gramscians (always in unison with their evil twins, the anti-Gramscians) [had] deformed Gramsci'.[105] In 2007 the author returned to the Sardinian thinker, with theses which appeared in some ways quite discontinuous from those he had proposed some years prior. Gramsci as a man and as a political thinker, Anglani claimed, had erred in everything, even if frequently scholars had not seen 'the absurdity' of Gramscian politics 'not only with respect to the problems and necessities of today but also with respect to Gramsci's own times'; the Sardinian intellectual could thus be studied – Anglani concluded – 'only from an "aesthetic" perspective'.[106] The author focussed mainly on a 1920s Gramsci, and the revolutionary Sardinian became associated with Maoist terrorism and 'Red Guards'.[107] The circle seemed to be definitively closed when in a book of some years later Anglani announced what seemed to him to now be Gramsci's real limits: 'his politics "in action" ... a sequence of wrong choices deriving from an unfounded and provisional analysis'.[108] This was because he had not been a reformist and socialist. Gramsci was a genius, but in the field of theory. In the field of practical politics, he was a disaster.

---

105   Anglani 1999, p. 24.
106   Anglani 2007, p. 44.
107   Anglani 2007, p. 128.
108   Anglani 2009, p. 27.

Contrary to Anglani, others expressed their conviction that Gramsci had not only been a great leader of his era, a Communist and Marxist who had opened the way for a new politics of the subaltern classes – even more than this, the author of the *Notebooks* was considered still vital for understanding the contemporary world and seeking to change it. This was, for example, the belief held by Giuseppe Prestipino, who observed with a subtle argument, that there had always really been *three Gramscis*:

> there is the Gramsci who lies buried in the ground, but whose memory and papers will be looked after. There is the Gramsci diligently poured over on the tables of philological experts, in the expectation that he could be embalmed as a great classic. And finally there is the living Gramsci from whom one cannot demand a response, but with whom instead one can enter into dialogue, a conversation that can project itself onto the problems of our own times.[109]

Only by starting from Gramsci could the contemporary *passive* revolution – which was for the author neo-liberal supremacy – be transformed[110] into *active* revolution, through a Gramscian 'intellectual and moral reform', thanks to the richness of the categories which had anticipated some of the traits of contemporary society, e.g. 'the Gramscian conception which sees the pairing of capital and labour included in the fullest divide between ruler and the subaltern subject 'adequate' to the contemporary (and truly "totalitarian") submission of every form of life (not only of work) to capitalist rationality and irrationality'.[111]

In his *Per Gramsci. Crisi e potenza del moderno* – 'For Gramsci: Crisis and Modern Power' – Alberto Burgio also established a strong link between Gramsci's own time and the present, focussing on the centrality of the processes of passive revolution. This focused on neoliberalism, 'Reagan and Thatcher's "conservative revolution"', which represented a true 'restoration', equal to the 'passive revolution of the twentieth-century established by Fascist regimes'.[112] Despite this, there was 'at least an *apparent* ability for capitalism to reach a consensus in this historic phase'.[113] Throughout, Burgio claimed, given that

---

109 Prestipino 2007, p. 117.
110 Prestipino 2007, p. 143.
111 Prestipino 2007, p. 99. Also see the same author's more recent Prestipino 2011, which is more a book *with* than *about* Gramsci.
112 Burgio 2007, p. 30.
113 Burgio 2007, p. 34.

such processes are 'ambivalent' and that 'passive revolution' has a 'dialectical nature' – with a 'relatively progressive' dimension'[114] as Gramsci himself emphasised – one could not ignore the fact that 'bourgeois modernity ... has granted labour a conscious subjectivity of its own strengths and irreducibly transformative nature'.[115] This was a line that included a strong and Gramscian 'optimism of the will'.

Pasquale Voza's book *Gramsci e la 'continua crisi'* – 'Gramsci and the "Continuing Crisis"' – focussed on the concept of passive revolution and its analytical potential in the contemporary epoch, and no less to the phenomena in Gramsci's own time and analysis, which tried to achieve a balance between rigorous analysis of the theses and the tendency to find a lesson for today that was neither purely philological not stuck in the past. For Voza too, the phenomenon of passive revolution was not ambivalent, but contained a dialectic. Yet they nevertheless proposed a basic weakness in revolutionary forces for Gramsci: there was thus a lack of that 'vigorous antithesis' on which Vazo correctly put great emphasis. But – the author specified – 'the utility of the argument of passive revolution remains in the ability to imagine an "active revolution" or better still "an anti-passive revolution"',[116] i.e. of subjectification, of the political constitution of the subject of antagonism and conflict', traversing the molecular processes with respect to which Voza emphasised the importance Gramsci laid on a new kind of intellectual and a political party.

It does not seem insignificant that the concept of passive revolution would become central to many of the reflections advanced by interpreters and scholars of Gramsci active on the left: the concept evidently came to be felt as the one most suited to contribute to explanations of decades of neoliberal hegemony. Carlos Nelson Countinho saw nonetheless a use of the concept which was too broad, claiming that 'rather than speaking about passive revolution, it would be useful to try and identify many phenomena of the neoliberal era within the concept of counter-reform', which also had 'its part to play, if perhaps marginally, in Gramsci's categorical arsenal'.[117] Indeed what was missing in the 'neoliberal era' was that typical capacity of hegemonic classes, through 'passive revolution', to accept moments of the reforms pushed for by the subaltern classes, instead demolishing their conquests and rights one by one. This did not mean, naturally, that there were no changes in this process: indeed, for

---

114 Burgio 2007, p. 38.
115 Burgio 2007, p. 77.
116 Voza 2008, p. 51.
117 Coutinho 2007, p. 21.

Gramsci 'the counter-indication of a process of counter-reform does not represent a complete absence of the new, but the great drive to conserve (indeed to restore) a range of possible changes'.[118]

For Raul Mordenti, author of *Gramsci e la rivoluzione necessaria* – 'Gramsci and the Necessary Revolution' – the focus was on how to '*use* Gramsci, and not only cite him'.[119] If 'Gramsci was a communist', as Mordenti wrote, arguing against his reduction to the level of a faint-hearted classic, he was a communist who reasoned by starting from a historical limitation: a rationale which was not of secondary relevance to revolutionaries in a new century. Above all, for Gramsci the revolution was 'contemporary – though neither imminent nor inevitable – which is to say that it is history's key term'.[120] Mordenti focussed at length on the peculiarity of Gramscian revolution. In his analysis of contemporary events (he defined Berlusconism as 'hegemony without hegemony'), Mordenti, along with the category of 'passive revolution', privileged the concept of *Brescianeismo*, seen as a 'characteristic of the national Italian *ethos*'.[121]

That Gramsci was a communist was also underscored by Luciano Canfora, arguing exactly with those parts of the former Communist Party who – just as the right-wing did – wanted to *cleanse* the Sardinian thinker from such an *imperfection*: 'removing this great figure from the history of communism excites the right wing, and also pleases some on the left who have been affected by a notorious and deep amnesia. Luckily there are still those who study history and those texts which Gramsci penned even while he was left to rot in a Fascist prison'.[122] The Gramscian category on which Canfora focused was that of 'Caesarism': the ambiguous role of a 'great personality' who, rising to power through a complex situation, provides an intrinsically anti-democratic solution to political crises.

A large part of Mordenti's book was also dedicated to managing the legacy of Gramsci as Togliatti had moulded it. The same subject was the focus of a book by Michele Maggi, *La filosofia della rivoluzione. Gramsci, la cultura e la*

---

118 Coutinho 2007, p. 26.
119 Mordenti 2007, p. 7. The book was reprinted in 2011 by Editori Riuniti university press. The citations here are to the first edition.
120 Mordenti 2007, p. 42.
121 Mordenti 2007, p. 120. In recent years an interesting collective reflection on the possible *use* of Gramsci in today's reality has been collected in the volume *Seminario* 2010, with essays by A. Burgio, R. Mordenti, M. Porcaro, G. Prestipino, L. Vinci and P. Voza. [Translator's note: the reference is to Antonio Bresciani (1798–1862), a conservative figure heavily criticised by De Sanctis in a work which Gramsci praised highly in the *Notebooks*].
122 Canfora 2007, p. 54.

guerra europea,[123] – 'The Philosophy of Revolution: Gramsci, Culture and the European War' – which was not *only* a monograph on Gramsci but also a sketch of Italian culture in the first decades of the twentieth century, in which a reconstruction of Gramsci's thought was bound up with a dense texture of people, ideas, situations, cultural current. This included Croce first and foremost, but also Gentile, the group around *Voce*, Gobetti and Guido Dorso. Some of the more interesting parts, in the book and the most debatable, were those dealing with Togliatti as protagonist. According to Maggi, following the well-known speech of 1950 on Giolitti, Togliatti had distanced himself from the positions of the *Ordine Nuovo* (as they had related both to Gramsci and Togliatti) in the 1920s. Recognising in Giovanni Giolitti a positive, reformist dimension in the Italy of his times, Togliatti – Maggi claimed – juxtaposed his view of politics as a compromise to a 'politics of an unattainable reality', that is to revolutionary politics. But the Italian left of the post-War period remained imprisoned in the myths of the 1920s, and the *Notebooks* themselves – Maggi maintained – did not deviate that much from this 'actionist' line. I do not believe this to be an convincing evaluation, as in Gramsci's thought there is a theory of revolution which, taking into account the morphological transformations of society and the state, removes itself from nominalist, outdated oppositions between reform and revolution. That is, a culture of beginning from reality itself so as to try and *radically* change it. It is in this direction that Togliatti also pushed matters, a move he had to effect after the fall of Fascism, in a framework, despite all appearances, which was extremely blocked and difficult.

In opposition to many of the authors cited above – Burgio, Mordenti, Prestipino – who agree over a positive evaluation of the *management* of Gramsci's legacy as carried out by Togliatti, for Cesare Bermani there existed a *hidden* Gramsci who had to be liberated, a Gramsci influenced by Bogdanov and Proletkult, assessing the folkloristic and workerist, 'popular creative spirit' of Sorel's influence, which Togliatti and the Italian communist tradition had hidden in order to construct *another* political theoretical tradition connected to with Leninism – but which in truth represented a deformation of Gramsci's thought. This was the thesis at the basis of the book *Gramsci, Intellectuals and Proletarian Culture*,[124] in which the author collated a series of essays written over the course of many decades of activity, relating to popular culture. There were points of interest in the book: Bermani summarised the information already noted, but often forgotten, of the influence of Croce with regards to the

---

[123] Maggi 2008.
[124] Bermani 2007.

Gramscian conception of folklore; or on the reading of Gramsci advanced by scholars such as Ernesto De Martino and Gianni Bosio, to whom the author was particularly indebted. But the anti-Togliattian *anger*, which brought Bermani even to accuse Gerratana of having artificially constructed the critical edition in a way which hid Gramsci's anti-Stalinism, risked covering over the positive results of his ethno-anthropological research. Bermani's book was not the only one which advanced new ideas regarding Gramsci and folklore. Mimmo Boninelli published in the same year *Frammenti indigesti*,[125] – 'Undigested Fragments' – a collection which spanned the works of the young Gramsci, his journalistic writings and politics, as well as the prison works, so as to identify 'folkloristic themes' in many aspects of his experience, from Sardinian to religion and popular superstitions, from proverbs to anecdotes and songs, to dialogic theatre, with as many 'chapters' as there were brief anthological choices: an important mapping out of Gramsci's attention to the material.

Another important monograph was that which the journal *Lares* reserved for *Gramsci ritrovato* – 'Gramsci Rediscovered' – edited again by Boninelli, along with Antonio Deias and Eugenio Testa,[126] which collected together contributions to two conferences held in Nuoro in September 2007 and October 2008. Among the interventions, those by Alberto Maria Cirese (who returned to Gramsci after his important writings of the 1960s and 1970s), Giorgio Baratta, Pietro Clemente, Clara Gallini, Miguel Mellino, Anne Showstack Sassoon, Cosimo Zene and others were important essays: a collective reflection which bore witness to the traditional presence of Gramsci in ethno-anthropological studies in Italy and the *confusion* of recent years, but also a sign of his reprisal, connected to the effects of post-colonial studies. Another sign of this new interest was the Italian translation of a book by the American scholar Kate Crehan on *Gramsci, Culture and Anthropology*,[127] confirming the position which Gramsci had gained within Anglophone anthropology and in studies of the relation between culture and power.

After many books of this kind, one cannot nevertheless neglect the volume by the Canadian Richard J.F. Day, an original production not only for its title: *Gramsci Is Dead*, the Italian translation of which was published in 2008. The book argued against a conception of politics as hegemony. It was not a new thesis, having itself a long theoretical tradition behind it, most of all that of 'spontaneous' anarchism (the original subtitle was *Anarchist Currents in the Newest Social Movements*), returning to some of the trends in the movements

---

125 Boninelli 2007.
126 Deias, Boninelli and Testa 2008.
127 Crehan 2010.

of the 1960s and 1970s, refusing politics in favour of *alternative* life choices, and above all to the Italy of the 'movement of '77', with its Nietzschean rise of 'immediacy' against every theory of mediation, institutional or otherwise. In the end, it also reprised some of the currents of the 'movement of movements' (or the *anti-globalisation movement*) to which the author made explicit reference. The attempt to construct a 'counter-hegemony' was, for Day, illusory, because it would mean accepting 'the hegemony of hegemony', that is a conception of politics according to which a significant change would be reached only by traversing the statist levers of control and through a politics of alliances. Rather, for the author there was a need to act in a 'non-hegemonic' way, 'questioning the basic logic of hegemony' and instead embracing '*affinity for affinity*, that is, for non-universalizing, non-hierarchical, non-coercive relationships based and mutual aid and shared ethical commitments'. One finds here, from a theoretical point of view, the full cultural arena of 'post-structuralism', in a particularly radical version which Day calls 'post-anarchism', the aim of which is to define a politics which 'can in fact lead to progressive social change that responds to the needs and aspirations of disparate identities'.[128] *Differences* are given irrefutable praise, with an inability to see in the dominant structures of the sociopolitical system a unique, holistic structure and from this also the impossibility to counteract it through an alliance of subaltern subjects formed around a project of a complete alternative. It is not enough, however, to recognise *affinity* and to make space for existentialist manifestations and the politics of insubordination, refusal and flight to undefined islands of alternative living modelled on Agamben's concept of 'the coming community'. In its iconoclastic charge, the author seems to have ignored how Gramsci had explained that there was no longer a Winter Palace to be stormed and that one has to reformulate the concept of revolution with a sense of process. And of course, Gramsci spoke of a society divided into classes. If one thinks that there are no longer classes, every discussion of hegemony becomes no more than, and remains, the vengeful battle of oppressed minorities on the basis of their *issues*, which do not, nonetheless, even graze the surface of capital's hegemony over all of society. This would signal not so much *Gramsci's* death, but rather the death of any real hypothesis for change.

---

128   Day 2005, pp. 9–10.

CHAPTER 12

Gramsci's Return (2009–12)

1   New Working Tools

Among other initiatives, the Gramscian year of 2007 saw *l'Unità* distribute a CD-ROM with a digital version of the *Notebooks* (Gerratana's 'critical edition') as a supplement to the newspaper issue of April 27 – edited by Dario Ragazzini, who had worked on this project for many years.[1] The work, containing all of Gramsci's notes, also included the advantage of allowing for important lexical research. This opened up a new frontier – the use of information technology in the study of Gramsci's texts, as had already been applied to many other authors.

In this context the IGS Italia announced in 2011 the creation of a site dedicated to a digital library of Gramscian texts – *GramsciSource* – through which it wanted eventually 'to put Gramsci's works at everyone's disposal (scholars, readers, enthusiasts, the simply curious) in a digital format, as well as information on his life and thought, the scientific and philological debate around his works and their different editions, translations, the history of their criticism and other aspects relating to Gramsci and his presence in the world today'. This was merely the moment of announcing the beginning of a long work, which had a great deal of potential for development. A digital copy had the advantage of proceeding gradually, continually expanding and improving the product, extending that which is *offered* to the reader. For example, one could not imagine the *GramsciSource* would have at first, or immediately after, the ability to offer 'all the works of Gramsci and their translation into many languages, the reproduction of the manuscripts of the principal works, the digitisation of various historic and critical texts on Gramsci'.[2] Furthermore, *digital libraries* are already available on-line for many authors.[3] *GramsciSource* began with making the *Notebooks* available, presenting the texts according to the material as ordered in the manuscripts of each notebook so as to maintain the practical

---

1   The daily newspaper *l'Unità*, in 2007, offered its readers the possibility of buying Gramsci 1997c together with the newspaper.
2   Translator's note: now available at http://quaderni.gramsciproject.org (accessed 14/02/2021).
3   Cf. for example that for Nietzsche (www.nietzschesource.org) and for Wittgenstein (www.wittgensteinsource.org).

reasons – bound up with the international diffusion of the 'critical edition' of 1975 – for the numbering of the notes as established by Gerratana, and verifying the transcription of the original text. This was in reality a new (digital) edition, which had the ability to provide the basis for dealing with many of the different print editions which had been and will continue to be focused on, from that Togliatti and Platone's to Gerratana's and the 'French edition' currently in the process of publication.

Beyond these digital tools, other more traditional but equally precise ones have been put at the disposal of Gramsci scholars in recent years. In 2008 the first volume of the *Bibliografia Gramsciana Ragionata* (BGR) was published,[4] initiated and directed by Angelo d'Orsi; another useful tool for finding one's way through the now vast sea of titles on Gramsci recorded is the *Bibliografia gramsciana online*, initiated and executed by John M. Cammett and now edited by Francesco Giasi and Maria Luisa Righi, which has superseded 19,000 titles.[5] The BGR in fact reports everything which has been published in Italian, providing in a few lines on the content of every book, essay or newspaper article. It is a work which is often indispensable in order to orientate readers, and above all students, who must now pick through so many studies on different aspects of Gramsci's biography or theoretical legacy.

In 2009 the *Dizionario gramsciano 1926–1937* was published, the final harvest of the long work of the seminar on the vocabulary of the *Notebooks* held by the IGS Italia,[6] expanded to include contributions by authors who had worked on Gramsci for a long period of time. There are more than 600 entries, written by over sixty scholars from different countries, spanning more than 900 pages. Every entry provided references to others which were logically connected to it, thus forming a lattice of indications and citations. The objective – as one reads in the *Preface* – was obviously not to 'simplify or "contain" Gramsci', nor to 'restore – in a systematic form – all of the richness of his ideas', but rather to identify *ways of reading* based on attention to the text, to its diachronic nature and polysemy. As such all the entries, above all the longer ones, were not only reports on different meanings which the terms assumed in the

---

4 D'Orsi 2008. It is hope that this will be supplemented by two further volumes: *II. 1966–1987* and *III. 1988–2007*.
5 Cf. www.fondazionegramsci.org (accessed 31 October 2021). Also see p. 237, above. An important contribution is also the additional bibliography made by Alessandro Errico and Michele Filippini for Italy and Marcus Green for the rest of the world: see respectively the sites of the Igs Italia and of the IGS.
6 Liguori and Voza 2009.

prison *corpus*, but also 'directories' that referred back to the principle places in Gramsci's prison writings in which every catchword was treated, in the awareness that 'an entry in a dictionary cannot give an account of all the richness of an author's thought, but can and ought to be a useful instrument to accompany the reader's discovery of it'.[7]

The entries in the *Dizionario gramsciana* were of three different kinds, distinguished by length and according to the importance of the different catchwords in the prison writings. Not only concepts but also the people who filled up Gramsci's pages were included, and not only the most studied categories ('Americanism', 'philosophy of praxis', 'hegemony', etc) but also questions and topics which had been focused on less, terms and expressions which appeared in Gramsci's writings with their own peculiar physiognomy (from '*aporia*' to 'arbitrariness', from 'unemployment' to 'laicism', from 'sport' to 'wishful thinking'). The attention to the text in all its dynamics was an attempt to help in the reconstruction of the 'developing rhythm of thought'; clearly the task and responsibility still remains for each individual interpreter.

In 2009 an '*anastatic* edition of the manuscripts' of the *Notebooks* was published,[8] edited by Gianni Francioni, with the collaboration of Giuseppe Cospito and Fabio Frosini. Inspired by the new French edition of the *Notebooks*, the '*anastatic* edition' of Gramsci's main work was designed for a public imagined to be broader than that of philologists and specialists;[9] but it was (and is) useful above all for an advanced student of the *Notebooks*. To be accurate, this was not a *facsimile* edition, as was and is desirable[10] and could be published in the remit of the 'national edition', with a great deal of scientific research, even if undoubtedly also available only at a very high price (understandably this would not be an edition for everyday use). The volumes published in 2009 instead reproduced the *content* of the original notebooks (Gramsci's writings) without nevertheless reproducing the colours of gradations of colour (of the notebooks,

---

7   Liguori and Voza 2009, p. 6.
8   The term 'anastatic' is used in a broad, not literal, sense: this was in fact a photographic reproduction of the *Notebooks*, in black and white.
9   It should not be forgotten that this was, as the newpaper *L'Unione sarda* put it, an 'edition for the newsstands', 'intended for a broad audience', even if following 'rigorous philological and critical work' (G. Vacca in Gramsci 2009, i, p. 17. Also see A. Accardo in Gramsci 2009, p. 3).
10 In the first edition of this book I had hoped for a 'photographic reproduction of the originals of the *Notebooks*, so as to allow a fully developed philological debate and a more rigorous checking by the scientific community on the inteprétations which have gradually come about'. Liguori 1996a, p. 252.

the inks, the prison stamps).[11] The format also differed slightly[12] and of course the kind of paper on which it was printed.

The thirty-three notebooks in which Gramsci had written were regrouped in sixteen volumes (to which were adjoined a first volume given over to introductory essays). Some volumes merged more notebooks together, skipping the pages that Gramsci had left blank, both at the start of the 'special notebooks' so as to write introductory notes at a later date, which were at times either not written on or did not take up all the space left for them; and also at the end of some of the notebooks, not all of which were filled up for various reasons.[13] A *facsimile* edition would help the reader to better grasp the fact that the notebooks used by Gramsci are not all essays, and not essays all of equal standing (indeed, there are some that only take up a very few pages). Volume 14 of the '*anastatic* edition', furthermore, was much larger than the others, hosting *Notebooks 10, 12, 13* and *18*, which had been written by Gramsci not in the normal small notebooks, but on large exercise books. The tenth notebook – the editors wrote – was a 'notebook with the format for accounts (20.8 by 26.7 cm)'[14] while *Notebooks* 10, 12 and 18 were 'notebooks of a format measuring 21.8 by 31.2 cm'.[15]

In the 'anastatic edition', Francioni – correctly observing a tradition of numbering the notebooks, in a way which immediately assisted readers already used to the numbering of the 'Gerratana edition' – respected the numbering which Gerratana had given the notebooks, but drafted a different chronological version, according to their (often presumed) starting dates, in a manner which correlated to the order with which they had been consigned to the prison – even though we know that they had been given to Gramsci 'in groups', neither one at a time nor all at once.

---

11   Luciano Canfora wrote: 'The facsimille edition would allow one to study even those paleographic details (colours of the ink, physical structure of the manuscript, etc.) that are fundamental for serious philological analysis'. L. Canfora, *Così Gramsci disobbedì a Marx*, in *Corriere della sera*, 28 August 2009.
12   The small difference of format were lost in this edition, both for the 'small' notebooks, which slightly differed among them, in the originals, being between 19 cm and 21 cm in height, with a base of more than 15 cm, and for the 'large notebooks', of which I will speak further down.
13   *Notebook* 18, for instance, was written only one the first three sides (out of 60). 'It is proposed to collect the notes of the first draft continually excluded, for reasons of space, from *Notebook* 13'. G. Francioni and G. Cospito in Gramsci 2009, xiv, p. 229.
14   G. Francioni and F. Frosini in Gramsci 2009, xiv, p. 1.
15   G. Francioni and G. Cospito in Gramsci 2009, xiv, p. 113. *Notebook D* was indeed a 'small album for planning (23 cm × 5.8 cm)'. G. Francioni in Gramsci 2009a, xiii, p. 191.

The 'anastatic edition' had the advantage of putting the reproduction of the texts as it had been left by Gramsci at the public's disposal, without those interventions which every editor could not but carry out,[16] and of which I have given some account (such as those made by Gerratana),[17] but which readers frequently tend to then forget, ingesting the text in the form in which it in presented to them in the printed work. For example, it is sometimes forgotten that the numbering of the paragraphs of the *Notebooks* in the 'critical edition' of 1975 are Gerratana's and not Gramsci's, or that some of the titles are redactions, including the title of the very well-known *Notebook 19* ('Unification'). And this is not to speak of the difficult of reproducing the format of Gramsci's text in a normal printed edition, with the conspicuous marginal notations that almost construct another column of text, for example the notes that in Gerratana's edition became the *beginning* of *Notebook 10* (*The philosophy of Benedetto Croce*) and which in reality one finds only at the *end* of the manuscript of that notebook; or the first nine lines (*Introduction*) of the 'Gerratana edition' which appear on the first three sides of the manuscript, situated in the columns on the right, in the margins and in texts parallel to the principle one, in what was originally a 'computational' large notebook.[18]

Undoubtedly the 'anastatic edition' had the merit of making the reader aware of the true character of Gramsci's manuscripts. Thanks to this, moreover, it was possible for the first time to read some of those parts excluded from the 1975 edition, those 'notes or personal points connected to the necessities of prison life ... lists of books, notes from letters or moments, accounts and various calculations',[19] but also offerings closer to Gramsci's political reflections – for example the underwriting of Italian treasury bonds region by region, or some of the German electoral results which Gramsci attentively noted:[20] all those parts of the manuscript remained unpublished because Gerratana had considered them useless for publication. Thus all the notebooks were prefaced by an *Introductory Note*, sometimes by Francioni, others along with Cospito, still others with Frosini, and divided into three sections – *Description, Chronology,*

---

16 And also without those interventions which one can – and should – avoid, such as the inversion of the first and second parts of *Notebook 10* effected by Gerratana.
17 V. Gerratana in Gramsci 1975, pp. xviii onwards.
18 Cf. Gramsci 1975, p. 1207 and Gramsci 2009, xiv, p. 229. It must be noted that Gerratana had always correctly signaled his editorial interventions, putting in the margin of his 'critical edition' corresponding page numbers to the manuscript and placing square brackets around these marginal or interlinear texts.
19 V. Gerratana in Gramsci 1975, pp. xxxviii.
20 Gramsci 2009, vi, pp. 19 and 25.

Content – essays which were extremely useful for stimulating reflections on the *Notebooks*, on their history, on the internal connections which bound them together, on Gramsci's intellectual labour. Last but not least, this version of Gramsci's manuscripts showed how the 'A text' had been crossed out in a way such as to indicate that it had been *archived*, not to be considered anything other than as a first draft. Gerratana had thus done a good job in presenting to the reader a smaller work, having warned the reader from the start of the differences from the B and C texts. The impact this had on encounters with the Gramscian manuscripts was perhaps to further relativise the A texts. That is not to say, obviously, that they ought not be studied in order to understand the evolution of the author's thought, but in the knowledge nonetheless that for Gramsci the C text represented an evolved and certainly *superior*, if nonetheless still not final, stage. None of this represented anything new in an absolute sense, but the 'anastatic' edition without doubt helped foster a new perspective on Gramsci's work in prison.

Among other introductory essays, the first volume included a contribution by Gianni Francioni, *Come lavorava Gramsci* – 'How Gramsci Worked' – which was useful not only for studying the author of the *Notebooks*, but also grasping Francioni's new method and some of the peculiarities of the critical edition of the *Notebooks* which he was in the process of preparing.[21] In the 'notes on the text' published in the *Notebooks of Translations*, which had been driven forward in 2007 by the 'national edition' (as well as thanks to the French edition of the *Notebooks*), Francioni had already outlined the guiding criteria for his edition of the 'theoretical notebooks' (yet to be published). His proposal was not to make available 'all of the basic material as given in sequence from the start of each notebook' to the reader because, in his view, Gramsci himself – in the process of compiling the *Notebooks* – had attempted to make separations in order to distinguish the notebooks of translations, the miscellaneous notebooks, and those on particular issues (*the Tenth Canto of the* Inferno, Croce, etc). In 1932 the prisoner had interrupted his translations and begun the monothematic 'special notebooks', making a second draft of his notes. Francioni's edition was thus meant to restore the complex geography of Gramsci's writings, *aside from the intentions* with which they had been written. The new edition would maintain more of the contemporary numbering of the *Notebooks* and would try and salvage the unity of their material, meaning that the material in notebooks

---

21   Useful information on this matter is also to be found in Cospito 2010, especially the essays by G. Cospito, F. Frosini, D. Kanoussi, G. Schirru. Other contributions in the volume, all on Gramscian topics, are by A. Burgio, F. Giasi, L. Mancini and G. Vacca.

4, 7, 8, 9, 10 and 11 would also have a different layout and numbering,[22] with the intention of re-establishing 'the internal chronology of the paragraphs'.[23]

The question nonetheless remained of those discussions raised in the 1990s: if one started from the conviction, as Francioni did, that it was impossible to restore the *Notebooks* to the reader as Gramsci had written them, according to their exact process of construction at the time, why not continue to use them as they had been passed on to us, that is, through the Gerratana edition with its retrieval of the original text, eliminating the small modifications which had been made or, if one preferred, providing the most faithful transcription possible of the manuscript, while adding the numbering of the notebooks and paragraphs, explicating the different hypotheses regarding the chronology in the critical apparatus? Their actual spatial setting as they have come down to is a given fact, while their setting according to an imagined hypothesis of Gramsci's intentions must always be exactly that, a *hypothesis*, to which one day another might be added, which would then give rise to another new edition of all of Gramsci's prison writings which we have inherited. The newly announced criteria, in contrast to that which Gerratana said in his own time, seem already to be an *interpretation* (not by accident has Francioni considered it possible to also decipher the 'modes of writing – often *unconscious* – that cut across the manuscripts').[24] Especially in the case of a 'national edition', which would want to be nothing less than a point of reference for all Gramscian specialists, the best solution would be a diplomatic, interpretative edition, which is to say the reproduction of the text handed down by the author, with minimal editorial interventions (the adding of numbering to the notebooks and notes) and a separate apparatus, containing the different philological interpretations.[25]

The *National Edition of the Works of Antonio Gramsci* began to be issued in 1997 with the first volume (in two books) containing the *Notebooks of Translation (1929–1932)*, edited by G. Cospito and G. Francioni. There then appeared, in 2009 and 2011 respectively, the volumes *Epistolary, 1. January 1906 – December*

---

22 The correspondence between many of Gerratana's proposals and those of the future Francioni edition (as it is called today) are to be found in Cospito 2011a.
23 G. Francioni in Gramsci 2007d, p. 846.
24 G. Francioni in Gramsci 2007d, p. 837.
25 This solution seems still more productive in the case of a 'digital edition' as promised by the Igs, but could also be useful for a printed edition. As regards the digital edition, Raul Mordenti has imagined the opportunity for a 'codified, diplomatic, interpretative edition' (EDIC), possible through electronic means, with links which refer immediately to other available sources or comments, line by line or even word by word. Cf. Mordenti 2001 and Mordenti 1999, pp. 169–90. In relation to the discussion over the 'Francioni edition', see above p. 237.

1922 and *Epistolary, 2. January – November 1923*.[26] The 'plan of the edition' proceeds in three sections: *Essays (1910–1926)*, directed by Leonardo Paggi; *Prison Notebooks*, directed by Gianni Francioni; *Letters*, directed by Chiara Daniele. In its turn the new edition of the *Notebooks* – as we learn from Gianni Francioni's note to the text in the coda to the second volume of the *Notebooks of Translations* – will be formed 'in three volumes, dedicated respectively to the notebooks of translations (which were excluded from the Gerratana edition), the miscellaneous notebooks (which include also the first drafts of the notes) and the monographic notebooks'.[27]

That the beginning of the publication of the *National Edition* was formed from the *Notebooks of Translations* fills an important lacuna; these notebooks – aside from being a constituent part of Gramsci's prison *opus*, counting 600 pages of manuscript out of a total 3,000[28] – were until 2007 almost entirely unpublished, because Gerratana had published only brief extracts in an appendix to his edition of the *Notebooks*. Gerratana's choice was in accordance with his conviction that the *Notebooks of Translations* were positioned 'clearly outside of the plan of work which Gramsci had in his draft of the *Notebooks*',[29] and merely 'intellectual nourishment'. The pioneering work of Lucia Borghese ought to be remembered for its strong counter-argument.[30] As Francioni and Cospito's choice correctly demonstrated, a 'national edition' had to strive for completeness – as Francioni had maintained from the beginning of the 1990s – especially for an author such as Gramsci, whose textual impact has still not exhausted. The reader requires the availability of a publication which has not already decided on the *theoretical* validity of these 'translation exercises' (as they have been known till now), in other words their relation to the *Notebooks*. Even based on the provisional remarks in Cospito's *Introduction* it would seem

---

26 Gramsci 2009b, Gramsci 2011c. The publication of the Gramscian epistolaries are predicted to take up eight volumes, and another for the *Carteggi paralleli (1926–1937)*. On some novelties contained in the unpublished volumes, cf. Righi 2011. In general, on the state of the advancement of the work and the research connected to the *National Edition*, see the entire issue of *Studi storici*, 2011, n. 4, with essays by M.L. Righi and C. Natoli on the pre-prison letters, C. Daniele on the prison correspondence, L. Rapone on the young Gramsci, G: Schirru on Gramsci as a linguist, G. Cospito and F. Frosini on the new edition of the *Notebooks*, and M. Lana on the use of the new 'quantitative methods' applied to the study of *style* in order to attribute articles from the 1910s and 20s.

27 G. Francioni in Gramsci 2007d, p. 835.

28 Cf. G. Cospito in Gramsci 2007d, p. 13. On the topic of the publication of the translations made in prison by the author of the *Notebooks*, it is worth noting the publication of Gramsci 2011d.

29 V. Gerratana in Gramsci 1975, pp. xxxvii–xxxviii.

30 See above p. 263 onwards.

that such validity would be important to any research into Gramsci's *sources*. The material that Gramsci chose has a bearing on other parts of his theoretical discourse, if only as a 'suggestion', or point of departure, a *springboard* for an interest more theoretically developed elsewhere.

2   On the 'Philosophy of Praxis'

The Gramsci of the *Notebooks* formed the focus of several recent books, even if in some cases as a crowning moment to work undertaken over a much longer period. Such work has frequently concentrated on issues of the relations between Gramsci and Marx, and to the Gramscian *philosophy of praxis*. This is the case with Francesca Izzo, for example, who claimed in a conference in December 2008:

> I think that, in Gramsci's youthful articles (up to 1924–25), Marx was only one of many authors to whom he turned in order to develop his personal vision of historic socialism, and not even the most influential ... Marx's thought, such as it was presented through the socialist tradition (with the exception of Labriola) seemed to him to be inapplicable to the historical conjuncture which had opened up with the War and, in order to give new life to it, he undertook the task of dusting off and refining it under the influence of Sorel's work and above all Neoidealism. In the *Notebooks* the scenario changes profoundly. Gramsci underwent a real 'return' to Marx, mediated by the critique of Neoidealist revisionism and the lessons of Leninism. There are a few Marxian texts that became the direct and irreplaceable source for his interpretation of Marxism in terms of the philosophy of praxis.[31]

Izzo developed this thesis and others on which she had been working for a time in a book which came out a little later, *Democrazia e cosmopolitismo in Gramsci* – 'Democracy and Cosmopolitanism in Gramsci'. Gramsci's turning to Marx was based on some basic presuppositions about this own political culture and the research for the reasons of the defeat of the workers' movement of the 1920s. Gramsci had considered his own times to be the epoch of the '*realisation* of revolution' because – according to Izzo – 'the parabola of the state'

---

31   F. Izzo in Di Bello 2011, pp. 81–82, which contains the acts of the conference held in Naples in 4–5 December 2008.

was then in decline, and the *Notebooks* were 'the contribution which Gramsci meant to make from prison in affirming a process which took "cosmopolitan democracy" as its pole star'.[32] One could thus glimpse behind the *Notebooks* the old idea of communism and internationalism ('in a historical conceptual framework dominated by the evaluation of Americanism in terms of passive revolution'), translated into 'a form of cosmopolitanism which conserved itself and developed the democratic roots of the modern state'.[33] Renaming the idea of communism as 'democratic cosmopolitanism' is clearly a method of bringing Gramsci 'up to date', as had already been done in 1997, supplanting the hypothesis of *political praxis*. A more convincing argument in the book was the reflection in Gramscian literature on Marx, highlighting the importance assigned by the Sardinian thinker to works such as *Poverty of Philosophy* and *The Holy Family*.

The issue of the specificity of the prison reflections was also central to the volume by Giuseppe Cospito, *Il ritmo del pensiero. Per una lettura diacronica dei 'Quaderni del carcere' di Gramsci* – 'The Rhythm of Thought: Towards a Diachronic Reading of Gramsci's *Prison Notebooks*' – which brought together various essays by the author around a profoundly unitary proposition. For Cospito, the 'young Gramsci' was in truth very distant from orthodox Marxism, as he decidedly refused every economic causation. It was only later that Gramsci had 'turned' towards the orthodox Marxism of the Third International, towards determinism, which became in the 1920s – as Gramsci himself would explain in the *Notebooks* – a 'formidable force of moral resistance' in a political conjuncture characterised by defeat.[34] It was within this remit that political parties had become the Sardinian thinker's 'nomenclature of the class', and Cospito identified in this the dependence of his politics on the structural, socio-economic facts of class. This *orthodox* phase lasted up to the prison years, and did not become any less in the early *Notebooks*. He had then had a 'return to Marx' as described by Izzo (and – as we will see – Frosini). According to Cospito, this *reawakening from the dogmatic slumber* happened gradually, resulting in the end – in *Notebooks* 7 and 8 (in the *Philosophy of Benedetto Croce*) – in a near-complete rejection of the role of economic structure. Politics thus became finally *liberated* from being considered only a product of economics. After a serious episode of bad health in March 1931 and a consequent interruption of his work, many of Gramsci's positions seemed to the author to change, to become less *courageous*. Equally the concept of hegemony was rethought

---

32 Izzo 2009, pp. 49–50.
33 Izzo 2009, p. 137.
34 Cospito 2011b, p. 71.

without much of its economic roots, even if in *Notebook 13* one could still read that, if 'hegemony is the political ethic, it cannot but have its foundations in the decisive function that the leading group exercises in the decisive nucleus that is economic activity'.[35]

Cospito's ideas at times ran the risk of imposing a predefined schema. One-off claims made by Gramsci are at times over-emphasised, and some of his positions taken against *economism* interpreted as rejection of the role played by the 'economic world' more generally. Cospito seems to make the 'determining factor in the last instance' interchangeable with a determining factor of a mechanical kind: the development of the 'economic world', for Gramsci becomes a form of objective situation, in which the subject is collapsed into an analysis of the 'relation of forces' within political development.[36] But this had different possibilities of action depending on given class relations: there are determining factors therefore, but only *in the last instance*. Furthermore, an analysis in terms of class is not necessarily economistic. Cospito's book did, nonetheless, contain an interesting note on 'how Gramsci worked': when, in the C Text, one finds claims that Gramsci should by then, according to Cospito at least, have *overcome*, Cospito advances the suspicion that the waning ill communist thinker had *mechanically* recopied the texts of the first draft and that the C Text therefore *lagged behind* the simultaneous B Text.[37] But – one asks oneself – would it really have been so much harder, for an ill man, to write from scratch, elaborating notes, points and thought of original titles, rather than to copy the texts so as to progressively modify them only later?

The whole reading advanced by the book with regards to Gramsci's *theoretical journey* in prison did not, however, force Cospito to claim that the prisoner was outside of Marxism and the communist movement: 'the hard – if indirect – critique he made of Stalinism did not induce him to renege in total on the Bolshevik revolutionary experience, nor on the perspective of a possible overcoming of the capitalist horizon'.[38] It ought to be added, furthermore, that *Il ritmo del pensiero* is not only full of notes of great interest, but also important for its methodological approach, which constitutes an exemplary case of reading the *Notebooks* diachronically, the most worthwhile model with which to read the prison writings, even if the desire to prove the usefulness of this method induced the author to propose an *extreme* interpretation and therefore, in the end, conclusions that are less than convincing.

---

35 Gramsci 1975, p. 1591.
36 C.N. Coutinho, *Rapporti di forza*, in Liguori and Voza 2009.
37 Cospito 2011b, p. 60.
38 Cospito 2011b, p. 157.

With two books published in 2009 and 2010, Fabio Frosini reprised and developed his interpretation of Gramsci already drafted in the volume of 2003[39] as well as in various essays, a reading founded on the centrality of Gramsci's *philosophical* reflections, on the bond between philosophy and politics, on the new relation established with Marx's thought in the prison works, and on an original reading of the relation between ideology and truth. The first of the two volumes, *Da Gramsci a Marx. Ideologia, verità e politica* – 'From Gramsci to Marx: Ideology, Truth and Politics' – brought together a series of previous writings only some of which focus on the Sardinian communist. The second, *La religione dell'uomo moderno. Politica e verità nei* Quaderni del carcere *di Antonio Gramsci* – 'The Religion of Modern Man: Politics and Truth in Antonio Gramsci's *Prison Notebooks*' – was more holistic and entirely dedicated to Gramsci, above all to his mature thought. In the first text, the author turned to read Marx *through* Gramsci, that is, from the importance that the latter assigned to the former's works of 1845–1850 and to the concept of *praxis* in the *Theses on Feuerbach*. It is in *praxis* that Gramsci had found the key to the originality of Marxism, its power to present itself not only as one philosophy among others but as a new way of understanding what philosophy truly means. Beginning with this originality, Gramsci – according to Frosini – grasped that in Marx there was a new conception of 'truth'. Frosini wrote that:

> The essence of Gramsci's work in the *Notebooks* is not therefore in the realisation of a new theory ... nor the development of a new detailed strategy ... but the project of a new approach to Marx capable of mobilising ... that which according to the author of the *Notebooks* was his true 'discovery': the redefinition of the concept of 'truth' in terms of 'praxis'.[40]

The book focused on the main passages of Gramsci's idiosyncratic reading of Marx, from the *Theses on Feuerbach* to the political works around 1848, to the *Preface of 1859*. Gramsci had advanced a theory of validity (the 'gnoseological validity of the superstructure'): 'thought would no longer be independent of that ideological web in which it has been expressed',[41] that is, independent of class relations.[42] For Frosini (as for Cospito) *historical materialism* could not give a specific account of politics, seemingly a non-decisive, ideological aspect

---

39 See above chapter 11 footnote 9.
40 Frosini 2009, p. 22.
41 Frosini 2009, p. 117.
42 On the topic of ideology, one should also note the newly re-published book of 1976: Fergnani 2011.

(that is, *superstructural*), even though it seems that for Marx it was always decisive in the moment itself. In a way which was quite separate from Cospito's conclusions, Frosini saw in the Gramscian theory of the relations of forces a way to overcome this *impasse*, a solution which 'allowed one to think through the unity of history as a process and politics of real struggle'.[43]

Frosini's reading of Gramsci brought to light some fundamental moments of the *Notebooks*, even if it allowed some important aspects of Marx to fall by the wayside. He proposed a reading that put one Marx 'into play' with another (the political Marx of praxis against Marx the scientist of historical materialist). In relation to Gramsci, such an interpretation removes a series of references which are in fact present in the *Notebooks* – not only to Engels[44] but also to *Capital* – and introduces a break between *historical materialism* and *the philosophy of praxis*, two subjects clearly shown to be connected in the *Notebooks*. Gramsci, I would argue, did not renege on historical materialism but, by rereading the *Preface of 1859* the light of the *Theses on Feuerbach*, emphasised the dialectic between base and superstructure, in the end rejecting (if only in part) the celebrated metaphor not because he thought that there was no fundamental role for 'structure' but because in such a metaphor it seems that only the base can *act*, without the effective *re-action* of the second element.

Frosini's following book, *La religione dell'uomo moderno*, is a work rich in both hermeneutics and theory, constructed on the basis of significant philological move. The author placed questions of *ideology* and *religion* at the centre of his research,[45] – concepts that Gramsci analysed above all in relation to Marx and to Croce – demonstrating the similarities between Gramsci and these authors (in relation to Marx: Gramsci began from the second of the *Theses on Feuerbach*, in which was posited the immanence of practical truth) and also the differences (above all the difference from Croce, but also from the Marx of *The German Ideology*). The ideology of the *Notebooks* was related to *truth*, as every form of knowledge is seen as 'internal to, and conditioned by, determinate social relations'.[46] *Truth* is intimately connected with praxis, politics and hegemony.

---

43 Fergnani 2011, p. 110.
44 Gramsci referred frequently to Engels as an authority on Marxism, not only his *Anti-Dühring*, but above all using Engels' reading of ideology and the 'final instance', which attempted to *correct* the Marx of the *Preface to A Contribution to the Critique of Political Economy* of 1859 (but on this I refer you to my own essay, *Engels. La presenza nei Quaderni* in Liguori 2006).
45 To Gramsci, religion was any belief 'capable of significantly moving a mass of people into action'. Frosini 2010, p. 40.
46 Frosini 2009, p. 21.

As he had claimed in his previous book, Frosini insisted on the importance of the substitution of the couplet 'structure and superstructure' with the theory of the 'balance of forces'. For Gramsci politics could not be superstructural, an *expression* of the economy,[47] but was connected to the 'balance of forces', both structural and superstructural. The centrality of the 'balance of forces' and of subjectivity removed every residual role from the 'base': everything is 'contingent'. 'It is not the dialects internal to the "real base" which determines the crisis, but the political struggle in terms of the relation of forces ... which, at a certain point, makes a "crisis" evident, one that in reality is always there', but which from time to time could be disactivated through hegemonic activity. And therefore the decisive proposal of a 'crisis' was the unification of subaltern subjects, and 'the construction of a common imagination of the subaltern, an imagination capable of unifying them in a common struggle'.[48]

In Frosini's discourse, great weight was given to emphasising the absence of any 'stadial' vision of history in Gramsci: history was instead described by the *immanence* which characterises the battle for hegemony. For the author 'Gramsci's theoretical effort lay precisely in the deconstruction of historical materialism',[49] aside from any conception of reality as political, partial and conflictual. History, for Gramsci's *philosophy of praxis*, is always interwoven with a specific 'relation of forces'. Marx and Machiavelli, then, were Gramsci's mediators, to be set alongside the problematic development found in the works of the late Althusser.

Frosini wanted to emphasise the new conception of Marxism that can be gleaned from the *Notebooks*. But in the end he not only documented the fact, by now quite clear, that Gramsci had profoundly reinterpreted Marxism (by making a dialectic of the relationship between structure and superstructure, assigning an unusual role to the 'superstructure') but also claimed that Gramsci had, in the course of his prison reflections, abandoned historical materialism – at least what was usually meant by this expression. The book went forward in this interpretative framework for many pages, evidencing a tendency within contemporary Gramscian studies to oppose the philosophy of praxis to historical materialism, even in the dialectical version which Gramsci offered to it. The suggestion is that Gramsci – who continued to consider himself a Marxist and

---

47   Against an 'expressive conception' of the relation between structure and superstructure, see Laclau and Mouffe 2011 [1985], and the following pages below. This kind of critique, originally against Hegelian Marxism, can also be found in the Althusser of *Reading Capital*. See above, p. 146.
48   Frosini 2009, p. 196.
49   Frosini 2009, p. 34.

a Communist – had *overcome* Marxism as we are used to thinking of it (the creation through a structural moment of subjective activities chosen from those *contingently* possible: this is Engel's 'determination in the final instance' to which Gramsci frequently referred). Frosini wanted to take seriously the question of the *Notebooks*: 'how is historical movement built on the structural base?'[50] But this seems to ignore the fact that even here, in the crucial eleventh notebook, Gramsci uses the term 'structure'. The 'philosophy of praxis' indicates Gramsci's positioning in the internal battle of Marxism, his struggle against economic determinism, his contribution to the development of a theoretical tradition which he did not abandon but developed, precisely because he demanded its continual development in relation to historical times and changes.

A part of the book quite different from some other readings in *La religione dell'uomo moderno* was when Frosini identified without hesitation that in 'passive revolution' there was a risk and not an opportunity for subaltern subjects. Indeed he evoked 'the risk of a passive revolution "from below"'.[51] Passive revolution could not have been the 'political program' of the Sardinian communist.[52] This, for Frosini, was an important claim, which had important implications for the present.

In Frosini's book one senses the constant influence of Laclau and Mouffe, who in recent years has found significant recognition in Italy, including in public discourse. It has been said of *Hegemony and Socialist Strategy* – written by Ernesto Laclau and Chantal Mouffe in the 1980s and published in Italy only in 2011, a famous but controversial work, representing an original mix of Derrida, Althusser and Gramsci – that, by explicitly distancing themselves from the author of the *Notebooks*, Laclau and Mouffe contributed not to the diffusion through the English speaking world of an awareness of Gramsci (even if the *Notebooks* are actually cited very little in the book itself) but, unfortunately, of a frequently disengaged use of him. The 'overcoming' of Marxism was necessary for the two authors, starting from the belief that 'many social antagonisms, many issues which are crucial to understanding contemporary societies, belong to fields of discursivity which are *external* to Marxism, and cannot be reconceptualized in the terms of Marxist categories'.[53] Nonetheless, building on that tradition, they criticised not only the more economistic versions, but also theories based on 'determination in the last instance', seeing the

---

50 Gramsci 1975, p. 1422.
51 Frosini 2009, p. 222.
52 Frosini 2009, p. 224.
53 Laclau and Mouffe 2011, p. 24 (English translation Laclau and Mouffe 2001, p. ix; preface to the second edition).

Gramscian category of hegemony as an awareness of Marxism's difficulty in explaining the 'contingency' of the structural base, and the attempt to find a solution to such a theoretical *impasse* on the level of political activity. What distanced the authors from Gramsci was the refusal to read society as symbolised by the struggle for hegemony between 'fundamental classes', which for Gramsci were the ultimate and undeniable subjects of hegemony itself. For Laclau and Mouffe there was in fact an *essentialist* theory in the *Notebooks* – and for this reason one that ought to be rejected – because it was based on a class subject. *Essentialism* means – for the two authors – identifying the identity of subjects 'ontologically', '*a priori*'. Instead, 'politics' had to give rise to a 'bloc' of antagonist subjects converging in a project of change described as 'radical democracy', which does not exclude *a priori* any kind of socialism, but which does nonetheless largely sidestep it.

Many of the interesting points of the book (such as the critique of the '*founding* character of the revolutionary act', in favour of the gradual character of change – the war of position – or the central theme of ideology, identities and subjects, of which a complex, dynamic and multifaceted description is provided) would have pleased Gramsci, for whom subjects are not pure expressions of the economy, even if equally they cannot evade it. Laclau and Mouffe thus posed very real problems in Marxism, but mapped out a way in which all micro-narrations and identities appeared on the same level through which to form 'bloc', a 'chain of equivalence', or rather a coalition between all movements in search of rights – via a procedure that is not entirely clear. And above all, for our current purpose here, one that is not present in Gramsci.

The books examined above privileged the Gramsci of the *Notebooks*. The research of Chiara Meta on the concept of 'pragmatism'[54] gave space to the young writings instead of the prison works, for the first time investigating the basis, in all its aspects, of the issue of the relation between Gramsci and one of this principle *sources* – pragmatism – that most American philosophy of the nineteenth and twentieth centuries, which had crossed the ocean, finding its place in anti-positivist culture and the re-evaluation of the subject which spread throughout Europe. The book documents very well the various roads by which pragmatism had made its way both into Italian culture at the beginning of the century, into Gramsci's young education and then his mature system of thought, that of the *Notebooks*. She provided an original version, different from how pragmatism appeared elsewhere, re-evaluated theoretically and historically, allowing for an open and mutual relation to the ideas of 'maturity' and 'originality', but without denying the distant influence of Gramsci's sources.

---

54 Meta 2010.

The influence of pragmatism on the young Gramsci had been manifold; the intellectual school had arrived in Italy through American pragmatism (especially William James's version). Meta distinguished between the more serious and mediated versions by Vailati and Calderoni in Italian pragmatism, and that 'magic', lively, irrational, even confused version proposed by Papini and Prezzolini. Delving into the culture of those years, the book reconstructed some of the less studied moments of Gramsci's education, including Annibale Pastore's courses on Labriola in 1914–1915. But it was above all Vailati's epistemology, according to the author, which had the strongest influence on Gramsci's education: Vailati laid emphasis on categories which would become central in Gramsci's later work – those of prediction, ideology, common sense, conformity, and translatability.

In the *Notebooks*, in the redefinition of Marxism which we find there, in fact, these and other themes remain evident through the confrontation with pragmatism, in first place with Hames and Vailati. The entire pedagogical aspect, the theory of personality and the 'conception of man', for example, is difficult to understand – Chiara Meta explained – without the relationship to pragmatism. But even the central theme of 'Americanism' derives from reflexions on pragmatism, fundamentally stimulated by focusing on the theoretical galaxy constituted by the theory of ideology, common sense and conformism. Nor should the reasons for the arguments against singular causation or anti-essentialism be forgotten, typical elements of pragmatist culture, which are among the elements – not by accident, perhaps – that characterise interpretations of Gramsci in the English language today.

3   Gramsci's 'Fortune'

In 2001 two books of great interest came out on the diffusion of Gramscian thought, concerning both its *history* and *geography*. In *Operazione Gramsci*, Francesca Chiarotto reconstructed the diffusion of Gramsci's fame and thought in the post-war period, meaning the 'operation' (it was not accident that the cover recalled that of a crime novel) by which Togliatti and the Communist Party purposefully introduced the Sardinian communist into Italian culture. The book's merit lay above all in the significant archival research on which it rested, through which the author wove together books, public speeches, letters and documents that had rarely been cited. According to Chiarotto:

> Togliatti, in a difficult balance between the tasks of maintaining autonomy from Stalinist directives and fidelity to the Soviet Union, made use

of Gramsci's persona and work with intelligence and without prejudice so as to confirm, alongside a Communist identity, the national nature of a party on the path of profound reorganisation ... Gramsci's work was utilised as the means by which to enter into dialogue with Italian society, an unavoidable reference for the 'New Party', one that was no longer a classically Leninist party, but one of the masses, respectful of the democratic constitution, a party which put nation before internationalism and which was Italian rather than Communist.[55]

The difficulty which came to pass already in the post-War period lay in the fact that Gramsci's writings are fragmentary and eclectic. Did they need to be published in the form in which they were found (as would indeed be done by Valentino Gerratana thirty years later, after the necessary critique that took a decade) or rendered more accessible and immediate, regrouped around themes and presented in a simplified form? The second hypothesis had prevailed, and if the chosen form had certain limits, it was probably the most apt for making Gramsci well known, and ensuring his wide diffusion (as Gerratana himself had maintained). The important element which Chiraotto documented was that the alternatives thought through by the Communist Party concerned not whether to publish all of the works or a censured version, but which form was the best for presenting the material in the objectively difficult form of the notes left by Gramsci: philological fidelity or a form which allowed it the greatest possible popularity? For the author, 'what this debate confirms most of all is the will to render Gramsci's thought available to the greatest number of readers, before any consideration about Stalinist directives, fears of excommunication or arguments about political opportunism'.[56]

The success of the 'operation' had been signalled by the assigning of the Premio Viareggio 1947 to the *Prison Letters*. Aside from the prize's founder, Leonida Repaci, Chiarotto focussed on the roles played by the two judges, the classicist Concetto Marchesi and the literary critic Giacomo Debendetti. The right wing reacted badly, bemoaning a Communist plot. And there were even those among Gramsci's admirers who sneered at the act: Cesare Pavese – who was the *magna pars* of Einaudi, as well as a member of the Communist Party – thought the award seemed a *deminutio*, for, he wrote in private, it was like seeing it go to Machiavelli or Cattaneo: Gramsci was too great for a literary award. Indeed, Gabriele Pepe had lamented the bourgeois aura of mediocrity which circulated

---

55   Chiarotto, 2011, p. 49.
56   Chiarotto, 2011, p. 91.

around the Premio Viareggio, so far from the style and interests of the Sardinian communist. In a private letter, on the contrary, Togliatti rejected with some force that the recognition was inappropriate for the *Letters*, adding that politics – whether to Gramsci's advantage or otherwise – had to be absent from any attempt to influence the judges.[57] From the Premio Viareggio onwards, 'operation Gramsci' went ahead not only because of purposeful cultural work but also because Gramsci's greatness was destined to impose itself even despite the 'iron curtain'.

In *Gramsci globale*, however, Michele Filippini[58] studied some of the aspects of Gramsci's international diffusion, combing a heightened awareness of contemporary Anglophone culture with a captivating narrative form. Here is the list of protagonists in the book, provided by the author in on the back cover:

> *Antonio Gramsci*, the protagonist. *Partha Chatterjee*, the Indian who heard the subalterns. *John Fonte*, the thinktank man. *Ranajit Guha*, the warden of Indian radical histories. *Stuart Hall*, the English-Jamaican who studied cultural phenomena. *Rush Limbaugh*, the conservative with the big audience. *James Thornton*, the mad preacher. *Cornel West*, the Christian, the Marxist, the Afro-American intellectual. *Raymond Williams*, the Welshman who understood popular culture.

For an informed reader this was enough to understand Filippini's objective: to investigate the mass culture which the more serious *thinkers* had engaged throughout the world on both left and right, in order to study not so much Gramsci and how he had been *interpreted* but rather how his thought had been *used* in times and places really quite distant from that in which it was born. And the range of such uses, which the book explored with great mastery, was indeed extremely varied. It ranged from American conservatives who wanted to combine Fox News and the 'Tea Party' to Thatcherism as studied by Stuart Hall and Birmingham cultural studies: two entirely different models of following hegemony 'from the right', according to an interpretation of Gramsci's theory of 'common sense'. She also studied the all-round activity of the preacher and pragmatist philosopher in the most prestigious American university, Cornel West, who had put himself in the shows of hip-hop musicians to develop the role of an 'organic intellectual' who consciously worked to reunify high and low culture so as to create a 'popular Gramscianism, a "Gramscianism of the

---

57 For a range of opinions on the attributions of the Premio Viareggio, see Chiarotto, 2011, pp. 34–36.
58 Filippini 2011.

people" which was part of the search of a popular creative spirit'.[59] One of Filippini's chapters focusses on the historiography of Indian progressives who have valued Gramsci's category of the 'subaltern' more than anyone, with a creative application of the notes on Italian Unification to the situation in post-colonial India. The book gave rise to many ideas, and the creative uses of Gramsci studied by Filippini could indeed have an importance for the Italian left regarding the political objective of its battle without losing sight of Gramsci's thought.

A quite different approach was taken by Lelio La Porta in his book on 'Antonio Gramsci and Hannah Arendt', which compared two very different authors, without attempting – as sometimes happens – to find points of similarity and convergence at all costs, but instead quite honestly clarifying through a detailed analysis that their theoretical and political paths did have some moments of intersection. The parallel with Arendt, one of the authors most appreciated today in the world of the *liberal* left, is also shown, in its own way, in the diffusion of the Sardinian thinker's fame. There nonetheless remain insuperable differences between the two thinkers: for example, 'an abyssal distance runs between the Gramscian democratic philosophy and Arendt's intellectual *sub specie*; for the latter the truth cannot change, for the former the truth is that from which politics starts in order for change to be possible'.[60] Or still more: for Arendt the model of revolution is provided by the American Revolution and, after that, the two English revolutions, while she regarded the French Revolution and that of Russia with open hostility, as two revolutionary experiences broken by both violence and the centrality which the 'social question' had had in these, instead of a discourse on the 'form of governance'. This demonstrated not only a total rejection of Marxism however, but also an inability – as La Porta explained – to grasp some of the concrete aspects of the Anglo-Saxon revolutionary experience.

4 Creative Uses

We have already mentioned Cornel West's *popular Gramscianism*. In Italy there have also been some attempts at a *creative and popular use* of Gramsci, in terms however less of politically translating the thinker as much as popularising his figure. It is not possible within the limits of this work to confront non-print works. This leaves out, therefore, Gramscian filmography, as important as it is,

---

59 Filippini 2011, p. 22.
60 La Porta 2010, p. 131.

beginning with Giorgio Baratta's film which we have already mentioned[61] and some musical renditions[62] but we ought note some of the theatrical attempts, for example *Cena con Gramsci* ('At Dinner With Gramsci') by Davide Daolmi (from an idea by Roberto Rampi), the text of which can be read in the volume *Nino: appunti per Antonio Gramsci 1937–2007*,[63] which was part of a cultural project (promoted, other than Rampi, by Marta Gallo and Elena Lah) which also included a website, an exhibition and a visual project. This was a cultural intervention that went beyond simply a theatrical text. 'What interests us here is to investigate ... communication and mass communication in particular ... We are interested in outlining an area of reflections to understand what has happened to a figure, a symbol so dense with meanings as Gramsci has been in the twentieth century'.[64] The response, wrote the art director Elena Lah, lay in an attempt to orchestrate a meeting between Gramsci and the pop art of Andy Warhol.[65] One should ask whether this does not run the risk, even with Gramsci – should one manage (something not to be discounted) to popularise his *image*, producing t-shirts, posters and lively, colourful representations as Lah has in this beautiful visual project – of reducing him to being 'under the sign of nothing', condemned to being confused with the most superficial objects, as happened to a persona as rich as that of Ernesto Che Guevera, for example.

However, the theatrical text of *Cena con Gramsci* by David Daolmi was a valid attempt to find a Gramsci who had recently returned to the scene: a single dense and rich act, which if the writing could seem at times not entirely accessible, was entertaining, interesting and importantly *disturbing*, in a way which would perhaps have pleased Gramsci, an admirer of the Futurists and the early Pirandello. The protagonist of the text was a student working on a university thesis on Gramsci, haunted by his enigmatic mystery and the figures of a long story that is hard to bring to life today. The conclusion of the young finalist was that, in order to pay homage to Gramsci, a thesis was not enough, nor just to study, but that it was necessary to *act*. A year later the project also gave rise to a graphic novel, a 'comic strip version' of the comedy, rewritten by Elettra Stamboulis and with illustrations by Gianluca Costantini. At the centre of one of the

---

61   Baratta was the originator and co-author of the documentaries *Gramsci l'ho visto così* (1988) and *New York e il mistero di Napoli. Viaggio nel mondo di Gramsci raccontato da Dario Fo* (1993). The sceenplay Del Fra and Mangini 1979 was published after the film of the same name directing by Del Fra in 1977.

62   The most well known are *Quello lì (compagno Gramsci)* by C. Lolli (1973) and *Rosa di Turi* by Radiodervish (19968).

63   Rampi 2007.

64   R. Rampi in Rampi 2007, pp. 14–15.

65   E. Lah in Rampi 2007, pp. 80–81.

more singular projects of the 'collective removal' of Gramsci at the end of the twentieth century – wrote Rampi in his introductory note – lies 'the event of a significant division ... There is another Gramsci, beyond that of the academy, who needs to be revived. It is appropriate that the arts, to whom he gave so much of his theoretical attention, should give him a new, contemporary, everyday and accessible rendering'.[66]

Gramsci *in comics* was not a total novelty. An 'Introduction to Gramsci', edited by the Argentinian scholar of Marxism, Néstor Kohan, had been enriched by the drawings of Miguel Rep[67] explaining Gramscian concepts for beginners. In 2011 an interesting 'fantasy biography of a little Gramsci' came out, written and drawn by Luca Paulesu.[68] The book – as intelligent as enjoyable – began from an inspired conceit: Gramsci was drawn as a child, but thinking and evaluating as an adult, indeed, as an adult Gramsci – a little like Linus and Charlie Brown in *Peanuts*. Little Antonio (*Nino*), that is, humourously demonstrated the awareness and structures of thought he would have as an adult. He showed a great awareness – and in Paulesu's drawings this came with a melancholic streak, both in design and in the words – of not only the physical troubles of a child, but also the destiny which awaited him as an adult, such as in the opening line: 'I am a Sardinian, a hunchback, and a communist too. I will breathe my last breath after a long period of suffering in prison. They call me Nino'.[69] What follows, image after image, is not so much a recounting of the facts, but rather an evocation of the familial and historiographical problems and events that remain undeciphered, as well as Gramscian thoughts and concepts. This was certainly not a comic strip for teenagers, and perhaps also not for adults totally ignorant of Gramscian questions (who could fully enjoy the joke, delivered with a sense of feeling and ambiguity on a par with the best of Altan's cartoons, by little Nino: 'My imaginary friend will be called Palmiro, but I don't want to have anything to do with him anymore if he gets my notebooks in a mess',[70] and of the whole analogy, if one does not already have some knowledge of Gramsci and his life?), but rather a critical, graphic biography, full of citations drawn from the works in and out of prison, and from reinterpretations of the principle concepts. In sum, an interpretation in itself – with the limits imposed on it by the genre – of the life and thought of the Sardinian communist, constructed through drawings as much as words.

---

66 R. Rampi in Stamboulis and Costantini 2011.
67 Kohan and Rep 2003.
68 Paulesu 2012.
69 Paulesu 2012, p. 25.
70 Paulesu 2012, p. 37.

A particular tone was given to the work by the fact that the author is the grandson of Teresina, Antonio's treasured sister, who had lived for a long time in Ghirlarza and had heard and reheard stories from his grandmother about Nino, his childhood, his tragic future. This *familial air* proved to be a source of precious memories as well as some new facts: Gramsci's young literary interests, his love for Tolstoy and *War and Peace* (from which came the joke: 'All the young Russians love the modern Prince!'),[71] or the reasons for his disagreements with his father Ciccillo (who had ruined the family more than once, with a spell in prison due to a deficit discovered in the office where he worked – but also a second time, by carelessly squandering a substantial inheritance from his wife through commercial errors, once again throwing the family out onto the street),[72] or the fact that the books which Nino studied elsewhere remain at the home of his parents, and remain partly dispersed among friends and family. And, as can be seen at various points in the text, there remain unpublished letters by Nino in the family's estate.

Returning to theatre – which, it ought not be forgotten, was one of the young Gramsci's great passions – Piero Zucaro also wrote a theatrical and unconventional text, *L'uomo di Turi* – 'The Turi Man',[73] focusing on the invented character *Unico* ('unique') an anarchist who Gramsci is said to have met during his prison years, and who he described in the *Letters* as an 'extreme individualist'.[74] What was in reality for Gramsci only a fleeting meeting became in Zucaro's drama (full or irony but also attentive not to distort the concepts and events of Gramsci's life, at least the most important ones) the Sardinian communist's *alter ego*, allowing the playwright to represent Gramscian ideas and events in the form of a dialogue. This was a representation which derived from the school of contemporary theatre, above all that of Peter Weiss. Zucaro recounted, among other matters, daily prison life from the point of view of the cell in which the two characters were enclosed. Between a game of cards, an apparition of Nino's mother and (*a la* Weiss) a theatrical representation of the whole prison, various points of fundamental Gramscian concepts were explicated. Beginning with the *Uomo di Turi*, Zucaro undertook a period of research and a theatrical workshop focused on Gramsci, which gave rise to a volume of texts (adaptations, scripts) and reflections from many participants.[75]

---

71 Paulesu 2012, p. 253.
72 Paulesu 2012, p. 50.
73 Zucaro 2008.
74 Letter to Tania Schucht 19 February 1927.
75 Zucaro 2011.

In terms of narratives inspired by Gramsci, we should also note *L'amore assente* – 'Absent Love' – by Adriana Brown, a novel focused on the personal and emotional events of Gramsci's life, on the love story which coincided, more or less, with that of the Schucht sisters.[76] The author was the grandchild of Nilde Perilli and – in order to sketch out her narrative, which moved from Gramsci's stay at Serebryany Bor (the Russian sanatorium where Gramsci first met Eugeni and then Gulia) through to the Sardinian communist's death – had used 'letters, notes and memories' of her relative. Nilde Perilli, who had already been a friend to Eugenia during her stay in Rome before WWI, had been the link between Antonio and Tania in the 1920s, and was the latter's friend and confidant in the years in which she remained in Italy to assist Gramsci. What importance did fiction have in the author's attempt at a reconstruction, and how much was it based on her relative's information (also to be taken with caution, as with all memories)? At times one can only have doubts regarding the reconstruction – especially in that there was some straightforward blunders, such as when one reads that in prison Gramsci was working on 'his program for a history of Italian literature'; at other times one has the impression of notes on the psychology or daily life of protagonists rich with knowledge of Gramsci's life, and Tania's. There were events which certainly Nilde (as well as the author) could know better than the contents of the *Notebooks*, such as, for example, the reasons for Tania's estrangement from her family. It is worth noting that the hypothesis sustained in the book, according to which Antonio had repeatedly broken off his emotional relationship which he had had with Eugenia as soon as he met the beautiful Iulca (Giulia), was confirmed a decade later by new historiographical research.[77]

5 Stories and Histories

If the books by Brown and Tancredi explicitly presented themselves as historical novels, there have also been narratives which, although presenting themselves as investigations or journalistic reconstructions, have a level of credibility a rung down from even some of the products of creative writing, recounting for the most part stories which seem aimed above all at outcry and scandal.

---

76 Brown 2002.
77 Righi 2011. While this book was with the editors for publication, Tancredi's novel on the same matter was published. Tancredi 2012.

The events between Antonio and Iulca are those which have been submitted to this treatment the most, for example by Bruno Vespa,[78] who we note only because he solicited a detailed response from Antonio Gramsci Jr., the son of Giuliano Gramsci. Replying to him in a newspaper, he wrote:

> First of all I have to say that I have not found any evidence of the 'fist of Stalin' which 'came down on' Gramsci's family in Russia. From the end of the 1920s, in accordance with general developments in the country, the Schucht family began to live a little better. Apollo received a spacious apartment in central Moscow and a personal pension. Many apparent 'sins' were not in his favour: a German of noble origins, an ex-emigrant, a friend of Lenin and finally stepfather to a heterodox Italian Communist. In 1933 this perfect 'enemy of the people' died calmly in the most prestigious hospital in the Soviet Union … In the 1930s, when almost no one in the family was working, Giulia, hindered by no one, regularly sent Tatiana large sums of money which served to help Gramsci … the only plausible hypothesis is that it was precisely the Soviet authorities themselves who were taking care to alleviate the sufferings of the 'condemned Trotskyist' imprisoned by Mussolini.[79]

These are comments of great interest to anyone involved in the polemics which continually recur regarding Gramsci and the more serious historiography of this argument. Gramsci Jr. *rehabilitated* the role played by Togliatti in helping Gramsci's family in Moscow and disproved the scandals which wanted to make Tatiana into an agent of Soviet services, charged with spying on her brother-in-law.[80] The subtle irony with which he dismantled the *eternal return* (certainly not unbiased) of much nonsense about Gramsci, and his relations with the USSR and the PCd'I, offered up by a politically oriented journalism[81] was not supported by sentimentality nor based on memory: Antonio Jr. had undertaken a series of investigations in Moscow among the family papers held by

---

78   Vespa 2007, p. 281.
79   A. Gramsci, Jr., *Quanti errori su mio nonno (Il libro di Vespa)*, in *l'Unità*, 20 November 2011.
80   On this, see the competence and irony, already in the 1980s, of Santucci 2011, pp. 70–3 (an article from 1983).
81   Caprara 2001, Lehner 2008. These are works full of unproved and implausible claims which – along with the 'historiographical campaign' begun in the 1980s by Craxi's PSI against Togliatti's memory – continuously, cyclically nourish the arguments of Italian political culture. The tone of a volume with quite distinct ambitions is not very different: Nieddu 2004.

the archives of the Communist movement, publishing two books which bring to light the history of the Schucht family and their relations with the Sardinian communist.[82]

The *historiographic* polemics over Gramsci continually recur in the press. In 2008 the shocking news had a wide circulation in the mass media (including occasionally in the evening TV news, something quite rare), although devoid of any substantial foundations, of Gramsci's 'death bed conversion': suffering in his hospital room, staring at an image of Saint Thérèse and the baby Jesus, the Sardinian communist had devoted himself to the image up to the point of wanting to kiss it. He then asked for the sacraments, and died.[83] This shocking news was, however, not new. Nor was it only a 'joke' – as someone wrote. It was part of the construction of a politically oriented intervention, which tried, indefensibly, to undermine the credibility of the opposite camp, at the expense of Gramsci and, above all, at the expense of historical truth, or at the very least of more serious historiographical research.

In more recent times there was a new episode: the attempt to represent the Sardinian thinker as an intolerant figure who, blinded by hatred, supported the cruellest political violence. Without any warning, a well-known author, Roberto Saviano, has renewed and spread[84] this thesis, taken from book *Gramsci e Turati: Le due sinistre* – 'Gramsci and Turati: The Two Lefts' – by Alessandro Orsini. The alternative traditions between the revolutionary and reformist lefts (a dichotomy which Gramsci had overcome in advance in the *Notebooks* through a conception of democracy as a process of the revolution) was revisited by the author in a Manichean light, across many pages void of documentary support. In the first place he made reference to the young Gramsci without any biographical or historical contextualisation. Using a method based on single, small and totally decontextualised quotations, he depicted him as the supporter of an indoctrinated sect who maintained that 'the true socialist is a man who only reads the Party press' and who 'does not need to look through or speak about books and journals which express views different from those of the Party'.[85] This is what Gramsci's life was reduced to in the period in which the Socialist press perhaps published more extracts from liberal thinkers than classics of Marxism, in which Croce's writings on *La città futura* were published and which, at least up to the Russian Revolution, could be considered a pupil of certain famous liberals, of Salvemini's pragmatism more than Marx. Many

---

82 Cf. Gramsci Jr 2008.
83 Allow me to recommend my own essay, Liguori 2009b.
84 R. Saviano, *Elogio dei riformisti*, in *la Repbblica*, 28 February 2012.
85 Orsini 2012, p. 70.

examples of Achille Loria's thought were contained in the book: from the claim that in 1916 Gramsci invited his readers to cultivate only 'communist ideas'[86] when communism was still not spoken about in the international workers' movement, through to the satisfied claim according to which after Gramsci's arrest he had stopped 'parrying' with his adversaries,[87] as if while contained within a Fascist prison he would have been able to criticise his political enemies and that this would not have been seen as a sign of opportunism or revenge. The author showed among other matters no knowledge of the 'critical edition' of the *Notebooks*, citing the thematic edition instead, something which today would not be permissible for a student submitting a paper for marking.[88]

The studies by Dario Biocca have also – as with Orsini's book – provoked vibrant polemics, mainly due to an error effected by the author himself. Advertising in *La Repubblica* an essay he had written for the journal *Nuova storia contemporana*[89] – in which he maintained that Gramsci, in order to obtain conditional freedom had invoked an article of law on a prisoner's 'repentance' and therefore had in the end given in to Fascism – Biocca showed that he had taken into consideration the penal code of 1889 and not that which was in place in 1930.[90] *Nuova storia contemporanea* immediately spotted the error and did not publish it: the original essay was split up and in the first issue of 2012 Biocca published *Casa Passarge: Gramsci a Roma (1924–26)*, a study on the rich German family from whom Gramsci had rented a room while in the capital. The study contained some interesting particulars on Gramsci's life in Rome, but also introduced useless and malicious doubts on the reasons for which the Sardinian communist had chosen such a living arrangement in preference to living together with his comrades. This had in fact been written about by Felice Platone in a less suspiscious era (1938): 'In Rome ... we found him a room with a German family, who offered a good guarantee of peace and calm'.[91] It was not Gramsci's choice, therefore, but that of his Party. In the third issue of

---

86 Ibid.
87 Orsini 2012, p. 67.
88 It might be that Orsini was fooled by the fact of having reached for the 'thematic edition' revised by Gerrantana in the 1970s for Editori Riuniti – a situation which can trick an inexperienced author.
89 D. Biocca, *Il 'ravvedimento' di Gramsci*, in *la Repubblica*, 25 February 2012.
90 This was shown immediately by P. (but N.) Naldi, *Quanti errori sulla vita di Gramsci*, in *l'Unità*, 2 March 2012. On Gramsci's 'repentance', and more generally on many 'historiographic legends' about the Sardinian communist, see the points made by Bruno Gravagnuolo: *Giochini sull'eroico Gramsci*, in *l'Unità*, 29 February 2012 and *Gramsci ravveduto? Ecco le prove di un falso teorema*, in *l'Unità*, 7 April 2012.
91 Platone 1938, p. 145.

Nuova storia contemporanea Boccia published another essay titled *I comunisti il carcere, la libertà condizionale* – 'The Communists, Prison and Conditional Freedom' – in which the error regarding the penal code was implicitly corrected (there was also a comparison between the old 'Codice Zanardelli' and the new 'Codice Rocco'[92]), but here he claimed that good conduct and repentance were nonetheless elements to be evaluated by the authorities for the concession of legal benefits, and that the demands by many communists who requested conditional liberty were rejected at exactly the time when Mussolini conceded 'Gramsci some clemency'.[93] In any case, the fact remains that Gramsci's 'repentance' was never proved (the evaluation of the prisoner's 'conduct' is another matter). Furthermore – as Joseph Buttigieg wrote in arguing against Biocca – one cannot understand 'why Mussolini would have kept his enemy's "repentance" a secret',[94] rather than use the news for propaganda, seeing that this had been his objective.

The history of Gramsci's prison years remains thus at the centre of interests both for scholars and the media. The studies on Gramsci from the years in Turin or the 1920s should, however, not be passed over. Among the first to be given mention is the essay by Michele Marseglia on *La formazione culturale di Antonio Gramsci (1910–1928)*;[95] ('Gramsci's Cultural Education') and then Luca Michelini's *Marxismo, liberalismo, rivoluzione: saggio sul giovane Gramsci 1915–1920* ('Marxism, Liberalism, Revolution: Essays on the Young Gramsci') which investigated the relations between the young Sardinian socialist and the culture of *liberismo* at the time (Einaudi and Pareto above all), contesting the opinion according to which one can 'speak of a real *liberal* phase in Gramsci's intellectual journey'.[96] The volume by Leonardo Rapone which dealt with the years spanning from 'his university apprenticeship to the factory councils', is also important, covering the controversy over the youthful sources, to the 'participation' in a journalistic activity full of battles and taking positions of great originality regarding Gramsci's early yet rich cultural sources. These ranged from the argument with the reformists of the PSI to his admiration for Salvemini, Neoidealism and *La Voce* (all part of a culture, to which Gramsci notably adhered, against Giolitti and the parliament of the time); to the Great War, a real watershed in Gramsci's life, as it was in facing the war, even before the Russian Revolution, that Rapone identified the moment of maturing in Gram-

---

92   Biocca 2012, pp. 45–46.
93   Biocca 2012, p. 74.
94   J. Buttigieg, *Non si fa storia senza documenti*, in *la Repubblica*, 19 March 2012.
95   Marseglia 2010.
96   Michelini 2011, p. 25.

sci's political thought, in the context of the development of mass society and the inability of the old leading liberal ruling classes to understand the radical changes involved. It was nonetheless after the October Revolution that Gramsci began to deepen his understanding of Marx's thought, when he had begun to sharpen 'a vision of history in which it was possible to justify and rationalise the effect of the Russian Revolution within the theoretical realm of Marxism'[97] and an original development of Soviet politics as an alternative to liberal democracy, which had to be begun and developed before the proletarian revolution.

Gramsci in the 1920s was also the subject of a book by Marcos Del Roio, focusing on Gramsci and the 'united front'.[98] The author diligently reconstructed the complex debate within the International which accompanied the newly adopted strategy – not without ambiguities, interpretative differences and periodic adjustments – beginning with the Third Congress of the Comintern (1921). Following the catastrophic failure of 'Left Communism', Gramsci had gradually assumed the 'united front' as a strategic option, overcoming the sectarian interpretations which were shared by many sects of the International and the Bordigist PCd'I;[99] the Sardinian communist had based his struggle against Bordiga on this new vision first, and only afterwards did it form the basis of his own construction of a strategy adapted to "the West".

6 The Political and Theoretical Journey of the Prison Years

The small volume by Franco Lo Piparo, *I due carceri di Gramsci. La prigione fascista e il labirinto comunista* – 'Gramsci's Two Prisons: The Fascist Prison and the Communist Labyrinth' – also provoked many discussions. In it, the author maintains the thesis by which the originality of Gramsci's thought would have taken him, in the last years of his life, outside of the PCd'I and Marxist and Communist theory and praxis. The book began with Gramsci's letter of 27 February 1933 to his sister-in-law Tania, in which Gramsci declared and made 'official, even if in a cryptic manner, his real estrangement – above all philosophically – from Communism as it was being realised'.[100] In this letter to Tania, in reality, Gramsci mainly speaks about the difficult and dramatic relations with his wife Giulia, even if remembering with some confusion the various reasons for his strong dissatisfaction about what the reactions of those around him (fam-

---

97   Rapone 2011, p. 272.
98   Del Roio 2010.
99   Del Roio 2010, p. 117.
100 Lo Piparo 2012, p. 17.

ily members and party comrades) who were not as close to him as he would have liked. As we have already seen, these represented the comments and outpourings of a man being tested physically and psychologically by prison and still more be his worsening health in Turi. Phrases and outpourings, however, which according to Lo Piparo would have been a 'metaphor' of a now compromised relation with the Soviet Union. From here the author deduced the fact that Gramsci had wanted to show his actual decision to separate himself from the Communist movement.

That relations between Gramsci and the Communist movement had been strained for two or three years has already been noted. There is indeed a hint of this in the letter in question. The idea, however, that Togliatti had been Gramsci's *real imprisoner* – as the author wanted to prove – has to be strongly rejected (just as in another part Lo Piparo still more paradoxically claimed that Mussolini 'protected Gramsci in prison'.)[101] Notwithstanding doubts and suspicions (over the famous letter by Grieco from 1928, to which we will return shortly), the Sardinian communist knew that his comrades had not abandoned him. This is evident from the continuation of the same letter where, writing of 'having blundered' Gramsci added: 'Nonetheless, I am quite convinced that this is not quite true, by your attitude and especially that of the lawyer'.[102] And furthermore, we might add, that of Sraffa, the means to the continued relations between the prisoner and Togliatti.

Furthermore, according to Lo Piparo, the letter which Sraffa had drawn up in the last days of the prisoner's life, with Gramsci's agreement, and had sent to him in the post, with which he wanted to ask permission to leave for Soviet Russia, was supposedly an extreme tactic by 'Togliatti and Stalin' (and Sraffa) 'to lead the Sardinian thinker into a second prison, a Communist one.[103] But how was it possible that they were fooled into thinking that Gramsci – who, according to Lo Piparo, had not been a Communist for four years – would obey a project which he did not agree with, given that the request would have to be signed by himself? No one, including Lo Piparo, has mentioned blackmail or intimidation of Gramsci's family in the USSR: a hypothesis which would be without foundation, as we have seen confirmed by the research of Antonio Gramsci Jr.

But the thesis of the book which actually catalysed so much debate was quite another: Lo Piparo – making much out of some claims made by various protagonists of the events, who after Gramsci's death, in some cases immediately

---

101   Lo Piparo 2012, p. 123.
102   Gramsci 1965, p. 690.
103   Lo Piparo 2012, p. 67.

after the end of the war, spoke of the 'thirty notebooks' or of 'thirty or so notebooks' – advanced the hypothesis that there was a notebook which had been hidden or destroyed by Togliatti, presumably because it was too heterodox. As is well known, there are 29 books of notes and jottings, four more of translations, as well as two unused, and one more used by Tania to draft a provisional index of the notes, a work which was soon interrupted. Aside from the fact that it was unlikely that Giulia, Tania or anyone else knew how to distinguish between the different kind of notebook, why – as Lo Piparo claimed – would Togliatti have destroyed this thirtieth, dangerous notebook in Italy and not, more prudently, in Russia, when it was only during the war that he had time to read Gramsci's complete manuscript?[104] The obvious intent of Lo Piparo is that of restoring the liberal democratic figure of Gramsci, finally freeing his life from any Communist connotation which still rendered him unpalatable to some tastes. Driven by this anxiety, the scholar even attributed Gramsci[105] with a claim about hegemony ('the supposed hegemony ... of a liberal democratic regime')[106] which in reality was Croce's philosophy as summarised by Gramsci.[107]

The theoretical and political journey of the prison years has formed one of the main focuses of Gramscian debates in recent years. The realisation of the fact that the reflections of the *Notebooks* had a diachronic development which requires reconstruction has propelled forward not only the study of the history of concepts contained therein, but the study of the history of the years following the arrest. In a deft and original way, Angelo Rossi located the evolution of the positions taken by the prisoner, particularly through connecting the *Letters* and the *Notebooks*, even if the results were not always convincing. Rossi had co-written a book with Giuseppe Vacca in 2007, 'Gramsci Between Mussolini and Stalin', exemplifying the new kind of approach. This offered significant material and important moments of reflection, as well as a series of

---

104   In various different arguments Gianni Francioni has also taken apart the theory of the missing notebook. G. Francioni, *La leggenda del quaderno 'rubato'*, in *l'Unità*, 2 February 2012.
105   Lo Piparo 2012, p. 109.
106   Gramsci 1975, p. 691.
107   In the same year, 2012, Carmine Donzelli republised a work from 1981 on the thirteenth Notebook (Gramsci 2012) with a new preface dedicated to a different matter. In it, the author repeated many of Lo Piparo's theses (except for the extreme situating of the Sardinian communist as a liberal democrat), claiming that Togliatti had tried to keep Gramsci in prison, using Tania and Sraffa as his guards. Over the years, Donzelli claimed, in the umpteenth reconstruction of what many agreed was a hypothesis unsupported by any serious confirmation – Togliatti would win over the former, but not the latter, as faithful agents of the Comintern.

interesting (if debatable) interpretative hypotheses. The four essays that made up the book were dedicated to the relation and communication between the imprisoned Gramsci and the Party; to the (unpublished) documents taken by Gennaro Gramsci after the 1930 visit to Turi, when he was invited by Togliatti to understand the political orientations of his brother; to the return to the issue of the 'constituent' ('the thorn in the side') with which Gramsci had devised during the meetings with other detained comrades, an alternative to the communist politics claimed in 1928–29; and analyses of 1933, the final year spent in Turi, and the hypothesis of the prisoner's liberation by means of inter-state negotiations.[108] But there were also other moments and historical events which were confronted in the volume, often with a sharp eye, such as the role of Sraffa, Grieco's letter of 1928, the attention with which Mussolini followed Gramsci's biography, the vigilance of the prisoner so that not a single gesture could be interpreted as a capitulation to Fascism. Sraffa's role was brought back, here not only as a friend to Gramsci – which had long been recognised – but also as an 'undercover' Communist, a militant to all effects, not formally a member exactly so as to be able to perform the tasks assigned to him (as was also the case with Gennaro Gramsci). Indeed – via means of an analysis of his correspondence with Tania – here Sraffa acquired a *leading* role, which implicitly reframed that of Gramsci's sister-in-law.

Another aspect of great interest was that of the codes of communication utilised by Sraffa, Togliatti and Tania on one hand and Gramsci on the other, to exchange messages with political content. In this part, co-written by the two authors, the book did not seem entirely convincing. It is clear that Gramsci's language, as a result of censorship, especially in the *Letters*, is full of double meanings and the consequent necessity to read between the lines. But despite this it is not possible to define a *code* in the strong sense of the word. In many cases one is dealing with transparent metaphors (such as that of Silvio Spaventa, a prisoner liberated thanks to international pressure), or of references to a barely veiled reality. It is clear also that if Gramsci debated Croce's role, he already shared a certain background and understanding with Togliatti, meaning that to discuss Croce in a certain way also constituted a confirmation of the 'politics of Lyons' and the analysis of Italian society which underlay it. That Gramsci's interlocutors were interested to decipher the opinions on current events is evident, as demonstrated in a letter from Sraffa to Togliatti,[109] in which he explained the desire to find themes of research 'whose political

---

108   Vacca and Rossi 2007. The first and fourth essays were by Rossi, the second and third by Vacca.
109   A. Rossi in Vacca and Rossi 2007, p. 40.

content could be made to pass under the guise of literature'. The only example given as an attempt to communicate in code related to Gramsci's study of the Tenth Canto of the *Inferno*. It should be noted however that Gramsci did not write so many pages on Dante and other aspects of Italian cultural history simply in order to throw off the censor and then write about politics; they were arguments that truly interested him. Nor can one imagine that he could have moulded his own interpretation of Dante to such external factors. And, at the same time, the content of such esoteric communications seems quite poor: the prisoner is meant to have had communicated that, like Cavalcante, he was concerned about the fate of his 'son', the Party. It is also doubtful that Gramsci would have wanted to pass for the hero, even if fighting for his own salvation.

Notwithstanding some confusions, it ought to be said that the hermeneutic work carried out by the authors is important for the documentary attention given to Gramsci's situation and his opposition – shown in many ways – to the aims prevalent within the ranks of the International. It provided convincing examples of critical excavation and certain interpretations of the correspondence indicated the richness opened up by a contextual reading of the whole epistolary and the prison papers in parallel: a work of no small merit.

The book has many other points of interest: Gramsci's attention to the evolving international situation, including in relation to the possibility of his own emancipation by means of an inter-state solution, the only possible way given the Sardinian communist's conviction that Fascism would never concede liberty to a prisoner if it seemed a success to the opposition (the responsibility of the failed liberation would thus be attributed to Stalin, who clearly 'had no interest in asking for his freedom').[110] There was also a reflection on question of the 'constituent' of which Gramsci had spoken in prison, and the problematic evaluation it contained for the *transitional phase* and the ends of transition itself more generally. On this topic, Vacca wrote: 'both the theory of hegemony developed in the *Notebooks* and the conception of "a new kind of democracy" implied the overcoming of the theory of the "revolutionary proletariat" and the "dictatorship of the proletariat", and thus means a reformulation of revolution as the "ultimate goal", if not its abandonment'.[111] The claim that Gramsci had, in prison, carried out a profound redefinition of the idea of revolution, distancing himself from the Bolshevik model with a series of original historical, political categories (hegemony, war of positions, etc), is incontestable. However, if what is meant instead is that in such a way Gramsci's 'ultimate goal' was no

---

110 Vacca and Rossi 2007, p. 9.
111 G. Vacca in Vacca and Rossi 2007, p. 157.

longer the overcoming of capitalist society, then something has been claimed which we do not find written in the *Notebooks*.

In 2010 Rossi published a new book, *Gramsci da eretico a icona* – 'Gramsci: From Heretic to Icon'. Two elements had already been present in the previous book: the method of analysis chosen for deciphering the prison Gramsci, and the importance assigned to the proposal for a constituent assembly. Rossi intersected the prison notes with the letters and the facts of the 'great and terrible world', as well as the testimonies of Terracini and other prisoners of Fascism, so as to lend full political importance to the prison reflections. The author thus reconstructed the first years after the arrest as continuations of the political battle, beginning with the celebrated letter of 1926. He claimed that the original activities were followed by a revision of thought which led Gramsci to develop a democratic communism 'of a kind different from that of the Third International'.[112] For this reason the proposal of the constituent seemed to be 'a radical rethinking of Communist theory and practice'.[113] Gramsci considered the 'turn' to be a 'deviation by the Party towards 'insurrectionalist', substantially extremist positions, in deference to the erroneous directives of the Comintern', which he rejected without breaking his solidarity to the Communist movement.[114] Gramsci had imagined – according to Rossi – a democratic, parliamentarian route, rather than a Soviet one, even if he simultaneously claimed 'the necessity of institutions and autonomous organisms of the "subordinate" classes'.[115] He did not accept, that is, liberal democracy *tout court*, but rather some of its values in view of an *Aufhebung*, an overcoming able to maintain its positive aspects. Aware that the PCd'I could not go forward without Soviet assistance, having understood that the new period of the PCUS and the International did not allow any more open discussion, Gramsci had chosen not to advance any direct confrontation with Stalinism, but he did not (and this was also the reason for having written the *Notebooks*) stop developing a different strategic path, one which was valid for Italy and the West.[116] Rossi shows the parallel journey of Gramsci's political battle of the early prison years and the contemporaneous texts of the first four notebooks. The crudeness of the Marxism prevalent in the Soviet Union was for Gramsci directly conditioned by the schematism of the International's politics. But he hoped that such theoretical crudeness – comparable with the early culture of the Reformation – would be followed by a

---

112   Rossi 2010, p. 28.
113   Rossi 2010, p. 17.
114   Rossi 2010, p. 18.
115   Rossi 2010, p. 106.
116   Rossi 2010, pp. 33–34.

revival similar to that undertaken by classic German philosophy, which had, in the final analysis, been inspired by the Reformation.

Rossi perhaps over emphasised Croce's role in Gramsci's formation, making the Neopolitan philosopher the absolute 'master with whom he continued to converse throughout his entire life'.[117] In contrast, the author considered Lenin one source with which 'the relation ... was without very tormented and difficult',[118] insisting on Gramsci's 'distance from Leninism'. There are, in this reading, two elements which remain confusing: an over-valuation of the role of neoidealist philosophy, as in reality Gramsci's formative background was influenced by a variety of factors, which contributed to its richness. Secondly, the relation with Lenin seems to be read almost entirely negatively. But while in prison Gramsci repeatedly recalled the teachings of the Russian Communist and the *Notebooks* do not take 'distance from Leninism' but (and here we simply repeat Togliatti's words in 1958) are a *translation* of Leninism, at the peak of advanced capitalist society. To *translate* effectively means to establish a critical, creative relation with the source, neither literally reproducing nor entirely negating it.

Democracy had been exiled by Fascism. There were no grounds for any possible 'insurrectionism', as stated at Lyons: these are the ways in which the Turi correspondence parallels the first notebooks, containing the construction of a new Marxism. Gramsci accelerated the moment of this new theoretical and political path in the crucial year of 1930. The attempt to form a framework in preparation for the recommencement of political struggle would fail partly due to the opposition from two 'professional revolutionaries' faithful to the line, Tosin and Lisa. Once thrown out of the Party after speaking to the 'centre', Athos Lisa would be a 'thorn in the side'. But, as Rossi proposed, perhaps Togliatti had "tweaked" Lisa's reports, removing Gramsci's dissent from them, thus contributing significantly to saving Gramsci, his Russian family, the Italian Party and possibly also himself from Stalinism.[119]

Rossi defended Togliatti's operations: his 'precautions' were necessary 'inasmuch as the Communist Party had to account to a *dominus*, Stalin, who would not admit an iota of autonomy'.[120] Gramsci himself was extremely cautious in prison, according to Lisa's account from many years later: 'I never heard Gramsci make any judgments about party politics. Every time a question of this kind was put to him, he responded without hesitation: "I think the politics of the

---

117   Rossi 2010, p. 55.
118   Rossi 2010, p. 57.
119   Rossi 2010, p. 81.
120   Rossi 2010, p. 125.

party are correct.'"[121] Furthermore, according to the author, Gramsci himself 'accepted the party's politics even if he did not share their political line'.[122] Thus he never exposed his dissent, while also without rejecting the idea of a different foundation for Communism and Marxism. The Sardinian communist remained a *congealed* symbol of anti-Fascism, awaiting his *resurrection* by Togliatti once he had returned to Italy,[123] free to build a new road to Socialism and to establish a new version of Marxism on the basis of Gramsci's ideas.

The most recent works on Gramsci of which we will give an account here are those on the prison years. Giuseppe Vacca's *Vita e pensieri di Antonio Gramsci* – 'The Life and Thought of Antonio Gramsci' – is perhaps the best result of an interpretative line we have already focused on. It is based on two convictions: that Gramsci's prison thought had a diachronic development which ought to be studied in its process of composition, and that the motor of the prison researches should be looked for in Gramsci's desire – in the mode and forms allowed to him – to pursue his political battles and, albeit carefully, continue to communicate with the Party through the use of a 'code' which was known by only very few – Togliatti and Sraffa most of all, but also by other leading members of the PCd'I (and partly by Tania and Giulia Schucht). The book constructed the first real history of Gramsci in prison, formed through an immense work of interconnecting the correspondence and many other sources, often unpublished ones.

Vacca's reading, as we have already seen in relation to the 2007 book, began from the constant search for a *hidden line of communication* between Gramsci and his interlocutors and therefore ran the risk of being possible only by unproven (in some cases also improbable) interpretations. The author did not fail to advance his claims with some caution, stating that to explain everything through the deciphering of a code for secret political communication would be reductive.[124] With this warning taken into account, Vacca's work remains very useful even if promoting an interpretation of Gramsci at times too inclined to unilaterally value elements of novelty over those of the tradition of the Third International. The book reached two important conclusions. First, that the prisoner's freedom could only have been effected on the level of state diplomacy, but it was simply not a political priority for the USSR to make an exchange with

---

121   Ibid.
122   Rossi 2010, p. 130.
123   Rossi 2010, p. 137.
124   'Gramsci's letters cover a host of topics from cultural history and practical philosophy, and it would be wrong to reduce their depth to merely politics in a strict sense'. Vacca 2012, p. 202.

a Fascist state which was on the rise, regardless of Gramsci's heterodoxy. This conviction had already been expressed, as we have seen, in the book written with Rossi in 2007 but the claim was now argued and reiterated in a much more articulate and convincing manner.

The second main point, on the other hand, seems to me partially new, an important specification with respect to Vacca's previous work: while in prison, Gramsci proceeded with a 'revision of Bolshevism', but 'his position was not that of a schism, placing him outside of Soviet Communism, but of a heterodox Communist who thought he could struggle from within to reform its foundations'.[125] As Vacca shows convincingly,[126] that Gramsci wanted to return to the Soviet Union to continue his political battles (here he was evidently deluded) and that a stay in Sardinia (his idea for when he would be released from penal detention) would be a *transitional phase*, and that afterwards he still imagined going to the land of Socialism.[127]

On the theoretical level, Vacca confirmed his participation in that group of authors who have maintained the total novelty (in different ways) of the philosophy of praxis with respect to historical materialism: 'Gramsci's reflections', he writes, 'aim for a development of a theory of the constitution of subjects freed from any form of determinism and this is what distinguishes his "philosophy of praxis."'[128] This was not a new conviction for Vacca, inasmuch as it returns to that of his *Gramsci e Togliatti* of 1991.[129]

'Gramsci in Prison and under Fascism' was also the subject of a work by Luciano Canfora which came out in May 2012.[130] The book confronted many issues: Gramsci's interpretations of Fascism and Croce,[131] the *Appello ai fratelli in camicia nera* of 1936, the history of Gramsci's legacy and its management by Togliatti, the story of the anarchist Ezio Taddei, who turned on Gramsci in 1937, the Communist historiography which he radically criticised. Canfora also returned to the letter written to Gramsci (as well as to Terracini and Scoccimarro) by Grieco in 1928, which induced the prisoner's anger and suspicion. Having argued for so long that the letter was a forgery by OVRA in order to 'provoke' Gramsci,[132] Canfora now wrote than in reality it had been written by its sig-

---

125 Vacca 2012, p. 211.
126 This thesis had already been articulated in Vacca 1999.
127 Vacca 2012, pp. 316–17.
128 Vacca 2012, p. 215n.
129 See above Chapter 9, after footnote 83.
130 Canfora 2012.
131 On the interpretation of Croce see Frosini 2012.
132 See p. 247. But also see Canfora 2008, where the theses of 1989 were revised with new arguments.

natory, Ruggero Grieco, and by him alone. Canfora did not exactly claim that Grieco was a traitor and a spy, but leaves the interpretation open: for what other motives would make him – and him alone – plot such a scheme? On whose behalf had Grieco enacted his *provocations* if not to help Fascism and sow division? All of the clues left by Canfora in fact lead one to believe that Grieco was a traitor, including the responsibility which the author attributed to him for the *Appello* of 1936.[133]

In my view, Canfora's new interpretation raises more questions than it answers. The 1928 letters had been written by Grieco, but surely the decision was wider (otherwise the 'provocateur' would not have been able to escape being quickly identified). They were clumsy, but they had no impact on the anti-Communist trials, nor were they submitted as evidence.[134] Furthermore, it is certain that the psychological and physical conditions of the prisoner had worsened, which explains why Gramsci had responded to the letter of 1928 with ever more serious suspicions, along with his fading hopes of freedom and life. Looking at the reasons for which Grieco (and Togliatti) would have written the letter, we are obviously in the field of conjecture. It is probable, however, that the premise was to communicate, foremost to Gramsci, that their battle against the opposition in the Soviet Union had ended with the victory of Stalin's majority, and that the PCd'I (already carrying an atmosphere of Trotskyism due to Gramsci's letter of '26) could no longer continue to play with fire, could no longer insist on disputing the new, and now irreversible, path. This was the 'coded' message. It is more probably therefore that Gramsci had erred in his response to the 'wicked letter': it was a rash mistake, but not a betrayal. As Vacca has argued, he remained in prison because Mussolini had no desire to free him without adequate compensation (as well as propaganda) and Stalin was not interested to pay such a price.

7 The Future Gramsci

The 'return of Gramsci': this was the headline in some newspapers, referring to the great mass of books, essays and newspaper articles dedicated to the Sardinian thinker at the end of 2011 and the first half of 2012. This was seen as an effect not only of the first decade of the century, in which there have been so many high-quality studies, but also a re-situating of Gramsci in an important

---

133 On this see Pistillo 2012.
134 On this see D'Alessandro 2009.

public position. Why has this happened? Why did the attempt to consign Gramsci to the archives fail for so many years ago, and why has there been instead not only a significant production of studies, but his significant reappearance in the media and public culture,[135] a presence missing for so long – even if this has sometimes happened in a superficial, rhapsodic and intermittent way, as so frequently happens in a world of information and culture industry? How has Gramsci intersected today with the identity and problems of at least a section of social, political and cultural subjects, still gaining interest, stances and polemics, whether for or against?

It has been said that in Italy there was no lack of attempts – in the first part of the 1990s – to try and 'forget Gramsci' (just as there were to 'forget Marx' or 'forget Berlinguer'), especially by a section of the political sphere anxious to excise every aspect of the Marxist and Communist tradition. It has also been said that this 'working hypothesis' failed for various reasons – in the first place because of the relevance of Gramsci's legacy and the position which he occupies in contemporary global culture. In one way or another today one has to take into account the Sardinian thinker, including within political and cultural spheres which thought they had not only buried Gramsci but dispersed his ashes, relegating him to the past. Instead today there is an attempt to develop Gramsci's theoretical legacy, comparing it with the contemporary positions of the moderate left – or, on the other hand, to apply it to reality and prove the legacy's value (both in method and substance) as an attempt to radically change political and social reality. Or, in yet another way, to 'learn from the enemy', as have the Neo-conservative American thinktanks for several decades. The greatness of a political thinker is seen in exactly this plurality of questions that revolve around him from diverse quarters. If Gramsci is a 'classic', he is a classic who still speaks to our world.

For these reasons one can say that Gramsci will continue to solicit interest and inspire important studies, in the direction of an ever great historical, philological and conceptual contextualisation of his thought, but also a non-dogmatic theoretical and political conversation. The risk is that on one hand this will only be specialist material, and on the other of making him banal and

---

135   The main moments of media communication aout Gramsci have most recently been two TV programmes which have received very high viewing numbers: the first for the Festival di Sanremo 2011, when (17 February) the actors Luca Bizzarri and Paolo Kessisoglu read Gramsci's celebrated article *Indifferenti* (published 11 February 1917). The second was the program *Quello che (non) ho* of 15 May 2012, in which Ettore Scola devoted a very real personal reflection, to great effect, on the *Prison Notebooks*. Both of the programs can be viewed on Youtube.

popularised. There ought to be an attempt to render him more readable for those who do not have the cultural tools available to a professional scholar. We do not need a 'Gramsci for all seasons' but a 'Gramsci for everyone', albeit on the basis of scientific and rigorous reliability. Both one and the other – the reduction of the distance between 'intellectuals' and 'people', and a seriousness of study – are tasks which we know would have certainly pleased Antonio Gramsci himself.

Bibliography

Adamo, S. (ed.) 2007, *Culture planetarie. Prospettive e limiti della teoria e della critica culturale*, Rome: Meltemi.

Agosti, A. 1996, *Palmiro Togliatti*, Turin: Utet.

Ajello, N. 1979, *Intellettuali e il PCI. 1944–1958*, Rome-Bari: Laterza.

Alcaro, M. *Dellavolpismo e nuova sinistra*, Bari: Dedalo.

Althusser, L. 1969, *For Marx* (trans. Ben Brewster), orig. 1965, London: New Left Books.

Althusser, L. 1971, 'Ideology and Ideological State Apparatuses', in *Lenin and Philosophy and Other Essays* (trans. Ben Brewster), orig. 1968, Monthly Review Press.

Althusser, L. and Balibar, É. 1997, *Reading Capital*, translated by B. Brewster and D. Fernbach, orig. 1965, London and New York: Verso.

Amendola, G. 1967, *Storia del Partito comunista italiano 1921–1943*, Rome: Editori Riuniti.

Amendola, G. 1978, *Rileggendo Gramsci*, in *Prassi rivoluzionaria e storicismo in Gramsci*, monographic notebook of *Critica marxista*, n. 3.

Anderson, P. 1977, *The Antimonies of Antonio Gramsci*, in *New Left Review*, n. 100.

Anglani, B. 1999, *Egemonia e poesia. Gramsci: l'arte, la letteratura*, Lecce: Manni.

Anglani, B. 2007, *Solitudine di Gramsci. Politica e poetica del carcere*, Rome: Donzelli.

Anglani, B. 2009, *Il paese di Pulcinella. Letteratura, rivoluzione, identità nazionale nel giovane Gramsci*, Bari: Palomar.

Asor Rosa, A. 1965, *Scrittori e popolo. Saggio sulla letteratura populista in Italia*, Rome: Samonà e Savelli.

Asor Rosa, A. 1973, *Intellettuali e classe operaia*, Florence: La Nuova Italia.

Asor Rosa, A. 1975, *La cultura*, in *Storia d'Italia*, vol. 4: *Dall'Unità a oggi*, Turin: Einaudi.

Asor Rosa, A. 1977, *Le due società. Ipotesi sulla crisi italiana*, Turin: Einaudi.

Auciello, N. 1974, *Socialismo ed egemonia in Gramsci e Togliatti*, Bari: De Donato.

Badaloni, N. 1962, *Marxismo come storicismo*, Milan: Feltrinelli.

Badaloni, N. 1967, *Gramsci storicista di fronte al marxismo contemporaeo*, in *Prassi rivoluzionaria e storicismo in Gramsci*, monographic notebook of *Critica marxista*, n. 3.

Badaloni, N. 1975, *Il marxismo di Gramsci*, Turin: Einaudi.

Badaloni, N. 1981, *Gramsci: la filosofia della prassi come previsione*, in *Storia del marxismo*, vol. III, Turin: Einaudi.

Badaloni, N. 1992, *Due manoscritti inediti di Sraffa su Gramsci*, in *Critica marxista*, n. 6.

Baldussi, A. and Manduchi, P. (eds.) 2010, *Gramsci in Asia e in Africa*, Cagliari: Aipsa.

Baratta, G. 2003, *Le rose e i quaderni. Il pensiero dialogico di Antonio Gramsci*, Rome: Carocci.

Baratta, G. 2007, *Antonio Gramsci in contrappunto. Dialoghi col presente*, Rome: Carocci.

Baratta, G. and Catone, A. (eds.) 1989, *Modern Times. Gramsci e la critica dell'americanismo*, Milan: Diffusioni '84.

Baratta, G. and Catone, A. (eds.) 1995, *Antonio Gramsci e il 'progresso intellettuale di massa'*, Milan: Unicopli.

Baratta, G. and Liguori, G. (eds.) 1999, *Gramsci da un secolo all'altro*, Rome: Editori Riuniti.

Barbagallo, F. 1992, *Socialismo e democrazia: la polemica tra Giolitti e Longo nel 1956*, in A. Agosti (ed.), *Luigi Longo. La politica e l'azione*, Rome: Editori Riuniti.

Battista, P. 1990, *Il nuovo Gramsci divide il Partito comunista italiano*, in *La Stampa*, 24 August.

Bedeschi, Giuseppe 1983, *La parabola del marxismo teorico in Italia*, Rome-Bari: Laterza.

Bellini, F. and Galli, G. 1953, *Storia del Partito comunista italiano*, Milan: Schwarz.

Bergami, G. 1977, *Il giovane Gramsci e il marxismo 1911–1918*, Milan: Feltrinelli.

Bermani, C. 2007, *Gramsci, gli intellettuali e la cultura proletaria*, Milan: Cooperativa Colibrì.

Berneri, C. 1964, *Scritti scelti di Camillo Berneri: Pietrogrado 1917-Barcellona 1937*, ed. by P.C. Masini and A. Sorti, Milan: Sugar.

Bertelli, S. 1980, *Il gruppo. La formazione del gruppo dirigente del Partito comunista italiano 1936–1948*, Milan: Rizzoli.

Berti, Giuseppe ("J") 1943, *Nel cinquantesimo compleano del compagno Ercoli*, in *Stato operaio*, nn. 2, 3 and 4.

Bianchi Bandinelli, R. 1962 (2nd edition), *Dal diario di un borghese*, orig. 1948, Milan: il Saggiatore.

Biocca, D. 2012, *I comunisti, il carcere e la libertà condizionale*, in *Nuova Storia Contemporanea*, n. 3.

Bobbio, N. 1955, *Politica e cultura*, Turin: Einaudi.

Bobbio, N. 1990, *Saggi su Gramsci*, Milan: Feltrinelli.

Bonetti, P. 1980, *Gramsci e la società liberaldemocratica*, Rome-Bari: Laterza.

Boninelli, M. 2007, *Frammenti indigesti. Temi folclorici negli scritti di Antonio Gramsci*, Rome: Carocci.

Bonomi, G. 1973, *Partito e rivoluzione in Gramsci*, Milan: Feltrinelli.

Boothman, D. 2004, *Traducibilità e processi traduttivi. Un caso: A. Gramsci linguista*, Perugia: Guerra.

Borghese, L. 1991, *Tia Alene in bicicletta. Gramsci traduttore dal tedesco e teorico della traduzione*, in *Belfagor*, n. 6.

Brennan, T. 2009, *Gramsci e gli Stati Uniti: un'esasperazione*, in M. Pala (ed.), *Americanismi. Sulla ricezione del pensiero di Gramsci negli Stati Uniti*, Cagliari: Cuec.

Broccoli, A. 1972, *Antonio Gramsci e l'educazione come egemonia*, Florence: La Nuova Italia.

Brown, A. 2002, *L'amore assente. Gramsci e le sorelle Schucht*, Turin: CET – Clerico editore.

Brunello, Y. 2007, *Identità senza rivoluzione. Stuart Hall interprete di Gramsci*, in *Critica marxista*, n. 5.

Buci-Glucksmann, C. 1976, *Gramsci e lo Stato*, orig. 1975, Rome: Editori Riuniti.

Burgio, A. and Santucci, A.A. (eds.) 1999, *Gramsci e la rivoluzione in Occidente*, Rome: Editori Riuniti.

Burgio, A. 2002, *Gramsci storico. Una lettura dei 'Quaderni del carcere'*, Rome-Bari: Laterza.

Burgio, A. 2007, *Per Gramsci. Crisi e potenza del moderno*, Rome: DeriveApprodi.

Cacciatore, G. 1999, *Gramsci: problemi di etica nei* Quaderni, in G. Vacca (ed.), *Gramsci e il Novecento*, ii, Rome: Carocci.

Calzolaio, V. (ed.) 1991, *Gramsci e la modernità*, Naples: Cuen.

Cambria, A. 1976, *Amore come rivoluzione*, Milan: SugarCo.

Cammett, J.M., 1989, *Bibliografia gramsciana (versione provvisoria)*, no location, no date, but 2010.

Cammett, J.M. (ed.) 1991, *Bibliografia gramsciana 1922–1988*, Rome: Editori Riuniti.

Cammet, J.M. and Righi, M.L. (eds.) 1995, *Bibliografia gramsciana. Supplement updated to 1993*, Rome: Fondazione Istituto Gramsci.

Canfora, L. 1989, *Togliatti e i dilemmi della politica*, Rome-Bari: Laterza.

Canfora, L. 2007, *Su Gramsci*, Rome: Datanews.

Canfora, L. 2008, *La storia falsa*, Milan: Rizzoli.

Canfora, L. 2012, *Gramsci in carcere e il fascismo*, Rome: Salerno editrice.

Capecelatro, E.M. and Carlo, A. 1972, *Contro la questione meridionale*, Rome: Samonà and Savelli.

Capitani, L. and Villa, R. (eds.) 1999, *Scuola, intellettuali e identità nazionale nel pensiero di Antonio Gramsci*, Rome: Gamberetti.

Caprara, M. 2001, *Gramsci e i suoi carcerieri*, Milan: Edizioni Ares.

Caracciolo, A. and Scalia, G. (eds.) 1959, *La città futura. Saggi sulla figura e il pensiero di Antonio Gramsci*, Milan: Feltrinelli.

Carbone, G. and Lombardo Radice, L. 1952, *Vita di Antonio Gramsci*, Rome: Edizioni di cultura sociale.

Carini, C. (ed.) 1995, *La rappresentanza politica in Europa tra le due guerre*, Florence: Cet.

Cassano, F. (ed.) 1973, *Marxismo e filosofia in Italia (1958–1971)*, Bari: De Donato.

Cavallaro, L. 2005, *Lo Stato dei diritti. Politica economica e rivoluzione passiva in Occidente*, Naples: Vivarium.

Cesari, S. 1991, *Colloquio con Giulio Einaudi*, Rome-Naples: Theoria.

Cessi et al 1973, *Studi gramsciani*, Rome: Editori Riuniti.

Chambers, I. (ed.) 2006, *Esercizi di potere. Gramsci, Said e il postcoloniale*, Rome: Meltemi.

Chiarante, G. 1987, *Società civile e riforma intellettuale e morale*, in *Critica marxista*, n. 2–3.

Chiarotto, F. 2011, *Operazione Gramsci. Alla conquista degli intellettuali nell'Italia del dopoguerra*, Milan: Bruno Mondadori.

Ciliberto 1982, *Filosofia e politica nel Novecento italiano. Da Labriola a 'Società'*, Bari: De Donato.

Ciliberto 1984, 'La battaglia delle idee' alla svolta degli anni sessanta, in *Togliatti nella storia d'Italia*, monographic volume of *Critica marxista*, n. 4–5.

Coen, F. 1977 (ed.), *Egemonia e democrazia. Gramsci e la questione comunista nel dibattito di Mondoperaio*, Quaderni di Mondoperaio, 1977.

Colletti, L. 1979a, Marxismo, in *Enciclopedia del Novecento*, vol. IV, Rome: Istituto dell'Enciclopedia Italiana.

Colletti, L. 1979b, *Tra marxismo e no*, Rome-Bari: Laterza.

Contemporaneo, 1987, Come rileggiamo Gramsci. A cinquant'anni dalla sua scomparsa, *Il Contemporaneo di Rinascita*, 1987, n. 30.

Cortesi, L. 1975, P. Togliatti, la svolta di Salerno e l'eredità gramsciana, in *Belfagor*, 1975, n. 1.

Corvisieri, S. 1969, *Trotskij e il comunismo italiano*, Rome: Samonà e Savelli.

Cospito, G. (ed.), 2010, *Gramsci tra filologia e storiografia. Scritti per Gianni Francioni*, Naples: Bibliopolis.

Cospito, G. 2011a, Verso l'edizione critica e integrale dei 'Quaderni del carcere', in *Studi storici*, n. 4.

Cospito, G. 2011b, *Il ritmo del pensiero. Per una lettura diacronica dei 'Quaderni del carcere'*, Naples: Bibliopolis.

Coutinho, C.N. 2001, Cultura e società in Brasile, in *Rivista di studi portoghesi e brasiliani*, n. 3.

Coutinho, C.N. 2004, Lessico gramsciano, in *Critica marxista*, n. 2–3.

Coutinho, C.N. 2006, *Il pensiero politico di Gramsci*, Milan: Edizione Unicopli.

Coutinho, C.N. 2007, L'epoca neoliberale: rivoluzione passiva o controriforma?, in *Critica marxista*, n. 2.

Crehan, K. 2010, *Gramsci, cultura e antropologia*, edited by G. Pizza, Lecce: Argo.

Croce, B. 1944, *Per la nuova vita dell'Italia. Scritti e discorsi 1943–44*, Naples: Ricciardi.

Croce, B. 1945a, Dell'arte delle riviste letterarie odierne, in *Quaderni della "Critica"*.

Croce, B. 1945b, *Pagine politiche*, Bari: Laterza.

Croce, B. 1947, Antonio Gramsci – Lettere dal carcere, in *Quaderni della "Critica"*, n. 8.

Croce, B. 1948, *Due anni di vita politica italiana (1946–1947)*, Bari: Laterza.

D'Orsi, A. 1999, Lo studente che non divenne 'dottore'. Gramsci all'università di Torino, in *Studi storici*, n. 1.

D'Orsi, A. and Chiarotto, F. (eds.) 2008, *Egemonia. Usi e abusi di una parola controversa*, Naples: Libreria Dante and Descartes.

D'Orsi, A. (ed.) 2008, *Bibliografia gramsciana ragionata, I: 1922–1965*, Rome: Viella.

D'Alessando, L.P. 2009, I dirigenti comunisti davanti al Tribunale speciale, in *Studi storici*, n. 2.

Daniele, C. 2005, *Togliatti editore di Gramsci*, Rome: Carocci.

Day, R.J.F. 2005, *Gramsci Is Dead: Anarchist Currents in the Newest Social Movements*, London and Toronto: Pluto Press and Between the Lines.

De Felice, F. 1971, *Serrati, Bordiga, Gramsci e il problema della rivoluzione in Italia 1919–1920*, Bari: De Donato.

De Giovanni, B. 1977, *Togliatti e la cultura meridionale*, in F. De Felice (ed.), *Togliatti e il Mezzogiorno*, acts of the convention held in Bari 2–4th November 1975, Rome: Editori Riuniti.

De Giovanni, B. 1981, *Il 'moderno Principe' fra politica e tecnica*, in *Critica marxista*, n. 3.

De Giovanni, B. 1983, *Sulle vie di Marx filosofo in Italia*, in *Il Centauro*, n. 9.

De Giovanni, B. 1985, *Il Marx di Gramsci*, in B. De Giovanni and G. Pasquino, *Marx dopo Marx*, Bologna: Cappelli.

De Giovanni, B., Gerratana, V. and Paggi, L. 1977, *Egemonia Stato partito in Gramsci*, Rome: Editori Riuniti.

Deias, A., Boninelli, G.M. and Testa, E. (eds.) 2008, *Gramsci ritrovato*, monographic edition of *Lares*, n. 2.

Del Fra, L. and Mangini, C. 1979, *Antonio Gramsci: i giorni del carcere. Un film come storia*, Milan: Ottoviano.

Del Noce, A. 1978, *Il suicidio della rivoluzione*, Milan: Rusconi.

Del Roio, M., 2010, *I prismi di Gramsci. La formula politica del fronte unico (1919–1926)*, Naples: La città del sole, no date, but 2010.

Di Bello, A. (ed.) 2011, *Marx e Gramsci. Filologia, filosofia e politica allo specchio*, Naples: Liguori.

Di Domenico, G. 1979, *Saggio su 'Società'*, Naples: Liguori.

Di Meo, A. 1986, *Trasformazione e modernizzazione: il caso della scienza italiana*, in *Critica marxista*, n. 2–3.

Donini, A. 1975, *Per la storia dei 'Quaderni' di Gramsci e sulla 'svolta di Salerno'*, in *Belfagor*, n. 4.

Dorso, G. 1925, *La rivoluzione meridionale*, Turin: Piero Gobetti editore.

Dorso, G. 1945, *La questione meridionale nel pensiero di Antonio Gramsci*, in *La rivoluzione meridionale*, Turin: Einaudi.

Durante, L. and Liguori, G. (eds.) 2012, *Domande dal presente. Studi su Gramsci*, Rome: Carocci.

Durante, L. and Voza, P. (eds.) 2006, *La prosa del comunismo critico. Labriola e Gramsci*, Bari: Palomar.

Fabre, G. 1990, *Correggere quei Quaderni*, in *Panorama*, 30 September.

Fergnani, F. 2011, *Antonio Gramsci. La filosofia della prassi nei Quaderni del carcere*, edited by A. Vigorelli and M. Zanantoni, Milan: Unicopli.

Fernández Buey, F. 1999, *La politica come etica del collettivo*, in Burgio and Santucci (eds.) 1999.

Ferretti, G.C. 1992, *L'editore Vittorini*, Turin: Einaudi.
Ferri, F. (eds.) 1977-1979 *Politica e storia in Gramsci*, 2 vols, atti del Convegno internazionale di studi gramsciani, Florence, 9-11 December 1977, Rome: Editori Riuniti.
Festa, F.S. 1976, *Gramsci*, Assisi: Citadella editrice.
Filippini, M. 2011, *Gramsci globale. Guida pratica alle interpretazioni di Gramsci nel mondo*, Bologna: Odoya.
Finelli, R. 2005, *Tra moderno e postmoderno. Saggi di filosofia sociale e di etica del riconoscimento*, Lecce: Pensa.
Finelli, R. 2012, *Antonio Gramsci. La rifondazione di un marxismo 'senza corpo'*, in P.P. Poggio (ed.), *L'altro Novecento: comunismo eretico e pensiero critico*, i, Milan: Jaca Book.
Fiori, G. 1966, *Vita di Antonio Gramsci*, Bari: Laterza.
Fiori, G. 1991, *Gramsci Togliatti Stalin*, Rome-Bari: Laterza.
Flores, M. and Gallerano, N. 1992, *Sul Partito comunista italiano. Un'interpretazione storica*, Bologna: il Mulino.
Fondazione Istituto Gramsci Piemontese (ed.) 1998, *Il giovane Gramsci e la Torino d'inizio secolo*, Turin: Rosenberg and Sellier.
Forenza, E. and Liguori, G. (eds.) 2012, *Valentino Gerratana 'filosofo democratico'*, Rome: Carocci.
Fortini, F. 1965, *Verifica dei poteri*, Milan: il Saggiatore.
Francioni, G. 1984, *L'officina gramsciana. Ipotesi sulla struttura dei 'Quaderni del carcere'*, Naples: Bibliopolis.
Francioni, G. 1992, *Il bauletto inglese. Appunti per una storia dei 'Quaderni' di Gramsci*, in *Studi storici*, n. 4.
Francioni, G. 1979, *Per la storia dei 'Quaderni del carcere'*, in Ferri (ed.) 1977-1979.
Fresu, G. 2005, *'Il diavolo nell'ampolla'. Antonio Gramsci, gli intellettuali e il partito*, Naples: La città del sole.
Frosini, F. 2003, *Gramsci e la filosofia. Saggio sui* Quaderni del carcere, Rome: Carocci.
Frosini, F. 2009, *Da Gramsci a Marx. Ideologia, verità e politica*, Rome: DeriveApprodi.
Frosini, F. 2010, *La religione dell'uomo moderno. Politica e verità nei* Quaderni del carcere *di Antonio Gramsci*, Rome: Carocci.
Frosini, F. 2012, *I* Quaderni *tra Mussolini e Croce*, in *Critica marxista*, n. 4.
Frosini, F. and Liguori, G. (eds.) 2004, *Le parole di Gramsci. Per un lessico dei 'Quaderni del carcere'*, Carocci: Rome.
Fubini, E. 1969, *Bibliografia gramsciana*, in Rossi 1969.
Fubini, E. 1979, *Bibliografia gramsciana 1968–1977*, in Ferri 1977-1979.
Garin, E. 1974, *Intellettuali italiani del XX secolo*, Rome: Editori Riuniti.
Garin, E. 1966, *Quindici anni dopo*, in E. Garin, *Cronache di filosofia italiana*, Bari: Laterza.
Garin, E. 1978, *Filosofia e scienza nel Novecento*, Rome-Bari: Laterza.

Garin, E. 1997, *Con Gramsci*, Rome: Editori Riuniti.

Garosci A. 1954, *Pensiero politico e storiografia moderna*, Pisa: Nistri-Lischi.

Germanetto, G. 1931, *Memorie di un barbiere*, preface by P. Togliatti, Brussels: Edizioni di cultura sociale.

Germanetto, G. 1945, *Memorie di un barbiere*, Rome: E.Gi.Ti.

Gerratana, V. 1972, *Ricerche di storia del marxismo*, Rome: Editori Riuniti.

Gerratana, V. 1974, *Intellettuali italiani del XX secolo: il problema del postfascismo*, in *Studi storici*, n. 3.

Gerratana, V. 1987, *La classicità di Antonio Gramsci*, in *Jonas. I Quaderni*, n. 1.

Gerratana, V. 1989, *Per la storia della prima edizione dei 'Quaderni del carcere'*, in *Critica marxista*, n. 6.

Gerratana, V. 1997, *Gramsci. Problemi di metodo*, Rome: Editori Riuniti.

Ghiro, A. 2012, *Gramsci e la psicologia. Tra patchwork e teoria scientifica*, Padua: Cleup.

Giacomini, R., Losurdo, D. and Martelli, M. (eds.) 1994, *Gramsci e l'Italia. Atti del convegno internazionale di Urbino, 24–25 January 1992*, Naples: La città del sole.

Giolitti, A. 1957, *Riforme e rivoluzione*, Turin: Einaudi.

Gobetti, P. 1924, *La rivoluzione liberale*, Bologna-Rocca S. Casciano-Florence: L. Cappelli.

Gobetti, P. 1960, *Scritti politici*, edited by P. Spriano, Turin: Einaudi.

Gramsci, A. 1949, *Americanismo e fordismo*, Milan: Universale economica.

Gramsci, A. 1963, *La cultura italiana del '900 attraverso le riviste: IV: L'Ordine Nuovo 1919–1920*, edited by P. Spriano, Turin: Einaudi.

Gramsci, A. 1964, *2000 pagine di Gramsci*, edited by G. Ferrata and N. Gallo, Milan: il Saggiatore.

Gramsci, A. 1965, *Lettere dal carcere*, edited by S. Caprioglio and E. Fubini, Turin: Einaudi.

Gramsci, A. 1966, *Socialismo e fascismo. L'Ordine Nuovo 1921–22*, Turin: Einaudi.

Gramsci, A. 1967a, *La formazione dell'uomo*, edited by G. Urbani, Rome: Editori Riuniti.

Gramsci, A. 1967b, *Scritti politici*, edited by P. Spriano. Rome: Editor Riuniti.

Gramsci, A. 1968, *Scritti 1915–1921*, edited by S. Caprioglio, Milan: I Quaderni de 'il Corpo'.

Gramsci, A. 1971, *Selections from the Prison Notebooks*, translated and edited by Q. Hoare and G. Nowell Smith, New York: International Publishers.

Gramsci, A. 1972, *L'alternativa pedagogica*, edited by M.A. Manacorda, Florence: La Nuova Italia.

Gramsci, A. 1974, *Per la verità. Scritti 1913–1926*, edited by R. Martinelli, Rome: Editori Riuniti.

Gramsci, A. 1975, *Quaderni del carcere*, critical edition of the Istituto Gramsci, edited by V. Gerratana, Turin: Einaudi.

Gramsci, A. 1978, *Some Aspects of the Southern Question*, in Q. Hoare (ed. and transl.), *Selections from Political Writings 1921–1926*, orig. 1926, London: Lawrence and Wishart.

Gramsci, A. 1984, *Il nostro Marx 1918-1919*, Turin: Einaudi.
Gramsci, A. 1992, *Lettere 1908-1926*, edited by A.A. Santucci, Turin: Einaudi.
Gramsci, A. 1994, *Scritti di economia politica*, edited by F. Consiglio and F. Frosini, Turin: Bollati Boringhieri.
Gramsci, A. 1996. *Lettere dal carcere 1926-1937*, edited by A.A. Santucci, Palermo: Sellerio.
Gramsci, A. 1997a, *Pensare la democrazia. Antologia dai 'Quaderni del carcere'*, introduced and edited by M. Montanari, Turin: Einaudi.
Gramsci, A. 1997b, *Filosofia e politica. Antologia dei 'Quaderni del carcere'*, introduced and edited by F. Consiglio and F. Frosini, Florence: La Nuova Italia.
Gramsci, A. 1997c, *Le opere. La prima antologia di tutti gli scritti*, edited by A.A. Santucci, Rome: Editori Riuniti.
Gramsci, A. 2004a, *La nostra città futura. Scritti torinesi (1911-1922)*, introduced and edited by A. d'Orsi, Rome: Carocci.
Gramsci, A. 2004b, *Il lettore in catene. La critica letteraria nei Quaderni*, edited by A. Menetti, Rome: Carocci.
Gramsci, A. 2007a, *Nel mondo grande e terribile. Antologia degli scritti 1914-1935*, edited by G. Vacca, Turin: Einaudi.
Gramsci, A. 2007b, *Pensare l'Italia*, edited by G. Vacca, edizione fuori commercio riservata ai lettori de l'Unità.
Gramsci, A. 2007c, *Scritti scelti*, edited by M. Gervasoni, Milan: Rizzoli.
Gramsci, A. 2007d, *Quaderni di traduzioni (1929-1932)*, edited by G. Cospito and G. Francioni, Rome: Istituto della Enciclopedia Italiana.
Gramsci, A. 2008a, *Contro l'indifferenza. Antologia per la scuola media superiore*, edited by L. La Porta and G. Prestipino, no location, SEAM.
Gramsci, A. 2008b, *Scritti sulla Sardegna*, edited by G. Melis, Nuoro: Elisso.
Gramsci, A. 2009a, *Quaderni del carcere. Edizione anastatica dei manoscritti*, edited by G. Francioni, Rome and Cagliari: Biblioteca Treccani and L'Unione Sarda.
Gramsci, A. 2009b, *Epistolario, 1. gennaio 1906-decembre 1922*, edited by D. Bidussa, F. Giasi, G. Luzzatto Voghera and M.L. Righi, Rome: Istituto della Enciclopedia italiana.
Gramsci, A. 2010a, *Cronache teatrali 1915-1920*, edited by G. Davico Bonino, Turin: Aragno.
Gramsci, A. 2010b, *Il Risorgimento e l'Unità d'Italia*, edited by C. Donzelli, Rome: Donzelli editore.
Gramsci, A. 2011a, *Odio gli indifferenti*, introduction by D. Bidussa, Milan: Chiarelettere.
Gramsci, A. 2011b, *Scritti per il Risorgimento*, preface and edited by P. Voza, Cosenza: Ottavomiglio.
Gramsci, A. 2011c, *Epistolario, 2. gennaio-novembre 1923*, edited by D. Bidussa, F. Giasi and M.L. Righi, Rome: Istituto della Enciclopedia italiana.

Gramsci, A. 2011d, *I racconti dei fratelli Grimm. Le traduzioni originali dai 'Quaderni del carcere'*, edited by N. Caleffi and G. Leoni, with an introductory essay by L. Borghese, Sassuolo: Incontri editrice.

Gramsci 2012, *Il moderno principe. Il partito e la lotta per l'egemonia. Quanderno 13. Noterelle sulla politica del Machiavelli*, edited by C. Donzelli, Rome: Donzelli editore.

Gramsci Jr., A. 2008, *La Russia di mio nonno. L'album familiare degli Schucht*, Rome: Nuova iniziativa editoriale.

Gramsci Jr., A. 2010, *I miei nonni nella rivoluzione. Breve storia della famiglia russa di Antonio Gramsci*, Rome: Edizioni riformiste.

Gramsci, A. and Schucht, T. 1997, *Lettere 1926–1937*, edited by C. Daniele and A. Natoli, Turin: Einaudi.

Gravagnuolo, B. 1990, *Il revisionista Gramsci*, in *Rinascita*, n. 20.

Gruppi, L. 1967, *Il concetto di egemonia*, in *Prassi rivoluzionaria e storicismo in Gramsci*, monographic notebook of *Critica marxista, n. 3*.

Gruppi, L. 1972, *Il concetto di egemonia in Gramsci*, Rome: Editori Riuniti.

Gruppi, L. 1984, *Introduzione* to P. Togliatti, *Opere*, vol. V: 1944–1955, Rome: Editori Riuniti.

Guiducci, R. 1956, *Socialismo e verità*, Turin: Einaudi.

Hall, S. 2006a, *Politiche del quotidiano. Culture, identità e senso comune*, introduced and edited by G. Leghissa, with a preface by G. Baratta, Milan: Il Saggiatore.

Hall, S. 2006b, *Il soggetto e la differenza. Per un'archeologia degli studi culturali e postcoloniali*, edited by M. Mellino, Rome: Meltemi.

Hobsbawm, E.J. 1987, *Per capire le classi subalterne*, in *Rinascita*, 28 February.

Ingrao, P. 1977, *Masse e potere*, Rome: Editore Riuniti.

Ingrao, P. 1990, *Le cose impossibili. Un'autobiografia raccontata e discussa con N. Tranfaglia*, Rome: Editori Riuniti.

Istituto Gramsci 1972, *Il movimento operaio italiano degli anni sessanta e la formazione teorico politica delle giovani generazioni*, Rome: Editori Riuniti.

Istituto Gramsci 1992, *Verbale della riunione del comitato di esperti del 6 maggio 1991*, in *Ig Informazioni*, n. 2, pp. 7–8.

Izzo, F. 2009, *Democrazia e cosmopolitismo in Antonio Gramsci*, Rome: Carocci.

Jocteau, G.C. 1973, *Sul concetto di egemonia in Gramsci e Togliatti*, in *Rivista di storia contemporanea*, n. 1.

Jocteau, G.C. 1975, *Leggere Gramsci. Guida alle interpretazioni*, Milan: Feltrinelli.

Kohan, N. and Rep, M. 2003, *Gramsci para principiantes*, Buenos Aires: Era naciente.

Kołakowski, L. 2005, *Main Currents of Marxism: Its Origins, Growth and Dissolution*, orig. 1975, Oxford: Oxford University Press.

La Porta, L. 2010, *Antonio Gramsci e Hannah Arendt. Per amore del mondo grande, terribile e complicato*, Rome: Aracne.

La Rocca, T. 1981, *Gramsci e la religione*, Brescia: Queriniana.

Laclau, E. and Mouffe, C. 2001, *Hegemony and Socialist Strategy*, Second edition, London: Verso.

Laclau, E. and Mouffe, C. 2011, *Egemonia e strategia socialista. Verso una politica democratica radicale*, Genova: il Melangolo.

Lehner, G. 2008, *La famiglia Gramsci in Russia. Con diari inediti di Margarita e Olga Gramsci*, Milan: Mondadori.

Leone de Castris, A. 1997, *Gramsci rimosso*, Rome: Datanews.

Lepre, A. 1998, *Il prigioniero. Vita di Antonio Gramsci*, Rome-Bari: Laterza.

Liguori, G. 1987, *Dieci anni di studi gramsciani in Italia (1978–1987)*, in *Oltre Gramsci, con Gramsci*, monographic volume of *Critica marxista*, n. 2–3.

Liguori, G. 1989, *La fortuna di Gramsci nel mondo*, in *Critica marxista*, n. 6.

Liguori, G. 1996a, *Gramsci conteso. Storia di un dibattito, 1922–1996*, Rome: Editori Riuniti. (First edition of the current volume).

Liguori, G. 1996b, *Dallo storicismo alla scoperta delle forme*, in *Il pensiero di Cesare Luporini*, Milan: Feltrinelli.

Liguori, G. 1996c, *Su alcune letture di Gramsci fuori d'Italia. Althusser, la 'scuola althusseriana', Kołakowski*, in M. Alcaro and V. de Nardo (eds.), *La filosofia italiana fuori d'Italia*, Quaderno di *Il contributo*.

Liguori, G. 2006, *Sentieri gramsciani*, Rome: Carocci.

Liguori, G. 2007, *Rileggendo Gramsci, tra filologia e divulgazione*, in *Critica marxista*, n. 3–4.

Liguori, G. 2009a, *La morte del PCI*, Rome: manifestolibri.

Liguori, G. 2009b, *La conversione di Gramsci e la creazione di un nuovo senso comune*, in *Historia Magistra*, n. 1.

Liguori, G. and Voza, P. (eds.) 2009, *Dizionario gramsciano 1926–1937*, Rome: Carocci.

Lo Piparo, F. 1979. *Lingua intellettuali egemonia in Gramsci*, Rome-Bari: Laterza.

Lo Piparo, F. 2012, *I due carceri di Gramsci*, Rome: Donzelli.

Longo, L. 1957, *Revisionismo nuovo e antico*, Turin: Einaudi.

Losurdo, D. 1990, *Gramsci, Gentile, Marx e le filosofie della prassi*, in B. Muscatello (ed.), *Gramsci e il marxismo contemporaneo*, Rome: Editori Riuniti.

Losurdo, D. 1997, *Antonio Gramsci dal liberalismo al 'comunismo critico'*, Rome: Gambaretti.

Luperini, R. 1971, *Gli intellettuali di sinistra e l'ideologia della ricostruzione*, Roma: Edizioni di Ideologie, 1971.

Luporini, C. 1973, *Il marxismo e la cultura italiana del Novecento*, in *Storia d'Italia*, Rome: Einaudi.

Luporini, C. 1974, *Dialettica e materialismo*, Rome: Editori Riuniti.

Luporini, C. 1979, *Gramsci e la religione*, in *Critica marxista*, n. 1.

Lussana, F. and Pissarello, G. (eds.) 2008, *La lingua\ le lingue di Gramsci e delle sue opere. Scrittura, riscritture, letture in Italia e nel mondo*, Soveria Mannelli: Rubbettino.

Macciocchi, M.A. 1974, *Per Gramsci*, Bologna: Il Mulino.

Maggi, M. 2008, *La filosofia della rivoluzione. Gramsci, la cultura e la guerra europea*, Rome: Edizioni di Storia e Letteratura.

Maitan, L. 1955, *Attualità di Gramsci e politica comunista*, Milan: Schwarz.

Manacorda, M.A. 1970, *Il principio educativo in Gramsci*, Rome: Armando.

Mancina, C. 1977, *Introduzione a L. Althusser, Freud e Lacan*, Rome: Editori Riuniti.

Mancina, C. 1980a, *Rapporti di forza e previsione. Il gioco della storia secondo Gramsci*, in *Critica marxista*, n. 5.

Mancina, C. 1980b, *'Il fronte ideologico': ideologia e istituzioni statali in Gramsci*, in *Prassi e teoria*, n. 7.

Marseglia, M. 2010, *La formazione culturale di Antonio Gramsci (1910–1928)*, Rome: Aracne.

Martelli, M. 1996, *Gramsci filosofo della politica*, Milan: Unicopli.

Martelli, M. 2001, *Etica e storia. Croce e Gramsci a confronto*, Naples: La città del sole.

Martinelli, R. 1995, *Storia del Partito comunista italiano*, VI, Turin: Einaudi.

Mastellone, S. (ed.) 1997, *Gramsci: i 'Quaderni del carcere'. Una riflessione politica incompiuta*, Turin: Utet libreria.

Mastellone, S. and Sola, G. (eds.) 1997, *Gramsci: il partito politico nei* Quaderni, Florance: Cet.

Mastrogregori, M. 2008, *I due prigionieri. Gramsci, Moro e la storia del Novecento italiano*. Genoa: Marietti.

Matteucci, N. 1951, *Antonio Gramsci e la filosofia della prassi*, Milan: Giuffrè.

Medici, R. 1990, *La metafora Machiavelli. Mosca Pareto Michels Gramsci*, Modena: Mucchi.

Medici, R. 2000, *Giobbe e Prometo. Filosofia e politica nel pensiero di Gramsci*, Florence: Alinea.

Melchiorre, V., Vigna, C. and De Rosa, G. (eds.) 1979, *Antonio Gramsci, il pensiero teorico e politico, la 'questione leninista'*, 2 vols, Rome: Città nuova editrice.

Meta, C. 2010, *Antonio Gramsci e il pragmatismo. Confronti e intersezioni*, Florence: Le Càriti.

Michelini, L. 2011, *Marxismo, liberismo, rivoluzione: saggio sul giovane Gramsci 1915–1920*, Naples: La città del sole.

Monasta, A. 1985, *L'educazione tradita*, Pisa: Giardini.

Mondolfo, R. 1955, *Intorno a Gramsci e alla filosofia della prassi*, Milan: Edizioni *Critica sociale*.

Mondolfo, R. 1968, *Umanismo di Marx*, Turin: Einaudi.

Montagnana, M. 1942, *Gli Scritti di A. Gramsci*, in *Stato operaio*, n. 3–4.

Montagnana, M. 1947, *Ricordi di un militante*, Milan: Fasani.

Montaleone, C. 1996, *La cultura a Milano nel dopoguerra*, Turin: Bollati Boringhieri.

Montanari, M. 2002, *Studi su Gramsci. Americanismo democrazia e teoria della storia nei* Quaderni del carcere, Lecce: Edizioni Pensa Multimedia.

Montanari, M. 2007, *Politica e storia. Saggi su Vico, Croce e Gramsci*, Bari: Publierre.

Mordenti, R. 1996, Quaderni del carcere *di Antonio Gramsci*, in A. Asor Rosa (ed.), *Letteratura italiana. Le opere*, vol. IV, Turin: Einaudi.

Mordenti, R. 1998, *Introduzione a Gramsci*, Rome: Datanews.

Mordenti, R. 1999, *Per l'edizione ipertestuale dello Zibaldone Laurenziano di Boccaccio (Plut. XXIX, 8)*, in *I nuovi orizzonti della filologia*, Rome: Accademia nazionale dei Lincei.

Mordenti, R. 2001, *Informatica e critica dei testi*, Rome: Bulzoni.

Mordenti, R. 2007, *Gramsci e la rivoluzione necessaria*, Rome: Editori Riuniti.

Mussolini, B. 1959, *Opera omnia*, vol. XXIX, Florence: La Fenice.

Nardone, G. 1971, *Il pensiero di Gramsci*, Bari: De Donato.

Natoli, A. 1990, *Antigone e il prigoniero. Tania Schucht lotta per la vita di Gramsci*. Rome: Editori Riuniti.

Natoli, C. 1995, *Gramsci in carcere: le campagne per la liberazione, il partito, l'Internazionale (1932–1933)*, in *Studi storici*, n. 2.

Natoli, C. 1999, *Le campagne per la liberazione di Gramsci, il Pcd'I e l'Internazionale (1934)*, in *Studi storici*, n. 1.

Natoli, C. 2000, *Fascismo democrazia socialismo. Comunisti e socialisti tra le due guerre*, Milan: Angeli.

Natta, A. 1967, *Il partito politico nei* Quaderni del carcere, in *Prassi rivoluzionaria e storicismo in Gramsci*, monographic notebook of *Critica marxista*, n. 3.

Natta, A. 1984, *Il Partito comunista italiano negli anni del centrosinistra*, in *Togliatti nella storia d'Italia*, monographic volume of *Critica marxista*, n. 4–5.

Natta, A. 1987, *Così Gramsci ci ha insegnato a innovare con coraggio. Intervista ad Alessandro Natta di Franco Ottolenghi e Giuseppe Vacca*, in *l'Unità*, 18 January 1987, republised in *Oltre Gramsci, con Gramsci*, monographic volume of *Critica marxista*, 1987, n. 2–3.

Nieddu, L. 2011, *Antonio Gramci. Storia e mito*, Venice: Marsilio.

Onofri, F. 1957, *Classe operaia e partito*, Bari: Laterza.

Orfei, R. 1965, *Antonio Gramsci coscienza critica del marxismo*, San Casciano: Relazioni sociali.

Orrù, E. and Rudas, N. (eds.) 2010, *Identità e universalità. Il mondo di Antonio Gramsci*, Cagliari: Tema.

Orsini, A. 2012, *Gramsci e Turati. Le due sinistre*, Soveria Mannelli: Rubbettino.

Paggi, L. 1970, *Gramsci e il moderno principe*, Rome: Editori Riuniti.

Paggi, L. 1974, *La teoria generale del marxismo in Gramsci*, in A. Zanardo (ed.), *Storia del marxismo contemporaneo. Annali Feltrinelli 1973*, Milan: Feltrinelli.

Paggi, L. 1984, *Le strategie del potere in Gramsci. Tra fascismo e socialismo in un paese solo 1923–1926*, Rome: Editori Riuniti.

Partito comunista italiano, 1956, *VIII Congresso del Partito comunista italiano. Atti e risoluzioni*. Rome.

Pasquinelli, C. 1977, *Antropologia culturale e questione meridionale*, Florence: La Nuova Italia.

Paulesu, L. 2012, *Nino mi chiamo. Fantabiografia del piccolo Antonio Gramsci*, Milan: Feltrinelli.

Paulesu Quercioli, M. (ed.) 1977, *Gramsci vivo nelle testimonianze dei suoi contemporanei*, Milan: Feltrinelli.

Paulesu Quercioli, M. 1991, *Le donne di Casa Gramsci*, Rome: Editori Riuniti.

Peregalli, A. 1978, *Il comunismo di sinistra e Gramsci*, Bari: Dedalo.

Perlini, T. 1974, *Gramsci e il gramscismo*, Milan: Celuc.

Petronio, G. and Paladini Musitessi, M. (eds.) 2001, *Marx e Gramsci. Memoria e attualità*, Rome: Manifestolibri.

Pierini, F. 1978, *Gramsci e la storiografia della rivoluzione. Studio storico-semantico*, Rome: Edizioni Paolini.

Pistillo, M. 1989, *Gramsci come Moro?*, Manduria-Bari-Rome: Lacaita.

Pistillo, M. 1991, *Un discorso sconosciuto di Togliatti su Gramsci del 1937*, in *Critica marxista*, n. 6.

Pistillo, M. 1996, *Gramsci-Togliatti. Polemiche e dissensi nel 1926*, Manduria-Bari-Rome: Lacaita.

Pistillo, M. 1996, *Mussolini-Gramsci: la destra alla ricerca di una identità culturale*, in *Critica marxista*, n. 1–2.

Pistillo, M. 2001, *Le difficili verità d'un lento assassinio*, Manduria-Bari-Rome: Lacaita.

Pistillo, M. 2012, *'Ai fratelli in camicia nera'. Grieco, il PCI e l'ultimo libro di Canfora*, in *Critica marxista*, n. 4.

Platone, F. 1938, *Gramsci*, Paris: Edizioni italiane di cultura.

Portelli, H. 1973, *Gramsci e il blocco storico*, Rome-Bari: Laterza.

Portelli, H. 1976, *Gramsci e la questione religiosa*, Milan: Mazzotta.

Potier, J-P. 1990, *Piero Sraffa*, Rome: Editori Riuniti.

Poulantzas, N. 1971, *Fascismo e dittatura*, orig. 1970, Milan: Jaca Book.

Poulantzas, N. 1975a, *Potere politico e classi sociali*, orig. 1968, Rome: Editori Riuniti.

Poulantzas, N. 1975b, *Classi sociali e capitalismo oggi*, orig. 1974, Milan: Etas libri.

Prestipino, G. 1979, *Da Gramsci a Marx. Il blocco logico-storico*. Rome: Editori Riuniti.

Prestipino, G. 1986, *Il socialismo in un solo mondo. Il lungo cammino dei comunisti italiani*, Rome: Ediesse.

Prestipino, G. 2000, *Tradire Gramsci*, Milan: Teti.

Prestipino, G. 2007, *Gramsci vivo e il nostro tempo*, Milan: Edizioni Punto Rosso.

Prestipino, G. 2011, *Diario di viaggio nelle città gramsciane*, Milan: Edizioni Punto Rosso.

Prezzolini, G. 1923, *La coltura italiana*, Florence: "La Voce".

Prezzolini, G. 1930, *La cultura italiana* (2nd edition), Milan: Corbaccio.

Prezzolini, G 1971, *Gobetti e La Voce*, Florence: Sansoni.

Proto, M. (ed.) 1999, *Gramsci e l'Internazionalismo. Nazione, Europa, America latina*, Manduria-Bari-Rome: Lacaita.

Ragazzini, D. 1976, *Società industriale e formazione umana nel pensiero di Gramsci*, Rome: Editori Riuniti.

Ragazzini, D. 2002, *Leonardo nella società di massa. Teoria della personalità in Gramsci*, Bergamo: Moretti & Vitali.

Ragionieri, E. 1976, *Palmiro Togliatti*, Rome: Editori Riuniti.

Rampi, R. (ed.). *Nino: appunti per Antonio Gramsci 1937–2007*, Milan: Infoarte.

Rapone, L. 2011, *Cinque anni che paiono secoli. Antonio Gramsci dal socialismo al comunismo (1914–1919)*, Rome: Carocci.

Riechers, C. 1975, *Antonio Gramsci: Marxismo in Italia*, Naples: Thélèma.

Righi, M.L. (ed.) 1995, *Gramsci nel mondo. Atti del convegno internazionale di studi gramsciani, Formia 25–28 Ottobre 1989*, Rome: Fondazione Gramsci.

Righi, M.L. 2011, *Gramsci a Mosca tra amori e politica (1922–1923)*, in *Studi storici*, n. 4.

Rolland, R. 1934, *Antonio Gramsci. Ceux qui meurent dans les prisons de Mussolini*, Paris: Imprimerie centrale.

Romano, S.F. 1945, *Storia della questione meridionale*, Palermo: Edizioni Pantea.

Romeo, R. 1974, *Risorgimento e capitalismo*, first edition: 1959, Bari: Laterza.

Rossi, A. 2010, *Gramsci da eretico a icona. Storia di un 'cazzotto nell'occhio'*, preface by B. De Giovanni, Naples: Guida.

Rossi, P. 1969 (ed.) 1969, *Gramsci e la cultura contemporanea*, Rome: Editori Riuniti (2 vols).

Russo, G. (ed.) 1978, *L'egemonia operaia. Ricostruzione di un dibattito*, Bologna: Cappelli.

Salvadori, M.L. 1970, *Gramsci e il problema storico della democrazia*, Turin: Einaudi.

Salvadori, M.L. 1978, *Eurocomunismo e socialismo sovietico*, Turin: Einaudi.

Salvadori, M.L. 2007, *Gramsci e il problema storico della democrazia*, 2nd edition, Rome:: Viella.

Santarelli, E. 1991, *Gramsci ritrovato 1937–1947*, Catanzaro: Abramo.

Santucci, A.A. (ed.) 1987a, *Letture di Gramsci*, Rome: Editori Riuniti.

Santucci, A.A. 1987b, *Antonio Gramsci 1891–1937. Guida al pensiero e agli scritti*, Rome: Editori Riuniti.

Santucci, A.A. 1989, *Le manifestazioni per il cinquantesimo anniversario della morte di Gramsci. Un bilancio*, in *Ig Informazioni*, n. 1.

Santucci, A.A. (ed.) 1995, *Gramsci in Europa* e *in America*, Rome: Laterza.

Santucci, A.A. 1996, *La 'filologia vivente': Eugenio Garin e il metodo di Gramsci*, in *The Italinist*, n. 16.

Santucci, A.A. 2001, *Senza comunismo. Labriola Gramsci Marx*, Rome: Editori Riuniti.

Santucci, A.A. 2005, *Antonio Gramsci 1891–1937*, edited by L. La Porta, Palermo: Sellerio.

Santucci, A.A. 2011, *Affermare la verità è una necessità politica. Scritti di Antonio Santucci*, edited by D. Giannone, Soveria Mannelli: Rubbettino.

Sassoon, D. 1980, *Togliatti e la vita italiana al socialismo*, Turin: Einaudi.

Sbarberi, F. (ed.) 1988, *Teoria politica e società industriale. Ripensare Gramsci*, acts of the convention undertaken at Turin, 10–12 December 1987, Turin: Bollati.

Sbarberi, F. 1986, *Gramsci: un socialismo armonico*, Milan: Angeli.

Schirru, G. (ed.) 2009, *Gramsci le culture e il mondo*, Rome: Viella.

Schucht, T. 1991, *Lettere ai familiari*, Rome: Editori Riuniti.

Sechi, S. 1974, *Movimento operaio e storiografia marxista*, Bari: De Donato.

Seminario su Gramsci 2010, Milan: Edizioni Punto Rosso.

Sereni, E. 1948, *Gramsci e la scienza d'avanguardia*, in *Società*, 1948, n. 1.

Sereni, E. 1949, *Scienza marxismo cultura*, Milan: Le edizioni sociali.

Serra, P. 1995, *Metafisica e storia*, Naples: Edizioni Scientifiche Italiane.

Spriano, P. 1960, *Torino operaia nella grande guerra*, Turin: Einaudi.

Spriano, P. 1967, *Storia del Partito comunista italiano*, vol 1: *Da Bordiga a Gramsci*, Turin: Einaudi.

Spriano, P. 1977a, *Gramsci e Gobetti*, Turin: Einaudi.

Spriano, P. 1977b, *Gramsci in carcere e il partito*, Rome: Editori Riuniti.

Spriano, P. 1979, *Intervista sulla storia del PCI*, edited by S. Colarizi, Rome-Bari: Laterza.

Spriano, P. 1980, *Il compagno Ercoli*, Rome: Editori Riuniti.

Spriano, P. 1986, *Le passioni di un decennio (1946–1956)*, Milan: Garzanti.

Sraffa, P. 1991, *Lettere a Tania per Gramsci*, with an introduction and edited by V. Gerratana, Rome: Editori Riuniti.

Stamboulis, E. and Costantini, G. 2011, *Cena con Gramsci*, no location: BeccoGiallo. (Also an e-book downloadable from www.unita.it).

Suppa, S. 1979, *Consiglio e Stato in Gramsci e Lenin*, Bari: Dedalo.

Tamburrano, G. 1963, *Antonio Gramsci. La vita. Il pensiero. L'azione*. Manduria-Bari-Rome: Lacaita.

Tancredi, L. 2012, *La vita privata di Giulia Schucht*, Macerata: Edizioni Ev.

Tasca, A. 1971, *I primi dieci anni del PCI*, Bari: Laterza.

Tega, W. (ed.) 1990, *Gramsci e l'Occidente. Trasformazioni della società e riforma della politica*, Bologna: Cappelli.

Terracini, U. 1975, *Sulla svolta*, edited by A. Coletti, Milan: Pietra.

Thomas, P. 2009, *The Gramscian Moment*, Leiden and Boston: Brill.

Togliatti, P. (ed.) 1938, *Gramsci*. Paris: Edizioni italiane di cultura.

Togliatti, P. 1949, *Pensatore e uomo d'azione*, in P. Togliatti, *Scritti su Gramsci*.

Togliatti, P. 1964, *Sul movimento operaio italiano*, edited by F. Ferri, Rome: Editori Riuniti 1964.

Togliatti, P. 1967a, *Gramsci*, edited by E. Ragionieri, Rome: Editori Riuniti.

Togliatti, P. 1967b, *Opere*, vol I: 1917–1936, edited by E. Ragionieri, Rome: Editori Riuniti.

Togliatti, P. 1971, *La formazione del gruppo dirigente del Partito comunista italiano nel 1923–1924*, Rome: Editori Riuniti.

Togliatti, P. 1974, *La politica culturale*, edited by L. Gruppi, Rome: Editori Riuniti.

Togliatti, P. 1979, *Opere*, vol. VI: 1935-44, edited by F. Andreucci and P. Spriano, Rome: Editori Riuniti.

Togliatti, P. 1984a, *Opere*, vol. V: *1944-1955*, edited by L. Gruppi, Rome: Editori Riuniti.

Togliatti, P. 1984b, *Opere*, vol. VI: *1956-1964*, edited by L. Gruppi, Rome: Editori Riuniti.

Togliatti, P. 2001, *Scritti su Gramsci*, edited by G. Liguori, Rome: Editori Riuniti.

Togliatti, P. 2010, *Corso sugli avversari. Le lezioni sul fascismo*, edited by F.M. Biscione, Turin: Einaudi.

Togliatti, P. 2014, *Sul fascismo*, edited and introduced by G. Vacca, Rome-Bari: Laterza.

Tortorella, A. 1987, *Consenso e libertà*, in *Critica marxista*, 1987, n. 2–3.

Trentin, B. 1996, *La città del lavoro*, Milan: Feltrinelli.

Tronti, M. 1987, *L'uomo Gramsci e i giovani d'oggi*, in *Jonas*, – 1 Quaderni, February.

Turi, G. 1990, *Casa Einaudi*, Bologna: Il Mulino.

Vacca, G. 1974, *Saggio su Togliatti e la tradizione comunista*, Bari: De Donato.

Vacca, G, 1976, *Alcuni temi della politica culturale di Togliatti*, in Cecchi, Leone and Vacca (eds.), *I corsivi di Roderigo*, Bari: De Donato.

Vacca, G. 1978, *Gli intellettuali di sinistra e la crisi del 1956*, Rome: Editori Riuniti.

Vacca, G. 1984, *La 'via italiana' e gli intellettuali (1956–1964)* in *Togliatti nella storia d'Italia*, monographic volume of *Critica marxista*, n. 4–5.

Vacca, G. 1985, *Il marxismo e gli intellettuali. Dalla crisi di fine secolo ai 'Quaderni del carcere'*, Rome: Editori Riuniti.

Vacca, G. 1989, *Gorbačëv e la sinitra europea*, Rome: Editori Riuniti.

Vacca, G. 1991, *Gramsci e Togliatti*, Rome: Editori Riuniti.

Vacca, G. 1994, *Togliatti sconosciuto*, published along with *l'Unità* of August 31st.

Vacca, G. (eds.) 1999a, *Gramsci e il Novecento*, 2 vols, Rome: Carocci.

Vacca, G. 1999b, *Gramsci a Roma, Togliatti a Mosca*, in C. Daniele (ed.), *Gramsci a Roma, Togliatti a Mosca. Il carteggio del 1926*, with an essay by G. Vacca, Turin: Einaudi.

Vacca, G. 1999c, *Appuntamenti con Gramsci*, Rome: Carocci.

Vacca, G. and Rossi, A. 2007, *Gramsci tra Mussolini e Stalin*, Rome: Fazio.

Vacca, G., Baroncelli, G.E., Del Poro, M., Schirru, G. (eds.), 2009, *Studi gramsciani nel mondo. Le relazioni internazionali*, Bologna: il Mulino.

Vacca, G., Schirru, G. and Capuzzo, P. (eds.) 2009, *Studi gramsciani nel mondo. Gli studi culturali*, Bologna: il Mulino.

Vacca, G. and Schirru, G. (eds.) 2009, *Studi gramsciani nel mondo. 2000–2005*, Bologna: il Mulino.

Vacca, G., Kanoussi, D., Schirru, G. (eds.) 2011, *Studi gramsciani nel mondo. Gramsci in America latina*, Bologna: il Mulino.

Vacca, G. 2012, *Vita e pensieri di Antonio Gramsci 1926–1937*, Turin: Einaudi.

Vander, F. 2002, *Che cos'è socialismo liberale? Rosselli, Gramsci e la rivoluzione in Occidente*, Manduria, Bari and Rome: Lacaita.

Vespa, B. 2007, *L'amore e il potere. Da Rachele a Veronica un secolo di storia italiana*, Rome and Milan: Eri and Mondadori.

Vinco, R. 1983, *Una fede senza futuro? Religione e mondo cattolico in Gramsci*, Verona: Mazziana.

Vittoria, A. 1992, *Togliatti e gli intellettuali. Storia dell'Istituto Gramsci negli anni Cinquanta e Sessanta*, Rome: Editori Riuniti.

Vivanti, C. 1978, *Egemonia/dittatura*, in *Enciclopedia*, vol. V, Turin: Einaudi.

Voza, P. 2008, *Gramsci e la 'continua crisi'*, Rome: Carocci.

Zanardo, A. 1987, *Per la cultura della sinistra*, in *Oltre Gramsci, con Gramsci*, monographic volume of *Critica marxista*, 1987, n. 2–3.

Zangheri, R. 1983, *Gramsci e la teoria del materialismo storico*, in *Critica marxista*, n. 5.

Zucaro, D. 1954, *Vita del carcere di Antonio Gramsci*, Milan-Rome: Edizioni Avanti!.

Zucaro, P. 2008, *L'uomo di Turi. Suggestioni da 'Lettere dal carcere' di A. Gramsci*, Cosenza: Falco Editore.

Zucaro, P. (ed.) 2011, *Aspettendo l'uomo di Turi*, Cosenza: Universal Book.

Index of Names

Accardo, Aldo   320n
Adamo, Sergia   301n
Adler, Max   212, 218
Adorno, Theodor W.   91
Agazzi, Emilio   117n, 119, 119n, 120, 120n
Agosti, Aldo   9n
Ajello, Nello   37n, 39n, 55n, 59n, 68n, 75n, 99n, 252n
Alatri, Paolo   55, 56, 56n
Albergamo, Francesco   72n
Alcaro, Mario   137n
Alicata, Mario   58, 58n, 67n, 72, 72n, 75n, 93, 93n, 102, 103, 103n, 104, 104n, 146, 146n
Alighieri, Dante   19, 27, 309n, 350
Aloisi, Massimo   72, 72n
Altan   339
Althusser, Louis   72, 117, 141, 144, 146, 146n, 147, 147n, 148, 159, 160, 164, 178, 179, 179n, 216n, 268, 331, 331n, 332
Amato, Giuliano   196, 196n
Amendola, Giorgio   10n, 11, 11n, 19, 31n, 75n, 96, 156, 157, 157n
Amendola, Giovanni   49
Amodio, Luciano   91
Amoretti, Giuseppe   28, 28n
Anderlini, Luigi   77n
Anderson Perry,   220, 220n, 221, 221n
Ansaldo, Giovanni   4n
Antonetti, Nicola   284n
Antoni, Carlo   66, 67n
Apitzsch, Ursula   301
Arcari, Antonio   86, 86n
Arendt, Hannah   337
Argentieri, Federigo   249n, 252, 268n
Aronowitz, Stanley   238
Asor Rosa, Alberto   4n, 36n, 40n, 57n, 94n, 99n, 102n, 140, 140n, 141, 153, 182, 183, 183n, 184, 184n, 201n, 207, 279
Auciello, Nicola   61n, 172, 172n, 173, 173n
Auletta, Francesco   308
Avigdor, Ezio   117n

Badaloni, Nicola   141, 142, 142n, 159, 160, 160n, 161, 175, 175n, 176, 176n, 203, 203n, 204, 204n, 205, 205n, 214, 214n, 215n, 241, 241n, 242, 243, 259n, 265n
Baget Bozzo, Gianni   66, 66n, 226n
Bagnoli Paolo   283
Bakhtin, Michail Michailovič   296
Balbo, Rosellina   192n
Baldussi, Annamaria   304n
Balibar, Étienne   146n, 267
Banfi, Antonio   33, 78
Baratta, Giorgio   244, 244n, 245n, 246n, 266n, 267, 267n, 268n, 269n, 273n, 277, 277n, 286, 288, 289, 289n, 290, 290n, 292n, 301, 301n, 303, 316, 338, 338n
Barbagallo, Francesco   xv, 98n
Barbusse, Henri   129
Barca, Luciano   100, 100n
Barcellona, Pietro   xv
Bartoli, Matteo   221, 222, 296
Battista, Pierluigi   9n
Bedeschi, Giuseppe   35n
Belinsky, Vissarion Grigor'evič   62
Bellini, Fulvio   81, 81n, 82, 82n, 83n
Benjamin, Walter   279
Bentham, Jeremy   246
Bergami, Giancarlo   227, 227n
Bergson, Henri   66n, 163
Berlinguer, Enrico   356
Berlinguer, Mario   49, 49n
Berlusconi, Silvio   302
Bermani, Cesare   315, 315n, 316
Bernari, Carlo   43, 43n
Berneri, Camillo   23, 23n
Bernstein, Eduard   250
Bertelli, Sergio   54n
Berti, Giuseppe   17, 31n, 80, 80n
Bertinotti, Fausto   275, 275n, 276, 277
Bertondini, Alfeo   117n
Bettini, Filippo   246n
Bianca, Omero   72n
Bianchi Bandinelli, Ranuccio   54, 54n
Bianco, Eugenio   13
Bianco, Vincenzo   11n
Bilenchi, Romano   92
Biocca Dario   344, 344n, 345, 345n
Biscione, Francesco M.   10n

INDEX OF NAMES

Bizzarri, Luca   356n
Bobbio, Norberto,   69n, 92, 93, 93n, 95, 95n,
    113, 133, 133n, 145, 147, 148, 149, 149n,
    150, 151, 152, 155, 169, 170, 171, 172, 174,
    175, 179, 191, 192, 192n, 193, 195, 195n, 201,
    203, 206n, 210, 210n, 246, 246n, 249,
    250, 250n, 251, 251n, 257, 270, 273
Bodei Remo   203n, 204, 204n, 240n, 272,
    273, 273n
Bogdanov, Aleksandr Aleksandrovič   315
Bonetti, Paolo   211, 211n
Boninelli, Mimmo   316, 316n
Bonomi, Giorgio   187, 187n
Bonomi, Ivanoe   49n
Boothman, Derek   288, 296, 296n, 301, 303
Bordiga, Amadeo   5, 6, 8, 18, 20, 21, 24, 25,
    41, 52, 81, 82, 83, 87n, 137, 138, 139, 166,
    184n, 228, 252, 300, 346
Borghese, Lucia   262n, 325
Borgia, Lucia   239n
Borrelli, Armando   72, 72n
Borrelli, Gianfranco   300
Bosio, Gianni   316
Bovero, Michelangelo   243, 243n
Bréal, Michel   296
Brecht, Bertolt   268
Brennan, Timothy   303, 304, 304n
Broccoli, Angelo   172n
Brondino, Michele   303
Brown, Adriana   341, 341n
Brown, Charlie   339
Bucci, Tonino   307n
Brunetti, Bruno   293n
Bruno, Giordano   19, 43, 62, 262
Bukharin, Nikolaj Ivanovič   69, 72, 113, 212,
    230n, 231, 246, 257, 265, 282, 309
Buci-Glucksmann, Christine   179, 179n, 180,
    180n, 181, 181n, 203n
Buonaiuti, Ernesto   44
Buozzi, Bruno   16
Burgio, Alberto   275, 275n, 277, 290n, 295,
    295n, 296, 296n, 300, 307n, 312, 313,
    313n, 314n, 315, 323n
Buttigieg, Joseph A.   xv, 238n, 244, 265n,
    267, 267n, 298n, 302, 303, 304, 304n,
    305n, 306, 345, 345n

Cacciari, Massimo   182, 252n
Cacciatore, Giuseppe   269, 269n, 289

Cadinu, Antonello   305
Cafagna, Luciano   122n, 246, 246n
Calabrò, Gaetano   284n
Calabi, Lorenzo   246
Calderoni, Mario   334
Calosso, Umberto   13, 13n, 23
Calvino, Italo   101, 101n
Calzolaio, Valerio   246
Cambria, Adele   188n
Cammett, John M.   xii, xiin, 162, 237, 319
Campanella, Tommaso   19, 43
Campanini, Massimo   303
Candeloro, Giorgio   122n, 123
Canetti, Elias   279
Canfora, Luciano   10n, 15n, 16n, 52, 127n,
    243, 247, 247n, 248, 248n, 314, 314n,
    321n, 354, 354n, 355
Cantimori, Delio   43, 43n, 53n
Cantoni, Remo   78, 78n, 79n
Capecelatro, Edmondo M.   186n
Capitani, Lorenzo   273n, 277n
Caprara, Massimo   342n
Caprioglio, Sergio   91, 124n, 189n, 262n
Capuzzo, Paolo   302, 304, 304n
Caracciolo, Alberto   113, 113n, 114, 114n, 115,
    117, 117n, 118, 118n, 119n, 120n, 226n
Carbone, Giuseppe   56, 56n, 88, 88n, 89
Cardia, Umberto   134n, 135, 246, 246n
Carducci, Giosuè   26, 27
Carini, Carlo   284n
Carli, Guido   206n
Carlo, Antonio   186n
Carpi, Umberto   246
Caruso, Sergio   283
Cassano, Franco   141n, 143n, 144n, 145n
Castellina, Luciana   267, 267n
Catone, Andrea   244n, 245n, 246n, 286
Cattaneo, Carlo   111, 335
Cavalcanti, Cavalcante   350
Cavallari, Giovanna   284n
Cavallaro, Luigi   299, 299n
Ceresa, Giuseppe   28n, 86
Cerroni, Umberto   113
Cesari, Severino   52n
Cesarini, Marco   92n
Cessi, Roberto   109n, 110, 110n, 111n, 112n,
    113n, 114n, 115n, 116n, 117n, 121, 121n,
    122n, 123n
Chabod, Federico   121, 154

INDEX OF NAMES

Chakravorty Spivak, Gayatri   301n
Chambers, Iain   301n, 303
Chatterjee, Partha   336
Cheddadi, Abdesselam   303
Chiarante, Giuseppe   235, 236n
Chiaromonte, Gerardo   75n
Chiarotto, Francesca   52n, 300n, 334, 335, 335n, 336n
Ciccarelli, Roberto   288n
Cicerchia, Carlo   117n, 118, 118n
Ciliberto, Michele   38n, 39n, 40n, 224, 224n, 225n, 241, 241n, 261n, 262n, 272, 272n
Cingari, Salvatore   300
Cirese, Alberto Maria   77n, 316
Clemente, Pietro   316
Coen, Federico   192n, 193n, 194n, 195n, 196n, 197n
Cohen, Jean L.   271, 271n
Colletti, Lucio   139, 139n, 141, 146, 195, 195n, 212, 212n, 213, 238, 239n, 232n
Collina, Vittore   283
Colombi, Arturo   74, 74n, 75
Cometa, Michele   301n
Compagna, Francesco   75n
Consiglio, Franco   286, 291
Constant, Benjamin   246
Costantini, Gianluca   338, 339n
Cortesi, Luigi   41n, 138, 138n
Corvisieri, Silverio   182n
Cospito, Giuseppe   220n, 288, 289n, 300, 320, 321n, 322, 323n, 324, 324n, 325, 325n, 327, 327n, 328, 328n, 329, 330
Cossu, Costantino   252n
Coutinho, Carlos Nelson   x, 238n, 267, 267n, 272, 272n, 289n, 294, 294n, 295, 295n, 306, 307n, 313n, 314n, 328n
Cox, Robert   270, 270n
Cozzi, Michele   250n
Craxi, Bettino   342n
Crehan, Kate   316, 316n
Crisafulli, Vezio   77, 77n, 78, 78n
Crispi, Francesco   133
Croce, Benedetto   XIV, 1, 1n, 3n, 4, 5, 34, 34n, 35, 35n, 36, 36n, 37, 37n, 38, 39, 42, 44, 46, 50, 52, 53, 53n, 54, 55, 56, 58, 60, 63, 64, 64n, 65, 65n, 66, 67, 67n, 68, 68n, 69, 71, 72, 99, 111, 116, 118, 119, 121, 129, 133, 150, 154, 155, 164, 176, 184n, 212, 217, 224, 226n, 227, 229, 240, 242, 250, 251, 257, 259, 264, 265, 278, 279, 291, 293, 299, 300, 315, 323, 330, 343, 348, 349, 352, 354, 354n
Cromwell, Oliver   123
Cucchi, Aldo   252
Curiel, Eugenio   43
Curti, Lidia   301n

Daolmi, Davide   338
Day, Richard J. F,   316, 317, 317n
Dal Sasso, Rino   113
D'Alema, Massimo   273n
D'Alessandro, Leone Pompeo   355n
D'Annunzio, Gabriele   83, 309n
Daniele, Chiara   17n, 43n, 61n, 259, 281, 282n, 325, 325n
Davidson, Alastair   267, 267n
De Caro, Raffaele   49n
De Clementi, Andreina   138, 138n, 139n, 139n
De Felice, Franco   165, 165n, 166, 166n, 167, 203n, 261n
De Gasperi, Alcide   133
De Giovanni, Biagio   36n, 40n, 58n, 60n, 198, 198n, 199, 199n, 200, 200n, 201, 201n, 202n, 203, 203n, 217, 217n, 240, 240n, 249n, 250, 250n
De Leon, Daniel   129
De Martino, Ernesto   76, 76n, 77, 77n, 316
De Mauro, Tullio   221, 221n, 246n, 267, 267n
De Murtas, Mario   262n
De Rosa, Gabriele   226n, 229
De Sanctis, Francesco   55, 58, 62, 64, 67, 68, 78, 103, 129, 143, 178, 284, 314n
Debenedetti, Antonio   251n
Deias, Antonio   316, 316n
Del Fra, Lino   338n
Del Noce, Augusto   217, 226, 226n, 227, 227n, 228, 228n, 229, 229n, 257
Del Roio, Marcos   346, 346n
Della Volpe, Galvano   72, 95, 113, 116, 117, 141, 142n, 146, 184, 192n
Dewey, John   238n
Di Biagio, Anna   300
Di Domenico, Giovanni   40n
Di Meo, Antonio   230n, 309, 309n

INDEX OF NAMES

Di Vittorio, Giuseppe   17
Diaz, Furio   193, 193n, 196, 196n, 238n
Dimitrov, Georgi   17n, 60, 61n, 255n
Donini, Ambrogio   19n, 73, 73n, 74
Donzelli, Carmine   348n
D'Orsi, Angelo   167n, 277n, 287, 287n, 291, 291n, 300, 300n, 308, 309, 309n, 319, 319n
Dorso Guido,   1, 4, 4n, 5, 31, 49, 49n, 315
Durante Lea   x, 188n, 288, 288n, 291n, 292, 292n, 293n, 301n, 303, 307n

Einaudi, Giulio   51, 52, 52n, 53n, 59, 59n, 89, 124n, 177, 183, 189, 189n, 214, 261, 262n, 271, 279, 335
Einaudi, Luigi   4, 345
Engels, Friedrich   8, 17, 47, 55, 62, 146, 212, 330, 330n
Ercoli, *see* Togliatti, Palmiro
Errico, Alessandro   288n, 307n, 319

Fabre, Giorgio   260n
Fagone, Virgilio   231n
Fasano, Pino   246n
Fattorini, Emma   226n
Fergnani, Franco   117n, 329n, 330n
Fernández Buey, Francisco   238n, 269, 269n, 286
Fernández Diaz, Osvaldo   238n
Ferrara, Gianni   243
Ferretti, Gian Carlo   37n, 246
Ferri, Franco   75n, 127n, 203n, 204n, 205n, 206n
Festa, Francesco Saverio   226, 226n
Fetscher, Iring   151
Filippini, Michele   128n, 267n, 288n, 289n, 219n, 336, 336n, 337, 337n
Finelli, Roberto   244, 244n, 245, 245n, 268, 268n, 269n, 285, 289n, 292, 292n, 293, 293n
Fiori, Giuseppe   9n, 132, 134, 134n, 135, 135n, 136, 136n, 139, 254, 254n, 255
Flores, Marcello   94n
Fontana, Benedetto   272, 272n, 302, 302n, 303, 303n
Fonte, John   336
Forenza, Eleonora   x, 189n, 278n, 288n, 303, 307n
Forgacs, David   238n, 301n

Fortini, Franco   77n, 91, 101, 102, 102n, 140n
Fortunato, Giustino   4, 44
Foucault, Michel   209, 304
Francese, Joseph   189n
Francioni, Gianni   190n, 221n, 225, 225n, 260, 260n, 261, 261n, 262, 263, 264, 264n, 265, 265n, 320, 321, 321n, 322, 323, 324, 324n, 325, 325n, 348
Fresu, Gianni   300, 300n
Freud, Sigmund   241
Frosini, Fabio   x, 262n, 265n, 285, 286, 288n, 289n, 290, 290n, 291, 292, 293, 293n, 308, 320, 321n, 322, 323n, 325n, 327, 329, 329n, 330, 330n, 331, 331n, 332, 332n, 354n
Fubini, Elsa   1, 1n, 124n, 162, 162n

Gaddi, Giuseppe   26, 26n
Galasso, Giuseppe   148, 153, 153n, 154, 226n
Galilei, Galileo   19, 43, 62
Gallerano, Nicola   94n
Galli, Giorgio   81, 81n, 82, 82n, 83n
Galli Della Loggia, Ernesto   195, 195n
Gallini, Clara   316
Gallo, Elisabetta   289n, 301
Gallo, Marta   338
Garibaldi, Giuseppe   19, 27, 43
Garin, Eugenio   31n, 34n, 39n, 110, 110n, 111, 148, 152, 152n, 153, 153n, 252, 252n, 277, 278, 278n
Garosci, Aldo   67, 67n
Garuglieri, Mario   85, 85n
Gennari, Egidio   11, 11n, 16
Gensini, Stefano   246
Gentile, Giovanni   3n, 5, 33, 36, 49, 63, 67, 102, 102n, 116, 118, 119n, 180, 217, 224, 226, 226n, 227, 227n, 240, 242, 293, 315
Germanetto, Giovanni   2n, 87n
Gerratana, Valentino   xv, 59n, 60n, 61n, 68, 68n, 113, 114, 115, 115n, 151, 151n, 164n, 177n, 178n, 180n, 189, 189n, 190, 190n, 196, 196n, 197, 198, 199, 199n, 201, 210, 223, 223n, 224, 225, 239n, 241, 241n, 247n, 259, 260, 261, 261n, 262n, 264, 264n, 265, 265n, 277, 278, 278n, 279, 280, 281, 288, 288n, 290, 290n, 298, 301n, 304, 304n, 305, 316, 318, 319, 321, 322, 322n, 323, 324, 324n, 325, 325n, 335

Gervasoni, Marco 310
Geymonat, Ludovico 33, 101, 101n, 113
Ghiro, Alessandro 298n
Giacomini, Ruggero 246n
Giannattasio, F. 65, 66n
Giasi, Francesco XIIn, 189n, 300, 308n, 319, 323n
Gill, Stephen 271, 271n
Gioberti, Vincenzo 116, 123, 140
Giolitti, Antonio 96, 96n, 97, 98, 98n, 99, 99n, 133, 252
Giolitti, Giovanni 315, 345
Gobetti, Piero XIV, 1, 1n, 2, 2n, 3, 3n, 4, 5, 19, 23, 24, 31, 36, 44, 64, 111, 129n, 197, 227, 309, 315
Gonzalez, Felipe 273n
Gorbachev, Michail 246, 256
Gramsci, Antonio jr. 188n, 342, 343n, 347
Gramsci, Delio 309
Gramsci, Francesco (Ciccillo) 340
Gramsci, Gennaro 135, 135n, 136n, 349
Gramsci Giuliano 309, 342
Gramsci Teresina 340
Gravagnuolo, Bruno 249, 250n, 344n
Graziadei, Antonio 83
Green, Marcus 302, 303, 307n, 319n
Grieco, Ruggero 5, 5n, 6, 6n, 9n, 10n, 13, 14, 15, 15n, 17, 22n, 27, 49, 49n, 73n, 247, 254, 259, 282, 347, 349, 354, 355
Grigor'eva Irina 238n
Gruppi Luciano 31n, 59n, 84n, 143, 143n, 151, 158, 158n, 159, 159n, 171, 171n, 172, 198n, 200
Gualtieri, Roberto 308
Guglielmi, Guido 246n
Guha, Ranajit 302, 302n, 336
Guiducci, Armanda 91, 117n
Guiducci, Roberto 91, 91n, 101, 102, 102n, 117n, 195, 195n
Guttuso, Renato 93, 93n

Hall, Stuart 267, 238, 290, 301, 301n, 302, 302n, 303, 336
Haug, Wolfgang Fritz 268, 268n, 285, 305
Hegel, Georg Friedrich Wilhelm 5, 8, 47, 55, 55n, 68, 113, 116, 117, 149, 151, 224, 272
Henriques, Luiz Sérgio 306
Hobbes, Thomas 239

Hobsbawm, Eric J. XII, XIIn, 203, 203n, 236, 236n, 238, 238n, 298n, 303
Hoggart, Richard 301
Holub, Renate 302

Ingrao Pietro 51n, 94n, 142n, 182, 187n, 192, 193, 193n, 198, 198n, 200, 201, 201n, 205, 206, 206n
Izzo Francesca 283, 308, 326, 326n, 327, 327n

James, William 334
Jervolino, Domenico 269, 269n
Jocteau, Gian Carlo 169, 169n
Judy, Ronald 302
Jünger, Ernst 241

Kanoussi, Dora 303, 304n, 305, 305n, 323
Kautsky, Karl 194, 211, 212, 218
Kebir, Sabine 267, 267n
Kessisoglu, Paolo 356
Kołakowski, Leszek 213, 213n, 250n
Kohan, Néstor 339, 339n
Korsch, Karl 146, 212
Khrushchev, Nikita Sergeevic 94, 100

La Porta, Lelio 194n, 298n 314, 337, 337n
La Rocca, Tommaso 230, 231n
Labriola, Antonio 20, 44, 58, 58n, 62, 69, 71, 78, 103, 117, 118, 119n, 129, 143, 144, 163, 177, 178, 178n, 217, 218, 224, 291, 292, 293, 300, 316, 334
Laclau, Ernesto 331n, 332, 332n, 333
Lama, Luciano 206, 206n, 207, 207n
Lana, M. 189n, 325n
Lay, Giovanni 127, 127n
Lehner, Giancarlo 252n, 342n
Lenin (Ul'janov) Vladimir Il'ic 16, 17, 18, 20, 49, 55, 60, 62, 69, 71, 78, 105, 106, 108, 109, 110, 114, 118, 120, 123, 130, 131, 133, 138, 146, 150, 151, 152, 155, 156, 157, 158, 165, 166, 170, 171, 172, 173, 174, 175, 176, 178, 179, 180, 186, 198, 199, 211, 212, 213, 219, 220, 221, 240, 267, 279, 299, 342, 352
Leone de Castris, Arcangelo 205, 205n, 246n, 274, 274n
Leonetti, Alfonso 6, 10, 12, 80, 125, 135, 252

INDEX OF NAMES

Lepre, Aurelio   281, 281n
Libertini, Lucio   53n
Liguori, Guido   188n, 189n, 194n, 213n, 220n, 231n, 237n, 238n, 243n, 249n, 266n, 267n, 268n, 269n, 273n, 278n, 282n, 287n, 288n, 289n, 290n, 306n, 310n, 319n, 320n, 328n, 330n, 343n
Limbaugh, Rush   336
Linus   339
Lisa, Athos   13, 126, 127n, 352
Livi, Augusto   49n
Livorsi, Franco   283, 284n
Lo Piparo, Franco   221, 221n, 222, 222n, 280n, 300, 346, 346n, 347, 347n, 348, 348n
Locke, John   239, 246
Lombardi, Franco   53n
Lombardo Radice, Lucio   34n, 72, 72n, 88n, 89
Longo, Luigi   11, 98, 98n, 99, 99n
Loria, Achille   344
Losurdo, Domenico   xv, 227n, 243, 266, 266n, 273, 273n, 274, 275n
Lucetti, Gino   13
Luhmann, Niklas   209
Lukács, Geòrgy   68, 91, 116, 117, 146, 212, 218
Lunacharsky, Anatolij   129
Lunghini, Giorgio   xv, 185n
Luperini, Romano   38n, 246n
Luporini, Cesare   33, 38n, 246n, 39, 39n, 55n, 60, 60n, 61, 76, 76n, 77, 77n, 110, 110n, 111, 112, 112n, 116, 117, 142n, 144, 145, 145n, 177, 177n, 178, 200, 200n, 230n, 231, 231n, 232, 232n, 251, 251n, 283
Lussana, Fiamma   304n, 305n, 306n
Luxemburg, Rosa   52, 146, 163

Macciocchi, Maria Antonietta   182, 188, 188n
Machiavelli, Niccolò   66, 68, 123, 236, 239, 269, 297, 331, 335
Macis, Enrico   254
Maggi, Michele   314, 315, 315n
Magnani, Valdo   252
Magri, Lucio   186, 187, 187n
Maitan, Livio   91, 92, 92n
Malandrino, Corrado   283
Manacorda, Gastone   73n, 74, 75n, 89, 108, 109n, 122n, 123, 123n
Manacorda, Mario Alighiero   172n, 244
Mancina, Claudia   146n, 179n, 198n, 205, 205n, 215, 215n, 216, 216n, 241, 241n, 249n, 250, 251n
Mancini, Lucia   323n
Manduchi, Patrizia   304n
Mangini, Cecilia   338n
Mangoni, Luisa   203n, 241, 242n
Mao Zedong   185, 187, 188, 188n
Marchesi, Concetto   335
Marramao, Giacomo   184, 184n, 185, 185n, 241, 241n
Marrone, Titti   250n
Marseglia, Michele   345, 345n
Martelli, Michele   299, 299n
Martí, José   308
Martinelli, Renzo   35n, 189n
Marx, Karl   5, 8, 17, 20, 47, 52, 55, 56, 62, 69, 86, 111, 112, 116, 117, 141, 143, 145, 146, 149, 150, 151, 152, 155, 170, 171, 174, 176, 178, 196, 198, 214, 216, 217, 221, 222n, 224, 227, 242, 249, 259, 259n, 266, 267, 275, 276, 277, 285, 286, 293, 326, 327, 329, 330, 330n, 331, 343, 356
Mastellone, Salvo   283, 283n, 284, 284n
Matteotti, Giacomo   12
Matteucci, Nicola   68, 69, 69n
Maturi, Walter   154
Matsuda, Hiroshi   267, 267n
Mayo, Peter   303
Mazzini, Giuseppe   19, 27, 43, 284
Medici, Rita   288, 297, 297n
Mehring, Franz   146
Meillet, Antoine   296
Melchiorre, Virgilio   229, 229n, 230, 230n
Mellino, Miguel   316
Meocci, Antonio   86, 86n
Merli, Stefano   137, 138n, 139, 139n, 140, 140n, 184, 185
Meta, Chiara   x, 288, 307, 333, 333n, 334
Mezzadra, Sandro   284, 284n
Michelini, Luca   345, 345n
Michels, Roberto   163, 246
Mila, Massimo   59n
Mill, John Stuart   246
Minucci, Adalberto   275, 275n
Mitarotondo, Laura   294n
Momigliano, Franco   44, 91
Monasta, Attilio   223, 223n
Mondolfo, Rodolfo   69, 69n, 70, 70n, 118
Montagnana, Mario   13, 31n, 87n

Montagnana, Rita   28n
Montaleone, Carlo   xv, 78
Montanari, Marcello   271, 271n, 283, 284, 284n, 285, 286
Morandi, Rodolfo   137, 140
Mordenti, Raul   x, 279, 279n, 280n, 301n, 314, 314n, 315, 324n
Moro, Aldo   248n
Morpurgo-Tagliabue, Guido   56, 56n
Mortellaro, Isidoro D.   274, 274n
Morton, Adam   303
Mosca, Gaetano   4, 246, 297
Mouffe, Chantal   331n, 332, 332n, 333
Muscetta, Carlo   55, 55n, 73n, 89, 89n, 246
Musil, Robert   279
Mussolini, Benito   14, 15, 15n, 16n, 40, 134, 184n, 227, 247, 282, 342, 345, 347, 348, 349, 355

Naldi, Nerio   308, 344n
Napolitano, Giorgio   75, 96, 170n, 309
Nardone, Giorgio   168, 186n, 169, 169n
Natoli, Aldo   188n, 248n, 258, 258n, 259, 280, 280n, 281
Natoli, Claudio   13, 283, 283n, 308, 325n
Natta, Alessandro   30n, 31n, 60, 60n, 61, 75, 157, 157n, 158, 158n, 233, 233n, 247n
Nieddu, Luigi   342n
Nietzsche, Friedrich Wilhelm   251, 317, 318n
Nogueira, Marco Aurélio   306

Occhetto, Achille   250
Omodeo, Adolfo   154
Onofri, Fabrizio   59n, 92n, 96n, 98, 98n
Orfei, Ruggero   226n
Orlando, Vittorio Emanuele   49n
Orrù, Eugenio   307n
Orsini, Alessandro   343, 343n, 344, 344n

Paggi, Leonardo   37n, 60n, 131n, 162, 162n, 163, 163n, 164, 164n, 165, 165n, 198, 199n, 205, 205n, 219, 219n, 220, 262n, 325
Pajetta, Gian Carlo   87, 87n
Pala, Mauro   304
Papa, Franca   283
Paladini Musitelli, Marina   285n, 286, 288, 291, 291n, 301n, 309, 309n
Palomba, F   273n
Panzieri, Raniero   137, 140

Papi, Fulvio   113
Papini, Giovanni   246, 334
Pareto, Vilfredo   2, 296, 297, 345
Paris, Robert   148 n, 305
Parodi, Giovanni   28n
Pascoli, Giovanni   26, 27
Pasquinelli, Carla   77n
Pastore, Annibale   334
Pastore, Ottavio   57n
Paulesu, Luca   339, 339n, 340n
Paulesu Quercioli, Mimma   188n, 197n
Pavese, Cesare   335
Pavone, Claudio   205, 205n
Péguy, Charles   129
Pellicani, Luciano   195, 195n
Pellico, Silvio   26, 86
Pepe, Gabriele   55, 55n, 335
Peregalli, Arturo   25n, 184n
Perilli, Nilde   341
Perlini, Tito   185, 185n, 186, 186n, 228
Pertini, Sandro   13, 41, 41n
Petronio, Giuseppe   113, 285, 285n
Piacentini, Ercole   86
Pierini, Franco   231n
Pierlandi,   23, 23n
Pintor, Luigi   186, 186n
Pissarello, G.   304n, 305n, 306n
Pistillo, Michele   xii, 13n, 18n, 248, 248n, 282, 282n, 355n
Pizzorno, Alessandro   91, 101, 102n
Platone, Felice   29n, 38, 38n, 43, 50, 50n, 59n, 73n, 75n, 80, 80n, 88, 88n, 223, 319, 344, 344n
Plekhanov, Georgij Valentinovic   212
Plotinus   262, 262n
Porcaro, M.   314n
Portelli, Hugues,   170, 170n, 226, 226n
Potenza, Nicola   14, 14n, 15n, 18
Potier, Jean-Pierre   7n
Poulantzas, Nicos   178, 178n, 179, 179n
Prestipino, Giuseppe   x, 222, 222n, 223, 242, 288, 297, 297n, 312, 312n, 314n, 315
Prezzolini, Giuseppe   xiv, 1, 3, 3n, 4, 246, 334
Procacci, Giuliano   154
Proto, Mario   274n
Punzo, Luigi   300

INDEX OF NAMES

Racinaro, Roberto   272, 273, 273n
Ragazzini, Dario   172n, 297, 297n, 298n, 318
Ragionieri, Ernesto   9n, 10n, 11n, 16n, 131n, 148, 155, 155n, 163
Rampi, Roberto   338, 338n, 339, 339n
Rapone, Leonardo   308, 325n, 345, 346n
Ravazzoli, Paolo   10, 80, 135
Ravera, Camilla   252
Reale, Eugenio   86, 86n
Rep, Miguel   399, 399n
Repaci   335
Revelli, Marco   276, 277, 277n
Ricardo, David   185, 259, 259n
Riechers, Christian   184, 184n, 228
Righi, Maria Luisa   XII, 188n, 237n, 258n, 319, 325n, 341n
Robespierre, Maximilien   3, 123
Rocco, Alfredo   345
Rodano, Franco   50, 50n
Roderigo Di Castiglia, *see* Togliatti Palmiro
Rolland, Romain   14, 14n, 26, 129
Romano, Salvatore Francesco   49, 49n, 92, 132, 133, 134
Romeo, Rosario   121, 121n, 122, 122n, 123, 153
Romita, Giuseppe   49n
Rorty, Richard   251
Rosengarten, Frank   238n, 267, 267n
Rosiello, Luigi   117n
Rossanda, Rossana   102, 102n, 103, 142, 143, 143n, 144, 144n, 145, 146n, 186, 186n, 253, 253n
Rosselli, Carlo   IX, 16, 26, 294n
Rossi, Angelo   8n, 22n, 127n, 135n, 136n, 348, 349n, 350n, 351, 351n, 352, 352n, 353n, 354
Rossi, Pietro   149n, 150n, 151n, 152n, 153n, 154n, 155n, 156n
Rousseau, Jean-Jacque   267
Rudas, Nereide   307n
Rusconi, Gian Enrico   243, 243n
Russo, Giovanni   206n, 207n
Russo, Luigi   54, 55, 55n, 87

Saba, Michele   49
Said, Edward   267, 290, 301, 303
Salinari, Carlo   67n, 73
Salvadori, Massimo L.   167, 167n, 168, 168n, 193, 193n, 194, 194n, 196, 196n, 198, 198n, 211, 211n, 249, 249n
Salvemini, Gaetano   4, 25, 110, 111, 123, 129, 343, 345
Santarelli, Ezio   31n, 53n
Santucci, Antonio A.   XIIn, XV, 209n, 237n, 238, 238n, 246n, 248n, 261, 262, 262n, 275, 275n, 278n, 287, 298, 298n, 299n, 342n
Sapegno, Natalino   148, 153, 153n
Sardo, Giuseppe,   49
Sartre, Jean-Paul   146, 186
Sasso, Gennaro   113, 252, 252n
Sassoon, Donald,   32, 285
Saviano, Roberto   343, 343n
Sbarberi, Franco   213, 213n, 245, 245n, 246n, 276, 276n
Scalfari, Eugenio   207, 207n
Scalia, Gianni   101, 117, 117n, 118n, 119n, 120n, 226n
Schiavone, Aldo   239, 239n
Schirru, Giancarlo   300, 301n, 302, 302n, 303, 303n, 304, 304n, 323n, 325n
Schmitt, Carl   209, 241
Schucht Apollon,   281, 342, 343
Schucht, Eugenia   188n, 341, 342, 343
Schucht, Giulia   188n, 258, 281, 309, 309n, 341, 342, 346, 353
Schucht, Tatiana (or Tania)   10, 188n, 258, 258n, 259, 261, 280, 280n, 281n, 340n, 341, 342, 343, 346, 348, 348n, 349, 353
Sciascia, Leonardo   248, 248n
Scoccimarro, Mauro   125, 247, 354
Scola, Ettore   356n
Secchia, Pietro   75
Sechi, Salvatore   52n
Semeraro, Giovanni   303
Sen, Amartya   303
Sereni, Emilio   59, 59n, 70, 71, 71n, 72, 73, 170n
Seroni, Adriano   113
Serra, Pasquale   163, 226n
Serra, Renato   129
Serrati, Giacinto Menotti   163
Showstack Sassoon, Anne   271, 272n, 301, 316
Sichirollo, Livio   113
Silone, Ignazio   IX, 12, 53, 53n, 80, 252
Soave, Sergio   308

Sola, Giorgio 284n
Sorel, Georges 4, 129, 163, 175, 176, 177, 177n, 220, 229, 246, 271, 315, 326
Sozzi, Gastone 19
Spano, Velio 13, 45
Spano Satta, Francesco 49
Spaventa, Bertrando 102, 102n, 103, 116
Spaventa, Silvio 349
Spini, Andrea 283
Spriano, Paolo 1n, 5n, 7n, 10n, 16n, 17n, 22n, 43n, 95n, 96n, 101, 101n, 113, 114, 114n, 115n, 124n, 127, 129, 129n, 130, 130n, 131, 131n, 156, 156n, 196, 196n, 197, 197n, 201, 201n, 202, 202n, 209, 209n, 243, 246, 247, 247n, 280
Sraffa, Piero 6, 7n, 10, 247, 258, 259, 259n, 260, 260n, 261, 285, 308, 347, 348n, 349, 353, 359
Stalin, (Džugasvili) Josif Visarionovic 11, 12, 13, 16, 17, 20, 23, 53, 57, 59, 62, 69, 71, 74, 84, 89, 105, 107, 114, 133, 247, 253, 254, 255, 256, 242, 247, 248, 350, 352, 355
Stamboulis, Elettra 338, 339n
Suppa, Silvio 212, 212n, 292, 293, 293n, 307n

Taddei, Ezio 16n, 354
Tamburrano, Giuseppe 117n, 120, 120n, 132, 132n, 133, 133n, 196, 196n
Tancredi, Lucia 341, 341n
Tasca, Angelo 11, 13, 13n, 17, 24, 24n, 25, 25n, 80, 81, 82, 82n, 83, 83n, 87n, 125, 126n, 137, 184n, 252, 254, 308
Tega, Walter 243n
Telò, Mario 243, 271, 271n
Terracini, Umberto 10, 10n, 125, 126, 247, 252, 351, 354
Testa, Eugenio 316, 316n
Texier, Jacques 151, 152, 152n, 242, 244, 285
Thomas, Peter x, 290n
Thornton, James 336
Tocqueville, Alexis de 246
Togliatti, Palmiro x, xiii, xv, 1, 1n, 4, 4n, 6, 6n, 7, 7n, 8, 8n, 9, 9n, 10, 11, 12, 13, 15, 16, 17, 17n, 18, 18n, 19, 19n, 20, 20n, 21, 21n, 22, 22n, 23, 24, 24n, 26, 27, 27n, 28n, 30, 31, 31n, 32, 32n, 33, 34, 34n, 35, 35n, 36, 36n, 37, 37n, 38, 39, 39n, 40, 40n, 41, 41n, 42, 42n, 43, 43n, 44, 44n, 45, 45n, 46, 46n, 47, 47n, 48, 48n, 49, 50, 50n, 51, 52, 54, 55, 57, 57n, 58, 58n, 59, 59n, 60, 60n, 61, 61n, 62, 62n, 63, 63n, 64, 64n, 65, 65n, 71, 73, 73n, 74, 75, 79, 80, 80n, 82, 83, 84, 84n, 85, 88, 89, 90, 90n, 91, 92, 94, 94n, 95, 95n, 96, 96n, 97, 98, 99, 99n, 100, 103, 105, 105n, 106, 106n, 107, 107n, 108, 108n, 109, 109n, 110, 110n, 111, 115, 117, 118, 120, 123n, 124, 124n, 125, 125n, 126, 126n, 127, 127n, 128, 129, 131, 133, 135, 136, 137, 138, 139, 140, 141, 142, 143, 146, 150, 150n, 155, 156, 157, 159, 163, 165, 169, 170, 171, 173, 174, 175, 176, 177, 178, 181, 185, 186, 187, 198, 189n, 192n, 197, 200, 223, 246, 247, 248, 252n, 253, 254, 254n, 255, 255n, 256, 258, 259, 281, 282, 283, 300, 314, 315, 319, 334, 336, 342, 342n, 347, 348, 348n, 349, 352, 353, 354, 355
Tolstoy, Lev 340
Tortorella Aldo xv, 205, 205n, 235, 235n, 269, 269n, 273n, 285n
Tosel, André 238n, 242, 244, 246, 268, 268n
Tosin, Bruno 352
Trentin, Bruno 275, 275n, 277
Tresso, Pietro 10, 25, 25n, 80, 135
Trostky, Lev Davidovic 52, 80, 92n, 248n, 254, 255
Trombetti, Gustavo 85, 85n, 86, 127, 127n
Tronti, Mario 113, 116, 116n, 117, 117n, 118, 119n, 182, 184, 184n, 226n, 234, 234n, 242, 242n, 309
Trostel, Willi 6
Tuccari, Francesco 284n
Tulli, Enrico 7
Turati, Filippo 239n, 343
Turi, Gabriele 53n

Urbani, Giovanni 172n

Vacca, Giuseppe xv, 8n, 10n, 17n, 19n, 22n, 36n, 37n, 38n, 40n, 43n, 52n, 61n, 62n, 99n, 100n, 101n, 102n, 103n, 104n, 105n, 127n, 135n, 136n, 173, 173n, 174, 174n, 175, 176, 188n, 189n, 201, 201n, 203, 204n, 218, 218n, 219n, 240n, 250, 250n, 255, 255n, 256, 256n, 257, 257n, 258, 258n, 260, 261n, 262, 262n, 269n, 270n, 271n, 272n, 273n, 276n, 277n, 281n, 282, 282n, 283, 300, 301, 303, 303n, 304, 304n, 308,

INDEX OF NAMES

308n, 310, 310n, 320n, 323n, 348, 349n,
350, 350n, 353, 353n, 354, 354n, 355
Vailati, Giovanni   296, 334
Valiani, Leo   43, 44, 177, 177n
Vander, Fabio   294n
Vattimo, Gianni   251, 251n
Veca, Salvatore   239n
Verdaro, Virgilio   25n
Verga, Giovanni   68
Vespa, Bruno   342, 342n
Vico, Giambattista   116, 224, 236, 262
Vigna, Carmelo   229
Villa, Roberto   273n, 277n
Vinci, Luigi   314n
Vinco, Roberto   231n
Vittoria, Albertina   52n, 73n, 74n, 75n, 189n
Vittorini, Elio   33, 37n, 39, 40, 40n, 51, 51n
Vivanti, Corrado   220n
Voltaire (Arouet François-Marie)   57
Voza, Pasquale   188n, 189n, 194n, 220n, 274, 274n, 288, 291, 291n, 292n, 293n, 301n, 307, 313, 313n, 314n, 319n, 320n, 328

Wahrol, Andy   338
Weber, Max   209, 239, 241
Weiss, Peter   340
West, Cornel   238, 238n, 336, 337
Williams, Raymond   301, 303, 336

Zanardo, Aldo   xv, 58n, 113, 234, 234n, 235, 235n, 239n, 242, 242n
Zangheri, Renato   122, 122n, 123, 123n, 216, 216n, 243, 268, 268n, 276, 276n
Zhdanov, Andrei Aleksandrovič   57, 68, 103
Zene, Cosimo   316
Zucaro, Domenico   88
Zucaro, Piero   340, 340n

Printed in the United States
by Baker & Taylor Publisher Services